Verlag
Dr. Dieter Winkler

Legasthenie: erkennen, verstehen, fördern

Beiträge zum 13. Fachkongress des Bundesverbandes Legasthenie 1999

Herausgegeben von
Gerd Schulte-Körne
in Zusammenarbeit mit dem Bundesverband Legasthenie e.V.

Verlag Dr. Dieter Winkler

Die Deutsche Bibliothek – CIP-Einheitsaufnahme

Legasthenie: erkennen, verstehen, fördern / hrsg. von Gerd Schulte-Körne in Zusammenarbeit mit dem Bundesverband Legasthenie e.V. – Bochum: Winkler, 2001

(Beiträge zum ... Fachkongress des Bundesverbandes Legasthenie ... ; 13)
ISBN 3-930083-77-9 kart
ISBN 3-930083-82-5 Gb

Printed in Germany

Inhaltsverzeichnis

1 Ursachen

1.1 Auditive Wahrnehmung

1.1.1 The functional neuroanatomy of reading and dyslexia: Clues from PET neuroimaging

Judith M. Rumsey and Barry Horwitz

Introduction

Neuroimaging provides a valuable tool for investigating the functional neuroanatomy of reading and its disorders. We used positron emission tomography (PET) to identify the neural pathways subserving reading in good readers and deviations in the use of those pathways in developmental dyslexia. Using O^{15}-labelled water as a tracer to measure regional cerebral blood flow, an indirect measure of neuronal activity, dyslexic men and normal control men were examined with tasks designed to contrast phonological and orthographic components of reading, thought to be differentially affected in dyslexia. Pronunciation (reading aloud) and lexical decision making were compared with a common baseline condition (visual fixation) and with each other to determine patterns of activation/deactivation („subtraction technique"). Covariance techniques were then applied to relate brain activity to levels of reading skill and to examine the functional connectivity of the left angular gyrus, a region of critical importance to reading.

Neuroimaging of pathways subserving phonological and orthographic components of reading

Phonological and orthographic processing constitute complementary components of reading skill. The phonological component involves the use of the speech code to store and retrieve information (Vellutino et al, 1995) and is involved in sounding out words. The orthographic component involves both visual analysis and the recognition of linguistic patterns (e.g., letter-sound invariances, sequential dependencies, structural redundancies, letter position frequencies) (Vellutino et al, 1995).

Whether these components are subserved by the same neural pathways and mechanisms or by different pathways and mechanisms is a matter of debate. Dissociations between the ability to read words with irregular spellings („exception words") and pseudowords in the acquired alexias have stimulated „dual route" models of reading that propose the existence of independent neural pathways and distinctly different mechanisms subserving orthographic and phonological processing (Coltheart et al, 1993). Conversely, connectionist models of reading (Seidenberg & McClelland, 1989; Plaut et al, 1996) have proposed that phonological and orthographic processing occur simultaneously in distributed neural networks. and that both words and pseudowords are processed within common local networks via a single interactive process.

Because phonological aspects of reading are disproportionately affected in developmental dyslexia, the neural pathways associated with these two components are of interest.

For this reason, the neural substrates of these components of reading skill were investigated through the use of pronunciation (reading aloud) and lexical decision making tasks in men with histories of normal development. The methods used are detailed in Rumsey et al (1997a) and abbreviated below.

Fourteen healthy, strongly right-handed, monolingual men, ages 18-40 years of age (M 25, SD 5), with educations ranging from a high school diploma to postgraduate degrees, were studied. Those with less than a college degree were oversampled. All were free of any history of developmental disorder, significant psychiatric disorder and substance abuse. All were of at least average intelligence and able to read with average or better speed and accuracy.

Pronunciation and lexical decision making were used to contrast phonological and orthographic processing and were evaluated against a common visual fixation condition, as well as against each other. Ten scans with 6.5mm within-plane resolution and 5.5mm axial resolution were obtained per subject. Each of the five tasks were presented twice, with novel items used for each run of the four reading tasks.

Visual fixation required subjects to fixate on a crosshair at the center of the computer monitor. Phonological pronunciation required pseudowords (e.g., phalbap, chirl) to be read aloud, thus forcing a reliance on rule-based grapheme-to-phoneme conversions. Orthographic pronunciation required words with irregular spellings and/or inconsistent pronunciations, which thereby violate phonological rules (e.g., pharaoh, choir), to be read aloud, forcing a reliance on visual familiarity. Phonological decision making required subjects to determine which of two visually-presented pseudowords (e.g., jope – joak, gaim – goam) sounded like a real word. Orthographic decision making required subjects to decide which of two visually-presented items (a real word or its pseudohomophone) (e.g., thurd – third, deep – deap) was in fact a real word.

Because phonological processing is slower than orthographic processing (Waters & Seidenberg, 1985) and because dyslexic men were expected to perform reading tasks more slowly than normal readers, a subject-paced design was used with a fixed interstimulus interval. Subject-paced designs are less sensitive to differences in the duration of cognitive processing required to perform a task (which are reflected in reaction times) and more sensitive to differences in the intensity of local neural processing than are fixed pace designs and thus are preferred for identifying differences in the use of neural mechanisms, particularly between patients and controls (D'Esposito et al, 1997). Subjects were allowed the time they needed to process the stimuli, but were encouraged to respond as quickly as possible, ensuring that both control and dyslexic men engaged in the cognitive processing required for task performance during most of the scanning time.

Statistical Parametric Mapping (SPM) was used to generate brain maps showing pixels that differed significantly between conditions within and between groups, an approach widely known as the „subtraction approach." Brain images from individual subjects were warped into a standard brain space, referenced to a Talairach atlas (Talairach & Tournoux, 1988), so that data could be averaged across individuals for group comparisons. Data were smoothed to adjust for variability in brain anatomy, and effects of whole brain blood flow were removed through the use of ratios of regional to whole brain blood flow. Statistical comparisons (Student t) were made on a pixel by pixel basis. A significance threshold of $p < .001$ was set for differences between visual fixation and each of the reading tasks. For more subtle comparisons, including differences between the phonological and orthographic versions of pronunciation and lexical decision making and for group comparisons, the threshold was set at $p < .01$. Nonetheless, most group differences were significant at $p < .001$.

Controls performed with greater than 90% accuracy on all but pseudoword reading (phonological pronunciation), on which they were 82% accurate. Their phonological processing was slower than was their orthographic processing, as indicated by longer reaction times ($p < .001$) on the phonological version of each task type.

All four reading tasks activated regions on both sides of the brain, but these activations were more intense on the left than on the right, in accordance with the expected lateralization of language function. Common to all four tasks was a ventral stream of activation from visual association areas in the left lingual gyrus into the fusiform gyrus, as well as activation of the left thalamus and left anterior cingulate gyrus.

Notable differences were seen in the patterns of activation elicited by pronunciation and lexical decision making. Lexical decision making, especially phonologic decision making, activated the left inferior frontal cortex near Broca's area, but did not activate Wernicke's area. Decision making also activated the inferior parietal region, particularly on the left. Pronunciation activated the left superior temporal cortex in the region of Wernicke's area, but did not activate the left inferior frontal region.

The patterns of activation were highly similar for the phonological and orthographic versions of each task type. For these comparisons, differences were seen in the intensity, rather than in the location, of the activations. Comparing the two pronunciation tasks, pseudoword pronunciation was more activating of left superior temporal cortex than was exception word pronunciation. Phonological decision making was more activating of left inferior frontal cortex than was orthographic decision making. While an understanding of the specific operations performed by these regions awaits further research, some working hypotheses are that phonological awareness is subserved by left temporoparietal regions (Petersen et al, 1989; Rumsey et al, 1992) and subvocal rehearsal and verbal working memory (involved in silent phonological decision making) by left frontal regions (Paulesu et al, 1993). Figure 1.1.1.1 summarizes the patterns of left-hemisphere cortical activation associated with the four reading tasks for the control men.

Deviations in posterior neural activity during reading in developmental dyslexia

Developmental dyslexia is believed to stem from core deficits in phonological awareness (Pennington et al, 1987; Wagner & Torgeson, 1987), which adversely affect both phonological decoding and orthographic processing (Castles et al, 1999; Fisher et al, 1999). While early diagnoses frequently lack stability (Shaywitz et al, 1994), children who are severely affected show a strong persistence of reading disabilities and phonological deficits into adolescence and adulthood (Maughan, 1995; Pennington et al, 1987), thus allowing these deficits to be studied in older subjects. Well established functional imaging methods (i.e., PET), when applied to adults, can serve an important role in identifying the neural circuitry involved in dyslexia and in generating focused hypotheses for further testing in subjects of different ages.

Early PET studies of dyslexic men used auditory (nonreading) tasks to avoid the potential confounds and interpretive dilemmas associated with poor reading. These studies showed reduced activation of left temporoparietal and superior temporal cortex during a phonological awareness task (rhyme detection), reduced activation of right frontal and temporal regions during a tonal memory task, and normal activation of left inferior frontal regions during a syntax task involving sentence comprehension (Rumsey et al, 1992, 1994a, b). These findings suggested deviations in the use of posterior language regions in dyslexia. To further investigate the functional neuroanatomy of dyslexia, men with clear childhood diagnoses of dyslexia, who continued to show clinically significant deficits in reading decoding, were examined with the PET methods described above. The tasks described above provided probes of both anterior and posterior regions involved in reading. Highlights of this dyslexia study are presented below and detailed in Rumsey et al (1997c).

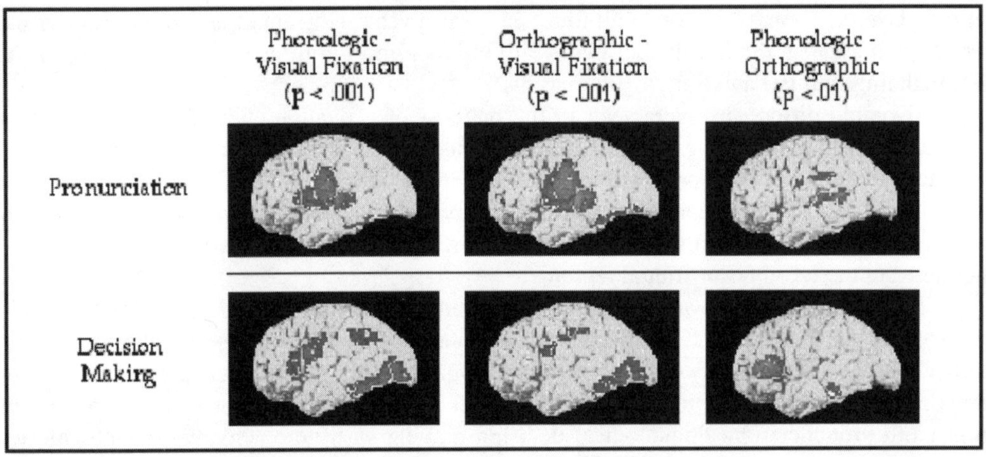

Figure 1.1.1.1 Regions activated by normal readers in and near the lateral surface of the left hemisphere during pronunciation and lexical decision making relative to a visual fixation control. Differences in the degree of activation elicited by the phonological and orthographic versions of these tasks are also shown. Adapted from Rumsey et al (1997a).

Seventeen healthy right-handed, monolingual dyslexic men of average or higher intelligence (Wechsler Adult Intelligence Scale-Revised IQs 90+), ages 18-40 years, were studied. The sample was matched to the control group on age, education, handedness (measured as a continuous variable), socioeconomic background and IQ. All dyslexic subjects had documented histories of childhood reading disorder and continued to show deficits in decoding, documented with a standardized, timed test of oral paragraph reading (Gray Oral Reading Test-Third Edition). Approximately half the sample continued to show deficits even in single word reading (Wide Range Achievement Test-Third Edition Reading score < 90). Comprehension of both spoken and written language was good for the entire sample, consistent with their histories of better spoken language development.

As expected, the dyslexic group performed less accurately and more slowly (with longer reaction times) than the control group across tasks. Nonetheless, they were fully engaged in all the tasks despite their difficulty. Their performance on the decision making tasks (approximately 85% accurate) was better than that on the pronunciation tasks, and their performance on the orthographic tasks better than that on the phonological tasks.

Relative to the control group, the dyslexic group showed more spatially extensive activation and deactivation across tasks and throughout the brain, perhaps reflecting the high level of difficulty they experienced. Larger areas of activation have been noted to accompany lower levels of skill in some studies (Raichle et al, 1994). Statistical tests for differences in the intensity of these activations/deactivations frequently did not meet significance, however.

Significant differences in task-related changes in blood flow were localized to the temporal and parietal lobes, as a result of reduced activation and unusual deactivation within these regions. During pronunciation, the dyslexic group showed reduced activation of the left superior temporal gyrus and failed to activate the right superior gyrus (activated by controls). Abnormalities seen in the dyslexic group were greater during phonological (pseudoword) pronunciation. Figure 1.1.1.2 provides a graphic summary of the patterns of activation/ deactivation exhibited by dyslexic and control men on the reading tasks and the differences between these groups.

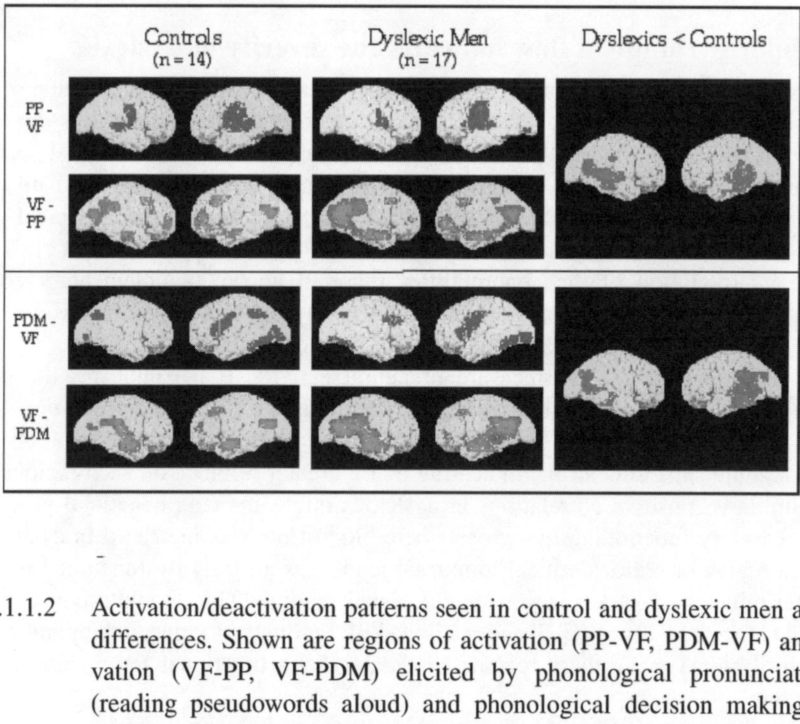

Figure 1.1.1.2 Activation/deactivation patterns seen in control and dyslexic men and group differences. Shown are regions of activation (PP-VF, PDM-VF) and deactivation (VF-PP, VF-PDM) elicited by phonological pronunciation (PP) (reading pseudowords aloud) and phonological decision making (PDM), relative to visual fixation (VF). Results for the orthographic tasks were similar, although less pronounced. Adapted from Rumsey et al (1997c).

In contrast to the reduced blood flow seen in these posterior language regions, the dyslexic group showed normal, robust activation of left inferior frontal cortex during lexical decision making and the same robust increase in left inferior frontal activation during phonological relative to orthographic decision making as was seen in the controls. During lexical decision making, the dyslexic group again showed reduced blood flow (relative to controls) in temporal cortex (superior and middle temporal gyri) and the angular/supramarginal region, particularly on the left. Differences were more pronounced for phonological than for orthographic decision making.

Regions of normal and/or increased activation included the left anterior cingulate gyrus (activated normally, but with somewhat higher values in the dyslexics) and the left and right insulae, where the dyslexic group showed a subtle increase in activation under some conditions. The anterior cingulate is thought to be involved in attention and response selection (Petersen et al, 1989). The left insula has been hypothesized to serve as a bridge connecting posterior and anterior language regions (Paulesu et al, 1996).

Thus, reductions in activation and blood flow seen in the dyslexic group were localized to bilateral superior/middle temporal and angular/supramarginal regions. Normal levels of activation were seen in left inferior frontal cortex. These results are generally consistent with results of earlier, fixed-pace auditory studies not involving reading. Thus, the functional correlates of impaired reading and phonological processing in dyslexia appear to primarily involve posterior portions of language networks involved in reading.

Left angular gyral blood flow indicates the severity of dyslexia

In developmental disorders such as dyslexia, symptoms result from the interaction of primary pathophysiology with experiential factors, making neuroimaging findings less direct reflections of brain pathology than is the case with lesions acquired in adulthood. Abnormal activation/deactivation patterns may reflect poor performance, a reliance on alternate cognitive strategies, compensatory activity and/or functional lesions, such as those associated with cortical anomalies of the sort reported in autopsy studies of dyslexia (Galaburda et al., 1985). To aid in the interpretation of the abnormalities reported above, complementary covariance techniques were applied to relate patterns of regional cerebral blood flow (rCBF) to the levels of reading skill demonstrated by dyslexic men and their controls.

By providing an indirect measure of neural activity, rCBF indicates the degree to which subjects use particular brain regions to perform a task. Those brain regions which are critical to normal reading might be expected to show positive correlations between levels of rCBF and reading skill in controls, indicating that a greater reliance on such regions benefits reading. Similarly, positive correlations in dyslexics might indicate beneficial processing or even compensatory functioning in regions where blood flow was increased in dyslexia. Conversely, if a region or regions critical to normal reading were truly dysfunctional in dyslexia, then greater reliance on such a region should impair reading. This should produce a negative correlation between levels of rCBF and reading skill. Findings of reduced temporal and parietal rCBF in dyslexia make these regions candidates for a functional lesion resulting in impaired reading.

Thus, to relate rCBF to reading skill, PET maps reflecting rCBF during each task condition were correlated with scores on two clinical tests of reading skill--the Wide Range Achievement Test-Third Edition (WRAT-3) and the Gray Oral Reading Test-Third Edition (GORT-3), as well as with performance accuracy during the scans, on a pixel-by-pixel basis within each group (Rumsey et al, 1997b; in press). Of particular interest were regions whose correlations differed significantly between groups in which controls showed significant positive correlations and dyslexics significant negative correlations.

These correlational analyses uniquely identified a region in/near the left angular gyrus as demonstrating such a pattern. The correlations for this region were uniformly positive and significant ($p < .01$) for the control group and uniformly negative, with most correlations significant, for the dyslexic group, compatible with an interpretation of the dysfunction of this region in dyslexia. Figure 1.1.1.3 contains sample scatterplots of these correlations.

Group differences in the correlations for this region were significant (p < .01) for all of the comparisons (3 reading measures x 5 blood flow maps).

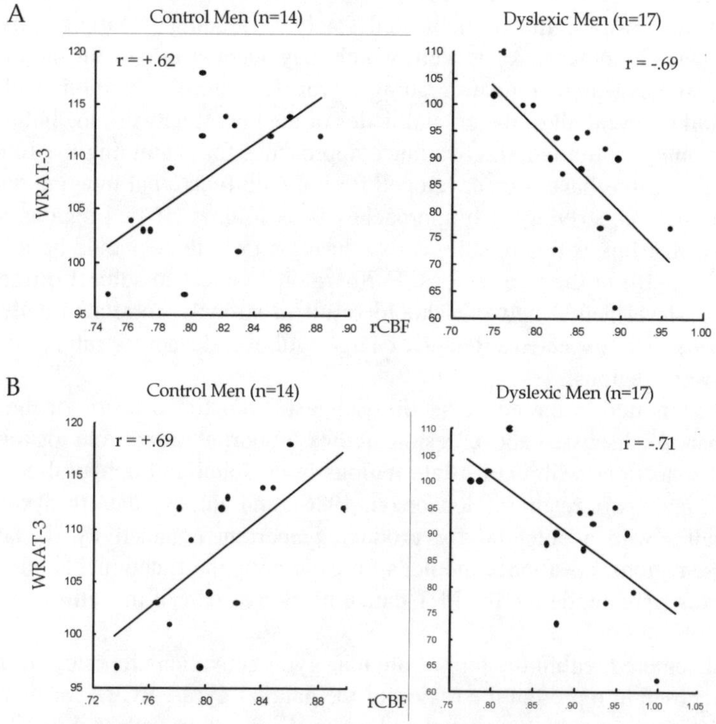

Figure 1.1.1.3 Sample scatterplots of correlations of left angular gyrus rCBF and reading skill. Higher rCBF was associated with better reading skill in controls, but with worse reading in dyslexic men. Results are shown for the Wide Range Achievement Test-Third Edition (WRAT-3) and were similar for other reading measures. Adapted from Rumsey et al (in press).

Within the control group, positive correlations indicated that greater reliance on this region was associated with better reading skill. Conversely, negative correlations in the dyslexic group indicated that greater reliance on this region was associated with worse reading skill, or more severe dyslexia. The findings reported here suggest a functional lesion involving the left angular gyrus in developmental dyslexia.

The literature on the acquired alexias has established the critical importance of this region in reading (Henderson, 1986). In developmental dyslexia, an autopsy study has reported cortical anomalies of probable prenatal origin (neuronal ectopias, architectonic dysplasias) affecting left perisylvian regions in particular (Galaburda et al, 1985). Galaburda et al (1985) hypothesized that such anomalies may impair brain function either directly and/or by forming improper connections with other brain regions involved in language and visual processing. Thus, the functional connectivity of the left angular region was also of interest.

Functional connectivity of the left angular gyrus in normal reading and dyslexia

Because written language is a recent addition to human communication, it is unlikely that a neural network has evolved that is dedicated solely to reading. Neurons activated during reading are engaged by other tasks as well, which may account in part for the fact that functional imaging studies which compare reading to various control conditions (subtraction approach) often fail to reveal all of the crucial nodes of the neural network mediating reading.

To overcome this limitation, covariance approaches for examining the functional connectivity of brain regions have been developed for use with functional imaging data (Horwitz, 1994). The rationale underlying such approaches is as follows: If two regions are anatomically linked and that link is functionally active during a task, there should be a high correlation between the rCBF in the two regions. Furthermore, subject-to-subject differences in the use of a systems-level neural network should result in strongly correlated activity between network elements. The expected effect is a large within-task, across-subject correlation in blood flow between regions.

The data reported in the above section suggest a functional lesion of the left angular gyrus in dyslexia. As discussed above, lesion studies support a critical role for this region and its functional connections with extrastriate regions in occipital and temporal cortex and posterior language regions in reading (Henderson, 1986), and autopsy data in dyslexia suggests cortical anomalies with a potential for producing aberrant connectivity (Galaburda et al, 1985). For these regions, covariance methods for examining the functional connectivity of the left angular gyrus were applied to the PET data collected as part of this effort (see Horwitz et al, 1998).

A voxel centered within the foci of angular gyral activations reported in the published literature was chosen to represent the region of the angular gyrus. RCBF for this voxel in the left and right hemispheres was correlated and mapped separately with that in all other voxels of the brain during each of the two pronunciation tasks (pseudoword and exception word reading) for each group separately. A statistical threshold was set at $p < .001$ (one-tailed). This corresponds to an r of .57 for controls and .52 for the dyslexic group. Group differences in these correlations were tested with a Z statistic (using a $p < .01$ threshold) following the conversion of r values to a normal distribution via a Fisher r-to-Z transformation.

Figure 1.1.1.4 illustrates some key results. Results for pseudoword reading in controls included large positive correlations between blood flow in the left angular gyrus and extrastriate visual areas in occipital and temporal cortex in the left hemisphere. These included a region at the junction of Brodmann's areas 19 and 37 that frequently includes the motion processing area V5/MT (Watson et al, 1993),[1] areas in the lingual and fusiform gyri (Brodmann's areas 18 and 20) shown to be activated during visual stimulation with letter and word-like stimuli (Nobre et al, 1994), the posterior portion of the left superior temporal gyrus (Brodmann's area 22), part of Wernicke's area, and a region in left inferior frontal gyrus (Brodmann's area 45), part of Broca's area. Results for exception word reading were similar to those for pseudoword reading, though somewhat reduced: Correlations with the left lingual and fusiform gyri were significant, but those with Wernicke's area and the inferior frontal cortex were just below our threshold for statistical significance. These results indicate that strong functional connectivity of visual association and language regions in the left hemisphere with the left angular gyrus is observed during normal reading. A lack of significant, comparable correlations with the homologous, right-sided angular gyrus within the right hemisphere indicates the greater engagement of the observed left-hemisphere network during in reading.

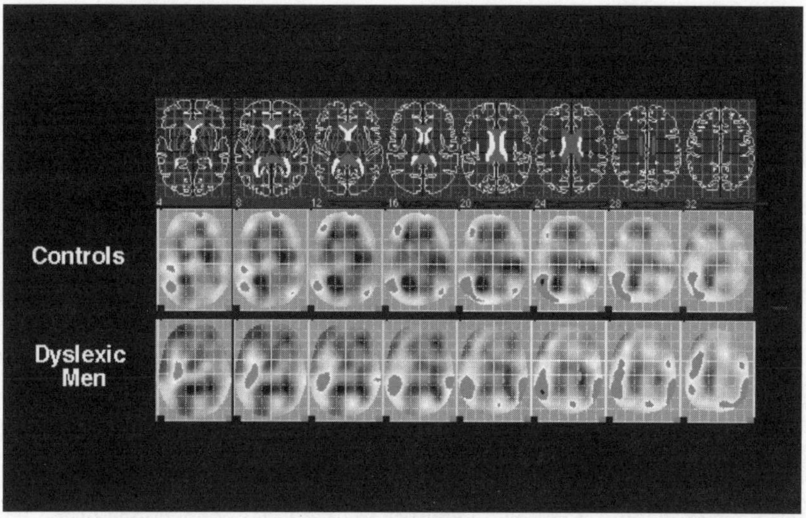

Figure 1.1.1.4 Correlations of rCBF for a reference voxel in the left angular gyrus (black dot on Talairach slice +24) with rCBF in all other voxels during phonological pronunciation (reading aloud of pseudowords). Shown are significant (p < .001) positive correlations for control and dyslexic men on selected axial slices. The approximate anatomy of each slice is shown in the top row of drawings.

Controls showed positive correlations, suggesting strong functional connectivity, with several left-sided visual association and language regions, including Brodmann's area 19 (slice +24), area 19/37 (slice +4), Wernicke's area (slice +8), and an area approximate to Broca's area (slice +16). The dyslexic group showed a striking lack of these same correlations, suggesting a functional disconnection of the left angular gyrus from these regions. In contrast, the dyslexic men showed many significant positive correlations with the right superior temporal (slices +16 and +20) and right inferior parietal regions (slices +24 and +28). Results for exception word reading were similar, but less pronounced. Adapted from Horwitz et al (1998).

In contrast, the dyslexic group showed no significant positive correlations of the left angular gyrus with the regions described above for pseudoword or exception word reading. These differences were marked, with the correlations for the above-mentioned regions significantly smaller for the dyslexic group for both pseudoword and exception word reading. In addition, the dyslexic group showed significantly higher correlations than did the controls in portions of right posterior cortex (e.g., inferior parietal, superior temporal regions). These differences correspond to regions of significant positive correlation in the dyslexic group and an absence of these correlations in controls (see Figure 1.1.1.4).

The lack of the normal correlations with left angular blood flow suggests the absence of normal functional connectivity in dyslexia. As a group, the dyslexic men were not using the same network to read as were controls. The presence of positive correlations with right posterior temporal/ inferior parietal regions not seen in controls further suggests an aberrant organization of posterior networks subserving reading in dyslexia.

Conclusions

The above results support several conclusions regarding reading: (1) Phonological and orthographic processing appear to engage a common neural network. A caveat rests with the limitations of temporal and spatial resolution available with our PET methods and intersubject averaging. (2) Pronunciation and silent lexical decisions differentially engage portions of the neural network involved in reading: Pronunciation activates superior temporal cortex; lexical decision making, the inferior frontal cortex and portions of inferior parietal cortex. Thus, decision making paradigms are unlikely to adequately reveal all the important nodes of the network involved in reading aloud. (3) Phonological processing is subserved predominantly by a network of left-sided regions in the superior temporal, inferior frontal, and inferior parietal cortices. The specific contributions of these regions in supporting reading requires further study, although other work suggests the involvement of left temporoparietal cortex in phonological awareness and left inferior frontal cortex in subvocal rehearsal and verbal working memory. (4) Positive correlations of rCBF with reading skill support an important role of the left angular gyrus in reading. (5) Reading activates functional connections of the left angular gyrus with left extrastriate regions in the occipital and temporal lobes, the left posterior superior temporal gyrus (Wernicke's area), and left inferior frontal gyrus.

Regarding dyslexia: (1) Abnormalities in patterns of activation/deactivation localize to posterior regions--bilateral temporal and inferior parietal regions--during both reading and lexical decision making, despite the fact that decision making predominantly activates anterior language regions. (2) Inverse correlations of rCBF with reading skill suggest that reliance on the left angular gyrus impairs reading. Greater reliance on this region is associated with worse reading, or more severe dyslexia. This in turn suggests a functional lesion of the left angular gyrus. (3) The absence of strong positive correlations of left angular blood flow with that in other visual association and language regions seen in controls is lacking in dyslexia, suggesting a disruption of the normal functional connectivity of this region. Aberrant positive correlations with right posterior regions further support a hypothesis of altered functional connectivity of the left angular region.

Footnote

A subsample of the controls and dyslexic men reported here were studied with functional magnetic resonance imaging with a paradigm designed to activate the visual motion area V5/MT. As reported in Eden et al (1996), a visual motion stimulus activated this region bilaterally in controls, but failed to do so in the dyslexic men, suggesting an abnormality in the magnocellular visual pathway.

References

Castles, A., Datta, H., Gayan, J. & Olson, R.K. 1999. Varieties of developmental reading disorder: Genetic and environmental influences. *Journal of Experimental Child Psychology* 72: 73-94.

Coltheart, M., Curtis, B. Atkins, P. & Haller, M. 1993. Models of reading aloud: Dual-route and parallel-distributed processing approaches. *Psychological Review* 100: 589-608.

D'Esposito, M., Zarahn, E., Aguirre, G. K., Shin, R. K., Auerbach, P. & Detre, J. A. 1997. The effect of pacing of experimental stimuli on observed functional MRI activity. *NeuroImage* 6: 113-121.

Eden, G.F., Van Meter, J.W., Rumsey, J.M., Maisog, J.M., Woods, R.P. & Zeffiro, T.A. 1996. Abnormal processing of visual motion revealed by functional brain imaging. *Nature* 381: 66-69.

Fisher, S.E., Marlow, A.J., Lamb, J., Maestrini, E., Williams, D.F., Richardson, A.J., Weeks, D.E., Stein, J.F. & Monaco, A.P. 1999. A quantitative-trait locus on chromosome 6p influences different aspects of developmental dyslexia. *American Journal of Human Genetics* 64: 146-156.

Galaburda, A.M., Sherman, G.F., Rosen, G.D., Aboitiz, F. & Geschwind, N. 1985. Developmental dyslexia: four consecutive patients with cortical anomalies. *Annals of Neurology* 18: 222-233.

Henderson, V.W. 1986. Anatomy of posterior pathways in reading: A reassessment. *Brain and Language* 29: 119-133.

Horwitz, B. 1994. Data analysis paradigms for metabolic-flow data: Combining neural modeling and functional neuroimaging. *Human Brain Mapping* 2: 112-122.

Horwitz, B., Rumsey , J.M. & Donohue, B.C. 1998. Functional connectivity of the angular gyrus in normal reading and dyslexia. *Proceedings of the National Academy of Sciences* 95: 8939-8944.

Maughan, B. 1995. Annotation: Long-term outcomes of developmental reading problems. *Journal of Child Psychology and Psychiatry* 36: 357-371.

Nobre, A.C., Allison, T. & McCarthy, G. 1994. Word recognition in the human temporal lobe. *Nature* 372: 260-263.

Paulesu, E., Frith, C.D. & Frackowiak, R.S.J. 1993. The neural correlates of the verbal component of working memory. *Nature* 362: 342-334.

Paulesu, E., Frith, U., Snowling, M., Gallagher, A., Morton, J., Frackowiak, R.S. & Frith, C.D. 1996. Is developmental dyslexia a disconnection syndrome? Evidence from PET scanning. *Brain* 119: 143-157.

Pennington, B.F., Lefly, D.L., Van Orden, G.C., Bookman, O.M. & Smith, S.D. 1987. Is phonology bypassed in normal or dyslexic development? *Annals of Dyslexia* 37: 62-89.

Petersen, S.E., Fox, P.T., Posner, M.I., Mintun, M. & Raichle, M.E. 1989. Positron emission tomographic studies of the processing of single words. *Journal of Cognitive Neuroscience* 1: 153-170.

Plaut, D.C., McClelland, J.L., Seidenberg, M.S. & Patterson, K. 1996. Understanding normal and impaired word reading: Computational principles in quasi-regular domains. *Psychological Review* 103: 56-115.

Raichle, M.E., Fiez, J.A., Videen, T.O., MacLeod, A.M., Pardo, J.V., Fox P.T. & Petersen, S.E. 1994. Practice-related changes in human brain functional anatomy during nonmotor learning. *Cerebral Cortex* 4: 8-26.

Rumsey, J.M., Andreason, P., Zametkin, A.J., Aquino, T., King, A.C., Hamburger, S.D., Pikus, A., Rapoport, J.L. & Cohen, R.M. 1992. Failure to activate the left temporoparietal cortex in dyslexia: An oxygen 15 positron emission tomographic study. *Archives of Neurology* 49: 527-534.

Rumsey, J.M., Andreason, P., Zametkin, A.J., King, A.C., Hamburger, S.D., Aquino, T., Hanahan, A.P., Pikus, A. & Cohen, R.M. 1994a. Right frontotemporal activation by tonal memory in dyslexia, an O-15 PET study. *Biological Psychiatry* 36: 171-180.

Rumsey, J. M., Horwitz, B., Donohue, B.C., Nace, K., Maisog, J.M. & Andreason, P. 1997a. Phonologic and orthographic components of word recognition: a PET-rCBF study. *Brain* 120: 739-760.

Rumsey, J. M., Horwitz, B., Donohue, B.C., Nace, K., Maisog, J.M. & Andreason, P. 1997b. Severity of dyslexia related to regional cerebral blood flow. *NeuroImage* 5(4): S570.

Rumsey, J. M., Horwitz, B., Donohue, B. C., Nace, K. L., Maisog, M. & Andreason, P. (1999) A functional lesion in developmental dyslexia: Left angular gyral blood flow predicts severity. *Brain and Language* 70: 187-204.

Rumsey, J.M., Nace, K., Donohue, B.C., Wise, D., Maisog, J. M. & Andreason, P. 1997c. A positron emission tomographic study of impaired word recognition and phonological processing in dyslexic men. *Archives of Neurology* 54: 562-573.

Rumsey, J.M., Zametkin, A.J., Andreason, P., Hanahan, A.P., Hamburger, S.D., Aquino, T., King, A.C., Pikus, A. & Cohen, R.M. 1994b. Normal activation of frontotemporal language cortex in dyslexia, as measured with oxygen 15 positron emission tomography. *Archives of Neurology* 51: 27-38.

Seidenberg, M.S. & McClelland, J.L. 1989. A distributed developmental model of word recognition and naming. *Psychological Review* 96: 523-568.

Shaywitz, S.E., Shaywitz, B.A., Fletcher, J.M., & Escobar, M.D. 1990. Prevalence of reading disability in boys and girls. Results of the Connecticut Longitudinal Study. *Journal of the American Medical Association* 264: 998-1002.

Talairach, J. & Tournoux, P. 1988. Co-Planar Stereotaxic Atlas of the Human Brain. Translated by M. Rayport. Thieme Medical Publishers, New York.

Vellutino, F., Scanlon, D.M., & Chen, D.S. 1995. The increasingly inextricable relationship between orthographic and phonological coding in learning to read: Some reservations about current methods of operationalizing orthographic coding. In *The Varieties of Orthographic Knowledge II: Relationships to Phonology, Reading and Writing*, ed. V.W. Berninger. Dordrecht, Netherlands: Kluwer Academic Publishers.

Wagner, R.K. & Torgeson, J.K. 1987. The nature of phonological processing and its causal role in the acquisition of reading skills. *Psychological Bulletin* 101: 193-212.

Waters, GS & Seidenberg, M.S. 1985. Spelling-sound effects in reading: Time-course and decision criteria. *Brain and Cognition* 13: 575-572.

Watson, J.D.G., Myers, R., Frackowiak, R.S.J., Hajnal, J.V., Woods, R.P., Mazziotta, J.C., Shipp, S. & Zeki, S. 1993. Area V5 of the human brain: evidence from a combined study using positron emission tomography and magnetic resonance imaging. *Cerebral Cortex* 3: 79-94.

1.1.2 Wie arbeitet das Gehirn beim Lesen? Die Möglichkeiten bildgebender Verfahren in der Forschung über Lese-Rechtschreibstörungen

Bernhard Blanz

1. Lese-Rechtschreibstörungen sind auch noch im Erwachsenenalter nachweisbar

Vor 20 Jahren wurde noch die Meinung vertreten, die Lese-Rechtschreibstörung (LRS) sei eine typische Störung des frühen Schulalters und bessere sich spätestens nach der Pubertät. In letzter Zeit besteht jedoch Einigkeit darüber, dass die LRS nicht nur eine schwerwiegende sondern auch sehr hartnäckige Störung ist; ohne spezifische Behandlung kann nicht mit einer Verbesserung gerechnet werden. Zwar lernen die meisten Betroffenen lesen und schreiben, ihre Lese- und Rechtschreibleistung bleibt aber auch noch im Erwachsenenalter deutlich schlechter als die von regulär Lesenden. Dies zeigen bspw. die Befunde von Bruck (1990), die die Lesegeschwindigkeit von Erwachsenen mit einer LRS im Vergleich zu gesunden Erwachsenen sowie gesunden Kindern untersuchte (Tabelle 1.1.2.1): Für das Lesen von Wörtern benötigen Erwachsene mit einer LRS im Durchschnitt etwa 400 Millisekunden mehr Zeit als gesunde Erwachsene und etwa 300 Millisekunden mehr als 12jährige gesunde Kinder.

	Erwachsene		Kinder 6. Klasse
	LRS	gesund	
Wörter	956	565	662
Non-Wörter	2019	882	839

Tabelle 1.1.2.1 Lesetempo in Millisekunden von Gesunden (Kinder und Erwachsene) und Erwachsenen mit LRS (Bruck 1990)

2. Assemblierte und adressierte phonologische Verarbeitung beim Lesen

Sicher ist, dass die LRS Ausdruck einer gestörten zerebralen Informationsverarbeitung ist; davon sind mindestens zwei Systeme betroffen, nämlich das visuelle sowie das sprachverarbeitende System. Im sprachverarbeitenden System spielt die phonologische Bewußtheit eine entscheidende Rolle. Mit phonologischer Bewußtheit wird die Fähigkeit bezeichnet, die einzelnen Laute oder Phoneme, aus denen Wörter zusammengesetzt sind, zu erkennen, zu analysieren und zu modifizieren. Diese phonologische Bewußtheit ist beim Leselernprozess entscheidend, beim Lesenlernen kommt es nämlich v.a. darauf an, orthographische Zeichen, also

Buchstaben, in Phoneme, also Laute, zu transformieren; die Laute werden dann zu Wörtern zusammengesetzt und weiterverarbeitet. Diese Lesestrategie der Graphem-Phonem-Zuordnung, auch als assemblierte phonologische Verarbeitung bezeichnet, wird insbesondere im Grundschulalter genutzt. Aber auch später, nämlich beim Lesen von sehr seltenen oder unbekannten Wörtern, muß auf sie zurückgegriffen werden; ihr Nachteil ist ihre Langsamkeit.

Deshalb wird sie mit zunehmender Leseroutine durch eine zweite, schnellere Lesestrategie abgelöst, nämlich die sogenannte adressierte phonologische Verarbeitung (Coslett et al. 1984). Diese ermöglicht das ganzheitliche oder lexikalische Erfassen von Wörtern und damit schnelleres Lesen. Bei dieser Lesestrategie spielt die phonologische Bewußtheit eine untergeordnete Rolle, sie hat aber als Voraussetzung, dass die zu lesenden Wörter bekannt und wie in einem Lexikon ganzheitlich abgespeichert sind. Deshalb kann diese Strategie am Beginn des Lesenlernens noch nicht eingesetzt werden; im Laufe der Leseentwicklung und mit zunehmender Routine wird der lexikalische Speicher jedoch immer umfangreicher und so die Voraussetzung für das Nutzen dieser schnelleren und damit überlegenen Lesestrategie geschaffen.

Ein häufig genutztes Paradigma zur Untersuchung dieser beiden unterschiedlichen Lesestrategien ist die Präsentation von regulären, sinnhaften Wörtern und von sogenannten Non-Wörtern, diese werden auch als Nonsens-Wörter oder Pseudo-Wörter bezeichnet. Non-Wörter sind aussprechbare aber sinnlose Buchstabenkombinationen, also Kunstwörter, wie bspw. das Non-Wort „FOLM“. Weil diese Non-Wörter unbekannt sind, können sie lexikalisch nicht gespeichert sein; im Unterschied zu sinnvollen Wörtern können sie deshalb nur mittels der langsameren Strategie der Graphem-Phonem-Zuordnung gelesen werden. Tabelle 1.1.2.1 zeigt für verschiedene Gruppen das durchschnittliche Lesetempo für Wörter und für Non-Wörter. Erwachsene mit und ohne LRS sowie gesunde Kinder lesen Wörter eindeutig schneller als gleichlange Non-Wörter. Dies weist darauf hin, dass unterschiedlich schnelle Lesestrategien genutzt werden.

3. Der LRS liegt eine Störung der assemblierten phonologischen Verarbeitung zugrunde

Seit einiger Zeit wird die Hypothese diskutiert, dass bei der LRS die assemblierte phonologische Verarbeitung, auf der die Graphem-Phonem-Zuordnung beruht, beeinträchtigt ist. Diese Hypothese wird durch den häufig replizierten Befund gestützt, dass Kinder, Jugendliche und auch Erwachsene mit LRS beim Lesen von Non-Wörtern mehr Schwierigkeiten haben als beim Lesen von Wörtern. Dies zeigt Tabelle 1.1.2.1 Für das Lesen von regulären, sinnhaften Wörtern benötigen Erwachsene mit LRS im Durchschnitt 400 Millisekunden länger als gesunde Erwachsene und etwa 300 Millisekunden länger als gesunde Kinder; das wurde bereits erwähnt. Für das Lesen von Non-Wörtern ist die Differenz zwischen Erwachsenen mit LRS und Gesunden mit mehr als 1100 Millisekunden aber weitaus größer. Dies zeigt die beträchtlichen Schwierigkeiten der Betroffenen mit LRS beim Non-Wort-Lesen: Auch bei Erwachsenen mit LRS ist die Graphem-Phonem-Zuordnung und damit die phonologische Verarbeitung noch deutlich beeinträchtigt. So ist das Lesen von Non-Wörtern ein sensiblerer Indikator für das Erkennen einer LRS im Erwachsenenalter als das Lesen von Wörtern.

4. Zerebrale Grundlagen der LRS

4.1 Hirnstrukturelle Befunde

Schon seit langem wird nach den hirnstrukturellen und hirnfunktionellen Grundlagen der LRS gesucht. Zahlreiche Befunde aus verschiedenen morphologischen, strukturellen und funktionellen Untersuchungen weisen dabei auf Beeinträchtigungen in den sprachverarbeitenden Gehirnstrukturen hin. So wurden in post-mortem-Untersuchungen an Erwachsenen mit LRS sogenannte Ektopien, also Anhäufungen untypischer Zellen im Bereich des Planum temporale gefunden (Galaburda, 1992). Ebenfalls im Bereich des Planum temporale wurden atypische Symmetrien beschrieben – bei regulär lesenden Rechtshändern findet sich zu 70% eine links-betonte Asymmetrie des Planum temporale und nur zu 10% eine rechts-betonte.

		Temporallappen	
	Alter	links > rechts	rechts > links
LRS	16,5	3	14
Lernbehindert	14,9	4	2
Gesund	16,5	9	3

Tabelle 1.1.2.2 Temporallappen-Asymmetrie und LRS: Eine MRT-Studie (Dalby et al, 1998)

Tabelle 1.1.2.2 zeigt Daten einer dänischen Studie. Hier wurden drei Gruppen von rechtshändigen Jungen im Jugendalter untersucht: Jugendliche mit LRS wurden verglichen mit lernbehinderten sowie normalbegabten Gleichaltrigen. Bei Jungen mit einer LRS wurde signifikant seltener eine linksseitige Asymmetrie des Temporallappens gefunden, im Gegensatz zu den gesunden sowie den lernbehinderten Jugendlichen, die die übliche linksseitige Asymmetrie in diesen Gehirnregionen aufwiesen. Allerdings gibt es auch Studien, die diese hirnstrukturellen Unterschiede zwischen Betroffenen mit einer LRS und Normallesenden nicht bestätigen konnten.

4.2 Hirnfunktionelle Befunde mit bildgebenden Verfahren bei Erwachsenen

Hirnfunktionelle bildgebende Untersuchungen weisen auf eine Involvierung sprachverarbeitender Hirnregionen beim Lesen hin. Fiez und Petersen (1998) haben Befunde aus neun Studien zusammengefaßt, in denen der Leseprozess mit bildgebenden Verfahren bei Gesunden untersucht wurde, überwiegend mittels PET. Zerebrale Aktivierungen beim lauten Lesen von Wörtern wurden erwartungsgemäß in der dominanten Hemisphäre occipital, insbesondere aber temporal und auch frontal gefunden, also in Gehirnregionen, in denen sprachgebundene Informationen verarbeitet werden. Vor dem Hintergrund, dass die zerebrale Sprachverarbeitung überwiegend der dominanten Hemisphäre zugerechnet wird, ist interessant, dass auch in der nicht-dominanten Hemisphäre Aktivierungsmuster beobachtet wurden, ebenfalls in sprachverarbeitenden Gehirnregionen. Ein wesentliches Ergebnis dieser Literaturübersicht ist, dass das Lesen von Wörtern in verschiedenen Untersuchungen zu ähnlichen Aktivierungsmustern geführt hat. Die Autoren weisen aufgrund dieser Befunde darauf hin, dass bildgebende funktionelle Untersuchungsmethoden ein maßgebliches Instrumentarium sind, um die zerebralen Prozesse beim Lesen umfassender verstehen zu können.

Zum besseren Verständnis der hirnfunktionellen Grundlagen der regulären und der gestörten Wortverarbeitung hat die Arbeitsgruppe um Shaywitz mit fMRT-Untersuchungen an Erwachsenen mit LRS wesentlich beigetragen (Shaywitz et al. 1996, 1998). Diese Arbeitsgruppe entwickelte ein ausgeklügeltes Paradigma mit steigenden Anforderungen an die phonologische Verarbeitung. In ihren Untersuchungen mußten verschiedene Entscheidungsaufgaben bearbeitet werden, nämlich rein visuelle Entscheidungsaufgaben ohne phonologische Verarbeitung (Tabelle 1.1.2.3, Nr. 1 und 2), phonologische Reim-Entscheidungsaufgaben (Nr. 3 und 4) sowie semantische Aufgaben (Nr. 5).

Entscheidungsaufgaben

1.	Do	\\V	and	\\V	match?
2.	Do	**bbBb**	and	**bbBb**	match?
3.	Do	**T**	and	**V**	rhyme?
4.	Do	**leat**	and	**jete**	rhyme?
5.	Are	**corn**	and	**rice**	in the same category?

Tabelle 1.1.2.3 Paradigma mit steigenden Anforderungen an die phonologische Verarbeitung (Shaywitz et al, 1998)

Es zeigte sich, dass gesunde Erwachsene bei phonologischen Aufgaben, bspw. beim Non-Wort-Reimen (Nr. 4, Tabelle 1.1.2.3), links inferior-frontale (Broca-Zentrum), links posterior-temporale (Wernicke-Zentrum) und links parieto-occipitale (Gyrus angularis) Hirnareale aktivierten. Bei Erwachsenen mit LRS fehlte dagegen sowohl die temporale als auch die parieto-occipitale Aktivierung. Dafür fand sich frontal eine signifikant deutlichere Aktivierung. Die Unteraktivierung temporo-parieto-occipitaler Strukturen bei Erwachsenen mit LRS belegt deren funktionelle Beeinträchtigung in Gehirnregionen, in denen visuell aufgenommene orthographische Informationen in phonologische Strukturen übersetzt werden. Die Autoren vermuten, dass die relative Überaktivierung links inferior-frontal eine kompensatorische Reaktion auf dieses funktionelle Defizit sein könnte. Andere hirnfunktionelle Untersuchungen zeigen vergleichbare Ergebnisse (Peterson, 1995; Rumsey, 1996).

4.3 Hirnfunktionelle Befunde mit bildgebenden Verfahren bei Kindern und Jugendlichen

Bisher wurden solche Untersuchungen mit bildgebenden Verfahren (PET, fMRT) ausschließlich bei Erwachsenen durchgeführt. Wegen der Entwicklungseinflüsse ist aber mehr als fraglich, ob solche an Erwachsenen erhobenen Befunde uneingeschränkt auf Kinder und Jugendliche übertragbar sind.

In unseren eigenen fMRT-Untersuchungen bei Kindern und Jugendlichen mit LRS fanden wir jedoch ähnliche Resultate (Georgiewa et al., 1999). Untersucht wurden 17 Kinder/Jugendliche mit LRS und 17 regulär lesende Gleichaltrige, sie waren nach Alter, Geschlecht und kognitiver Leistungsfähigkeit parallelisiert. Tabelle 1.1.2.4 zeigt die ausgeprägte Diskrepanz zwischen nonverbaler kognitiver Leistungsfähigkeit und den Lese- bzw. Rechtschreibfähigkeiten in der LRS-Gruppe.

	LRS (n=17)	**Kontrollen (n=17)**	**p**
Alter	13;5	14;3	.33
Jungen	8/17	8/17	1.00
IQ	109	104	.23
Lese-IQ	79	106	<.001
Rechtschreib-IQ	74	93	<.001

Tabelle 1.1.2.4: Lese- und Rechtschreibleistungen von Kindern mit LRS und gesunden Kontrollen (Georgiewa et al. 1999)

Bei Aufgaben, die assemblierte phonologische Verarbeitung verlangen, nämlich beim Non-Wort-Lesen und bei einer Transformationsaufgabe (hier besteht die Aufgabe darin, den ersten Buchstaben eines Wortes an das Ende zu verschieben und die Silbe „-ein" anzuhängen; auf diese Weise wird das Wort „Blume" in „Lumebein" verändert), zeigten regulär lesende Kinder und Jugendliche signifikante Aktivierungen links-frontal im Bereich des Broca-Zentrums sowie links-temporal. Kinder und Jugendliche mit einer LRS aktivierten diese Gehirnregionen jedoch nicht.

So zeigen zerebrale Aktivierungsstudien vergleichbare Resultate sowohl für Kinder und Jugendliche als auch für Erwachsene mit LRS; alle beschriebenen Befunde weisen auf eine Störung im phonologischen Verarbeitungssystem hin. Wenn funktionelle Defizite im sprachverarbeitenden System auch noch bei Erwachsenen mit LRS nachweisbar sind, stellt sich die Frage, wie die Betroffenen mit LRS trotzdem Lesen und Schreiben lernen. Müssen bspw. kompensatorische Prozesse angenommen werden oder findet eine Art Nachreifung statt?

5. Die Behandlung von Kindern und Jugendlichen mit LRS ist verbesserungsbedürftig

Auch wenn solche Fragen noch ungeklärt sind, eröffnen die neurofunktionellen Befunde Möglichkeiten, die Behandlung von Kindern und Jugendlichen mit LRS zu verbessern.

Günstig ist sicherlich, die phonologischen Defizite im Rahmen von Übungsbehandlungen stärker und spezifischer zu fördern.

	Strehlow et al. (1999)	**Schulte-Körne et al. (1998)**	**Overmeyer et al. (1999)**
Alter (Jahre)	8,8	9,7	11,7
Jungen vs. Mädchen	16 / 9	14 / 3	8 / 8
IQ	101	102	108
Fallkriterium	1 Standardabweichung	1 Standardabweichung	2 Standardabweichungen
Intervention bei	Betroffenen	Eltern	Betroffenen
Methode	2 Programme	Schärfung und Dehnung	fehlerorientiert
Kontakte	30	24	20
Dauer	12 Monate	24 Monate	10 Monate
Rechtschreibleistung[1]			
vor Behandlung	35,3	37,1	31,4
nach Behandlung	39,8	40.6	35,4
Verbesserung	4,5	3,5	4,0

[1]in T-Wertpunkten

Tabelle 1.1.2.5 Vergleich von Rechtschreib-Übungsprogrammen

Die Behandlung von Kindern und Jugendlichen mit LRS ist ein langwieriger und schwieriger Prozeß. So zeigen die Resultate von drei verschiedenen Therapiestudien zwar vergleichbare, insgesamt aber nur mäßige Verbesserungen der Rechtschreibleistungen, nämlich zwischen 3,5 und 4,5 T-Wertpunkten. Dies kann bedeuten, dass die LRS generell nur sehr schwer beeinflußbar ist, dieser Befund kann aber auch heißen, dass die optimalen Förderungsmöglichkeiten noch nicht gefunden wurden. Hier besteht zweifellos noch Forschungsbedarf; klar ist aber auch, dass die Verbesserung der Interventionsansätze nur dann gelingen kann, wenn die zerebralen Grundlagen der LRS besser verstanden werden. Dabei sind bildgebende Verfahren inzwischen unverzichtbar geworden.

Literatur:

Bruck M: Word-recognition skills of adults with childhood diagnoses of dyslexia. Developmental Psychology. 1990; 26: 493-454

Coslett HB, Gonzalez-Rothi L, Heilmann KM: Reading: Dissociation of the whole-word and phonologic routes. Brain and Language. 1984; 24: 20-35

Dalby MA, Elbro C, Stodkilde-Jorgensen H: Temporal lobe asymmetry and dyslexia: An in vivo study using MRI. Brain and Language. 1998; 62: 51-69

Fiez JA, Petersen SE: Neuroimaging studies of word reading. Proc Natl Acad Sci. 1998; 95: 914-921

Galaburda AM: Neurology of developmental dyslexia. Curr Opin Neurol Neurosurg. 1992; 5: 71-76

Georgiewa P, Rzanny R, Hopf JM, Knab R, Glauche V, Kaiser WA, Blanz B: FMRI during in word processing in dyslexic and normal reading children. Neuroreport (1999, in press)

Peterson BS: Neuroimaging in child and adolescent neuropsychiatric disorders. Am Acad Child Adolesc Psychiatry. 1995; 34: 1560-1576

Rumsey JM: Neuroimaging in developmental dyslexia. A review and conceptualization. In: Lyon GR, Rumsey JM, eds: Neuroimaging. A window to the neurological foundations of learning and behavior in children. Baltimore, London, Toronto, Sydney: Paul H. Brookes; 1996: 57-78

Schulte-Körne G, Deimel W, Remschmidt H: Das Marburger Eltern-Kind-Rechtschreibtraining – Verlaufsuntersuchung nach zwei Jahren. Zeitschrift für Kinder- und Jugendpsychiatrie 1998; 26: 167-173

Shaywitz SE, Shaywitz BA, Pugh KR, et al. The neurobiology of developmental dyslexia as viewed through the lens of functional magnetic resonance imaging technology. In: Lyon GR, Rumsey JM, eds. Neuroimaging. Baltimore, London, Toronto, Sydney: Paul H. Brookes; 1996: 79-94

Shaywitz SE, Shaywitz BA, Pugh KR, et al: Functional disruption in the organization of the brain for reading in dyslexia. Proc Natl Acad Sci. 1998; 95: 2636-2641

Strehlow U, Haffner J, Busch G, Pfüller U, Rellum T, Zerahn-Hartung C: An Schwächen üben oder durch Stärken ausgleichen? Vergleich zweier Strategien in der Förderung von Kindern mit einer umschriebenen Lese-Rechtschreib-Schwäche. Zeitschrift für Kinder- und Jugendpsychiatrie und Psychotherapie 1999; 27: 103-113

1.1.3 Auditive Verarbeitungs- und Wahrnehmungsstörungen und Legasthenie

Martin Ptok

Auditive Verarbeitungs- und Wahrnehmungsstörungen (AVWS)

Definition

Störungen der auditiven Verarbeitung und Wahrnehmung lassen sich grob nach Lehnhardt [18] einteilen in Störungen, die vom Ganglion spirale bis zum unteren Vierhügel lokalisiert sind, und solche, die rindennahe Abschnitte betreffen. Eine weitere, in der klinischen Routine gebräuchliche Einteilung differenziert Störungen des zentralen Hörens weiter [13, 19, 21] in:

- *Störungen des zentralen Hörens = Auditive Wahrnehmungs- und Verarbeitungsstörung (AVWS)*
- *Zentrale Fehlhörigkeit*
- *Zentrale Schwerhörigkeiten*

Der im angloamerikanischen Schrifttum zu findende Begriff „central auditory processing disorders" (CAPD) wird definiert als „Defizite bei einem oder mehreren zentralen auditorischen Prozessen, die verantwortlich sind für die Generierung auditorisch evozierter Potentiale sowie für die folgenden Verhaltensweisen: Geräuschlokalisation und -lateralisation; auditorische Diskrimination; auditorische Mustererkennung; zeitliche Aspekte des Hörens einschließlich der zeitlichen Auflösung, der zeitlichen Maskierung und der zeitlichen Abfolgeerkennung; der auditorischen Performanz mit verstümmelten akustischen Signalen" [4].

Pathophysiologie

Die Arbeitshypothese des hierarchischen Stufenmodells der auditiven Verarbeitung und Wahrnehmung gilt derzeit in der Literatur als anerkannt. Hiernach muss der Gesamtprozess des Hören (Informationsverarbeitung) bis hin zur Stufe des „Outputs" (Sprechen, Schreiben) als hierarchisch gegliederter Stufenprozess betrachtet werden (s. hierzu u.a. 9, 22, 23, 28):

Grob kann unterschieden werden, dass zunächst sprachliche und nicht-sprachliche Signale gleichwertig (ohrspezifisch und binaural) verarbeitet werden. Hierbei werden Frequenz, Zeit, Intensität, Phase des akustischen Signals erkannt. Diese Funktionen lassen sich annäherungsweise der Kochlea und den zentralen Bahnen im Hirnstamm bis zum Corpus geniculatum zuordnen. Dieser Verarbeitung schließt sich eine Analyse durch höhere (kognitive) Funktionen (Wahrnehmung) an. Aufmerksamkeit und Gedächtnis haben hier im Gegensatz zu den vorbewußtlichen Verarbeitungsschritten einen deutlichen Einfluß. Schließlich findet eine Analyse phonetischer oder nichtsprachlicher Signale statt. Eine solche Verarbeitung und Wahrnehmung kann dann zur regelrechten Verwertung (Sprachproduktion, alphabetisches – nicht zwangsläufig orthographisch richtiges! – Schreiben) führen.

Basierend auf diesem Stufenmodell lassen sich Defizite der Informationsverarbeitung in Bezug auf die Sprachverarbeitung wie folgt definieren:

low-level Defizite (Extraktion akustischer Merkmale)

phonetische Defizite (Extraktion phonetischer Merkmale)
phonologische Defizite (Phonemidentifikation, -diskrimination)
lexikalisch-semantische Defizite (Wort- und Bedeutungserkennung)
morphologisch-syntaktische Defizite
Defizite der verschiedenen metalinguistischen Bewußtheiten
Produktionsdefizite (ggf. einschließlich artikulomotorischer und graphomotorischer Defizite).

Prävalenz

Die Prävalenz solchermaßen diagnostizierten auditiven Verarbeitungs- und Wahrnehmungsstörungen wird auf 2-3% aller Kinder und auf bis zu 20% aller älteren Erwachsenen geschätzt [4]. Sicher ist, dass AVWS (bzw. CAPD) isoliert oder in Kombination mit anderen Störungen auftreten können (siehe DAMP-Symptomkomplex-12)

Diagnostik

Zur Diagnostik von AVWS sind eine Reihe von Testmethoden vorgeschlagen worden (s. z.B. 1-3, 5, 10, 16, 17, 24), aufgrund praktischer Gesichtspunkte wird für die Routinediagnostik in der Klinik immer eine Auswahl zu treffen sein. Das diagnostische Vorgehen ist allerdings derzeit weder im angloamerikanischen noch im deutschsprachigen Raum einheitlich, allerdings sind deutliche, neurophysiologisch bzw. psychoakustisch beeinflusste Tendenzen erkennbar.

Therapie

Zur Therapie wurden Reihe von Verfahren (übende Verfahren, apparative Verfahren, medikamentöse Behandlung etc.) vorgeschlagen (siehe hierzu z.B. 2, 5, 6, 13, 16, 17, 26, 27, z.T. mit weiteren Literaturhinweisen), die allerdings überwiegend auf Fallberichten oder Erfahrungsberichten beruhen.

Legasthenie

Im Gegensatz zur auditiven Verarbeitungs- und Wahrnehmungsstörung ist die Lese-Rechtschreibstörung definiert als eine „umschriebene Beeinträchtigung der Lese-und Rechtschreibfähigkeiten, die nicht allein durch das Entwicklungsalter, durch unkorrigierte optische oder akustische Beeinträchtigung oder unangemessene Beschulung erklärbar ist. Sie ist nicht Folge anderer Störungen (wie z.B. Intelligenzminderung, grober neurologische Defizite, unkorrigierter Seh- oder Hörstörung oder emotionaler Störungen), aber sie kann zusammen mit diesen auftreten. Häufig treten andere klinische Symptome (wie z.B. Aufmerksamkeitsstörung oder Störungen des Sozialverhaltens) oder andere Entwicklungsstörungen (wie umschriebene Entwicklungsstörungen motorischer Funktionen oder des Sprechens und der Sprache) gemeinsam auf (s. hierzu u.a. 25). Sie gilt also als entwicklungsbiologisch und zentralnervös bedingte Störung des Erlernens des Lesens und Schreibens alphabetischer Schriftsprache (29).

Im Mittelpunkt der Legasthenieforschung stand zunächst die Erforschung der Ursachen bzw. die Erforschung jener Teilprozesse, die für das Erlernen des Schreibens und Lesens erforderlich sind (Teilleistungsschwächen). Es wurde dann zunehmend deutlich, dass bei legasthenen Kindern Probleme in der Zuordnung unterschiedlicher Lautvarianzen zu Phonemen und deren Repräsentanz durch Buchstaben bestehen. Die hierfür geforderte Leistung, nämlich die bewusste Lautanalyse, um den Code der gesprochenen Sprache in den Code der Schriftsprache zu transferieren (sprachlautanalytische–kognitive!) Feinoperationen – deren Fehlen beim Sprechen nicht unbedingt zu einer Kommunikationsstörung führt), gilt bei Legasthenikern als eingeschränkt bzw. gestört.

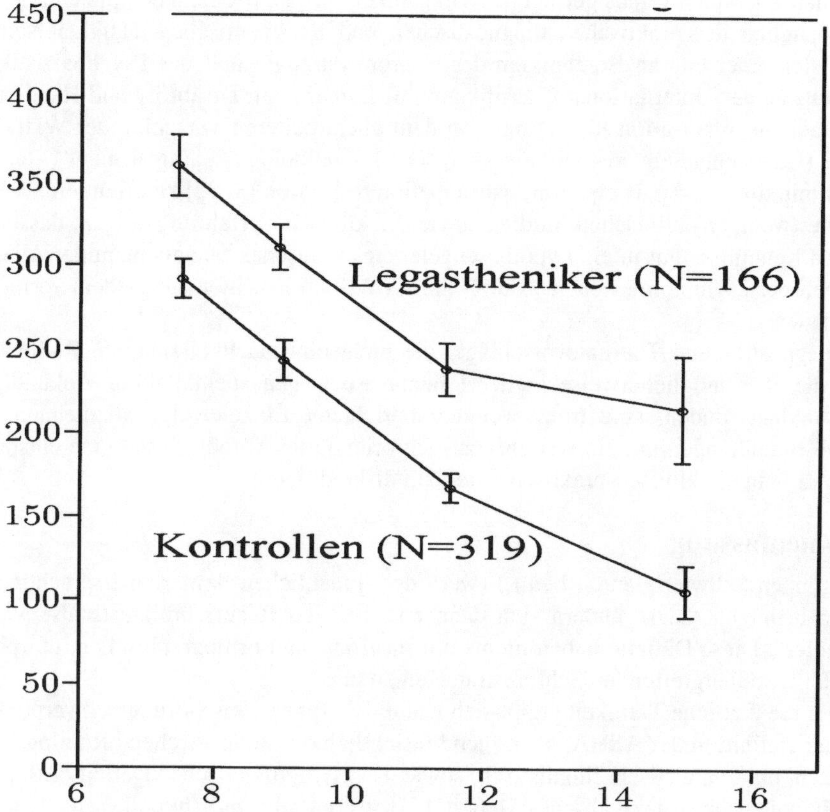

Abb. 1.1.3.1 Basale Fähigkeiten der auditiven Verarbeitung und Wahrnehmung bei Kindern mit / ohne Legasthenie. Auf der x–Achse ist das Alter der Kinder aufgetragen, auf der Y-Achse der Wert (ohne Einheit), der sich aus der Summierung von 5 Testergebnissen (Frequenzauflösung, Intensitätsauflösung, temporale Kodierung, monaurale Reihung, binaurale Reihung) ergibt. Deutlich ist zu sehen, dass mit zunehmendem Alter sowohl bei normalen wir bei legasthenen Kindern die basalen auditiven Verarbeitungsfähigkeiten immer besser werden, und dass legasthene Kindern einen Rückstand von ca. 2-3 Jahre aufweisen.

Ausblick

Klinisch wie wissenschaftlich sind die vielen offenen Fragen zur AVWS sowie zur Legasthenie unbefriedigend. Wie in vielen Bereichen der Medizin (s. hierzu u.a. die Cochrane-Library), beruhen also derzeit diagnostische wie therapeutische Maßnahmen auf einer Reihe von Hypothesen (hierarchisches Stufenmodell der auditiven Verarbeitung und Wahrnehmung, Abgrenzbarkeit von „bottom up“ versus „top-down“ Prozessen, Wirksamkeit von störungsspezifischen Therapien versus geringerer Wirksamkeit unspezifischer Therapien etc.).

Bezüglich der praktischen diagnostischen und therapeutischen Tätigkeit scheint es sinnvoll, sich einerseits an Ergebnissen der Neurophysiologie und der Psychoakustik sowie andererseits an der „International Classifikation of Impairment, Disability and Handicap“ der Weltgesundheitsorganisation [8, 31] bzw. an dem überarbeiteten Vorschlag der WHO gemäß ICIDH-2 (Unterscheidung in „Disease or disorder / pathology“, „impairment“, „activity / activity limitation“ und participation / participation restriction [8, 32] zu orientieren.

Die (wenigen) klinischen Studien sowie die klinische Erfahrung zeigen, dass sich die bisherigen Kenntnisse gut in ein hypothesengeleitetes klinisches Management der AVWS und damit auch der „symptomatischen“, durch die AVWS verursachten Legasthenieformen integrieren lassen.

Diagnostik- und Therapievorschläge, die nicht eine nachvollziehbare Rationale aufweisen, die aber möglicherweise in der Laienpresse wegen spektakulärer Ankündigungen großen Anklang finden, sind trotz eventuell berichteter Einzelerfolge abzulehnen, da sie ernsthafte Bemühungen um ein wissenschaftlich orientiertes Vorgehen und eine entsprechende Integration in die klinisch-praktische Medizin diskreditieren.

Zusammenfassung

AVWS können Schwierigkeiten beim Erwerb der sprachlichen bzw. schriftsprachlichen Fähigkeiten bedingen. Diese äußern sich dann z.B. bei den Rechtschreibtests als „Wahrnehmungsfehler“. Diese Defizite haben nichts mit insuffizienten orthographischen, morphematischen oder wortübergreifenden Schreibstrategien zu tun.

Für die ärztliche Tätigkeit ergibt sich u.a. die Aufgabe, den Störungsschwerpunkt (z.B. gemäß der Definition der ASHA, aber auch hinsichtlich des auditorischen „Routings“ (nichtlinguistisch, prä–linguistisch, linguistisch) sowie das „symptomatische“ Defizit (z.B. phonetisches, phonologisches, lexikalisches Defizit 15) zu ermitteln und (hypothesengeleitet) Therapievorschläge zu unterbreiten.

Literatur

1. Arnold GE (1951) Die Untersuchung zentraler Hörstörungen mit neuen Hörprüfmethoden. Arch Ohren-, Nasen-, und Kehlkopfheilkunde 157:521
2. Bellis TJ (Hrsg.) (1996) Assessment and management of central auditory processing disorders in the educational setting – from science to practice. Singular, San Diego
3. Bess FH, Humes LE (1995) Audiology – the fundamentals, 2. Aufl.. Williams & Wilkins, Baltimore
4. Chermak GD, Hall JW, Baran JA, Sloan C, Musiek;FE (1997) Diagnosis and mamagement of CAPD and ADHD.
5. Chermak GD, Musiek FE (1997) Central auditory processing disorders – new perspectives. Singular, San Diego

6. Cramer B (1990) Verhaltenstherapeutisches Trainingsprogramm für fehlhörige Kinder. Deutsche Gesellschaft für Verhaltenstherapie, Tübingen
7. Dougherty RF, Cynader MS, Bjornson BH, Edgell D, Giaschi DE (1998) Dichotic pitch: a new stimulus distinguishes normal and dyslectic auditory function. NeuroReport 9:3001-3005
8. Frattali CM (1998) Assessing functional outcomes: an overview. Sem Speech Hear 19 (3):209-221
9. Fujisaki H, Kawashima T (1970) Some experiments on speech perception and a model for the perceptual mechanisms. (Ann. Rep. Eng. Res. Instit.; 29, Univ. Tokyo, Faculty of Engineering)
10. Greiner G, Conreaux C (1977) Neurogene und zentrale Hörstörungen. In: Berendes J, Link R, Zöllner F (Hrsg.) Hals-Nasen-Ohrenheilkunde in Praxis und Klinik, 2. Auflage, Band III/3. Thieme, Stuttgart
11. Hari R, Kiesila P (1996) Deficit of temporal auditory processing in dyslexic adults. Neurosci Lett 205:138-140
12. Hellgren L, Gillberg IC, Bagenholm A, Gillberg C (1994) Children with deficits in attention, motor control and perception (DAMP) almost grown up: psychiatric and personality disorders at age 16 years. J Child Psychol Psychiatry 35:1255-1271
13. Hesse G, Nelting M, Brehmer D, Lemmermann E, Ptok M (1998) Benefit-, Effektivitäts- und Effizienznachweis therapeutischer Verfahren bei zentral-auditiven Verarbeitungs- und Wahrnehmungsstörungen. Sprache-Stimme-Gehör 22:194-198
14. Jansen H, Mannhaupt G, Marx H, Skowronek H (1999) Bielefelder Screening zur Früherkennung von Lese-Rechtschreibschwierigkeiten (BISC). Hogrefe, Göttingen, Bern, Toronto, Seattle
15. Jerger J (1997) Rethinking global behavioural tests of central auditory processing. Asha 7:3-6
16. Katz J, Stecker N, Donald H (Hrsg.) (1992) Central auditory processing – a transdisciplinary view. Mosby, St. Louis
17. Lauer N (1999) Zentral-auditive Verarbeitungsstörungen im Kindesalter – Grundlagen – Klinik – Diagnostik – Therapie. Thieme, Stuttgart
18. Lehnhardt E (1996) Praxis der Audiometrie, 7.Auflage Georg Thieme Verlag, Stuttgart, New York
19. Ptok M (1997) Das schwerhörige Kind. Dt Ärztebl 1997;94:A-1932-1937
20. Ptok M, Fischer B (2000) Auditory low level deficits in children with dyslexia. ARO Midwinter Meeting Astracts 23:(Im Druck)
21. Ptok M, Ptok A (1996) Audiometrie im Säuglings- und Kindesalter, Teil 4: Untersuchungen zur auditiven Verarbeitung und Wahrnehmung. HNO Aktuell 4:271-276
22. Sawusch JR (1977) Peripheral and central processes in selective adaptation of place of articulation in stop consonants. J Acoust Soc Am 62:738-750
23. Sawusch JR, Gagnon DA (1995) Auditory coding, cues, and coherence in phonetic perception. J Exp Psychol Hum Percept Perform 21:635-652
24. Schorn K, Stecker M (1994) Hörprüfungen. In: Naumann HH, Helms J, Herberhold C, Kastenabuer C (eds) Oto-Rhino-Larnygologie in Klinik und Praxis, Band 1. Thieme, Stuttgart
25. Schulte-Körne G, Ptok M (1998) Lese-Rechtschreibstörung (Editorial). Sprache-Stimme-Gehör 22:1-2
26. Signer M (1979) Hörtraining bei auditiv differenzierungsschwachen Kindern, 2. Aufl.. Haupt, Stuttgart
27. Sloan C (1986) Treating auditory processing difficulties in children. Singualar, San Diego
28. Sussman JE (1993) Focused attention during selective adaptation along a place of articulation continuum. J Acoust Soc Am 93:488-498
29. Warnke A, Wewetzer C, Grimm T (1998) Lese-Rechtschreibstörungen: Begriff – neurobiologische Befunde – Prognose. Sprache-Stimme-Gehör 22:3-7
30. Witton C, Talcott JB, Hansen PC, Richardson AJ, Griffiths TD, Rees A, Stein JF, Green GG (1998) Sensitivity to dynamic auditory and visual stimuli predicts nonword reading ability in both dyslexic and normal readers. Curr Biol 8:791-797

31. World Health Organization (1980) International classification of impairments, disabilities and handicaps.
32. World Health Organization (1997) International classification of impairment, disability and handicap (ICIDH-2).
33. Wright BA, Lombardino LJ, King WM, Puranik CS, Leonard CM, Merzenich MM (1997) Deficits in auditory temporal and spectral resolution in language-impaired children. Nature 387(6629):176-178

1.1.4 Die Normalität der primären Sprachentwicklung – mögliche Zusammenhänge mit der Lese-Rechtschreib-Störung (Legasthenie)

Eberhard Kruse

Unsere Sprache ist bekanntlich die einzige spezifisch menschliche Leistung, wichtigstes Instrument unserer Kommunikation und letztlich Basis unseres gesamten Bildungssystems. Um so erstaunlicher ist deshalb, wie selbstverständlich im allgemeinen von dem normalen Erwerb der Sprache und der sekundären Sprachleistungen des Lesens und Schreibens ausgegangen wird. Fragt man, warum wir unsere „Muttersprache", bei uns also Deutsch sprechen, erhält man meist schulterzuckend zur Antwort, weil wir halt hier wohnen. Dies ist sicherlich zutreffend, aber deswegen noch längst nicht hinreichend für den normalen Erwerb der Lautsprache.

Sprache – und hierauf werde ich später noch kurz eingehen – Sprache ist ein funktionelles Endprodukt, und als solches abhängig von kritischen Vorentwicklungen und Vorleistungen. Die Kenntnis der *Normalität* in der Entwicklung solcher kritischen Vorentwicklungen und Vorleistungen stellt meines Erachtens generell das beste Raster dar zur Früherkennung von Normabweichungen und hierüber zur gezielten Frühförderung mit anerkannt besten Förderungsresultaten.

Hierfür liefert die Pädaudiologie ein beeindruckendes Beispiel, führt doch jede zu spät, d.h. nach dem 6. Lebensmonat erkannte angeborene Hörstörung zwangsläufig zu einer mehr oder minder gravierenden Störung auch der Sprachentwicklung. Dies ist theoretisch weithin bereits Allgemeinwissen, wobei die bundesdeutsche Früherfassungs-Realität allerdings eine noch sehr deutlich andere Sprache spricht. Dabei wissen wir heute, daß Kinder, deren Hörstörung bis spätestens zum 6. Lebensmonat diagnostiziert wurde, bei entsprechender sinnesspezifischer Förderung entweder einen normalen natürlichen Spracherwerb aufweisen bzw. eine ihrer individuellen Intelligenz entsprechende Sprachentwicklung. (23)

Umgekehrt aber – und diesen Weg möchte ich nun mit Ihnen gehen – umgekehrt machen sich aber solche Hörstörungen sehr früh in Abweichungen insbesondere der *präverbalen Sprachentwicklung* bemerkbar, deren Beachtung uns meines Erachtens beispielsweise recht sicher eine nun in der Tat *rechtzeitige* Diagnostik angeborener Hörstörungen deutlich innerhalb des 1. Lebenshalbjahres erlauben würde im Unterschied zu allen jahrzehntelangen Versuchen der Neugeborenen-Untersuchungen und apparativen Vorsorge-Screenings innerhalb der kindlichen Vorsorge-Untersuchungen. (14)

1. Bedeutung der präverbalen Sprachentwicklung

Die umfangreiche Literatur über die frühe Phase des Spracherwerbs, die präverbale Sprachentwicklung des 1. Lebensjahres, bezieht sich entweder auf prosodische Spektralanalysen und Beschreibung insbesondere emotionaler, interaktionaler oder linguistischer Charakteristika der Schrei- und Lall-Periode (5,7,8,15,16,17,18,19) oder aber auch spezieller auf die eigentliche Lall-Entwicklung, nun aber undifferenziert und typischerweise mit Gewichtung vor allem der 2. Lallphase. (11)

Diese eher formal-deskriptive Beschreibung der Lallphase findet sich im wesentlichen unverändert seit den Klassikern von Fröschels (9) und Seeman (20) über das Handbuch von Luchsinger und Arnold (2; s.a. 16) bis hin in die heutige Generation der fachbezogenen Lehrbücher (3,4,22), ohne daß hieraus neue Konzepte einer Frühförderung sprachentwicklungsgestörter bzw. sprachentwicklungsgefährdeter Kinder entwickelt worden wären. Man hört vielmehr noch allzu oft, daß eine Sprachtherapie erst jenseits des 4. Lebensjahres notwendig sei, es wird sogar gelegentlich vor allzu frühen Interventionen gewarnt angesichts angeblicher Spontanremissionen. (21) Das ungute Wort einer „Spätentwicklung" scheint immer noch fröhliche Urständ zu feiern, und dies wohl nicht ganz unabhängig von den aktuellen Wirrungen einer „Gesundheits-Reform".

Nach unserer Ansicht (14) vollzieht sich dem gegenüber die Sprachentwicklung *entscheidend* in den ersten 4 Lebensjahren, was eine Sprachdiagnostik und ggf. Sprachtherapie notwendigerweise zwischen 0 und 4 Jahren zur Folge haben muß, der Phase der „primären Sprachentwicklung". (13)

1.1 Sprache als funktionelles Endprodukt

Wie erwähnt, betrachten wir Sprache als ein *funktionelles Endprodukt*, das entsprechend kritischer Vorentwicklungen und Vorleistungen bedarf.

Historisch betrachtet, wurde Ende der 60-iger Jahre mit dem Konzept der *Teilleistungsstörungen* (10) deutlich, daß Sprache ohne hirnfunktionellen Kontext nicht hinreichend zu diagnostizieren und folglich auch nicht hinreichend zu therapieren war. In diesen Kontext gehört auch die Definition einer Legasthenie als folgenschwerer Störung der sekundären Sprachleistungen. Seitdem zählt die neuro- bzw. entwicklungspsychologische Testung zum differentialdiagnostischen Standard-Inventar, was angesichts der kindlichen Kooperationsbedingung regelhaft allerdings erst jenseits des 4. Lebensjahres nutzbar war und ist, aus unserer Sicht also wiederum deutlich zu spät.

Entscheidend neue Impulse resultierten für uns dann in den 80-iger Jahren aus den Arbeiten der St. Gallener Arbeitsgruppe um Frau Affolter (1), die aufbauend auf dem entwicklungspsychologischen Modell von Piaget die Bedeutung der *Wahrnehmung* herausgestellt hat, insbesondere die für uns seinerzeit absolut neue Gewichtung der Taktil-Kinästhetik für Physiologie und Pathologie der kindlichen Entwicklung generell und der Sprachentwicklung im Besonderen. Es klingt für uns heute geradezu trivial, daß die angemessene Information und ein entsprechendes Instruktionsverständnis Voraussetzung sein müssen für ein Teilleistungs-Handeln und somit auch für die testgebundene Diagnostik.

Um nun aber wiederum etwas wahrnehmen zu können, benötigen wir in unserer hier thematisierten Betrachtungsweise sprachspezifische *Sinnesreize* als Voraussetzung jeglicher, zumal kommunikativer Interaktion mit unserer jeweiligen Umgebung. Die kritischen Entwicklungsperioden insbesondere der für die Sprachentwicklung wesentlichen Sinnessysteme des Fühlens und des Hörens, aber auch für das als erstes und bislang am besten erforschte Seh-System liegen nach heutiger Kenntnis im 1. Lebensjahr, nach persönlicher Überzeugung im ersten Lebens-Halbjahr. (14)

Aus dieser Abfolge wird nun nachvollziehbar, warum unseres Erachtens die Diagnostik und Therapie einer Sprachentwicklungsstörung innerhalb der ersten 4 Lebensjahre, der „primären Sprachentwicklung", zu erfolgen hat, und eben nicht erst jenseits des 4. Lebensjahres an dem dann fast für jeden Laien entwicklungsauffälligen funktionellen Endprodukt.

1.2 Normalität der präverbalen Sprachentwicklung

Postnatal – und hierauf möchte ich mich beschränken – postnatal beginnt die Sprachentwicklung mit der *„Schreiperiode"*, dem allbekannten „ersten Schrei". Aus sprachfunktioneller Sicht handelt es sich dabei um die *Phonation* als Klangbasis des Sprechens zum Transfer über die kommunikative Distanz hin zum Interaktionspartner.

Um die funktionelle Bedeutung dieser frühen Phase für die Wahrnehmungs- und Sprachentwicklung zu verdeutlichen, sei zunächst auf die nachfolgende Entwicklungsstufe verwiesen, die *Lallperiode.* unterteilt in 2 Abschnitte, der „1. bzw. 2. Lallphase". Diese Lall-Entwicklung wird m.E. weithin noch erheblich unterschätzt in ihrer Relevanz nicht nur für den Verlauf der Sprachentwicklung, sondern vor allem für die Frühdiagnostik von *Wahrnehmungsstörungen* und der kindlichen Entwicklung insgesamt.

2. Entwicklungsphysiologische Aspekte des Lallens

Zur Normalität der Lall-Entwicklung sind 3 Aspekte besonders hervorzuheben:

1. ist das Lallen eine originäre Entwicklungsleistung des *Kindes*, keine Nachahmung einer Vorgabe von Erwachsenen. Offensichtlich handelt es sich bei der Auslösung um die Aktivierung einer *Anlage*, eines Moduls im Sinne der linguistischen Theorie des Nativismus. (12)
2. ist das Lallen offensichtlich *weltweit identisch*, also zunächst völlig unabhängig von der jeweiligen Sprachumgebung. Jedenfalls gibt es wohl kein chinesisches, englisches oder deutsches Lallen; es gibt nur „das" Lallen als wohlgemerkt kindsspezifischer Leistung.
3. ist das Lallen nicht gleich bei Geburt vorhanden, sondern entwickelt sich erst ab etwa dem 2. Lebensmonat. Die Frage nach dem „Warum" läßt sich prinzipiell immer in der gleichen Weise beantworten, daß dann nämlich für die Entwicklung einer spezifischen Leistung kritische *Vorentwicklungen* stattfinden müssen.

Was sind nun diese notwendigen Vorleistungen für das Lallen, was passiert in diesem frühen Alter vorher?

2.1 Entwicklungskritische Vorleistungen des Lallens

Wie bereits angedeutet, erfolgt als erstes die *Phonation* als ein akustisches Signal, das allseits bekannte Aktionen, oftmals Hektik in der unmittelbaren Umgebung des Kindes stimuliert mit zunächst haptischer bzw. taktil-kinästhetischer und visueller Wahrnehmbarkeit.

Zweitens findet die frühe Ernährung statt, funktionell vor allem das *Saugen* und *Schlucken*, anders ausgedrückt: ein Training der orofacialen und speziell nun der *intraoralen Motorik.*

Die Kombination dieser beiden Vorleistungen ergibt dann das *Lallen.*

2.3 Entwicklung der intraoralen Sensomotorik

Das Training der intraoralen Motorik beim Saugen und Schlucken bedeutet nun wiederum *Koordination, Optimierung* und *Automatisierung* als Prinzipien des Lernens. *Lernen* benötigt seinerseits mindestens 2 Komponenten, zum einen die *Aktion*, hier also die Motorik, zum anderen ein *Feedback* über eben diese Aktion, über den Effekt dieser Motorik.

Diese Zusammenhänge kennzeichnet man mit dem Begriff der *„Sensomotorik"*, hier also der „intraoralen Sensomotorik". Die Rückmeldung erfolgt in diesem Falle *taktil-kinästhetisch*, über unser Fühlsystem, als taktil-kinästhetische Wahrnehmung. Damit wird ein funktioneller Regelkreis etabliert, mit dem das Kind seine eigene Entwicklung stimuliert im Sinne der Koordination, Optimierung und Automatisierung.

Störungen dieses Regelkreises haben prinzipiell nur 2 Ursachen: entweder eine Störung der *Aktion*, hier der Motorik, beispielsweise als Lähmungen, oder aber bei regelrechter Motorik Störungen der *Sensorik* als hier nun einer *Fühlstörung*, einer Sinnesstörung.

Störungen der kommunikativ relevanten Sinnesmodalitäten haben bekanntlich jeweils eine mittelgradige und eine maximale Ausprägung. Im Hörsystem wäre die mittelgradige Störung bekanntlich die Schwerhörigkeit, im Sehsystem die Sehbehinderung. Die maximale Ausprägung wäre im Hörsystem die Gehörlosigkeit, im visuellen System die Blindheit. Im Fühlsystem könnte unseres Erachtens das „hyperkinetische Syndrom" einer mittelgradigen und der „Autismus" der maximalen Ausprägung einer *taktil-kinästhetischen* Störung entsprechen.

Spezifischer Marker zur Früherkennung einer taktil-kinästhetischen Störung ist deshalb die meist deutliche *Verzögerung* im Beginn der Lallperiode. Zugleich wird eine mehr oder minder ausgeprägte *Ernährungsstörung* offenkundig, meist als „Schluckstörung" mit der Notwendigkeit gelegentlich auch einer Sonden-Ernährung und der Indikation zur logopädischen Therapie im Sinne der orofacialen Regulationstherapie nach Castillo-Morales mit intraoraler Stimulation.

2.4 Erste Lallphase oder Entwicklung der auditiven Eigenwahrnehmung

Wie geht es nun weiter mit der normalen Sprachentwicklung, wenn also das Lallen zeitgemäß eingetreten ist? Wiederum erfolgt ein *Lernvorgang* mit typisch kindlicher Prägung, gekennzeichnet nämlich durch beneidenswerte *Kreativität* und spontanen *Explorationsdrang*. (1,18)

Das Lallen beinhaltet eine Schallproduktion als Aktion, die zur Auslösung des Lernvorganges wiederum ein Feedback benötigt. Dieses Feedback nutzt naturgemäß für ein Schallereignis den auditiven Modus mit hier also der Entwicklung der auditiven Wahrnehmung, noch spezieller: der *auditiven Eigenwahrnehmung*.

Der Effekt dieser auditiven Eigenwahrnehmung ist ebenfalls kindstypisch die Aktions-Wiederholung, aber eben keine langweilig einfache Wiederholung, sondern nun eine *kreative* Variabilität und Explorationsfreude mit dem Ergebnis nicht nur eines quantitativen Zuwachses des Lallens, sondern auch der zunehmenden qualitativen Differenzierung.

Diese Kombination mit Zunahme des Lallens sowohl in quantitativer wie qualitativer Hinsicht nennen wir *„Lallcrescendo"*, und dieses Lallcrescendo tritt normalerweise zeitlich zwischen dem 3. bis 5. Lebensmonat auf. Fehlt dieses Lallcrescendo, liegt eine Störung dieses *auditiven* Regelkreises vor mit wiederum nur 2 prinzipiell möglichen Ursachen:

Entweder handelt es sich um eine periphere Hörstörung, die wir heute hinreichend sicher spätestens nach der Geburt objektivieren können, oder um eine Störung der Sensorik, hier also der auditiven Wahrnehmung bzw. der auditiven Eigen- oder Selbstwahrnehmung.

Die *Schlußfolgerung* muß hier also lauten: fehlt das Lallcrescendo, ist unverzüglich eine Hördiagnostik erforderlich, kein – aus meiner Sicht gar nicht existentes – Hörscreening, sondern eine fachärztliche, d. h. heute eine phoniatrisch-pädaudiologische *Diagnostik*. Je nach Ergebnis wäre die therapeutische Konsequenz entweder die Hörgeräteversorgung bzw. Cochlea-Implantation mit hörspezifischer Frühförderung oder aber bei peripherer Normalhörigkeit ein auditives Wahrnehmungstraining, was ebenfalls in dieser frühen Altersstufe durchaus methodisch leistbar ist.

Mit Kenntnis des Lallcrescendos verfügen wir somit über ein ausgesprochen sicheres Instrument zur absolut rechtzeitigen Früherfassung angeborener kindlicher Hörstörungen.

2.5 Zweite Lallphase oder Entwicklung der auditiven Fremdwahrnehmung

Erst jetzt, etwa zu Beginn des 2. Lebenshalbjahres, kommen nun endlich wir Erwachsenen in der Sprachentwicklung des Kindes zum Zuge, indem wir nämlich regelhaft und ohne jede Ausnahme etwas ganz Typisches und absolut Richtiges tun: wir begeben uns auf das Entwicklungsniveau des Kindes, d.h.: wir lallen mit. Im Ergebnis nun lallen nun zwei als Voraussetzung für den nächsten Entwicklungsschritt, der *präverbalen Interaktion.*

Diese präverbale Interaktion (18) kann nur gelingen, wenn das Kind eine neue Leistung zu entwickeln beginnt, nämlich die *auditive Fremdwahrnehmung*. Es beginnt auditiv wahrzunehmen, daß nicht nur es selbst, sondern auch die anderen mit ihrem Lallen einen Schall produzieren. Hieraus entsteht ein strukturierter und systematischer *Interaktionsrhythmus* im Sinne eines „Frage-Antwort-Verhaltens". Das Kind lallt und wartet dann, bis der Erwachsene widerlallt, und erst dann setzt das Kind wieder ein usw. usf.

Das *systematische* Auftreten dieses Interaktionsrhythmus gilt uns bislang in Ermangelung einer objektiven Meßbarkeit als Beleg für die dann offenbar entwickelte auditive Fremdwahrnehmung als notwendiger Voraussetzung für eine Entwicklung in die Sprache der Umgebung. Erst mit der entwickelten auditiven Fremdwahrnehmung, also etwa ab dem 5.-6. Lebensmonat beginnt der Weg in die Sprache der Umgebung, in unsere *„Muttersprache"* Erst jetzt, mit Beginn des 2. Lebenshalbjahres, können nun endlich wir Erwachsenen *eigen-aktiv* in die Gestaltung der Sprachentwicklung des Kindes eingreifen mit Induktion von Silbenverdoppelungen wie „ma-ma" oder „pa-pa", den *„Lallworten"* als allerdings weiterhin *präverbalen* Lautäußerungen.

2.6 Übergang Lallperiode/Einwort-Phase

Während ein Kind mit kongenital hochgradiger Hörstörung bzw. Resthörigkeit die 2. Lallphase über die alternative Sinnes-Kombination visuell / taktil-kinästhetisch fast unauffällig absolvieren kann, bleibt ihm der Übergang in die eigentliche *verbale* Phase, die Phase der „Einwort-Sätze", ohne therapeutische Hilfe versperrt.

Dieser Übergang sollte normalerweise um das 1. Lebensjahr herum, also um den 1. Geburtstag herum erfolgen mit physiologischer Varianz allerdings bis etwa spätestens zum 15. Lebensmonat und nicht, wie meist noch in der Literatur angegeben, bis zum 18. Lebensmonat. (13) Anderenfalls wäre hier nämlich allerspätestens eine Hördiagnostik höchst dringlich, da im pathologischen Fall sich die Diagnostik einer angeborenen Hörstörung um fast 1 Jahr verspätet hätte bei wohlgemerkt mit Kenntnis des Lall-Crescendos an sich möglicher früherer Diagnostik. *Ein* verpaßtes Jahr in dieser hochdynamischen Entwicklungsphase reduziert gravierend das individuelle Optimum in der Sprachentwicklung eines Kindes mit allen weiteren Nachteilen einer solchen unnötigen, *vermeidbaren* Deprivation.

3. Verbale Phase der primären Sprachentwicklung

Ist der Übergang in die verbale Phase allerdings regulär gelungen, wird man sich an dem Fortgang der Sprachentwicklung vom Einwort über Zwei- und Mehrfach-Wörtern bis hin zu komplexen Sätzen und kindlichem Erzähldrang orientieren mit besonderer Beachtung etwa der Altersstufe um das 3. Lebensjahr mit seiner physiologischen Sprechunflüssigkeit als stottersensibler Risikophase. Abschluß der primären Sprachentwicklung wäre der 4. Geburtstag, also das vollendete 4. Lebensjahr mit dann normaler Artikulation aller Laute, meines Erachtens auch der S-Laute, und einer altersgemäßen kindlichen Grammatik (6); kurzum: ein solches Kind müßte für Fremde einwandfrei verstehbar sein.

Natürlich folgt dann noch eine sekundäre Phase der Sprachentwicklung bis hin zum Abschluß im Alter von ca. 12 bis 14 Jahren, dem Zeitpunkt der fixierten hirnfunktionellen Dominanz.

4. Prinzipien der Wahrnehmungsentwicklung

Entscheidende Voraussetzung für eine normale und natürliche Sprachentwicklung ist somit zusammenfassend die Normalität der *Wahrnehmungsentwicklung*. Ohne normale Wahrnehmung kann sich keine „Muttersprache" entwickeln, bleibt die Sprachentwicklung zumindest defizitär.

Nach Piaget umfaßt die normale Wahrnehmungsentwicklung 3 Komponenten:
die Entwicklung *Modalität* als Ausreifung der einzelnen Sinnessysteme,
die Entwicklung der *Intermodalität* mit Verknüfung der einzelnen Sinnesmodalitäten, und
die Entwicklung der *Serialität* als 3. Wahrnehmungsdimension in Raum und Zeit.

Intermodalität und Serialität basieren auf der *Modalität*, auf der normalen Ausreifung jedes einzelnen funktionsrelevanten Sinnessystems, für die Kommunikation also vorrangig des Fühlens, des Hörens und des Sehens. Störungen der Modalität führen demnach zwangsläufig zu Störungen in der Intermodalität und wohl auch der Serialität

Sinnesstörungen müssen deshalb *früh* diagnostiziert und *früh* therapiert werden unter Beachtung nämlich ihrer *„sensitiven oder kritischen Entwicklungsperioden"*, die für alle Sinnessysteme im 1. Lebensjahr liegen, vermutlich sogar im 1. Lebenshalbjahr. (14) Von den angeborenen Hörstörungen wissen wir längst, wie effektiv sich eine so frühe Förderung insbesondere auf die Qualität der natürlichen Sprachentwicklung auswirkt. (14,23)

Diagnostik von Wahrnehmungsstörungen ist also gleichzusetzen mit sehr, sehr früher Diagnostik, einer primär fachärztlichen Diagnostik, noch präziser: einer phoniatrisch-pädaudiologischen Diagnostik. (14) Sind schon Hörstörungen in dieser frühen Altersstufe deutlich weniger auffällig als Sehstörungen, haben wir derzeit noch ungleich größere Probleme in der Frühdiagnostik taktil-kinästhetischer Störungen.

5. Relevanz der primären Sprachentwicklung für die Legasthenie

Vor diesem Hintergrund insbesondere der präverbalen Sprachentwicklung und ihrer engen Verknüpfung mit der kommunikationsspezifischen Wahrnehmungsentwicklung werden auch denkbare Zusammenhänge mit der Störung der *sekundären Sprachleistungen* des Lesens und der Rechtschreibung, der Legasthenie erkennbar. Offensichtlich handelt es sich nämlich auch bei der Legasthenie um die Störung eines „funktionellen Endprodukts", das zwar in aller Regel erst in der 2. Grundschulklasse, also im Alter von 8 – 9 Jahren diagnostiziert wird, vermutlich aber ungleich früher entstanden sein könnte, nämlich möglicherweise in der Phase insbesondere der *serialen* Wahrnehmungsentwicklung und somit wiederum deutlich innerhalb des 1. Lebensjahres.

Wir möchten deshalb mit diesen Ausführungen – und unter Verweis auf eine offensichtlich sinnvolle Kooperation mit unserem Gebiet der Phoniatrie und Pädaudiologie als hochspezialisierter Fachmedizin für Kommunikationsstörungen – die Aufmerksamkeit insbesondere der Legasthenie-Forschung auf die Analyse dieser frühen vorsprachlichen Entwicklungsphasen lenken. Wir erwarten hieraus nicht nur direkte Stimuli für neue präventive Therapieansätze, sondern durchaus auch neue Einsichten in die Pathophysiologie und Aetiopathogenese der Lese- und Rechtschreib-Störung.

Literatur

1. Affolter, F.: Wahrnehmung, Wirklichkeit und Sprache. Neckar-Verlag, Villingen-Schwenningen, 1987
2. Arnold, G.E.: Die Sprache und ihre Störungen. In: Luchsinger, R., Arnold, G.E.: Handbuch der Stimm- und Sprachheilkunde, Band 2. 3. Auflage. Springer, Wien New York, 1970
3. Biesalski, P., Frank, F. (Hrsg) Phoniatrie – Pädaudiologie. 2. Auflage. Thieme, Stuttgart New York, 1994
4. Böhme, G. (Hrsg) Sprach-, Sprech-, Stimm- und Schluckstörungen, Bd. 1. 3. Auflage. Fischer, Stuttgart Jena Lübeck Ulm, 1997
5. Bruner, J.S.: Wie das Kind sprechen lernt. Hans Huber, Bern 1987
6. Clahsen, H.: Normale und gestörte Kindersprache. Linguistische Untersuchungen zum Erwerb von Syntax und Morphologie. Benjamins, Amsterdam 1988
7. D´Odorico, L., Cassibba, R., Salerni, N. (1997) Temporal relationships between gaze and vocal behavior in prelinguistic and linguistic communication. J. Psycholing Res. 26:539-556
8. Elias, G., Broerse, J. (1996) Developmental changes in the incidence and likelihood of simultaneous talk during the first two years: a question of function. J. Child Lang. 23:201-217
9. Fröschels, E.: Lehrbuch der Sprachheilkunde. 2. Auflage. Deuticke, Leipzig Wien, 1925
10. Graichen, J. (1973) Teilleistungsschwächen, dargestellt an Beispielen aus dem Bereich der Sprachbenutzung. Z. Kinder-Jugendpsychiat. 1:113-143
11. Grimm, H.: Störungen der Sprachentwicklung. Hogrefe, Verlag für Psychologie, Göttingen Bern Toronto Seattle, 1999
12. Kanngießer, S.: Anlagebedingungen und Devianzen der Sprachbeherrschung. In: Kriz, J. (Hrsg) Sprachentwicklungsstörungen. Theoretische Modelle und therapeutische Praxis. Patholinguistica 13. Wilhelm Fink, München, 1984
13. Kiese-Himmel, C. (1999) Überlegungen zur psychologischen Frühdiagnostik von Sprachentwicklungsstörungen. Kindheit und Entwicklung 8:92-99
14. Kruse, E.: Aufgaben und Probleme interdisziplinärer Frühförderung aus der Sicht der Phoniatrie und Pädaudiologie. In: Kröhnert, O. (Hrsg) Modelle interdisziplinärer Frühförderung zur Begabungsentfaltung auf der Grundlage eines hörgerichteten Spracherwerbs. Stiftung zur Förderung körperbehinderter Hochbegabter, Vaduz, 1991
15. Mandler, J.M.: Preverbal representation and language. In: Bloom, P., Peterson, A., Nadel, L., Garrett, M.F. (eds) Language and Space. MIT Press, Cambridge/MA London 1996
16. Martin, J.A.M.: Voice, Speech, and Language in the Child: Development and Disorder. Arnold, G.E., Winckel, F., Wyke, B.D. (eds) Disorders of Human Communication. Bd. 4. Springer, Wien New York 1981
17. Morgan, J.L. (1996) A rhythmic bias in preverbal speech segmentation. J. Memory Lang. 35:666-688
18. Papousek, H., Papousek, M.: Preverbal communication in humans and the genesis of culture. In: Segerstrale, U., Molnar, P. (eds.) Nonverbal Communication. Where nature meets culture. Erlbaum, Maheah/NJ, 1997
19. Schöler, H., Fromm, W., Kany, W. (Hrsg) Spezifische Sprachentwicklungsstörung und Sprachlernen. Univ.-Verlag Winter, Programm Edition Schindele, Heidelberg, 1998
20. Seeman, M.: Sprachstörungen bei Kindern. 3.Auflage. Volk und Gesundheit, Berlin, 1969
21. Tigges-Zuzock, C., Kohns, U. (1995) Sprachdiagnostik und Therapieindikation in der pädiatrischen Praxis. Der Kinderarzt 26:358-365

22. Wirth, G.: Sprachstörungen, Sprechstörungen, Kindliche Hörstörungen. Deutscher Ärzte-Verlag, Köln, 1994
23. Yoshinaga-Itano, C., Sedey A.L., Coulter, D.K., Mehl, A.L. (1998) Language of early- and later-identified children with hearing loss. Pediatrics 102:1161-1171

1.1.5 Sprachwahrnehmungsdefizite – ein Handicap für das Lesen- und Schreibenlernen

Helmut Breuer[1]

LRS schon in der Schultüte?

Mit welchem Erfolg ein Kind sprechen, später schreiben und lesen lernt und welche laut- und schriftsprachliche Kompetenz es dabei erreicht, hängt von psychosozialen und reifungsbedingten neurophysiologischen Bedingungen ab. *(Dummer-Smoch, L., 1996, 1993)*

Es ist sicher kein Zufall, dass alle Kinder der Welt normalerweise zwischen dem fünften und siebenten Lebensjahr damit beginnen, die schriftliche Form ihrer Muttersprache zu erlernen. Sie beherrschen zu diesem Zeitpunkt alle diejenigen sensomotorischen Fähigkeiten, um die sinnlich-wahrnehmbaren Modalitäten der gesprochenen Sprache zu differenzieren und zu realisieren. Die automatisierte Beherrschung dieser sprachbezogenen Wahrnehmungsleistungen ist eine notwendige Voraussetzung, um den Inhalt sprachlicher Zeichen zu erschließen. Ohne genaues Wahrnehmen von Sprache ist ein Verstehen von Sprache nicht möglich.

Am Ende des Vorschuljahres beherrschen die Kinder auch die für den Erwerb der Schriftsprache notwendigen lautsprachlichen Grundfertigkeiten auf der Laut-, Wort- und Satzebene. Auf der **Lautebene** wird vom Schulanfänger eine normgerechte Artikulation verlangt, damit er verstanden werden kann. Sprechmotorische Sicherheit benötigt er auch, um später beim Lesen- und Schreibenlernen Lautzeichen in Schriftzeichen und umgekehrt umsetzen zu können. Auf der **Wortebene** ist ein altersentsprechender Wortschatz nötig. Sein Reichtum bildet eine Grundlage für das Sprachverstehen und damit für die Weite und Tiefe des Denkens. Der verfügbare Wortschatz repräsentiert das Kommunikations- und Wissenspotential, eine Voraussetzung für den Lernerfolg in der Schule. Auf der **Satzebene** wird vom Schulanfänger verlangt, dass er seine Gedanken grammatisch-syntaktisch, d. h. logisch folgerichtig ausdrücken kann. Das setzt eine altersgemäße und automatisierte Beherrschung der Satzbildungsregeln und – wie beim Wortschatz – ein funktionierendes Sprachgedächtnis voraus. *(Breuer, H., und Weuffen, M., 1990)*

Eine prophylaktische Förderstrategie zur Einschränkung von Lernschwierigkeiten im Anfangsunterricht wird demzufolge einmal auf das individuelle Niveau der Sprachwahrnehmungsleistungen, zum anderen auf das lautsprachliche Niveau des Kindes gerichtet sein. Beide sind miteinander verbunden. In diesem Beitrag stehen die Sprachwahrnehmungsfunktionen, ihre Diagnose und Förderung im Vorschulalter und frühen Schulalter im Vordergrund.

Lernschwierigkeiten am Schulanfang

Etwa 14 bis 15% aller ABC-Schützen haben am Schulanfang massive Schwierigkeiten beim Lesen- und Schreibenlernen. Eigentlich sind es anfangs mehr. Während aber einige diese Schwierigkeiten mit Unterstützung ihrer engagierten Eltern und Lehrer überwinden und sie als Episoden bald vergessen, beginnen sie für die anderen zum ständigen Begleiter zu wer-

---

1 Dieser Beitrag fasst die Inhalte von Vortrag und Praxisseminar des Verfassers auf dem 13. Fachkongress zusammen.

den. Die Eltern sind ratlos, zumal in der bisherigen Entwicklung der Kinder vor dem Schuleintritt keine Anzeichen für ein Versagen in der Schule zu erkennen waren. Tief enttäuscht sind die Kinder, weil sie von den Misserfolgen ganz unerwartet betroffen werden, denn auch sie waren stolz darauf, endlich ein Schulkind zu sein. Es beherrscht auch sie der Gedanke: wer lesen, schreiben und rechnen kann, ist kein kleines Kind mehr. *(Kossow, H.-J., 1991)*

Darauf hinzuwirken, den Kindern am Schulanfang derartige Enttäuschungen möglichst zu ersparen, ist aus vielen Gründen notwendig, denn für ein Kind in diesem Alter haben *Lernerfolge* am Schulanfang den Charakter von *Lebenserfolgen* – mit allen damit verbundenen Konsequenzen für Befindlichkeit und Selbstbewusstsein, für Eigeninitiative und Risikobereitschaft. Ein Kind, dem die ersehnten Lernerfolge verwehrt bleiben, erlebt Frustrationen und Drangsale, weil es seine elementaren psychosozialen Grundbedürfnisse nach Liebe und Geborgenheit, nach Lob und Beistand, nach Erfahrungsgewinn, neuem Wissen und Können, nach Selbsttätigkeit und Eigenbestimmung nicht befriedigt bekommt.

Nicht alle Kinder, denen das Lesen- und Schreibenlernen in der Schule unerwartet Schwierigkeiten macht, haben verständnisvolle Eltern und Lehrer. Oft wird ihnen mangelnder Fleiß und Wille unterstellt, doch damit haben ihre Lernprobleme anfangs überhaupt nichts zu tun. Weil sich eine Lese-Rechtschreibschwäche – bei normaler Intelligenz des Kindes – erst im Grundschulunterricht zu erkennen gibt, werden spezielle Fördermaßnahmen in der Regel erst dann eingeleitet, wenn die Symptome des Versagens deutlich, hartnäckig und lange genug auftreten. Der Gedanke, dass es u. U. besser und möglich ist, den betreffenden Kindern vorbeugend zu helfen, spielt gegenwärtig noch kaum eine Rolle. Dabei stimmt jedermann der Erkenntnis zu, dass jedes Entwicklungsproblem eine Vorgeschichte hat, also in vorhergehenden Etappen der Entwicklung verwurzelt ist und entwicklungsfördernde Interventionen hier einsetzen müssen. Im Unterschied zu pädagogisch-psychologischen Problemlagen ist es bei medizinischen ganz selbstverständlich, vorbeugende Maßnahmen (Hygiene, Impfungen, Ernährung usw.) durchzuführen, um später eventuell auftretende Konfliktsituationen zu vermeiden. Im pädagogischen Bereich wird gegen prophylaktische Maßnahmen mit dem Argument vorgegangen, man würde den Kindern die Unbeschwertheit ihres Lebens nehmen und übersieht dabei, dass es nicht auf eine Förderung irgendwann ankommt, sondern zur rechten Zeit und mit dem richtigen Inhalt.

Zur Häufigkeit unerwarteter Schwierigkeiten beim Lesen- und Schreibenlernen

Um diese Frage zu beantworten, wurden 925 Lehrer, die 23.454 Schüler in den Klassen 1 und 2 unterrichten, befragt, wie viele ihrer Schüler beim Lesen- und Schreibenlernen unerwartet Probleme haben. Das Ergebnis zeigt Tabelle 1.1.5.1

Eine nächste Befragung von 40 Grundschullehrern hatte zu klären, wie viele Schüler es mit **beständigen** Lese-Rechtschreibproblemen zu tun haben. Es ging dabei darum, den Anteil jener Schüler zu ermitteln, die ohne eine besondere Förderung beim Lesen- und Schreibenlernen ihre Schwierigkeiten nicht zu überwinden imstande sind. Aus der Tabelle 1.1.5.2 geht hervor, dass sich dieser Anteil am Ende der Klasse 2 auf etwa 14 bis 15% reduziert hat.

Vergleiche mit Erhebungen in anderen Ländern zeigen, dass die ermittelten Anteile tendenziell gleich sind. Auch international ist der Anteil von Jungen unter der Gruppe der ABC-Schützen mit Lernschwierigkeiten deutlich höher als der der Mädchen. Das Problem der Schwierigkeiten ist offensichtlich weniger von didaktischen Besonderheiten oder vom Schulsystem abhängig. *(Ruoho, K., 1990, 1997)*

Anteil von Schülern 1. und 2. Klassen mit unerwarteten Schwierigkeiten beim Lesen- und Schreibenlernen	
Schwierigkeiten unterschiedlichster Art hatten von den 23.454 Schülern	26,5%
davon Mädchen	39,0%
davon Jungen	61,0%

Tabelle 1.1.5.1

Anteil von Kindern mit beständigen Schwierigkeiten beim Lesen und Schreibenlernen	
Von den in die Befragung einbezogenen 1.059 Schülern betrifft das	14,2%
davon Mädchen	38,0%
davon Jungen	62,0%

Tabelle 1.1.5.2

Die beim Schuleintritt bestimmende Lernmotivation bzw. die Grundeinstellung praktisch aller Schulanfänger gegenüber der Schule, dem Lernen usw. ist positiv. In der ersten Schulwoche wurden von uns Kinder (sie hatten alle vorher einen Kindergarten besucht) gefragt (im Rahmen einer Unterhaltung), wo es besser sei, im Kindergarten oder in der Schule. Abbildung 1.1.5.3 zeigt die Ergebnisse von 2 Klassen mit 48 Schülern. Die Befragung wurde nach dem ersten Schuljahr wiederholt. Es zeigt sich, dass die positive Primärmotivation gegenüber der Schule bei einigen Schülern abgeschwächt ist bzw. verloren geht. Das ist für die weitere Schullaufbahn dieser Kinder eine zusätzliche Belastung. *(Behrndt, S.-M., und Steffen, M., 1996)*

Die Funktion der sprachbezogenen Wahrnehmungen im Ensemble der Lernvoraussetzungen am Schulanfang.

Sprachwahrnehmungsdefizite subtilerer Art belasten den Schreib-Lese-Lernprozess, bleiben im Vorschulalter aber oft unerkannt. Als Beispiel dafür sei die Fähigkeit des Kindes genannt, klangähnliche Vokale und Konsonanten hörend zu differenzieren. Hat ein Schulanfänger noch Schwierigkeiten, die klangähnlichen aber bedeutungsunterscheidenden Konsonanten „g“ und „d“ im Inlaut der Wörter „Nagel“ und „Nadel“ zu unterscheiden, dann handelt er dennoch im Vorschulalter richtig, weil er sich an der Gesamtsituation orientiert. Bestimmte Situationscharakteristika helfen ihm gewissermaßen zu erkennen, welches Wort gesprochen wurde. Je intelligenter ein Kind ist, desto besser kann es im Spiel solche (phonematischen) Informationslücken schließen. Seine Schwäche bleibt unerkannt. Beim Lernen in der Schule fehlen u. U. diese zusätzlichen Orientierungen. Fehler sind die Folge.

Emotionale Beziehung von Schulanfängern gegenüber der Schule
(Angaben in%)

Schule wird erlebt	1. Schulwoche	Ende des 1. Schulhalbjahres
	97,5	50,0
	2,5	30,0
	---	20,0

Abb. 1.1.5.3

Folgende Sprachwahrnehmungsleistungen sind für das Erfassen und Realisieren der sinnlich-warnehmbaren Modalitäten der Laut- und Schriftsprache erforderlich:

1. Die Fähigkeit zur optischen Differenzierung und graphomotorischen Realisierung sprachlicher Zeichen

Die optische Differenzierungsfähigkeit ist weniger für den Erwerb der Lautsprache, dafür aber besonders wichtig für den Erwerb der Schriftsprache. Blindgeborene Kinder lernen bekanntlich nur gering verzögert sprechen, weil ihnen das Mundbild als Anhaltspunkt sprechmotorischer Nachahmung fehlt.

Einige Bemerkungen zur Abbildung 1.1.5.3: Die beiden Tassen sind unabhängig davon, ob der Henkel rechts oder links gerichtet ist, in ihrer Bedeutung gleich. Die Raum-Lage-Modalität für den Henkel (auf der einen Seite, auf der anderen Seite) ist unwesentlich, braucht vom Kind nicht beachtet zu werden. Die Lage des „Bogens“ aber erhält beim Lesen- und Schreibenlernen eine entscheidende Bedeutung. Von seiner Raum-Lage-Modalität hängt es ab, ob es sich um ein „b“, „d“, „q“ oder „p“ handelt. In ähnlicher Weise erhalten Häufigkeits-, Größen-, Richtungs- und andere optische Details ihren besonderen Wert, um sprachli-

Die optische Differenzierungsfähigkeit

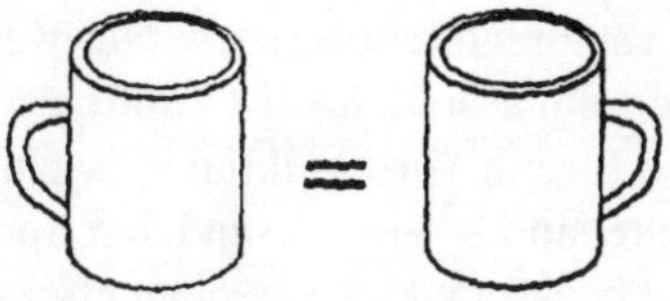

d ≠ b m ≠ n

p ≠ q

ℓ ≠ l

27 ≠ 72 69 ≠ 96

HAUS **RAND** **WAND**
HAUS BAND WAND
LAUS **SAND**
RAUS **LAND**

Modalitäten:
Raum-Lage (hier, dort, oben, unten, vorn, hinten, daneben ...)
Richtung (rauf, runter, gerade, rund, eckig ...)
Größe (größer, kleiner, kürzer, länger, weit, nah, eng, breit ...)
Häufigkeit (mehr, weniger ...)
usw.

Abb. 1.1.5.4

che Zeichen in ihrer Code-Funktion zu identifizieren. Am Schulanfang haben etwa 14% der Kinder mit der Beachtung dieser Modalitätsunterschiede Schwierigkeiten. Einige von ihnen überwinden dieses Handicap im Prozess des Lesen- und Schreibenlernens. Anderen gelingt das ohne eine spezielle Förderung nicht. Da aber das Übertragen optischer Zeichen in akustische Zeichenreihen und umgekehrt, also das Umsetzen von Gesprochenem in Geschriebenes ohne eine genaue visuelle Differenzierung nicht möglich ist, kann eine ungenaue optische Differenzierungsfähigkeit den Lese-Schreiblernprozess behindern. Die Entwicklung der optischen Differenzierungsfähigkeit verläuft beim Kind relativ sprach-unabhängig. Es lernt optische Modalitäten unter den Bedingungen einer normalen Anregungssituation beim Bauen, Basteln, Malen, Kneten, Puzzeln, Hantieren usw. im alltäglichen Spiel allerdings nur dann beherrschen, wenn diese Modalitäten auch versprachlicht werden. Nur wenn die sprachlichen Bezeichnungen gedächtnismäßig gespeichert sind, sind sie für künftiges Handeln verfügbar. Dafür ist die sprachliche Anregungssituation für ein Vorschulkind so wichtig.

Optische Sprachwahrnehmungsdefizite sind – wie alle anderen Sprachwahrnehmungsschwächen – nur in der Einheit von Tun und begleitendem Sprechen effektiv zu überwinden.

Auf dem Prüfstand von Längsschnittuntersuchungen wurde ein Screening für pädagogisches und medizinisches Fachpersonal zur Diagnose von Sprachwahrnehmungsdefiziten entwickelt und psychometrisch abgesichert. *(Breuer, H., und Weuffen, M., 1990, 1997).* Die Items für die Analyse der optischen Differenzierungsfähigkeit z. B. fünf- bis sechsjähriger Kinder berücksichtigen Modalitäten, die für das Erlernen der Schriftzeichen wichtig sind. Das Kind hat folgende Vorlagen nacheinander abzumalen:

Die Bewertung hängt davon ab, ob das Kind die charakteristischen Merkmale der Figuren wiedergibt. Für vier- bis fünfjährige und sechs- bis siebenjährige Kinder gestalten sich die Anforderungen anders. Zu den Verfahren, zur Instruktion und Auswertung siehe a. a. O.

Bemerkenswert ist, dass sich gerade im letzten Vorschuljahr die optisch-graphomotorische Differenzierungsfähigkeit sehr dynamisch entwickelt. Während ein Jahr vor Schuleintritt erst etwa 24% der Fünf- bis Sechsjährigen das für die Aneignung der Schriftsprache benötigte Niveau erreicht haben (also von dieser Lernvoraussetzung schon mit 5 Jahren mit dem Lese- und Schreibenlernen beginnen könnten), haben zum Zeitpunkt des Schulanfangs 86% der ABC-Schützen das erforderliche Niveau erreicht. Das letzte Vorschuljahr stellt demnach für die Ausformung der optisch-graphomotorischen Differenzierungsfähigkeit eine ausgesprochen sensible Phase und damit einen günstigen Zeitpunkt für prophylaktische Fördermaßnahmen dar. Das bestätigte sich in vergleichenden Längsschnittuntersuchungen. Anliegen der optisch-graphomotorischen Förderung ist es, das Kind bei unterschiedlichsten Tätigkeiten zur bewussten Beachtung und Ausführung optischer Details zu führen. Das Frostig'sche Konzept der Wahrnehmungsförderung gibt hierfür ausgezeichnete Orientierungen. Für die Förderung eignen sich besonders das Zeichnen und Malen mit Farbstiften, Tusche, ohne und mit Begrenzungen im Raum; Arbeiten mit Plastilin, Buntpapier, Formfiguren; Faltübungen, Bauen, Basteln; Form- und Farbübungen mit Kreisen, Dreiecken, Vierecken, Rechtecken, Stäbchen; Ausschneideübungen, Reißübungen; Zusammensetzen und Aufkleben der ausgeschnittenen und gerissenen Teile; Puzzle-Spiele, Kugeln und Steckmusterspiele; Lottospiele, Suchspiele, Murmeln, Zielwerfen usw.

Die Förderung dieser und anderer Basisfunktionen im Vorschulalter, besonders auch im Kindergarten, hat den unschätzbaren Vorteil, dass die bevorzugte Zuwendung durch die Erzieherin vom Kind als Auszeichnung und etwas Positives erlebt wird. Eine Förderung bzw.

Nachhilfe nach erlebten Misserfolgen in der Schule hat es dagegen mit einer ganz anderen emotionalen Befindlichkeit des Kindes zu tun.

2. Die phonematische Differenzierungsfähigkeit

Für das Sprechen-, Lesen- und Schreibenlernen benötigt das Kind die Fähigkeit, klangähnliche Vokale und Konsonanten zu differenzieren. Es sind oft nur sehr feine Unterschiede im Klangbild, die über die bezeichneten Bedeutungsunterschiede entscheiden. Wer z. B. zwischen einem gesprochenen und gehörten „g" und „d" oder zwischen der Länge des Vokals „a" in den Wörtern „Nagel" und „Nadel" bzw. „Kamm" und „Kahn" nicht zu unterscheiden vermag, hat nicht nur Verstehensschwierigkeiten, sondern auch Probleme beim Umsetzen von Lautzeichen in Schriftzeichen. Viele Rechtschreibfehler haben hier ihren Ausgangspunkt. (Siehe Abbildung 1.1.5.5)

Die phonematische Differenzierungsfähigkeit

Beispiele:

Kamm-Kahn **Uhr-Ohr**

Bahn-Bein **backen-baden**

Nagel-Nadel **waschen-naschen**

Modalitäten:
Klangähnliche aber bedeutungsunterscheidende Vokale und Konsonanten

(subtile Schwächen sind vor der Schule nicht zu bemerken)

Abb.1.1.5.5

Die Qualität der phonematischen Differenzierungsfähigkeit lässt sich nicht mit Hörschwellenmessungen bestimmen, weil diese Hörleistung sich in einem Komplex sprachlicher, nichtsprachlicher, situativer Kontexte und kommunitiv-personaler Beziehungen zu bewähren hat. Diese spezifische Hörleistung des Menschen übt die Kontrollfunktion bei der Realisierung von Sprechlauten aus und spielt eine wichtige Rolle beim Differenzieren melodischer und rhythmischer Modalitäten beim Sprechen. Diese Code-Träger werden in ihrer Bedeutung für das Erfassen sprachlicher Inhalte und Strukturen oft unterschätzt.

Zum Zeitpunkt des Schuleintritts weisen etwa noch 15% der Kinder phonematische Schwächen auf. In der Gruppe der Schüler, die später als Legastheniker diagnostiziert wurden, beträgt der Anteil mit phonematischen Schwächen 88% (!). Besonders betroffen sind außerdem jene Kinder, die im Vorschulalter lautsprachliche Auffälligkeiten zeigten. Obwohl bei Schulbeginn lautsprachlich unauffällig, also logopädisch erfolgreich behandelt, stellen sie einen großen Teil der Schüler mit Lese-Rechtschreibschwächen im Anfangsunterricht.

Weil sich die phonematische Differenzierungsfähigkeit in der Phase des Sprechenlernens sehr dynamisch ausformt, müsste eine Förderung bereits **vor** dem letzten Vorschuljahr erfolgen.

Phonematische Differenzierungsschwächen lassen sich mit der „Differenzierungsprobe" (a. a. O.) ermitteln. Auf dem Prüfstand von Längsschnittuntersuchungen haben sich die nachstehend aufgeführten Phonemvergleiche bewährt. Sie werden vom Kind mittels bildlich dargestellter klangähnlicher Begriffspaare gefordert. Dieses Verfahren hat sich in der logopädischen Praxis seit langem als effektiv erwiesen. Es geht auf Schilling und Schäfer (1962) zurück und wurde von Theiner (1968) weiterentwickelt.

Zur Diagnose der phonematischen Differenzierungsfähigkeit werden bei fünf- bis sechsjährigen Kindern folgende Phonemvergleiche genutzt:

Probeaufgabe	Keller	-	Teller
	Kopf	-	Topf
Prüfaufgaben	Tanz	-	Gans
	Sack	-	satt
	krank	-	trank
	backen	-	baden
	Kanne	-	Tanne
	Nagel	-	Nadel
	Kamm	-	Kahn
	Tasse	-	Tasche
	Wache	-	Wasche

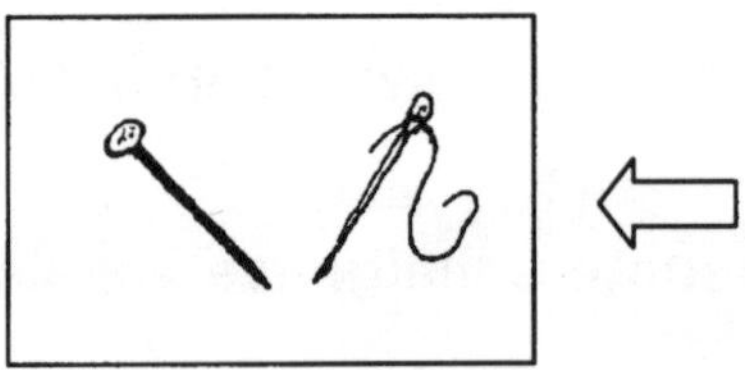

Abb. 1.1.5.6

Eine vorschulische Förderung der phonematischen Differenzierungsfähigkeit ist möglich. Dabei kommt es darauf an, spielerische Tätigkeiten mit entsprechenden Herausforderungen zum genauen Hinhören und begleitenden Versprachlichungen in einer Atmosphäre positiver emotionaler Befindlichkeit durchzuführen. Hörübungen mit geschlossenen Augen zum Unterscheiden verschiedenster Geräusche (Papierknistern, Schlüsselrasseln, Schereklappern, Schalterknipsen ...); Nachahmen von Tierstimmen; Erraten von unterschiedlichen Inhalten in geschüttelten Streichholzschachteln; Flüsterspiele, stille Post; Sprechspiele, Kinderverse; Laute heraushören usw. können in den Spielalltag im Kindergarten individuell gezielt eingebaut werden.

3. Die sprech-kinästhetische Differenzierungsfähigkeit

Sprechen und Schreiben erfordern eine komplexe und präzise fein- und feinstmotorische Koordination. Es gibt wohl kaum einen komplizierteren Bewegungsvollzug vom Menschen zu erlernen, als das Sprechen. Das vitale Bedürfnis zur Kommunikation, zur Nachahmung, ständige Sanktionen, Anregungen und sofortige Korrekturen, sprechende Vorbilder und eine positive emotionale Beziehung zu ihnen sind dabei entscheidende Triebkräfte. *(Hoffmann, H., und Koschay, E., 1996)*

Die kinästhetische Differenzierungsfähigkeit ist Voraussetzung für die Herausbildung automatisierter sprech- und schreibmotorischer Muster. Das schließt die normgerechte Artikulation, die richtige Reihenfolge und Vollständigkeit der Laute ein (siehe Abbildung 1.1.5.6) Beim Schreibenlernen in der Schule orientiert sich das Kind nicht nur am Wortklangbild des Lehrers. An der Analyse der gehörten und zu schreibenden Lautstruktur eines Wortes sind immer eigene Artikulationsbewegungen des Kindes aktiv beteiligt. Wenn das eigene sprechmotorische Muster (bedingt durch schlechte sprachliche Vorbilder) ungenau, unvollständig ist oder überflüssige Laute enthält, schreibt das Kind zwangsläufig fehlerhaft. Sprechmotorische Mängel machen sich beim Lesenlernen weniger bemerkbar, weil das Kind von der Buchstabenfolge her gelenkt wird.

Die sprech-kinästhetische Differenzierungsfähigkeit

Beispiele:

Schneemann	**Polizei**
Sneemann	**Pulizei**
Neemann	**Polizerei**
Scheemann	**Polizeier**
Schleemann	

Modalitäten:
Reihenfolge, Vollständigkeit, Richtigkeit der Lautbildung (Auslassungen, Hinzufügungen, Ersetzen durch andere Laute, Vertauschen, Stammelfehler)

Abb. 1.1.5.7

Etwa 11% der Kinder eines Einschulungsjahrganges beginnen das Schreiben- und Lesenlernen mit sprech-kinästhetischen Unsicherheiten auf der Lautebene. Im Rückschlussverfahren wurden bei legasthenischen Schülern am Schulanfang in 85% (!) der Fälle derartige Mängel festgestellt. Bei der Gruppe von Kindern mit Lese-Rechtschreibschwierigkeiten dominieren demnach Defizite im phonematischen und kinästhetischen Bereich. Diese sind bei ihnen im letzten Vorschuljahr z. T. stärker ausgeprägt als bei später als lernbehindert diagnostizierten Schülern. Während bei Lernbehinderten im Rückschlussverfahren im Vorschulalter globale, massive und stark förderresistente Sprachwahrnehmungsdefizite ermittelt wurden, tendieren spätere legasthene Kinder zu partiell-massiven Ausfällen im phonematischen und kinästhetischen Bereich. Das Niveau der Lautsprache kann dabei sehr unterschiedlich sein, während es bei späteren Lernbehinderten fast immer schwach ist.

In den ersten Lebensjahren weist das sprechmotorische Niveau eines Kindes enge Beziehungen zu seinem allgemeinen Motorik-Niveau auf. Kinder, die schon frühzeitig ein gutes sprechmotorisches Niveau erreichen, weisen durchweg gute Motorik-Quotienten auf. Sehr heterogen ist dagegen die Streubreite im Motorik-Quotienten bei künftigen Schulanfängern mit schwachen sprechmotorischen Leistungen. *(Lehmann, W., Breuer, H., Steingart, K.-M., 1980)*

Die Sprechkinästhesie hat insofern einen besonderen Stellenwert im Ensemble der Sprachwahrnehmungen, weil sie die gedächtnismäßige Speicherung sprachlicher Gebilde wesentlich unterstützt. Der Spracherwerb Gehörloser wäre ohne kinästhetische Sprechspuren nicht möglich. Beim Lesenlernen kommt es sehr darauf an, Kinder mit Leselernschwierigkeiten immer wieder laut lesen zu lassen, weil damit die bewusste Kontrolle der kinästhetischen Gliederung unterstützt wird.

Im Rahmen des Screenings „Differenzierungsprobe" wird die sprechmotorische Sicherheit geprüft, indem die Kinder nach linguistischen Gesichtspunkten ausgewählte Wörter mit artikulatorischen Klippen nachsprechen. Diese Wörter dürfen den Kindern nicht geläufig sein, weil sonst bereits eine sprechmotorische Automatisierung bestehen würde.

Die Prüfwörter für die Altersstufe 5 bis 6 lauten:

Post - kutsche
Alu - minium
Schell - fisch - flosse

Sprechmotorische Mängel sind nicht nur motorisch verursacht. Sie können auch auf Schwächen in der phonemisch-auditiven Rückkoppelung beruhen. Deshalb ist auch dieser Wahrnehmungsbereich sorgfältig zu prüfen. In der Förderung ist eine Verbindung beider Wahrnehmungsbereiche zweckmäßig. Das hat sich in der Behandlung von Stammlern, Aphasikern und lese-rechtschreibschwachen Kindern als effektive Strategie bewährt.

Die sensible Phase für die Ausformung der sprechmotorisch-kinästhetischen Differenzierungsfähigkeit liegt vor dem 5. Lebensjahr. Spätestens im letzten Vorschuljahr sind Artikulationsmängel zu beseitigen. Wenn beim Schuleintritt noch fehlerhaft artikuliert wird, bedeutet das ein schweres Handicap für den Lese-Schreiblernprozess.

Zur Förderung: Damit die Kinder ihre Sprechorgane funktionell immer besser beherrschen lernen, kommt es auf spaßige, lustbetonte und herausfordernde Sprechsituationen an. Im Mittelpunkt stehen dabei Zungen-, Lippen- und Atemübungen. Vom Zungenturnen über Zungenbrecher bis zum Kamm- und Seifenblasen blasen, von Brummlippchen über Lockerungsübungen für Zunge und Lippen bis zu Kinderreimen, Abzählversen und Sprechspielen mit Zungenbrechern gibt es viele Möglichkeiten. Das Bedürfnis zur motorischen Aktivität und die unvoreingenommene Beziehung zu eigenen Mängeln im Vorschulalter drängen geradezu nach einer Verbindung von Bewegung und Sprechen. Hand- und Gebärdenzeichen können die Förderung sehr unterstützen. *(Dummer, L., und Hackethal, R., 1984)*

Wie jede Sprachwahrnehmungsförderung, so „strahlt" auch die kinästhetische auf andere Wahrnehmungsbereiche aus. Transfereffekte lassen sich auf das Niveau der phonematischen und rhythmischen Differenzierungsfähigkeit nachweisen.

4. Die melodische Differenzierungsfähigkeit

Melodisch-intonatorische Modalitäten fungieren in allen Sprachen (unterschiedlich stark) als Code-Träger. Gleiche Wörter und Sätze drücken unterschiedliche Inhalte, Erwartungen oder emotionale Beziehungen in Abhängigkeit ihres intonatorischen „Untertextes“ aus. Es kommt nicht nur darauf an, **was** gesagt wird, sondern auch **wie** es gesagt wird. Gleiche Wörter und Sätze können sachlich-mitteilend, zweifelnd, drohend, bittend, abweisend oder fragend sein.

Für das Lernen im Anfangsunterricht hat die Fähigkeit eines Kindes, melodisch-intonatorische Feinheiten in der Sprache des Lehrers zu erfassen, zunächst Bedeutung für die Synchronie des Mitdenkens. Der Lehrer drückt mit seiner Stimmführung aus, ob ein Gedanke abgeschlossen ist oder ob er weitergeführt wird. Mit der Stimmführung werden gedankliche Höhepunkte, wichtige Informationen angekündigt, wird Aufmerksamkeit erzeugt usw.. Ein Kind, das diese prosaischen Modalitäten nicht erfasst, lässt sich in seiner geistigen Aktivität und Aufmerksamkeit nicht wie gewünscht führen. Kenntnislücken und Verständnisschwierigkeiten beim Erfassen entfalteteter Gedanken sind die Folge.

Intonatorische Modalitäten beim Sprechen drücken außerdem emotionale Beziehungen zum Kommunikationspartner, zu Aufgaben und Ereignissen, aber auch eigene Befindlichkeiten aus (siehe Abbildung 1.1.5.8). Wenn man davon ausgeht, dass die Eigenaktivität eines Kindes, sein Neugier- und Risikoverhalten, sein Selbstvertrauen und seine Ansprechbarkeit von seiner emotionalen Befindlichkeit abhängen, muss man den „emotionalen“ Signalen, die der Lehrer mit der Art seiner Stimmführung aussendet, große Bedeutung für das Lernverhalten und den Lernerfolg der Schüler zumessen. Die melodische Differenzierungsfähigkeit – sie ist nicht identisch mit Musikalität – beginnt sich früh zu entwickeln. Schon im Mutterleib reagiert das Kind auf melodische Merkmale in der Sprache der Mutter anders als auf jene anderer Menschen. Der Säugling lernt es sehr schnell, melodische Nuancen in der Stimme seiner Mutter als das Ankündigen von Bedürfnisbefriedigung oder -verweigerung zu unterscheiden. In seinem Schreien setzt er das Gelernte um.

Im Niveau der melodischen Differenzierungsfähigkeit zeigen sich zwischen Vier- und Sechsjährigen kaum Unterschiede. Deshalb ist die Zeit im Vorschulalter für das Erlernen einer Fremdsprache so wichtig. Wer eine andere Sprache nach dieser melodisch-sensiblen Phase erlernt, erreicht in ihr kaum die intonatorische Qualität wie in der Muttersprache. Für die Integration von Ausländerkindern sind ihr Alter bei der Begegnung mit dem anderen Sprachmilieu und die Möglichkeiten zur sprachlichen Kommunikation von großer Bedeutung.

Etwa 11% der Schulanfänger haben Schwierigkeiten, intonatorische Modalitäten zu erfassen. Sie sind dadurch nicht sensibel genug, semantische Strukturen und Feinheiten zu erkennen. Das sind aber Grundlagen des folgerichtigen Denkens. Es ist verwunderlich, dass diese kognitive Basisfunktion in den üblichen Intelligenzprüfverfahren praktisch keine Rolle spielt. Das trifft bedauerlicherweise auch auf die rhythmische Differenzierungsfähigkeit zu. Ihre Negierung in Intelligenzprüfverfahren für jüngere Kinder wiegt besonders schwer.

Für die Früherkennung und damit für die Frühförderung melodischer Differenzierungsschwächen mussten ebenfalls Möglichkeiten aus dem Alltagsverhalten der Vorschulkinder genutzt werden. Dabei spielte die Überlegung eine Rolle, dass alle Völker ihre Jüngsten mit Wiegen- und Kinderliedern vertraut machen. Diese stimmen in der Einfachheit der Melodieführung und des Rhythmus überein. Genau hier liegen die Anreize, um die Fähigkeit zur Differenzierung sprachmelodischer Modalitäten ausbilden zu können. Wiegen- und Kinderlieder tragen also nicht nur zum aktuellen Wohlbefinden (in Verbindung mit Schaukelbewegungen usw.) des Kindes bei. Sie bereiten außerdem die sensomotorische Beherrschung der prosaischen Code-Träger beim Sprechen vor. Auch wenn die Mutter mit ihrer Singstimme mit Profisängern auf Kassetten nicht konkurrieren kann, übt sie, verbunden mit fürsorglichen Körperkontakten, eine viel nachhaltigere Wirkung auf die emotionale und intellektuelle Entwicklung ihres Kindes aus.

Die melodische Differenzierungsfähigkeit

Beispiele:

Komm her!

Komm her?

Emotion, Denken, Synchronie

Modalitäten:
Tonunterschiede, Tönstärke, Tonlängen, Tonmodalitäten, Melodieführung

(Melod. Differenzierung bedeutet nicht Musikalität!)

Abb. 1.1.5.8

Im Screening wird vom Kind das Singen eines einfachen, ihm bekannten Kinderliedes gefordert. Dazu sind Kinder in diesem Alter gern bereit, wenn der Untersucher eine entsprechende Atmosphäre zu schaffen vermag.

Bei der Förderung von Kindern mit Schwächen in der melodischen Differenzierungsfähigkeit ist – ähnlich wie bei der rhythmischen Differenzierungsfähigkeit – mit spektakulären Sofortergebnissen nicht zu rechnen. Das hängt u. a. mit der Verwurzelung dieser Leistung in den frühesten Lebensetappen des Kindes zusammen. Die Förderung verlangt viel Geduld und Ausdauer. Wichtig ist eine Atmosphäre bzw. eine Umgebung des Kindes, in der Melodisches eine Rolle spielt, in der eben gesungen wird. Eine permanente Geräuschkulisse durch Radio und Fernsehen stellt dafür keinen Ersatz dar. Singen, wenn möglich mit Musikinstrument begleiten, Lieder summen und pfeifen, Nachsingen von Melodieabschnitten, Liederraten nach Vorgabe weniger Töne, Nachsingen eigener Melodiefolgen, Erkennen von Tonhöhenunterschieden, Imitieren von Tierlauten, Kammblasen, Töne unterscheiden (laut – leise, hoch – tief, kurz – lang); mit Klangstäbchen, Triangel oder Tamburin begleiten, Nachahmen von Zweitonfolgen (Kuckuck) und Dreiklängen, Hören von Musik, Sing- und Kreisspiele, Melodieimprovisationen zu dargestellten Situationen usw. haben nachweisbar gute Fördereffekte.

5. Die rhythmische Differenzierungsfähigkeit

Wenn von Rhythmus gesprochen wird, denken die meisten Menschen an die Verbindung von Rhythmus und Musik. Es gibt zwar keine Musik ohne Rhythmus, jedoch gibt es Rhythmus ohne Musik. Biologische Rhythmen wie Herzschlag, Atmung, Wechsel von Aktivität und Ruhe, aber auch optische, motorische, taktile, akustische Musterfolgen sind zu nennen.

Während die bisher besprochenen Sprachwahrnehmungsleistungen mehr oder weniger die Differenzierung von einzelnen Modalitäten zu sichern haben, obliegt der rhythmischen Differenzierung die Zusammenschau, die Erfassung der Beziehungen von Modalitäten zu strukturierten Ordnungen. Diese Leistung stellt besondere Anforderungen an Analyse- und Syntheseprozesse, Grundlagen des Denkens. Die Fähigkeit, Regelhaftigkeiten in Strukturen zu erfassen, innere Beziehungen und Ordnungen zwischen den Zeichen zu erkennen und zu gestalten, für Regelhaftigkeiten, Schwerpunkte, Akzentuierungen, metrische Verhältnisse sensibel zu sein, bestimmt qualitative Merkmale des Denkens. Die rhythmische Differenzierungsfähigkeit spielt für schulisches Lernen offensichtlich eine wichtige Rolle. Dazu ein Beispiel aus einer unserer Längsschnittuntersuchungen (siehe Tabelle 1.1.5.9). Von den 648 Schülern, die vom letzten Vorschuljahr bis ans Ende der Klasse 10 in eine Untersuchung zur Erkundung prophylaktischer Möglichkeiten zur Einschränkung unerwarteter Lernschwierigkeiten im Anfangsunterricht einbezogen waren, wurde bei 32 Schülern mit sehr gutem Schulerfolg und 22 Schülern mit schwachem Schulerfolg am Ende des 10. Schuljahres das Niveau der rhythmischen Differenzierungsfähigkeit kurz vor Schuleintritt zum Schulerfolg in Beziehung gesetzt. Die Ergebnisse sprechen für sich. Alle in der Schule besonders erfolgreichen Schüler begannen ihre Schullaufbahn mit einer völlig intakten rhythmischen Sicherheit. Die Vergleichsgruppe der weniger erfolgreichen Schüler begann ihre Schullaufbahn ausnahmslos mit mehr oder weniger großen Mängeln. Diese Untersuchungsergebnisse werden durch Befunde von Lernbehinderten eindeutig bestätigt.

Die Fähigkeit, den Rhythmus in der Sprache als Kodeträger zu erkennen und beim Sprechen einzusetzen, ist als Indikator dafür anzusehen, ob das Kind die innere Struktur, die sprachlichen Wort- und Satzschemata und die feineren Unterschiede und Subtilitäten der Bedeutung erfassen kann. Rhythmische Differenzierungsfähigkeit hat eine konstituierende Funktion für die sprachliche Kompetenz. Ohne die Fähigkeit, rhythmische Gliederungen zu erfassen, mangelt es an der Sensibilität für Regelhaftigkeiten und metrische Verhältnisse. Die Beziehung zu mathematischen Grundfertigkeiten wurde auf dem Prüfstand von Längsschnittuntersuchungen bestätigt.

Der Begriff Strukturierung beinhaltet auch die Wortwahl und die Stellung der Wörter innerhalb des Satzes. Rhythmische Kode-Merkmale führen zum Sinn einer Aussage, heben die semantischen Höhepunkte hervor. Auch beim Schreibenlernen sind seriale Ordnungen (z. B. die Reihenfolge der Buchstaben) zu beachten. Auf den hohen Stellenwert der rhythmischen Differenzierungsfähigkeit im Ensemble sprachbezogener Wahrnehmungsleistungen wurde meine Mitarbeiterin Frau Dr. Weuffen bei der Therapie erwachsener Aphasiker aufmerksam. Wenn vor der Behandlung die rhythmische und die melodische Differenzierungsfähigkeit auf dem Niveau der Screening-Anforderungen noch intakt waren, konnte für die sprachliche Rehabilitation eine gute Prognose gestellt werden. Fehlten diese Voraussetzungen, war die Therapie langwierig und oft wenig erfolgreich. Thiele, R. *(zitiert bei Kainz, F. 1954, S. 115)* spricht in diesem Zusammenhang bereits davon, dass die Unfähigkeit, einen Reihenrhythmus zu produzieren, eine besonders tiefe Abbaustufe der sprachlichen Ausdrucksfähigkeit anzeigt.

15% der Schulanfänger beginnen ihre Schullaufbahn mit Unsicherheiten in der rhythmischen Differenzierung. Wie außergewöhnlich stark die richtige Strukturierung von Sätzen (Satzbildung) von der rhythmischen Differenzierungsfähigkeit abhängt, zeigt sich bei agrammatisch sprechenden Vorschulkindern. 87% von ihnen weisen Defizite in dieser kognitiven Basisfunktion auf.

Das rhythmische Differenzierungsniveau im Vorschulalter bei erfolgreichen und weniger erfolgreichen Schülern

Rhythmisches Differenzierungs-niveau im letzten Vorschuljahr	Schulerfolg nach Klasse 10: **erfolgreich**	**wenig erfolgreich**
+	100%	0%
+ /–	0%	9%
-	0%	91%

Tabelle 1.1.5.9

Die rhythmische Differenzierungsfähigkeit

Beispiele:

König Arthur ist Sieger.
König Arthur ist Sieger.
König Arthur ist Sieger.
König Arthur ist Sieger.
Der Lehrer sagt der Schüler ist ein Esel.

Modalitäten:
Betonung, Pausen, Strukturierung

Abb. 1.1.5.10

Als geeignete Items für die Früherkennung von Defiziten in diesem Wahrnehmungsbereich wurden im Ergebnis von Längsschnittuntersuchungen nachzuklatschende Rhythmen ermittelt.

(Siehe Abbildung 1.1.5.10) Diese simple erscheinenden Aufgaben besitzen eine hohe prognostische Sicherheit. Sie erfüllen drei wichtige Strukturierungsanforderungen.

Es müssen

a) Modalitäten (kurz – lang, betont – schwächer betont)
b) Mengen (simultan bis vier Elemente)
c) Ordnungen (Wechsel zwischen den Modalitäten)

erkannt werden.

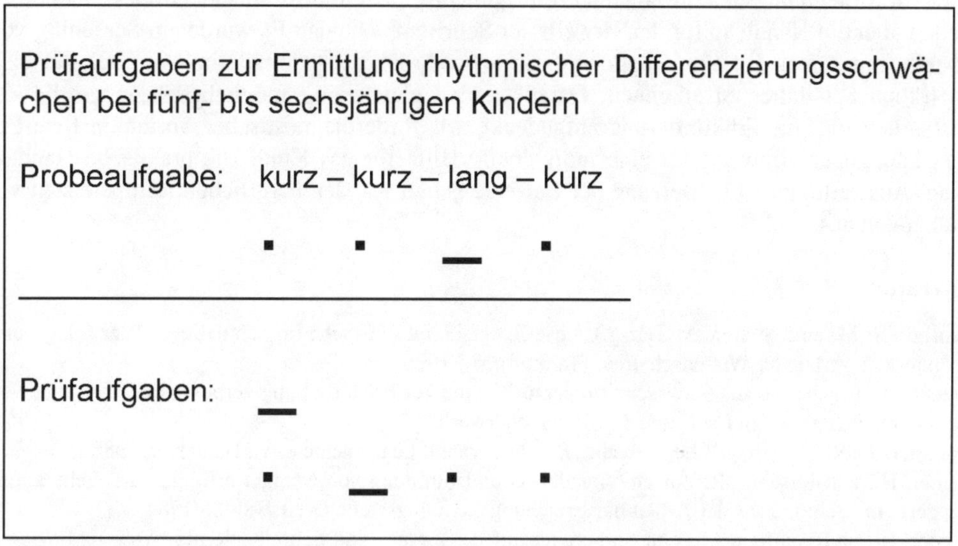

Abb. 1.1.5.11

Obwohl rhythmische Differenzierungsschwächen nur schwer zu überwinden sind, haben Förderbemühungen Erfolg, wenn sie zum richtigen Zeitpunkt (also möglichst im Vorschulalter) und in der Einheit von motorischer, melodischer und rhythmischer Aktivierung durchgeführt werden. Da die rhythmischen Modalitäten eine maßgebliche konstituierende Funktion für das Sprachgedächtnis besitzen – also für die Vorratskammer des Verstandes – kommen entsprechenden Anregungen im Vorschulalter eine wichtige Förderrolle zu. In diesem Zusammenhang sind besonders Kinderreime, Abzählverse einzuordnen. Sie machen den Vorschulkindern nicht nur viel Freude, sie lassen sich auch wegen ihres Rhythmus gut behalten. Davon profitiert das Sprachgedächtnis. Es ist eine wichtige Mitgift aus dem Vorschulalter für das Lernen in der Schule und danach.

Zu den Fördermöglichkeiten gehören: Lieder klatschen, zuerst dabei summen, schließlich nur klatschen; Namen, Wörter, Sätze silbenweise klatschen oder mit anderen Bewegungen verbinden; Übungen mit Tamburin, Klangstäbchen; Sätze mit unterschiedlicher Betonung sprechen; Malen und Bewegen nach Musik; Tanzen, Turnen; Bewegungen mit Silbensprechen verbinden, Reihenübungen: Muster zeichnen, legen, flechten, bauen; Klatschrhythmen wiederholen; Koordination von Sprechen und Bewegen, Abzählverse nutzen, Gehen bei vorgegebenem Rhythmus; mit Partner überkreuz klatschen; Reime auswendig lernen; mit Taschenlampe morsen; mit der Trillerpfeife Rhythmen nachpfeifen; Reimwörter suchen; Tempovarianten befolgen; Silben zählen, auf Kärtchen suchen; Wörter erfinden, Silben anhängen usw..

Zusammenfassung:

Das Sprechen-, Lesen- und Schreibenlernen des Kindes ist u. a. an die Fähigkeit gebunden, Sprache in ihren optischen, phonematischen, kinästhetischen, melodischen und rhythmischen sinnlich-wahrnehmbaren Modalitäten, die als Kode-Träger für den sprachlichen Inhalt fungieren – präzise und automatisiert sensomotorisch zu differenzieren und zu imitieren. Subtile Sprachwahrnehmungsdefizite bleiben im Alltagsverhalten des Vorschulkindes unerkannt, stellen aber ein Handicap für den Erwerb der Schriftsprache dar. Es wurde ein Screening vorgestellt, mit dessen Hilfe es möglich ist, Sprachwahrnehmungsdefizite im Vorschulalter bzw. im frühen Schulalter zu erkennen. Dabei werden gleichzeitig mögliche pädagogische Zugriffstellen für eine Frühförderung aufgedeckt. Als förderdiagnostisches Verfahren liefert es dem Pädagogen Hinweise für eine individuelle Hilfe für das Kind. Die praktische Handhabung, Auswertung und Umsetzung der Befunde gehen von den beruflichen Kompetenzen von Pädagogen aus.

Literatur

Behrndt, S.-M., und Steffen, M. (Hrsg.): Lese-Rechtschreibschwäche im Schulalltag. Peter Lang Europäischer Verlag der Wissenschaften, Frankfurt/M., 1996

Breuer, H.: Ergebnisse aus Längsschnittuntersuchungen zur Früherfassung verbosensomotorischer Voraussetzungen für den Laut- und Schriftspracherwerb.

Dummer-Smoch, L. (Hrsg.): Legasthenie, Bundesverband Legasthenie e. V., Hannover, 1988

Breuer, H., und Kasten, M.: Zur emotionalen Grundstimmung von weniger erfolgreichen Schulanfängern, in: Beiträge aus der Arbeit der Erziehungsberatungsstelle Greifswald, 6/1984

Breuer, H., und Weuffen, M.: Gut vorbereitet auf das Lesen- und Schreibenlernen, Volk und Wissen, Berlin 1990

Breuer, H., und Weuffen, M.: Lernschwierigkeiten am Schulanfang, Beltz, Weinheim und Basel, 1999

Dummer-Smoch, L.: Korrektur der neuen Lesedidaktik und Berücksichtigung legasthener Schwächen, in: Behrndt und Steffen (a.a.O.), 1996

Dummer-Smoch, L.: Die Diagnostischen Bilderlisten. Veris, Kiel, 1993

Dummer-Smoch, L., und Hackethal, Renate: Kieler Leseaufbau. Veris, Kiel, 1984

Hoffmann, H., und Koschay, E.: Erarbeitung einer „LRS-spezifischen Lesehilfe" für Kinder mit einer Lese-Rechtschreibschwäche, in: Behrndt und Steffen, a.a.O., 1996

Kainz, F.: Psychologie der Sprache. Enke, Stuttgart, 1954

Kossow, H.-J.: Leitfaden zur Bekämpfung der Lese-Rechtschreibschwäche. Übungsbuch mit Kommentaren. Verlag der Wissenschaften, Berlin, 19XX

Lehmann, W., Breuer, H., Steingart, K. M.: Beziehungen zwischen Motorik und Verbosensomotorik im Vorschulalter. Ärztl. Jugendkunde 71, Heft 2, 1980

Ruoho, K.: Prophylaktische Möglichkeiten zur Einschränkung unerwarteter nicht defektiver Lernschwierigkeiten – Probleme und Ergebnisse in Finnland, in: Behrndt und Steffen, a.a.O., 1996

Ruoho, K.: Zum Stellenwert der Verbo-Sensomotorik im Konzept prophylaktischer Diagnostik der Lernfähigkeit bei finnischen Vorschulkindern im Alter von sechs Jahren. University of Joensuu, Joensuu, 1990

Schäfer, H., und Schilling, A: Beiträge zur Prüfung der pertiellen akustischen Lautagnosie bei stammelnen Kindern mit einem Lautagnosieprüfverfahren. Arch. Ohr-, Na.- und Kehlk.-Heilk., 2, 1962

Theiner, Ch.: Untersuchungen zur phonematischen Differenzierungsfähigkeit. Die Sonderschule, 1. Beiheft, 1968

1.1.6 Beeinträchtigungen der phonologischen Verarbeitung – ein wesentliches Handicap für das Lesenlernen

Karin Landerl

1. Relevanz der phonologischen Verarbeitung für den Schriftspracherwerb

Die zentrale Rolle, die der phonologischen Verarbeitung, also der Verarbeitung der Sprachlaute, beim Lesen und Rechtschreiben zukommt, ergibt sich aus der Struktur unseres Schriftsystems. Alle gängigen Schriftsysteme bilden linguistische Segmente, die beim Sprechen produziert werden, durch visuelle Zeichen ab. In Logogrammschriften (z.B. Chinesisch) steht ein Schriftzeichen für ein gesamtes Wort, in Silbenschriften (z.B. Japanisch) werden die Sprachsilben durch unterschiedliche Schriftzeichen repräsentiert. Alphabetische Schriften wie die deutsche verlangen die höchste linguistische Kompetenz von ihren Nutzern, weil hier die einzelnen Laute der gesprochenen Sprache, die Phoneme, durch Buchstaben oder Buchstabengruppen, die Grapheme abgebildet werden. Phoneme sind zwar bedeutungsunterscheidend (<u>Wind</u> und <u>Kind</u> unterscheiden sich lautlich nur durch das erste Phonem), sie sind aber an und für sich bedeutungslos. Das lesenlernende Kind, das bisher damit beschäftigt war, die Bedeutung der Wörter und Phrasen seiner Muttersprache korrekt zu interpretieren, muss also nun erstmals seine Aufmerksamkeit bewusst auf den strukturellen Aufbau des Sprachsystems richten, d.h. es muss die sog. phonologische Bewusstheit erwerben. Es muss entdecken, dass alle Wörter seiner Muttersprache aus einem relativ kleinen Satz von Phonemen aufgebaut sind, dass etwa der /a/-Laut in <u>Affe</u> dem /a/-Laut in <u>Hand</u> entspricht, obwohl die beiden Laute nur bedingt ähnlich klingen (in <u>Hand</u> wird das /a/ nasalisiert gesprochen, weil dem Vokal ein Nasallaut folgt). Hat das Kind erst einmal das Grundprinzip von Alphabetschriften verstanden, so ist in weiterer Folge der Erwerb der Buchstabe-Laut-Zuordnungen nur mehr eine Frage der Zeit. Gibt es aufgrund einer defizitären phonologischen Verarbeitung allerdings Schwierigkeiten beim Erwerb der phonologischen Bewusstheit, so wird dieser Erwerb mühevoll. Buchstaben, die für phonologisch ähnliche Laute stehen (z.B. /d/ und /t/, /n/ und /m/) können schlecht auseinandergehalten werden, in schweren Fällen werden die Buchstabe-Laut-Zuordnungen als für das Kind bedeutungslose artikulatorische Gebärden gelernt, ohne dass erfasst wird, dass diese mühsam gelernten Mundstellungen den Sprachlauten entsprechen, die das Kind tagtäglich produziert und hört.

Sprechen ist nicht das Produzieren einer Abfolge von Lauten. Vielmehr werden die einzelnen Sprachlaute, die Phoneme, miteinander verschliffen und als artikulatorische Einheiten wie Silben, Morpheme, Wörter und Propositionen produziert. So ist etwa bei der Artikulation der Silbe /pa/ die Zungenstellung während der Artikulation des /p/-Lautes anders (nämlich tiefer im Mundraum) als bei Artikulation des /p/-Lautes der Silbe /pi/. Dieser Prozess der Koartikulation ist es, der unsere Sprache so effizient macht, der aber das lesenlernende Kind vor ein großes Problem stellt, wenn es beim lautierenden Lesen diesen natürlichen Sprachprozess künstlich nachahmen soll. Dem lautierenden Lesen kommt im Schriftspracherwerb eine zentrale Bedeutung zu, weil er es dem Kind ermöglicht, die zahlreichen unbekannten Wörter, mit denen es ständig konfrontiert ist, selbstständing zu erlesen. Umgekehrt müssen beim lautorientierten Schreiben aus dem Sprachfluss die einzelnen Phoneme in der korrekten Reihenfolge heraus gefiltert werden, obwohl das akustische Signal kaum Anhaltspunkte für diesen Segmentationsprozess gibt – häufig sind nicht einmal Wort- oder Satzgrenzen akustisch deutlich erkennbar, geschweige denn einzelne Laute. Insbesondere die Segmentation von komplexen Konsonantenabfolgen (z.B. Pflanze, Strand) ist linguistisch durchaus anspruchsvoll und gelingt bei Vorliegen von Defiziten in der phonologischen Verarbeitung oft nur denkbar schlecht.

Für einen kompetenten, flüssigen Leseprozess ist die Strategie des lautierenden Lesens zwar eine wesentliche, wahrscheinlich sogar unverzichtbare Komponente, diese Strategie alleine reicht aber auf Dauer nicht aus, weil sie aufwendig ist und viel Zeit in Anspruch nimmt. Kompetente Leser bauen im Lauf der Zeit ein umfassendes orthographisches Gedächtnis auf, in dem Gedächtniseinträge für Wortschreibungen gespeichert werden. Wörter oder Wortteile, die in diesem orthographischen Speicher repräsentiert sind, müssen nun nicht mehr mühevoll lautierend erlesen werden, sondern können schnell und automatisch direkt wiedererkannt werden. Auch für eine kompetente Rechtschreibung ist eine rein lautorientierte Schreibstrategie auf Dauer nicht ausreichend. Vielmehr greifen wir auch hier auf unseren orthographischen Gedächtnisspeicher zu, aus dem wir die korrekte Wortschreibung zumeist automatisch und ohne viel Aufwand abrufen können.

Schwierigkeiten beim Aufbau eines derartigen orthographischen Gedächtnisspeichers sind ein zentrales Symptom der spezifischen Lese-/Rechtschreibschwäche. Das Lesen bleibt auffällig langsam und mühevoll und die Schreibungen betroffener Kinder sind zwar weitgehend lauttreu, entsprechen aber häufig nicht den Konventionen der deutschen Rechtschreibung. Aktuelle Theorien der Worterkennung besagen, dass kompetente Leser Schriftwörter im Gedächtnis speichern, indem sie eine multiple Vernetzung zwischen der Gedächtnisrepräsentation für das Schriftwort und der für das Sprechwort aufbauen (Ehri, 1992; Perfetti, 1992). Man kann sich das stark vereinfacht so vorstellen, dass sich die Schriftwortrepräsentation auf den bereits vorhandenen Gedächtniseintrag für das entsprechende Sprachwort darauf setzt. Diese multiple Vernetzung umfasst unter anderem auch Verbindungen zwischen den einzelnen Buchstaben und den korrespondierenden Lauten oder zwischen häufig vorkommenden Vor- und Nachsilben wie *ver-* und *-heit* und deren Verschriftlichung. Schriftwörter, für die derartige multipel vernetzte Gedächtnisrepräsentationen vorhanden sind, können ohne mühevolles Zusammenlauten direkt und automatisch gelesen und orthographisch korrekt geschrieben werden. LRS-Kinder haben massive Schwierigkeiten, derartige Schriftwortrepräsentationen aufzubauen, weil die multiple Vernetzung mit der Sprechwortrepräsentation nicht gelingt.

2. Evidenz für ein phonologisches Defizit als Ursache der LRS

Lesen und Rechtschreiben sind also komplexe psycholinguistische Tätigkeiten. Liegen bei einem Kind Defizite in der phonologischen Verarbeitung vor, so ist es nicht verwunderlich, dass auch der Schriftspracherwerb problematisch sein wird. Von den derzeit diskutierten Theorien zur Verursachung von spezifischer Lese-/Rechtschreibschwäche ist die These des phonologischen Defizits als zentrale Ursache dieser Störung die empirisch am besten belegte Konzeption. Sie ist inzwischen weitgehend anerkannt und hat etwa auch bereits Eingang in die Definition dieser umschriebenen Entwicklungsstörung gefunden. So heißt es etwa im Internationalen Statistische Manual der Weltgesundheitsorganisation (ICD10): „Kinder mit einer umschriebenen Lese-/Rechtschreibstörung haben in der Vorgeschichte häufig eine umschriebene Entwicklungsstörung des Sprechens und der Sprache. Eine sorgfältige Beurteilung der Sprachfunktionen deckt oft entsprechende subtile, gegenwärtige Probleme auf." (Dilling, Mombour & Schmidt, 1993, S. 275).

Für den anglo-amerikanischen Raum hat Vellutino (1979) bereits vor zwei Jahrzehnten die Evidenz in bezug auf kognitive Defizite bei spezifischer Leseschwäche zusammengetragen und überzeugende Belege für Defizite in der phonologischen Verarbeitung gefunden, während für Defizite in anderen Bereichen der kognitiven Verarbeitung (visuelle Differenzierung, Raumlageorientierung, Intermodalität, Serialität) kaum empirische Evidenz vorliegen. Ich möchte Ihnen nun kurz die Befunde einer Studie präsentieren, in der wir der Frage nach kognitiven Defiziten bei deutschsprachigen leseschwachen Kindern nachgegangen sind (Wimmer, Mayringer & Landerl, 1998).

In dieser umfassenden Studie wurden nicht nur die phonologischen Fertigkeiten sondern auch andere kognitive Verarbeitungsprozesse einer Gruppe von Kindern am Ende der 2. Schulstufe (N=27), die bereits massive Schwierigkeiten beim Lesen und Rechtschreiben zeigten, mit einer Kontrollgruppe von gleichaltrigen Kindern verglichen, die eine normale Schriftsprachentwicklung aufwiesen (N=20). Die Entwicklung dieser Kinder war bereits vom Zeitpunkt der Einschulung an beobachtet worden, sodass auch von diesem frühen Messzeitpunkt Befunde vorliegen, welche kognitiven Fertigkeiten die Kinder für den Schriftspracherwerb mitbrachten. Abbildung 1.1.6.1 zeigt die Effektstärken für die diversen kognitiven Aufgaben. Effektstärken zeigen, wie groß der Unterschied zwischen den Mittelwerten der LRS-Gruppe und der Kontrollgruppe sind. Eine Effektstärke von -1 bedeutete, dass der Mittelwert der LRS-Gruppe eine Standardabweichung unter dem der Kontrollgruppe liegt, d.h. wir sprechen von einem bedeutungsvollen Unterschied. Eine Effektstärke, die gegen 0 geht zeigt dagegen, dass kein wesentlicher Unterschied zwischen den beiden Gruppen vorliegt. In Abb. 1.1.6.1 sind die durchgeführten Aufgaben nach der Größe der Effektstärke sortiert. Außerdem sind die Effektstärken jener Aufgaben, für die linguistisch-phonologische Verarbeitungsprozesse eine Rolle spielen, schwarz aufgetragen, während die Effektstärken der rein nonverbalen Aufgaben in weiß gehalten sind.

Abb. 1.1.6.1 zeigt deutlich, dass es v.a. bei jenen Aufgaben auffällige Unterschiede gibt, bei denen Sprachverarbeitung eine Rolle spielt. Das größte Defizit der LRS-Kinder zeigte sich beim „Schnellen Benennen". Diese Aufgabe besteht darin, dass eine Abfolge von abgebildeten Objekten, Farbtupfern oder Ziffern so schnell wie möglich benannt werden müssen. Dass LRS-Kinder bei derartigen Aufgabenstellungen langsamer sind als Kinder mit normalen Leseentwicklungen, hat sich bereits in vielen Studien gezeigt. Eine gängige Interpretation ist, dass die LRS-Kinder geringfügig länger brauchen, um die phonologischen Worteinträge in ihrem mentalen Lexikon aufzurufen. Auch Nachsprechen von Pseudowörtern differenzierte hochsignifikant zwischen den beiden Gruppen. Korrektes Nachsprachen eine Pseudowortes wie MAWIMO oder BOWIBA erfordert eine kompetente Sprachperzeption, eine kurzzeitige Speicherung der unbekannten Lautabfolge im Gedächtnis und eine artikulatorisch korrekte Wiedergabe – bei Vorliegen eines phonologischen Defizits sind Schwierigkeiten bei derartigen Aufgabenstellungen nicht weiter verwunderlich. Bei der Aufgabe Pseudonamen lernen, für die die Kinder die erfundenen Namen (FILO, KOGAN und SPURK) für drei visuell gut unterscheidbare Phantasietiere lernen sollten, waren die LRS-Kinder ebenfalls stark beeinträchtigt. Offenkundig hatten die Kinder große Schwierigkeiten, die unbekannten Lautabfolgen zu speichern und wiederzugeben.

Keine Unterschiede zwischen der leseschwachen und der Kontrollgruppe zeigten sich bei den nonverbalen Aufgaben, die als weiße Balken aufgetragen sind. Zu Beginn der ersten

Klasse, also noch vor Einsetzen des Leseunterrichts, wurde eine Aufgabe zur visuellen Suche durchgeführt. Den Kindern wurde ein Blatt mit auf Zeilen angeordneten gezeichneten Äpfeln vorgelegt, die eine unterschiedliche Orientierung haben. Das Kind muss so schnell wie möglich alle Äpfel durchzustreichen, deren Stiel nach oben zeigt, und die Äpfel, deren Stiel in eine andere Richtung zeigt, ignorieren. Diese Aufgabe erfordert also eine adäquate visuelle Differenzierung und Raumlageorientierung. Die leseschwachen Kinder hatten mit dieser Aufgabenstellung keinerlei Schwierigkeiten, sie bearbeiteten die Apfel-Aufgabe ebenso so präzise und genau so schnell wie die Kinder, die später keinerlei Leseschwierigkeiten entwickelt haben.

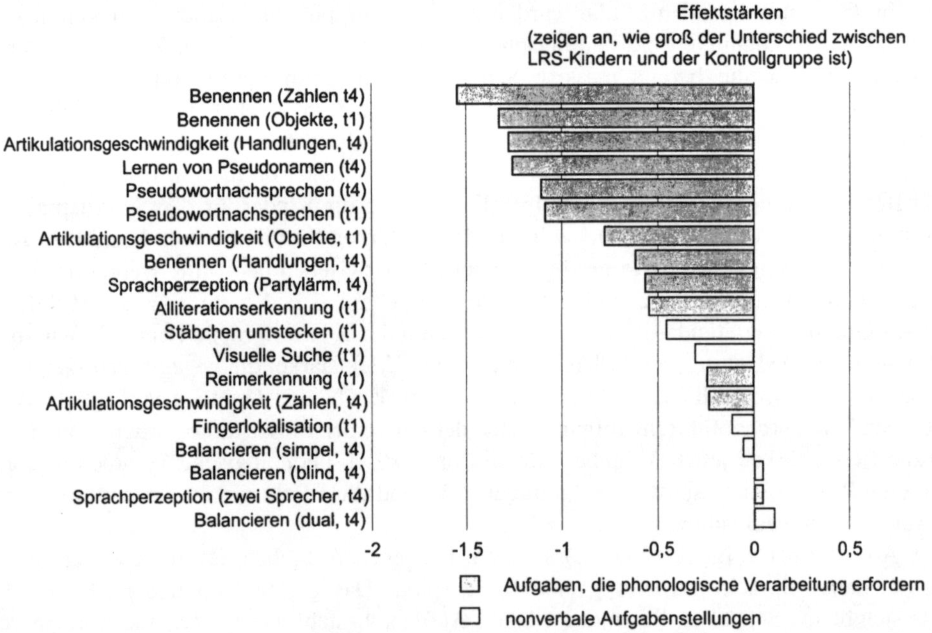

Abb.1.1.6.1 Kognitive Defizite bei LRS-Kindern aus Wimmer, Mayringer & Landerl (1998)

Eine Aufgabe, die eine gute körperliche und motorische Integration erfordert, ist die Balancieraufgabe. Das Kind muss für 30 s auf einem Bein auf einem Balken balancieren und es wird beobachtet, wie stark es schwankt bzw. wie oft es vom Balken steigen muss. Interessanterweise zeigte sich in keiner der drei durchgeführten Bedingungen auch nur der geringste Unterschied zwischen den leseschwachen und den normallesenden Kindern. Die Leseschwierigkeiten können also kaum durch motorische Defizite oder mangelnde Integration der beiden Körperhälften verursacht sein.

Zusammenfassend zeigt diese Studie also, dass auch bei deutschsprachigen Kindern mit Lese-/Rechtschreibschwäche ein Defizit in der phonologischen Verarbeitung vorliegt, während für Defizite in anderen Bereichen der kognitiven Verarbeitung keine Hinweise gefunden werden konnten.

3. Weitere Befunde zur Relevanz der phonologischen Verarbeitung für den Schriftspracherwerb

Arbeiten unserer Forschergruppe in Salzburg zeigen, dass bei englischsprachigen Kindern der Leseerwerb langsamer verläuft als bei deutschsprachigen (Landerl & Wimmer, 1998) und dass englischsprachige Legastheniker wesentlich massivere Beeinträchtigungen der Lesefertigkeiten aufweisen als deutschsprachige (Landerl, 1996; Landerl, Wimmer & Frith, 1997). Insbesondere die Fertigkeit des lautierenden Lesens, welche deutschsprachige Kinder normalerweise bereits in den ersten Monaten des Leseerwerbs erlernen und welche selbst von legasthenen Kindern – zum Teil stark verzögert und mit Hilfe von intensivem Training – mühvoll, aber kompetent beherrscht wird, bereitet englischsprachigen Kindern oft bis in die dritte und vierte Schulstrufe große Schwierigkeiten und kann von legasthenen Kindern oft nur bei kurzen, einfachen Buchstabenabfolgen umgesetzt werden. Landerl (1996) berichtet etwa, dass zwölfjährige deutschsprachige Legastheniker dreisilbige Pseudowörter (z.B. atledent, Prositrie) zwar nur sehr langsam, aber mit recht hoher Lesegenauigkeit bewältigen konnten. Nur knapp über 20% der Items wurden falsch gelesen. Eine Gruppe von gleichaltrigen englischsprachigen Kindern konnte dagegen über 70% der präsentierten Pseudowörter nicht korrekt lesen. Deutsch und Englisch verwenden dasselbe Alphabet, also können diese Unterschiede nicht mit der visuellen Verarbeitung zusammenhängen. Die beiden orthographischen Systeme unterscheiden sich aber deutlich in bezug auf ihre phonologische Transparenz. Die deutsche Orthographie zeichnet sich durch eine hohe Konsistenz der Buchstabe-Lautzuordnungen aus, die offenbar selbst von Kindern mit phonologischem Defizit verhältnismäßig gut erfasst wird. In der englischen Orthogaphie steht ein- und derselbe Buchstabe oft für sehr unterschiedliche Laute (z.B. hand, garden, hate, ball – vgl.dazu dt. Hand, Garten, Hass, Ball). Die zahllosen unregeläßigen Schreibungen erschweren es englischsprachigen Kindern zusätzlich, zu erfassen, wie genau dieses komplexe Schriftsystem ihre Muttersprache abbildet. Diese Befunde zeigen also ebenfalls, dass Unterschiede in den Leseleistungen vor allem auf Unterschiede in der phonologischen Verarbeitung zurückzuführen sind.

Eine weitere Gruppe von Befunden, die die zentrale Rolle der phonologischen Verarbeitung für den Schriftspracherwerb aufzeigt, sind Studien die zeigen, dass zwischen den phonologischen Fertigkeiten zum Zeitpunkt der Einschulung und der späteren Leseleistung ein enger Zusammenhang besteht (Überblick bei Schneider, 1989). Diese Tatsache hat sich die Bielefelder Forschungsgruppe zu Nutze gemacht und hat ein Screeningverfahren entwikkelt, das bereits bei Schuleintritt die Identifikation von Kindern ermöglicht, bei denen ein erhöhtes Risiko vorliegt, dass sie Leseschwierigkeiten entwickeln könnten (Bielefelder Screening, Jansen, Mannhaupt, Marx & Skowronek, 1999).

Eine dritte Befundgruppe, die die Bedeutung der phonologischen Verarbeitung belegt, sind Trainingsstudien. Trainingsprogramme zur Verbesserung der phonologischen Verarbeitung in der Vorschulzeit wirken sich positiv auf den Verlauf des Schriftspracherwerbs aus. Für den deutschen Sprachraum sind hier insbesondere die Arbeiten der Würzburger Forschergruppe um Prof. Schneider zu nennen, deren umfassend evaluiertes phonologisches Trainingsprogramm für das letzte Kindergartenjahr inzwischen auch publiziert wurde (Küspert & Schneider, 1999).

Als vierte und letzte Befundgruppe möchte ich schließlich auf die zunehmende Zahl von neurophysiologischen Untersuchungen hinweisen, die zeigen, dass bei Kindern mit spezifischen Lese-/Rechtschreibschwierigkeiten insbesondere in jenen Gehirnarealen neurologische Auffälligkeiten festzustellen sind, die für die Sprachverarbeitung zuständig sind. Derartige Befunde werden im Rahmen dieser Tagung von prominenten internationalen Vertretern dieser Forschungsrichtung vorgestellt werden (z.B. Schulte-Körne, 1999; Shaywitz & Shaywitz, 1999).

Für die praktische Arbeit mit spezifisch lese-/rechtschreibschwachen Kindern sind diese Befunde natürlich ausgesprochen bedeutsam. Natürlich kann für den Einzelfall nicht ausgeschlossen werden, dass zusätzlich zu einem phonologischen Defizit auch noch andere kognitive Defizite vorliegen, die einen negativen Einfluss auf die problematische Situation des Kindes haben. Für die Behandlung lese-/rechtschreibschwacher Kinder muss aber unbedingt berücksichtigt werden, dass die phonologische Verarbeitung fast immer eine Schwachstelle darstellt und dass Schwächen in diesem Bereich sich stark negativ auf das Lesen- und Rechtschreibenlernen auswirken.

Literatur

Dilling, H., Mombour, W. & Schmidt, M.H. (Hrsg.) (1993). Internationale Klassifikation psychischer Störungen, ICD-10, Kapitel V (F) Klinisch-diagnostische Leitlinien (2. korrigierte Aufl.). Bern: Huber.

Ehri, L. C. (1992). Reconceptualizing the development of sight word reading and ist relationship to recoding. In P. Gough, L.C. Ehri, & R. Treiman (Eds.), Reading acquisition (pp. 107-143), Hillsdale, NJ: Erlbaum.

Jansen, H., Mannhaupt, G., Marx, H. & Skowronek, H. (1999). Bielefelder Screening zur Früherkennung von Lese- und Rechtschreibschwierigkeiten (BISC). Göttingen: Hogrefe.

Küspert, P. & Schneider, W. (1999). Hören, lauschen, lernen: Sprachspiele für Kinder im Vorschulalter. Würzburger Trainingsprogramm zur Vorbereitung auf den Erwerb der Schriftsprache. Göttingen: Vandenhoeck & Ruprecht.

Landerl, K. (1996). Legasthenie in Deutsch und Englisch. Frankfurt: Peter Lang.

Landerl, K., & Wimmer, H. (1998). Lesenlernen bei deutsch- und englischsprachigen Kindern. Normaler und gestörter Leseerwerb. In R. Weingarten & H. Günther (Hrsg.), Schriftspracherwerb (S. 82-97); Baltmannsweiler: Schneider Verl. Hohengehren.

Landerl, K., Wimmer, H. & Frith, U. (1997). The impact of orthographic consistency on dyslexia: A German – English comparison. Cognition, 63, 315-334.

Schneider, W. (1989). Zur frühen Vorhersage von Leseleistungen. Zeitschrift für Pädagogische Psychologie, 3, 157-168.

Schulte-Körne, G. (1999, Oktober). Hirnanatomische und hirnphysiologische Korrelate zur Legasthenie. 13. Fachkongress des Bundesverbandes Legasthenie, Würzburg.

Shaywitz, S.E. & Shaywitz, B. (1999, Oktober). Functional disruption in the organization of the brain for reading in dyslexia. 13. Fachkongress des Bundesverbandes Legasthenie, Würzburg.

Perfetti, C. (1992). The representation problem in reading acquisition. In P.B. Gough, L.C. Ehri, & R. Treiman (Eds.), Reading acquisition (pp.145-174). Hillsdale, NJ: Erlbaum.

Vellutino, F.R. (1979). Dyslexia: Theory and research. Cambridge, MA: MIT Press.

Wimmer, H., Mayringer, H., & Landerl, K. (1998). Poor reading: a deficit in skill-automatization or a phonological deficit? Scientific Studies of Reading, 2 (4), 321-340.

1.1.7 The 'Phonological Representations' Hypothesis in Dyslexia

Usha Goswami

The processes involved in the development of spoken language are becoming increasingly well understood. For example, the ability to recognise and categorise spoken words as similar or different is increasingly recognised as a key factor in spoken language development. This has led to a greater understanding of the developmental importance of language games in helping the child to specify key aspects of the sound patterns of their language. For example, nursery rhymes have an important developmental function in English (Goswami, 1995). Related research has shown that dyslexic children may have particular difficulties in coding the sound patterns of familiar words in their mental lexicons. This has become known as the 'phonological representations' hypothesis.

Lexical Development

A simple view of the way in which individual words or lexical forms are coded in the brain is shown in Figure 1.1.7.1. When children first begin to acquire spoken language, in infancy, their spoken vocabularies consist of rather few words. Each word, however, is represented in terms of certain semantic features ('Daddy' may refer to a person of a certain sex and size) and also in terms of certain phonological features (the child can recognise that 'Daddy' is a different word from 'doggy'). At this developmental timepoint, the motor programme for producing the word 'Daddy' is probably quite underspecified, and the child may say 'Dada' or 'Da' when intending to name 'Daddy'. Small vocabulary size at this time may also lead toddlers to 'over-extend' the words that they do know, and the child may use their word for 'Daddy' to refer to visitors like the milkman and the postman, and to uncles and other adult males as well.

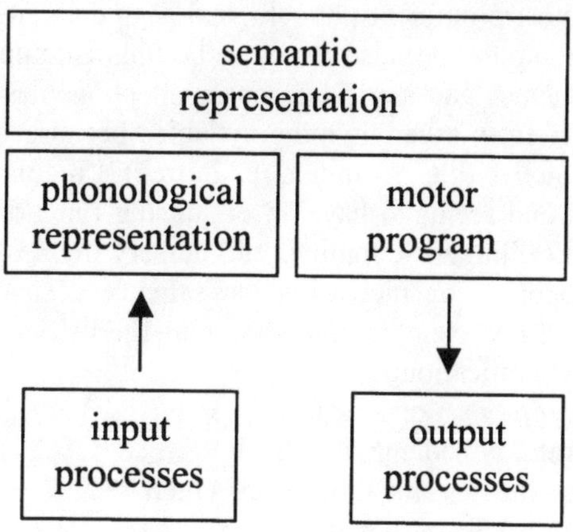

Figure 1.1.7.1

Most children go through a dramatic burst in naming activity between the ages of 1 and 2 years. Spoken vocabulary suddenly grows exponentially (by the age of 6, the average child comprehends 14,000 words, see Dollaghan, 1994). Although the phonological output typically remains imprecise (sometimes only a regular caretaker can decode the child's intended meaning), children at this point in development are rapidly acquiring more and more words which of course sound more and more similar to each other. There is considerable developmental pressure to represent these words in the brain in a way that will distinguish them from other words and allow the child to recognise them accurately and quickly during speech comprehension. For example, an English 2-year-old probably knows the similar-sounding words 'cot', 'cat' and 'cut', 'hot', 'not' and 'lot', and 'cough'. All of these words differ from 'cot' by a single phoneme (a phoneme is the smallest unit of sound that changes the meaning of a word – for example, 'cot' and 'cat' differ in their medial phoneme). In order to distinguish between these very similar-sounding words both quickly and accurately, child linguists argue that children must begin to represent the sequences of sounds that constitute each known word in their brains. They must represent the 'segmental phonology' of the words that they know.

Phonological Representations

A number of sources of evidence suggest that segmental phonology is represented at an increasingly fine-grained level as development proceeds. Children's first words are thought to represent fairly global phonological characteristics. Early in language development, the child needs to discriminate relatively few unique words, and so quite holistic representations of phonological forms will suffice (e.g., Ferguson, 1986; Juscyk, 1993). However, as more and more words are acquired, children are thought to begin to represent the number of syllables in a word, and the 'onsets' and 'rimes' in each syllable. This process may begin as early as age 2.

The syllable is thought to be the primary linguistic processing unit for many European languages, as it is distinguished by a number of auditory cues including rhythm and stress. Within the syllable, the most prominent phonological segments are the onset and the rime. One syllable rhymes with another because it shares the linguistic unit called the <u>rime</u>, which comprises the vowel phonemes and any final consonant phonemes (e.g., t/ea-tr/ee; br/ight-k/ite). One syllable differs from other rhyming syllables because the phonemes before the vowel (the <u>onset</u>) are distinctive (e.g., /t/ in tea, /tr/ in tree). Linguistically, the rime is a very salient phonological unit, and seems to have an organising function for English phonology. Many of the language games, linguistic routines and nursery rhymes of early childhood act to emphasise segmental phonology by increasing the salience of phonological segments like syllables, onsets and rimes. For example, many popular English nursery rhymes have strong rhythms that emphasise syllabification:

Hump-ty Dump-ty sat on a wall
Hump-ty Dump-ty had a great fall
All the king's hor-ses and all the king's men
Could-n't put Hump-ty to-geth-er again.

and many popular nursery rhymes contrast both rhyming words ('Baa Baa Black Sheep' rhymes 'wool' with 'full') and highly similar but non-rhyming words (it also rhymes 'dame' with 'lane'):

Baa Baa Black Sheep
Have you any wool?
Yes sir, yes sir

Three bags full.
One for my master
And one for my dame
And one for the little boy
Who lives down the lane.

This process of re-representing the segmental phonology of individual words has been called 'lexical restructuring' (Metsala & Walley, 1998). The restructuring process is thought to be relatively word-specific. It will depend on the child's overall vocabulary size and also on the rate of expansion of that vocabulary. Children with large vocabularies who are rapidly acquiring lots of new words would be expected to experience greater pressure for restructuring, and consequently to have represented the syllables, onsets and rimes in many of the words in their vocabularies. Lexical restructuring will also depend on word frequency or familiarity. Words that are encountered many times are more likely to have been restructured, because the child needs to access them rapidly and accurately on so many occasions. Finally, lexical restructuring will depend on the number of similar-sounding words in the lexicon ('neighbourhood density'). Words in 'dense' neighbourhoods (words like 'cot', with many similar-sounding neighbours) should experience most pressure for restructuring, as they must be distinguished from a large number of other extremely similar words. Words in 'sparse' neighbourhoods, which must only be distinguished from a small number of other extremely similar words, should experience less pressure for restructuring. The characteristics of these phonological neighbours should also affect the restructuring process. Work in my laboratory has shown that, on average, 50% of the phonological neighbours of any monosyllabic word in English are rime neighbours. For example, the word 'cot' has 41 neighbours, of which 23 are rime neighbours. The word 'cook' has only 17 neighbours, of which 9 are rime neighbours. The fact that the majority of phonological neighbours for most words are rime neighbours means that the rime is an important organisational unit for English phonology (see Kessler & Treiman, 1997, for a converging linguistic analysis).

Learning to Read and Spell

Learning to read and spell has a profound effect on the segmental structure of the child's phonological representations. Prior to being taught to read and write, it is thought that most children have only represented the onsets and rimes in spoken words. These phonological units are sufficient to distinguish between all the words in the spoken language. However, learning to read requires the child to analyse spoken language at a finer grain —that of the phoneme. Because alphabetic letters correspond to phonemes, learning an alphabetic code teaches the child that words can also be represented as sequences of phonemes. Spelling may be particularly important in this respect, as the act of spelling forces the child to analyse each sound in a given word in sequence, thereby performing a phonemic analysis. Given this intimate relationship between reading and phonemic representation, it is interesting that children who are learning to read 'transparent' alphabetic codes that have a 1:1 correspondence between letters and sounds for reading (such as German) quickly become fluent in reading, and also develop good 'nonsense word' reading skills (they can accurately decode novel forms like 'tegwop'). Children who are learning to read English, a non-transparent alphabetic code, develop these skills far more slowly (e.g., Frith, Landerl & Wimmer, 1998; Goswami, Gombert & De Barrera, 1998; Goswami, Porpodas & Wheelwright, 1997; Wimmer & Goswami, 1994). Dyslexic children, particularly those learning to read a non-transparent orthography like English, seem to develop these skills particularly slowly, and may have difficulty in reaching a level sufficient to support fluent reading and writing.

Phonological Representations in Dyslexia

There is increasing evidence that dyslexic children experience a specific difficulty with the representation of segmental phonology. Many dyslexic children develop extensive spoken vocabularies and show no overt signs of speech output difficulties. Nevertheless, when their phonological system is placed under pressure, for example by the need to explicitly compare or manipulate segments of phonology (as in the oddity task, when the child must identify the 'odd word' in a triple like fan, cat, mat, or the Spoonerism task, when the child must substitute word onsets so that Sonne Mond becomes Monne Sond, see Bradley & Bryant, 1978; Landerl, Frith & Wimmer, 1997), dyslexic children in all languages exhibit phonological processing difficulties. It is now thought that these 'phonological awareness' difficulties stem from imprecisions and inadequacies in the ways that speech sounds are represented in the dyslexic brain.

For example, dyslexic children show poor nonsense word repetition in phonological memory tasks that require them to repeat nonsense words like ballop and thickery. Repeating nonsense (novel) word forms requires the child to set up new phonological representations, using segments of known words (like allop from 'gallop'). Developmental dyslexics are also slower to recognise familiar words on the basis of acoustic input. For example, they require more acoustic-phonetic information than age-matched controls to recognise familiar words from sparse neighbourhoods in speech 'gating' tasks. In such tasks, incremental 'gates' or segments of speech from word-onset are presented through headphones (Metsala, 1997). On the output side, developmental dyslexics show deficits in fine-grained measures of speech production such as the distinctness of vowel articulation (Elbro, Borstrom & Petersen, 1998). They also show word finding problems in 'confrontation naming' tasks (in which simple pictures must be named on demand), even though they are very familiar with the items in the pictures. Their problems are particularly marked when the familiar names are long and of low frequency, and thus correspond to phonological forms that have been encountered less frequently and that also require the accurate specification of more phonological segments (see Goswami, Schneider & Scheurich, 1999, for German; Swan & Goswami, 1997a, for English). Finally, dyslexic children find rapid 'automatized' speeded naming tasks difficult. These tasks require the child to name familiar items presented in lists (such as digits) as quickly as possible, thereby accessing and outputting what should be well-practiced and so well-specified phonological forms („nine, two, five, ...). Despite the familiarity of these phonological forms, the need to access and output the same forms repeatedly under time pressure stresses the child's phonological system, leading to poor performance.

Perhaps counter-intuitively, reading actually helps to specify phonological information for dyslexic children. In our study (Swan & Goswami, 1997a), we investigated the phonological characteristics of the word finding deficit in a group of 12-year-old dyslexic children with a reading age of 9 years 6 months. We found that the dyslexic children were more likely than age-matched (CA) and reading-level matched (RL) control children to produce naming errors for familiar words that were phonologically similar to the target (e.g., cog for clog). The dyslexic children's errors were more likely to share the initial phoneme with the target (32%, CA = 20%, RL = 16%), to share the correct number of syllables (47%, CA = 31%, RL = 27%), and to share the correct number of phonemes (22%, CA = 12%, RL =

14%). This suggests that the dyslexic children had rather imprecise or phonologically immature phonological representations of the familiar target words (the control children tended to make visual or semantic errors, such as saying 'shoe' for clog). Further, the dyslexic children were better at reading the target words than at naming them in response to a picture. This pattern was not found for the control children, and suggests that the act of decoding print was helping the dyslexic child to specify inadequate or missing portions of their phonological representations of familiar words.

Interestingly, phonological awareness in dyslexic children can be age-appropriate if the quality of the child's phonological representations is taken into account. Swan and Goswami (1997b) studied phonological awareness deficits at the syllable, onset-rime and phoneme levels in dyslexic children both before and after taking the representational quality of the individual words used in these tasks into account for each child. Their measure of representational adequacy was the accurate naming of familiar words to pictures (child says „clog" for clog). They found no phonological deficits at the syllable and onset-rime levels in comparison to both CA and RL controls when performance was scored only for words that had adequate phonological representations. In contrast, phonological awareness deficits at the phoneme level for adequately-represented items were found in comparison to both control groups. This suggests that spoken words with adequate phonological representations had been restructured to the onset-rime level by the dyslexic children, at an age-appropriate level.

However, although performance at the phoneme level improved greatly once the adequacy of the dyslexic child's phonological representations for individual words was taken into account (e.g., from 38% correct to 69% correct for an initial phoneme matching task), it did not reach the level of the control children (e.g., CA group improved from 71% to 93% correct, RL group from 58% to 84% correct, in the same task). It is not surprising that performance in phonemic awareness tasks improves for all children when performance is measured for words for which the child has a well-specified phonological representation. This suggests that lexical restructuring to the phoneme level is indeed taking place as age and reading ability increase. However, it is surprising that the performance of dyslexic children was worse than that of younger RL controls for words that had adequate phonological representations in the phoneme tasks only. As noted earlier, the representation of fully-specified phoneme-level information is thought to depend on reading and spelling experience. For the dyslexic children, it seems likely that despite having the same level of single word reading as the RL control children, they had read less overall (because of Matthew effects, see Stanovich, 1986) and so their lexical restructuring had progressed more slowly both because they had had less feedback from print and because they had a phonological processing difficulty.

Basic Auditory Processing Deficits?

Studies that have attempted to uncover basic auditory processing deficits to explain this apparently selective difficulty in representing phonological forms in memory have so far produced mixed results. Typically, a basic processing task will show dramatic impairments for some dyslexic children, and no apparent impairment for others, despite extremely careful subject selection. Thus some dyslexic children have great difficulty with 'minimal pairs' tasks that require the discrimination of similar-sounding words (e.g., smack-snack), yet others do not (Adlard & Hazan, 1998). Some dyslexic children find phoneme categorisation and repetition tasks very difficult (e.g., discriminating between or repeating /b/ and /d/), and others do not (e.g., Manis et al., 1997; Reed, 1989). Some dyslexic children find temporal order judgements very difficult. Typically, such tasks require them to decide whether a high tone preceded a low tone or vice versa. Accordingly, it has been proposed that dyslexia is caused by temporal processing deficits, but this view is quite controversial (e.g., Tallal, 1980). For example, Mody et al. (1997) have shown that dyslexic children who find it difficult to discriminate phonemes like ba/da show no deficit in a nonspeech analogue task that makes the same temporal processing demands (based on sine wave speech). Thus far, most auditory processing deficits that have been found appear to be specific to linguistic stimuli. However, the lack of uniformity across subjects is puzzling, and is an obvious challenge for future research.

Convergent Evidence from Brain Imaging Studies

Evidence from brain imaging work is consistent with the view that the key difficulty in dyslexia is a weakness in the representation of phonological information. The phonological processing system spans a number of cortical and subcortical regions in the brain, including frontal, temporal and parietal cortex. Studies of aphasia long ago revealed the importance of Broca's area (frontal cortex) and Wernicke's area (posterior superior temporal gyrus) for the motor production and receptive aspects of speech respectively, and the lateralisation of language-related processes to the left hemisphere is equally well-documented.

Interpretation of functional neuroimaging studies of dyslexia is complicated by the fact that only adult developmental dyslexics can be scanned, which means that the brain's compensatory responses to any initial disorder may account for some of the patterns of task-related activity that are found. Nevertheless, despite seemingly inconsistent results in early studies, localisation of phonological mechanisms in the temporoparietal junction and abnormalities in activation surrounding this junction in adult developmental dyslexics during phonological processing tasks have been documented by a number of research groups (see Eden & Zeffiro, 1998, for review). When performing tasks like rhyme judgement, rhyme detection, and word and nonsense word reading, dyslexic subjects show reduced activation in temporal and parietal regions, particularly within the left hemisphere.

A Speculative Developmental Analysis of Phonological Development in-Dyslexia

On the basis of the evidence discussed in this paper, the following proposals can be made concerning the development of phonological representations in dyslexia. Dyslexic children, like all children, begin acquiring a spoken vocabulary in infancy, and like all children they experience increasing developmental pressure to specify accurately the phonological segments in words as they learn more and more similar-sounding words. For most words, they develop adequate phonological representations that specify the onsets and rimes in the words, but this requires substantially more practice and experience with the spoken word forms than it does for children with no phonological processing deficit. For some words, dyslexic children do not develop adequate phonological representations, perhaps because of subtle input-related processing deficiencies that are not yet well-understood, or perhaps because they have a selective deficit in representing the input (the input may be processed accurately by the brain but not stored accurately). The imprecision of these representations of spoken word forms lead to a number of problems, the most marked of which concern reading and spelling acquisition. Dyslexic children who are learning to read and spell transparent orthographies like German can read and spell relatively accurately, but they do so extremely slowly. Dyslexic children who are learning to read and spell non-transparent orthographies like English read and spell inaccurately, and extremely slowly. The challenge for research is to understand more completely why some spoken word forms are represented accurately while others are not, for individual children. If factors like overall neighbourhood density, number of rime neighbours and age of acquisition turn out to characterise which words do and do not have well-specified phonological representations in dyslexic children, then this would have obvious implications for remediation. For example, intensive tuition could target words from dense neighbourhoods, or words with many rime neighbours. Our current research is investigating the importance of these factors in the development of phonological awareness in both normal and dyslexic children.

Bibliography

Adlard, A., Hazan, V. (1998). Speech perception in children with specific reading difficulties (dyslexia). Quarterly Journal of Experimental Psychology, 51A: 153-177.

Dollaghan, C.A. (1994). Children's phonological neighbourhoods: Half empty or half full? Journal of Child Language, 21, 257-271.

Eden, G.F., Zeffiro, T.A. (1998). Neural systems affected in developmental dyslexia revealed by functional neuroimaging. Neuron, 21: 279-282.

Elbro, C., Borstrom, I., & Petersen, D.K. (1998). Predicting dyslexia from kindergarten: The importance of distinctness of phonological representations of lexical items. Reading Research Quarterly, 33, 36-60.

Ferguson, C.A. (1986). Discovering sound units and constructing sound systems: It's child's play. In J.S. Perkell & D.H. Klatt (Eds.), Invariance and variability in speech processes (pp. 36-51). Hillsdale, NJ: Erlbaum.

Frith, U., Wimmer, H., & Landerl, K. (1998). Differences in phonological recoding in German- and English-speaking children. Scientific Studies of Reading, 2, 31-54.

Goswami, U. (1995). Rhyme in Children's Early Reading. In R. Beard (Ed.), Rhyme, Reading and Writing, pp. 62-79. London: Hodder & Stoughton.

Goswami, U. (in press). Phonological representations, reading development and dyslexia: Towards a cross-linguistic theoretical framework. Dyslexia.

Goswami, U., Bryant, P.E. (1990). Phonological Skills and Learning to Read. Hillsdale, NJ: Lawrence Erlbaum.

Goswami, U., Gombert, J., & De Barrera, F. (1998). Children's Orthographic Representations and Linguistic Transparency: Nonsense Word Reading in English, French and Spanish. Applied Psycholinguistics, 19, 19-52.

Goswami, U., Porpodas, C., & Wheelwright, S. (1997). Children's orthographic representations in English and Greek. European Journal of Psychology of Education, 12 (3), 273-292.

Goswami, U., Schneider, W., & Scheurich, B., (1999). Picture naming deficits in developmental dyslexia in German. Developmental Science, 2, 53-58.

Jusczyk, P.W. (1986). Toward a model of the development of speech perception. In J.S. Perkell & D.H. Klatt (Eds.), Invariance and variability in speech processes (pp. 1-33). Hillsdale, NJ: Erlbaum.

Jusczyk, P.W. (1993). From general to language- specific capacities: The WRAPSA model of how speech perception develops. Journal of Phonetics, 21, 3-28.

Landerl, K., Wimmer, H., & Frith, U. (1997). The impact of orthographic consistency on dyslexia: A German-English comparison. Cognition, 63, 315-334.

Manis, F.R., McBride-Chang, C., Seidenberg, M.S., Keating, P., Doi, L.M., Munsun, B., & Petersen, A. (1997). Are speech perception deficits associated with developmental dyslexia? Journal of Experimental Child Psychology, 66, 211-235.

Metsala, J.L. (1997). Spoken word recognition in reading disabled children. Journal of Educational Psychology, 89, 159-169.

Metsala, J.L., & Walley, A.C. (1998). Spoken vocabulary growth and the segmental restructuring of lexical representations: Precursors to phonemic awareness and early reading ability. In J.L. Metsala & L.C. Ehri (Eds.), Word Recognition in Beginning Literacy, pp. 89-120. Hillsdale, NJ:Erlbaum.

Mody, M., Studdert-Kennedy, M., & Brady, S. (1997). Speech perception deficits in poor readers: Auditory processing or phonological coding? Journal of Experimental Child Psychology, 64, 199-231.

Swan, D., & Goswami, U. (1997a). Picture naming deficits in developmental dyslexia: The phonological representations hypothesis. Brain & Language, 56, 334-353.

Swan, D., & Goswami, U. (1997b). Phonological awareness deficits in developmental dyslexia and the phonological representations hypothesis. Journal of Experimental Child Psychology, 66, 18-41.

Tallal, P. (1980). Auditory temporal perception, phonics and reading disabilities in children. Brain & Language, 9: 182-198.

Wimmer, H. (1993). Characteristics of developmental dyslexia in a regular writing system. Applied Psycholinguistics, 14, 1-33.

Wimmer, H., & Goswami, U. (1994). The influence of orthographic consistency on reading development: Word recognition in English and German children. Cognition, 51, 91-103.

1.2 Visuelle Wahrnehmung

1.2.1 Visuelle Probleme bei Kindern mit Legasthenie[1]

W. D. Schäfer

Zusammenfassung

Der aktuelle Wissensstand zur Legasthenie, das Sehen betreffend, besagt, dass Störungen in der Sehbahn oder im Sehzentrum angenommen werden. Kleine Hilfen (kontrastreiche große Schrift, Zeitzuschlag bei Arbeiten) mildern diese Probleme. Krankhafte Befunde beider Augen sind nicht die Ursache der Legasthenie. Um aber klare Bilder zum Sehzentrum weiterzuleiten, sollten auch geringe Fehler von Brechkraft oder der Augenbeweglichkeit durch Brillen korrigiert werden, falls die Betroffenen dies akzeptieren.

Geschichtliche Entwicklung

Vor gut 25 Jahren berichtete Hoffmann (1973) über 50 Schüler einer Legasthenieklasse, von denen er bei 40 pathologische Augenbefunde beobachtete. Dieses waren 28 mal Hyperopien[2] beider Augen, 19 mal Exophorien und 17 mal Konvergenzschwächen (Mehrfachnennungen waren möglich). Andere Refraktions- und Motilitätsstörungen gab es viel seltener. Man vermutete einen Zusammenhang von Hyperopie, Exophorie und Konvergenzschwäche mit der Legasthenie. Diese Zusammenhänge konnten in der Folgezeit aber nicht nachgewiesen werden.

Für Verwirrung sorgten Untersuchungen von Pestalozzi (1986), der über Heilungen der Legasthenie durch Prismentherapie bei 30 von 46 Patienten berichtete. Dies führte zu einer sehr kontroversen Diskussion, besonders in der Schweiz. Eine Klärung brachte die Untersuchung von 20 legasthenen, von Pestalozzi mit Prismenbrillen versorgten Kindern durch Schwarz (1992) in der Abteilung für Logopädie der Universität Zürich. Es zeigte sich, dass die Ergebnisse sowohl beim Lesen als auch beim Rechtschreiben etwas schlechter waren als bei einer Vergleichsgruppe der Klinik. Pestalozzi (1992) dementierte daraufhin seine frühere Mitteilung zur Heilung von Legasthenikern. Weitere Klärungen brachte die Grundlagenforschung zur Genese und Reihenuntersuchungen Betroffener und nicht Betroffener.

Ursachen

Die Genese der Legasthenie ist noch nicht sicher geklärt. Studien aus den letzten Jahren deuten jedoch auf eine zentrale Ursache hin. Dazu gehören die Obduktionsbefunde von Galaburda (1986), der im Gehirn (mittlerer Nucleus geniculatus des Thalamus) von Betroffenen kleinere Zellen als bei Vergleichspersonen nachgewiesen hat. Man vermutet deshalb, dass Höreindrücke nur verlangsamt wahrgenommen werden können. Ähnliche Phänomene für die Sehbahn haben mehrere Autoren dargestellt (s. Breitmeyer, 1995). So reagierten die magno-

---

1 Teile dieses Beitrages wurden mit freundlicher Genehmigung des borgmann-publishing Verlages, Hohe Straße 39, 44139 Dortmund, entnommen aus: W. D. Schäfer u. H. Mühlendyck: Legasthenie und okulär bedingte Lesestörungen, in: P. Haase: Schreiben und Lesen – sicher lehren und lernen, S. 121-132, borgmann, Dortmund 2000.

2 Fachausdrücke werden in einem Glossar am Ende der Arbeit erklärt

zellulären Zellen der Sehbahn im VEP von Legasthenikern auf schnellbewegte optische Reize und geringem Kontrast mit verminderten Antworten. Es komme zu einem Überlappen oder „Verschmieren“ der Bilder, so dass beim Lesen die Buchstaben nicht mehr exakt getrennt werden können. Neuere PET-Untersuchungen (Eden et al., 1996) zeigen, dass Aktivitätsunterschiede nicht nur im Sprachzentrum, sondern auch im kortikalen Sehzentrum nachzuweisen sind. Für einen Teil der familiären Legasthenien wurde der Genort für die Störung oder für Teilaspekte der Störung auf den Chromosomen 15 und 6 nachgewiesen (Grigorenko et al, 1997).

Kontrollstudien

Weitere Belege dafür, dass es sich bei der Legasthenie nicht um ein Problem der Augen handelt, brachten Kontrollstudien der letzten Jahre. Von besonderer Bedeutung ist eine schwedische Untersuchung (Ygge et al, 1993a,b). Die Autoren konnten aus einer Gesamtzahl von über 2000 Schülern jeweils 86 legasthene und 86 „Kontroll“-Schüler aussuchen. Beide Gruppen bildeten „passende Paare“, wobei das Alter (Mittelwert 9 Jahre, 5 Monate), das Geschlecht (68 männlich, 18 weiblich), die Klasse (jeweils zweite) und der Intelligenzquotient berücksichtigt wurden. Nicht einbezogen wurden mehrsprachige Kinder und solche, die die Untersuchung ablehnten, aber auch kranke oder mit Medikamenten behandelte Kinder.

Es ergaben sich keine signifikanten Unterschiede für die Funktionen: Augenstellung, Fusion, Stereopsis, Refraktion, Akkommodation, okuläre Dominanz, Augenbewegungen. Lediglich bei der Sehschärfe (Mittelwerte: 0.98 und 1.06) und bei der Kontrastempfindlichkeit waren Legastheniker schlechter als Nicht-Legastheniker. Die Autoren verwendeten allerdings übliche Sehschärfenteste mit Zahlen und Buchstaben und sie vermuten - so wie wir - dass dies der Grund für die Unterschiede sein könne. Deshalb verwenden wir den C-Test nach Hohmann und Haase (1981), bei dem die Lage der Lücke in einem schwarzen Ring erkannt werden muss.

In einer eigenen Studie (Schäfer, 1997) wurden 341 Kinder mit Legasthenie und Lernstörungen untersucht. 74% waren männlich und 26% weiblichen Geschlechts. Das Durchschnittsalter betrug 9,7 und 9,5 Jahre. Auch hier ergaben sich für die untersuchten Teilfunktionen der Augen keine Unterschiede zu Nichtbetroffenen. So erreichten 69% eine volle Sehschärfe beider Augen, während bei 31% die Sehschärfe der Augen unter dem Normbereich (19%) lagen oder ein Auge deutlich schlechter als das andere war (12%).

Untersuchung

Die Untersuchung durch den Augenarzt (Schäfer, 1995) besteht aus dem kompletten Befund beider Augen. Dabei ist eine objektive Refraktionsbestimmung in Zykloplegie auch im Pubertätsalter sowie ein pleoptisch-orthoptischer Status erforderlich. Besonderer Wert muss auf verdecktes Schielen und die Messung des Nahpunktes der Akkommodation gelegt werden.

Die genaue Bestimmung der Akkommodation ist sehr wichtig, da Mühlendyck (1999) annimmt, dass bis zu 10% der Schulkinder Störungen in diesem Bereich haben können. Typisch dafür ist die Hypoakkommodation. Hierbei funktioniert die Einstellung der Linse der Augen auf unterschiedlich weit entfernte Sehobjekte nicht altersentsprechend. Besonders das Lesen in der Nähe, aber auch der rasche Wechsel von Fern- und Nahsehen (z.B. Abschreiben von der Tafel) bereitet den Schülern große Probleme. Sie klagen über Kopf- und Augenschmerzen und wollen überhaupt nicht mehr lesen. Diese Veränderung kann man sich als vorzeitige Alterung einer Funktion des Körpers vorstellen. So kann die Akkommodation eines zehnjährigen Kindes etwa der eines 35- oder 50-jährigen Erwachsenen entsprechen.

Neben dem Lesen mit jedem Auge einzeln und dann mit beiden Augen für Ferne und Nähe, sind einfache Lese- und Schreibteste, mit dem man sich ein Bild über die Fähigkeiten des Kindes machen kann, hilfreich. Leseproben werden auch benutzt, um die Auswirkung geplanter Brillenverordnungen oder geänderter Brillen auszuprobieren, ebenso wie die probeweise Gabe von bifokalen Brillen oder Prismenbrillen.

Okuläre Therapie

Das Prinzip der Behandlung besteht darin, schon kleinere Störungen der Augen - falls die Kinder dies akzeptieren - durch Brillen zu korrigieren, um eine möglichst scharfe Abbildung im Sehzentrum zu erhalten. Bei der Therapie hat sich der Ausgleich auch geringer Refraktionsanomalien - besonders bei Astigmatismus - bewährt. Es werden bequeme, kindgerechte Brillen mit Nasensteg und Imperialbügel (Gespinstbügel) verordnet. Allerdings sind manche Kinder (ca. 1/5) durch zuviele andere Behandlungsmaßnahmen entmutigt und nicht mehr zum Brillentragen bereit, obwohl objektiv eine Verbesserung der Sehschärfe oder der beidäugigen Zusammenarbeit festzustellen ist.

Bifokale Brillen werden bei Akkommodationsschwäche, aber auch bei Esophorien mit akkommodativer Komponente im Nahbereich verordnet. Wichtig ist ein großes Nahsegment. Die Erfahrung lehrt, dass die betroffenen Kinder diese Brillen gerne tragen, weil etwa bei Hypoakkommodation die Beschwerden schlagartig behoben sind. Bewährt hat sich auch die Verordnung von Bifokalbrillen einfach nur zur Textvergrößerung (Lupeneffekt). Die Nahaddition bei Bifokalbrillen beträgt je nach Befund zwischen +1,5 und +3,0 Dioptrien (cm/m).

Bei Konvergenzschwäche und einigen Formen der Exophorie haben sich Prismenbrillen bewährt. Es sind bis etwa 5 Prismendioptrien (cm/m) Basis innen pro Glas erforderlich. Bei den etwas komplizierteren Störungen im Zusammenspiel zwischen Akkommodation, Fusion und Konvergenz können neben bifokalen Gläsern auch zusätzliche Prismen erforderlich werden. In Ausnahmefällen sind dann auch mehrere Untersuchungstermine erforderlich.

Brillenverordnungen sind allerdings nicht immer erforderlich. In unserer Studie (Schäfer, 1997) war dies nur bei 58% der Untersuchten erforderlich. Dies mag verwundern, da von den Kindern oft über Verschwommensehen, Augenschmerzen, Tränen, Lichtscheu, Kopfschmerzen oder Schwindel geklagt wird. Auch die Beobachtungen der Eltern und Lehrer an den Kindern mit Augenzwinkern, Augenreiben oder Stirnezusammenziehen bei Lese- und Schreibaufgaben ist kein sicherer Hinweis für krankhafte Augenbefunde.

Die Ergebnisse beim Tragen von Bifokal- und Prismenbrillen sind durchweg gut (Schäfer, 1997). Auch der Anteil der Kinder, die diese speziellen Brillen nicht tragen möchten, ist geringer als bei Verordnung einfacher Brillen. Bei etwa 1% der Untersuchten muss mit einer Augenmuskeloperation gerechnet werden. Diese Zahl entspricht etwa der, die für alle nichtlegasthenen Kinder angenommen wird.

Kleine Hilfen

Wichtig sind auch die kleinen Hilfen im täglichen Leben und in der Schule. So sollten die Kinder immer möglichst gut und groß gedruckte Arbeitsvorlagen (Matrizen, Fotokopien) mit kontrastreichem Druck und großer Schrift erhalten. Wenn kein gutes Vervielfältigungsgerät zur Verfügung steht, sollte der Lehrer sein Originalblatt dem legasthenen Schüler zur Verfügung stellen. Das Lesen mit Abdecken von Textteilen durch den Zeigefinger oder durch Anwendung einer Schablone[2], die nur das zu lesende Wort freigibt (Fahle, 1997) gehört ebenfalls zu diesen Hilfen. Bewährt hat sich auch eine Leselupe in Form eines Stabes, die jeweils eine Zeile stärker vergrößert. Können die Kinder damit oder mit einer „Briefmarkenlupe“, die es in jedem Haushalt gibt, besser lesen, empfiehlt es sich, die Verordnung einer bifokalen Brille zu überlegen. Ein Schülertisch mit verstellbarer Platte, ein bequemer ergonomisch geformter Stuhl und eine gute Beleuchtung (Tischlampe) sind weitere wichtige Hilfen. Bei schulischen Arbeiten sollten die Kinder einen Zeitzuschlag erhalten. Dieser kann bei 20 bis 50% oder mehr liegen, je nach Betroffenheit des Schülers und den Anforderung an Lesen und Schreiben. Auch die Nutzung des zweiten Sinneskanales (Gehör), der bei Legasthenikern auch irritiert sein kann, erleichtert das schulische Arbeiten. So kann der Text einer Aufgabe dem Schüler über ein Diktaphon (Walkman), das vom Lehrer besprochen wird, übermittelt werden. Das simultane Abspielen des Textes und das gleichzeitige Lesen erleichtert das Verstehen erheblich, außerdem wird durch den Kopfhörer zusätzlich noch das Hintergrundgeräusch der Klasse gedämpft.

Nicht gesicherte Behandlungsmethoden

Bei der Beurteilung neuer Therapien muss immer der Placebo-Effekt und der Einfluss zusätzlicher Behandlungsmaßnahmen berücksichtigt werden. Ein sehr dominanter Therapeut wird übergute Ergebnisse bewirken (Fahle, 1997). Man erkundige sich auch, ob die Kosten von der Krankenkasse übernommen werden. Nur bei erfolgversprechenden neuen Therapien geschieht dies.

Antisakkaden-Training

Fischer (1997) beobachtete, dass bei 2/3 der Legastheniker sogenannte „Express-Sakkaden“ häufiger und schneller ausgeführt wurden. Es handelt sich um Blick-Ziel-Bewegungen mit sehr kurzer Latenz. Muss bei Auftauchen eines Signales aber in die Gegenrichtung geblickt werden, dann treten Fehler bei den „Antisakkaden“ auf. Nach Training mit einem besonderen Gerät, kommt es zu einer deutlichen Verbesserung dieser Funktion. Diese Behandlung wurde bis jetzt noch nicht von anderen Autoren übernommen, da Zweifel bestehen, ob durch ein Antisakkaden-Training langfristig ein besseres Lesen zu erreichen ist.

MKH-Methodik

Die Mess- und Korrektionsmethodik nach H.-J. Haase wird besonders von Pestalozzi propagiert und beruht auf dem Polatest (Zeiss). Die Befürworter nehmen an, dass zumindest eine Teilursache der Legasthenie durch fehlerhaftes beidäugiges Sehen und latentes Schielen der Augen bedingt ist. Die Kritik besagt jedoch, dass der Polatest methodische Fehler hat (Lang, 1992; Mühlendyck et al, 1993; Gerling, 1998, 1999) und als subjektiver Test für Kinder ungeeignet ist. „Subjektiv“ bedeutet, dass das Kind Angaben machen muss, was sehr schwierig ist. Außerdem ergeben sich zu viele Esophorien, die dann mit Prismen auskorrigiert werden. Verstärkungen dieser Prismen und Prismenneuverordnungen sind nicht selten. Deshalb besteht auch ein vermehrtes Risiko von Augenmuskeloperationen, wenn die Prismenstärke deutlich über 5 Dioptrien pro Glas hinausgeht. Die Kosten der Behandlungen werden von den

2 Kindgerechte Lesehilfe-Schablonen hat Ulrich Butz, Schönfeldstr. 3, 76131 Karlsruhe, Tel.: 07 21/69 15 19 entwickelt.

Krankenkassen nicht übernommen. Keine Einwände bestehen gegen eine Vollkorrektur von Refraktionsanomalien mit Brillen. Die Bestimmung kann aber nur in Zyloplegie erfolgen. Die Tendenz der Augenärzte ist deshalb „objektive" Verfahren zu verwenden, die im Gegensatz zu den subjektiven Methoden auf der Beobachtung des Kindes beruhen.

Augendominanz

Stein et al (1985) und Otto (1989) haben beobachtet, dass legasthene Kinder keine fixierte Augendominanz haben. Ursache sei ein alternierendes Zentralskotom, wodurch die Lesestörung begründet sei. Stein sah dies bei zwei von drei Kindern. Deshalb wird die längere Okklusion eines Auges über sechs Monate bis zwei Jahre empfohlen, um durch Schaffung eines dominanten Auges Leseverbesserung zu bewirken. Lang (1992) kritisiert u.a., dass ein alternierendes Zentralskotom nicht nachgewiesen sei. Bishop (1989) hat die Daten von Stein durchgesehen und fand keinen Beweis dafür, dass die Okklusionsbehandlung die Lesefähigkeit verbessert hat. Durch die lange Okklusionstherapie mit Unterbrechung des beidäugigen Sehens muss bei 49% der Behandelten eine Augenmuskeloperation vorgenommen werden (Otto, 1989).

Irlengläser

Helen Irlen beschrieb 1983 als einen Faktor, der zur Legasthenie führen könne, das „Scotopic-Sensitivity-Syndrome". Die Betroffenen seien beim Lesen durch Verformung (distortions) gestört, bei denen sich Buchstaben und Wörter des Textes bewegen, wobei auch der weiße Hintergrund Teile des schwarzen Druckbildes überstrahlen könne. Durch Herausfiltern störender Anteile des Lichtspektrums mit farbigen Folien oder Brillen (es gibt über 100) könnten diese Distortions beseitigt werden. Gerling und Kommerell (1997) halten eine spezifische Wirksamkeit der Farbfilter bei Legasthenie nicht für belegt. Ein überzeugendes pathophysiologisches Konzept fehle. Da es auch zustimmende Literatur gibt, vermuten die Autoren einen unspezifischen Effekt (Placebo). Dieser beruht wohl darauf, dass jeder Mensch eine Lieblingsfarbe hat. Wird ein Lesetext damit unterlegt, kann dies als angenehmer empfunden werden.

Rasterbrille

Von verschiedenen Seiten wird immer wieder eine Rasterbrille empfohlen. Es handelt sich um eine Brille mit schwarzen Gläsern. Etwa alle 3 mm findet sich ein kleines Loch zum Durchsehen. Damit soll die Mikro-Sakkadentätigkeit der Augen angeregt werden. Sakkaden sind rasche Blicksprünge zwischen Folgebewegung der Augen. Die Mikrosakkaden laufen unbewusst ab zum Schutz des Sehpurpurs vor Ausbleichung (Toxler-Effekt). Durch die Anwendung dieser Brillen kommt es zur Kontrastminderung mit Reduktion der Sehschärfe und zu Fusionsstörungen (Schäfer, 1998). Dadurch können Heterophorien dekompensieren und eine Diplopie bewirken. Wegen der schlechten Sicht leiden die Kinder sehr, die diese Brillen tragen müssen.

Rat des Augenarztes an Eltern und Betroffene

Bei Legasthenie, Legasthenieverdacht, Dyskalkulie oder bei anderen Lernstörungen sollte die beschriebene, ausgiebige augenärztliche Untersuchung erfolgen. Es gibt besonders an Kindern interessierte Augenärzte, die meist eine Sehschule haben, in der Orthoptistinnen arbeiten. Wegen häufiger Sprach- und Hörstörungen sollten Betroffene bei einem Pädaudiologen (spezialisierter HNO-Arzt) vorgestellt werden. Besonders wichtig ist eine allgemeine Untersuchung des Kindes durch einen Kinder- und Jugendpsychiater oder einen besonders interessierten Pädiater.

Parallel dazu muss der Kontakt zur Schule und dem Schulpsychologen aufgenommen werden. Zusammen mit dem Gutachten des Kinder- und Jugendpsychiaters wird dann das weitere Vorgehen geklärt. Es können schulische und häusliche Fördermaßnahmen genügen, oft ist aber eine außerschulische Einzeltherapie erforderlich. Eltern und Betroffene müssen sich zum Thema Legasthenie sachkundig machen. Der Bundesverband Legasthenie, Königstraße 32, 30175 Hannover, der seit 25 Jahren besteht, hilft dabei.

Glossar wichtiger Fachausdrücke

Akkommodation	Einstellung der Linse des Auges auf die jeweilige Sehentfernung
Astigmatismus	Hornhautverkrümmung oder Brennpunktlosigkeit; Brechungsfehler des Auges, wobei das fixierte Objekt nicht als Punkt abgebildet wird.
Diplopie	Doppelbildwahrnehmung
Esophorie	latentes Innenschielen
Exophorie	latentes Außenschielen
Fusion	Überlagerung und Verschmelzung der Bilder beider Augen.
Heterophorie	latente Abweichung der Augenachsen
Hyperopie	Weitsichtigkeit
Hypoakkommodation	zu geringe und nicht altersentsprechende Einstellung der Linse des Auges auf ein nahes Objekt
Konvergenz:	gleichsinnige Bewegungen beider Augen nach innen beim Fixieren naher Objekte
magnozelluläre Bahnen	Über diese „M-Bahnen" werden schnell bewegte Reize von geringem Kontrast zum Sehzentrum in der Sehbahn fortgeleitet
Myopie	Kurzsichtigkeit
MKH	Mess- und Korrektionsmethodik nach H.-J. Haase; strittige Methode zur Feststellung und Behandlung von Augenabweichungen
Okklusion	Verschluss eines Auges mit Pflaster oder Folien zur Verbesserung der Sehschärfe des anderen Auges.
PET	Positronen-Emissions-Tomographie; bildgebendes Verfahren, das die Beurteilung der Stoffwechselaktivität des untersuchten Gewebes erlaubt
pleoptisch-orthoptischer Status	Untersuchung der sensorischen und motorischen Funktionen der Augen einzeln und der beidäugigen Funktionen für Ferne und Nähe
Polatest (Zeiss)	Test zur Überprüfung des beidäugigen Sehens
Prismendioptrien	1 Prismendioptrie (cm/m) bedeutet, dass ein Lichtstrahl von einem Glas in 1 m Abstand um 1 cm abgelenkt wird
Refraktion	Brechkraft des Auges

Sehpurpur	Farbstoff in der Netzhaut der im Hellen ausbleicht und sich im Dunkeln regeneriert.
Stereopsis	räumliches Sehen
Strabismus	manifestes (= sichtbares) Schielen der Augen
VEP oder VECP	visuell evozierte (cortikale) Potentiale; Hirnrindenpotentiale, die nach Lichtblitzen oder Schachbrettmustern abgeleitet werden
Zentralskotom, alternierend	wechselnde Unterdrückung der Seheindrücke des Zentrums beider Augen.
Zykloplegie	medikamentöse Lähmung des Ziliarmuskels, wodurch es zur Lähmung der Akkommodation kommt.

Literatur

Bishop DVM (1989): Unfixed reference, monocular occlusion, and developmental dyslexia - a critique. Br J Ophthalmol 73, 209-215

Breitmeyer BG (1996): Forschungsergebnisse zur Rolle zweier Verarbeitungskanäle im Seh- und Hörsystem beim Lesen und bei Lesestörungen. In: Dummer-Smoch L: Legasthenie, 28-42. Bundesverband Legasthenie, Hannover

Eden GF, VanMeter JW, Rumsey JM, Maisog JM, Woods RP, Zeffiro TA (1996): Abnormal processing of visual motion in dyslexia revealed by functional brain imaging. Nature 382, 66-69

Fahle M (1997): Legasthenie als Störung der visuellen Wahrnehmung. Z prakt Augenheilkd 18, 111-116

Fischer B, Biscaldi M (1995): Blicksprünge legasthenischer Kinder bei nicht-kognitiven Aufgaben. In: Legasthenie, 65-72. Bundesverband Legasthenie, Hannover

Galaburda AM (1986): Legasthenie - Einblick in biologische Interaktionen. In: Dummer-Smoch L: Legasthenie, 17-26 Bundesverband Legasthenie, Hannover

Gerling J, Ball M, Bömer T, Bach M, Kommerell G (1998): Fixationsdisparation am Pola-Zeigertest: nicht repräsentativ für die Augenstellung unter natürlichen Sehbedingungen. Klin Monatsbl Augenheilkd 212, 226-233

Gerling J.: Beruhen Abweichungen an den Testfiguren bei der Messmethodik nach H.-J. Haase auf Fixationsdisparation? 24. Strab. Seminarwoche, Bad Schandau 17.9.99

Gerling J, Kommerell G (1997): Irlen-Farbfilter: Spezifische Wirksamkeit bei Legasthenie nicht erwiesen. Z prakt Augenheilkd 18, 117-124

Grigorenko EL, Wood FB, Meyer MS, Hart LA, Speed WC, Shuster A, Pauls DL (1997): Suspectibility loci for distinct components of developmental dyslexia on chromosomes 6 and 15.Am J Hum Genet 60, 27-39

Hofmann K (1973): Augenfehler bei Legasthenikern. Klin Monatsbl Augenheilkd 162, 101-103

Hohmann A, Haase W (1981): Entwicklung der Sehschärfe beim Menschen - ein neuer Test mit standardisierten Einzel- und Reihenoptotypen. In: Arbeitskreis Schielen 13, 131-136. Berufsverband der Augenärzte Deutschlands, Düsseldorf.

Irlen H (1991): Reading by the colors: Overcoming dyslexia and other reading disabilities through the Irlen method. Avery, Garden City Park, New York

Lang J (1992): Zur Behandlung der Legasthenie mit Okklusion oder Prismen. Klin Monatsbl Augenheilkd 200, 596-598

Mühlendyck H, Rüssmann W, Reinboth JJ (1993): Der 4-Prismendioptrien-Basis-innen-Test in der Diagnostik von Exophorien mit Asthenopie und Kompensation über die akkommodative Konvergenz. Ophthalmologe 90, 6-10

Otto J, Egli A, von Frisching D, Klicpera C (1989): Legasthenie. edit. Otto, OPOS, St. Gallen

Pestalozzi D (1986): Über die Behandlung von heterophoren Legasthenikern mit Fixationsdisparation mittels Prismenvollkorrektion. Klin Monatsbl Augenheilkd 188, 471-473

Pestalozzi D (1992): Weitere Beobachtungen von Legasthenikern mit Prismenkorrektion. Klin Monatsbl Augenheilkd 200, 614-619

Schäfer WD (1995): Augenärztliche Hilfen bei Legasthenie. In: Legasthenie, 84-93. Bundesverband Legasthenie, Hannover

Schäfer WD (1997): Okuläre Befunde und Therapie bei Legasthenie. Z prakt Augenheilkd 18, 103-109

Schäfer WD (1998): Visuelle Wahrnehmung bei Legasthenie. Sprache, Stimme, Gehör 22, 13-16

Schwarz C (1992): Ist das Tragen von Prismenbrillen eine sinnvolle Maßnahme zur Behandlung von Legasthenie? Klin Monatsbl Augenheilkd 200, 599-611

Stein J, Fowler S (1985): Effect of monocular occlusion on visuomotor perception and reading in dyslexic children. Lancet 69-73

Ygge J, Lennerstrand G, Axelsson I, Rydberg A (1993 a): Visual functions in a Swedish population of dyslexic and normally reading children. Acta Ophthalmol 71, 1-9

Ygge J, Lennerstrand G, Rydberg A, Wijecoon S. Pettersson BM (1993 b): Oculomotor functions in a Swedish population of dyslexic and normally reading children. Acta Ophthalmol 71, 10-21

1.2.2 Die Abbildung von Lesematerial auf der Netzhaut

Susanne Trauzettel-Klosinski , Jens Reinhard , Manfred Mackeben , Ute Dürrwächter und Gunther Klosinski

Einleitung

Es war das Ziel dieser Pilotstudie, bei legasthenischen und normal lesenden Kindern die Bewegungen der Stelle des schärfsten Sehens relativ zu dem direkt auf die Netzhaut gescannten Lesematerial während des Lesens zu erfassen. Außerdem war es ein Anliegen, für diese Untersuchung Kinder mit „reiner" Legasthenie ohne zusätzliche Störungen auszuwählen und die Diagnose vorher durch psychologische Testverfahren zu verifizieren. Die Ergebnisse sollen zu einem besseren Verständnis von Lesestrategien und der spezifischen Schwierigkeiten von Legasthenikern beitragen.

Physiologische *visuelle* Voraussetzungen für die Lesefähigkeit

Der Lesevorgang besteht aus Blickhaltephasen, in denen das Auge auf einer Buchstabengruppe ruht und aus Blicksprüngen (Sakkaden), die das Auge zur nächsten Textstelle bringen. Bei der Registrierung von Augenbewegungen und ihrer Darstellung über die Zeit entsteht ein regelmäßiges Treppenstufenmuster.

Zur Erkennung von Buchstaben einer bestimmten Größe ist ein entsprechendes Auflösungsvermögen der benutzten Netzhautstelle erforderlich. Dieses ist an der Stelle des schärfsten Sehens (Fovea) am höchsten und nimmt mit zunehmender Entfernung vom Netzhautzentrum rasch ab. Deshalb wird stets nur ein begrenztes Areal des Textes zu beiden Seiten des Netzhautzentrums scharf gesehen - und zwar je ca. zwei Grad nach rechts und links des Fixationspunktes. Dieser Bereich wird in der Literatur als minimales Lesegesichtsfeld (Aulhorn 1953, Trauzettel-Klosinski 1997, Trauzettel-Klosinski et al. 1994 b), Buchstabenerkennungsbereich (Rayner 1975) oder „visual span" (Legge et al. 1997) bezeichnet. Um den nächsten Teil des Textes scharf zu sehen, muß das Auge einen Blicksprung machen. Durch parafoveale Informationsaufnahme kann das gesamte Wahrnehmungsareal („perceptual span") während einer Halteposition aber bis zu 5 Grad in Leserichtung erweitert werden (McConkie and Rayner 1976).

Methode

Mit Hilfe eines Scanning Laser Ophthalmoskops (SLO) wurden Bilder der Netzhaut erzeugt, die gleichzeitig auch die Stimuli (Fixationsmarken, Einzelworte verschiedener Länge, Texte und Piktogramme) zeigten. Dadurch können die Stelle des schärfsten Sehens, der retinale Abbildungsort der Stimuli , Augenbewegungen und Sprache simultan registriert und auf Videoband aufgenommen werden (Trauzettel-Klosinski et al. 1994 a). Wörter und Texte wurden laut gelesen. Die SLO-Methode bietet also den Vorteil, daß man in jedem Moment auf der Netzhaut des Patienten genau sehen kann, wo dieser hinschaut (Abb. 1.2.1. 1).

Untersuchte Personen

Zehn legasthenische Kinder (Alter: Mittelwert und Standardabweichung: 13,1 +/- 1,6 Jahre) und 12 normal lesende Kontrollkinder (13,2 +/- 1,5 Jahre) wurden psychologisch getestet

(Diagnose einer Lese- und Rechtschreibstörung nach ICD 10) und augenärztlich voruntersucht. Einschlußkriterien waren: Alter 11-15 Jahre, normaler Augenbefund (inclusive neuroophthalmologischer und orthoptischer Befund), mindestens durchschnittliche Intelligenz, keine zusätzlichen Störungen - sodaß eine Gruppe von „reinen" Legasthenikern ausgewählt werden konnte.

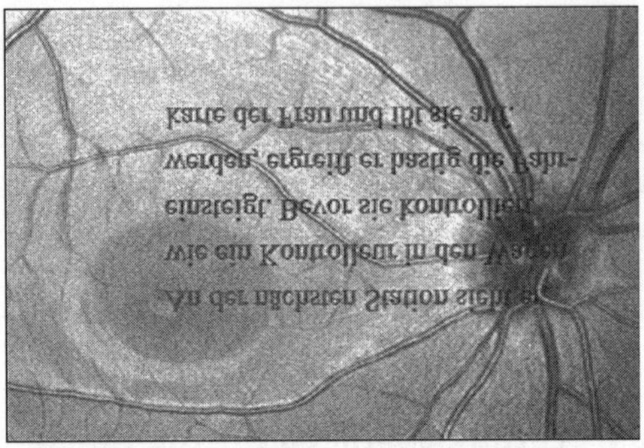

Abb. 1.2.2.1 Mit Hilfe des Scanning Laser Ophthalmoskops werden die Netzhaut und gleichzeitig der darauf gescannte Text dargestellt (für den Untersucher umgekehrt abgebildet). Die Versuchsperson fixiert gerade mit der Stelle des schärfsten Sehens (Fovea) den ersten Buchstaben links unten „A". Auf einem Videoband können die Augenbewegungen über den Text exakt aufgezeichnet werden.

Ergebnisse

Fixationsstabilität

Beim Fixieren eines Fixationskreuzes gab es in beiden Gruppen Kinder, die sehr ruhig und andere, die etwas unruhiger fixierten. Im Gruppenvergleich gab es keine Unterschiede (Mittel der Standardabweichungen der mittleren Augenposition: L = +/- 0,048; N = +/- 0,051)

Einzelwortlesen

Beim Lesen von einzelnen Wörtern nahm die Anzahl der Sakkaden mit zunehmender Wortlänge in beiden Untersuchungsgruppen zu, bei den Legasthenikern jedoch wesentlich stärker als bei den Kontrollkindern (Vorwärts: L: 101 +/- 34; N: 51 +/- 11 bzw. Rückwärts: L: 47 +/- 27; N: 28 +/- 7).

Abb. 1.2.2.2 zeigt die Augenbewegungen eines normal lesenden (links) und eines legasthenischen Kindes (rechts) während des lauten Lesens von Einzelwörtern. Der graue Balken links unten an der Ordinate zeigt jeweils die Zeit an, in der das Wort ausgesprochen wird. Bei dem 2-Buchstaben-Wort „er" macht das Kontrollkind 1 Sakkade, das legasthenische Kind keine. Das zentriert dargebotene Wort „aber" wird vom normalen Kind nach 1 Rückwärtssakkade laut vorgelesen, vom legasthenischen Kind nach 1 Rückwärts- und 1 Vorwärtssakkade. Das Wort „jungenhaft", ebenfalls zentriert dargeboten, wird vom Kontrollkind

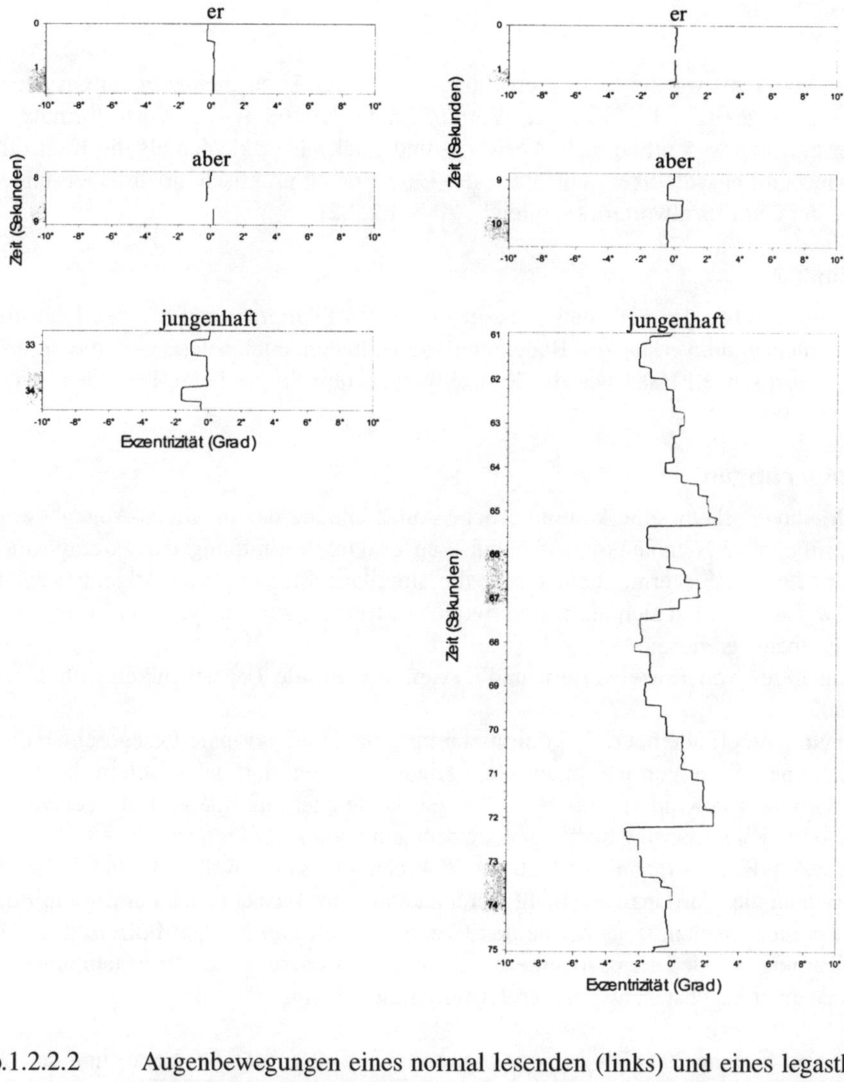

Abb.1.2.2.2 Augenbewegungen eines normal lesenden (links) und eines legasthenischen Kindes (rechts) beim lauten Lesen von Einzelwörtern (Foveaposition in Abhängigkeit von der Zeit). Die grauen Balken bezeichnen die Zeit, in der das Wort ausgesprochen wird. Einzelheiten siehe Text.

nach 1 Rückwärts- und 1 Vorwärtssakkade nach ca. 1 Sekunde vorgelesen. Das legasthenische Kind macht zahlreiche Vorwärts- und Rückwärtssakkaden, tastet das Wort dabei mehrfach ab, liest es nach etwa 5 Sekunden falsch vor und schließlich nach 12 Sekunden richtig.

Außerdem zeigte sich, daß auch die Größe des Blicksprungs (Sakkadenamplitude) mit zunehmender Wortlänge zunahm. Dies galt für beide Gruppen, wenngleich in geringerem

Maße für die Legastheniker (lineare Korrelation: L: r = 0,934; N: r = 0,992). Dies bedeutet, daß das Wahrnehmungsareal („perceptual span") dynamisch an die Wortlänge angepaßt werden kann (Mackeben et al.).

Textlesen

Beim Lesen von Text war die Lesegeschwindigkeit bei den Legasthenikern im Gruppenvergleich stark herabgesetzt (L: 77 +/- 22 Wörter/Minute; N: 168 +/- 22 Wörter/Minute). Legastheniker machten wesentlich mehr Vorwärts- und Rückwärtssakkaden als die Kontrollkinder. Bei manchen Legasthenikern entsprach der Lesevorgang praktisch einem Buchstabieren, ähnlich wie bei den Einzelwörtern (vergleiche Abb. 1.2.2.2).

Piktogrammlesen

Erste Ergebnisse haben gezeigt, daß es beim Lesen von Piktogrammen bei den Legasthenikern neben solchen, die verlängerte Benennungszeiten hatten, auch solche gab, die die Piktogramme genauso schnell lasen wie die Kontrollkinder, obwohl sie beim Textlesen ganz besonders langsam waren.

Schlußfolgerungen

Die SLO-Methode erlaubt eine kontinuierliche Aufzeichnung der Fixations-Augenbewegungen unter simultaner Netzhautkontrolle und eine exakte Bestimmung der Foveapositionen während des Lesens. Sie ermöglicht ferner die simultane Messung von Augenbewegungen und Sprache. Das SLO hat sich als ein wertvolles Instrument zur Analyse von Lesestrategien bei der Legasthenie erwiesen.

Beim Lesen von Einzelwörtern und Texten wiesen alle Legastheniker pathologische Befunde auf.

Die Normalbefunde bei der Fixationsstabilität sowie die normale Lesegeschwindigkeit für Piktogramme bei einigen legasthenischen Kindern zeigen, daß das Problem der hier untersuchten Gruppe von Kindern mit „reiner" Legasthenie eher auf eine gestörte Textverarbeitung als auf eine Fehlsteuerung der Augenbewegungen zurückzuführen ist.

Ein wesentliches Ergebnis ist, daß das Wahrnehmungsareal während einer Halteposition dynamisch an die Wortlänge angepaßt werden kann. Die Tatsache, daß der diesem Befund zugrunde liegende Mechanismus bei beiden Gruppen vorhanden ist, läßt hoffen, daß zielgerichtetes Training bei den Legasthenikern zu einer Vergrößerung des Wahrnehmungsareals und damit zu einer Verbesserung der Leseleistung führen kann.

Unterstützt von Fortüne 294 (Forschungsprogramm der Universität Tübingen) und der Deutschen Forschungsgemeinschaft (DFG Zr 13/1)

Literatur

Aulhorn E (1953) Über die Fixationsbreite und Fixationsfrequenz beim Lesen gerichteter Konturen. Pflügers Arch Physiol 257: 318-328

Legge GE, Ahn SJ, Klitz TS, Luebker A (1997) Psychophysics of reading - XVI. The visual span in normal and low vision. Vision Res 37 (14): 1999-2010

Lennerstrand G, Ygge J (1992) Dyslexia; ophthalmological aspects 1991. Acta Ophthalmol (Copenh) 70 (1): 3-13

Mackeben M, Trauzettel-Klosinski S, Reinhard J, Dürrwächter U, Klosinski G. Dynamic perceptual span revealed by single word reading in dyslexics and normal children. Vision Res, eingereicht

McConkie GW, Rayner K (1976) Asymmetry of the perceptual span in reading. Bull Psychonom Soc 8: 365-368

Rayner K (1975) The perceptual span and peripheral cues in reading. Cognitive Psychol 7: 65-81

Trauzettel-Klosinski S, Teschner C, Tornow RP, Zrenner E (1994 a) Reading strategies in normal subjects and in patients with macular scotoma - assessed by two new methods of registration. Neuro-Ophthalmology 14: 15-30

Trauzettel-Klosinski S, Teschner C, Tornow RP, Zrenner E (1994 b) Die Bedeutung des zentralen Gesichtsfeldes für die Lesefähigkeit und Rehabilitation Sehbehinderter. Spektrum Augenheilk 8: 128-134

Trauzettel-Klosinski S (1997) The significance of the central visual field for reading ability and the value of perimetry for its assessment. In: Wall M, Heijl A (Hrsg) Perimetry Update. Amsterdam, New York, Kugler, S 417-426

Warnke A (1990) Legasthenie und Hirnfunktion. Huber, Bern

1.3 Gedächtnis

1.3.1 Arbeitsgedächtnisleistungen bei Legasthenie – Wie generell ist das Defizit?

Evelin Witruk

1 Funktionsprinzipien des Arbeitsgedächtnisses und ihre Bedeutung für das Lesen und Schreiben

Die komplexen psychischen Leistungen des Lesens und des Schreibens setzen aufeinander aufbauende perzeptive und kognitive Verarbeitungsschritte sowie erhaltende und integrierende Funktionen des Arbeitsgedächtnisses mit dem Zugriff zum Langzeitgedächtnis voraus. Für das Arbeitsgedächtnis liegt die Analogie zu einer „Werkstatt" auf der Hand: Durch Wahrnehmungsleistungen eingehende Information muß kurzzeitig erhalten werden und zur aktiven Bearbeitung zur Verfügung gehalten werden. Gleichzeitig werden Vergleichs- und Suchprozesse im Langzeitgedächtnis gestartet, deren Ergebnisse ebenfalls ins Arbeitsgedächtnis aktiviert werden und dort eine Integration mit den wahrnehmungsseitig eingegangen Informationen erfolgt.

Gehen wir mit Klix (1984) davon aus, daß die Prozeduren des Arbeitsgedächtnisses in zweifacher Hinsicht wirksam werden:

1. bei der Verarbeitung von Wahrnehmungsinhalten und
2. bei der Bearbeitung von abgerufenen Inhalten aus dem Langzeitgedächtnis. Das Arbeitsgedächtnis startet die Informationssuche und die Operationssuche im Langzeitgedächtnis und verarbeitet die Kopien der dort abgerufenen Informationen.

Abgerufene automatisierte Programme und kontrolliert eingesetzte Prozeduren und Strategien werden auf die kopierten Informationen im Arbeitsgedächtnis angewendet. Die Funktion des Arbeitsgedächtnisses liegt damit sowohl in der Speicherung von Ausgangsinformationen und Zwischenergebnissen als auch in deren Verarbeitung im Sinne des Abarbeitens von Lösungsalgorithmen und ist damit von fundamentaler Bedeutung für Lese- und Schreibprozesse.

Mechanismen, welche die Aufrechterhaltung der eingegangenen und der abgerufenen Information im Arbeitsgedächtnis ermöglichen, werden von Baddeley und Hitch (1974) sowie von Gathercole und Baddeley (1993) beschrieben. Sie gehen von drei Komponenten des Arbeitsgedächtnisses aus:

- einer modalitätsunspezifischen, kapazitätsbegrenzten Zentralen Exekutive, welche den Abruf aus und den Zufluß in das Langzeitgedächtnis sowie die Verarbeitung und Speicherung von eingehenden Informationen realisiert.
- Des weiteren werden zwei modalitätsspezifische, ebenfalls kapazitätsbegrenzte Teilsysteme unterschieden, die unter der Kontrolle der Zentralen Exekutive stehen und auf die Verarbeitung von Sprache bzw. visueller Informationen spezialisiert sind (phonologische Schleife und visuell-räumliche Schleife). Über automatisiert ablaufende Rehearsalprozes-

se können somit modalitätsspezifische Informationen zur weiteren Bearbeitung innerhalb der zentralen Exekutive zur Verfügung gestellt und bereitgehalten werden.
- In den Modellen von Goldman-Rakic (1998) und Petrides (1994) wird innerhalb der visuell-räumlichen Schleife differenziert in die Speicherung des räumlichen Bezuges (Wo-System) und in den Objektbezug (Was-System), welche physiologisch mit unterschiedlichen Netzwerken realisiert werden.

Die Funktionen der Zentralen Exekutive können nach Cowan (1995) differenziert werden nach ihrem Anteil an automatisierten bzw. kontrollierten Exekutivprozessen. Automatisierte Exekutivprozesse können weitgehend unbewußt und mit geringem psychischem Aufwand realisiert werden, wie das zum Beispiel bei automatischer Worterkennung und dem dann möglichen Wortlesen möglich ist. Kontrollierte Exekutivprozesse erfordern eine bewußte Planung von Handlungsschritten, wie das zum Beispiel beim Erlesen eines Wortes durch Buchstaben-Lautzuordnungen und anschließender Synthese der Fall ist.

Neuro-anatomische Grundlagen dieser Arbeitsgedächtnisfunktionen sind hinsichtlich der Zentralen Exekutive nach Goldman-Rakic (1998) nachgewiesen in präfrontalen kortikalen Arealen, die ein interaktives Netzwerk zusammen mit posterioren kortikalen Arealen bilden. Durch dieses Netzwerk werden Kontroll- und die Koordinierungsfunktionen von Behaltens- und Verarbeitungsprozessen realisiert. Modalitätsspezifische Speicherleistungen werden in anderen kortikalen Arealen angenommen. So geht Goldman-Rakic (1998) davon aus, daß räumliche Informationen (Wo-System) in posterioren, dorsalen Kortexarealen erhalten werden, während Objektinformationen (Was-System) in posterioren, ventralen Arealen gespeichert werden. Ähnliche Vernetzungslokationen wurden von Mecklinger und Müller (1996) für Objekt- und Rauminformationen beim Menschen gefunden. Rösler et al. (1997) belegen mit neuropsychologischen Daten die Domainenspezifik von Leistungen des Arbeitsgedächtnisses bei visueller Informationspräsentation. In einer ersten Studie fanden sie bei Abrufprozessen aus dem Langzeitgedächtnis zu räumlichen Informationen Aktivierungen des parietalen Kortex, während verbale Abrufprozesse mit Aktivierungen des linksfrontalen Kortex verbunden waren. Eine weitere Studie zeigte, dass die Topographie arithmetischer und semantischer Arbeitsgedächtnisleistungen (N400-Effekt) weitgehend übereinstimmen und vor allem die Aktivierung centro-parietaler Regionen betreffen. Bei Aufgaben, die eine mentale Rotation von Buchstaben erforderten, konnte eine Negativierung über dem parietalen Kortex nachgewiesen werden, deren Amplitude mit dem Rotationsaufwand zunimmt. Syntaxverarbeitende Arbeitsgedächtnisleistungen konnten in einem weiteren Experiment von Rösler et al. (1997) in Form phasischer Negativierung über dem linken anterioren Kortex nachgewiesen werden.

Auch die Erhaltens- und Bearbeitungsleistungen auditiver Informationen in der phonologischen Schleife erscheinen nach Befunden von Schröger (1995) domainenspezifisch realisiert zu werden, da topographische Differenzierungen der aktivierten Hirnregionen nach Richtung, Frequenz, Lautstärke und Periodizität des auditiven Reizes elektrophysiologisch belegbar sind.

Lesen und Schreiben werden auf der Grundlage modalitätsspezifischer Erhaltens- und Bearbeitungsleistungen sowie auf der Grundlage von permanenten Vergleichs- und Abrufprozessen im Langzeitgedächtnis und Modalitätswechseln realisiert.

Einschränkungen von Arbeitsgedächtnisleistungen bei Legasthenikern sind mit verschiedenen Paradigmen und Materialarten sowohl bei auditiver als auch bei visueller Reizrepräsentation nachgewiesen worden. Hinsichtlich visuell-räumlicher Legasthenie Defizite des Arbeitsgedächtnisses liegen differenzierende Befunde vor. So und Siegel (1997) fanden Defizite bei Kanadischen und Chinesischen Legasthenikern bei visuellen Arbeitsgedächtnisaufgaben (Freies Reproduzieren von Wortlisten). Ellis (1981) berichtet über vier visuelle Gedächtnisvergleichsexperimente auf der Grundlage des „Posner Paradigmas" mit unterschiedlichen Materialarten, in denen er keine Legastheniker Defizite fand, wenn die beiden Reize nicht benennbar waren. Waren die visuellen Vergleichsreize phonologisch ähnliche Buchstaben, zeigten sich signifikante Legastheniker Defizite. Er interpretiert seine Ergebnisse als Benennungsdefizit. Auch Vellutinos (1987) Ergebnisse sprechen gegen ein generelles visuelles Arbeitsgedächtnisdefizit. Seine legasthenischen Kinder konnten z. B. für sie unbekannte, hebräische Worte und Buchstaben genauso gut reproduzieren wie normallesende Kinder der Kontrollgruppe. Handelte es sich um Listen englischer Worte, gelang ihnen die Reproduktion signifikant schlechter. Seine Interpretation bezieht sich auf ein seriales Defizit der Legastheniker bei der Speicherung und dem Abruf linguistischer Informationen. Auch Barnea et al. (1994) fanden Legastheniker Defizite bei Hebräisch sprechenden Kindern vor allem bei lexikalischen, visuellen Reizserien. Willows et al. (1993) fanden bei visuellen Gedächtnisvergleichen von Buchstaben, des für die Kinder unbekannten hebräischen Alphabetes Legastheniker Defizite bei der Genauigkeit und der Geschwindigkeit, welche bei jüngeren Kindern (6 Jahre) stärker vorlagen als bei älteren Kindern (8 Jahre). Kompensationseffekte von Defiziten des visuellen Arbeitsgedächtnisses konnten auch in unserer Studie von Witruk und Rosendahl (1999) bei visuellen Vergleichs- und visuell seriellen Reproduktionsaufgaben nachgewiesen werden. Hier zeigten sich im Längsschnitts- und im Querschnittsvergleich von 7-jährigen und 9-jährigen Legasthenikern mit steigendem Alter deutliche Angleichungen an die Kontrollgruppe, welche bei phonologischen, seriellen Reproduktionsaufgaben nicht auffindbar waren.

Hinsichtlich der Defizite des phonologischen Arbeitsgedächtnisses erscheint die Befundlage eindeutiger und weniger differenziert. Das hier am häufigsten verwendete Paradigma ist die sogenannte Gedächtnisspanne für Zahlen, Worte und Pseudoworte. Legastheniker Defizite in phonologischen Fertigkeiten und im phonologischen Arbeitsgedächtnis werden von Siegel und Linder (1984) für kanadische Kinder beschrieben, Ho und Bryant (1997) können diese phonologischen Defizite für englische und chinesische Legastheniker bestätigen. Gathercole und Baddeley (1993) fanden bei 8-, 11- und 15-jährigen legasthenischen Kindern Entwicklungsverzögerungen hinsichtlich der Artikulationsgeschwindigkeit, des Nachsprechens von Nichtworten sowie der Gedächtnisspanne für Worte. Phonologische Defizite, die bei 8- und 11-jährigen Legasthenikern nachweisbar waren, sind bei den 15-jährigen Kindern nicht mehr erkennbar. Damit kann man auch bezogen auf das phonologische Arbeitsgedächtnis von einer, wenngleich später einsetzenden Kompensationstendenz sprechen. Aus dieser Sicht wären dann die Befunde, die auf phonologische Arbeitsgedächtnisdefizite vor dem 15. Lebensjahr verweisen, eher als Entwicklungsverzögerungen interpretierbar.

Befunde zu Defiziten der phonologischen Schleife scheinen mit relativ hoher Konsistenz vorzuliegen. Defizite der visuell-räumlichen Schleife erscheinen stark materialabhängig zu sein, treten möglicherweise nur dann in Erscheinung, wenn es sich um benennbare Reize handelt. Dann wiederum könnten sie mit der phonologischen Umkodierung und der phonologischen Schleife zusammenzuhängen.

Ordnen wir die von uns angenommenen Arbeitsgedächtnisdefizite legasthenischer Kinder in das Mehrebenenmodell ein, so lassen sich diese auf der Ebene sekundärer Ursachen lokalisieren, auf deren Grundlage die Ausformung der Primärsymptomatik im Sinne individuellen Lese-und Rechtschreibversagens erfolgt.

2 Ziel- und Fragestellungen unserer Experimente

Lesen und Schreiben realisieren sich über hochkomplexe und adaptive Prozesse der Wahrnehmung, der Aufmerksamkeit sowie verschiedener kurz- und langfristiger Gedächtnisfunktionen. Damit besteht die zentrale Zielstellung der vorzustellenden Experimente darin, die Bedeutung und das Ausmaß möglicher Arbeitsgedächtniseinschränkungen bei legasthenischen Kindern zu prüfen. Die konzeptionelle Differenzierung von Arbeitsgedächtnisleistungen geschieht auf der Grundlage des Modells von Baddeley und Hitch (1974) bezüglich ihrer Modalitätsspezifik eingehender und zu erhaltender Informationen sowie auf der Grundlage des Modells von Cowan (1995) hinsichtlich des Anteils automatisierter versus kontrollierter Exekutivprozesse bei der Handlungs-/Antwortgenerierung.

Es sollen im folgenden drei experimentelle Studien vorgestellt werden, deren Fragestellungen ausgerichtet sind auf die Sprachsystemabhängigkeit, die Modalitäts- und Materialabhängigkeit sowie den Einfluß kontrollierter versus automatisierter Exekutivprozesse auf Arbeitsgedächtnisleistungen jeweils intelligenz-, alters- und klassenstufenhomogenisierter Stichproben legasthenischer und normallesender Kinder der 3. Klassenstufe. Dabei wurden experimentell gut erprobte Paradigmen in experimentelle Designs (adaptive Arbeitsgedächtnisexperimente, Sternberg-Experimente, sukzessive Gedächtnisvergleiche) überführt.

3 Sprachsystemabhängigkeit von Arbeitsgedächtnisleistungen legasthenischer und normallesender Kinder

Den Einfluß des Sprachsystems auf die Ausformung von Arbeitsgedächtnisleistungen bei legasthenischen und normallesenden Kindern untersuchten wir mit adaptiven Arbeitsgedächtnisexperimenten (Witruk und Ho, 1999), welche individuelle, schwierigkeitsangepaßte Bearbeitungswege erlauben und welche visuelle und auditive Vergleichs- und Reproduktionsleistungen analysieren. Es werden jeweils mit einer Zeitbegrenzung von 5 Minuten Aufgaben mit steigendem Schwierigkeitsgrad dargeboten. Nach einer Falschantwort wird drei Stufen im Schwierigkeitsniveau zurückgegangen, so daß die individuellen Leistungsgrenzen schnell erreicht werden aber keine Überforderung des Kindes eintreten kann. Die Aufgaben fußen auf dem „Same-Different Paradigma" und auf dem „Serial Recall Paradigma" und werden zum einen visuell und zum anderen auditiv präsentiert. Im Aufgabenteil A werden Punktmuster verwendet, welche in der Anzahl der Punkte erweitert werden. Die Entscheidung über Gleichheit/Ungleichheit ist über einen Gedächtnisvergleich mit einem zweiten Punktmuster zu treffen. Im Aufgabenteil B werden Tonfolgen hoher und tiefer Töne mit steigender Anzahl von Tönen präsentiert und es muß wiederum über Gleichheit/Ungleichheit über einen Gedächtnisvergleich mit einer zweiten Tonfolge entschieden werden. Die Aufgabenteile C und D verwenden als Antwortmodus die serielle Reproduktion zum einen eines Linienmusters mit steigender Anzahl von Linien (C) und zum anderen Tonfolgen steigender Länge bestehend aus hohen und tiefen Tönen, die auf der Tastatur mechanisch reproduziert wurden. Als abhängige Variablen wurden Genauigkeitsparameter des Arbeitsgedächtnisses als Anzahl der bearbeiteten Aufgaben, der gemittelte Wert der höchsten, individuell erreichten Schwierigkeitsstufen (lokale Maxima) sowie die individuell erreichte, höchste Schwierigkeitsstufe sowie Zeitparameter des Arbeitsgedächtnisses als Reaktions- und Reproduktionszeiten für richtige und falsche Lösungen erfaßt.

Wir verglichen diese Arbeitsgedächtnisleistungen bei legasthenischen und normallesenden Kindern in Leipzig und in Hong Kong. Die Stichproben wurden parallelisiert nach Alter, Klassenstufe (3. Klasse) und Intelligenz und es wurden 20 Legastheniker in Hong Kong und 42 in Leipzig sowie 20 normallesende Kinder in Hong Kong und 79 in Leipzig in die Untersuchung einbezogen. Ein Intelligenztest (CFT 1) und ein Lesetest (in Deutschland der Züricher Lesetest) wurden vor dem Experiment appliziert.

Die Ergebnisse zeigen die signifikante Überlegenheit der chinesischen Kinder in allen Zeitparametern der vier adaptiven Experimente (Abb. 1.3.1.1). Ihre Vorteile in den Genauigkeisparametern sind nur bei Aufgaben mit auditiver Reizpräsentation und der Nutzung der phonologischen Schleife signifikant nachweisbar.

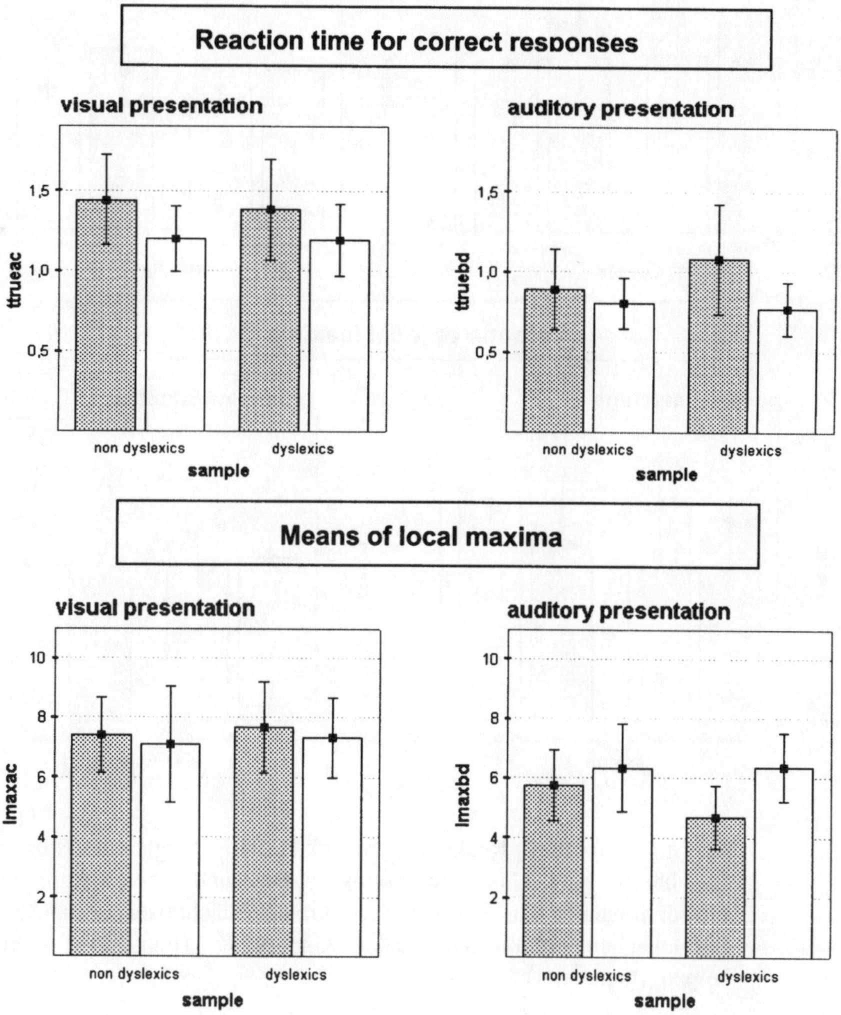

Abb. 1.3.1.1 Reaktionszeit und Reaktionsgenauigkeit bei visuellen und auditiven Arbeitsgedächtnisanforderungen legasthenischer und normallesender Kinder aus Hong Kong (weiß) und Leipzig (gepunktet)

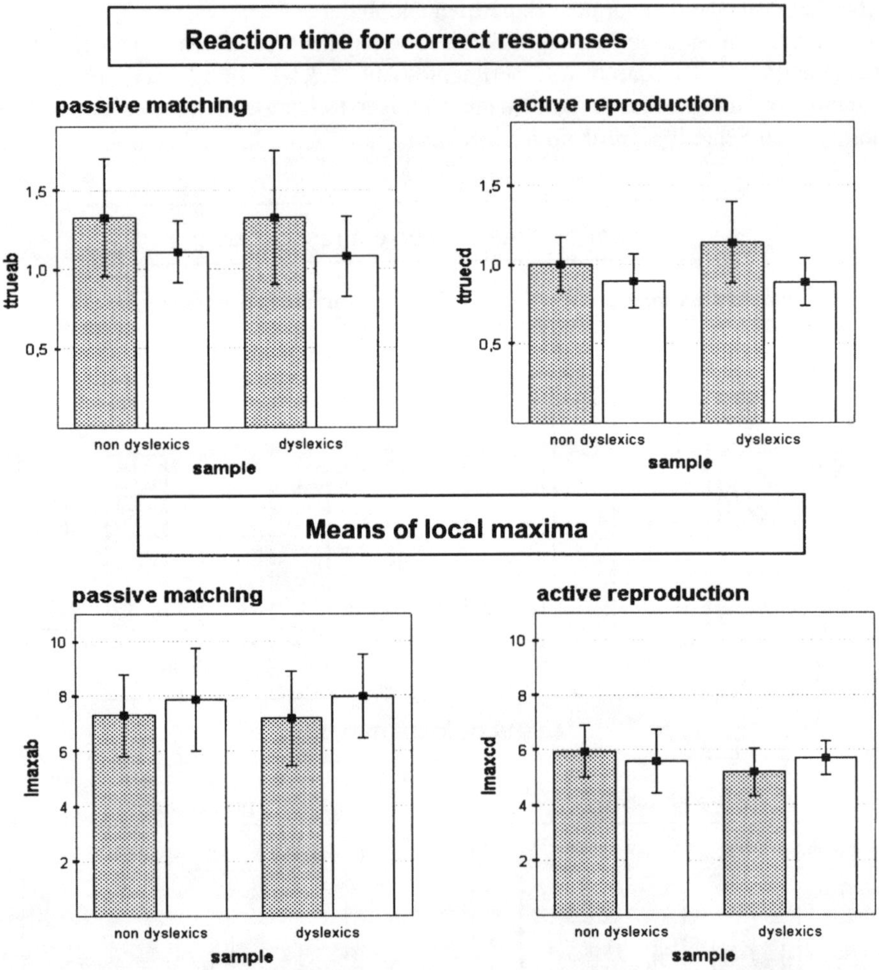

Abb. 1.3.1.2 Reaktionszeit und Reaktionsgenauigkeit bei Vergleichsleistungen mit Gleichheits- bzw. Ungleichheitsentscheidung und aktiven Reproduktionsanforderungen in den vier adaptiven Arbeitsgedächtnisexperimenten bei legasthenischen und normallesenden Kindern aus Hong Kong (weiß) und Leipzig (gepunktet)

Eine Diskriminierung zwischen legasthenischen und normallesenden Kindern ist signifikant nur für die deutschen Stichproben möglich und ist am stärksten ausgeprägt bei auditiver Reizpräsentation und bei Aktivierung stark kontrollierter Prozesse wie der aktiven Reproduktion von Reizsequenzen.

Die Ergebnisse belegen den starken Einfluß des Sprachsystems auf die Ausbildung von Arbeitsgedächtnisleistungen. Das zum großen Teil monosyllabische chinesische Sprachsystem mit seiner geringen Differenzierung von Silben macht für die mündliche Kommunikation eine Höhenmodulation der Silben (im Kantonesischen mit 9 Variationen der Silbe) sowie darüber hinaus eine enorme Ausnutzung des Kontextes erforderlich. Diese Kontextnutzung bedeutet, dass das Erlernen der chinesischen Sprache begleitet wird von einem „natürlichen“ und hoch effizienten Training des Arbeitsgedächtnisses, so daß in den von uns untersuchten Bereichen keine Legastheniedefizite erkennbar waren. Das deutsche Sprachsystem realisiert durch multisyllabische Wortkonstruktionen und Wortzusammensetzungen mit Ausnahme der Homophone eine Bedeutungseindeutigkeit auf Wortebene. Das Verstehen der deutschen, gesprochenen Sprache ist damit weniger auf die Kontextnutzung und damit das kurzzeitige Erhalten kurzer Einheiten im Sinne monosyllabischer Worte ausgerichtet. Wir können deshalb die signifikanten Leistungsnachteile der deutschen Kinder in den auditiven Experimenten bezüglich der Genauigkeit und der Geschwindigkeit des Antwortens als Ergebnis eines geringer ausgeprägten „natürlichen“ Trainings durch mündliche Kommunikation interpretieren, bei dem allerdings signifikante Leistungsdefizite der Legastheniker vor allem bezogen auf auditive Reizpräsentationen und am stärksten kombiniert mit aktiver Reproduktionsanforderung zutage treten.

4 Modalitäts- und Materialabhängigkeit von Arbeitsgedächtnisleistungen bei legasthenischen und normallesenden Kindern

Die besondere Betroffenheit auditiver bzw. phonologischer Wahrnehmungs- und Erhaltensleistungen bei deutschen Legasthenikern konnten wir auch mit den Ergebnissen unserer auf der Grundlage des „Sternberg-Paradigmas“ realisierten Arbeitsgedächtnisexperimente (Gräntzel und Jähn, 1997, Witruk und Schuster, 1997) bestätigen. Die Sternberg Anforderung prüft dabei Suchprozesse im Arbeitsgedächtnis, wobei sich die Zeit bis zur Entscheidung über die Zugehörigkeit bzw. Nichtzugehörigkeit eines Targetitems zu einer zuvor präsentierten Itemliste zusammensetzt aus der Reizkodierungszeit, der seriellen Vergleichszeit, der Entscheidungszeit sowie der Zeit für die motorische Reaktion. Diese komplex zusammengesetzte Antwortzeit nimmt nach Sternberg (1975) mit dem Umfang der Liste um ein Item jeweils um 38 msec zu und zeichnet sich bei negativen Sets (Targetitem war nicht enthalten) durch eine erschöpfende Suche über allen Items der Liste aus, während bei positiven Sets (Targetitem war in der Liste enthalten) eine selbstabbrechende Suche einsetzt. Wir prüften derartige Erhaltens-, Such- und Exekutivprozesse des Arbeitsgedächtnisses bei visueller und auditiver Präsentation von Worten (einsilbig mit vier Buchstaben, z. B. BAUM) und Pseudoworten (ebenfalls einsilbig mit vier Buchstaben, z. B. TARK) mit Listenlängen von 2 bis 5 Items. Dem Experiment lag damit ein vierfaktorieller Variablenplan zugrunde, nach welchem die Gruppenzugehörigkeit, die Materialart, die Präsentationsmodalität und die Listenlänge variiert wurden. Als abhängige Variablen wurden die Antwortzeiten und die Fehlersummen bestimmt. Die Parallelisierung der legasthenischen (n=21) und der normallesenden Kinder (n=21) erfolgte nach Alter, Klassenstufe (3. Klasse) und Intelligenz (gemessen mit dem CFT 1).

Die Ergebnisse belegen für die visuell präsentierten Merk- und Suchaufgaben keine signifikanten Gruppenunterschiede für Reaktionszeiten und Fehlerwerte, allerdings waren Fehler und Zeiten bei Pseudoworten signifikant in beiden Stichproben erhöht.

Signifikante Leistungsdefizite der Legastheniker zeigten sich ausschließlich bei auditiver Präsentation von Worten und Pseudoworten hinsichtlich der Fehlerraten.

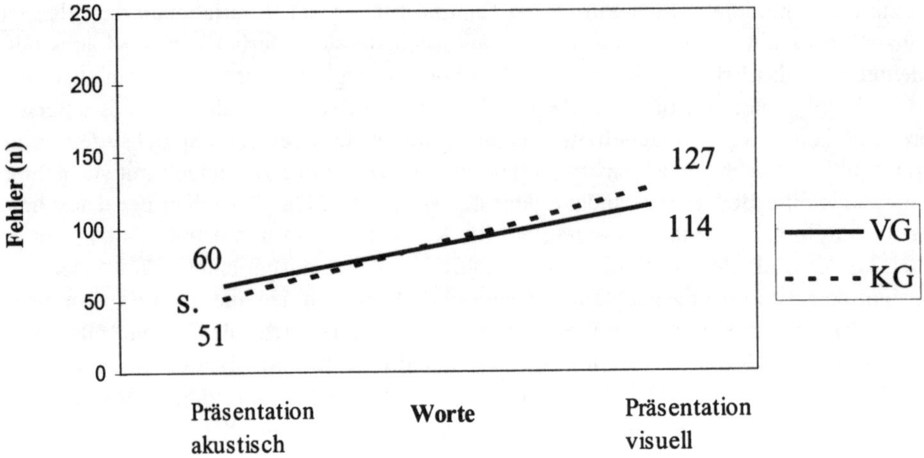

27

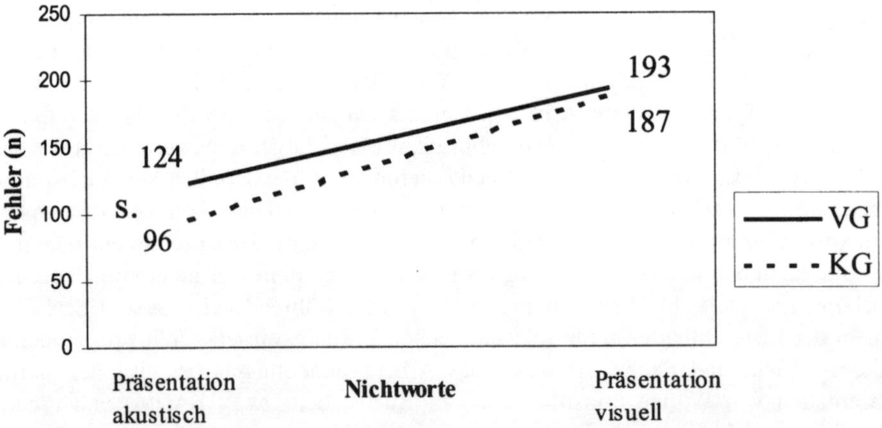

Abb. 1.3.1.3 Modalitäts- und Materialabhängigkeit von Arbeitsgedächtnisleistungen bei legasthenischen (Versuchsgruppe VG) und normallesenden (Kontrollgruppe KG) Kindern

In den verlängerten Reaktionszeiten zeigen sich auch, allerdings nur tendenziell Defizite der Legastheniker.

Drei Subtypen von Legasthenikern lassen sich auf der Grundlage der Modalitätsspezifik der Arbeitsgedächtnisleistungen unserer Sternberg-Experimente unterscheiden, wobei hierzu die individuellen Abweichungen der legasthenischen Kinder vom einfachen Standardabweichungsbereich der Antwortzeiten und der Fehlersummen der Kontrollgruppe bei auditiver und visueller Präsentation der Items zugrundegelegt wurden. Bei 28,6% unserer legasthenischen Kinder fanden wir dominierende visuelle Arbeitsgedächtnisdefizite, bei 38,1% waren es demgegenüber auditive bzw. phonologische Defizite, die vor allem die phonologische Schleife des Arbeitsgedächtnisses betrafen. Bei 33,3% unserer Legastheniker waren beide Modalitäten etwa gleichrangig gestört, was auf Defizite der phonologischen und der visuell-räumlichen Schleife verweist.

Die Ergebnisse belegen die Dominanz auditiver bzw. phonologischer Defizite von Arbeitsgedächtnisleistungen, welche vorrangig der phonologischen Schleife zuzuordnen sind.

5 Spezifische Materialabhängigkeiten visueller Arbeitsgedächtnisleistungen bei legasthenischen Kindern

Die Defizite im visuellen Arbeitsgedächtnisbereich erscheinen subtiler und noch stärker materialtyp- und –komplexitätsabhängig. Sie könnten nur einen Subtyp der Legastheniker betreffen, was kontroverse Ergebnisse erklärbar machen würde. Mit unserem dritten Experiment (Witruk, Lachmann und Graeve, 2000) untersuchten wir visuelle Vergleichsleistungen zweier, sukzessiv präsentierter visueller Reize unterschiedlicher Materialart (Buchstaben, Fünf-Punktmuster, Strichmuster) und unterschiedlicher Komplexität bei legasthenischen (n=24) und normallesenden (n=18) Kindern. Es handelte sich um „Same-Different-Aufgaben“ mit einer Präsentationszeit von 500 msec. für den ersten Reiz und einem Interstimulusintervall von ebenfalls 500 msec. zum zweiten Reiz. Reaktionszeiten und Fehlerraten wurden als abhängige Variablen erfaßt.

Die Ergebnisse zeigen hinsichtlich der Genauigkeits- und der Geschwindigkeitsparameter ein divergierendes Bild (siehe Abbildung 1.3.1.3).

Die Materialeffekte sind in beiden Gruppen mit ähnlichem Muster signifikant, d.h. die Vergleiche der Punktmuster waren in beiden Gruppen mit den höchsten Fehlerraten und den längsten Reaktionszeiten verbunden. Der bei den normallesenden Kindern zu beobachtende Leistungsvorteil mit signifikant kürzesten Reaktionszeiten und den geringsten Fehlerraten beim Vergleich von Buchstaben ist bei den legasthenischen Kindern nicht erkennbar. Das verweist auf Strategieunterschiede in der Nutzung des lexikalischen Kodes und der damit verbundenen Benennbarkeitsvorteile der normallesenden Kinder. Das bestätigt die Befunde von Ellis (1981) und Remschmidt und Warnke (1995).

Während wir hinsichtlich der Genauigkeitsleistungen signifikante Defizite der legasthenischen

Kinder vor allem bei Buchstaben und Punktmustern finden, zeigen sich keine signifikanten Reaktionszeitunterschiede. Die legasthenischen Kinder reagieren sogar tendenziell bei allen drei Materialarten schneller und zeigen damit einen partiellen Leistungsvorteil, der mit einer erhöhten Impulsivität und / oder als Kompensations- bzw. Trainingseffekte interpretierbar ist.

Diskussion

In den vorgestellten Experimenten wurden Arbeitsgedächtnisleistungen differenziert auf der Grundlage des Modells von Baddeley und Hitch (1974) bezüglich ihrer Modalitätsspezifik eingehender und zu erhaltender Informationen sowie auf der Grundlage des Modells von Cowan (1995) hinsichtlich des Anteils automatisierter versus kontrollierter Exekutivprozesse bei der Handlungs-/Antwortgenerierung. Dabei ging es um die Frage, inwieweit Legastheniker von normallesenden Kindern hinsichtlich verschiedener Funktionen des Arbeitsgedächtnisses abweichen und damit um die Frage, ob es sich um Legastheniker Defizite handelt und wie generell bzw. modalitäts-, material- und domainenspezifisch diese sind.

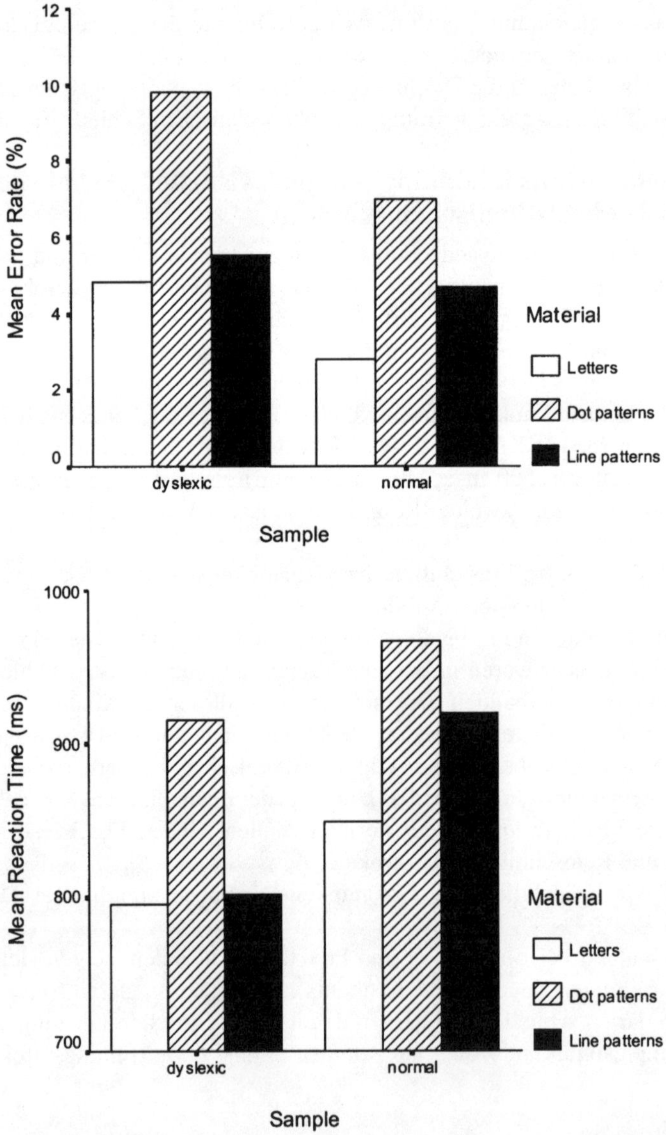

Abb. 1.3.1.4 Vergleich von Genauigkeitsleistungen und Reaktionszeiten legasthenischer und normallesender Kinder bei unterschiedlich schriftsprachlich relevantem Material

Die Ergebnisse der drei Experimente bestätigen nicht die Annahme eines generellen Arbeitsgedächtnisdefizits, sondern verweisen auf Modalitäts- und Materialabhängigkeiten, auf den Einfluß des Sprachsystems sowie die Bedeutung kontrollierter versus automatisierter Exekutivanforderungen auf die Arbeitsgedächtnisleistungen legasthenischer Kinder.

Wir können damit die ohnehin konsistentere Befundlage zu Defiziten der phonologischen Schleife bei Legasthenikern bestätigen, die offenbar den größten Teil der Lagastheniker betreffen (71,4% der Legastheniker Stichprobe nach der Subtypenanalyse im Experiment 2) und welche im Vergleich zu Defiziten der visuell-räumlichen Schleife stärker ausgeprägt erscheinen. Damit ist auch erklärbar, daß im Experiment 1 die deutschen legasthenischen Kinder am stärksten diskriminierbar waren von normallesenden, gleichaltrigen Kindern durch die phonologischen Arbeitsgedächtnisaufgaben mit hohem Grad an kontrollierten Exekutivprozessen (Serielles Reproduzieren). Auch im Experiment 2 zeigten sich signifikante Leistungsdefizite der Legastheniker sich ausschließlich bei auditiver Präsentation von Worten und Pseudoworten hinsichtlich der Fehlerraten.

Defizite der visuell-räumlichen Schleife erscheinen auch nach unseren Befunden des Experimentes 3 stark materialabhängig zu sein. Die von uns gefundenen signifikant höheren Fehlerraten der legasthenischen Kinder bei Buchstaben und Punktmustern betrafen demnach komplexere, visuelle Reizmuster, was die Ergebnisse von Casco und Prunetti (1996) bestätigen würde. Zum anderen sind sie bezogen auf den erschwerten lexikalischen Zugriff beim Vergleich von Buchstaben gut mit den Resultaten von Ellis (1981) und seiner Benennbarkeitshypothese erklärbar.

Der Zusammenhang von frühen, elementaren auditiven und visuellen Wahrnehmungsleistungen (z. B. Kontrastsensitivität und Persistenz) zu den späten, hochkomplexen Prozessen des Arbeitsgedächtnisses ist experimentell für die Legasthenieforschung noch ungeklärt. Darum rankt sich die Frage, ob und wie stark die Defizite des Arbeitsgedächtnisses von Defiziten der frühen Wahrnehmungsprozesse geprägt werden.

Die im Experiment 1 nachgewiesene Sprachsystemabhängigkeit von Arbeitsgedächtnisleistungen bestätigt erstmals den Überlegenheitseffekt der Chinesen auch für das Kindesalter. Für erwachsene Chinesen sind bessere Arbeitsgedächtnisleistungen für die phonologische Schleife z. B. durch Lau und Hoosain (1999) sowie Chincotta und Underwood (1997) sowie für die visuell-räumliche Schleife z. B. durch Lass (1995) nachgewiesen worden. In unserem Experiment 3 zeigte sich in den Zeitparametern eine generelle Chinesische Überlegenheit bezüglich visueller und auditiver Aufgaben. In den auditiven Aufgaben ließ sich darüber hinaus auch eine Genauigkeitsüberlegenheit der Chinesen erkennen. Unsere Befunde sprechen für eine stärkere Überlegenheit der Chinesischen Kinder bezüglich der Leistungen der phonologischen Schleife, aber gleichzeitig für eine, wenn auch geringere Überlegenheit bezüglich der visuell-räumlichen Schleife. Die Ergebnisse sind interpretierbar als Effekte eines durch das chinesische Sprachsystem initiierten „natürlichen" Arbeitsgedächtnistrainings durch mündliche Kommunikation und die damit erzwungenen kognitiven Prozesse des Sprachverstehens und der Sprachproduktion. Die festgestellte starke sprachbezogene Trainingsabhängigkeit von Arbeitsgedächtnisleistungen ist gut vergleichbar mit den von Gathercole und Baddeley (1993) nachgewiesenen altersbezogenen Kompensationseffekten der phonologischen Schleife sowie mit den von Witruk und Rosendahl (1999) gefundenen Kompensationseffekten der visuell-räumlichen Schleife.

Damit ist die im Titel formulierte Frage nach der Generalität des Defizites in dreifacher Hinsicht zu differenzieren: Wir können mit unseren vorliegenden Befunden eine Modalitätsspezifik, eine Materialspezifik sowie eine Sprach- bzw. Trainingsabhängigkeit von Arbeitsgedächtnisleistungen bei Legasthenikern konstatieren.

Literatur

Baddeley, A. D. und Hitch, G. (1974). Working memory. In G. Bower (Ed.), *Recent advances in learning and motivation.* 8, New York: Academic Press.

Barnea, A., Lamm, O., Epstein, R. und Pratt, H. (1994). Brain potentials from dyslexic children recorded during short-term memory tasks. *International Journal of Neuroscience*, *74*, 227-237.

Casco, C. und Prunetti, E. (1996). Visual search of good and poor readers: Effects with targets having single and combined features. *Perceptual and Motor Skills*, 82, 1155-1167.

Chincotta,D. und Underwood, G. (1997). Digit span and articulatory suppression: A cross-linguistic comparison. *European Journal of Cognitive Psychology*, 9, 1, 89-96.

Cowan, N. (1995). Attention and memory: An integrated framework. Oxford: Oxford University Press.

Ellis, N. (1981). Visual and name coding in dyslexic children. *Psychological Research*, 43, 201-218.

Gathercole, S. E. und Baddeley, A. D. (1993). Working memory and language. East Sussex, Hove, Lawrence Erlbaum Associates Ltd.

Goldman-Rakic, P. S. (1998). The prefrontal landscape: Implications of functional architecture for understanding human mentation and the central executive. In A. C. Roberts et al.(Eds), *The prefrontal cortex: Executive and cognitive functions.* New York: Oxford University Press.

Gräntzel, B. und Jähn, A. (1997). Untersuchung zur Arbeitsgedächtnisleistung von legasthenischen Kindern bei akustischer und visueller Darbietung von Worten und Nichtworten. Unveröffentlichte Diplomarbeit, Universität Leipzig, Institut für Angewandte Psychologie.

Ho, C. S.-H. und Bryant, P. (1997). Phonological Skills Are Important in Learning to Red Chinese. *Developmental Psychology*, 33, 6, 946-951.

Klix, F. (1984). Über Wissensrepräsentation im menschlichen Gedächtnis. In F. Klix (Ed.), *Gedächtnis, Wissen, Wissensnutzung* (pp. 9-73). Berlin, VEB Deutscher Verlag der Wissenschaften.

Lau, C. W. & Hoosain, R. (1999). Working memory and language difference in sound duration: A comparison of mental arithmetic in Chinese, Japanese, and English. *Psychologia: An International Journal of Psychology in the Orient*, 42, 3, 139-144.

Lass, U. (1997). Einfluß von Sprache auf Verarbeitungsprozesse im Kurzzeitgedächtnis - eine experimentelle Untersuchung mit deutschen und chinesischen Probanden. In G. Lüer & U. Lass (Eds.), *Erinnern und Behalten.* Göttingen, Vandenhoeck & Ruprecht.

Mecklinger, A. und Müller, N. (1996). Dissociations in the processing of „what" and „where" information in working memory: An event-related potential analysis. *Journal-of-Cognitive-Neuroscience.* Sep; Vol 8(5): 453-473.

Pedrides, M. (1994). Functional specialization within the dorsolateral frontal cortex. *Revue de Neuropsychologie.* 4, 3, 305-325.

Remschmidt, H. und Warnke, A. (1995). Zur visuellen und sprachlichen Informationsverarbeitung bei lese-rechtschreibschwachen Kindern im Längsschnitt. *Kinder- und Jugendpsychiatrie*, 23, Suppl. 1, 27.

Rösler, F. et al. (1997). Gedächtnisspuren im EEG. *Zeitschrift für Experimentelle Psychologie*, XLIV/1, 4-37.

Schröger, E. (1995). Processing of auditory deviants with changes in one vs. two stimulus dimensions. *Psychophysiology*, 32, 55-65.

Share, D. L. (1994). Deficient phonological processing in disabled readers implicates processing deficits beyond the phonological module. In K. P. van den Bos, L. S. Siegel, D. J. Bakker und D. L. Share (Eds.), *Current directions in dyslexia research.* Lisse: Swets und Zeitlinger.

Siegel, L. S. und Linder, B. A. (1984). Short-Term Memory Processes in Children With Reading and Arithmetic Learning Disabilities. *Developmental Psychology*, 20, 2, 200-207.

So, D. und Siegel, L. S. (1997). Learning to read Chhinese: Semantic, syntactic, phonological and working memory skills in normally achieving and poor Chinese readers. *Reading and Writing: An Interdisciplinary Journal*, 9, 1-21.

Staffel, P. und Witruk, E. (1999). In E. Witruk und T. Lachmann (Eds.), *Basic Mechanisms of Language and Language Disorders.* Leipziger Universitätsverlag, Leipzig.

Sternberg, S. (1975). Memory scanning. New findings and current controversies. *Quarterly Journal of Experimental Psychology*, *27*, 1-32.

Vellutino, F. R. (1987). Dyslexia. *Scientific American*, 256, 3, 1-42.

Willows, D. M., Kruk, R. S. und Corcos, E. (Eds.) (1993). Visual processes in reading and reading disabilities. Hillsdale: Lawrence Erlbaum Associates.

Witruk, E. (1993). Memory Deficits of Dyslexic Children. In P. Tallal, A. M. Galaburda, R. R. Llindas und C. von Euler (Eds.), Temporal information processing in the nervous system. Special reference to dyslexia and dysphasia. *Annals of the New York Academy of Sciences*, 682, 430-435, New York, The New York Academy of Sciences.

Witruk, E. und Ho, C. S.-H. (1999). Dyslexia and working memory in different language systems. Konferenzabstract und Vortragsmanuskript zum *5th Annual Meeting of the Society for Scientific Study of Reading*, Montreal, April 1999.

Witruk, E. und Schuster, U. (1997). Working memory in dyslexic children. Abstract und Vortragsmanuskript *4th World Congress on Dyslexia*, 23-26 September 1997, Halkidiki, Greece.

Witruk, E. und Rosendahl, W. (1999). Modalitäts-und Anforderungsspezifik von Arbeitsgedächtnisleistungen bei Legasthenikern. In *Kongreßbericht der XXIII. Arbeits- und Fortbildungstagung der Deutschen Gesellschaft für Sprachheilpädagogik e.V.*, Würzburg 1999.

Witruk, E. (1999). Working memory performance in dyslexic children. In E. Witruk und T. Lachmann (Eds.), *Basic Mechanisms of Language and Language Disorders.* Leipziger Universitätsverlag, Leipzig.

Witruk, E., Lachmann, T. und Graeve, J. (2000). Visual matching with different types of material in dyslexic and nondyslexic children. *The Official Journal of the Society for Scientific Study of Reading*, Lawrence Erlbaum Ass. Publ. Mahwah, New Jersey, London.

1.4 Allgemein

1.4.1 Einführung in die Legasthenieforschung für Laien

Mechthild Firnhaber

In der Vorankündigung für diese Arbeitsgruppe haben Sie folgende seltsam klingende Worte gelesen: Planum temporale, Ektopien, Dysplasien, Broca- und Wernicke-Zentrum, sensorische Integration, zentrale Fehlhörigkeit, zentrale Hörbahn, Vorläuferfunktion, Wahrnehmungs-störungen, Dysgrammatismus, Sprachentwicklungsstörungen und vieles mehr.

Wenn Sie das alles so hören, wird es Ihnen gehen wie mir damals vor fast 30 Jahren, als meine Söhne zur Schule kamen und bald feststand, dass sie eine sehr schwere Form der Legasthenie hatten: confused on a higher level, verwirrt auf höherem Niveau. Deshalb: Was soll das alles? Was bedeuten diese vielen Fremdwörter, was bedeuten die medizinischen Forschungsergebnisse für unsere Kinder? Ich will versuchen, dies für Sie verständlich und durchsichtig zu machen.

Zunächst einmal – und das habe ich bei den vielen Ihnen fremd klingenden Wörtern noch unterschlagen – zunächst möchte ich also doch kurz erwähnen, dass die „echte“ Legasthenie meist erblich bedingt ist. Es gibt viele Familien, in denen sich die Legasthenie seit Generationen vererbt und „heimisch“ fühlt, so wie das seit 3 Generationen in meiner Familie der Fall ist.

Man vermutet die verantwortlichen Gene auf den Chromosomen 6 und 15, neuerdings auch auf Chromosom 2, wie molekulargenetische Untersuchungen zeigten.

Viele Autoren im In- und Ausland haben ausgedehnte familiäre Studien durchgeführt, von denen ich hier besonders die Arbeiten des Genetikers Prof. Grimm (Würzburg) und des Kinder- und Jugendpsychiaters Dr. Schulte-Körne (Marburg) erwähnen möchte, nicht zuletzt auch deshalb, weil meine große Familie mütterlicherseits daran teilgenommen hat.

Es scheint nun auch so zu sein, dass das Gen auf Chromosom 6 relevant für phonologische Prozesse ist und der Genort für die nicht-phonologischen Anteile, also z. B. für die visuellen Fähigkeiten, auf dem Chromosom 15 zu finden ist.

Vielleicht ist das die Erklärung dafür, dass nicht alle Legastheniker identische Schwierigkeiten haben und nicht alle gleich stark betroffen sind. Wir wissen zwar schon viel, aber eben doch leider noch nicht alles.

Beginnen wir nun – und für Ihr Verständnis ist dies unerlässlich – mit den Forschungsergebnissen von Prof. Galaburda aus den 80er und 90er Jahren.

Er fand in den Gehirnen verstorbener Legastheniker, dass schon im Mutterleib (ca. im 4. Schwangerschaftsmonat) beim Fötus bestimmte Hirnzellen nicht weiter reifen (also ihre normale Form nicht erreichen – Dysplasien) bzw. nicht in die Hirnrinde wandern (Ektopien), wie sie es eigentlich sollten. Diese Veränderungen betreffen nun in der Hauptsache die Sprachregion in der linken Hirnhälfte, das heißt, ein Legastheniker hat dort teilweise weniger Zellen zur Verarbeitung von Signalen zur Verfügung, einige sind zu klein oder auch zu langsam arbeitend und manche sind auch nicht besonders gut geordnet.

Dies alles führt offensichtlich dazu, dass das sogenannte Planum temporale links, also die Region der linken Hirnhälfte, in der überwiegend das sensorische Sprachzentrum und das Hörzentrum liegen, bei Legasthenikern kleiner ist. Dies führt zu einer Symmetrie der Hirnhälften, obwohl bei Rechtshändern normalerweise die linke Hirnhälfte stärker und führend sein sollte (Asymmetrie).

Durch all diese Fehlfunktionen entstehen bei der Sprachverarbeitung, also beim Hören und Verarbeiten, unter anderem auch besonders bei schnell aufeinander folgenden Lauten und Signalen, Probleme.

Ähnlich gelagert sind auch die Schwierigkeiten bei der visuellen Verarbeitung, denn auch hier spielen nicht ordnungsgemäße Zellen eine wichtige Rolle.

Vielfach ist außerdem noch die normale Hemmung, der alle unsere Wahrnehmungen unterliegen, bei Legasthenikern nicht sehr ausgeprägt. Deshalb kann sowohl beim Hören als auch beim Sehen einiges „durcheinander purzeln".

Und leider ist das noch nicht alles. Wir wissen, dass manche Kinder auch eine sogenannte „zentrale Fehlhörigkeit" haben. Auf dieses Problem müssen wir näher eingehen, denn es ist vielfach eine der Hauptursachen von Sprachentwicklungsstörungen und der Legasthenie, obwohl natürlich längst nicht alle Legastheniker eine zentrale Fehlhörigkeit haben.

Leider kann man mit einer normalen Hörprüfung beim HNO-Arzt ein solches Problem nicht nachweisen. Legastheniker haben meist ganz normale Hörkurven. Man findet beim HNO-Arzt also nichts Auffälliges. Deshalb muss bei einem Verdacht auf eine zentrale Fehlhörigkeit ein Pädaudiologe aufgesucht werden. Die meisten Pädaudiologen finden sich an Uni-Kliniken, nur wenige sind niedergelassen.

Bei der zentralen Fehlhörigkeit liegen die Störungen im Nervennetz der zentralen Hörbahnen. Eigentlich fallen diese Kinder schon früh auf durch große Geräuschempfindlichkeit oder durch verspätetes und undeutliches Sprechen. Sie scheinen nicht zuzuhören, verstehen „Banane" statt „komm mal" und lassen sich durch jeden Piep ablenken. Als Erwachsene können Sie sich deshalb in lauter Umgebung nicht aufs Lesen konzentrieren und als Schüler können sie die Stimme des Lehrers nicht vom Geräuschpegel der Klasse unterscheiden. Sie leiden bis zur Erschöpfung unter lauten Klassen. Deshalb müssen diese Kinder immer vorne sitzen, aber nie mit dem Rücken zu den Mitschülern, sondern seitlich und nie am Fenster, wo andere Geräusche lauern und sie ablenken.

Häufig haben diese Legastheniker auch noch Störungen im rhythmischen und melodischen Bereich, was sich natürlich auch auf die Sprachverarbeitung und die Beherrschung der Schriftsprache auswirkt. Deshalb ist eine Förderung auf diesem Gebiet so früh wie möglich angezeigt.

Sprachentwicklungsstörungen, besonders in Legasthenikerfamilien, in denen die Legasthenie erblich nachgewiesen ist, sollte man immer ernst nehmen und rechtzeitig behandeln. Das bedeutet, dass unter Umständen schon das „Lallen" eines Säuglings auffällig sein kann und auch ein verspätetes Sprechenlernen, die schon erwähnte verwaschene Sprache und ein Dysgrammatismus, d. h., dass Kinder einen Satz nicht nach grammatikalischen Regeln aufbauen können.

Übrigens will ich Ihnen in diesem Zusammenhang auch die medizinischen Bezeichnungen für die Sprachzentren nennen: Das Broca-Zentrum ist zuständig für die motorischen Anteile der Sprache, das Wernicke-Zentrum für die sensorischen Bereiche, also, dass wir begreifen, was wir lesen und hören, und dann ist da noch die sogenannte Insel.

Es gibt eine sehr interessante amerikanische Studie, veröffentlicht in der Zeitschrift „Nature", die zeigt, dass Legastheniker bei Sprachaufgaben nur ihr „Broca-Zentrum" belasten. Dies bedeutet, dass ein Sprachzentrum überbelastet ist. Man spricht auch von einem Dysconnection-Problem, weil die Verständigung zwischen den Sprachzentren offensichtlich nicht oder nur sehr verzögert funktioniert.

So kann ich mir auch die Verständnisprobleme beim Lesen erklären. Wir wissen, dass für Legastheniker Lesen und Verstehen des Gelesenen meist zwei unterschiedlich verlaufende Vorgänge sind. Im Moment des Lesens haben sie es noch nicht verstanden. Das könnte auf das „Verständigungsproblem" zwischen den Sprachzentren zurückzuführen sein. Und wir verstehen nun schon eher, warum normal begabte Kinder nicht gleich begreifen, was sie da eben gelesen haben.

Kommen wir noch einmal auf die visuelle Wahrnehmungsstörung zurück, die ich nur sehr verkürzt dargestellt habe, weil ihr Anteil viel geringer ist als die der auditiven Wahrnehmung mit der zentralen Fehlhörigkeit. Aber auch bei der visuellen Wahrnehmung hat man in der Zeitschrift „Nature" interessante Experimente veröffentlicht. Man hat bei sich bewegenden Mustern, wie sie ja das Buchstabenlesen auch darstellen, bei Legasthenikern und Kontrollkindern unterschiedliche Hirnaktivitäten festgestellt. In bestimmten Bereichen gab es bei Legasthenikern keinerlei Aktivitäten im Gegensatz zu den Nicht-Legasthenikern.

Dazu kommt, dass allein schon der Lesevorgang hohe Anforderungen stellt an die Aufmerksamkeit eines Legasthenikers. Neuere augenärztliche Untersuchungen zur Lesegeschwindigkeit bewiesen eindeutig, wieviel mehr Zeit und Mühe ein Legastheniker aufwenden muss, um Texte zu erlesen. So zeigen diese aktuellen wissenschaftlichen Studien deutlich, mit welch' enormen Schwierigkeiten Legastheniker zu kämpfen haben.

Von entwicklungsneurologischer Seite wird auch schon die Auffassung vertreten, dass die verzögerte Verständigung, die man zwischen den Sprachzentren fand, auch in anderen Wahrnehmungsbereichen vorhanden ist. Ruf-Bächtiger geht davon aus, dass es eine allgemein „verzögerte Erfassungsspanne" gibt.

Seit langem vermuten wir auch schon, dass es zwischen den beiden Hirnhälften bei vielen Legasthenikern offensichtlich nur zu einer mangelhaften Zusammenarbeit kommt. Leider wissen wir darüber noch viel zu wenig. Interessant ist in diesem Zusammenhang, wie griechische Forscher herausfanden, dass der die beiden Hirnhälften verbindende Balken an einigen Stellen bei Legasthenikern weniger Nervenvernetzungen aufweist. Das könnte bedeuten, dass tatsächlich die Wahrnehmungsbereiche von rechter und linker Hirnhälfte an einigen Stellen nicht richtig vernetzt sind und sich allein deshalb schon nicht ordnungsgemäß entwickeln konnten oder geordnet zusammenarbeiten. So könnte man sich vorstellen, wie es zu der sogenannten gestörten sensorischen Integration kommen kann.

Die gestörte sensorische Integration ist sicher vielen von Ihnen schon geläufig, besonders, wenn Sie Eltern von schwer betroffenen Kindern sind, die unter Umständen schon vor der Schule eine sogenannte SI-Behandlung bei einer Ergotherapeutin hatten. Um die sensorische Integration zu verstehen, erinnern wir uns an unsere verschiedenen Sinnesfunktionen wie Sehen, Hören, Riechen, Fühlen. Überall kann es leider zu Störungen kommen:

1. Störung der visuellen Wahrnehmung
2. Störung der akustischen Wahrnehmung
3. Störung der Grob- und Feinmotorik
4. Störung des taktilen Sinnes (Berührungssinn)
5. Störung der Kinästhetik (Muskelbewegungssinn)
6. Störung des Vestibulärsystems (Gleichgewicht)

Aus den letzten drei Sinnesbereichen (4, 5, 6) ergibt sich die sogenannte Körperwahrnehmung, d.h. wir erhalten daraus diejenigen Signale, die notwendig sind, um uns selbst zu spüren und damit wir uns dann entsprechend bewegen und handeln können.

Bei der gestörten sensorischen Integration können also unter Umständen so manche Wahrnehmungsbereiche nicht in Ordnung sein.

Die ersten beiden Wahrnehmungsstörungen haben wir schon besprochen, aber auch die Grob- und Feinmotorik (3) ist unter Umständen betroffen, oft auch nur teilweise. So kann zum Beispiel die Feinmotorik des Mundes so gestört sein, dass ein Säugling nicht richtig saugen kann und bis über das dritte Lebensjahr hinaus sabbert, d. h. Speichelfluss hat. Es kann sein, dass er nicht oder nicht richtig gelallt hat und auch verspätet sprechen lernte. Gleichzeitig kann aber die Feinmotorik der Finger ganz ausgezeichnet funktionieren. Wenn also die Feinmotorik des Mundes ganz offensichtlich gestört ist, muss es nicht zwangsläufig sein, dass auch die Feinmotorik der Finger ebenso gestört ist. Es sind eben oft nur Teilbereiche nicht in Ordnung, aber genau dies kann das Zusammenspiel oder die regelrechte Entwicklung aller Sinnesfunktionen behindern, so als wenn beim Zahnrad ein Rädchen fehlt. Dann hakt es eben!

So ist auch die Körperwahrnehmung aus verschiedenen Sinneswahrnehmungen (4, 5, 6) zusammengesetzt und gerade hier kann die Störung auch nur eines Sinnesbereiches, z. B. des taktilen Sinnes, die normale Zusammenarbeit stören. Ein treffendes Beispiel von einem erwachsenen Legastheniker: Wenn er, so berichtet er, eine volle U-Bahn-Station betritt und seine Augen dann nicht mehr die fehlende taktile Information der Füße über den Muskelbewegungssinn an das Gleichgewicht ausgleichen können (weil er eben die Füße nicht mehr sehen kann), fühlt er sich, als sei er betrunken, als würde er schwanken. Ähnlich geht es ihm, wenn er durch einen Raum voller Menschen gehen muss. Durch die gestörte Körperwahrnehmung weiß er nicht, ob er irgendwo anstößt, denn er hat kein Gefühl dafür, wo sein Körper anfängt bzw. aufhört. Er gehört zu der Generation, in der man von gestörter sensorischer Integration noch nichts wusste und der deshalb auch nicht behandelt wurde.

Für Kinder bedeutet dies eine ungeheure Belastung, da sie sich ihre gestörte Wahrnehmung ja nicht erklären können und erst lernen müssen, damit zu leben. Manches schwer betroffene Kind hat eine sogenannte Dyspraxie, das heißt, dass es eine motorische und sensorische Entwicklungsverzögerung oder auch –störung haben kann, eine zusätzlich belastende Situation, wenn es damit unbehandelt eingeschult wird. Leider erkennen Kinderärzte, Orthopäden und auch sogar Kinderneurologen, die sich mit dieser Materie nicht intensiv beschäftigt haben, diese Störung oft gar nicht. Die Eltern werden vertröstet und so wird nicht rechtzeitig, d. h. schon vor der Schule behandelt.

Für Prof. Breuer haben diese Wahrnehmungsverzögerungen noch eine besondere Bedeutung. Er nennt einige davon „Vorläuferfunktion" (optische Differenzierung, phonematische Differenzierung, kinästhetische Differenzierung, melodische Differenzierung, rhythmische Differenzierung), die gut funktionieren müssen, wenn ein Kind zur Schule kommt. Dass diese Wahrnehmungsleistungen für den Sprach- und Schriftspracherwerb unerlässlich sind, sollte eigentlich allen bekannt sein. Leider haben aber auch die Erzieher in den Kindergärten nur wenige oder gar keine Kenntnisse und Eltern schon gar nicht. So werden immer wieder Kinder eingeschult, die längst vorher hätten behandelt werden müssen. Mit dem Test von Prof. Breuer im Vorschul- und Schulalter ließen sich grobdiagnostisch schnell Fehlfunktionen feststellen und auch behandeln.

Literatur:

Ayres, J.: Bausteine der kindlichen Entwicklung (über die Sensorische Integration), Springer-Verlag, 1992

Bielefeldt, E.: Tasten und Spüren, wie wir bei taktil-kinästhetischer Störung helfen können, Reinhardt-Verlag, 1991

Brand, Breitenbach, Maisel: Integrationsstörungen, Würzburg, Verlag Maria-Stern-Schule des Marienvereins, 1986

Breuer, H., Weuffen, M.: Gut vorbereitet auf das Lesenlernen und Schreibenlernen?, Barth-Verlag, Leipzig, 1990

Breuer, H., Weuffen, M.: Lernschwierigkeiten am Schulanfang, Beltzpraxis, 1993

Englbrecht, A., Weigert, H.: Lernbehinderungen verhindern. Unterrichtspraxis Grundschule, Diesterweg, 1994

Firnhaber, M.: Legasthenie und andere Wahrnehmungsstörungen – Wie Eltern und Lehrer helfen können, Fischer Taschenbuch, 1996, 2. erweiterte Auflage

Günther, H.: Wahrnehmungsauffällige Kinder in der Grundschule, Klett-Verlag, 1998

Kesper/Hottinger: Mototherapie bei Sensorischen Integrationsstörungen, Reinhardt-Verlag, 1993

Meister Vitale, B.: Lernen kann phantastisch sein. Kinderleichtes Lernen durch optimalen Einsatz beider Gehirnhälften, Synchron-Verlag, 1988

Miske-Fleming, D.: Theorie und Methode zur Behandlung von perzeptionsgestörten Kindern, Verlag modernes lernen, Schriftenreihe, 1987

Simon, W.: Befund: Legasthenie, Neue Ergebnisse für die Praxis, Schwanenverlag, 1981

Schenk-Danzinger, L.: „Legasthenie" Zerebralfunktionelle Interpretation, Reinhardt-Verlag, 1991

1.4.2 Das Verständnis raumzeitlicher Begriffe beim fünf- und sechsjährigen Kind und ihre Bedeutung für die schulische Leistung

Lucien Bertrand

Das Problem der Lesefertigkeit oder des schriftlichen Spracherwerbs beim Kind hat im Wandel der Zeit sehr unterschiedliche Erklärungsmomente erfahren. Von den Arbeiten von FERREIRO und DOWNING wissen wir, dass das Kind, um die Fertigkeit des Lesens und Schreibens zu erlernen, das Wesen und die Funktionen der geschriebenen Sprache verstanden haben muss, um dabei Erfolg zu haben.

Ich möchte kurz auf die Arbeiten von Emilia FERREIRO, einer langjährigen Mitarbeiterin von PIAGET, eingehen. Bei Kindern im Vorschulalter stellt sie vier Entwicklungsstadien fest, die ich hier der Klarheit halber in drei Etappen zusammengefasst habe:

In einem 1. Stadium versteht das Kind nicht, dass Zusammenhänge zwischen dem Aufbau der gesprochenen und der geschriebenen Sprache bestehen

Im zweiten Stadium, den FERREIRO das Silbenstadium nennt, versteht das Kind den Zusammenhang zwischen gesprochener und geschriebener Sprache, doch gebraucht es zur Darstellung einer Silbe oder Wortes ein Zeichen (oder Buchstabe)

Im dritten Stadium, den sie alphabetisches oder phonographisches Stadium nennt, hat das Kind verstanden, dass jedem Phonem ein Buchstabe entspricht.

Das Interesse an diesen Arbeiten besteht darin, dass der Leseprozess vom Standpunkt des Kindes gesehen wird und das Erlernen der Schrift von der Vorstellung ausgeht, die sich das Kind vom Schreibvorgang macht und nicht von der Tatsache, ob ein Wort richtig oder falsch geschrieben ist. Das Herausstreichen dieser kontinuierlichen Entwicklung der Strategien erlaubt uns nicht mehr, die Lernstörung unter den üblichen Aspekten zu sehen.

Ehe ein Kind das Lesen beherrschen kann, muss es also den Sinn und den technischen Aufbau der geschriebenen Schrift verstanden haben. Vernachlässigt man diese kognitive Erwerbsphase, bleibt die Leseleistung des Kindes schwach und stockend, weil das Kind nicht begriffen hat, welche dynamischen Prozesse das Lesenlernen von ihm verlangt. Wir wissen, dass die Schrift eine kodifizierte, visuelle Wiedergabe der gesprochenen Sprache ist. In der Schule wird allzu oft angenommen, das Kind wüßte das auch schon. Selten werden effektiv diese Voraussetzungen in den Lernprogrammen angeboten, sie werden ganz einfach als schon beim Kind vorhanden vorausgesetzt. Man nimmt in der ersten Klasse an, dass das Kind ein gewisses linguistisches Verständnis aufweist, dass es weiß, dass z.b. ein Redeschwall in Teile unterteilt werden kann, dass abstrakte visuelle Zeichen etwas Akustisches bedeuten. Es muss wissen, was ein gesprochenes Wort, was ein geschriebenes Wort ist, was Phoneme und Buchstaben sind. Um lesen zu lernen, muss das Kind also strukturelle und funktionelle Konzepte verstanden haben, die es sich selbst aneignen muss.

Vor kurzer Zeit hat der Nobelpreisträger Gabriel GARCIA MARQUEZ bei einem Kongress über die spanische Sprache den Widerstand der Kongressteilnehmer provoziert, als er vorschlug, die Rechtschreibung der spanischen Sprache abzuschaffen und den Leuten zu erlauben, ihre Sprache nach eigenem Gutdünken ohne Regelsystem zu schreiben. Er wurde fast des Saales verwiesen. Dabei ist es jedoch nicht schwierig, zu verstehen, was MARQUEZ sagen wollte: Die Sprache ist in ihrem Ansatz diskriminatorisch, weil sie den Benutzer der Sprache in zwei Lager teilt: einerseits diejenigen, welche eine Sprache mit allen Finessen beherrschen und die anderen, welche sie nur schwerfällig anwenden. Der eine schreibt eine korrekte Sprache, der andere läuft Gefahr, wegen seines Defizits, weil er nicht „richtig“ schreibt oder spricht, bestraft zu werden.

Diese Bestrafung beginnt allzu oft in der Grundschule, wo das Kind generell mit tragischen Lernmethoden konfrontiert wird: die Sprache wird nur sehr selten als Kommunikationsinstrument mit seiner intuitiven und subjektiven Sensibilität gelehrt, aber mit einem ganzen Werk von strikten, unerbittlichen Regeln, welche dem Wunsch des Kindes nach Kommunikation und Austausch nicht gerecht werden. Das Befolgenmüssen dieser orthographischen Regeln vernichtet die Freude, welche das Schreiben vermitteln könnte. Weil man den emotionalen Inhalt und die individuelle Bedeutung der Sprache vernachlässigt, zerstört man durch den absoluten Charakter der Regeln schlussendlich, was man zu schützen vorgibt: nämlich die Sprache selbst.

Einige werden sich wohl fragen, warum ich mich so lange auf diese Erklärungen über die Sprache selbst einlasse. Ganz einfach, um mit meinen nun folgenden Ausführungen nicht den Anschein zu erwecken, Sprache bestände allein aus raumzeitlichen Aspekten, die es im Falle von Problemen zu beheben genüge, um dem Kind das Lesen und Schreiben bei zu bringen. Das Erlernen der Sprache ist raumzeitlichen Regeln unterworfen: **auch, aber nicht nur**. Beim Umsetzen der gesprochenen Sprache in geschriebene Sprache, beim Diktat z.B., wird ein zeitlicher Vorgang in einen räumlichen Rahmen gestellt; beim Lesen wird dieser Rahmen nach festen räumlichen Regeln durchgesehen und in zeitliche Strukturen umgesetzt. Die raumzeitlichen Aspekte des Lesens und Schreibens sind also unverkennbar.

In diesem Kontext möchte ich nun eine Untersuchung vorstellen, welche in Luxemburger Vorschulklassen durchgeführt wurde und in der Zwischenzeit an der Uni Hannover im Fachbereich Erziehungswissenschaften, Psychologie der Behinderten, überprüft wurde und die Resultate auch bestätigt wurden.

Das Anliegen der Arbeit bestand in der Überprüfung der hauptsächlich in der französischen Literatur hervorgehobenen Zusammenhänge zwischen dem raumzeitlichen Entwicklungsstand eines Kindes im Alter von fünf und sechs Jahren und seiner Schulleistung. Es scheint mir sinnvoll, hier darauf hinzuweisen, daß die französische Literatur sowohl auf dem Gebiet der psychomotorischen Therapie als demjenigen der sonderpädagogischen Förderung von einer direkten Wechselbeziehung zwischen dem Raum-Zeit-Entwicklungsstand und einer entsprechenden Schulleistung ausgeht. **Raum und Zeit gelten dabei als die beiden Parameter, welche unseren geistigen Fähigkeiten erlauben, Erfahrungen zu machen und dieselben zu speichern.**

Die raumzeitlichen Begriffe als Voraussetzung für schulische Leistung wurden dabei im Kontext anderer Entwicklungsparameter in einer über zwei Jahre andauernden empirischen Längsschnittuntersuchung bei 250 Vorschulkindern überprüft.

Die Berücksichtigung bestehender Theorien, vornehmlich von PIAGET und WALLON, prägt die Auswahl neuer genereller Verfahren, die einerseits zur Prüfung der raumzeitlichen Wahrnehmung und Vorstellung, andererseits des Verständnisses ihrer Zusammenhänge dienen.

Man kann aus den Theorien ableiten, daß erst die Handlung im Raum, - damit verstehe ich nicht nur den räumlichen Raum, sondern auch den Zeitraum -, das Verständnis für räumliche Zusammenhänge ermöglicht. Darum haben wir versucht, neues Untersuchungsmaterial dort zu entwickeln, wo das bestehende nicht unseren Vorstellungen von aktivem Handeln entsprach. Die gleichen Überlegungen stellten wir an für den zeitlichen Raum mit seiner Periodizität und wählten auch hier aktive Untersuchungsformen auf dem Gebiet der Rhythmik aus. Rhythmik verbindet ja die beiden Komponenten der zeitlichen Wahrnehmung miteinander: die Ordnung und die Dauer.

Weitere Variablen sozialer, kognitiver und motorischer Kompetenzen wurden mit einbezogen, um auch aus diesen drei Bereichen eventuelle Gewichtungen der Zusammenhänge mit der allgemeinen Schulleistung festzustellen

Die Untersuchung des Raumes wurde in den den drei Wahrnehmungsräumen - akustisch, taktil, visuell - entsprechenden Aspekte geführt, zwei zusätzliche Untersuchungen prüften das aktive und passive Sprachverständnis räumlicher Begriffe sowie die räumliche Strukturierungsfähigkeit. Räumliche Zusammenhänge werden mittels der Prüfung der akustischen Wahrnehmung (AKURA), der taktilen Wahrnehmung (TAKRA), der visuellen Wahrnehmung (VIRA), des passiven (RABEG-A) und des aktiven (RABEG-B) Wortschatzes räumlicher Bestimmungswörter sowie der Raumstrukturierungsfähigkeit (RASTRU) geprüft. Es handelt sich dabei um neu geschaffene Verfahren, außer bei VIRA, wo es bei der Fülle von bestehenden Verfahren auf dem Gebiet des visuellen Raumes nicht angebracht schien, ein weiteres neues Verfahren zu entwickeln und wir dabei auf das aus HAWIK bestens bekannte Verfahren der KOHSschen Würfel, zwar mit anderen aus Frankreich her bekannten Items, zurückgriffen.

Die Verfahren, welche das Zeitverständnis prüften, basierten auf einer motorischen Wiedergabe vorgetragener Zeitstrukturen unter den Aspekten von Dauer und Ordnung. Die zeitliche Dauer wurde anhand der rhythmischen Anpassungsfähigkeit (RHYAN), die zeitliche Ordnung durch die rhythmische Nachahmungsfähigkeit (RHYNA) geprüft. Die komplexe Raum-Zeit-Verknüpfung (RAZEI) wurde ohne räumliche Anhaltspunkte geprüft. Ich werde jetzt im Detail auf die einzelnen Verfahren eingehen.

Alle Verfahren dienen der Erhebung der unabhängigen Variablen, wobei die Schulleistung als abhängige Variable gilt. Die Schulleistung wurde im folgenden Jahr am Ende des ersten Schuljahres durch das Einsammeln der Schulnoten in den Hauptfächern: Lesen, Schreiben und Rechnen bewertet.

Zur **Erfassung des akustischen Raumes** (Akura) wurde ein Verfahren entwickelt, bei dem die Versuchsperson eine Geräuschquelle durch Unterscheiden einer Reihe von 20 akustischen Reizen im Raum lokalisieren sollte. Die Geräuschquelle war das auf Stereoband aufgenommene Heulen der Sirene eines Interventionswagens. Fünf verschiedene Spieleinsatzwagen wurden in 0,5 m Entfernung von der Versuchsperson im Halbkreis auf dem Tisch aufgestellt, um dem Kind einen Anhaltspunkt für die Lokalisierung der Geräuschquelle zu geben.

Zur taktilen Erfassung einer räumlichen Anordnung (TAKRA) wurde in einem Ausschnitt ein Plättchen von 6x6 cm Größe eingelegt, auf dem eine bestimmte Anzahl von Muggelsteinen (zwischen zwei und sechs) in einer bestimmten räumlichen Anordnung aufgeklebt ist. Durch verhängte Eingänge an einer Hausfassade konnte das Kind mit beiden Händen ins „Innere des Hauses“ gelangen und die Anordnung ertasten. Auf einem Streifen von 6x6 cm großen Fotos sollte es dann nach Ertasten des Plättchens unter fünf angebotenen Bildern die ertastete Anordnung erkennen und zeigen.

Die Prüfung des visuellen Raumes (Vira) wurde anhand der KOHSschen Würfel durchgeführt. Der Test prüft die visuelle Analyse- und Synthesefähigkeit der Versuchsperson für räumliche Strukturen. Das Kind soll geometrische Zeichnungen, die ihm auf einer farbigen Unterlage gezeigt werden anhand von vier identischen farbigen Würfeln nachbilden. Hier die sieben Items in verkleinerter Form.

Bei der **Prüfung der Kenntnisse der Raumlage von Objekten** (RABEG-A), sowie **des Erwerbs der vier räumlichen Bestimmungswörtern**: von oben, von unten, von vorne, von hinten (RABEG-B) handelt es sich um eine doppelte Untersuchung, wobei der erste Teil der Prüfung – wie schon gesagt -den passiven Erwerb und der zweite Teil den aktiven Gebrauch der Bestimmungswörter der Raumlage von Gegenständen prüft.

Zwecks Feststellung dieses Erwerbs wird auf farbige Bilder von Gegenständen aus dem täglichen Wahrnehmungs- und Handlungsbereich des Kindes zurückgegriffen, wobei natürlich keine äußeren räumlichen Anhaltspunkte auf den Bildern zu sehen sein dürfen. Jedes Item der Bilderserie besteht aus fünf Fotos, wobei das erste Foto der Identifizierung des Gegenstandes dient. Der Gegenstand ist auf diesem Bild von der Seite zu sehen. Auf der anderen Seite sind Aufnahmen des gleichen Gegenstandes in vier unterschiedlichen räumlichen Lagen einzusehen, wobei die Darbietungsreihenfolge der einzelnen Bilder durch Zufall bestimmt ist.

Bei den fünf ersten Versuchen, die zur Prüfung des passiven Erwerbs dienen, wird dem Kind immer die gleiche Frage gestellt: „**Wo** siehst du (Name des Gegenstandes) von oben? - von vorne? - von hinten? - von unten?"

Bei den fünf folgenden Items wird das Kind, nach einem vorausgehenden Erklärungsbeispiel, aufgefordert, die räumlichen Bestimmungswörter: Von oben, unten, vorne, hinten, selbst zu gebrauchen mit der Frage: „**Von wo** siehst du (Name des Gegenstandes) hier?"

Bei der **Prüfung der räumlichen Strukturierungsfähigkeit** (RASTRU) soll das Kind nach einem Stellungswechsel von der einen zur anderen Seite eines Tisches, einem Stellungswechsel von 180° also, einen vor seinen Augen unter einen von neun im Quadrat aufgestellten undurchsichtigen Bechern versteckten Spielgegenstand wiederfinden und dadurch seine Raumstrukturierungsfähigkeit unter Beweis stellen. Bei dieser Untersuchung ist natürlich beim Kind das Verständnis der Objektpermanenz vorausgesetzt, wovon man in dem Alter ja ausgehen kann.

Zur Durchführung nimmt der Versuchsleiter an der schmalen Seite eines Tisches Platz und achtet darauf, daß keine zusätzlichen Gegenstände auf der Tischplatte der Versuchsperson irgendwelche Anhaltspunkte bieten können. An der dem Versuchsleiter entgegengesetzten Seite steht ein Schirm, der das Kind beim Wechsel von der Stellung vor dem Tisch (Vp1) zur Stellung hinter dem Tisch (Vp2) (oder umgekehrt) daran hindert, die Becher beständig zu beobachten.

Bei der ersten Aufgabe steht das Kind in Vp1 und wechselt zu Vp2, wo es seine Antwort gibt. Bei der nächsten Aufgabe steht es in Vp2 und geht nach Vp1, um die Antwort zu geben, usw.

Das Verständnis zeitlicher Strukturen wurde anhand von vier Verfahren geprüft:

Spontantempo, rhythmische Nachahmung und rhythmische Anpassung, sowie einer kombinierten Aufgabe raumzeitlicher Einheit.

Das **natürliche oder spontane Tempo (Spontem)** läßt sich beim Menschen beobachten, wenn er in der ihm eigenen, wohl neurologisch bedingten Frequenz mit dem Finger auf den Tisch oder mit dem Fuß auf den Boden klopft.

Die Messung der Fähigkeit, zeitliche Strukturen bei Eigentempo zu erwerben, wird in dieser Arbeit in Anlehnung an von STAMBAK gemachten Untersuchungen durchgeführt. Weil nur geringe Angaben über das Spontantempo in der untersuchten Altersgruppe bestehen, wurde versucht, durch Auswechseln der Unterlage, auf welche das Kind mit einem Tamburinschlegel klopfte, die Bedingungen der Untersuchung abzuändern und durch diese Abänderung

Informationen über das Bestehen des Spontantempos bei dieser Altersgruppe zu gewinnen. Ich will vorausschicken, dass die Existenz des Spontantempos für diese Altersgruppe nachgewiesen werden konnte, was uns erlaubte, die Fähigkeiten der rhythmischen Nachahmung und der rhythmischen Anpassung mit den ausgewählten Verfahren zu überprüfen.

Die Prüfung der **Nachahmungsfähigkeit rhythmischer Strukturen** (**Rhyna**) wird in ähnlicher Form in Frankreich im Zusammenhang mit Lesestörungen angewendet und dient gerne unter anderen Verfahren als eine Art Reifetest zur Prüfung der Lese- und Rechtschreibfertigkeit.

Hier die Rhythmen, welche dem Kind akustisch und visuell dargeboten werden.

a) oo .. oo .. oo
b) o . oo ...... o . oo ...... o . oo
c) o . ooo . oo .... o . ooo . oo .... o . ooo . oo
d) o . oo . o . ooo .... o . oo . o . ooo .... o . oo . o . ooo

Die **Prüfung der rhythmischen Anpassungsfähigkeit** (**Rhyan**) prüft die großmotorische Anpassungsfähigkeit des Kindes an ein Fremdtempo. Diese Prüfung wird mittels einem Metronom ohne Schlegel durchgeführt, wobei dem Kind ein bestimmtes Tempo angegeben wird, auf welchen es sich dann im Raum bewegen soll.

Die nun folgende Aufgabe könnte sowohl bei der Raum- als auch bei der Zeitwahrnehmung vorgestellt werden und nimmt in der Untersuchung eine besondere Stellung ein. Sie prüft als einzige die **Einheit von Raum und Zeit** (**Razei**) durch die Bewertung der Geschwindigkeit einer vorgetragenen Melodie. Dabei wird nicht wie bei PIAGET auf räumliche, sondern auf zeitliche Anhaltspunkte zurückgegriffen. Zweimal wird dem Kind eine Aufnahme einer auf Klavier vorgetragenen Melodie vorgespielt, jedoch mit unterschiedlicher Geschwindigkeit. Die Versuchsperson soll sagen, ob das Motiv das zweite Mal genau so schnell, schneller oder langsamer vorgetragen wird. In Wirklichkeit ist die zweite Darbietung niemals gleich schnell und der Unterschied in der Länge der beiden Darbietungen wird von Item zu Item geringer. Soweit zu den entwickelten Verfahren.

Ich habe schon darauf hingewiesen, daß wir noch andere Entwicklungsparameter des Kindes in die Untersuchung mit einfließen haben lassen, ich werde sie nur der Vollständigkeit halber erwähnen: Geschlecht und Alter des Kindes, Zahl der Geschwister, Rang des Kindes in der Geschwisterreihe,Beruf des Vaters / der Mutter.Dabei wurde der Beruf nur in dem Falle in Betracht gezogen, wo er auch ausgeübt wurde.

Mit Bewertungsskalen wurden Dimensionen gemessen, wie verbale Fähigkeit, motorische Entwicklung, Intelligenz, soziales Verhalten, schulische Anpassung und Konzentrationsfähigkeit.

Folgende Fragestellungen wurden überprüft:

Können Korrelationen zwischen einem raumzeitlichen Entwicklungsstand und der allgemeinen Schulleistung festgestellt werden?

Gibt es Anhaltspunkte für eine Korrelation zwischen einem allgemeinen motorischen Entwicklungsstand und der Schulleistung?

Haben andere Parameter, wie soziale Herkunft z.b., den gleichen oder eventuell einen größeren Einfluß auf die Schulleistung als der raumzeitliche Entwicklungsstand?

Zur Beantwortung der ersten Frage haben wir in einer ersten „kleinen" Regressionsanalyse die Korrelationen zwischen den die raumzeitliche Entwicklung betreffenden Verfahren als unabhängige Variablen und der erzielten Schulleistung des Kindes in der ersten Klasse als abhängige Variable für die untersuchte Population berechnet. Dabei ergibt sich allein für VIRA --also die visuelle Raumanalyse-- ein signifikanter Wert, während alle übrigen raumzeitlichen Werte aus der Gleichung ausscheiden. Daraus haben wir geschlussfolgert, dass offensichtlich individuelle Faktoren bei der Vorhersage der Schulleistung eine wesentlich größere Rolle spielen als die spezifischen Faktoren, zu welchen das Raum-Zeit-Verständnis gehört.

Angesichts dieses Resultates gingen wir zur dritten Frage über mit der Hypothese, daß ein größerer Prozentsatz der Gesamtvarianz von übergeordneten Variablen wie Bildungsniveau der Eltern, Geschlechtszugehörigkeit, usw. erklärt würde. Die sogenannte „große" multiple Regressionsanalyse der Summenvariablen der Untersuchung, die von einer Interkorrelation sämtlicher Daten ausgeht, bestätigt dann auch, daß das **Verständnis der Sprache sowie die aktive Ausdrucksfähigkeit** des Kindes seine Schulleistung in signifikanterer Weise als die visuelle Differenzierungsfähigkeit beeinflussen.

Dabei findet auch unsere zweite Frage eine Antwort in dem Sinne, daß bei den Interkorrelationen der zur Verfügung stehenden Daten das motorische Entwicklungsniveau des Kindes für die Schulleistung keinen statistisch signifikanten Wert erzielt.

Die Generalität und Spezifizität der Raum-Zeit-Variablen für eine entsprechende Schulleistung läßt sich in unserer allgemeinen Untersuchungsgruppe nicht oder nur sehr bedingt nachweisen. Wir schlußfolgern daraus, daß die Raum-Zeit-Variablen im Gesamt der Entwicklung aller Kinder nicht die hohe Bedeutung haben, die ihnen oft - vornehmlich in der französischen Literatur - zugestanden wird. Die Theoriebildung scheint eher eine Theorie der Entwicklung von Kindern mit Entwicklungsstörungen oder -verzögerungen zu sein als von einer Gesamtbevölkerung. Man scheint in der französischen Literatur wohl eher von einem klinisch betrachteten Patientengut auszugehen.

Aus diesen angestellten Überlegungen heraus überprüften wir eine Alternativhypothese: „**Die Zusammenhänge zwischen einem raumzeitlichen Entwicklungsstand und einer entsprechenden Schulleistung lassen sich nur bei Kindern mit Entwicklungsstörungen feststellen**".

Wir vergleichen zur Überprüfung dieser Hypothese in einem Extremgruppenvergleich die besten und die schwächsten Schüler unserer Stichprobe. Erfaßt wurden die von diesen beiden Gruppen erzielten Werte. Dabei sind die Unterschiede, außer bei SPONTEM - Spontantempo - hochsignifikant und bezeugen, daß ein Festigen raumzeitlicher Begriffe in der heil- oder sonderpädagogischen Praxis seinen Platz hat.

Eine anschließende multiple Regressionsanalyse der von den schwachen Schülern erzielten Werte läßt interessante Schlüsse zu zwischen einem entsprechenden Entwicklungsstand des Raum-Zeit-Verständnisses und der Schulleistung bei Schülern, welche Lernschwierigkeiten aufweisen. Dabei erscheinen die drei Variablen:

Verständnis räumlicher Begriffe - RABEG
Taktiler Raum - TAKRA
Raum-Zeit-Einheit - RAZEI

mit hohen Beta-Gewichten in der Gleichung und erklären fast 75% der gesamten Varianz. Dabei zeigt die multiple Regressionsanalyse klar die Bereiche auf, welche bei Kindern mit Schwierigkeiten zwecks Verbesserung der Lernvoraussetzungen indiziert sind.

Für die Praxis mit Kindern, welche Entwicklungsstörungen zeigen, läßt sich aus den erzielten Resultaten die Schlußfolgerung ziehen, daß es sinnvoll ist, in Spielsituationen das Verständnis des Raumes als dreidimensionales Koordinatensystem durch einen adäquaten, gehäuft angebotenen Gebrauch sprachlicher Begriffe zu fördern,

durch die Kombination taktiler und visueller Sinneserfahrungen auf dem Gebiet räumlicher Strukturen kognitive Lernprozesse zu initiieren oder zu festigen,

durch ein kindgemäßes Angebot von rhythmischen Spielen und Klatschübungen, kombiniert mit Temposteigerungen und -verlangsamungen bei Bewegungsabläufen das Verständnis des Kindes für die zeitliche Dauer von Ereignissen zu üben.

Hiermit erfahren die sonderpädagogischen Maßnahmen Bestätigung, bei welchen Kindern mit Lernschwierigkeiten Programme angeboten werden, die auf die allgemeine Verbesserung der Voraussetzungen zum Erlernen der Kulturtechniken zielen, anstatt auf die spezifische Behebung bestimmter Fehler.

2 Diagnostik

2.1 Frühe Diskrepanzdiagnose oder Screening der „Phonologischen Bewusstheit“

Lisa Dummer-Smoch

1 Vernachlässigung diagnostischer Maßnahmen – ein Rückblick

Nicht nur diagnostische, sondern auch frühdiagnostische Möglichkeiten wurden im Schulsystem lange Zeit vernachlässigt. Dazu haben verschiedene Auffassungen beigetragen. Am nachhaltigsten aber hat sich die wissenschaftliche Kontroverse zum Thema Legasthenie in den 70er Jahren ausgewirkt.

Bereits seit den Arbeiten von Valtin (1970) und Angermaier (1974) wurde das klassische Legasthenie-Konzept (Legasthenie als anlagebedingte, „isolierte“ Lese-Rechtschreibschwäche bei sonst guter Begabung und Lernfähigkeit) in den Erziehungswissenschaften in Frage gestellt. Die beiden Wissenschaftler waren an großen Gruppenuntersuchungen interessiert, die mit den erstmals zur Verfügung stehenden Rechtschreibtests durchgeführt werden konnten.

Der vorher an Hunderten von Fällen diskrepanter Lese-Rechtschreibschwäche inhaltlich und beschreibend definierte Begriff der „isolierten Lese-Rechtschreibschwäche“, der sich auf Kinder bezog, die allein wegen erschwerten Lesenlernens und später wegen ihrer unzureichenden Rechtschreibung in ihren Schullaufbahnen scheiterten, obwohl ihre Intelligenz sie für höhere Schulabschlüsse geeignet erscheinen ließ, wurde von einer neuen Generation von Wissenschaftlern kurzerhand ersetzt durch zwei statistische Zahlenwerte und zwar „aus wissenschaftstheoretischen und arbeitssökonomischen Gründen“ (Müller 1979, S. 81). Mit den beiden Zahlenwerten erfasste man die 5% schwächsten Rechtschreiber, sofern sie durchschnittlich intelligent waren (Müller 1966, Valtin 1970) oder unter Einbeziehung auch minderbegabter Schüler (Angermaier 1974). Diese Vorgehensweise nannte man eine ***„operationale Definition***“, weil auf diese Weise genau beschrieben werden konnte, mit welchen Tests Schüler zu untersuchen seien und nach welchen Kriterien sie als lese-rechtschreibschwach gelten sollten, um sie ggf. in der Schule zu berücksichtigen. Die Uneinheitlichkeit und Willkürlichkeit dieser quasi-diagnostischen Kriterien erwies sich später, als man das Kriterium für die Rechtschreibleistung auf Prozentrang 15 anhob und damit nicht mehr nur die 5% sondern die größere Gruppe der 15% schwächsten Rechtschreiber erfasste. Auf eine zahlenmäßige Diskrepanz zwischen den beiden Leistungen Intelligenz/Rechtschreibung (auch „gleitende Diskrepanz“ genannt) wurde hinfort nicht mehr geachtet. Da der Prozentrang 15 einem IQ von 85 entspricht, wurden zumindest in dieser größeren Gruppe eine Reihe von Kindern mit zahlenmäßig geringen Diskrepanzen als lese-rechtschreibschwach bezeichnet, obwohl sie es nach der Diskrepanz-Diagnose nicht gewesen wären.

Rudolf Müller, der die ersten Rechtschreibtests entwickelt und als erster diese operationale Definition angewandt hatte, erkannte sehr wohl, dass dadurch „der Begriff der Legasthenie erheblich erweitert (wurde), so dass die unter diese Definition subsumierten Schriftsprachestörungen äußerst heterogen in Erscheinungsform und Verursachung sind“ (Müller 1979, S.81).

Diese Erweiterung des Legasthenie-Begriffs sollte verhindern, dass in der Schule nur eine Gruppe von lese-rechtschreibschwachen Kindern gefördert würde, nämlich diejenigen

Kinder, die nach der klassischen Definition eher aus günstigeren Elternhäusern kamen und eher gut und überdurchschnittlich intelligent waren.

Dabei wurde allerdings nicht verstanden, dass Ausschlusskriterien einer Definition (als Legastheniker sollen nicht die minderbegabten, nicht die milieubenachteiligten, nicht die primär verhaltensgestörten Kinder gelten), nicht zugleich bedeuten, dass die Schule für diese, von der Legastheniediagnose ausgeschlossenen Gruppen nichts tun dürfe! Wer z.B. für sprachbehinderte Kinder schulische Hilfen fordert, spricht sich damit nicht gegen angemessene Hilfen für hör- oder sehbehinderte Kinder aus! Die Schule muss selbstverständlich für alle lese-rechtschreib-schwachen Kinder etwas tun. Aber jede dieser Gruppen benötigt unterschiedliche Hilfen!

Durch die „operationalen" Diagnose-Kriterien wurde die Legasthenie-Diagnose auf den Kopf gestellt: Die beiden Zahlenwerte bildeten das in seiner Schullaufbahn allein wegen seiner schwachen Lese- und/oder Rechtschreibleistung gefährdete und von Entmutigungen bedrohte Kind nicht mehr ab. Die operationale Definition schloss nunmehr alle Gruppen lese-rechtschreibschwacher Kinder ein, die man vorher unterschieden hatte – ein wohl einmaliger Vorgang in der Wissenschaft. Man könnte sagen, es wurden Birnen, Äpfel und Quitten in einen Topf geworfen, sofern sie nur eine bestimmte Größe nicht überschritten, um herauszufinden, was man über Äpfel wissenschaftlich aussagen könne! In der Wissenschaft geht es normalerweise um die Differenzierung von zunächst nur vorwissenschaftlich und grob gefassten Begriffen, nicht jedoch, wie es hier geschah, um die Zusammenfassung vorher bereits unterschiedener Sachverhalte. Und die operationale Definition schloss andererseits faktisch einen beträchtlichen Teil legasthener Schüler aus. Es wurde nicht erkannt, das selbst Schüler mit einem Prozentrang von 25 und mit noch besserer Rechtschreibung die Rechtschreibnote 5 erhalten können, zumal in Realschulen und Gymnasien. Nach der älteren Definition wären diese Schüler bei entsprechend höherer Intelligenz als Legastheniker zu diagnostizieren gewesen.

Die neuen Auffassungen, die schnell in die Öffentlichkeit und über entsprechende Empfehlungen der Kultusministerkonferenz schon 1978 auch in die Schulen drangen, hatten mehrere Folgen:

Die älteren, an der Diskrepanzdefinition orientierten ***Erlasse*** wurden Bundesland für Bundesland durch neue Erlasse ersetzt. Sie sprachen nur noch von „Schülern mit besonderen Schwierigkeiten beim Erlernen des Lesens und Rechtschreibens". Sie sahen die Lese-Rechtschreibschwächen der Kinder als ein Problem des Erstlese-Unterrichts an, dem durch binnendifferenzierte (nicht spezifische) Hilfen, die jeder Deutsch- oder Klassenlehrer (ohne spezifische Fortbildung) geben konnte, zu begegnen war. Mit diesen Hilfen sollte – bis auf Extremfälle, die nicht weiter definiert wurden – jede Lese-Rechtschreibschwäche bis zum Ende der Grundschulzeit zu beheben sein.

In der ***Grundschulpädagogik*** wurde die Auffassung übernommen, es handle sich beim Leselern-versagen um eine „Schwäche der Schule" und nicht um eine „Schwäche im Kind". Man ging davon aus, dass es keine behinderten Leselernprozesse gab und infolgedessen machten diagnostische oder frühdiagnostische Maßnahmen keinen Sinn. Sie führten vermeintlich nur zu einer „Etikettierung" der betroffenen Kinder. Eine solche Etikettierung sollte auch dadurch vermieden werden, dass Noten in den ersten beiden Schuljahren abgeschafft wurden. In den Berichtszeugnissen war tunlichst positiv auszudrücken, was das Kind konnte bzw. welche Fortschritte es gemacht hatte, und zwar nicht bezogen auf den Klassenmaßstab. Diesem „Notenschutz" sind in der Tat positive Aspekte abzugewinnen, zumal die

Lehrer/innen nicht mehr eine globale Fachnote zu erteilen haben und sie sich mit den individuellen Lernfortschritten des Kindes und nicht mehr mit seinen Fehlern auseinander setzen müssen. Da aber weder diagnostische Hinweise aus Beobachtungen noch einfachste lerndiagnostische Instrumente eingesetzt wurden, blieb ein Leselernversagen und die Art des Versagens unter diesen Voraussetzungen oftmals unerkannt.

Eine andere Folge war, dass die ***Lesedidaktiker*** sich den Argumenten der Grundschulpädagogen anschlossen: Behinderungen im Lernprozess des Kindes wurden nicht mehr vermutet, also auch nicht mehr erkannt, sondern im Sinne der Erklärungen „milieubedingtes Desinteresse am Lesen“ (lesefernes Elternhaus) oder „noch fehlende kognitive Reife für das Lesenlernen“ interpretiert.

In ihrem Buch „Mehr Zeit für die Schrift“ bestreitet z.B. Mechthild Dehn (1988), dass spezifische Übungen, wie sie z.B. früher in den LRS-Klassen und in Fördergruppen von erfahrenen Sonderschullehrern durchgeführt wurden, überhaupt helfen können: „Denjenigen Kindern, die solche lautliche Analyse nicht leisten können, ist kaum mit Hörübungen zu helfen; denn die so genannte akustische Differenzierungsschwäche ist meist ein kognitives Problem, keine Frage genauen Hörens: Diese Kinder wissen nicht, worauf sie ihre Aufmerksamkeit richten sollen, ***weil sie keine kognitiven Schemata ausgebildet haben“*** (1988, S. 182). Damit rückte, in wissenschaftlicher Verklausulierung, die Vermutung, wer nicht lesen lernen könne, sei dumm, wieder in den Bereich des Denkbaren. Ganz ähnliche Argumentationen finden sich bei Brügelmann (u.a. Brügelmann und Dummer 1987) und anderen Lesedidaktikern: Lesenlernen ist „Denkentwicklung“. Denken aber, das wurde offenbar übersehen, ist mit Intelligenz verbunden.

Zweitens stellte Mechthild Dehn angesichts der Tatsache, dass es in ihrer Untersuchung am Ende der 4. Klasse immer noch Kinder gab, die unter dem Niveau von Erstklässlern lasen und schrieben, die nachdenkliche Frage: „...ob wir nicht früher aufmerksam werden können auf solche grund-legenden Schwierigkeiten, die die Kinder in ihren Schreibungen unbekannter Wörter zu erkennen geben, wenn wir ihnen Gelegenheit dazu geben würden. Vielleicht bliebe ihnen dann ... mancher Misserfolg erspart“ (1988, S.53). Dem ist zuzustimmen. Logische Konsequenz dieses Gedankens aber wäre die Forderung nach Früherkennung solcher auf Dauer versagender Kinder. Dem stand jedoch die Furcht vor „Etikettierung“ im Wege.

2 Die neue Diskussion um Früherkennung und Frühförderung

Die Entwicklung ging allerdings weiter, vor allem unter dem Eindruck, dass nach wie vor, trotz der neuen Bemühungen leseschwachen Kindern zu helfen, eine nicht unbeträchtliche Zahl von Schülern im Verlauf der Schulzeit nicht lesen lernten. Im Jahr 1985 fand in der Universität Bielefeld eine Arbeitstagung von Psychologen und Lesedidaktikern statt, die den Anstoß gab zur Entwicklung eines Screening-Verfahrens, mit dessen Hilfe erschwerte Lesenlernprozesse vorausgesagt werden sollten. Grundlage dieses Screenings waren Vorstellungen über die „Phonologische Bewusstheit“ als einer wesentlichen Leselernvoraussetzung.

Die phonologische Bewusstheit wurde bereits von Bosch, dem großen Lesedidaktiker der Vor- und Nachkriegszeit, erkannt und beschrieben als Fähigkeit des Kindes im Einschulungsalter, „Sprache als Sprachgebilde zu vergegenständlichen“ (Bosch 1961 S. 69 f.). Er gab Schulanfängern das „Rätsel“ auf: „Welches Wort ist länger, klitzeklein oder groß?“ Um die richtige Antwort geben zu können, mußte das Kind sich vom Bedeutungsgehalt des Wortes lösen und lautliche Aspekte berücksichtigen. Diese Fähigkeit wird heute als „Phonologische

Bewusstheit“ bezeichnet. Ausreichende Leselernvoraussetzungen im Sinne der phonologischen Bewusstheit werden angenommen, wenn die Kinder ein Jahr vor der Einschulung in der Lage sind, sich vom Inhaltsaspekt eines gesprochenen Wortes zu lösen und sich u.a. auf die Länge/Kürze des Wortes (seine Silbenzahl) im Vergleich mit einem anderen, auf seinen Anfangslaut und ein zu diesem Wort passendes Reimwort zu konzentrieren. Eine Reihe von Untersuchungen aus dem In- und Ausland stützen inzwischen die Vermutung, dass man den Leselernweg aller Leseschwachen – unabhängig von einer Legasthenie-Diagnose – durch Früherfassung und eine entsprechendes Training der Leselernvoraussetzungen im Sinne der Phonologischen Bewusstheit deutlich erleichtern kann.

2.1 Die Untersuchungen von Borstrøm und Elbro

Borstrøm und Elbro (1997) trainierten in Dänemark Kinder legasthenischer Eltern (experimentelle Risikogruppe) im Vergleich mit einer Kontrollgruppe nicht trainierter Kinder legasthenischer Eltern (Risiko-Kontrollgruppe) und mit einer Kontrollgruppe von Kindern nicht-legasthener Eltern (Kontrollgruppe 2). Das Trainingsprogramm schloss zusätzlich zu den Aufgaben der phonologischen Bewusstheit Informationen über die Artikulationsstellung beim Sprechen der Laute ein. Am Ende des Trainings hatten die Risikokinder Fortschritte in der Phonologischen Bewusstheit gemacht, die zwar unter der Leistung der Kontrollgruppe 2 lagen, der Zuwachs im Vergleich mit der Ausgangsleistung war jedoch in beiden Gruppen etwa gleich hoch. Die Risiko-Kontrollgruppe, die anfangs etwa gleiche Leistungen zeigte wie die Risiko-Experimentalgruppe, verbesserte sich ohne Training auch, jedoch weniger stark als die trainierte Risikogruppe. Am Anfang der Klasse 2 zeigten sich vergleichbare Unterschiede zwischen den Gruppen im Lesetest (s. Tabellen 2.1.1 und 2.1.2).

	R-TG	R-KG	KG 2
Anzahl der Kinder	36	52	48
korrekt gelesene Wörter	64,2	51,3	84,6
Standard-Abweichungen	36,9	35,3	60,7

Tabelle 2.1.1 Mittelwerte richtig erlesener Wörter, Anfang Klasse 2, der Risiko-Trainingsgruppe (R-TG), der nicht trainierten Risiko-Kontrollgruppe (R-KG) und der nicht trainierten Kontrollgruppe von Kindern nicht-legasthener Eltern (KG 2)

Die Leistungen der Experimentalgruppe lagen mit durchschnittlich 64,2 richtig gelesenen Wörtern zwischen den besseren Leistungen der Kontrollgruppe 2 (84,6) und den schwächeren Leistungen der nicht trainierten Risiko-Gruppe (51,3). Von den 52 nicht trainierten Risiko-Kindern wurden 21 (40%) als „leseschwach“ klassifiziert (= Prozentrang ≤10). Von den trainierten Risiko-Kindern erwiesen sich nur 6 von 36 (17%), in der Kontrollgruppe allerdings nur 4 von 44 Kindern (8%) als lese-schwach.

	R-TG	R-KG	KG 2
N	36	52	48
Leseschwache (PR < 10)	6	21	4
Leseschwache in%	17%	40%	8%

Tabelle 2.1.2 Anzahl der als „leseschwach“ klassifizierten Kinder auf dem Niveau der 10% schwächsten Leseleistungen Anfang Klasse 2

Neben dem beeindruckenden Erfolg des Trainings bleibt aber festzuhalten, dass 6 Kinder der trainierten Gruppe (17%) keine ausreichenden Leseleistungen erreichten. Die Annahme liegt nahe, dass in diesen Fällen der Schweregrad der biologischen Handikaps therapieresistent ist und/oder ein anderes Training als das phonologische erfordert hätte.

2.2 Die Bielefelder Längsschnittstudie

In einer Bielefelder Längsschnittstudie (Jansen und Skowronek, 1997) hat man festgestellt, dass Kinder, die Anzeichen für unzureichende phonologische Bewusstheit ein Jahr vor der Einschulung erkennen ließen, bis zum Ende ihrer Schulzeit überwiegend zu den schwächeren Lesern und Rechtschreibern gehörten. Im neunten Schulbesuchsjahr (s. Tabelle 2.1.3 a + b) befanden sie sich mehrheitlich auf Hauptschulen, in Gesamtschulen oder Lernbehindertenschulen (2 von 28). Nur drei von 28 Risikokindern besuchten das Gymnasium, davon zwei mit einem Jahr Überalterung.

Das bedeutet, dass zwar der Stand der Phonologischen Bewusstheit starken Einfluss auf den Lernerfolg bei der Aneignung der Schriftsprache hat, dass aber von noch größerer Bedeutung ist, wie das Schulsystem mit schwächeren Rechtschreibleistungen umgeht: Die Rechtschreibleistung am Anfang der zweiten Klasse kann geradezu als Voraussage für den Schulerfolg gelten! Leider wurden Intelligenzdaten zu den Ergebnissen nicht mitgeteilt.

Zählt man die um zwei Jahre überalterten Schüler (ausgenommen Realschüler und Gymnasiasten) und die Sonderschüler zusammen, so ergibt sich in der Gesamtgruppe der mit einem Risiko für den Schriftspracherwerb behaftete Schüler ein Prozentsatz von 21,4% (4 von 28) Schulversagern, für die Tabelle 2.1.3 a + b: Die Stichprobe der Bielefelder Studie im 9. Schulbesuchsjahr.

Offen bleiben muss, wie viele von ihnen tatsächlich minderbegabt sind oder aber über schwache Rechtschreibleistungen nur entmutigt wurden. In der Gruppe mit guten Leselernvoraussetzungen beträgt dieser Anteil nur 2,4% (2 von 83) und keiner dieser Schüler besuchte eine Sonderschule.

Schulart	Kl. 7	KL. 8	Kl. 9	?	in%
Gym	-	2	1	3	**10,7**
Real	1	2	1	4	28,6
Ges	1	2	7	10	35,7
H	3	5	1	9	32,1
So	–	1	1	2	**7,1**
?	5	12	11	28	100
in%	19,9	42,9	39,3	100	//////////

Tabelle 2.1.3 a) Die Risikogruppe

Schulart	Kl. 7	KL. 8	Kl. 9	?	in%
Gym	-	3	37	40	**48,2**
Real	1	6	15	22	26,5
Ges	–	2	10	12	14,5
H	2	3	4	9	10,8
So	–	–	–	–	**0,0**
?	3	14	66	83	100
in%	3,6	16,9	79,5	100	//////////

Tabelle 2.1.3 b) Die Gesamtgruppe ohne Risikogruppe

2.3 Die Würzburger Untersuchungen

Eine Würzburger Studiengruppe (Schneider et al.1998) hat unausgelesene Kindergartenkinder im letzten Vorschuljahr mit Aufgaben der phonologischen Bewusstheit trainiert, so dass sie bei Schul-eintritt bessere Leselernvoraussetzungen hatten als Kinder ohne dieses Training. Am Ende der zweiten Klasse wurden der DRT 2 und ein Lesetest, die Würzburger Leise Leseprobe durchgeführt.

Die Ergebnisse sind eindrucksvoll: In einer der Studien zeichneten sich bis zum Ende der zweiten Klasse die Effekte des vorschulischen Trainings deutlich ab. Insbesondere der Vergleich der Kinder, die in den anfangs durchgeführten phonologischen Tests als

„Risikokinder" (die 25% schwächsten) eingestuft wordenwaren, läßt das Training als überaus erfolgreich erkennen.

Bezieht man die Zahlen auf die jeweiligen Gesamtgruppen, so sind noch 6,8% der trainierten Kinder (13 von 190) am Ende der 2. Klasse nach dem DRT 2 dem Niveau der 15% schwächsten Rechtschreiber zuzuordnen. In der nicht trainierten Kontrollgruppe allerdings sind es mehr als doppelt so viele, nämlich 16, 8% (26 von 154 Kindern).

	Trainierte Gruppe	Nicht trainierte Kontrollgruppe
Anzahl der „Risikokinder" mit PR = 25 im Vortest zur Phonologischen Bewusstheit	57 (von N = 190) (30% von 190)	33 (von N = 154) (21% von 154)
richtig geschriebene Wörter	Ø 18,26 (PR 60)	Ø 13,39 (PR 39)
Anzahl der Kinder mit PR = 15 im DRT 2	13 von 57 Kindern (3% von 57 Kindern)	26 von 33 Kindern (79% von 33 Kindern)
Anteil an der Gesamtgruppe	6,8% von 190 Kindern	16,9% von 154 Kindern

Tabelle 2.1.4 Die Leistungen der Risikokinder aus Trainings- und Kontrollgruppe im DRT 2 (nach Schneider et. al 1998, Tab.2 a , 4 b und 7 b).

Die Differenz zwischen trainierter Gruppe und nicht trainierter Kontrollgruppe auf dem Niveau der „Risikokinder" gibt zu Fragen Anlass: Könnte der relativ hohe Anteil der heute in den Schulen als rechtschreibschwach auffallenden Kinder nicht allein auf legasthene Schwächen sondern zu einem bedeutenden Teil darauf zurückzuführen sein, dass heute aufwachsende Kinder bis zum Einschulungsalter eher auf Bilder eingestellt sind als auf Sprache? Dann bedeutet ein phonologisches Training eine notwendige Kompensation für eher generell unterentwickelte Leselernvoraussetzungen. Der Unterschied zwischen nur knapp 7% schwächster Leistungen (im DRT 2) in der trainierten Gruppe und knapp 17% in der nicht trainierten Kontrollgruppe spricht für diese Annahme.

Wie weit dieses Training auch Teilleistungsschwächen genetischer oder schädigungsbedingter Art hat ausgleichen können, ist noch ungewiss. Man müsste die fast 7% der weniger erfolgreichen, wenngleich trainierten, Risikokinder genauer anschauen, um zu erfahren, welche Ursachen bei ihnen zu einem verminderten Erfolg im Schriftspracherwerb geführt haben – trotz des Trainings.

Eine weitere Frage stellt sich zur Diskrepanzgruppe: Sind in der Gruppe der besseren Rechtschreiber (Prozentrang ≤ 15) trotz des Trainings Diskrepanz-Legastheniker auszumachen oder konnte das Training die ursprünglichen Schwächen so ausgleichen, dass keine Probleme mehr entstanden sind? Wie bereits gesagt, können Legastheniker trotz besserer Rechtschreibleistungen zumal in Realschulen und Gymnasien versagen. Dieser Frage müßte bis in die 5. und 6. Klasse hinein nachgegangen werden, weil sich eine Diskrepanzlegasthenie bei höherer Intelligenz oder besserer Förderung erst in weiterführenden Schulen zeigt.

3 Früherkennung und Frühförderung – eine alte Forderung neu gesehen

Mit den Würzburger Untersuchungen zur „Phonologischen Bewusstheit“ stellt sich die Frage der Frühdiagnose neu: Wenn die „Phonologische Bewusstheit“ eine der wesentlichen Leselernvoraussetzungen darstellt, müssten entsprechende Aufgaben in Form eines Trainings auch zum Schulbeginn noch diagnostische Funktion haben. Man würde durch die gezielte Beobachtung während der Aufgabenlösung erkennen, welche Kinder mit dem Leselernprozess beginnen können, und welche vorab ein längeres Training der „Phonologischen Bewusstheit“ brauchen.

In dieser Gruppe könnte man durch längere Beobachtung frühe Hinweise etwa auf zentrale Fehlhörigkeit, visuomotorische oder visuelle Teilleistungsschwächen erkennen, den Eltern fachärztliche Untersuchungen empfehlen, daraufhin den Leselernprozess in kleineren Schritten organisieren und ihn mit spezifischen Hilfen begleiten.

Es wäre schön, wenn sogleich in allen Bundesländern und in allen Kindergärten ein Training der phonologischen Bewusstheit durchgeführt werden könnte, um die Gruppe der Leselernversager zu minimieren. Es gibt Kultusministerium, die sich für diesen Förderansatz interessieren.

Gleichwohl bleibt es an vielen Orten und in den meisten Schulen dabei, dass ein solches Training dem Schuleinritt noch nicht vorausgegangen ist. Als pragmatische Lösung , den Leselernprozess effektiver zu gestalten, schlage ich daher ein Minimum an Förderdiagnostik vor, das vor allem verhindern soll, dass Schulanfänger, die den Zugang zum Lesenlernen nicht finden, über das erste Schulhalbjahr hinaus unerkannt bleiben. Allzu häufig werden sie, wenn sie Fibeltexte auswendig vortragen, als gute Leser eingestuft. Und in der Tat unterscheidet sich ihr „Lesen“ für den unbefangenen Beobachter nicht von dem Lesen derjenigen Kinder, die bis Weihnachten lesen gelernt haben.

Über die Beobachtungen und ein entsprechendes Training in der Anfangsphase des Lesenlernens hinaus sollte jedoch eine förderdiagnostische Begleitung des Leselernprozesses selbst erfolgen, um ein beginnendes Versagen frühzeitig zu erkennen und rechtzeitig mit Hilfen eingreifen zu können. Die Frage der Diskrepanzdiagnose stellt sich unter diesen Voraussetzungen erst später, vor allem im Hinblick auf Schullaufbahnentscheidungen.

3.1 Beobachtungsspiele zur phonologischen Bewusstheit

Diese Beobachtungsspiele wurden in Anlehnung an das in Würzburg (Schneider und Mitarbeiter) entwickelte vorschulische Training der phonologischen Bewusstheit zusammengestellt. Mit diesen Spielen – durchgehend Memories – kann in den ersten Wochen nach der Einschulung beobachtet werden, welche Kinder mit dem Erkennen von Reimen, mit der Silbenzahl eines gesprochenen Wortes und mit dem Heraushören von Anfangslauten noch Schwierigkeiten haben. In diesen Fällen empfiehlt es sich, die Spiele gezielt zum Training der noch nicht entwickelten oder behinderten Fähigkeiten einzusetzen.

Um Schülern zu helfen, die die Leselernvoraussetzungen im Sinne der phonologischen Bewusstheit im Einschulungsalter noch nicht erlangt haben, sollten sich die Lehrkräfte zusätzlich mit Aufgaben-stellungen vertraut machen, die Schneider und Mitarbeiter für ein vorschulisches Training erarbeitet und eingesetzt haben (Küspert und Schneider 2000). Durch teilnehmende Beobachtung kann die Lehrerin feststellen, welche Kinder ihrer Anfangsklasse dann die phonologische Bewusstheit erreicht haben.

Führt jedoch dieses Training nicht zu den erwünschten Fortschritten, sollten – in einem zweiten Schritt – mit der Differenzierungsprobe von Breuer und Weuffen (1993) die Sprachwahrnehmungsleistungen überprüft werden. Gegebenenfalls ist dann zunächst mit Aufgaben zu üben, die Breuer und Weuffen in ihrem Buch empfehlen, bevor man sich der phonologischen Bewusstheit wieder zuwendet. Weiter ist zu empfehlen, dass alle hinsichtlich der phonologischen Bewusstheit auffälligen Kinder psychomotorisch und sprachheilpädagogisch überprüft und auch einem Augen- und einem Hals-Nasen-Ohrenarzt vorgestellt werden.

Kinder, die Aufgaben zur phonologischen Bewusstheit zu lösen vermögen, können mit dem eigentlichen Leselehrgang, d.h. mit der alphabetischen Strategie beginnen.

Das hier empfohlene Spielmaterial hat diagnostische und therapeutische Funktion: Es dient sowohl zur Erfassung des Anfangsstandes durch die am Spiel teilnehmende und beobachtende Lehrkraft, als auch zum Trainieren der noch unausgebildeten Leistung. Es beschränkt sich auf Reimpaare, Wortpaare mit gleichem Anlaut und Wortpaare mit gleicher Silbenlänge.

Alle Spiele (bisher im unveröffentlichten Manuskript vorliegend) sind als Memories gestaltet. Sie werden als „Aufdeck-Memories“ gespielt. Das heißt, eine Karte, die einmal aufgedeckt wurde, bleibt offen liegen. Der erste Spieler deckt zwei Karten auf. Wenn er sie nicht gemeinsam ablegen kann, deckt der zweite Spieler zwei weitere Karten auf und hat nun die Auswahl aus vier Karten. Wenn auch diesmal keine zusammenpassenden Karten dabei sind, deckt der dritte Spieler wiederum zwei Karten auf. So erweitern sich die Vergleichsmöglichkeiten Schritt für Schritt. Alle Mitspieler müssen alle offen liegenden Bildwörter immer wieder artikulieren, um z.B. auf gleiche Anfangslaute oder gleiche Silbenzahl zu achten.

Die Eltern derjenigen Kinder, die in diesen Spielen Schwierigkeiten erkennen lassen, sollten von der Lehrkraft informiert werden. Man führt sie in die Memory-Spiele ein und bittet sie, diese zu Hause mit den Kindern regelmäßig zu spielen. Dazu gehört auch die Anweisung, bei den Silbenkarten das jeweils aufgedeckte Bild-Wort vom Kind silbenweise sprechen zu lassen und für jede Sprechsilbe einen Setzstein oder Knopf auf den Tisch zu legen. Auf diese Weise ist die Silbenzahl auch visuell zu erfassen.

Da die Spiele sich auf Anlaute mit dehnbaren Konsonanten beschränken, ist die Anforderung an das Heraushören der Laute relativ leicht. Sie kann weiter erleichtert werden, wenn man Lautgebärden dazu einsetzt und ggf. einen Spiegel zur Kontrolle der eigenen Mundstellung beim Sprechen der kritischen Laute.

3.2 Frühe Überprüfungen der Lernfortschritte

Viele der heute in der deutschen Lesedidaktik vertretenen Modelle gehen auf Frith/Günther (Günther 1989) zurück. Danach gehen dem eigentlichen Leselernprozess zwei aufeinander folgende Vorleistungen voraus: Das Kritzeln von „Briefen“, mit dem das Kind die Erwachsenen nachahmt, ohne Laute und Buchstaben zu kennen. Auf der nächsten Stufe versucht es Firmenlogos und den eigenen Namen sowie Wörter wie „Mama“ und „Papa“ aus dem Gedächtnis niederzuschreiben. Es ist dies eine rein visuelle Leistung. Das Kind kennt zwar Buchstaben, kann sie aber noch nicht mit Lauten in Verbindung bringen. So entstehen charakteristische Fehler wie „OCOA OCLA“ für „COCA COLA“.

Der eigentliche Beginn des Leselernprozesses zeichnet sich ab, wenn das Kind anfängt, die alphabetische Strategie anzuwenden, d.h. Laut für Laut zu schreiben. Nun weiß es, dass Buchstaben für Laute stehen und dass man aus dem gesprochenen Wort eine Lautreihe

„heraushören“ und die entsprechende Buchstabenreihe aufschreiben muss. Auf diesem Lernniveau interessieren noch nicht die Unregelmäßigkeiten der deutschen Schriftsprache. Daher sollte der Lernstand mittels so genannter lautgetreuer Wörter überprüft werden, indem man den Kindern entsprechende Bilder vorlegt. Auch auf dieser Stufe kommt es zu charakteristischen Fehlern: Zunächst schreiben die Kinder das Wort unvollständig, aber mit Buchstaben, deren Laute im Wort vorkommen (PP für Papa). Später, bei vollständiger geschriebenen Wörtern, können orthografische Regeln noch nicht eingehalten werden (Bine, Hunt). Solche lautgetreuen Falschlösungen sollten auf dieser Stufe jedoch im Sinne der alphabetischen Strategie als positiv bewertet werden.

Der nächste Schritt der Erfolgskontrollen im Leselernprozess besteht aus diesen Gründen in der mehrfachen Kontrolle des Leselernstandes der Erstklässler bis etwa zu den Weihnachtsferien mit der Fragestellung: „Haben sie den Zugang zur alphabetischen Strategie gefunden?“ Es kommt darauf an, festzustellen, ob sie lautgetreu schreiben – unvollständig oder schon vollständig – bzw. ob ihre Schreibungen noch Buchstaben enthalten, deren Laute im gesprochenen Wort nicht vorkommen. In diesem Fall sind sie in einer Sackgasse logographemischer Schreibungen gelandet. Man muss bei ihnen die Laut-Buchstabenverbindungen noch einmal erarbeiten und sichern – am besten mit Hilfe der Lautgebärden (Dummer-Smoch 1989a, 1989 b).

Für diese frühen Erfolgskontrollen handelt es sich um Bilderlisten und Unsinnsätze, die von der Lehrkraft zu dem von ihr benutzten Fibellehrgang oder zur Eigenfibel selbst erstellt werden müssen. Die Lehrgänge sind zu unterschiedlich, als dass man ein allgemein geeignetes Material veröffentlichen könnte. Daher stellen die folgenden Ausführungen lediglich Anregungen dar für Möglichkeiten der Überprüfung.

Schon nach den ersten sechs bis acht Wochen im Leselernprozess kann man aus den Wörtern, die in der Fibel verwendet werden, zweisilbige Wörter auswählen, die als Bild darstellbar sind und deren Silben aus Konsonant-Vokal in der ersten und aus Konsonant-Vokal oder Konsonant-Vokal-Konsonant in der zweiten Silbe bestehen (Na-se, Fe-der). Wörter wie „ruft“ oder „filmt“ eignen sich nicht!

Mit solchen Bildern erstellt man kurze Listen, in denen am Zeilenanfang die Bilder stehen, damit in derselben Zeile das Wort dazu geschrieben werden kann. Die Auswertung der Schreibungen erfolgt nach vier Fehlerkategorien, wie sie auch in den Diagnostischen Bilderlisten (Dummer-Smoch 1993) benutzt werden. Auf diese Fehlerkategorien wird (L, WD, WT, WR), auf die unter 4.3 näher eingegangen.

Als Trainingsmaterial kann man Memories herstellen: Jeweils auf zwei Kärtchen schreibt man die beiden Silben eines Wortes. Auf die Rückseite der beiden Silbenkärtchen malt man das entsprechende Bild. Gespielt wird, indem alle Silben sichtbar und die Bilder verdeckt auf dem Tisch liegen. Wer im Spiel an der Reihe ist, nimmt eine Silbe auf, liest sie und dreht die Karte um. Anhand des Bildes kann das Kind nun feststellen, welche Silbe noch fehlt und diese suchen. Das Bild auf der Rückseite der zweiten Silbenkarte bestätigt den Erfolg! Danach ist das nächste Kind an der Reihe.

Auch „Unsinn-Fragen“ oder „Unsinn-Sätze“ können zu diesem frühen Zeitpunkt schon zur Überprüfung wie zum Training eingesetzt werden, wenn man die einfach strukturierten Wörter aus der Fibel benutzt, zum Beispiel:

Rufen Ameisen ? (+) (-)
Laufen Nasen ? (+) (-)
Malen Rosen ? (+) (-)

Als Antwort kann ein „(+)“ für „ja“ und ein „(-)“ für „nein“angekreuzt werden. So ist leicht festzustellen, ob das Kind richtig gelesen hat.

Beispiele für einen konsequenten Leseanfang mit dehnbaren Konsonanten und einfacher Wortstruktur finden sich im Übungsheft „Laute, Silben, Wörter“ von Dummer-Smoch (1996).

3.3 Die Diagnostischen Bilderlisten zur Beobachtung des Leselernprozesses

Für Lernerfolgskontrollen im Leselernprozess wurden drei Diagnostische Bilderlisten entwickelt: Für die Mitte der ersten Klasse (DBL-F), für das Ende der 1. Klasse (DBL 1) und für die Mitte der zweiten Klasse (DBL-2).

Die DBL-1 wurde als erste konstruiert und ursprünglich im „Kieler Leseaufbau“ veröffentlicht. Sie sollte zum einen der Diagnose von Leselernversagen am Ende der ersten Klasse dienen, aber danach auch der Erfolgskontrolle bei der Förderung der als schwer leseschwach erkannten Kinder nach dem „Kieler Leseaufbau“. Die Diagnostischen Bilderlisten DBL-F und DBL 2 entstanden später. Sie wurden jeweils im Zusammenhang mit bestimmten Untersuchungsvorhaben entwickelt.

Wie bereits angedeutet, unterscheiden sich die Diagnostischen Bilderlisten von Erfolgskontrollen, die manchen Fibellehrgängen beigegeben sind und von Rechtschreibtests in drei Punkten:

a) Die Verfahren prüfen fibelunabhängig die alphabetische Strategie und bieten klassenübergreifende Orientierungsnormen an. Damit geben sie der einzelnen Lehrkraft auch eine Rückmeldung zur Qualitätssicherung ihres Unterrichts.
b) Die Verfahren arbeiten stressfrei: Das Kind kann im eigenen Tempo, unabhängig von einem Diktierenden schreiben. Es kann daher nicht in Zeitdruck geraten.
c) Lese-Rechtschreibschwächen sind oft mit einer zentralen Fehlhörigkeit verbunden Esser 1994 und Wurm-Binse), die u.a. dazu führt, dass ähnliche Konsonanten und Kurzvokale nicht unterschieden werden können. Ebenso erschwert die Fehlhörigkeit auch das Sprachverstehen in halligen oder mit anderen Sprachgeräuschen erfüllten Räumen erheblich. Daher ist es wichtig, dass das Kind sich allein an der Bildvorgabe und seiner eigenen Artikulation orientieren kann. Das Verfahren schließt Hörfehler aus.

3.3.1. Die DBL-F (Mitte Klasse 1, Februar/März)

Die DBL-F (Frühform der DBL) entstand auf Anregung eines Schulrats, der nach positiven Erfahrungen mit der Frühförderung von Kindern mit Leselernschwächen schon in der zweiten Hälfte der ersten Klasse nunmehr nach einer Möglichkeit der Früherfassung um die Mitte der ersten Klasse suchte.

In einer Untersuchung, die mehr als 40 Klassen einschloss, wurden Prozentrangnormen für die 28. bis 29. Schulwoche nach Schuljahrsbeginn (März) erstellt. Die Stichprobe setzte sich aus 567 Jungen und 612 Mädchen zusammen, die alle altersgerecht die erste Klasse besuchten. Kinder, die bereits überaltert waren, z. B. nach einer Zurückstellung oder durch Wiederholung der ersten Klasse, und Kinder mit nicht-deutscher Muttersprache wurden in die Normierungsstichprobe nicht aufgenommen.

Als Faustregel (Orientierungswert) gilt, dass Kinder der spezifischen Förderung bedürfen, deren Fehlerschwerpunkt im Bereich der WD-Fehler liegt und die mehr als 7 der 14 Wörter falsch schreiben.

3.3.2 DBL-1 (Ende Klasse 1/Anfang Klasse 2)

Die DBL 1 und mehrere ihrer Vorformen sollten ursprünglich der Überprüfung des Lernstandes im Lesen/Schreiben am Ende der ersten Klasse dienen. Es erschien notwendig, zu diesem Zeitpunkt mit einem Siebungsverfahren alle Kinder zu erfassen, damit kein vermeintlich guter Leser, der nur die Fibel auswendig gelernt hatte, unerkannt bliebe.

Zum andern aber sollte die DBL 1 den Vergleich zwischen Klassen ermöglichen, die mit Lautgebärden lesen gelernt hatten, gegenüber Kontrollklassen mit herkömmlichem Fibelunterricht. Da der Unterschied zwischen beiden Gruppen eher im Bereich der 25% schwächsten Leser und/oder Schreiber vermutet wurde, nicht jedoch bei den 25 bzw. 5% besten Lesern/Schreibern, mußte ein Messinstrument gefunden werden, das durch relativ leichte Aufgabenstellung die Unterschiede zwischen leistungsschwächeren Schülern deutlicher hervortreten läßt.

Für die DBL 1 liegen aus einer Untersuchung mit mehr als 2.000 Schülern der 1. Klasse und mehr als 1300 Schülern der 2. Klasse Indizes für Trennschärfe und Schwierigkeit der Aufgaben vor. Prozentrangnormen wurden für 2167 altersgerecht eingeschulte Erstklässler für das Ende des Schuljahrs (Juni/Juli) errechnet. Überalterte Kinder, d. h. Zurückgestellte und daher verspätet Eingeschulte sowie Wiederholer der ersten Klasse und Kinder mit nicht-deutscher Muttersprache wurden in die Normierungsstichprobe nicht aufgenommen.

Eine zweite Normtabelle enthält die Prozentrangnormen für die 5. bis 8. Woche nach Schuljahrsbeginn in der zweiten Klasse (September/Oktober) aus 1252 Schüler-Protokollen dieser DBL.

3.3.3 Die DBL 2 (Mitte Klasse 2, Februar/März)

Die DBL 2 schließlich diente zunächst nur in der Einzelförderung der Feststellung qualitativer Fehler-schwerpunkte. Sie wurde vorerst ohne Normen benutzt. Die individuellen Fehlerschwerpunkte – Auslassungen bei Konsonantverbindungen, Umstellungen der Reihenfolge oder Fehler bei der Differenzierung ähnlicher Laute – erlauben, bei Schülern aus zweiten und dritten Klassen individuelle Förderansätze zu bestimmen. Aus einer Untersuchung mit 262 Schülern aus zweiten Klassen wurden zusätzlich Orientierungsnormen (Prozentrangnormen für die Mitte des zweiten Schuljahrs) gewonnen.

3.4 Die Fehlerkategorien

In allen drei Bilderlisten kommt es nur darauf an, ob die Kinder alle Laute im gesprochenen Wort wiedergegeben haben, und zwar entsprechend den rechtschriftlichen Möglichkeiten, die in der deutschen Schriftsprache für den jeweiligen Laut zur Verfügung stehen. Es geht um die erfolgreiche Anwendung der alphabetischen Strategie, noch nicht um orthografisch korrekte Schreibungen. So gelten z.B. die Schreibungen Hose – Hohse – Hoose als gleichwertig im Sinne der Anforderung, obwohl nur die erste Schreibung korrekt ist. Ebenso dulden wir die Schreibungen Hunt, Elefand, Lokomotiewe u.ä.

3.4.1 Die quantitative Auswertung: Wortfehler

Für jedes Wort wird bestimmt, ob es lautverändernde Fehler enthält oder nicht. Als Wortfehler zählen wir dann die in diesem Sinne falsch geschriebenen Wörter, nicht jedoch Schreibungen wie Hohse, Hunt oder Wige. Auch die Groß- und Kleinschreibung wird nicht berücksichtigt. Der Gesamtzahl der Wortfehler ordnet man anhand der Tabellen den entsprechenden Prozentrang zu.

Als kritisch gelten Fehlerzahlen von 10 und mehr in der DBL-F und von 20 und mehr in der DBL 1. Eine solche Fehlerzahl deutet nach unserer Erfahrung auf Stagnation der Lernprozesse. Betroffene Kinder sollten ggf. schon um die Mitte der ersten Klasse bzw. zu Beginn der zweiten in irgendeiner Form einen „Intensivkurs Lesen“ absolvieren. Ohne gezielte und kompakte Hilfe stehen diese Kinder in der Gefahr, analphabetisch zu bleiben, mit den bekannten gravierenden psychischen Folgen.

3.4.2 Die qualitative Auswertung: vier Fehlerkategorien

Da wir uns in den Diagnostischen Bilderlisten auf ein relativ einfach strukturiertes Wortmaterial stützen, das bis auf wenige Ausnahmen der Lautanalyse leicht zugänglich ist, da wir ferner die Probleme der Dehnung und Dopplung vermeiden, kommen wir mit vier Fehlerkategorien aus. Diese vier Kategorien besitzen nach unserer Erfahrung diagnostische Relevanz: sie verhelfen uns zum Förderansatz beim einzelnen Kind.

3.4.2.1 L = lautgetreue Lösungen

Wörter, in denen nur lautgetreue, aber orthographisch nicht korrekte Schreibungen vorkommen, (Schine, Hohse) werden nicht als Fehlerwörter gezählt. Die lautgetreuen Verstöße spielen aber für die qualitative Auswertung eine wichtige Rolle. Sie signalisieren die Güte der Schreibungen: Wer einen hohen individuellen Prozentsatz an lautgetreuen Lösungen aufweist, hat eine gute Basis im Lesen erworben und wird auch mit den später zu bearbeitenden Rechtschreibproblemen weniger Schwierigkeiten haben.

3.4.2.2 WD = Fehler der Wahrnehmungsdurchgliederung

Immer dann, wenn dem Lautbestand eines Wortes etwas hinzugefügt wurde oder wenn Laute fehlen, signieren wir „WD“. Für unleserliche Schreibungen, die keine Beziehung zum Lautbestand des gemeinten Wortes erkennen lassen (Nirel für Hose z.B.) geben wir 4 WD-Verstöße, um eine Gewichtung für den Schweregrad des Versagens zu erhalten.

Bei dieser Fehlerkategorie achten wir allerdings auf unterschiedliche Schweregrade:

a) Keine Beziehung zum Lautbestand des Wortes, Aneinanderreihungen von Buchstabenformen: Moleir – Hund, Ts – Wiege, ateirimene – Haus
   In diesen Schreibungen drückt sich aus, dass das Kind noch nicht den Zugang zur alphabetischen Strategie gefunden hat. Es ist nicht „auf dem Weg zur Schrift“ (Brügelmann). Es stagniert auf der Stufe logographischer Schreibungen, da es noch keine Laut-Buchstabenverbindungen erworben hat.
b) Rudimentäre (unvollständige) Schreibungen, bei denen aber Anfangslaute schon überwiegend und Endlaute gelegentlich getroffen werden: Drine für Daumen, Schal für Schaukel, Ulu für Nadel. In diesen Schreibungen zeigen sich erste Ansätze sicherer Laut-Buchstabenverbindungen. Es droht dennoch Stagnation im Leselernprozess, wenn nicht alsbald individuell gezielte Hilfe einsetzt.
c) Skelettschreibungen: Unvollständige Schreibungen, in denen aber das „Skelett“ des Wortes schon erkennbar ist. Es kommen fast ausschließlich Laute vor, die das gesprochene Wort enthält: Bsn für Besen, Kaml für Kamel, Rakt für Rakete.

Dieses Kind steht am Anfang der alphabetischen Strategie. Es ist schon „auf dem Weg zur Schrift". Steht es aber bereits am Ende der ersten oder in der Mitte der zweiten Klasse und ist es gar überaltert, so braucht es gleichfalls dringend Hilfe. Die Klasse arbeitet ja schon auf einem viel höheren Niveau!

3.4.2.3 WT-Fehler der Wahrnehmungstrennschärfe

Dies sind Verstöße, die auch bei vollständiger Wiedergabe des Lautbestandes im Wort vorkommen. Sie treten häufiger auf, sobald einem lese-rechtschreibschwachen Kind weniger Auslassungen unterlaufen. Die häufigsten Fehler dieser Art, die im 2. bis 4. Schuljahr die Schreibungen lese-recht-schreibschwacher Kinder geradezu charakterisieren können, bestehen in Vertauschungen von
a-o, m-n, n-r, t-f, H-k, h-k (visuelle Fehler), z.B. Kanel statt Kamel;
o-u, e-i, ü-ie, ö-e, b-p, d-t, g-k , w-f (auditive Fehler), z. B. Huse statt Hose, Babakei statt Papagei, Lewe statt Löwe.

Wir kennzeichnen aber auch andere Ersetzungen, die diesen beiden Gruppen nicht zuzuordnen sind, mit „WT", weil wir uns aus pragmatischen Gründen auf vier Kategorien beschränken wollen.

3.4.2.4 WR-Fehler der Wahrnehmungsrichtung

Es sind dies die Fehler, die früher als „legastheniespezifisch" bezeichnet wurden. Sie kommen aber, wie schon Schenk-Danzinger betonte, seltener beim Schreiben, am ehesten beim Lesen im indivi-duellen Fehlerprotokoll lese-recht-schreibschwacher Kinder vor, zwar unter folgenden Bedingungen:
in der 2. und 3. Klassenstufe,
wenn man Wörterlisten zu lesen gibt (keine Texte! Kontext hilft Fehler vermeiden!),
die solche Vertauschungen provozieren (Biene-Beine z.B.).

In den Fehlerprotokollen der Diagnostischen Bilderlisten finden wir allerdings bei einzelnen Kindern auch solche Schreibfehler. Wir unterscheiden Spiegelbildfehler (b-d, ie-ei, p-q: Zeige statt Ziege, danane statt banane); Drehfehler oder Rotationen (d-g, b-g, a-e: Reden statt Regen, Waben statt Wagen); Reihenfolge- oder Sequenzfehler (Kamle statt Kamel, Segimo statt Eskimo).

Da sehr häufig alle diese Fehler bei ein- und demselben Kind auftreten, halten wir eine getrennte Signierung nicht für notwendig.

4 Die Diskrepanz-Diagnose

Die sogenannte „Diskrepanzdiagnose", die erst bei Schülern der zweiten, dritten oder (in Schleswig-Holstein) der vierten Klasse mit zwei Testverfahren durchgeführt wird, kann sich bereits auf informell beobachtete Diskrepanzen stützen, wenn von Anfang an Beobachtungen festgehalten wurden, z.B. auch auf gute Rechenleistungen bei erschwertem Zugang zum Lesenlernen. Eine spätere testdiagnostische Überprüfung bestätigt in diesen Fällen dann lediglich den frühen Verdacht einer Diskrepanzlegasthenie. Bei der Anwendung entsprechend differenzierter Intelligenztests (Kaufmann-ABC-Test, PSB, HAWIK-R z.B.) können Schulpsychologen darüber hinaus Informationen über die individuellen Teilleistungsschwächen gewinnen, so dass ein angemessener Förderansatz für den Aufbau der Rechtschreibung und später für das Erlernen der Fremdsprachen gefunden werden kann. Insofern sollten sich ein frühes Screening der „Phonologischen Bewusstheit“, Lernerfolgskontrollen im Leselernprozess (gleichfalls als Screenings durchzuführen) und anschließende testdiagnostische Untersuchungen ergänzen.

Die Diskrepanzdiagnose ist wichtig für Kinder, die begonnen haben, sich wegen ihrer Schwierigkeiten beim Lesen- und Schreibenlernen für dumm zu halten. In diesen Fällen sollte die Diskrepanz-Diagnose frühzeitig, möglichst bis zum Ende der zweiten Klasse erfolgen. Wenn das betroffene Kind aber keine Selbstwertprobleme entwickelt, weil Eltern und Schule ihm seine Begabungen in anderen Bereichen bestätigen und die Rechtschreibfehler mit Gelassenheit hinnehmen, dann bedarf es der Diskrepanz-Diagnose erst in der 4. Klasse. Im Hinblick auf die weitere Schullaufbahn ist zu diesem Zeitpunkt nötig abzuwägen, und zwar unter Berücksichtigung der Stärken und Schwächen im Intelligenzprofil, welche Schulart zu wählen ist. Dazu muss man die Größe der Diskrepanzen zwischen den schriftsprachlichen Leistungen und den besseren Leistungen im Intelligenztest kennen. Manchmal ist es für ein gut begabtes, aber schwer legasthenes Kind besser, nicht über das Gymnasium, sondern zunächst über die Realschule oder über die Hauptschule zu einem Schulabschluss zu gelangen um danach ggf. den nächst höheren Abschluss im beruflichen Schulwesen anzustreben. In anderen Fällen ist der direkte Weg über ein Gymnasium richtiger.

Allerdings haben es die Schüler, die den direkten Weg gehen, im Gymnasium schwerer, weil sie hinsichtlich ihrer Rechtschreibung mit der Rechtschreib-"Elite“ verglichen werden. Demgegenüber stehen sie z.B. in einer Gesamtschule zumindest während der 5. bis 7. Klasse im Vergleich mit den Leistungen der gesamten Altersgruppe. Dadurch fällt die Rechtschreibnote besser aus. Außerdem müssen Legastheniker in Gymnasien damit rechnen, dass ein vorher gewährter „Notenschutz“ in der Studienstufe nicht mehr gewährt wird: Kürzlich erhielt ein legasthener Schüler in Schleswig-Holstein in der 11. Klasse des Gymnasiums, der in Mathematik die Note 2, in Physik die Note 1 und in Latein die Note 2 hatte, in einer Englischarbeit die Note 5. die sogenannte „Sperrklausel“ wirkt sich hier wörtlich aus: Sie versperrt ihm die leistungsgerechte Benotung (Inhalt der Arbeit war 2-), weil wegen der Rechtschreibnote 6 nur eine Gesamtnote 5 erteilt werden darf. Über dieses Rechenexempel sollten die Gymnasien allerdings einmal ernsthaft nachdenken, auch unter dem Aspekt des Artikels 3 im Grundgesetz: Niemand darf wegen einer Behinderung benachteiligt werden.

Literatur

Angermaier, M.: Sprache und Konzentration bei Legasthenie. Göttingen: Hogrefe 1974.

Angermaier, M. (Hg.): Legasthenie – Das neue Konzept der Förderung lese-recht-schreibschwacher Kinder in Schule und Elternhaus. Frankfurt a. M., Fischer 1976.

Borstrøm, I. u. Elbro, C.: Prevention of Dyslexia in Kindergarten: Effects of Phoneme Avareness Training with Children of Dyslexic Parents. In:Hulme, Ch. And Snowling, M (Eds.): Dyslexia: Biology, Cognition and Intervention.Whurr Publishers Ltd. London 1997

Bosch, B.:Grundlagen des Erstleseunterrichts. Ratingen: Henn, 1961.

Breuer, H. und Weuffen, M.: Lernschwierigkeiten am Schulanfang. Weinheim, Beltz, 1993.

Brügelmann, H. und Dummer, L.: Vom „3lft“ zum „Elefat“: Was heißt hier Leseschwäche? In: Balhorn, H. und Brügelmann, H. (Hrsg.): Welten der Schrift in der Erfahrung der Kinder. Konstanz, Faude, 1987.

Dehn, M.: Zeit für die Schrift. Lesenlernen und Schreibenkönnen. Bochum, Kamp, 1988.

Dummer-Smoch, L.: Lautgebärden im Erstleseunterricht. In: dgs-Landesgruppe Rheinland-Pfalz (Hg.): Förderung Sprachbehinderter – Modelle und Perspektiven. Hamburg, Wartenberg, 1989b, S. 44-56.

Dummer-Smoch, L.: Die Diagnostischen Bilderlisten. Handanweisung, Kiel: Veris, 1993.

Dummer-Smoch, L.: Laute, Silben, Wörter. Kiel, Veris 1996.

Günther, K. B. (Hg.): Ontogenese, Entwicklungsprozeß und Störungen beim Schriftspracherwerb. Heidelberg, Edition Schindele 1989.

Ingenkamp, K. (Hrsg.): Lese- und Rechtschreibschwäche bei Schulkindern. Bericht über eine Fortbildungs- und Arbeitstagung vom 11. Bis 4. Januar 1965 in der Kongreßhalle in Berlin. Weinheim, Berlin, Basel: Beltz, 1966.

Jansen, H. und Skowronek, H.: Abschlußbericht zum Forschungsprojekt: Lese-Rechtschreibschwäche und funktionaler Analphabetismus in der Sekundarstufe I. Universität Bielefeld, Fakultät für Psychologie und Sportwissenschaft, Abteilung Pädagogische Psychologie, 1997.

Küspert, P.& Schneider, W.: Hören, lauschen, lernen. Göttingen: Hogrefe 2000^2

Müller, R.: Über die Entwicklung diagnostischer Rechtschreibtests für 2. und 3. Klassen. In: Ingenkamp, K. 1966.

Müller, R.: Therapierelevante Diagnose der Legasthenie. In: Ebel, V., Bundesverband Legasthenie (Hrsg.): Legasthenie. Bericht über den Fachkongreß 1978. Bonn: Reha-Verlag 1979.

Schenk-Danzinger, L.: Legasthenie. Zerebral-funktionelle Interpretation. München, Ernst Reinhardt, 1991.

Schlee, J.: Legasthenieforschung am Ende? München, Urban und Schwarzenberg 1976.

Schneider, W., Roth, E., Küspert, P. und Ennemoser, M.: Kurz- und langfristige Effekte eines Trainings der sprachlichen (phonologischen) Bewußtheit bei unterschiedlichen Leistungsgruppen: Befunde einer Sekundäranalyse. Zeitschrift für Entwicklungspsychologie und Pädagogische Psychologie, 30 (1), 26 – 39.

Valtin, R.: Legasthenie – Theorien und Untersuchungen. Weinheim, Berlin, Basel: Beltz 1970.

2.2 Psychologische Diagnostik bei Lese- und Rechtschreibstörungen

Volker Ebel

Der hier vorgelegte Text ist das überarbeitete Manuskript des Vortrages, der auf dem Würzburger Kongress gehalten wurde. Seine Grundlage ist ein umfangreicheres Papier zum Thema, das von einer Arbeitsgruppe der Sektion Klinische Psychologie im Berufsverband Deutscher Psychologen erarbeitet und vom Gesamtverband als Grundsatzpapier „Legasthenie – ein umfassender Auftrag für Psychologen" angenommen wurde. Federführend für das Projekt waren der Vortragende und der Diplom-Psychologe Andreas Köhnke unter Mitarbeit der Kollegen Anton Häusler, Ulrike Oesch und Christoph Werres.

1 Lesen und Schreiben als integrativer Prozess

Lesen und Schreiben sind komplexe kognitive Fähigkeiten, die das ungestörte Zusammenspiel vieler zugrunde liegender Teilfähigkeiten erfordern. Ist eine dieser Teilfähigkeiten nur unzureichend entwickelt oder deren integratives Zusammenwirken gestört, so ist die Gefahr groß, dass es zu einer schriftsprachlichen Entwicklungsstörung kommt.

So müssen für das Erlernen des (Recht-) Schreibens insbesondere

- Wortklangbilder in die Lautbestandteile zerlegt werden können (Lautanalysefähig-keit);
- geringfügige Klangunterschiede zuverlässig erkannt werden (auditive Diskriminationsfähigkeit);
- Wörter laut oder leise mitartikuliert werden können, da durch die artikulatorische bzw. kinästhetische Analyse des Wortes die Lautanalyse unterstützt wird (Mundmotorik, kinästhetische Wahrnehmungsfähigkeit);
- den analysierten Lauten die entsprechenden Schriftzeichen zugeordnet werden. Hierzu ist es notwendig, dass die graphische Gestalt der Buchstaben sicher erinnert und visuell vorgestellt werden kann;
- Schriftzeichen in Schreibbewegungen umgesetzt werden können. Die Bewegungsplanung und -koordination muss ebenso ungestört sein, wie die kinästhetische Wahrnehmung der Handmotorik und das Zusammenspiel von Kraft, Muskeltonus und Bewegung.

Für das Erlernen des Lesens

- müssen Buchstaben visuell erfasst und unterschieden werden können (visuelle Diskriminationsfähigkeit);
- muss die Raumlage der einzelnen Buchstaben berücksichtigt werden (Raumlageerfassung);
- müssen Schriftzeichen unabhängig von ihrer Größe und Form sicher identifiziert wer-den (Formkonstanz);
- müssen die den Buchstaben zugehörigen Lautmuster abrufbar sein;

- müssen die schrittweise in Laute übersetzten Schriftzeichen kurzzeitig in der richtigen Reihenfolge erinnert und zu einem Wortklangbild aneinandergereiht werden können (auditives Kurzzeitgedächtnis und Lautsynthesefähigkeit);

2 Das Erscheinungsbild der Störung

Von Beginn an fallen die betroffenen Kinder dadurch auf, dass ihnen die Umwandlung von Schriftzeichen in Sprachlaute und umgekehrt nicht oder nur unzureichend gelingt. Das Zusammenschleifen von Lauten zu Wortklangbildern gelingt ihnen oft ebenso wenig wie das Zerlegen von Wortklangbildern in Laute. Häufig werden Buchstaben verwechselt, die ähnliche Laute abbilden (z.B. d und t, o und u) oder visuelle Ähnlichkeit aufweisen (z.B. b und d, u und n).

Das für den Anfangsunterricht bedeutsame lautierende Lesen und lautgetreue Schreiben wird dadurch nachhaltig beeinträchtigt. Bereits wenige Wochen nach der Einschulung wird die Stagnation in der Entwicklung der schriftsprachlichen Fertigkeiten erkennbar, und der Abstand zu den sich ungestört entwickelnden Mitschülern wächst stetig an.

Im weiteren Verlauf fällt beim Lesen eine niedrige Lesegeschwindigkeit, das Auslassen, Ersetzen, Verdrehen oder Hinzufügen von Wörtern oder Wortteilen und das Vertauschen von Wörtern im Satz oder von Buchstaben in den Wörtern auf. Auch im Leseverständnis zeigen sich Defizite. In der Rechtschreibung kommt es – neben zahlreichen Regel- und Dehnungsfehlern – zu Verdrehung, Umstellung, Auslassung und Einfügung von Buchstaben im Wort. In höheren Klassen überwiegt die Rechtschreibproblematik gegenüber den Leseschwierigkeiten und die Regelfehler nehmen relativ zu.

3 Hauptursachen des gestörten Schriftspracherwerbs

Lange Zeit wurden visuelle Wahrnehmungsstörungen als die Hauptursache der Lese- und Rechtschreibstörung betrachtet. Insbesondere die Annahme einer visuellen Diskriminations- und Gliederungsschwäche und einer ausgeprägten Raumlagelabilität galten als Grundphänomen der Legasthenie. Nach heutigem Wissensstand kann jedoch davon ausgegangen werden, dass bei der übergroßen Mehrzahl der betroffenen Kinder phonologische Verarbeitungsstörungen und bei etwa 5 bis 10% visuelle Wahrnehmungsstörungen einen ungestörten Schriftspracherwerb behindern.

Schon die Tatsache, daß 60 bis 70% der legasthenen Kinder bereits im Kleinkind- und Vorschulalter durch Sprachentwicklungsstörungen auffallen, kann als Hinweis auf spezifische sprachbezogene Verarbeitungsstörungen gewertet werden. Aber auch bei legasthenen Kindern mit anamnestisch unauffälliger Sprachentwicklung deckt eine sorgfältige Untersuchung oft spezielle Probleme bei der kognitiven Verarbeitung der Lautstruktur der Sprache auf.

Wissenschaftlich ist gut gesichert, dass besonders häufig

- legasthene Kinder über eine unzureichende Fähigkeit verfügen, Wörter als aus lautlichen Einheiten bestehend wahrzunehmen und analytisch und synthetisch damit umzugehen (phonologische Bewußtheit). Dieses Defizit ist bereits im Vorschulalter z. B. durch die Unfähigkeit, Wörter in Silben zu klatschen, Reimpaare zu erkennen, den Anlaut eines Wortes zu benennen oder gedehnt vorgesprochene Worte zu erkennen nachweisbar.

- es den betroffenen Kindern außergewöhnlich schwerfällt unmittelbar zuvor gehörte Zahlenketten oder Pseudowörter nachzusprechen. Die kurzzeitige Merkfähigkeit für serielle auditive Reize ist eingeschränkt.
- für legasthene Kinder der Zugriff auf die im mentalen Lexikon gespeicherten Inhalte beeinträchtigt ist. Das äußert sich z.B. in der verzögerten Benennung von bildhaft dargestellten Objekten.

Neben den häufig auftretenden phonologischen und gelegentlich beobachtbaren visuellen Verarbeitungsstörungen fallen legasthene Kinder gehäuft auch durch fein- und grobmotorische Koordinations-, taktil-kinästhetische Wahrnehmungs- und Aufmerksamkeitsstörungen auf.

4 Das psychosoziale Wirkungsgefüge Legasthenie und seine langfristigen Auswirkungen

Das unerwartete Versagen beim Erlernen des Lesens und Rechtschreibens, der stets negativ ausfallende Vergleich mit den Mitschülern und die enttäuschten bis vorwurfsvollen Reaktionen der Lehrer und Eltern treffen das Kind in seiner gesamten Persönlichkeit. Die Tatsache, in einer allseits als wichtig erachteten Leistungsanforderung zu versagen, führt zu einem Einbruch in das Vertrauen in die eigene Leistungsfähigkeit und zu einem Verlust des Selbstwertgefühls. Viele der betroffenen Kinder entwickeln als Reaktion auf das geschädigte Selbstwerterleben auffällige Verhaltensmuster, um sich auf anderen Wegen im sozialen Umfeld zu behaupten oder sich den kränkenden Leistungsanforderungen zu entziehen. Leistungsversagen und auffälliges Verhalten drohen zu einem Teufelskreis zu werden. Resignation und der Verlust der Lernmotivation bergen die Gefahr, dass sich das anfänglich auf das Lesen und Schreiben beschränkte Versagen nun auch auf andere Schulfächer ausdehnt. Oft ist dann der Weg in eine Sonderschule für lernbehinderte oder verhaltensgestörte Kinder vorgezeichnet und die Gesamtentwicklung der Persönlichkeit gefährdet.

In einer vom Zentralinstitut für seelische Gesundheit in Mannheim durchgeführten Un-tersuchung konnte – wie in anderen Studien auch – gezeigt werden, dass nahezu die Hälfte der legasthenen Kinder bereits im Alter von acht Jahren sekundäre psychische Störungen entwickelt hat. Bei Kindern, die bereits im Vorschulalter durch grobmotorische Unruhe und Aufmerksamkeitsprobleme auffielen, kommt es zu einer deutlichen Symptomverschärfung. Neben Hyperaktivität, Konzentrationsstörungen und aggressiven Verhaltensmustern sind psychosomatische Symptome und depressive Verstimmungen gehäuft zu beobachten. Langzeituntersuchungen zeigen auch, dass lese- und rechtschreibgestörte Kinder nicht nur gehäuft zusätzliche psychische Störungen entwickeln und eine oft suboptimale Schullaufbahn absolvieren, sondern dass auch die langfristige soziale Integration gefährdet ist. So waren in der bereits erwähnten Mannheimer Studie 25% der legasthenen Kinder im Jugendalter delinquent. Das lese- und rechtschreibgestörte Kind ist somit in besonderem Ausmaß in seiner gesamten Entwicklung gefährdet und von seelischer Behinderung bedroht.

5 Allgemeine Fragen zur Diagnostik der LRS

Wenn nun Eltern und Lehrkräfte Ursachen, Auswirkungen und Zusammenhänge eines gestörten Lernprozesses nicht erkennen können und unangemessen auf die Leistungsdefizite reagieren, wird das Problem für alle vergrößert. Um einem Betroffenen und seinen relevanten Beziehungspersonen wirksam und angemessen bei der Bewältigung dieser Problematik helfen zu können, ist eine gründliche psychologische Diagnostik unverzichtbar. Sie ist ein ganzheitlicher interaktiver Prozeß und somit mehr als das Zusammentragen von statistischen Testergebnissen. Die Leistungsdiagnose im engeren Sinne ist immer eingebettet in die individuelle Persönlichkeitsentwicklung der Betroffenen. Sie ist durch die Auswirkungen des gestörten Lernprozesses im Erleben des Kindes beeinflusst. Diese Auswirkungen müssen im diagnostischen Prozess berücksichtigt werden. Diagnostik bezieht sich zudem ja im allgemeinen auf nachfolgende fördernde oder therapeutische Interventionen. Also muss auch die weitere Entwicklung des Betroffenen mit der größtmöglichen Sicherheit antizipiert werden können, um die geeigneten Interventionsformen zu finden. All das verlangt eine besondere psychologische Kompetenz, nur durch ein Studium der wissenschaftlichen psychologischen Grundlagen und entsprechende Praxiserfahrungen erworben werden kann. Der diagnostische Prozess muss deshalb Fachleuten mit entsprechender gründlicher Ausbildung vorbehalten bleiben. Er kann auch nicht an Hilfskräfte delegiert werden. Auch eine Trennung von Diagnostik und Therapie bringt Probleme mit sich. So können zum Beispiel wesentliche Verhaltensbeobachtungen verloren gehen, die Aufschluss über das Zustandekommen einer Leistung geben können.

5.1 Diagnostische Ziele

Die diagnostischen Verfahren dienen zunächst der Frage, ob eine „umschriebene Entwicklungsstörung schulischer Fertigkeiten“ vorliegt. Darüber hinaus soll sie Fragen der Ursachen, des Erscheinungsbildes und der Auswirkungen klären und gegebenenfalls Behandlungsziele festlegen helfen.

5.2 Probleme der Diagnostik

Wegen der Polyätiologie und der verschiedenartigen Erscheinungsformen der Lese- und Rechtschreibstörungen sowie der unterschiedlichen Auswirkungen auf Erleben und Verhalten der Betroffenen ist schon die genaue Grenzziehung zwischen lese- und recht-schreibgestörten und nicht gestörten Kindern problematisch. Diagnostische Leitlinien, zum Beispiel in der Internationalen Klassifikation psychischer Störungen (ICD 10), fordern deshalb allgemein, dass Lese- und Rechtschreibleistungen „unter dem Niveau liegen, das aufgrund des Alters, der allgemeinen Intelligenz und der Beschulung zu erwarten ist“. Hauptmerkmal ist danach eine deutliche Beeinträchtigung in der Entwicklung von Fertigkeiten, die Lesen und regelhaftes Schreiben ermöglichen; die Beeinträchtigung darf aber nicht auf unzureichenden Unterricht, auf geistige Behinderung, auf Schwerhörigkeit, Sehstörungen oder neurologische Krankheiten zurückzuführen sein.

Diese Diskrepanzdefinition setzt also allgemeine intellektuelle Leistungsmöglichkeiten in eine abhängige Beziehung zur Qualität von Lese- und Rechtschreibleistungen. Es müssen demnach individuelle Leistungen auf den angeführten Gebieten gemessen und in Beziehung zur den erwartungsgemäßen Leistungen einer repräsentativen Gruppe der Gesamtpopulation gesetzt werden. Dies geschieht gemeinhin mit Testverfahren, die entsprechende statistische Werte liefern können.

Definitionen nach rein teststatistischen Werten sind nun aber aus guten Gründen fragwürdig:

- Rechtschreibtests sind sehr unscharfe diagnostische Methoden. Ihre statistische Absicherung ist schwierig, ihre Prozentränge streuen stark.

- Die Rechtschreibleistungen von lese- und rechtschreibschwachen Kindern sind instabil. Kinder, die innerhalb von acht Tagen mit demselben Rechtschreibtest zweimal getestet werden, haben häufig recht unterschiedliche Ergebnisse.
- Ein Kind, das wegen eines bestimmten Prozentranges als lese- und rechtschreibgestört definiert wird, kann nicht zum ungestörten Kind erklärt werden, sobald sein Testergebnis – z. B. durch therapeutische Maßnahmen – einen Grenzwert übersteigt, der als Definitionsmerkmal angesehen wird.
- Ein statistisches Ergebnis ist eine Momentaufnahme, über dessen Genese noch nichts ausgesagt ist. Wenn zum Beispiel ein Kind nach jahrelangen belastenden Übungssituationen mit seiner Rechtschreibleistung einen bestimmten Prozentrang erreicht hat, schließt dies nicht aus, daß es einige Monate zuvor nur einen wesentlich niedrigeren Prozentrang erreicht hätte, wenn es denn untersucht worden wäre.
- Ein rein statistisch festgelegtes Definitionskriterium berücksichtigt die Begleitsymptomatik nicht. Auch wenn das Versagen im Lesen und Schreiben für die Diagnose entscheidend ist, wird der psychologische und psychotherapeutische Interventionsbedarf vor allem auch durch das neurotisierende Potential eines gestörten Lernprozesses bestimmt. Psychische Störungen, die dauerhaft als Angst, Selbstwertkonflikt, psychosomatische Symptomatik oder als andere Verhaltensauffälligkeit im Zusammenhang mit schwachen Lese- und Rechtschreibleistungen auftreten, sind aus klinisch psychologischer Sicht ein Definitionsmerkmal für eine Lese- und Rechtschreibstörung. Dies gilt gerade auch, wenn psychische Beeinträchtigungen in den Ferien deutlich zurückgehen oder gar verschwinden.

Eine Diskrepanzdefinition nach Testwerten im Rechtschreib- und im Intelligenztest kann eigentlich nur für Forschungszwecke akzeptiert werden, wenn damit eine vergleichbare Population gesichert werden soll. Für eine klinisch-psychologische Definition kann ein Wert im Rechtschreibtest, der z. B. unter dem Prozentrang 15 liegt und ein sprachfreier IQ, der z. B. über 85 liegt, allenfalls als Orientierungshilfe gelten. Für eine genauere Diagnose einer beeinträchtigenden Störung sind deshalb umfangreichere diagnostische Interventionen notwendig.

6 Spezifische Diagnostik

6.1 Diagnostik des schriftsprachlichen Entwicklungsstandes

6.1.1 Lesen

Diagnostisches Ziel ist es, Ursachen für gestörte Verarbeitungsprozesse sprachlicher Reize zu erkennen. Dazu gehört insbesondere mangelhaft ausgebildetes Phonembewusstsein, das sich meist in Schwierigkeiten bei der Lautanalyse und Lautsynthese äußert.

6.1.1.1 Buchstaben lesen

(Buchstabentafeln enthalten u.a. der Züricher Lesetest und der Salzburger Lese- und Rechtschreibtest – SLRT. Aufschlußreicher sind Buchstabentafeln, die alle Einzelbuchstaben und Diphtonge mehrfach enthalten, um Unsicherheiten und Rateprozesse deutlicher zu machen.. Buchstaben lesen gibt auch Hinweise auf mögliche Schwierigkeiten bei der visuellen Informationsverarbeitung. Durch die Unabhängigkeit vom Kontext lassen sich hiermit häufig Unsicherheit in der Dekodierung auch dann noch feststellen, wenn der Leseprozess bei zusammenhängenden Texten kaum noch gestört erscheint.

6.1.1.2 Wörter lesen

(z.B. Salzburger Lese- und Rechtschreibtest, Zürcher Lesetest)

6.1.1.3 Texte lesen. (s.o.)

6.1.1.4 Pseudowörter lesen

Lese- und rechtschreibgestörte Kinder haben hierbei meist auch dann noch anhaltende Schwierigkeiten, wenn ihre Leseschwäche schon weitgehend abgebaut ist. Die Schwäche in der Fähigkeit zur Buchstabensynthese und in der phonologischen Bewusstheit wird hier wieder manifest. Solche Pseudowörter enthält der SLRT.

6.1.2 Schreiben

Diagnostisches Ziel ist es, den gestörten Rechtschreibprozeß qualitativ und quantitativ zu erfassen. Die Testergebnisse bieten die Möglichkeit einer individuellen Fehleranalyse.

6.1.2.1 Wörter schreiben

(Z.B. standardisierte Rechtschreibtests wie DRT, SLRT, WRT)

6.1.2.2 Texte schreiben

Diagnostisch aufschlußreich sind freie Texte, die die Kinder selbst erfinden sollen.

6.1.2.3 Buchstabendiktat

6.1.2.4 Abschreiben

6.1.2.5 Analyse der schulischen Bewertungen

6.2 Diagnostik der Sprachentwicklung

Störungen in der Sprachentwicklung vor der Einschulung sind, auch wenn sie diskret verlaufen oder den Eltern bei der Entwicklung ihres Kindes nicht aufgefallen sind, ein fakultatives Merkmal für die Diagnose einer Lese- und Rechtschreibstörung. Durch geeignete diagnostische Verfahren zur Sprachentwicklung – wie zum Beispiel neuropsychologische Tests – werden sie häufig auch noch bei älteren Kindern, Jugendlichen oder Erwachsenen aufgedeckt, die sich in ihrer Alltagssprache von Gleichaltrigen nicht mehr unterscheiden.

Besondere Aufmerksamkeit erfordern isolierte Artikulationsstörungen sowie expressive und rezeptive Sprachstörungen. Sie müssen in ihrer Ätiologie erfaßt werden. Hinweise auf relevante Sprachentwicklungsverzögerungen können auch ein deutlich eingeschränkter Wortschatz oder unzureichende Sprachstrukturen geben.

6.2.1 Standardisierter Sprachentwicklungstest

Relevante Hinweise auf Störungen in der Sprachentwicklung geben bereits kurze psychologische Testverfahren wie „Zahlen nachsprechen“ (enthalten im K-ABC; HAWIK-R und im Psycholinguistischen Entwicklungstest – PET), „Laute verbinden“ (PET), die „Differenzierungsprobe“ nach Breuer und Weuffen, der „Mottier-Test“ und andere Verfahren, die die Schwierigkeiten in der akustischen Informationsverarbeitung aufzeigen. Rezeptive Sprachstörungen manifestieren sich häufig in den Untertests „Wortverständnis“ und „Wörterergänzen“ des PET. Eine umfassendere Diagnostik ermöglichen psychologische Sprachentwicklungstests wie der „Heidelberger Spachentwicklungstest“.

Die Ergebnisse dieser psychologischen Testverfahren geben wichtige Hinweise auf die Notwendigkeit, spezifische Interventionsverfahren einzusetzen, die die Basisfunktionen für den Lese- und Rechtschreibprozess aufbauen und stärken.

6.3 Intelligenzdiagnostik

6.3.1 Standardisierter Intelligenztest

Die Anwendung von Intelligenztests soll sicherstellen, dass das defizitäre Lese- und Rechtschreibsystem eines Kindes nicht Hinweis auf eine allgemeine Intelligenzminderung ist. Anwendbar sind deshalb solche Verfahren, die hinreichende Aussagen über die intellektuellen Leistungsmöglichkeiten eines Kindes oder Jugendlichen im Vergleich zu statistisch abgesicherten Normen auf der jeweiligen Altersstufe machen können. Verfahren, die gut zwischen sprachfreien und sprachgebundenen Aufgaben differenzieren, sind besonders geeignet. Das gilt gerade auch für Verfahren mit Untertests, die lese- und rechtschreibgestörte Probanden aufgrund ihrer Defizite nur eingeschränkt bearbeiten können (K-ABC; Prüfsystem für Schul- und Bildungsberatung – PSB, Adaptives Intelligenz Diagnosticum – AID). Bei einer Bewertung der so gewonnenen statistischen Daten – zum Beispiel durch einen IQ – muß dieser Umstand aber gebührend berücksichtigt werden.

Da, wie erwähnt, ein niedriger statistischer Wert, wie z.B. ein „unterdurchschnittlicher“ Intelligenzquotient, über sein Zustandekommen nichts Sicheres aussagen kann, ist in solchem Fall eine qualifizierte psychologische Differentialdiagnostik unverzichtbar. Sie sollte auch hinreichend gesicherte Aussagen über die emotionalen, situativen oder per-sönlichkeitsbezogenen Anteile einer schwachen Testleistung gestatten.

Die Ergebnisse differenzierender Intelligenztests geben darüber hinaus aber auch oft Hinweise auf gut entwickelte intellektuelle Leistungsbereiche, die in einer Behandlung kompensatorisch berücksichtigt werden sollten.

Eine qualifizierte Intelligenzdiagnostik setzt also ein umfassendes psychologisches Fachwissen voraus, das eine entsprechende wissenschaftliche psychologische Ausbildung erfordert. Kenntnisse in Anwendung und Auswertung allein genügen nicht, und Mängel im diagnostischen Prozess haben häufig schwerwiegende Folgen für Betroffene.

6.4 Diagnostik anderer Leistungs- und Verhaltensbereiche

Lese- und Rechtschreibstörungen sind häufig begleitet von Störungen in anderen Lei-stungsbereichen. Oft fallen Verzögerungen in der motorischen Entwicklung, Aufmerk-samkeitsdefizite, Unsicherheiten in der Lateralität oder visuomotorische Beeinträchtigungen auf.

Hinweise ergeben sich besonders aus der Anamnese oder aus Verhaltensbeobachtungen während des Untersuchungsprozesses.

Die polyätiologischen Erkenntnisse zum LRS-Problem machen diagnostische Interventionen in verschiedenen Leistungsfeldern nicht nur notwendig, um Hypothesen zu den Ursachen der Störung zu bilden, sondern auch, um gezielte therapeutische Interventionen zu ermöglichen.

6.5 Diagnostik sekundärer neurotischer Störungen

Lese- und Rechtschreibstörungen stellen für Betroffene oft schon im frühen Schulkindalter eine hohe Belastung durch die unterschiedlichen und meist beeinträchtigenden sozialen Prozesse dar, die sie im sozialen Umfeld auslösen. Da betroffene Kinder die Belastungssituation während der Schulzeit im allgemeinen durchgehend erleben, wirkt die dauerhafte Konfliktsituation symptomverstärkend im Sinne eines Teufelskreises: Es entsteht ein Bedingungsgefüge, in dem sich Ursachen und Wirkung der Störung mischen und gegenseitig verstärken. Damit sind meist Ängste mit erheblichen Selbstwertverletzungen verbunden. Dieser negative systemische Prozeß kann sich verselbständigen und schließlich zum Ausgangspunkt einer schweren Persönlichkeitsstörung werden.

Häufig manifestiert sich die Belastungsstörung bei Kindern als Motivationsverlust, Abwehr gegenüber Anforderungen, auffälliges aggressives Verhalten auch gegenüber Beziehungs-personen, Leistungsangst oder in psychosomatischen Begleitsymptomen.

Zur Diagnose sekundärer Belastungsstörungen stehen vor allem zahlreiche allgemeine und spezifische Fragebogenverfahren (z.B. Angst-Fragebogen für Schüler (AFS), Hanes-Skala, Aussagen-Liste zum Selbstwertgefühl für Kinder und Jugendliche (ALS), Leistungsmotivationstest für Jugendliche (LMT-J) und Interviews (DIPS), aber auch einige projektive Verfahren (z.B. Satzergänzungstest, Familie in Tieren, Verfahren zur Analyse von Familienbeziehungen) zur Verfügung.

6.6. Anamnese und Exploration

Eine symptomorientierte Anamnese wird vor allem die möglichen Störungen im frühesten Kindesalter, die Entwicklung relevanter Bereiche wie Sprache, Motorik, Aufmerksamkeit, soziales Verhalten, Aufälligkeiten in Kindergarten und Schule umfassen. Die Exploration gibt Auskunft über die gegenwärtige Problemlage aus der unterschiedlichen Sicht des betroffenen Kindes und seiner Beziehungspersonen. Das legasthene Störungsbild von Kindern, die unter problematischen Lebensumständen aufwachsen, verschärft häufig die familiäre Konfliktlage insgesamt deutlich mit wiederum negativen Rückwirkungen auf das Kind. Die häuslichen Verhältnisse müssen deshalb in angemessener Form exploriert werden. Auch hierfür sind in der psychologischen Forschung und Praxis zahlreiche Fragebögen und strukturierte Interviews vor allem für Eltern, aber auch für Lehrkräfte entwickelt worden (z.B. MEI, DIPS, DEF). Ein Modell für eine systemische Diagnostik haben Betz und Breuninger entwickelt und im „Teufelskreis Lernstörungen" dargestellt.

Dass Lese- und Rechtschreibstörungen familiär gehäuft auftreten können, sollte in der Anamnese berücksichtigt werden.

6.7 Medizinische Zusatzdiagnostik

Die ärztliche Diagnostik ist gefordert, um organische Beeinträchtigungen oder neurologische Störungen aufzudecken oder auszuschließen. Dazu gehören Untersuchungen peripherer Beeinträchtigungen im akustischen und visuellen Bereich und Abklärungen organischer Begleiterscheinungen.

6.8. Therapiebegleitende Diagnostik

Unverzichtbar während der psychologischen Behandlung einer Lese- und Rechtschreibstörung ist schließlich eine therapiebegleitende Verlaufsdiagnose,

- die Behandlungsergebnisse darstellbar macht,
- die aus den Untersuchungsergebnissen abgeleitete Hypothesen verifiziert oder modifiziert,
- die Probleme lösen hilft, die erst im Laufe des Behandlungsprozesses deutlich werden
- und auf neue Interventionsmöglichkeiten oder notwendige Methodenänderungen hinweist.

Für Diagnostik, aber auch für Prävention und Therapie der umschriebenen Lese- und Rechtschreibstörung und ihrer psychopathologischen Folgewirkungen bietet die Psychologie alle wesentlichen wissenschaftlichen Grundlagen. Das Studium der Psychologie und eine spezifische Fortbildung ist deshalb die beste Voraussetzung, um das komplexe Störungsbild wirksam behandeln zu können.

2.3 Neuropsychologische Diagnostik bei lese-rechtschreibschwachen Kindern

Erwin Breitenbach

1 Einleitung

Die Neuropsychologische Diagnostik als anwendungsbezogener Teilbereich der Neuropsychologie, wird meist dann veranlasst, wenn eine zerebrale Schädigung neurologisch nachgewiesen wurde oder ein Verdacht darauf besteht. Neurologische und neuropsychologische Untersuchungsmethoden ergänzen sich oder, genauer formuliert, meist werden neurologische Untersuchungen im Rahmen der neuropsychologischen Diagnostik mit psychologischen Methoden fortgesetzt. Ziel der neuropsychologischen Diagnostik ist es, Leistungsminderungen im Zusammenhang mit hirnorganischen Beeinträchtigungen zu überprüfen. Mit Hilfe differenzierter Testverfahren werden einzelne Funktionsbereiche (sprachliche Kommunikation, Handlungsplanung, Wahrnehmung, Gedächtnis, usw.) untersucht, die bestimmten Hirnarealen zuzuordnen sind. Für das Kindesalter haben solche Zusammenhänge von Gehirn und Verhalten jedoch nur eine begrenzte Bedeutung, da es sich selten um umschriebene Störungen handelt und zusätzlich fortlaufende entwicklungsbedingte hirnorganische Veränderungen zu berücksichtigen sind. Dennoch hat auch die neuropsychologische Diagnostik im Kindes- und Jugendalter die Aufgabe und Möglichkeit, Stärken und Schwächen deutlich zu machen, um damit einerseits Hinweise für spezifische therapeutische Ansätze zu liefern und andererseits Prognosen über zukünftige schulische und berufliche Möglichkeiten zu erstellen.

2 Neuropsychologische Diagnostik als Förderdiagnostik

Für die sonderpädagogische Praxis lassen sich derzeit in unserer Gesellschaft vier klar voneinander unterscheidbare diagnostische Fragestellungen ausmachen: die deskriptive Diagnostik, die Selektionsdiagnostik, die Integrationsdiagnostik und die Förderdiagnostik.

Eine sich ständig stellende Aufgabe in unserer Gesellschaft ist die Verteilung vorhandener Ressourcen. Dazu müssen Kriterien geschaffen werden, anhand derer die Zuteilung vorgenommen werden kann. Im Bereich der Sonderpädagogik ist es aus diesem Grund notwendig, Behinderungen oder Verhaltens- und Lernstörungen möglichst exakt zu beschreiben, um die Verteilung sonderpädagogischer Ressourcen wie zum Beispiel zusätzliche Förderung und Therapie, zusätzliche Lehrerstunden usw. vornehmen zu können. Im Rahmen einer **deskriptiven Diagnostik** wird festgestellt, ob ein Kind einer solchen Kategorie (Geistige Behinderung, Lese-Rechtschreibschwäche, ...) zugeordnet werden kann, was dann seinen Anspruch auf die Zuweisung entsprechender Ressourcen rechtfertigen würde.

In einem mehrgliedrigen Schul- und Bildungssystem stellt sich zwangsläufig die Frage nach der Zuweisung und Selektion. Unterschiedliche Schultypen und unterschiedliche Bildungs- und Ausbildungseinrichtungen stellen unterschiedliche Anforderungen an Kinder und Jugendliche. Die **Selektionsdiagnostik** überprüft, inwieweit Fähigkeiten und Kompetenzen von Kindern und Jugendlichen diesen Anforderungsprofilen entsprechen und liefert somit Hilfen bei Fragen nach der geeigneten Schullaufbahn oder Berufswahl.

Durch das Ziel der Integration von Menschen mit Behinderungen in unsere Gesellschaft werden Fragen nach Integrationsmöglichkeiten und nach zu schaffenden Bedingungen für diese Integration gestellt. Die **Integrationsdiagnostik** analysiert nicht problematische Verhaltensweisen oder Lernsituationen mit der Absicht, Förderstrategien und Lernhilfen zu entwickeln, sondern geht der Frage nach, inwieweit ein Mensch mit einer bestehenden, nicht veränderbaren Behinderung am gesellschaftlichen Leben in größtmöglichem Umfang teilhaben kann.

Lern- und Entwicklungsprozesse sind gekennzeichnet durch das Überwinden von Lernhemmungen, Lernhindernissen unterschiedlichster Art. Zur Analyse solcher Lernbehinderungen und zum Auffinden geeigneter Hilfen und Fördermaßnahmen bedarf es der **Förderdiagnostik**. Die hier vorzustellende neuropsychologische Diagnostik ist als reine Förderdiagnostik zu verstehen. Es gilt individuelle Stärken und Schwächen eines Kindes aufzudekken, um herauszufinden, unter welchen Lernbedingungen und mit welchen Lernhilfen die nächsten Entwicklungs- und Lernschritte zu realisieren sind.

Wie der Begriff Förderdiagnostik schon nahelegt, bilden Diagnostik und Förderung hier eine untrennbare Einheit in einem fortschreitenden Entwicklungs- und Lernprozess. Es werden Daten und Fakten erhoben, die in einem unmittelbaren Zusammenhang zu pädagogischen Interventionen stehen.

Im folgenden soll nun dieser förderdiagnostische Prozeß näher beschrieben werden: Aus seinem didaktischen Wissen heraus macht ein Lehrender einem Kind oder Jugendlichen ein Lehrangebot, um ein bestimmtes Lernziel zu erreichen. Er weiß zum Beispiel, wie Kinder normalerweise das Schreiben, Lesen oder Rechnen lernen und gestaltet entsprechend sein Lehren. Trifft er mit seinem Angebot beim Lernenden auf Lernbereitschaft und Lernmotivation, so wird das Kind sich auf sein Lehrangebot einlassen. An verschiedenen Stellen des Lehr-Lernprozesses können jedoch beim Lernenden aus den unterschiedlichsten Gründen Lernschwierigkeiten, Lernhemmungen auftreten, die das Kind alleine nicht überwinden kann. Der Lehrende ist nun gezwungen, den Lehr-Lernprozeß an dieser Stelle zu analysieren, um zu verstehen und um aus diesem Verstehen heraus dem Lernenden Hilfen zur Überwindung seiner Lernhemmungen anbieten zu können. Es entsteht für den Lehrenden damit eine spezifische diagnostische Fragestellung.

Der Lehrende besitzt einerseits ein allgemeines Wissen über Lehren und Lernen, über den Verlauf einzelner Erwerbsprozesse und über Lernhindernisse sowie andererseits auch bereits ein bestimmtes Wissen über den Lernenden und dessen individuelle Lernbedingungen. Auf dieser Wissensbasis entwickelt der Lehrende erste Hypothesen über mögliche Gründe und Bedingungen für das Entstehen der Lernhemmung beim Lernenden. So kann zum Beispiel ein Lehrer, dessen Schüler übermäßig viele Rechtschreibfehler im Diktat unterlaufen, die Vermutung haben, diese große Fehlerzahl hänge mit einer mangelnden Kenntnis der Rechtschreibregeln, mit einer zu gering entwickelten auditiven Gliederungsfähigkeit oder auch mit einer zu geringen Merkfähigkeit für sprachliches Material zusammen.

Im nächsten Schritt wird der Lehrende versuchen, seine Hypothesen zu überprüfen, indem er geeignete diagnostische Verfahren auswählt und sie durchführt. So könnte der Lehrer in obigem Fall die Rechtschreibfehler seines Schülers systematisch nach einzelnen Kategorien ordnen und auf diese Weise sehen, ob dieser Schüler im Laufe eines Diktates tatsächlich gehäuft gegen einzelne Rechtschreibregeln verstößt oder in welchem Ausmaß ihm typische Fehler unterlaufen, die auf mangelhafte auditive Verarbeitung hinweisen.

Bestätigen die diagnostischen Informationen die Vermutungen des Lehrenden nicht, findet der Lehrer in unserem Beispiel keine Hinweise auf eine mangelnde Regelkenntnis oder die angenommenen Schwächen in der auditiven Informationsverarbeitung, muß er neue Hypothesen über den möglichen Bedingungshintergrund suchen und diese dann wiederum überprüfen. Besagter Lehrer wird vielleicht nun Vermutungen darüber anstellen, ob die Lernsituation in seiner Klasse für den betreffenden Schüler ungünstig ist. Schenkt er ihm genügend Aufmerksamkeit und Zuwendung? Traut er ihm unter Umständen zu wenig zu und gibt vorschnell Unterstützung, sodass der Schüler zu selten Lernerfolge erlebt, die er sich selbst und seinem Können zuschreiben kann? Mit Hilfe einer gezielten Unterrichtsbeobachtung durch einen Kollegen oder eine Kollegin könnte der Lehrer beispielsweise versuchen, diese Hypothesen zu überprüfen, um so zu einem veränderten Lehrangebot zu kommen.

Erhärtet sich jedoch der ursprüngliche Verdacht über den Bedingungshintergrund der Lernhemmung, wird der Lehrende auf dieser Basis Hypothesen über nächste Entwicklungsschritte und entsprechende Fördermaßnahmen entwerfen. Er wird sich überlegen, in welchen weiteren Lernschritten und mit welchem neuen Lehrangebot er seinem Schüler beim Überwinden der vorhandenen Lernhemmung helfen kann.

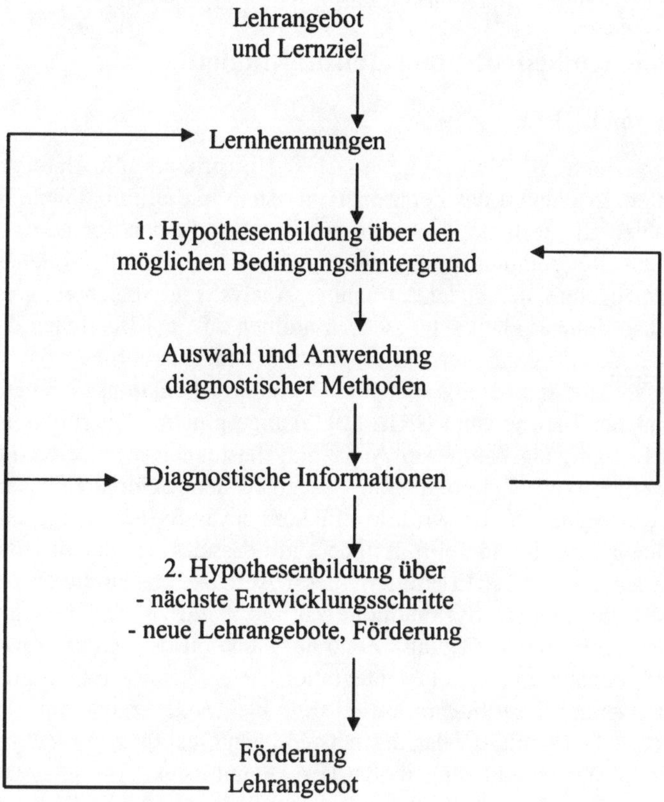

Abb. 2.3.1 Darstellung des förderdiagnostischen Prozesses

Setzt er sein neues Lehrangebot in die Tat um, kann er beobachten, inwieweit der Schüler auf dieses Angebot zugreift und wie er mit dem veränderten Lehrangebot seine Lernhemmungen überwindet und zum Beispiel im Prozess des Schreibenlernens fortschreitet. Der Lehrende erfährt auf diese Weise, ob seine Hypothesen, das neue Lehrangebot betreffend, erfolgreich und damit richtig waren. Gleichzeitig beinhaltet diese Erfahrung eine Reihe neuer diagnostischer Informationen über das Lernen des Schülers, die der Lehrende bei der weiteren Gestaltung seines Lehrangebotes, beim Festlegen nächster Entwicklungs- und Lernschritte sowie bei der Auswahl neuer Hilfen berücksichtigen wird. Es kann jedoch auch der Fall eintreten, daß sich im Rahmen des neuen Lehr- und Förderangebotes neue Lernhemmungen einstellen, die ihrerseits wieder einer Analyse bedürfen.

Förderdiagnostik wird verstanden als ein Prozess, in dem fortlaufend Hypothesen aufgestellt und überprüft werden. Zunächst beziehen diese sich auf mögliche Ursachen und Bedingungen für die vorliegenden Lern- und Entwicklungsprobleme. Daran schließen sich Hypothesen über etwaige Lern- und Förderhilfen an, deren Umsetzung in praktische Förderung zeigt, in wieweit sie das Erreichen der nächsten Lern- und Entwicklungschritte ermöglichen.

Die neuropsychologische Förderdiagnostik findet ihre Hypothesen mit Hilfe der aus Teilfunktionen bestehenden funktionellen Systeme und untersucht die Teilfunktionen mit der Methode der Variation der Aufgabenstellung.

3 Untersuchen bedeutsamer Teilfunktionen

3.1 Theorie von LURIA

LURIA (1973) versucht, die Bedeutung einzelner Hirnstrukturen in eine ganzheitliche Sichtweise einzubetten. Er gliedert das Zentralnervensystem in drei funktionale Einheiten. Zur ersten Einheit zählen alle Teile des Zentralnervensystems, die den Tonus, Aktivierung und den Grad der Bewußtheit regulieren. In der zweiten Einheit werden alle Teile des Zentralnervensystems zusammengefaßt, die an der Aufnahme, Analyse und Speicherung von Informationen beteiligt sind. Die dritte Einheit setzt sich zusammen aus den Bereichen des Zentralnervensystems, die mit der Programmierung, Regulation und Ausführung von Aktivitäten befaßt sind. An jeder Verhaltensäußerung sind immer alle drei Funktionseinheiten beteiligt. Damit ist das Kernstück der Theorie von LURIA (1973) angesprochen: die funktionellen Systeme.

Bei der Bewältigung komplexer Anpassungsleistungen, wie Lesen oder Schreiben, arbeiten viele weitgestreute Zellgruppen in verschiedenen Gehirnarealen auf verschiedenen Funktionsebenen zusammen. Es wird so ein komplexes System aufgebaut, bestehend aus zahlreichen Untersystemen und Teilfunktionen, mit dessen Hilfe die anstehende Aufgabe bewältigt werden kann. Nach der Erledigung dieser Aufgabe, stehen die einzelnen Teilfunktionen und Subsysteme für neue Systembildungen und damit zur Erledigung neuer komplexer Anpassungsleistungen zur Verfügung. Zentrale Funktionsweise des Zentralnervensystems scheint also die schnelle und korrekte Integration vieler Subsysteme zu größeren Gesamtsystemen zu sein. Gelingt diese Integrationsleistung nicht, oder stehen einzelne Teilfunktionen nicht im erforderlichen Umfang oder der notwendigen Qualität zur Verfügung, kommt es zu entsprechenden Leistungsminderungen oder Lernhemmnissen.

Die neuere neurologische Forschung liefert Befunde, die LURIA's Modellvorstellung der funktionellen Systeme grundsätzlich stützen. PUGH et al. (1996) gehen zum Beispiel bei ihren Forschungsbemühungen von der Annahme aus, daß für den Leseprozess orthographische, phonologische und lexikalisch-semantische Teilfähigkeiten bedeutsam sind. Dabei meint orthographisch alle Prozesse der Identifikation von Buchstaben, phonologisch die Gesamtheit aller Vorgänge zur Erkennung der phonemischen Bausteine der Sprache und lexikalisch-semantisch alle Prozesse, die zum Erkennen der Wortbedeutung nötig ist. Sie ließen sich weiter von der Vorstellung leiten, daß sich mit jeder dieser Teilfähigkeiten ein System neurologischer Substrate in Verbindung bringen läßt. Fasst man die für unser Anliegen interessierenden Ergebnisse zusammen, lässt sich festhalten: Mit der Zunahme der Aufgabenkomplexität und Aufgabenschwierigkeit geht auch eine Zunahme der aktivierten Hirnmasse einher und an jeder Teilfertigkeit scheint ein Netz unterschiedlicher Hirnregionen beteiligt zu sein.

Es muss jedoch auch darauf hingewiesen werden, dass in der Studie von PUGH et al. (1996) wie auch in zahlreichen anderen (zum Beispiel HORWITZ et al. 1998, PAULESU et al. 1996, RUMSEY et al. 1997) enorm komplexe Aktivierungsmuster gefunden wurden, die eine große Zahl von Hirnarealen umfassen. Das Herstellen von Beziehungen zwischen Funktionen und Hirnarealen gestaltet sich extrem schwierig. Allein das Konstrukt der phonologischen Verarbeitung besteht, wie RUMSEY et al. (1997) zeigen konnten, aus einem großen System von Teilfertigkeiten und erscheint über viele Hirnregionen verteilt. Angesichts der Plastizität vor allem des Gehirns von Kindern und Jugendlichen (BOOKHEIMER/DAPRETTA 1996) erweist sich eine solche Funktionsverteilung derzeit als kaum vorstellbar. Noch problematischer wird das Herstellen von Orts-Funktions-Zusammenhängen, werden Studien zu gestörten Lese- oder Schreibprozessen mit einbezogen.

Das im folgenden zu beschreibende funktionelle System zum Schriftspracherwerb muss deshalb aus neurologischer Sicht als eine stark vereinfachende Grobstruktur angesehen werden, die sich nur in sehr eingeschränktem Maße auf neurologische Forschungergebnisse stützen kann.

3.2 Funktionelles System zum Schriftspracherwerb

Da eine Beschreibung des gesamten funktionellen Systems an dieser Stelle den Rahmen sprengen würde, sollen beispielhaft die Teilfunktionen aus dem Bereich der auditiven Verarbeitung erläutert werden.

Damit spezifische und feste Beziehungen zwischen Vorstellungen und sprachlichen Lautgestalten, also Wörtern entstehen können, müssen zunächst zwei Teilprozesse, nämlich das Erkennen feiner Klangunterschiede (Diskrimination) und gleichzeitig das Ignorieren solcher Unterschiede (Konstanzerleben), integriert werden. Das Kind muss lernen, verschiedene Geräusche und Lautgebilde voneinander zu unterscheiden. Diese Fähigkeit wird im Laufe der Entwicklung mehr und mehr verfeinert, so dass sogar sehr ähnlich klingende Geräusche und Laute differenziert werden können. Diskriminiert wird jedoch nicht nur nach der Kategorie gleich-verschieden, sondern auch danach, ob etwas schneller, langsamer, höher oder tiefer gesprochen wird. Diese wahrgenommenen Unterschiede sind von Anfang an für das Kind bedeutungstragend. Eine höhere, eher leise Stimme wird von den meisten Säuglingen als angenehm erlebt, während tiefe und laute Stimmen eher Angst einflößen. Auditive Differenzierungsleistungen sind so von Anfang an eine wichtige Grundlage für das Deuten und Verstehen vorsprachlicher und später auch sprachlicher Umweltereignisse.

Gleichzeitig mit diesem feinen Diskriminationsvermögen entwickelt sich eine gegenläufige Fähigkeit. Die Kinder lernen, kleine durchaus wahrnehmbare Unterschiede zu ignorieren. Das Wort „Auto“ klingt jedesmal anders, je nachdem ob der Opa, die Mutti oder der kleine Bruder es aussprechen. Es wird in einer anderen Tonlage, Lautstärke und vielleicht sogar in einer anderen mundartlichen Einfärbung ausgesprochen. Trotz dieser feinen Unterschiede muß das Wortklangmuster „Auto“ jedesmal als dasselbe vom Kind wahrgenommen werden.

SCHNEIDER et al. (1994) sehen aufgrund ihrer umfangreichen Forschungsarbeiten in der phonologischen Bewussttheit, das heißt dem Bewusstsein und dem Zugang zur phonologischen Struktur von Sprache, eine wesentliche Voraussetzung für den Schriftspracherwerb. KÜSPERT (1998) fand bei der Sichtung vorliegender Studien, daß phonetisches Rekodieren im Arbeitsgedächtnis stattfindet. Die Bedeutung des Arbeitsgedächtnisses wird offensichtlich, wenn man sich vergegenwärtigt, daß ein Leseanfänger beim Erlesen eines Wortes zunächst jeden Buchstaben einzeln in das entsprechende Phonem dekodieren muss. Diese einzelnen Phoneme müssen solange im Arbeitsgedächtnis präsent sein, bis alle Laute des zu lesenden Wortes abgerufen sind und nun zu einem Wort zusammengfügt werden können.

Erste Begriffsbildung Wiedererkennensgedächtnis Aktivierung Aufmerksamkeitssteuerung	Repräsentanz im Gedächtnis Codierung, Decodierung – Langzeitgedächtnis (semantisches, phonematisches, ortographisches Lexikon) – Arbeitsgedächtnis – Abrufprozesse
Visuelles System – Diskrimination – Konstanzerleben – Figur-Grundwahrnehmung – räuml. Orientierung	Auditives System – Diskrimination – Konstanzerleben – Figur-Grundwahrnehmung – Phonematische Analyse – Arbeitsgedächtnis
Feinmotorische Regulation – Artikulation (Phonation, Atmung, Prosodie) – Graphomotorik – Okulomotorik	Sequentielle Regulation – Segmentierung – Zeitteilung – Sequenzgedächtnis – Automatisierung
Pausen und Unterbrechungen Start- und Stoppregeln Temporegulation	Halte-, Stell- und Gleichgewichtsreaktionen Muskeltonus
Arbeitsgedächtnis	Motivation sozial-emotionale und organismische Bedingungen

Abb. 2.3.2 Zusammenstellung der am Schriftspracherwerb beteiligten Teilfunktionen oder Untersysteme

In der Regel sind wir immer von einer Geräuschkulisse bestehend aus mehr oder weniger deutlichen Geräuschen und Stimmen umgeben. Um gezielt sprachliche Klanggestalten aufzunehmen, müssen wir die Fähigkeit entwickeln, einzelne, für die momentane Situation wichtige Geräusche oder Stimmen aus der Geräuschkulisse herauszufiltern, was uns mit Hilfe der Figur-Grundunterscheidung gelingt. Viele Lehrkräfte kennen Kinder, die zum Beispiel Arbeitsaufträge, die an die gesamte Klasse gerichtet sind, nicht verstehen, und deswegen sehr oft nachfragen. Manche dieser Kinder warten auch ab, bis die anderen mit dem Arbeiten begonnen haben und erschließen sich dann über die Beobachtung der Mitschüler die sprachlich gegebene Aufgabenstellung. Ursache für diese Schwierigkeit kann unter anderem auch eine nicht ausreichend entwickelte auditive Figur-Grundwahrnehmung sein.

Die Teilfunktionen eines funktionellen Systems dienen in der neuropsychologischen Förderdiagnostik als Grundlage für eine erste Hypothesenbildung über mögliche Ursachen und Bedingungen der vorliegenden Lernbehinderungen.

3.3 Qualitative Analyse psychometrischer Verfahren

Mit Hilfe einzelner Subtests oder Aufgabenstellungen aus psychometrischen Verfahren lassen sich die entsprechenden Teilfunktionen auf unterschiedlichem Niveau, unterschiedlich komplex und in unterschiedlichem Zusammenhang überprüfen.

Wiederum beispielhaft sollen hier einige Subtests angeführt werden, die sich dazu eignen, die spezifischen Teilfunktionen aus dem Bereich der auditiven Informationsverarbeitung zu analysieren:

* **Auditive Diskrimination**

Subtests aus Testverfahren:

Breuer/Weuffen:	Phonematische Differenzierung
Mottier-Test	
TÜKI:	Bereich H1: Wortverständnis
	Bereich J2: Reproduzierende Sprache
DRT 2/3:	Fehlerart Trennschärfe (WT)
	Fehlerart Wortdurchgliederung (WD)
TAW:	Einzelgeräusche
	Geräuschdiskrimination
	Wortlängen
	Klangeigenschaften
	Silben
Sedlak/Sindelar:	Unterscheiden von Wortpaaren
	Unterscheiden von Paaren sinnloser Wörter
DIAS:	Aufgabengruppe D und S (Unterscheiden)
Küspert:	Transfertest zur phonologischen Bewußtheit
BISC:	Laut-zu-Wort-Vergleich
	Silbensegmentierung

* **Auditives Konstanzerleben**

Subtests aus Testverfahren:

TAW:	Reimwörter
Küspert:	Reimaufgabe

BISC:	Reimproduktion Reimvergleich

* **Auditive Figur-Grundwahrnehmung**

Subtests aus Testverfahren:

TAW:	Geräuschdiskrimination Sprach-Geräuschdiskrimination
Sedlak/Sindelar:	Heraushören
DIAS:	Aufgabensammlung D und S (Figur-Grund)

4 Variation der Aufgabenstellung

Zusätzlich zur Auswahl der Aufgabenstellungen vor dem Hintergrund funktioneller Systeme besteht die neuropsychologische Förderdiagnostik noch aus einem Verfahren, das den Umgang mit den Aufgabenstellungen beschreibt: die Variation der Aufgabenstellung. Diese Methode ist in der Entwicklungstheorie von WYGOTSKI (1978, 1987) begründet.

4.1 Theorie von WYGOTSKI

Zentraler Gedanke in der Entwicklungstheorie von WYGOTSKI (1978, 1987) ist die Zone der proximalen Entwicklung. Sie wird von ihm definiert als Distanz zwischen dem aktuellen Entwicklungsniveau eines Kindes, welches bestimmt ist durch seine Fähigkeit, Probleme selbständig zu lösen und einer höheren Ebene als möglicher Entwicklung, bestimmt durch die Fähigkeit, Probleme unter Anleitung zu lösen. Die Distanz zwischen aktuellem Entwicklungsstand und potientieller Entwicklung überwindet das Kind mit Hilfe kompetenter Personen (Eltern, ältere Geschwister, Lehrer, ...). Die kompetente, sachkundige Person baut bei ihrer Hilfestellung auf bereits vorhandene Fähigkeiten und Fertigkeiten auf und konfrontiert das Kind mit Aktivitäten und Aufgaben, die ein Kompetenzniveau erfordern, das über dem aktuellen Fähigkeitsniveau liegt, aber dennoch im Bereich des dem Kind Möglichen. Sie baut Brücken zwischen den vorhandenen und neuen Fertigkeiten und Fähigkeiten. Kinder beobachten andere Menschen oder werden zum Beispiel von Erwachsenen oder anderen Kindern auf wichtige Aspekte einer Situation aufmerksam gemacht. Kinder fragen nach neuen, ihnen unbekannten Dingen und Sachverhalten und werden im Gespräch aufgeklärt. Ein älteres Geschwister unterstützt den kleineren Bruder beim Erlernen des Radfahrens, indem es neben diesem herläuft und ihn im Gleichgewicht hält. Eltern ermutigen ihr Kind, auf dem Spielplatz zum Schaukeln. Sie wählen dabei eine Schaukel, die sehr dicht über dem Boden hängt, schieben das Kind nur ganz wenig an oder setzen sich zunächst selbst auf die

Schaukel und nehmen das Kind auf ihren Schoß. Sie schaffen auf diese Weise einen benutzerfreundlichen Kontext, der ihrem Kind das Erlernen des Schaukelns möglich macht und erleichtert. Gleiches tut ein Vater, der an das Fahrrad seines Kindes, das Fahrradfahren lernen möchte, Stützräder montiert. Anleitung kann sowohl implizit als auch explizit sein. Lernen erfolgt in der Beschäftigung mit Aufgaben, an denen eine kompetente Person in irgend einer Form beteiligt ist und wird so zu einem natürlichen Nebenprodukt dieser Beschäftigung.

Förderdiagnostik hat unter diesem Gesichtspunkt nicht mehr die Aufgabe, lediglich den momentanen Entwicklungsstand festzustellen, sondern in der diagnostischen Situation soll auch der Lern- oder Entwicklungsprozess, der unter der Einwirkung eines kompetenteren Erwachsenen vonstatten geht, mit einbezogen werden. Der Erwachsene provoziert über seine Hilfestellungen diesen Lernprozess und macht auf diese Weise die Zone der nächsten Entwicklung sichtbar. Diese nächsten unter kompetenter Hilfe zu bewältigenden Entwicklungs- und Lernschritte bilden dann auch die Ausgangsbasis für weitere Fördermaßnahmen.

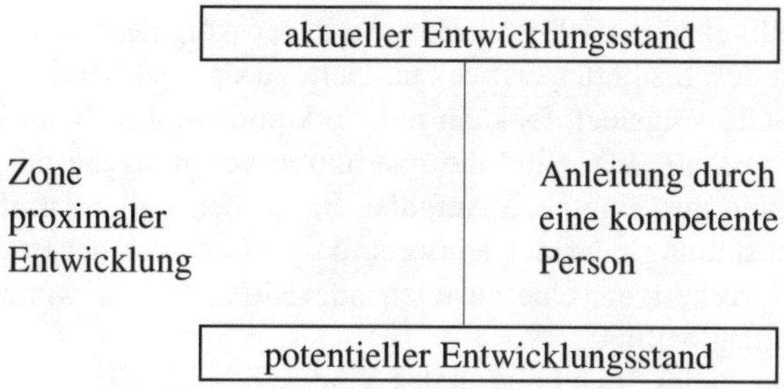

Abb. 2.3.3 Darstellung der Zone proximaler Entwicklung nach WYGOTSKI

WYGOTSKI (1974) geht von dem bekannten und unumstrittenen Sachverhalt aus, daß ein Kind, das angeleitet wird und dem Hilfen angeboten werden, immer mehr leisten und schwierigere Aufgaben lösen kann als alleine. Diese Fähigkeit, von bisher Gelerntem ausgehend, Neues mit Unterstützung aufzunehmen ist für WYGOTSKI (1974) entscheidender für die Beurteilung der geistigen Entwicklung als das lediglich Feststellen des momentanen Entwicklungsstandes. Er konnte in seinen Untersuchungen zeigen, dass zum Beispiel zwei Kinder die gleiche Anzahl von Aufgaben richtig lösen konnten. Bei einem herkömmlichen diagnostischen Vorgehen hätte man für beide Kinder den gleichen Entwicklungsstand konstatiert. Bot man ihnen jedoch bei schwierigeren, von ihnen selbständig nicht lösbaren Aufgaben, entsprechende Hilfen an, bewältigten diese beiden Kinder unterschiedlich viele und unterschiedlich schwierige Aufgabenstellung. WYGOTSKI (1974) schlussfolgert daraus, daß diese beiden Kinder anscheinend nicht auf dem gleichen geistigen Niveau stehen und ihr Entwicklungsstand eben nicht gleich ist. Vielmehr unterscheiden sie sich sehr deutlich in ihren Zonen der nächsten Entwicklung, was in seinen Untersuchungen auch Unterschiede im schulischen Lernen bedingte. Er zieht daraus den Schluss, „daß die Zone der nächsten Entwicklung für die Dynamik der intellektuellen Entwicklung und den Leistungsstand eine unmittelbarere Bedeutung besitzt als das gegenwärtige Niveau ihrer Entwicklung" (WYGOTSKI 1974, S. 237).

Aus dieser Sichtweise erwächst der Förderdiagnostik die Aufgabe, herauszufinden, welche Aufgaben ein Kind unter welcher Anleitung bewältigen kann, um damit Hinweise zu geben, was dem Kind wie als nächstes gelehrt werden kann.

4.3 Allgemeine Hinweise zur Aufgabenvariation

Für das methodische Vorgehen schlug bereits WYGOTSKI (1974) vor, die herkönmmlichen Testverfahren nicht gänzlich zu verwerfen, sondern die dort zu findenden Aufgaben zu benutzen, und sobald ein Kind bei der Lösung scheitert, entsprechende Hilfen zu geben; das heißt die Aufgabenstellung so lange zu variieren, bis das Kind zu einer Lösung fähig ist. Durch die Aufgabenvariation werden Hilfestellungen gesucht, die einem Kind das Durchschreiten der proximalen Zone der Entwicklung ermöglichen. Die gefundenen Hilfen stellen Förderstrategien dar, die ein Fortschreiten des Kindes in seinem Lernen und seiner Entwicklung ermöglichen.

Folgende grundsätzliche, bei vielen Aufgabenstellungen verwendbare Variationsmöglichkeiten sind denkbar:

* Verlängerung der Bearbeitungszeit
* mehrmaliges Wiederholen der Instruktion
  Beispiel: Im Grundintelligenztest CFT 1 werden Aufgaben vorgelegt, bei denen sich die Items über zwei Seiten des Testheftes erstrecken. Dem zu untersuchenden Kind wird jedoch immer nur eine Seite vorgelegt. Es kann nun vorkommen, dass beim Übergang von der einen auf die andere Seite dem Kind die Instruktion verlorengeht, oder es den Eindruck gewinnt, es komme nun eine neue Aufgabe. In solchen Fällen ist allein die Wiederholung der Augabenstellung oder der Hinweis, dass es auf der neuen Seite genauso weitergeht wie auf der vorherigen, eine ausreichende Hilfe, die zur weiteren erfolgreichen Aufgabenbewältigung beiträgt.
* Anpassen der Instruktion an das Sprachniveau des Kindes
  Beispiel: Im Subtest zur Figur-Grundwahrnehmung des FEW (Frostigs Entwicklungstest der visuellen Wahrnehmung) werden die Kinder aufgefordert, eine in anderen Figuren versteckte zu „umreißen". Bei Sprachverständnisschwierigkeiten hilft oft bereits die Formulierung „mit dem Stift um die Figur herumfahren".
* Vergrößerung der Vorlagen
* Pausen einlegen, kurze Arbeistphasen, Verteilen der Aufgaben auf mehrer Tage
* Experimentierphase zulassen
* Aufgaben in Teilschritten anbieten
* Vormachen, Aufgaben beispielhaft lösen
* Reduzieren der Reizvielfalt
  Beispiel: Zur Bearbeitung des ersten Subtests im CFT 1 wird dem Kind eine Seite des Testheftes vorgelegt, auf der über 70 Zeichen und Bildchen in acht Reihen angeordnet sind. Es kann nun sein, daß ein Kind durch diese Reizfülle verwirrt ist. Deckt man den größten Teil der Vorlage mit einem weißen Blatt Papier ab, wird diesem Kind ein erfolgreiches Bearbeiten möglich.
* Sprache als Strukturierungshilfe einsetzen
  Beispiel: Der Hamburg-Wechsel-Intelligenztest für Kinder (HAWIK-R) enthält den Subtest Bilder ordnen. Dabei werden dem Kind mehrere Bildkärtchen vorgelegt, die eine Geschichte erzählen. Allerdings stimmt die Reihenfolge der Bildkärtchen nicht. Das Kind soll nun die Bildkärtchen so ordnen, dass sich eine in sich stimmige Geschichte ergibt. Bietet das Kind als Lösung eine unlogische Reihenfolge an, kann man es bitten, die vor ihm liegende Geschichte zu erzählen. Einigen Kindern fallen beim Umsetzen ihrer Geschichte in Sprache die logischen Ungereimtheiten auf und sie korrigieren ihre Lösung.

Nimmt man solche Variationen in der Aufgabenstellung vor, ist natürlich eine quantitative Auswertung nicht mehr möglich, da die Normierung psychometrischer Verfahren an eine möglichst exakte Standardisierung gebunden ist.

Dafür erhält der Untersucher aber sehr schnell eine Reihe wichtiger Hinweise über die individuellen Lernbedingungen eines Kindes. Wird die Untersuchung immer dann beendet, wenn das Kind die Aufgaben nicht mehr lösen kann, so hat der Untersucher für die weitere Förderung kaum verwertbare Erkenntnisse gewonnen. Streng genommen weiß er nur: er hat dem Kind zum Beispiel eine Reihe von Bildchen vorgelegt und es war nicht in der Lage, diese in eine logische Reihenfolge zu bringen. Findet er aber über die Variation der Aufgabenstellung heraus, dass die Versprachlichung zur korrekten Lösung führt, kann er dieses Wissen von nun an bei ähnlichen Aufgaben hilfreich einsetzen. In gleicher Weise können auch die anderen einfachen und allgemeinen Variationen diagnostisch interpretiert werden und zu konkreten Hilfestellungen führen.

4.3 Spezifisches Beispiel

In vorliegenden spezifischen, praktisch verwertbaren Beispielen werden die Aufgabenstellungen systematisch variiert. Dies bedeutet, daß sich die Variation der Aufgabenstellung an klar definierten Kategorien oder Merkmalen orientiert.

GRAICHEN (1975) erläutert die Methode der systematischen Aufgabenvariation anhand eines Fallbeispiels und zeigt dabei die unterschiedlichen Interpretationsmöglichkeiten der möglichen Fehlleistungen. Er stellt einem fünfjährigen Jungen im Verlauf des Kramer-Intelligenztests folgende Aufgabe: 20 Holzperlen liegen in einer Schachtel vor dem Kind und es soll dem Untersucher vier Perlen geben.

1. Reagiert das Kind weder auf die sprachliche Aufforderung noch auf die Geste der aufgehaltenen Hand, könnte eine autistische Störung vorliegen, die mit weiteren Aufgaben untersucht werden müsste. So wäre an dieser Stelle zu klären, ob das Kind seine Mitarbeit beispielsweise nur bei sprachlichen Aufgaben verweigert oder nur bei bestimmten Personen oder grundsätzlich immer.
2. Geht das Kind zwar auf die Aufforderung ein und gibt eine Perle, fängt dann aber an die Perlen im Raum herumzuwerfen, steht auf und wendet sich anderen Gegenständen zu usw., wäre das unter Umständen ein Hinweise auf eine Schwäche in der Oberprogrammsteuerung mit einem Verlust der Aufgabenstruktur, die bei anderen Aufgabenstellungen ebenfalls zu beobachten sein müsste.
3. Das Kind lässt sich auf die Aufgabenstellung ein und bleibt auch im Programm, entnimmt der Schachtel jedoch eine falsche Anzahl von Perlen.

3.1. Eine erste Hypothese zur Erklärung dieser Fehlleistung könnte das Vorliegen einer peripheren Hörbehinderung sein. Dem Kind wird deshalb die gleiche Aufgabe noch einmal mittels Gestik gestellt und die Anzahl der Perlen mit den Fingern gezeigt. Einem schwerhörigen oder gar tauben Kind würde die Lösung der Aufgabe nun sofort gelingen.

3.2. Auch auf die gestische Aufforderung gibt das Kind die falsche Anzahl von Perlen, was auf eine Lernminderung in diesem kognitiven Bereich aufmerksam macht. Als nächstes wird das Kind aufgefordert, zu zählen („Wie weit kannst Du denn schon zählen"). Das Kind nennt nun zum Beispiel verschiedene Zahlwörter aber in falscher Reihenfolge. Hier könnte man eine Sprachentwicklungsstörung vermuten, die zurückzuführen ist auf Schwierigkeiten bei der Bildung von Übergangswahrscheinlichkeiten und einem daraus resultierenden Problem beim Abruf sprachlicher Elemente in der richtigen Reihenfolge. Dies erschwert möglicherweise auch den Aufbau eines konstanten Mengenbegriffes, was ein Abzählen-können voraussetzt.

3.3. Das Kind gibt die Zahlenfolge in der richtigen Reihenfolge wider, aber das Abzählen gelingt nicht sicher. Dies wird sichtbar, wenn die gleiche Anzahl von Perlen, wie sie im freien Zählen erreicht wird, vor dem Kind aufgereiht wird, und es gebeten wird sie zu zählen. Zeigt das Kind völlig asynchron zum Nennen der Zahlwörter auf die Perlen, indem sein zeigender Finger weiterwandert ohne dass ein Zahlwort genannt wird oder umgekehrt, könnte die Schwierigkeit hier in der Koordination von Bewegungsabläufen und Denkvollzügen liegen.

Es ließe sich aber auch noch vermuten, dass dieses Kind in anderen motorischen Leistungen auffällig ist und ihm die Koordination verschiedener motorischer Systeme schwerfällt. Diesem Verdacht wird nachgegangen, indem von ihm eine Reihe diadochokinetisch fortgesetzter, manueller Übungen gefordert werden.

Am Ende seiner Ausführungen weist GRAICHEN (1975) noch darauf hin, dass es für solche Aufgabenvariationen kein festes Kochbuch geben kann, sondern dieses Vorgehen nur durchführen kann, wer ein breites Fachwissen parat hat.

Weitere Anregungen zur Variation der Aufgabestellungen finden sich in der Tübinger Luria-Christensen Neuropsychologischen Untersuchungsreihe für Kinder (TÜKI) sowie bei KORNMANN und RÖSSLER (1986) und KORNMANN (1986)

5 Zusammenfassung

Eine neuropsychologisch orientierte Förderdiagnostik besteht aus zwei Teilen. Einmal führt das funktionelle System, das zum vorliegenden Problem erstellt wird, zu wissenschaftlich abgesicherten Hypothesen über die möglichen Teilfunktionen, die dieses Problemverhalten bedingen könnten. Beispielhaft wurde dies für den Schriftspracherwerb aufgezeigt. Daran anschließend sucht der Diagnostiker nach geeigneten Aufgabenstellungen zur Überprüfung der einzelnen Teilfunktionen, die er in der Fülle der vorliegenden Überprüfungsverfahren finden kann.

Im zweiten Teil der neuropsychologisch orientierten Förderdiagnostik überprüft er seine Ausgangshypothesen mit den ausgewählten Aufgabenstellungen und sucht über die Variation der Aufgabenstellung nach geeigneten Hilfs- und Fördermöglichkeiten.

Literatur

Bookheimer, S.Y. u. Dapretto, M. Functional Neuroimaging of Language in Children: Current Directions and Future Challenges. In Thatcher, R.W., Lyon, G.R., Rumsey, J. u. Krasnegor, N. (Hg.), Developmental Neuroimaging: Mapping the Development of Brain and Behavior. San Diego 1996, 157-167

Graichen, J. Kann man legasthenische und dyskalkulatorische Schulschwierigkeiten voraussagen? Praxis der Kinderpsychologie und Kinderpsychiatrie 24, 1975, 52-57

Horwitz, B., Rumsey, J.M. u. Donohue, B.C. Functional connectivity of the angular gyrus in normal reading and dyslexia. Proceeding of the National Academy of Sciences of the USA 95, 1998, 8939-8944

Kornmann, R. Förderdiagnostisch orientierte Variation der Testbedingungen bei ausgewählten Aufgaben des HAWIK. Zeitschrift für Heilpädagogik 37, 1986, 674-684

Kornmann, R. u. Rössler, G. Variation der Untersuchungsbedingungenals förderdiagnostisches Prinzip am Beispiel eines Verfahrens zur Prüfung der Fähigkeit zur Lautunterscheidung. In Kornmann, R., Meister, H. u. Schlee, J. (Hg.), Förderdiagnostik. Konzept und Realisierungsmöglichkeiten. Heidelberg 1986, 102-106

Küspert, P. Phonologische Bewußtheit und Schriftspracherwerb. Zu den Effekten vorschulischer Förderung der phonologischen Bewußtheit auf den Erwerb des Lesens und Rechtschreibens. Frankfurt 1998

Luria, A.R. The working brain. An Introduction to Neuropsychology. London 1973

Paulesu, E., Frith, U., Snowling, M., Gallagher, A., Morton, J., Frackowiak, R. u. Frith, C. Is developmental dyslexia a disconnection syndrome? Evidence from PET scanning. Brain 119, 1996, 143-157

Pugh, K.R., Shaywitz, B.A., Shaywitz, S.E., Constable, R.T., Skudlarski, P., Fulbright, R.K., Bronen, R.A., Shankweiler, D.P., Katz, L., Fletcher, J.M. u. Gore, J.C. Cerebral organization of component processes in reading. Brain 119, 1996, 1221-1238

Rumsey, J.M., Nace, K., Donohue, B., Wise, D., Maisog, J.M. u. Andreason, P. A Positron Emission Tomographic Study of Impaired Word Recognition and Phonological Processing in Dyslexic Men. Archives of Neurology 54, 1997, 562-573

Schneider, W., Vise, M., Reimers, P. u. Blaesser, B. Auswirkungen eines Trainings der sprachlichen Bewußtheit auf den Schriftspracherwerb in der Schule. Zeitschrift für Pädagogische Psychologie 8, 1994, 177-188

Wygotski, L.S. Denken und Sprechen. Frankfurt 1974

Wygotski, L.S. Mind in Society: The Development of Higher Psychological Processes. Cambridge 1978

Wygotski, L.S. Ausgewählte Schriften. Band 2: Arbeiten zur psychischen Entwicklung der Persönlichkeit. Köln 1987

Testverfahren:

BISC	Bielefelder Screening zur Früherkennung von Lese-Rechtschreib-schwierigkeiten
Breuer/Weuffen	Lernschwierigkeiten am Schulanfang.Weinheim 1994
DIAS	Diagnostisches Inventar auditiver Alltagshandlungen
DRT 2/3	Diagnostischer Rechtschreibtest für die Klassen 2 und 3
Küspert	Phonologische Bewußtheit und Schriftspracherwerb. Ffm. 1998
Mottier-Test	Teil des Züricher Lesetests
Sedlak/Sindelar	Hurra ich kann's. Wien 1994
TAW	Test zur auditiven Wahrnehmung
TÜKI	Tübinger-Luria-Christensen Neuropsychologische Untersuchungsreihe für Kinder

2.4 Die Legasthenie-Diagnostik durch den Schulpsychologen

Ingrid Buchhorn

1 Der LRS-Erlass als Voraussetzung schulpsychologischen Handelns

Bei der Arbeit der Schulpsychologin mit lese- und rechtschreibschwachen Kindern ist die Berücksichtigung des in Nordrhein-Westfalen geltenden Erlasses des damaligen Kultusministeriums mit dem Titel „Förderung von Schülerinnen und Schülern bei besonderen Schwierigkeiten im Erlernen des Lesens und Schreibens (LRS)" vom 19.07.91 unerlässlich (Richtlinien von 1991).

Die Grundschullehrer haben demgemäß eine wichtige und anspruchsvolle Aufgabe zu erfüllen, die in der Praxis nicht häufig genug betont werden muss, besonders wenn es um die Einrichtung von Förderkursen geht.

Die Vermittlung der Kulturtechniken des Lesens und Schreibens ist vorrangig eine Aufgabe der Grundschule; die Weiterentwicklung der in der Grundschule erworbenen Fähigkeiten des Textelesens, -verständnisses und der Rechtschreibleistungen müssen die weiterführenden Schulen übernehmen.

Die Grundschullehrer haben den Lese- und Rechtschreibunterricht sorgfältig nach den Richtlinien und Lehrplänen durchzuführen und die Entwicklung des Lernprozesses „gründlich abzusichern".

Diese Aufgaben gelten gemeinhin als selbstverständlich und werden auch von der Grundschule immer wieder gegenüber nichtschulischen Einrichtungen betont.

Im Einzelnen werden dann im Erlass von den Grundschullehrern – wie ich meine – sehr differenzierte Aufgaben verlangt. Sie sollen die Kinder ihrer Klasse gründlich und intensiv bezüglich ihres Leistungsniveaus und ihrer Lernfortschritte beobachten.

Bei der Durchführung des Lese- und Schreiblehrgangs sollen sie die spezifischen Sprach- und Sprechfähigkeiten der einzelnen Kinder „gezielt" fördern, desweiteren ihre visuellen und auditiven Wahrnehmungsfähigkeiten, ihre grob- und feinmotorischen Koordinationsfähigkeiten entwickeln, um Schwierigkeiten beim Erlernen des Lesens und Schreibens zu verhindern.

Dies setzt umfangreiche, gut fundierte, psychologische Kenntnisse der individuellen Problematik der Kinder bei ihren Rechtschreibproblemen voraus. Weiter werden in den Förderkatalog auch allgemeine Lernvoraussetzungen aufgenommen, die die Lehrkraft zu beachten hat: z. B. Steigerung der Lernfreude, des Selbstvertrauens, der Konzentration, der Denkfähigkeit und der Umgang mit Misserfolg.

Über die zu ergreifenden Fördermaßnahmen wird folgendes ausgeführt: Sie sollen zu einem frühen Zeitpunkt einsetzen und über einen „angemessenen" Zeitraum durchgeführt werden, um die Entstehung der Lernschwierigkeiten zu verhindern und zu beheben. Mit den Eltern sollte ein reger Austausch über die Lernerfolge ihrer Kinder stattfinden.

Die Fördermaßnahmen – seien es solche im Rahmen des differenzierten Unterrichts oder aber auch als zusätzliche über die Stundentafel hinaus – fordern anspruchsvolle Lernanalysen für jedes betroffene Kind: Schulische, soziale, emotionale, kognitive und physiologische Bedingungen des Lern- und Arbeitsverhaltens sollen berücksichtigt werden.

Ebenso sollen die Förderziele – wie bereits oben beim normalen Unterricht angesprochen – vielfältige Aspekte aufnehmen: die Groß-, Fein- und Graphomotorik, visuelle und auditive Wahrnehmung, sprachliche Fähigkeiten und generelle Merkfähigkeit, Konzentration.

Dies zu den hochgesteckten Zielen des Erlasses, die sowohl eine sorgfältig durchgeführte Diagnostik als auch gezielte Fördermaßnahmen einschließen.

Wie sieht die Ist-Situation aus?
Nach meiner Umfrage Ende September 1999 sind von den 28 Grundschulen Hamms an 18 Grundschulen Förderkurse außerhalb der Stundentafel für das Schuljahr 1999/2000 eingerichtet worden (das sind 64% der Schulen mit insgesamt 55 Kursen, durchschnittlich 2 pro Schule in den Klassen 2, 3 und 4, Gruppenstärke 6 bis 10 Kinder)

Die inhaltliche Gestaltung der Fördermaßnahmen erfolgt überwiegend nach einem Konzept der Regionalen Schulberatungsstelle der Stadt Hamm, das vor zehn Jahren entwickelt und in den folgenden Jahren den kooperierenden Schulen vorgestellt wurde (Buchhorn, I., 1998).

Das Konzept berücksichtigt insbesondere den Förderaspekt der auditiven Wahrnehmungsdifferenzierung und die Gliederungsfähigkeit.

Als Gründe für eine Beschränkung bzw. die Nichteinführung von LRS-Kursen wird die personelle Problematik an den Schulen genannt. Generell wird von den Schulen ein größerer Bedarf an notwendigen Unterstützungsmaßnahmen durchaus erkannt; es wird sowohl im Schulbereich als auch in der Öffentlichkeit eine kontinuierliche Verschlechterung der Lese- und Rechtschreibfähigkeiten der heranwachsenden Generation beklagt, dennoch wird meines Erachtens die Notwendigkeit einer verstärkten Förderung aber nicht in ausreichendem Maße umgesetzt.

In der Schulberatungsstelle und den anderen Beratungsstellen der Stadt zeichnet sich entsprechend ein hoher Förderbedarf ab. Circa 25 bis 30 Prozent der Eltern führen als Anmeldegrund die Lese- und Rechtschreibproblematik ihrer Kinder an, die zum großen Teil von schwerwiegenden psychischen Problemen begleitet werden. Dieser hohe Bedarf steht in einem Mißverhältnis zu den schulischen Fördermaßnahmen, die trotz langjähriger Bemühungen von Seiten der Beratungsinstitutionen nicht ausgeweitet wurden. Offensichtlich gibt es institutionelle Bedingungen, an denen eine ausreichende Versorgung der LRS-Kinder scheitert.

Das sind meines Erachtens häufig Gründe in der unterschiedlichen Wahrnehmung von Eltern und Lehrer/Schulen bezüglich der LRS-Problematik der Kinder:

- von den oft unendlichen Bemühungen der Eltern bei den Hausaufgaben ihrer Kinder bekommen die Lehrer wenig mit.
- das Auswendiglernen von Diktaten durch häusliches Üben oft bis ins 4. Schuljahr hinein,
- die relativ günstigen Ergebnisse der „fleißigen“ Schüler und Schülerinnen verstellen dann den Blick der Lehrkräfte in Bezug auf das Ausmaß der Lese- und Rechtschreibstörung der betroffenen Kinder.
- Nicht unerwähnt bleiben soll die noch immer unaufgeklärte Einstellung von einzelnen Lehrkräften gegenüber dem Phänomen der Lese- und Rechtschreibstörung. Sie wird häufig gar nicht als existent und wissenschaftlich unbegründet gesehen oder man findet

noch „Uraltkonzepte" von der „b-p"-Vertauschung als typische und einzig anerkanntes Störungsbild der LRS in den Köpfen vor.

2 Die diagnostischen Maßnahmen der Schulberatungsstelle

Der Erlass sieht in besonders schwierigen Fällen die Einschaltung von Schulpsychologen vor. Sie sollen beratend tätig sein, etwa bei der Diagnose-Feststellung einer LRS und gegebenenfalls LRS-Kinder fördern.

Ganz allgemein bemühen sich die Psychologen der Schulberatungsstelle darum, zu einem möglichst frühen Zeitpunkt das Lese- und Schreibversagen festzustellen, deren Schwere und Ausmaß zu bestimmen und die spezifischen Schwierigkeiten des Störungsbildes zu ermitteln.

Die Ergebnisse der testpsychologischen Untersuchungen und weiterer diagnostischer Informationen werden, wenn die Eltern zustimmen, an die betreffenden Lehrkräfte weiterzugeben.

2.1 Die bei der LRS-Diagnose angewandten Testverfahren

Die folgenden Lese- und Rechtschreibtests werden neben einer ausführlichen Intelligenzdiagnostik in der Schulberatungsstelle der Stadt Hamm angewandt:

Lese- und Rechtschreibtests
(in der Regionalen Schulberatungsstelle Hamm angewandt)

Vorschulbereich

Abkürzung	Verfahren	Inhalte der Verfahren	Testalter	Autoren	Verlag
DP I	Schuleingangsdiagnostik am Schulanfang – Verfahren zur Diagnose sprachbezogener Wahrnehmungsleistungen von älteren Vorschul-kindern und von Schülern mit Lernschwierig-keiten	Überprüfung der optisch-graphomotorischen, akustisch-phonematischen, kinästhetisch-artikulatorischen, melodischen und rhythmischen Differenzierungsfähigkeit	5- bis 6-jährige Kinder	H. Breuer und M. Weuffen	Beltz-Verlag
BISC	Bielefelder Screening zur Früherkennung von Lese- und Rechtschreibschwierigkeiten	Pseudowörter-Nachsprechen, Reimen, Wort-Vergleich-Suchaufgabe, Laute-Assoziieren, Farben benennen von Objekten, richtige Farben benennen von Objekten, Laute heraushören	a. 10 Monate vor der Einschulung, b. 4 Monate vor der Einschulung	H. Jansen, G. Mannhaupt, H. Marx, H. Skowronek	Hogrefe-Verlag

Grundschulbereich

Ab-kürzung	Verfahren	Inhalte der Verfahren	Testalter	Autoren	Verlag
DBL Frühform	Diagnostische Bilderliste – Frühform	Wörter zu dargestellten Bildern schreiben	ca. 8 Monate nach der Einschulung	L. Dummer-Smoch	Veris-Verlags-GmbH
DBL	Diagnostische Bilderliste Form A, B	Wörter zu dargestellten Bildern schreiben	Ende 1. Kl., Anfang 2. Kl.	L. Dummer-Smoch	Veris-Verlags-GmbH
ZLT	Zürcher Lesetest	Wortlisten und Lesetexte	ab 4. Monat 2. Schuljahr	H. Linder, H. Grissemann	Huber-Verlag
ZLVT	Zürcher Leseverständnistest	Lesetexte mit Bildvorlagen, Satzauswahl, Handlungs-Testaufgaben	4. bis 6. Schuljahr	H. Linder, H. Grissemann, H. Marx	Huber-Verlag
Knuspel-L	Knuspels Leseaufgaben	Hörverstehen, Rekodieren, Dekodieren und Leseverstehen	Ende 1. bis Ende 4. Schuljahr	H. Marx	Hogrefe-Verlag
TGR ½	Test Grundanforderungen Rechtschreibung	Feststellung der Rechtschreib- und Lesefertigkeit, Analyse der Rechtschreibschwierigkeiten	Ende der 1. bis Mitte der 2. Kl.	P. Rathenow und D. Peh	Beltz-Verlag
RST 1	Rechtschreibtest	Wortlücken in Sätzen ergänzen	Ende 1. Kl., Anfang 2. Kl.	P. Rathenow, U. Raatz	Beltz-Verlag
DRT 2	Diagnostischer Rechtschreibtest	Wortlücken in Sätzen ergänzen	Ende 2. Kl., Anfang 3. Kl.	R. Müller	Beltz-Verlag
DRT 3	Diagnostischer Rechtschreibtest	Wortlücken in Sätzen ergänzen	Ende 3. Kl, Anfang 4. Kl.	R. Müller	Beltz-Verlag
DRT 4	Diagnostischer Rechtschreibtest	Wortlücken in Sätzen ergänzen	Mitte 4. Kl.	M. Grund, G. Haug, C. L. Naumann	Beltz-Verlag
WRT 4 – 5	Westermann-Rechtschreibtest	Wortlücken in Sätzen ergänzen	Mitte 4. Kl.	P. Rathenow	Westermann-Verlag
TEKO	Testbatterie zur Erfassung kognitiver Operationen	Substanzerhaltung (SE), Zahlerhaltung (ZE), Klasseninklusion (KI), Matrizen (MA), Raumlage (RL), Asymmetrische Sereation (AS), Ordinale Zuordnung (OZ), Reihenfolge (RF)	5;0 bis 8;0 Jahre	W. Winkelmann	Westermann-Verlag

Abb. 2.4.1 Lese- und Rechtschreibtests (in der Regionalen Schulberatungsstelle Hamm angewandt)

2.1.1 Ausführungen zum Bielefelder Screening zur Früherkennung von Lese- und Rechtschreibschwierigkeiten (BISC)

Ich halte es für wichtig, zwei neue Verfahren der LRS-Diagnostik vorzustellen und näher zu erläutern, deren wissenschaftlichen Ansätze meines Erachtens gut fundiert sind.

Das **BISC** (Jansen, H., Mannhaupt, G., Marx, H. und Skowronek, H., 1999) ist ein Verfahren zur Früherkennung von Lese- und Rechtschreibschwierigkeiten, das bereits vor dem Eintritt in die Schule einsetzbar ist. Es überprüft schon vor der Phase des Schriftspracherwerbs die mit diesen Lernprozessen verknüpften spezifischen Fähigkeiten und Fertigkeiten. Damit können dann Vorhersagen über den zukünftigen Erfolg beim Erlernen des Lesens und Schreibens gemacht werden. Die sogenannten Prädiktoren gelten als mit hoher Wahrscheinlichkeit zutreffende Vorhersagefaktoren (= 92,2%, Marx, H., Jansen, H., 1999).

Es sind vor allem die Aspekte der lautlichen Qualitäten der gesprochenen Sprache und das auf sprachliche Qualitäten bezogene Aufmerksamkeitsverhalten und der Gedächtniszugriff, die auf dem Prüfstand stehen.

Das **BISC** enthält Aufgaben, die

- eine Einsicht in die phonologische Struktur der Sprache und Analyse-/Synthesefähigkeiten phonologischer Einheiten erfordern.
- Reimwörter erkennen: z.B.: Weg – Steg, Kind – Glas,
  Silben-Segmentieren: z.B.: fin – den, Fe – der – ball
  Anlaut zu Wörtern finden: z.B.: au – Auto, ei – Oma,
  Laute zu einem Gesamtwort zusammenfügen: z.B.: Ei – s, M – aus
- die die schnelle Abrufbarkeit von Assoziationen zwischen Bildobjekten und Farben erfassen. Sie stellen ähnliche Anforderungen an das Kind wie die schnelle Abrufbarkeit von Laut-/Buchstabenentsprechungen des Schulkindes („Schnelles-Benennen-Farben“: z.B: Salat – grün, Tomate – rot)
- die das Behalten vorgegebener phonetischer Strukturen (unterschiedlich lange Silbenfolgen) und ihre entsprechend korrekte Wiedergabe erfordern (Pseudowörter – Nachsprechen: z.B.: Sam – bam – bu – la) die eine Steuerung der Aufmerksamkeit auf visuell vorgegebene Strukturen und das Erkennen relevanter Unterschiede anhand von Vergleichen dieser Strukturen verlangen (ein Testwort soll mit mehreren Wörtern verglichen werden: z. B. „Laut“ –mit Laut – Laub – Leid – Land)

2.1.2 Ausführungen zu Knuspels Leseaufgaben (Knuspel-L)

Der **Knuspel-L** (Marx, H., 1998) ist ein Verfahren zur Feststellung des Niveaus grundlegender Lesefertigkeiten und des Leseverständnisses (als Einzel- und Gruppentest einsetzbar). Mit ihm können Aussagen über den Zusammenhang und die Abhängigkeit von verschiedenen Lesefertigkeiten gemacht werden. Das Modell, das dem Testaufbau zugrunde liegt, bezieht neben speziellen Lesefertigkeiten auch das Hörverstehen mit ein und berücksichtigt insbesondere drei spezifische Lesefertigkeiten:

1. Lesen als Rekodierung,
2. Lesen als Dekodierung,
3. Lesen als Verstehen von schriftsprachlichen Äußerungen

zu 1: Mit Rekodierfähigkeit wird die Verarbeitung von Schriftsymbolen zu intern repräsentierten phonologischen Informationen verstanden. Das erlesene Wort muss dabei vom Kind – selbst bei einer exakten Übertragung der Schriftinformation in ihre lautliche Repräsentation einschließlich einer normgerechten Aussprache – nicht unbedingt verstanden werden.

Damit die Rekodierung gelingt, müssen eine Vielzahl von Fertigkeiten vorhanden bzw. ausgebildet sein. Ich nenne nur einige:

Buchstabenkenntnis, Diskriminationsfähigkeit für Zeichengestalten und für deren entsprechende phonetische Realisierungen, Gedächtnis für Graphem- und Phonemkorrespondenzen, Fähigkeit des Segmentierens, Sprachentwicklungsstand und intellektuelle Fertigkeiten.

Geprüft wird das Rekodieren anhand ein- oder zweisilbiger, orthografisch korrekt geschriebener Wortpaare, die abhängig von ihrer Schreibweise entweder gleich oder verschieden ausgesprochen werden. Das Kind hat die Aufgabe zu entscheiden, ob die angebotenen Wortpaare gleich klingen oder nicht.

zu 2: Zunächst muss als Voraussetzung die Rekodierungsfähigkeit gegeben sein, nämlich die korrekte Umsetzung von Schriftsymbolen in die entsprechenden phonologischen Repräsentanzen. Diese müssen es erlauben, dass nun zusätzlich die Erfassung der Wortbedeutung möglich ist.

Als Voraussetzungen gelten hierbei die korrekte Aussprache des Wortes, das orthografische Wissen und der Zugriff zum semantischen Bestand der Sprache.

Aufgabe des Kindes ist es zu prüfen, ob die 40 dargebotenen Wörter mit unbekannter Schreibweise als semantisch sinnvolle Wörter – bei korrekter Rekodierung – gelten können oder nicht.

zu 3: Mit dem Lesen als Verstehen schriftsprachlicher Äußerungen ist auf der Basis der Re- und Dekodierfähigkeit das Erfassen von Sinnzusammenhängen auf der Satz- und Textebene gemeint. Komplexe Textstrukturen wie Wortwahl, Grammatik, Syntax und inhaltlichen Kenntnisse müssen in den Verarbeitungsprozess mit einbezogen sein.

Die Auswertungsmöglichkeiten des Tests sind vielfältig. Es können Vergleiche zwischen Hörverstehen und dem Verstehen schriftsprachlicher Äußerungen vorgenommen werden und Vergleiche zwischen dem sogenannten Knuspel-Score I „Vorläuferfertigkeit für das verstehende Lesen“ und dem Knuspel-Score II, der Lesefähigkeit. Darüber hinaus sind weitere, sehr detaillierte Untersuchungsmöglichkeiten der Lesefertigkeit und Lesefähigkeit von Kindern möglich.

2.2 Fehleranalyse am Beispiel von 4 Rechtschreibprotokollen

Anhand der Rechtschreibprotokolle von vier Kindern, die der Schulberatungsstelle vorgestellt wurden, werde ich nun auf die Schwierigkeiten der Kinder genauer eingehen.

Zunächst komme ich auf die Schreibprobleme zu sprechen, die bei ca. 10 Prozent der Kinder im 1. Schuljahr auftreten und mit Wahrnehmungsfehlern bezeichnet werden. Diese setzen sich in weiteren Schuljahren fort, insbesondere dann, wenn keine speziellen Fördermaßnahmen vorgenommen werden.

Das Protokoll der Diagnostischen Bilderliste von Nico nach einem Jahr Lese- und Schreiblehrgang belegt eindrucksvoll seine Schwierigkeiten in der auditiven Wahrnehmung.

Es sind insbesondere die Fehler, die aufgrund mangelnder phonologischer Bewußtheit und von Problemen mangelnder Segmentierungsfähigkeit entstanden sind. Sie ermöglichten ihm keine adäquate Analyse der Lautstruktur von vorgegebenen Wörtern.

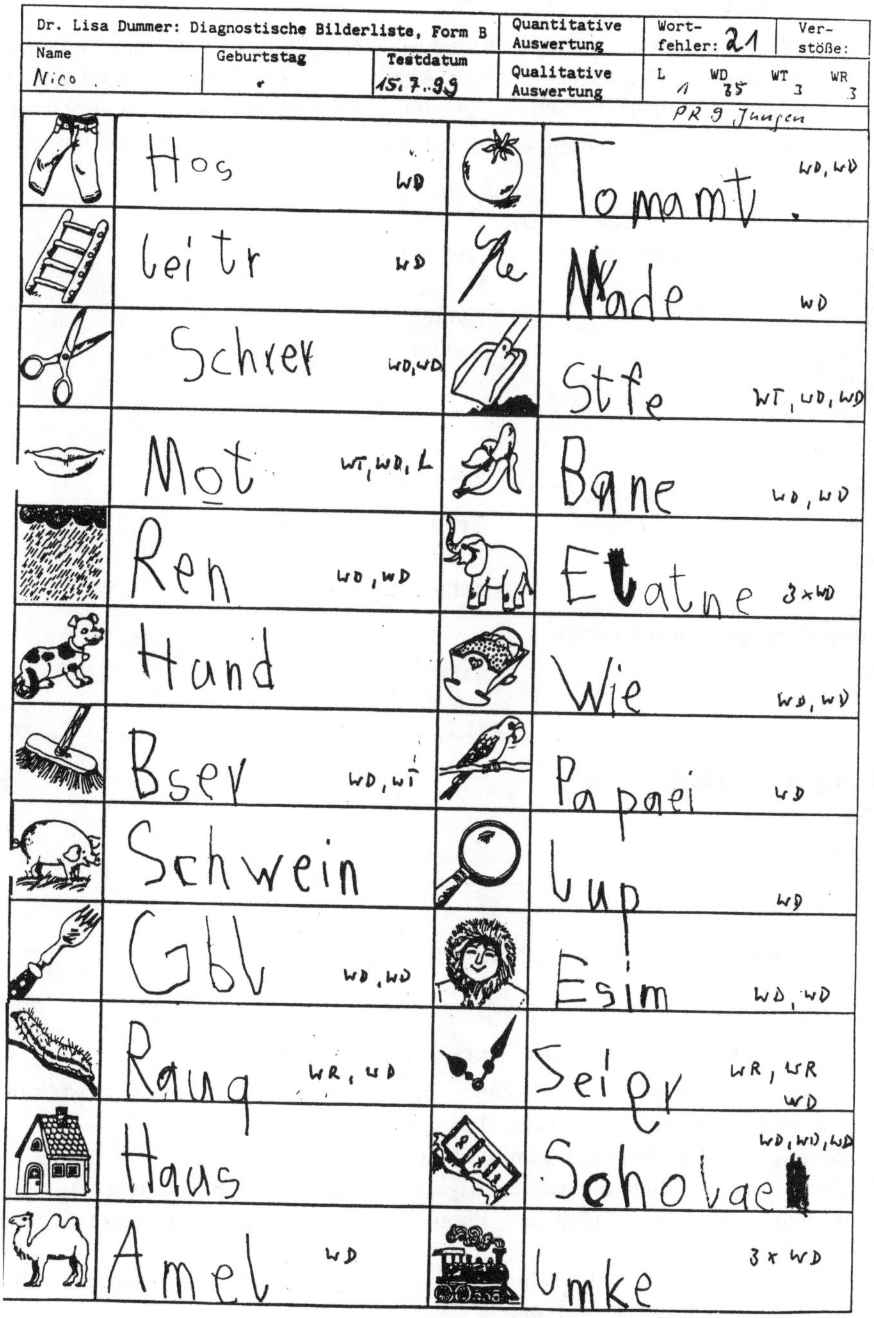

Dr. Lisa Dummer: Diagnostische Bilderliste, Form B			Quantitative Auswertung	Wort-fehler: 21	Ver-stöße:
Name: Nico	Geburtstag	Testdatum: 15.7.99	Qualitative Auswertung	L 1, WD 35, WT 3, WR 3	
				PR 9 Jungen	

Wort	Fehler	Wort	Fehler
Hos	WD	Tomamt	WD, WD
leitr	WD	Nade	WD
Schrer	WD, WD	Stfe	WT, WD, WD
Mot	WT, WD, L	Bane	WD, WD
Ren	WD, WD	Eatne	3 x WD
Hand		Wie	WD, WD
Bser	WD, WT	Papaei	WD
Schwein		lup	WD
Gbl	WD, WD	Esim	WD, WD
Raug	WR, WD	Seier	WR, WR, WD
Haus		Soholae	WD, WD, WD
Amel	WD	Umke	3 x WD

Abbildung 2: Diagnostische Bilderliste, Nico

Abb. 2.4.2 Diagnostische Bilderliste, Nico

2.2.1 Fehlerarten der Diagnostischen Bilderliste

Die Abbildung 2.4.3 Fehlerarten der Diagnostische Bilderliste führt die einzelnen Fehlerkategorien auf und nennt Beispiele, während in der Abbildung 2.4.4: Kriterien des Lese- und Schreibversagens im 1. Schuljahr die Schwierigkeiten der Kinder beim Lesen und Schreiben nach einem Jahr Unterricht nach phänomenologischen Gesichtspunkten umfassend dargestellt werden.

1. Wortdurchgliederungsfehler (WD):

reduzierter Wortumfang	erweiterter Wortumfang
Schin__	Hasen
Has__	Kammel
Leitr	Laeiter
Bane	
Rakte	
Schokld	

2. Wahrnehmungstrennschärfe (WT):

Kabel	Tefel
Gapel	Saun
Panane	Schukulade

3. Wahrnehmungsrichtung (WR):

Wagne	Magen
Rakeet	aun
Besne	Gadel

4. Lautgetreue Schreibweise:

hant
munt
Schine
Lokomotiwe

Abb. 2.4.3 Fehlerarten der Diagnostischen Bilderliste

Kriterien des Schreibversagens im 1. Schuljahr

- Phonem-Graphem-Korrespondenzen können nicht vorgenommen werden (das Prinzip wird nicht erkannt, Anbieten von „Scheinlösungen“)
- Die Kodierung erfordert überdurchschnittlich viel Zeit.
- Die Kodierung erfolgt fehlerhaft (von niedriger bis zu hoher Fehlerbandbreite)
  1. aufgrund mangelnder Fähigkeit, Phonemstrukturen vollständig zu analysieren (➔ „Wortskelette“)
  2. aufgrund mangelnder Fähigkeit, die Reihenfolge der Phoneme innerhalb einer Struktur zu erkennen (➔ Serialität)
  3. aufgrund mangelnder Fähigkeit, einzelne Phoneme trennscharf wahrzunehmen.
  4. aufgrund mangelnder Fähigkeit, die grafischen Zeichen zur Verfügung zu haben bzw. sie korrekt wiedergeben zu können.

Abb. 2.4.4 Kriterien des Schreibversagens im 1. Schuljahr

Zu den in der Liste der Kriterien für das Schreibversagen genannten „**Wahrnehmungsfehlern**" kommen im Verlauf der folgenden Grundschuljahre die sogenannten **Regelfehler** hinzu, so dass das Fehlerrepertoire der LRS-Kinder recht umfangreich werden kann. Die Auflistung ist selbstverständlich abhängig von den in den Tests verwandten Prüfwörtern des DRT 2, 3 und 4.

In den folgenden Fehlerprotokollen der Kinder Sebastian, André und Sabrina nach 2, 3 und 4 Schuljahren kann man sehr deutlich die Bandbreite der Fehlerarten – spezifisch für jedes Kind – sehen:

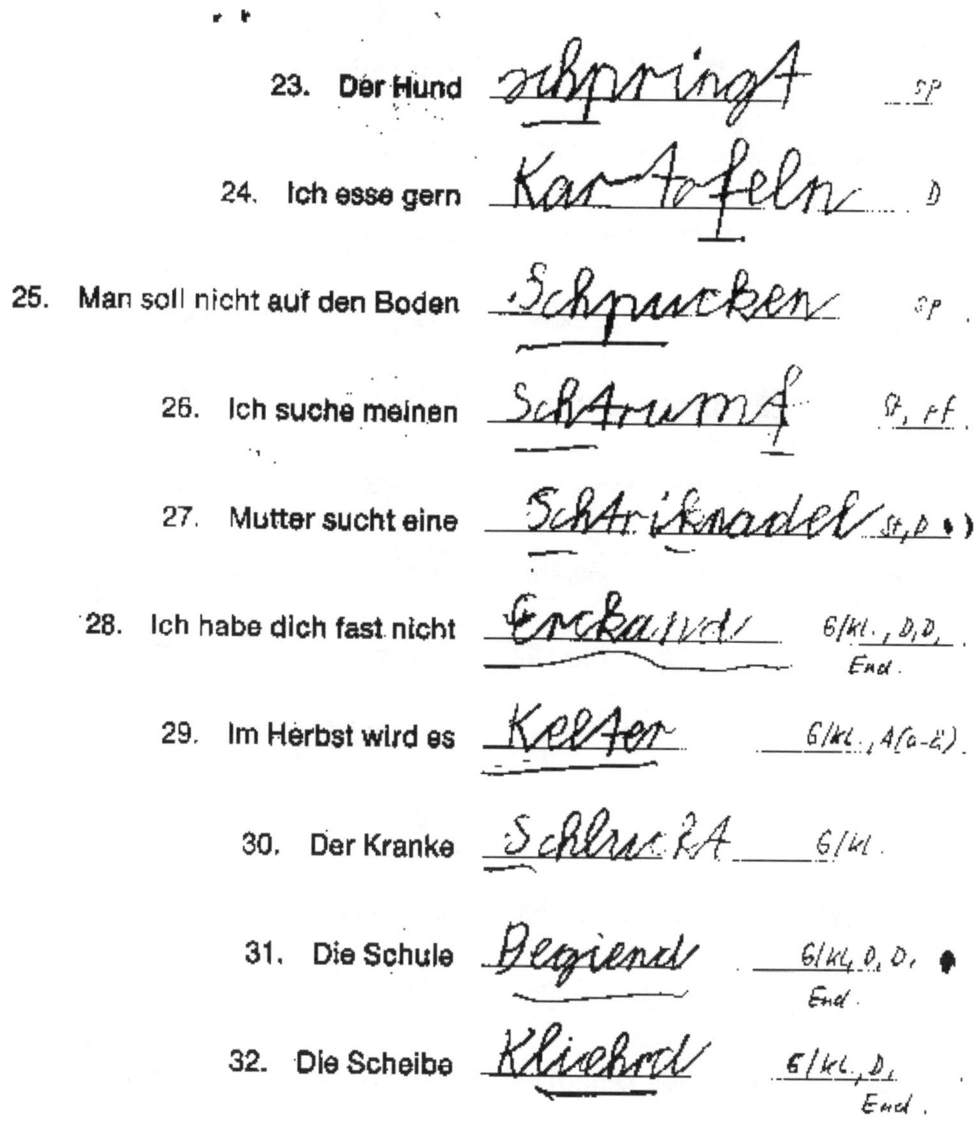

Abb. 2.4.5 DRT 2-Protokoll 3. Seite, Sebastian

16. Ich kaufe für Mutti einen	strauß	G/kl., s-ß
17. Wir lassen die Gläser	klengen	G/kl., e-i
18. Die Fische	schwimen	D
19. Opa leidet an einer schweren	krankheit	G/kl.
20. Der Wagen wirbelt viel	schtaub	G/kl., St
21. Das Boot	sing	A (g-k)
22. Dichter Schnee	felt	A (a-ä), D
23. Das Messer ist	schtumf	st, n-m, pf
24. Sabine	wingt	A (g-k)
25. Die Tür	knelt	G/kl., a-e, D
26. Karin	fersteht	v-f
27. Fritz	rumt	s-z, nk = (A: g-k)
28. Dein Geschenk macht mich	glüglich	g-k, D
29. Er ging	Ckwer	qu
30. Der Dieb kommt ins	Gefenis	WD, WD = ng

Abb. 2.4.6 DRT 3-Protokoll 2. Seite, André

1. Maria kauft ein neues Kleit — A(d-t) .
2. Die Urlauber Hoffen — G/k — auf sonniges Wetter.
3. Er Schipt — G/k, D, A(b-p) — sein Auto zur Werkstatt
4. Ißt du gerne Qrak — Qu, W) ?
5. Im Herbst fahlen — D — die Blätter.
6. Welche Meinung hast du hierzu?
7. Das Kind Flegt — G/k, Pf — seine Tiere.
8. Wir Trefen — G/k D — uns um 6.00 Uhr.
9. Möchtest du das Eis Brobiren — p-b, G/K ?
10. Bert kauft ein kariertes Hemt — A(d-t) .
11. Die Kinder sitzen Fri[illegible]ch — G/k, D — im Garten.
12. Der Hausmeister beseitigt den Schmuz — tz .
13. Das Paket Wigt — G/k, D — fünf Pfund.
14. Du sollst die Straße am Zebrastreifen Überfu[illegible] !
G/k, qu

Abb. 2.4.7 DRT 4-Protokoll 1. Seite, Sabrina

Die daran anschließende Aufstellung zeigt die potentiellen Fehlerarten gemäß den Prüfwörtern der Tests DRT 2, 3 und 4, die je nach Kind in der entsprechenden Bandbreite vorkommen können:

Fehleranalyse (ab dem 2. Schuljahr)

Wahrnehmungsfehler

Wahrnehmungsdurchgliederungsfehler
Auslassungen und Hinzufügungen von Lauten/Buchstaben,
später häufig: „-ng“ als „n“ oder „g“ wiedergegeben,
„pf“ als „f“ wiedergegeben

Wahrnehmungstrennschärfe

überwiegend	e – i
Anfangsfehler	o – u
Verwechslungen	m – n
im Wort	ö – ü
	ch_1 – r
	ch_2 – sch
	s – ß – z – tz
Verwechslungen	g – k
beim Anlaut/	d – t
Silbenbeginn	b – p
	w – f

Wahrnehmungsrichtung
am häufigsten b/d-Vertauschungen

Regelfehler

Groß- und Kleinschreibungsfehler

Dehnungs- und Dopplungsfehler

Ableitungsfehler

Schreibkonventionsfehler

v – f	scht – st
ai – ei	schp/schb – sp
kw – qu	
i/ü – y	

Abb. 2.4.8 Fehleranalyse anhand von DRT-Protokollen

In der nun folgenden Abbildung 2.4.9 wird der Gesamtumfang der testpsychologischen Untersuchung von vier Kindern dargestellt.

Name/ Alter	**Klasse**	**Tests**			**Beurteilung im Zeugnis**
		Schreiben	**Lesen**	**Intelligenz**	
Nico 7;0 Jahre	Anfang 2. Schuljahr	DBL, Form B Wortfehler 21, PR = 9	1. Knuspel-L: Vorläuferfertigkeit PR = 14,4 2. ZLT: Laute eu, ch, pf unbekannt, kann zweisilbige Wörter der Wortliste 1 nicht erlesen	CPM = IQ 125 CFT = IQ 122 (103/125)	Lesebereich: liest nur auswendig Gelerntes zum Diktat: schreibt Geübtes nicht fehlerfrei Mathematik: beherrscht den Zahlenraum 0 bis 20 sicher
Sebastian 8;10 Jahre	Anfang 3. Schuljahr	DRT 2, PR = 3, PR-Band 3 – 4	1. Knuspel-L: Vorläuferfertigkeit, T-Wert = 42, PR = 21; Lesefähigkeit, T-Wert = 40, PR = 16 3. ZLT: Lesetext Zeit: PR = 26 – 50, Fehler: PR = 11 – 15	CPM = IQ 124 KFT 1- 3 = IQ 115/112	Lesen: soll täglich lesen üben, Rechtschreibung: hohe Fehlerzahl (WD-, WT-Fehler) auch in geübten Diktaten Mathematik: Im Zahlenraum bis 1000 sicher, benötigt noch viel Zeit
André 10;5 Jahre, wiederholte das 2. Schuljahr	Anfang 4. Schuljahr	DRT 3 PR = 1, PR-Band 1 – 2		CPM = IQ 96 KFT 1 – 3 = IQ 91 – 94	Rechtschreiben: 5 Mathematik: 5 Lesen: 2 Deutsch: 4
Sabrina 11; 6 Jahre Wiederholung des Schuljahr erforderlich	Ende 4. Schuljahr	DRT 4 PR-Band 0 – 1	Knuspel-L: Vorläuferfertigkeit, T-Wert = 39, PR = 14,6 Lesefähigkeit, T-Wert = 29, PR = < 3	CFT 20 = nicht lernbeh. K-ABC = durchschnittliches Ergebnis, Problem: auditives Kurzzeitgedächtnis	Rechtschreiben: 6 Deutsch: 5 Lesen: 5 Sachkunde: 5 Mathematik: 4

Abb.2.4.9 Gesamtergebnisse der testpsychologischen Untersuchungen von 4 Kindern

3 Vereinbarungen zur Verbesserung der Situation der LRS-Kinder mit der Schule

Bevor ich auf die Vereinbarungen zu sprechen komme, die ich als Schulpsychologin mit der Lehrkraft treffen kann, um die Situation des LRS-Kindes zu verbessern, muss noch erwähnt werden, dass der oben genannte Erlass eine Notengebung für die Leistungen in der Rechtschreibung und im Lesen zwingend vorschreibt, d. h. ab 3. Schuljahr 1. Halbjahr bis zum Ende des 4. Schuljahres stehen also Noten in den Zeugnissen als Ziffern ausgedrückt.

Ein Begleittext im Zeugnis dazu kann allerdings die Bemühungen und Fortschritte des Kindes zusätzlich erwähnen und so die Härte der Benotung etwas abmildern.

1. Welche Maßnahmen kann die Grundschule im Rahmen des LRS-Erlasses neben den gezielten Fördermaßnahmen ergreifen, um die psychischen Belastungen der lese- und rechtschreibschwachen Kinder zu reduzieren?
   - stärkere Gewichtung der mündlichen Leistungen in Deutsch und in Sachkunde
   - das Schreiben differenzierender Diktate (Grundtexte ohne Erweiterungstexte)
   - besondere Vereinbarungen bei den Hausaufgaben in Deutsch (weniger oder spezielle Hausaufgaben, Beschränkung des Zeitvolumens)
   - Vorlesenlassen kürzerer Texte
   - beim Aufsagen von Gedichten: kürzere und genau festgelegte Textpassagen
   - Hervorheben guter Leistungen in anderen Fächern
2. Als günstige Faktoren für die Bereitschaft der Lehrer, die oben genannten Maßnahmen umzusetzen, erlebe ich in meiner Tätigkeit als Schulpsychologin folgende:
   - die allgemeine Leistungsfähigkeit des Kindes ist zufriedenstellend, ausreichende Leistungen erweisen sich dagegen als ungünstig
   - die Eltern zeigen deutlich Interesse an der Verbesserung der Teilleistungsschwäche des Kindes und halten Kontakte zu Lehrern, holen Übungsvorschläge und allgemeine Ratschläge ein
   - die Hausaufgaben werden regelmäßig angefertigt, ggf. in der abgesprochenen Kürzung
   - die Eltern organisieren eine außerschulische Förderung
   - die soziale Integration des Kindes in der Klasse ist als positiv zu bezeichnen
3. In welchem Fall sind überhaupt die oben genannten Erleichterungen für das Kind anzustreben?
   - nur in Absprache mit den Eltern, dem Kind und Lehrern
   - nur dann, wenn es feststeht, dass die leichteren Anforderungen vom Kind akzeptiert werden,
   - es gibt Kinder, für die die Erleichterungen in den Anforderungen schlimmer sind als z. B. eine schlechte Note im Diktat unter normalen Konkurrenzbedingungen
   - wenn die Eltern entweder von der Schule die Einrichtung einer Fördermaßnahme zusätzlich zu den Unterrichtsstunden verlangen oder wenn sie selbst außerschulische Maßnahmen ergreifen.

Die Ausstellung einer Bescheinigung mit der Maßgabe, die im Runderlass dargelegten Ausführungen über die Beurteilung eines LRS-Kindes zu berücksichtigen, wird im Grunde genommen nur relativ selten in der schulpsychologischen Praxis vorgenommen.

Gründe dafür sind einmal persönliche Absprachen mit den Lehrern, die Lese- und Rechtschreibleistungen im Sinne des Erlasses entsprechend umzusetzen – diese sind wirkungsvoller. Nur dann, wenn für den Lehrer die Ausstellung einer Bescheinigung als rechtlich fundiertes Dokument notwendig erscheint, wird das folgende Schreiben – je nach Fall in entsprechender Variation – ausgestellt.

Regionale Schulberatungsstelle der Stadt Hamm

Heinrich-Reinköster-Straße 6

59065 Hamm

Bescheinigung

Nach den Ergebnissen der testdiagnostischen Untersuchung vom ___________ liegt bei ______________________, geb. ________________ eine besondere Schwierigkeit im Erlernen des Rechtschreibens (LRS) im Sinne des RdErl. d. Kultusministeriums vom 19.07.91 vor.

Ich bitte, die Rechtschreibleistungen nicht in die Beurteilung der schriftlichen Arbeiten und Übungen im Fach Deutsch oder in einem anderen Fach mit einzubeziehen.

Der Anteil des Rechtschreibens ist bei der Bildung der Note im Fach Deutsch zurückhaltend zu gewichten (s.a. RdErl).

Mit freundlichen Grüßen

I. Buchhorn

Diplom-Psychologin

Abb.2.4.10 LRS-Bescheinigung der Regionalen Schulberatungsstelle der Stadt Hamm

Zum Abschluß dieses Berichts möchte ich es nicht unerwähnt lassen, dass nach einer gründlichen diagnostischen Beurteilung der LRS-Kinder eine Förderung im Lesen und Schreiben nach einem von der Schulberatungsstelle in Hamm entwickelten Lese- und Schreibaufbau erfolgt, der sowohl die Wahrnehmungsprobleme als auch die Schwierigkeiten der LRS-Kinder mit den Rechtschreibregeln berücksichtigt, wenn es unsere Kapazität (2,5 Stellen) zulässt.

Literatur

Breuer, H., Weuffen, M.: Lernschwierigkeiten am Schulanfang – Schuleingangsdiagnose zur Früherennung und Frühförderung, Weinheim/Basel, Beltz-Verlag, 4. Auflage 1997

Buchhorn, I.: Lese- und Schreibaufbau – Texte und Übungen (4 Bände, Einführung, Lösungsheft) Regionale Schulberatungsstelle der Stadt Hamm, 9. Auflage, 1998

Dummer-Smoch, L., Hackethal, R.: Handbuch zum Kieler Leseaufbau, Kiel, Veris-Verlag, 2. Auflage 1988

Grissemann, H., Baumberger, W.: Zürcher Leseverständnistest für das 4. bis 6. Schuljahr (ZLVT 4. –6.) Bern, Huber-Verlag, 1986

Grissemann, H.: Zürcher Lesetest Bern, Huber-Verlag, 1981

Jansen, H., Mannhaupt, G., Marx, H., Skowronek, H.: Bielefelder Screening zur Früherkennung von Lese- und Rechtschreibschwierigkeiten (BISC), Göttingen, Hogrefe-Verlag, 1. Auflage 1999

Marx, H.: Knuspels Leseaufgaben – Knuspel-L Göttingen, Hogrefe-Verlag, 1998

Marx, H., Jansen, H.: Möglichkeiten und Grenzen der Früherkennung und Vorhersage von Lese-Rechtschreibschwierigkeiten Skript, Universität Bielefeld, 1999

Müller, R.: Diagnostischer Rechtschreibtest DRT 2 – Leistungstest für 2. Klassen Weinheim, Beltz-Verlag, 2. Auflage 1983

Müller, R.: Diagnostischer Rechtschreibtest DRT 3 – Leistungstest für 3. Klassen Weinheim, Beltz-Verlag, 3. Auflage 1991

Müller, R.: Diagnostischer Rechtschreibtest für 4. Klassen – DRT 4 Weinheim, Beltz-Verlag, 1994

Peh, D., Rathenow, P.: Test Grundanforderungen Rechtschreibung für die 1. und 2. Klasse – TGR 1/ 2 Weinheim, Beltz-Verlag, 1984

Rathenow, P., Raatz, U., Rechtschreibtest RST 1 Frankfurt/Main, Beltz-Verlag, 1973

Rathenow, P.: Westermann Rechtschreibtest 4/5 Braunschweig, Georg-Westermann-Verlag, 1. Auflage 1979

Richtlinien zur Förderung von Schülern bei besonderen Schwierigkeiten im Erlernen des Lesens und Rechtschreibens (LRS): Bereinigte Amtliche Sammlung der Schulvorschriften (BASS) des Landes Nordrhein-Westfalen, 14-01 Nr. 1, 1991

Winkelmann, W.: Testbatterie zur Entwicklung kognitiver Operationen, TEKO Braunschweig, Georg-Westermann-Verlag, 1. Auflage 1975

2.5 Die Würzburger Leise Leseprobe (WLLP)

Petra Küspert und Wolfgang Schneider

Hintergründe zur Entwicklung der WLLP

Die WLLP entstand im Rahmen der Forschungsprojekte zur phonologischen Bewusstheit am Lehrstuhl für Psychologie IV der Universität Würzburg (vgl. den Beitrag von W. Schneider in diesem Band). Hier wurde ein Testverfahren benötigt, mit dem sich ab dem Ende des ersten Schuljahres die Leseleistung der Kinder und somit die Effekte der vorschulischen Förderung überprüfen ließen. Die Suche nach einem geeigneten standardisierten Lesetest verlief allein von der Anzahl verfügbarer Lesetests her zufrieden stellend; es gab schon zum damaligen Zeitpunkt (etwa Mitte 1995) eine beachtliche Menge an Lesetests auf dem Markt. Bei genauer Durchsicht der Tests zeigte sich jedoch schnell eine ganze Reihe gravierender Kritikpunkte, die die Verwendbarkeit und den Wert der vorliegenden Testverfahren deutlich schmälerten:

Fast alle Verfahren sind sowohl hinsichtlich des Wortmaterials als auch hinsichtlich der Normierungsdaten veraltet.

Ein weiteres Manko dieser Tests liegt darin, dass die meisten der Verfahren nur schuljahresspezifisch verwendbar sind, also nur in einer Klassenstufe durchgeführt werden können. Gerade im Grundschulbereich wäre es jedoch bedeutsam, die Entwicklung der Lesefertigkeit mit einem einzigen Instrument kontinuierlich über mehrere Klassenstufen hinweg zu erfassen, um die individuellen Leistungszuwächse genau abbilden zu können. Ein solches schuljahresübergreifend verwendbares Verfahren würde überdies den direkten Vergleich von Forschungsergebnissen verschiedener Länder und Sprachräume ermöglichen.

Darüber hinaus basieren die meisten verfügbaren Verfahren auf einer unzureichenden Standardisierung. Bei vielen Lesetests sind die Normierungsdaten nur sehr unvollständig aufgeführt bzw. ermöglichen nur grobe Abschätzungen von Leistungsbereichen. Außerdem wurden die Normen häufig an sehr kleinen Eichstichproben gewonnen.

Ein weiterer Kritikpunkt an den verfügbaren Verfahren besteht in deren mangelnder Ökonomie. Die meisten Lesetests sind nur in Einzelsitzungen von etwa einer Schulstunde Dauer durchzuführen. Gerade für die Anwendung im Forschungsbereich spielt die Ökonomie eines Tests eine bedeutende Rolle, da hier in der Regel mit großen Stichproben gearbeitet wird. Hier wird also ein Lesetest benötigt, der bei einer kurzen Bearbeitungszeit im gesamten Klassenverband durchführbar ist. Ein solcher Test ist natürlich auch im schulischen Alltag, etwa zur Auswahl von Kindern, die einer besonderen Förderung bedürfen, von großem Nutzen.

Zusammenfassend machten wir damals die Feststellung, dass für den deutschen Sprachraum kein Lesetest vorliegt, der in ökonomischer Weise die Leseleistung schuljahresübergreifend erfasst und zufrieden stellend normiert bzw. hinsichtlich der Testgütekriterien Reliabilität und Validität überprüft ist.

Dank finanzieller Förderung durch die Deutsche Forschungsgemeinschaft konnte mit der Entwicklung eines neuen Lesetests, der diesen Anforderungen genügen sollte, begonnen werden. Bis zur heutigen Zeit gab und gibt es natürlich auch in der Lesetestlandschaft einige erfreuliche Entwicklungen, es kamen und kommen auch von anderen Autoren neue und wertvolle Testverfahren hinzu, wie beispielsweise der Salzburger Lese- und Rechtschreibtest (Landerl, Wimmer & Moser, 1999), Knuspels Leseaufgaben (Marx, 1997) oder der Hamburger Lesetest für 3. und 4. Klassen (HAMLET 3-4; Lehmann, Peek & Poerschke, 1997). Die WLLP hat auch inmitten dieses nunmehr erweiterten Angebots ihren festen Platz, da sie sorgfältig entwickelt und überprüft wurde, ausnehmend ökonomisch ist und überdies von den meisten Kindern nicht als Test, sondern als Wettspiel mit Bildern erlebt wird.

Zu den Grundlagen der WLLP: Modelle der Leseentwicklung

Seit den 80er Jahren wurde eine Reihe von Modellen konzipiert, die die Entwicklung der Lesekompetenz, also den Weg zum Analphabeten zum kompetenten Leser, beschreiben. All diesen Modellen ist gemein, dass in der Anfangsphase des Leselernprozesses das synthetische Lesen, also das lautierende Lesen, das Zusammenlauten, von größter Bedeutung ist. Das heißt: die Kinder kennen die Buchstaben-Laut-Beziehungen und *er-lesen* die Wörter Buchstabe für Buchstabe, Laut für Laut. Im weiteren Verlauf der Leseentwicklung spielt zunehmend die automatische, direkte Worterkennung eine Rolle. Für das geschriebene Wort ist nun bereits eine Gedächtnisrepräsentation eingespeichert, das Wort kann sofort als Ganzes erkannt und schnell gelesen werden. Hier finden wir einen deutlichen Unterschied zwischen durchschnittlichen Lesern und leseschwachen Kindern: leseschwache Kinder sind auch bei Wörtern hoher Vorkommenshäufigkeit vielfach nicht in der Lage, diese automatisch und schnell abzurufen, sondern müssen über synthetisches Lesen die Aussprache generieren, um schließlich zur Bedeutung eines Wortes zu gelangen. Diese komplexen Vorgänge gehen natürlich zu Lasten des Lesetempos; entsprechend zielt die WLLP auf die Erhebung der Lese*geschwindigkeit* ab.

Beschreibung der WLLP

Die WLLP wurde in Anlehnung an den im skandinavischen Raum weit verbreiteten Lesetest OS 400 (Søegård & Petersen, 1974) entwickelt. Die WLLP ist ein Gruppentest und dient der Überprüfung der Leseleistung über die Erfassung der Lesegeschwindigkeit in den Klassenstufen 1 bis 4. Der Test besteht aus insgesamt 140 Items (Testaufgaben); bei jedem Item ist ein Wort leise zu lesen und dann in einer Reihe von vier Bildern dasjenige anzustreichen, das dem Gelesenen entspricht. Unter diesen vier Bildern befinden sich neben dem Zielwort Abbildungen phonologisch ähnlicher bzw. mit dem Zielwort in semantischer Beziehung stehender Wörter.

Die zu lesenden Wörter sind ein- bis viersilbig. Um Unterschiede im Wortschatz der Kinder als Störvariable zu eliminieren, wurde nur Wortmaterial verwendet, das Grundschulkindern geläufig ist.

Bei der WLLP handelt es sich um einen Speed Test; entsprechend steht den Kindern eine gewisse Zeitspanne (5 Minuten in allen Klassenstufen) zur Bearbeitung zur Verfügung, und als abhängige Variable dient die Anzahl der in dieser Zeit korrekt bearbeiteten Items. Wie bei Speed Tests üblich sind die einzelnen Aufgaben von geringer Schwierigkeit, und Leistungsunterschiede zeigen sich über die Geschwin-digkeit, mit der die Kinder arbeiten.

Der Zeitaufwand für die Durchführung der WLLP setzt sich zusammen aus der Bearbeitungszeit von 5 Minuten und der Zeit für Instruktion und Austeilen/Einsammeln und beträgt insgesamt ca. 15 Minuten. Zur Auswertung stehen Schablonen zur Verfügung. Der Testrohwert errechnet sich durch Subtraktion der Anzahl von Auslassungen und Fehler von der Zahl insgesamt bearbeiteter Items. Die WLLP liegt in 2 Pseudo-Parallelformen A und B vor.

Reliabilität und Validität der WLLP

Im Jahr 1997 war es dank der finanziellen Unterstützung durch die Deutsche Forschungsgemeinschaft möglich, die WLLP in groß angelegten Studien umfassend hinsichtlich der Gütekriterien Reliabilität und Validität zu überprüfen und an einer repräsentativen Stichprobe zu eichen.

Für die Reliabilität (Zuverlässigkeit) des Tests ergaben sich über die Paralleltestmethode (N=175) Werte zwischen r=.82 und r=.93. Über die Retest-Methode (N=513, Intervall 14 Wochen) ergaben sich Reliabilitätskoeffizienten zwischen r=.75 und r=.88. Somit ist der WLLP eine durchaus zufriedenstellende Zuverlässigkeit zu bescheinigen.

Zur Überprüfung der Validität (Gültigkeit) der WLLP führten zwischen 67 und 74 Versuchspersonen pro Klassenstufe neben diesem Test weitere, bereits etablierte Verfahren (z.B. Diagnostischer Lesetest zur Frühdiagnose von Lesestörungen (DLF 1-2; Müller, 1984), Bremer Lesetest für 3. und 4. Klassen (BLT 3-4; Niemeyer, 1976), Lesetestserie (Biglmaier, 1969)) durch, um den Zusammenhang zwischen den Leistungen in den altbewährten Tests und dem neuen Verfahren zu klären. Die WLLP korreliert in allen Klassenstufen hoch mit den entsprechenden Einzelverfahren. Auch die Zusammenhänge zwischen den Leistungen in der WLLP und der Lehrerbeurteilung bzw. der Deutschzensur sind durchaus zufriedenstellend, so dass die WLLP als valides Verfahren zur Erfassung der Leseleistung von Grundschülern bezeichnet werden kann.

Die Eichung der WLLP

Für die Erstellung der Normen zur WLLP konnten die Daten von insgesamt 2820 Schülern der Klassenstufen 1 bis 4 aus sieben deutschen und einem österreichischen Bundesland herangezogen werden. Die Eichung fand gegen Ende des Schuljahres statt, entsprechend liegen für die WLLP Prozentrangnormen mit Gültigkeit für die letzten drei Monate der Jahrgangsstufen 1 bis 4 vor.

Einsatzbereiche der WLLP

Die WLLP ist im gesamten Grundschulbereich einsetzbar. Grundlegende Voraussetzung ist die Beherrschung der Buchstabe-Laut-Beziehungen, dies ist spätestens zum Ende des ersten Schuljahres der Fall. Die WLLP prüft das leise Lesen, welches der natürlichen Lesesituation wesentlich mehr entspricht als das laute Vorlesen. Über die WLLP wird speziell die Lesegeschwindigkeit erfasst; über die Lesegenauigkeit, also die Fehler, die ein Kind beim Lesen macht, und auch über das Leseverständnis werden keine Aussagen gemacht. Einzig die Lesegeschwindigkeit als Teilkomponente der Lesekompetenz wurde als abhängige Variable gewählt, da sich in der neueren Forschung zeigte, dass in relativ regulären Orthographien wie dem Deutschen sich durchschnittliche Leser von schwachen Lesern vornehmlich in Hinblick auf das Lesetempo unterscheiden, kaum aber hinsichtlich der Lesegenauigkeit. Das heißt: auch schwache Schüler sind in der Lage, alles zu lesen, sie kommen dabei jedoch wesentlich langsamer voran. Aber auch in den höheren Grundschulklassen, in denen vermehrt das Leseverständnis fokussiert wird, ist die Wortlesegeschwindigkeit eine basale Komponente, denn ein beeinträchtigtes Textverständnis ist in der Regel die Folge des langsamen und mühevollen

Zusammenlesens. Wir gehen also davon aus, mit der Lesegeschwindigkeit eine grundlegende Fertigkeit zu erfassen, die einen guten Indikator für die Lesefähigkeit insgesamt darstellt.

Die WLLP ist in verschiedenen Bereichen anwendbar: so dient sie als Forschungsinstrument, bewährt sich in der schulpsychologischen Diagnostik und ist auch im Schulalltag einsetzbar, etwa um den Leistungsstand einer Klasse zu bestimmen, bzw. als grobes „Screening", als eine Art Grobsieb, mithilfe dessen sich leistungsschwächere Schüler im Klassenverband herausfiltern lassen.

Auf die Grenzen des Anwendungsbereiches der WLLP soll gesondert hingewiesen werden: Obwohl die WLLP auch Hinweise auf Problembereiche der einzelnen Schüler zu geben vermag, ist zu empfehlen, für die reliable Beurteilung individueller Schwächen in den Teilfertigkeiten des Lesens noch ein Einzelverfahren nachzuschieben. Auch wenn es darum geht, diagnosegeleitete Fördermaßnahmen zu konzipieren, wäre es sinnvoll, im Anschluß bei diesen schwächeren Kindern noch ein Einzelverfahren hinzuzuziehen, welches eine genaue qualitative Analyse der Lesefehler ermöglicht.

Literatur:

Biglmaier, F. (1969). Lesetestserie. München: Reinhardt.

Landerl, K., Wimmer, H. & Moser, E. (1997). Der Salzburger Lese- und Rechtschreibtest (SLRT). Göttingen: Hogrefe.

Lehmann, R.H., Peek, R. & Poerschke, J. (1997). Hamburger Lesetest für 3. und 4. Klassen (HAMLET 3-4). Göttingen: Hogrefe.

Marx, H. (1998). Knuspels Leseaufgaben (Knuspel-L). Göttingen: Hogrefe.

Müller, R. (1984). Diagnostischer Lesetest zur Frühdiagnose von Lesestörungen (DLF 1-2). Weinheim: Beltz.

Niemeyer, W. (1976). Bremer Lesetest für 3. und 4. Klassen (BLT 3-4). Bremen: Herbig.

Søegård, A. & Petersen S.P.B. (1974). ORDSTILLELÆSNINGSPRØVE OS-400. Kopenhagen: Dansk Psykologisk Forlag.

2.6 Lesediagnose mit der Hamburger Leseprobe (HLP 1-4)

Peter May

1 Kurzbeschreibung

Die *Hamburger Leseprobe* (HLP 1-4) ist ein Verfahren zur Erfassung der Lesefertigkeit und zur Analyse von Leseprozessen *vom ersten bis zum vierten Schuljahr*, bei Kindern mit gravierenden Leseschwierigkeiten teilweise auch darüber hinaus. Die HLP wurde 1992 zunächst als Hamburger Version entwickelt und wird seitdem in allen Hamburger Grundschulen für die Bestimmung der Leseleistung – insbesondere im Rahmen der Diagnose von Lese-Rechtschreib-Schwierigkeiten – eingesetzt. Aufgrund der zunehmenden Nachfrage auch aus anderen Bundesländern nach einem modernen Lesetest wurden Vergleichsdaten für in anderen Bundesländern erhoben, so dass die HLP nun als Lesetest mit bundesdeutschen Vergleichswerten vorliegt.[1]

Die HLP-Testmappe enthält

- das *Manual für die HLP* mit ausführlicher Beschreibung des Materials, mit Anleitungen für Durchführung und Auswertung, einschließlich der Beschreibung und Interpretation von Beispielen, sowie mit allen Vergleichstabellen
- *Vorlagen* für alle Geschichten und Wörterlisten
- *Protokoll-Listen* für alle Geschichten und Wörterlisten
- *Auswertungsbögen* für die quantitative und die qualitative Auswertung

2 Diagnosekonzept

Die HLP ermöglicht es, zwei Ziele der pädagogischen Diagnostik miteinander zu verbinden, die sich bei den früheren Lesetests in der Regel widersprachen: Das Beobachten von Leseprozessen unter *alltagsnahen Bedingungen* und das Gewinnen von *Vergleichsmaßstäben* zur Beurteilung der Förderbedürftigkeit besonders schwacher Leselerner.

Dies wird in der HLP durch folgende *Prinzipien* realisiert:

(1) Die HLP enthält *Texte, deren Inhalt und Wortschatz den Erfahrungen der Kinder entsprechen*. Sie werden deshalb von den Kindern mit Interesse gelesen und inhaltlich als gehaltvoll verstanden. Obwohl sie hinsichtlich Umfang, Schwierigkeitsgrad und Komplexität für Vergleichszwecke konzipiert und bearbeitet wurden, wirken die Texte nicht gekünstelt oder abgehoben.

(2) Die HLP enthält neben *Texten*, die die *Fähigkeit der Kinder zum Verstehen einer Geschichte* erfassen, auch Listen von *Einzelwörtern*, die es erlauben, die *Strategien der Kinder zum Entschlüsseln von Wörtern* ohne Einbettung in einen Kontext zu beobachten. Die Wörterlisten enthalten nur Nomen, die den Kindern von der Bedeutung her vertraut sind. Sie vermeiden seltene Wörter und optisch ähnliche Wortstrukturen, die häufig auch bessere Leser zu Fehlern provozieren.

---

1 Die HLP ist ab Frühjahr 2000 erhältlich beim Verlag für pädagogische Medien, Unnastr. 19, 20253 Hamburg, Tel. 040-4903737.

(3) Die HLP erlaubt die analysierende *Beobachtung und Dokumentation der Lernentwicklung beim Lesen* über einen langen Zeitraum (*zweites bis viertes Schuljahr*) mit einem *einheitlichen Konzept*. Damit entfällt die Schwierigkeit, Ergebnisse unterschiedlicher Beobachtungs- und Testinstrumente aufeinander beziehen zu müssen. Ermöglicht wird diese Lernbeobachtung durch die Bereitstellung mehrerer *Parallelformen*, die hinsichtlich Textsorte, Aufgabenschwierigkeit und Länge vergleichbar sind. Für alle Parallelformen liegen *Vergleichswerte für die Leseleistung zu mehreren Zeitpunkten* aus verschiedenen Klassenstufen vor, so dass die Lernfortschritte einzelner Kinder ggf. über Jahre dokumentiert werden können. Dies erleichtert auch die Beurteilung der Leselernentwicklung in Berichtszeugnissen.

(4) Das Hauptanliegen der HLP ist die Analyse von Leseprozessen jener Kinder, deren Lernentwicklung sich kritisch gestaltet. Deshalb umfasst die HLP insbesondere solche *Leseaufgaben, die für die Beobachtung von schwachen Lesern geeignet sind.* Um Überforderungen der schwachen Leser zu vermeiden, kann die Lesediagnose schon mit einer einzigen leichten Geschichte und/oder einer einfachen Wörterliste abgeschlossen werden, da Vergleichswerte für jede Einzelgeschichte/ Wörterliste zu verschiedenen Zeitpunkten vorliegen. Darüber hinaus enthält die HLP aber auch schwierigere Leseaufgaben, die für durchschnittliche und bessere Leser noch Herausforderungen darstellen oder mit denen Lernfortschritte von ehemals schwachen Lesern erfasst werden können. Die HLP umfasst *Geschichten mit vier Schwierigkeitsstufen* und *Wörterlisten mit zwei Schwierigkeitsstufen.*

(5) Die HLP ist ein Verfahren für die *Einzelbeobachtung*, mit dem der *Prozess des Erlesens und Sinnerfassens* differenziert analysiert werden kann. Den Kindern werden die einzelnen Geschichten vorgestellt, sie betrachten (bei den leichten Geschichten) zunächst das Bild, und im Gespräch mit der Lehrerin bilden sie erste Hypothesen über den zu erwartenden Inhalt. Die Kinder haben dann die Wahl, den Text erst leise für sich zu lesen oder ihn gleich laut vorzulesen.

Dies ermöglicht die Berücksichtigung der individuellen Gewohnheiten und befreit die Kinder von künstlichen Einschränkungen durch die Testsituation. Der Leseprozess selbst wird durch Protokollbogen und optional mit einem Tonband dokumentiert. Anschließend findet ein kurzer Dialog zwischen Lehrerin (Testleiter/in) und Kind über den Inhalt des Gelesenen statt, damit festgestellt werden kann, inwieweit die Kinder diesen verstanden haben.

(6) Die *Auswertung der HLP* umfasst nicht nur globale Punktwerte zur Kennzeichnung der *Leseleistung* und der *Lesegeschwindigkeit*, sondern ermöglicht eine *qualitative Analyse des Leseprozesses* mit Hilfe eines vorgegebenen Auswertungsbogens. In diese qualitative Analyse geht die Erfahrung ein, dass das Erlesen eines unbekannten und für das Kind noch schwierigen Textes als eine Art *Problemlöseprozess* aufzufassen ist, der verschiedenartige Teilprozesse umfasst. Für das Gesamtergebnis werden deshalb auch nicht die Fehler, die das Kind beim Lesen macht, gezählt, sondern die einzelnen Wörter werden mit Hilfe einer Punktskala bewertet, so dass auch *Teillösungen* des Kindes in die Beurteilung der Leseleistung eingehen.

Aus der Analyse der Vorgehensweisen des Kindes beim Erlesen ergeben sich *Gesichtspunkte für die weitere Förderung*, die im Anleitungsheft mit ausführlichen Beispielen von Kindern erläutert werden.

(7) Ein besonderes Kennzeichen der HLP ist das gewollte *Einbeziehen der Interaktion zwischen Lehrerin und Kind* beim Erlesen. Die Kinder werden beim Lesen nicht sich selbst

überlassen, und die Lehrerin ist nicht nur distanzierte Testleiterin, sondern *als Helferin* soll sie *gezielt in den Prozess der Lösungssuche eingreifen* und dem Kind Hinweise für das weitere Vorgehen geben. Dadurch wird einerseits die Lesesituation psychologisch günstig gestaltet und Leistungsblockaden bei prüfungsängstlichen Kindern vorgebeugt. Andererseits erlaubt diese gezielte Interaktion die Analyse der *Lesesituation als Teil eines beginnenden Förderprozesses*. Die Lehrerin erfährt, inwieweit das Kind in der Lage ist, steuernde und korrigierende Hinweise in den eigenen Lösungsprozess zu integrieren. Und sie kann ihre eigenen Hilfen hinsichtlich der Angemessenheit überprüfen und korrigieren.

(8) Die HLP wurde in einer *umfangreichen Längsschnittstudie entwickelt und erprobt*, in welcher die Leselernentwicklung von ca. 560 Hamburger Kindern vom ersten bis vierten Schuljahr parallel zu ihrer Lernentwicklung im Rechtschreiben beobachtet wurde. Durch Ergänzung der Normierung in mehreren Bundesländern liegen nun *bundesweite Vergleichswerte zur Leseleistung* in mehreren Parallelformen der Geschichten von *sieben verschiedenen Zeitpunkten* vor.

3 Verlauf

3.1 Zur Entwicklung des Rechtschreibniveaus bei Grundschulkindern unter Beachtung verschiedener Einflussfaktoren

Selma-Maria Behrndt, Martina Steffen, Michael Becker

Rahmenbedingungen

Die Bilanz der Jahre 1989 bis 1999 in Mecklenburg-Vorpommern hinsichtlich der LRS-Diagnostik, -Beratung und -Förderung zeigt deutlich, dass sich die gemeinsamen Anstrengungen für den Aufbau einer schulischen Förderung für Schüler mit Schwierigkeiten im Lesen und Schreiben gelohnt haben. Es ist gelungen, diese schulische Förderung landesweit flächendeckend umzusetzen. Waren es 1992 etwa 35% der LRS-Schüler mit einer spezifischen Förderung in Schulen Mecklenburg-Vorpommern, so wird heute der LRS-Erlaß in den Bereichen Beratung, Diagnostik und Förderung in vollem Umfang umgesetzt.

Künftig wird es weiter notwendig sein, die LRS-Förderstrategie immer wieder neuen wissenschaftlichen Erkenntnissen und schulischen Bedingungen anzupassen. Folgende Aspekte sind dabei zu beachten:

Die Umsetzung einer schulischen LRS-Diagnostik und Förderung ist im Bereich der Schule eine sensible Größe. Die Erfahrungen der alten Bundesländer zeigten dies.

In der Kultusministerkonferenz besteht immer noch eine relative Resistenz gegenüber dem Begriff „Legasthenie".

In und zwischen den Disziplinen Medizin, Psychologie und Pädagogik werden immer noch kontroverse Diskussionen um den LRS-Begriff geführt. Verunsicherungen mit entsprechenden schulpraktischen Auswirkungen bezüglich der Notwendigkeit und Machbarkeit einer schulischen LRS-Förderung sind die Folge.

Die Längsschnitterhebungen zur Entwicklung des Rechtschreibniveaus im Grundschulbereich in Mecklenburg- Vorpommern sind unter **schulpraktischen** Aspekten konzipiert und ausgewertet worden. Die Ergebnisse dieser Untersuchungen müssen dabei mit der Entwicklung der LRS-Förderstrategie insgesamt in diesem Zeitraum in Beziehung gesetzt werden. Folgende Punkte erwiesen sich dabei als grundlegend:

Die Förderung der LRS-Schüler basiert auf einem inzwischen bundesweit anerkannten Konzept zur Fortbildung der LRS-Lehrkräfte.

Bewährt haben sich auch in der schwierigen Phase des Aufbaus neuer Verwaltungsstrukturen die LRS- Leiteinrichtungen innerhalb der Staatlichen Schulämter, die sich als Mittler zwischen theoretischem Anspruch und schulpraktischer Realisierbarkeit verstehen. Die Koordination der Beratung, Diagnostik und Förderung sowie die Abstimmung in schwierigen Situationen und die Organisation der Multiplikatorentätigkeit sind wichtige Aufgaben dieser LRS-Leiteinrichtungen.

Die schulaufsichtliche Umsetzung hat sich ebenfalls als wichtige Rahmenbedingung erwiesen. Die Verbindung von schulrechtlichen Voraussetzungen mit qualitativen Parametern unter schulaufsichtlicher Begleitung stellt sich als ein Knotenpunkt für die flächendeckende Realisierung der LRS-Förderung dar. Dabei ist zu beachten, dass sich für eine qualitätsgerechte Förderung die Verteilung der LRS-Förderstunden nach dem individuellen Förderbedarf der Schüler und an Lehrer mit lrs-spezifischem Fortbildungsprofil richten muss und nicht nach freien Stundenkapazitäten anderer Lehrkräfte.

Eine Arbeitsgruppe zur ständigen Fortschreibung des seit 1992 gültigen LRS-Erlasses und der Hinweise und Anmerkungen unterstützt die Bemühungen zur Entwicklung einer gut funktionierenden schulischen LRS-Förderung.

Folgende Formen der LRS- Förderung haben sich in den letzten Jahren bewährt:

Binnendifferenzierte Förderung

Sie ist als Möglichkeit für Schüler mit vorübergehenden oder leichteren Problemen unter Berücksichtigung der individuellen Leistungen zu sehen. Obwohl die Anzahl dieser Schüler den weitaus größten Anteil aller Grundschüler mit Schwierigkeiten im Lesen und Schreiben der Klassenstufen 1 bis 4 ausmacht, gestaltet sich die binnendifferenzierte Förderung am kompliziertesten. So ist für die Lehrer beispielsweise die Berücksichtigung der individuellen Lernvoraussetzungen, des unterschiedlichen Leseverhaltens und des Lesetempos der Schüler immer mit dem Ziel bedeutsam, noch nicht erworbene Fähigkeiten und Fertigkeiten im Unterricht systematisch zu entwickeln. Die Leistungsbewertung und –feststellung sollte nach pädagogischem Ermessen erfolgen und dem aktuellen Leistungsstand des einzelnen Schülers angepasst sein. Innerhalb des binnendifferenzierten Unterrichts ist bewusst auf zielgleiche Vorgehensweisen zu verzichten.

Förderung in Kleingruppen

Der LRS-Erlaß ermöglicht für Schüler der Klassenstufen 2 bis 4 mit dem Verdacht des Vorliegens einer Lese-Rechtschreibschwäche und darüber hinaus nach Beendigung der Grundschulzeit, die Förderung in einer Kleingruppe. Der individuelle Förderanspruch bezieht sich hier auf Schüler, bei denen eine Teilleistungsstörung im Lesen und Schreiben in der Form vorliegt, dass allein eine binnendifferenzierte Förderung nicht ausreichend ist. Der klassen- und/oder jahrgangsübergreifende Förderunterricht wird in Gruppen von drei bis sechs Schülern durch LRS-Lehrkräfte realisiert.

Die LRS-Kleingruppenförderung hat sich insgesamt als wichtige Säule innerhalb der Gesamtstrategie erwiesen, setzt aber auch ein Abwägen zwischen Fördermöglichkeit, Notwendigkeit und vorhandenen Mitteln voraus.

Formen der Intensivförderung

Sie werden für Schüler angeboten, bei denen andere Fördervarianten nicht erfolgreich waren. Dies betrifft den weitaus geringeren Teil der Schüler mit einer LRS (ca.1%). Für Schüler, bei denen der Erwerb der Schriftsprache trotz binnendifferenzierter Förderung im Anfangsunterricht der Grundschule vollständig zu scheitern droht, ist eine Intensivförderung in selbständigen LRS-Kleinklassen möglich. In ihnen unterrichten Grundschullehrkräfte, die in Fortbildungskursen durch das L.I.S.A. in den Bereichen Beratung, Diagnostik und Unterricht auf diese Aufgaben speziell vorbereitet werden. Die Auswahl dieser Schüler erfolgt im Rahmen einer prozessorientierten Diagnostik. Grundlage für den Unterricht in diesen Kleinklassen ist die modifizierte Rahmenrichtlinie für den Lese-Rechtschreiblehrgang in selbständigen LRS-Kleinklassen der Klassenstufen 2 und 3 an Grundschulen.

Als weitere Formen der Intensivförderung gelten die Kleingruppen mit erhöhtem Förderbedarf, der an der Stammschule realisiert wird sowie die Förderung in Halbjahreskursen sowie Intensivkurse z.B. an der Diagnostik- und Therapieschule (Klinikschule) ambulant oder auch mit stationärer medizinischer Betreuung.

LRS-Förderung nach Einzelfallentscheidungen in allen Klassenstufen

Einzelfallentscheidungen im Grund-, Haupt- und Realschulbereich haben sich für Schüler mit komplexen psychischen Störungsbildern, für Schüler mit kumulierenden Schwierigkeiten und für Schüler mit schwersten LRS-Erscheinungsbildern, bewährt..

Generell gilt, dass die Erfassung und Förderung von Kindern mit Schwierigkeiten im Lesen und in der Rechtschreibung **präventiv**, also in der Anfangsphase des Schriftspracherwerbs bereits in Klasse 1, spätestens am Ende der 2. Klasse realisiert werden muss (Feststellung des Umfangs des Förderbedarfs, Festlegen der Organisationsformen und Methoden der Förderung).

Von entscheidender Bedeutung für die qualitativ erforderliche Beratung, Diagnostik und Förderung stehen in diesem Zusammenhang die

- Sicherung einer modernen, zeitgemäßen Fortbildung auf der Grundlage neuester wissenschaftlicher Erkenntnisse,
- flächendeckende Öffentlichkeitsarbeit zur Entwicklung der LRS-Förderstrategie für Eltern, LRS-Lehrkräfte, Schulleiter zum Beispiel über Infohefte,
- Berechtigung zur Beratung, Diagnostik und Förderung für Lehrkräfte aller Schularten sowie Personal mit sonderpädagogischer Aufgabenstellung (PmsA)
- in LRS-Kleinklassen laut LRS-Erlaß mit den entsprechenden Zertifikaten
- jährlichen zentralen **LRS-Fortbildungstage** für Multiplikatoren (LRS-Lehrkräfte, Schulpsychologen, Schulräte).

Zur Entwicklung des Rechtschreibniveaus

Die Gesamtpopulation umfaßte die Schüler der 2. Klassen der Jahrgänge 1993/94, 1994/95, 1995/96 unter längsschnittlichem Aspekt bis zur 5. Jahrgangsstufe (siehe Untersuchungsplan) in Mecklenburg-Vorpommern insgesamt.

Aus diesen Populationen gingen jeweils repräsentative und ausgewählte Stichproben hervor. Die ausgewählten Stichproben gliedern sich in:
Stichprobe 1: gute Rechtschreibleistungen in den Erhebungen,
Stichprobe 2: schwächere Rechtschreibleistungen in den Erhebungen,
Stichprobe 3: Rechtschreibleistungen bei Förderschülern.

Die Auswertung der Stichproben 1 und 2 konnte aus personellen und finanziellen Gründen nur im 1. Jahrgang bis zur Klasse 4 erfolgen. Dafür wurden, zum Teil mit Hilfe weiterer Projekte, sehr differenzierte Analysen einzelner Schülergruppen (Schulversuch, Fehlhörigkeitsprojekt) und innerhalb einer Stadt durchgeführt. Ergebnisse, die die genannte Population tangieren, gehen in den Bericht ein.
In Abb.3.1.1 wird die Vernetzung der Populationen veranschaulicht:

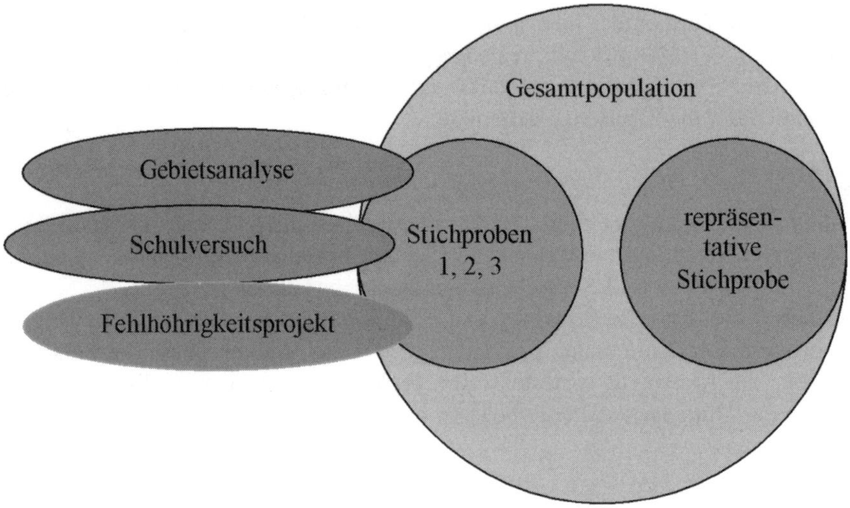

Abb. 3.1.1 Vernetzung der Populationen

Längs- und Querschnittsvergleiche

Wie aus Abb. 3.1.1 ersichtlich, erfolgten neben den quantitativen Erhebungen des Rechtschreibniveaus in den Jahrgangsstufen 2, 3, 4, 5 Kohortenvergleiche hinsichtlich der Rechtschreibfertigkeiten verschiedener Bildungsjahrgänge unter Beachtung solcher Einflussgrößen, wie z. B. Geschlechts- und Altersunterschiede, Schullaufbahn, Schultyp, Klassengröße, Lehr- und Lernmethoden, Art der Förderung, Verhaltensauffälligkeiten und ihre Bedeutung im Kontext der Intervention bei Lese-Rechtschreibschwierigkeiten.

In diesem Beitrag wird nur auf den Aspekt des Fördereinflusses eingegangen.

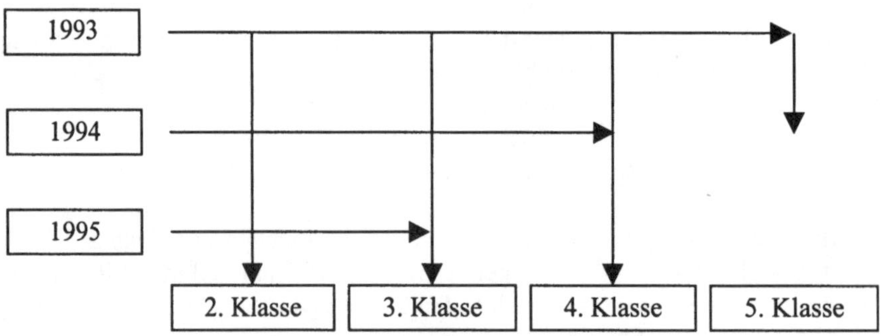

Abb. 3.1.2 Übersicht über Längs- und Querschnittsvergleiche

Zur Erfassung des Niveaus der Rechtschreibfertigkeiten wurden Screeningverfahren eingesetzt bzw. mußten entwickelt werden. Zur Abklärung von Einflussfaktoren kamen auch Fragebögen mit 5-stufigen Schätzskalen zu Lehr- und Lernmethoden zum Einsatz. Weiterhin wurden Zensuren einbezogen. In den Protokollbögen waren ebenfalls Angaben zur Art der Förderung enthalten.

Erhebungsinstrumente

Die Instruktionen, Untersuchungsmaterialien und Auswertungskriterien wurden in einer Handreichung vom Landesinstitut für Schule und Ausbildung (Schwerin 1998) veröffentlicht.

Untersuchungszeitpunkt 1 und 2 (September bzw. März Klasse 2)	– Diagnostische Bilderliste „Forschungsgruppe Frühförderung 1993 bis 1998 M-V" in Anlehnung an Dummer-Smoch (Diagnostische Bilderliste) – eine Rechenarbeit
Untersuchungszeitpunkt 3 und 4 (April Klasse 3 bzw. Klasse 4)	– Wortdiktat „Forschungsgruppe Frühförderung 1993 bis 1998 M-V" in Anlehnung an Kossakowski – Bilderliste in den allgemeinen Förderschulen – Fragebogen zur Erfassung der methodisch-didaktischen Gestaltung des muttersprachlichen Unterrichts – Zensuren in den Fächern Lesen, Rechtschreibung und Mathematik
Untersuchungszeitpunkt 5 (April Klasse 5)	– Wort- und Satzdiktat „Forschungsgruppe Frühförderung 1993 bis 1998 M-V" – Zensuren in den Fächern Deutsch, Englisch und Mathematik – überarbeitete Bilderliste in den 2. Klassen der allgemeinen Förderschule

Tabelle 3.1.1 Erhebungsinstrumente

Gesamtübersicht über die Populationen

Die mit den Screeningverfahren (Tab. 3.1.1) ermittelte Rechtschreibentwicklung innerhalb der repräsentativen Stichproben der Jahrgänge 1993, 1994 und 1995 ist in Tabelle 3.1.2 dargestellt. In die Analyse sind jeweils ca. 800 Schüler eines Jahrganges (502 Schüler in Klasse 5) einbezogen. In den folgenden Tabellen entspricht *sehr gut* einem Prozentrang > 75 und *sehr schwach* einem Prozentrang ≤ 10.

Population	Untersuchungszeitpunkt									
	September 2. Klasse		März 2. Klasse		April 3. Klasse		April 4. Klasse		April 5. Klasse	
	sehr gut	sehr schwach	sehr gut	sehr schwach	sehr gut	sehr schwach	sehr gut	sehr schwach	sehr gut	sehr schwach
1993	27,4	11,0	36,8	10,2	27,5	9,8	30,2	9,9	33,6	9,6
1994	31,7	9,4	25,5	9,1	26,6	9,2	35,3	9,5		
1995	29,2	10,4	35,6	9,7	26,8	8,1				

Tabelle 3.1.2 Quantitative Entwicklung des Rechtschreibniveaus in den repräsentativen Stichproben (Angaben in Prozent)

Betrachtet man die Ergebnisse im *Längsschnitt,* so ist festzustellen, dass der Anteil der sehr guten Rechtschreiber der Population 1993 vom September 2. Klasse bis zum April 5. Klasse von 27,4 auf 33,6% zunimmt. Der Gipfel in der 2. Erhebung ist auf den zu diesem Zeitpunkt sehr niedrigen Schwierigkeitsgrad der Diagnostischen Bilderliste zurückzuführen. Im umgekehrten Verhältnis dazu verringert sich der Anteil der sehr schwachen Rechtschreiber von 11,0 auf 9,6% in Klasse 5.

In der Stichprobe des Jahrganges 1994 ist der Anteil von sehr guten Rechtschreibern von Klasse 2 (31,7%) zu Klasse 4 (35,3%) ebenfalls gestiegen. Der Anteil der sehr schwachen Rechtschreiber ist annähernd konstant geblieben.

Für den Jahrgang 1995 ist festzustellen, dass der Anteil der sehr schwachen Rechtschreiber im Zeitraum 2. Klasse bis 3. Klasse kontinuierlich abnimmt und erreicht mit 8,1% im April der 3. Klasse den niedrigsten Wert im Vergleich zu allen Erhebungszeitpunkten.

Einfluss der Förderung

Im Ergebnis der ersten Auswertung ist eine positive und eine negative Stichprobe bezogen auf das Erhebungsgebiet gebildet worden. Es waren also Regionen zu erkennen, in denen insgesamt bessere oder im anderen Fall schlechtere Gesamtergebnisse erreicht worden sind.

In der positiven Stichprobe sind die Ergebnisse demnach signifikant besser als im Durchschnitt der repräsentativen Stichprobe gewesen, in der negativen Stichprobe dagegen schlechter. Folgenden These wurde in bezug auf die Förderung geprüft:

Gibt es Unterschiede in dem Einsatz einer spezifischen LRS-Förderung zwischen diesen beiden Gebieten?

Zunächst ein Überblick hinsichtlich der spezifischen Förderung insgesamt:

Art der Förderung	Population 1993	
	4. Klasse	5. Klasse
Binnendifferenzierung	16,8	3,6
allgemeine Förderung	18,4	8,0
LRS-Förderung	6,5	8,2

Tabelle 3.1.3 Art der spezifischen Förderung in Klasse 4 und 5 in der Population 1993 (Angaben in%)

Der Frage, in welchem Ausmaß schulische Förderung für die schwächsten Rechtschreiber realisiert wird, soll wie in Abbildung 3.1.3 dargestellt, nachgegangen werden. Folgende Verknüpfungen ergeben sich: Wurden Schüler mit einem schwachen Rechtschreibniveau in Klasse 2 in der Klasse 3 bzw. Schüler mit einem schwachen Rechtschreibniveau in Klasse 3 in Klasse 3, 4 und 5 gefördert? Lassen sich Unterschiede im Umfang der Förderung zwischen der positiven und der negativen Stichprobe finden?

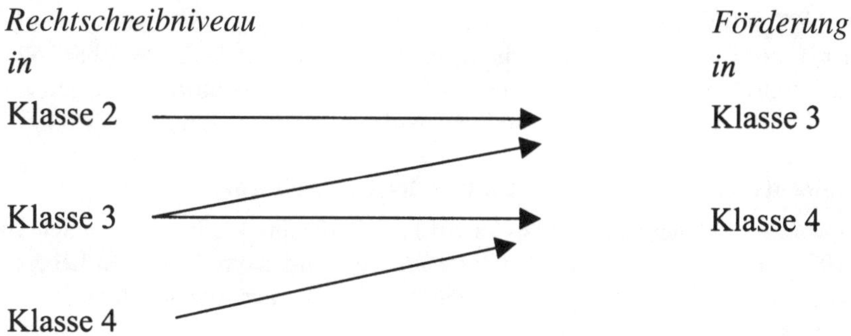

Abb. 3.1.3 Dargestellte Beziehungen zwischen schulischer Förderung und schwachem Rechtschreibniveau

Schulische LRS-Förderung wird in der Regel am Ende des vorausgegangenen Schuljahres beantragt. Der Zusammenhang zwischen dem Niveau der Rechtschreibung in der 2. Klasse und der Einbeziehung der Schüler in die Förderung in Klasse 3 stellt sich in den beiden Stichproben wie folgt dar:

In der Tabelle 3.1.4 wird sichtbar, daß nur ein geringer Teil der schwachen Rechtschreiber aus Klasse 2 in der negativen Stichprobe spezifischen LRS-Förderunterricht (4,8%) erhielt. Der Anteil der spezifischen Förderung ist in der positiven Stichprobe um das fast achtfache höher (35,6%).

Von den Schülern, die in der 3. Klasse schwache Rechtschreibleistungen aufwiesen und zur positiven Stichprobe gehörten, wurden 67% gefördert (davon 22,3% LRS-Förderung). Von den schwachen Rechtschreibern in der negativen Stichprobe wurden dagegen nur 38%

der Schüler in eine Förderung einbezogen (davon 6,9% LRS-Förderung). Das Ergebnis belegt, dass in der Region mit insgesamt besseren Rechtschreibleistungen wesentlich mehr für die Förderung schwacher Rechtschreiber getan wurde. In der Region mit insgesamt schwächeren Rechtschreibleistungen ist deutlich weniger LRS-Förderung angeboten worden. Im Rahmen dieser Untersuchungen konnte nicht festgestellt werden, ob dieser Unterschied eine Frage der schulischen Erfassung und Interpretation der Schwierigkeiten darstellt und demnach Förderstunden in der negativen Stichprobe auch nicht beantragt wurden.

Art der Förderung	Stichproben Population 1993	
	positiv	negativ
Binnendifferenzierung	0	0
Allgemeine Förderung	35,7	38,1
LRS-Förderung	35,6	4,8

Tabelle 3.1.4 Zusammenhang zwischen schwachem Rechtschreibniveau (PR≤10) Klasse 2 und Art der Förderung in Klasse 3

Eine ähnliche Tendenz wie in der positiven Stichprobe 1993 ist hinsichtlich des Einsatzes spezifischer Förderung in der repräsentativen Stichprobe 1993 nachweisbar. 52,8% der schwachen Rechtschreiber wurden gefördert. In der 4. Klasse bekamen 61,7% der schwachen Rechtschreiber eine spezifische Förderung (davon 21% LRS-Förderung).

Rechtschreibentwicklung unter dem Einfluss der Intensivförderung

Analysiert wurden Schüler der Intensivförderklassen, die im Rahmen eines Schulversuchs 1995 bis 1997 nach Beendigung der 1. Klasse mit der Förderform begonnen haben. Parallel wurden Erhebungen bei den Schülern durchgeführt, die erst nach 2 Schuljahren in die spezifische Intensivförderform kamen, also ein Jahr älter waren.

Die Population, die nach Beendigung der 1. Klasse in die Förderform aufgenommen wurde, steigt direkt in die 2. Klasse auf (im folgenden o.W.- ohne Wiederholung-). Die Population, die erst nach der 2. Klasse in die Intensivförderung aufgenommen wird, wiederholte die 2. Klasse in Form eines Dehnjahres (im folgenden m.W.- mit Wiederholung).

Bei der Auswahl der Populationen ist auf eine Gleichverteilung der intellektuellen Leistungsdispositionen im Mittelwert geachtet worden.
Tabelle 3.1.5 soll eine Übersicht der verschiedenen Populationen geben:

Population 1995 **o.W.** bedeutet also im folgenden, dass die Schüler 1995 **nach Beendigung der 1. Klasse** in die Intensivförderform Klasse 2 aufgenommen wurden. Für die Population 1995 **m. W.** gilt, das die Schüler 1995 *nach Beendigung der 2. Klasse* ebenfalls in eine Intensivförderform Klasse 2 kamen. Die Populationen 1996 und 1997 sind entsprechend zu betrachten.

In den Populationen 1995 und 1996 mit und ohne Wiederholung wurden im Rahmen der prozessbegleitenden Diagnostik jeweils drei Erhebungszeitpunkte (Beginn der Intensivförderung, Ende der 2. Klasse und der 3. Klasse) analysiert. Für die Population 1997 lagen nur zwei Messpunkte vor. Die Leistungen der Schüler sind in vier Bereiche eingeteilt worden:

Populationen	Anzahl der Schüler innerhalb der Jahrgänge		
	1995	1996	1997
ohne Wiederholung der 2. Klasse	22	22	23
mit Wiederholung der 2. Klasse	16	24	24
Normalpopulation	23		
Gesamt	61	46	47

Tabelle 3.1.5 Übersicht der Populationen des Schulversuchs

A → PR > 50 gutes Niveau
B → PR < 50 im Bereich von Schwierigkeiten bis durchschnittliches Niveau
C → PR < 10 im Bereich einer Störung liegend
D → PR < 1 völliges Versagen
Gemessen wurde das Rechtschreibniveau in der 2. und 3. Klasse jeweils anhand eines Wort- (Lory) und eines Satzdiktates (Bauer). Beide Verfahren sind in der Schweiz normiert worden und über den Schulpsychologischen Dienst in St. Gallen zu beziehen.

Für die 1.Klasse galten die bereits vorgestellten Erhebungsmöglichkeiten (Behrndt/ Steffen/Watzek 1996).

Die Entwicklung der Schüler mit einem sehr schwachen Ausgangsniveau (C und D, n =110) soll zunächst in Tabelle 3.1.6 dargestellt werden. Ihr ist zu entnehmen, dass fast dreiviertel der jüngeren Schüler überhaupt keinen Zugang zur Schriftsprache zum Zeitpunkt der Ausgangsdiagnostik am Ende der 1. Klasse gefunden hatten (71,2%). Bei den älteren Schülern sind es etwas weniger gewesen (63,4%). Trotzdem erreichten fast 21% der jüngeren Schüler ein gutes Entwicklungsniveau auf der Wortebene zum Ende der 3. Klasse. Bei den älteren Schülern waren es nur 15%. Kein Schüler beider Populationen lag noch im Prozentrangbereich kleiner 1. Im elementaren Bereich konnte also bei den Schülern, die zu einem früheren Zeitpunkt in eine Intensivförderung kamen, ein höherer Leistungszuwachs erzielt werden.

Betrachtet man die Bewältigung von Anforderungen, bei denen für richtiges Schreiben ein schon höher entwickeltes Automatisierungsniveau vorausgesetzt wird, ergeben sich die Ergebnisse nach dem Satzdiktat (Bauer) (Tabelle 3.1.7).

Aus der Tabelle 3.1.7 ist zu entnehmen, dass keiner dieser Schüler am Ende der 3. Klasse in einem Prozentrangbereich zu finden ist, der unter 1 liegt. Der Anteil der Schüler in dem Prozentrangbereich größer als 50 (A) ist bei den älteren Schülern (mit Wiederholung) höher.

Bereits Ende der 2. Klasse ist zu erkennen, dass die positive Entwicklung der Rechtschreibfähigkeiten auf der Satzebene bei ihnen weiter fortgeschritten ist. Allerdings verläuft die Entwicklung, gemessen an der Alternorm, nicht kontinuierlich. Während bei den Jüngeren der Anteil von Schülern mit einem besseren Niveau immer größer wird, nimmt bei den Älteren der Anteil der Schüler, die noch in einem Bereich mit massiven Störungen liegen, wieder zu (43,7%).

	Ausgangsdiagnostik		Ende Klasse 2		Ende Klasse 3	
Niveaustufen	o.W.	*m.W.*	o.W.	*m.W.*	o.W.	*m.W.*
A	0,0%	*0,0%*	21,2%	*29,5%*	20,9%	*15,0%*
B	0,0%	*0,0%*	28,8%	*29,5%*	51,2%	*55,0%*
C	28,8%	*36,4%*	43,9%	*31,8%*	27,9%	*30,0%*
D	71,2%	*63,6%*	6,1%	*9,1%*	0,0%	*0,0%*

Tabelle 3.1.6 Entwicklung der Schüler mit massivem Rechtschreibversagen auf der Wortebene im Längsschnitt (o.w. = ohne Wiederholung, m.w. = mit Wiederholung der Klasse)

	Ausgangsdiagnostik		Ende Klasse 2		Ende Klasse 3	
Niveaustufen	o.W.	*m.W.*	o.W.	*m.W.*	o.W.	*m.W.*
A	0,0%	*0,0%*	6,1%	*13,6%*	4,7%	*15,0%*
B	0,0%	*0,0%*	37,9%	*49,0%*	55,8%	*41,3%*
C	28,8%	*31,8%*	47,0%	*31,8%*	39,5%	*43,7%*
D	71,2%	*68,2%*	9,1%	*5,6%*	0,0%	*0,0%*

Tabelle 3.1.7 Entwicklung der Schüler mit massiven Rechtschreibversagen auf der Satzebene im Längsschnitt (o.w. = ohne Wiederholung, m.w. = mit Wiederholung der Klasse)

Perspektiven für eine schulische LRS-Förderung

Die Ergebnisse der Projekte zeigen, dass eine schulische Frühförderung positive Auswirkungen auf die Entwicklung des Rechtschreibniveaus der Schüler in den untersuchten Gebieten in Mecklenburg-Vorpommern hat.

Im Sinne einer Qualitätssicherung im Bereich der Schulen sollte es zukünftig möglich sein, noch bestehende Unterschiede zwischen einzelnen Gebieten (siehe positive und negative Stichprobe) durch den Ausbau des Fördernetzes auszugleichen.

Um positive Erfolge zu bewahren sowie eine qualitativ hochwertige LRS-Förderung in Mecklenburg-Vorpommern insgesamt zu sichern, werden im folgenden dafür notwendige Parameter markiert:

Für Schüler mit Schwierigkeiten im Lesen und Schreiben soll im gesamten Grundschulbereich eine **prozessbegleitende Förderdiagnostik** mit dem Ziel erfolgen, individuelle Schwierigkeiten rechtzeitig zu erkennen und durch Veränderung und/oder Ergänzung der Förderpläne die erforderlichen Schritte zur Kompensierung der Schwachstellen einzuleiten.

Auf wesentliche Punkte der prozessbegleitenden LRS-Förderdiagnostik sei im folgenden eingegangen, da die Kritik der traditionellen Legasthenieförderung sich nach Grissemann (1996) vor allem auf folgende Punkte konzentrierte:

- Ausrichtung auf normierte Schulleistungstests zur Feststellung der Förderbedürftigkeit
- Ausrichtung auf legasthenietypische Fehler
- Ausrichtung auf Basalfunktionen
- Fehlende Ausrichtung auf die Prozesse des Lesens und Schreibens.

Mit der Konzipierung der Frühförderung (Schulversuch) ist davon ausgegangen worden, dass wesentliche Ziele der LRS- Förderung zum einen der Abbau der Schriftsprachschwierigkeiten und zum anderen die Bereitstellung von Techniken sind, die einen positiven Transfereffekt auf andere Lernsituationen ermöglichen, so dass die Gesamtsituation der LRS-Schüler verbessert wird.

Auf diesem Weg ist es für die Förderlehrer unumgänglich, ihre Ziele immer wieder zu kontrollieren und zu spezifizieren. Borchardt (1996) beschreibt im Zusammenhang mit Faktoren, die einer Verbesserung des Förderunterrichtes dienen, dass eine für die jeweiligen Kinder treffende Schwierigkeitsdosierung der Aufgaben von größter Bedeutung sei. Für eine Optimierung des Förderunterrichtes seien auch die Diagnose relevanter Lernvoraussetzungen und eine kontinuierliche unterrichtsbegleitende Diagnose von zentraler Bedeutung.

Schulleistungstests bieten für den Lehrer die Möglichkeit, unabhängig von dem Niveau der Klasse, den individuellen Leistungsstand zu bestimmen. Bei Klassen mit einem relativ homogenen Leistungsprofil, LRS-Klassen, kommt diesem Faktor sicherlich ein besonders hoher Stellenwert zu.

Prozessbegleitung bezieht sich also vor allem auf den Lese- und Schreiblernprozess. Da nicht immer auf psychometrisch abgesicherte Verfahren zurückgegriffen werden konnte, war es auch Anliegen des Schulversuchs, didaktisch bewährte Methoden und Verfahren der LRS-Lehrer einzubeziehen.

Die Diagnose relevanter Lernvoraussetzungen ist Bestandteil der Eingangsdiagnostik für die Intensivförderklassen. Zur Aufhellung des Bedingungsgefüges der schulischen Schwierigkeiten werden neben aktuellen schulischen Leistungen auch frühere Bedingungen einbezogen.

Das Niveau des Lesens und Schreibens ist in diesem Rahmen zu messen, um entsprechend der Phasen des Schriftspracherwerbs (Scheerer-Neumann 1989) fördern zu können.

Beobachtungen der LRS-Lehrer hinsichtlich der Lern- und Leistungsmotivation, der sozialen Kompetenz und der eingesetzten Lernstrategien gehören ebenfalls zu einer prozessorientierten LRS-Förderdiagnostik.

Das Schema der Abb. 3.4 soll den förderdiagnostischen Prozess in den LRS- Intensivförderformen verdeutlichen.

Folgende Grundaussagen lassen sich aus den Ergebnissen des „Schulversuchs 1995 bis 1999“ zur weiteren Entwicklung der LRS-Förderstrategie formulieren:

- Früherkennung und Frühförderung sind Voraussetzung für eine zielgerichtete Intensivförderung der Schüler mit massiven Schwierigkeiten im Lese-Rechtschreibprozess.

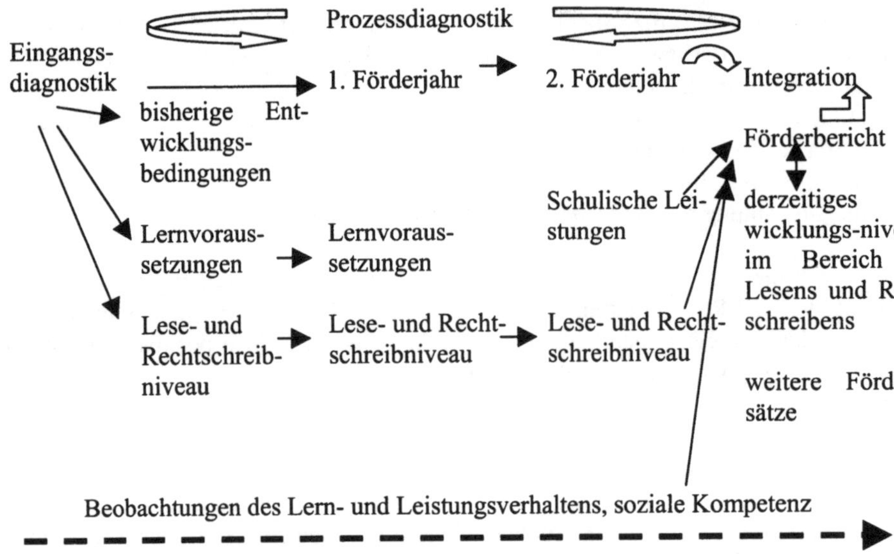

Abb 3.1.4 Förderdiagnostischer Prozess in den LRS- Intensivförderformen

- Beratung, Diagnostik und fachkompetente Förderung für Schüler mit massiven Schwierigkeiten im Lesen und Rechtschreiben sind unverzichtbare Bedingungen für die im Schulversuch praktizierte Intensivförderung.
- Innerhalb der Intensivförderung sind durch ein ausgebautes Adaptionsverfahren die Schüler mit erheblichen Schwierigkeiten auf den Reintegrationsprozess in ihre Stammklasse vorzubereiten.
- Innerhalb der Intensivförderung sind offene Lernsituationen methodisch-didaktisch aufzubereiten und so zu nutzen, dass Handlungskompetenzen des Einzelnen persönlichkeitsformend unterstützt werden können.
- Die Intensivförderung ist im Kontext mit dem sozialen Lernen im Umfeld der interkulturellen Erziehung eine Chance für die zunehmende Befähigung des Einzelnen, auch in schwierigen Situationen unterschiedliche Interessen wahrzunehmen.
- Die Intensivförderung erfordert den Einsatz von Personal mit sonderpädagogischer Aufgabenstellung im unterrichtsbegleitenden Bereich, um die ganzheitlichen Lernsituationen durch spielerische und anwendungsbezogene Handlungssituationen unter Einsatz variierter Materialien zu stützen. Folgender Grundsatz muss gelten: Was im Unterrichtsprozess aufgebaut wird, muss durch ganzheitliche Maßnahmen gesichert werden.
- Die Intensivförderung erhöht den Anspruch auf Durchlässigkeit allgemeinbildender Schulen für Schüler mit erheblichen Schwierigkeiten im Lesen und Rechtschreiben in allen Jahrgangstufen.
- Die Potenzen der Intensivförderung können in die methodisch-didaktische Gestaltung des förderorientierten Unterrichts in Diagnoseförderklassen einbezogen werden.
- Die Intensivförderung ermöglicht für Schülern mit erheblichen Schwierigkeiten eine adäquate Anbahnung berufsorientierter Fähigkeiten und den individuellen Zugang in die Arbeitswelt.

- Die Intensivförderung erfordert eine ausgeprägte schülerbezogene Teamarbeit der Lehrkräfte und dem Personal mit sonderpädagogischer Aufgabenstellung einer Einrichtung, den Fachleuten und Erziehungsberechtigten.

Die Ergebnisse der zweijährigen Intensivförderung belegen die Notwendigkeit des Einsatzes analytisch- synthetischer Unterrichtsverfahren, die hier innerhalb des Kieler Lese- und Rechtschreibaufbaus sowie der Förderstrategie nach Kossow zum Einsatz kamen.

Literaturergänzung:

Landesinstitut für Schule Aus und Weiterbildung: Erhebungsmaterialien der Forschungsgruppe „Frühförderung1993 bis 1998“. Handreichung vom Landesinstitut für Schule und Ausbildung. Schwerin 1998.

3.2 Verlaufsuntersuchungen zur schulischen Förderung von Kindern mit Legasthenie

Christian Klicpera und Barbara Gasteiger-Klicpera

Bevor wir mit der Darstellung der Anliegen und Probleme schulischer Förderung legasthener Kinder, wie sie sich aus Verlaufsuntersuchungen ergeben, beginnen, ist es sinnvoll, sich mit der Frage auseinanderzusetzen, warum eine spezielle Förderung von Kindern mit Lese- und Rechtschreibschwierigkeiten durch die Schule erfolgen soll. Unserer Ansicht nach legen mehrere Gründe nahe, darin eine vordringliche Aufgabe der Schule zu sehen.

Wegen der Bedeutung des Lesens und Schreibens für den weiteren Lebensweg der Kinder und insbesondere die berufliche Entwicklung (Mikulecky & Drew, 1991) muß es ein besonderes Anliegen der Schule sein, den Kindern eine sichere Basis in der Beherrschung der Schriftsprache zu vermitteln.

Die Fähigkeit zum Lesen und Schreiben stellt eine der wichtigsten Voraussetzungen zur Teilhabe am gesellschaftlichen Leben in einem größeren Gemeinwesen dar. Demokratisches Leben ist wesentlich darauf angewiesen, dass keine Gruppe in ihrer Fähigkeit zur Teilnahme am Leben der Gemeinschaft wesentlich behindert wird.

Die Fähigkeit zum Erlernen des Lesens und Schreibens ist individuell recht unterschiedlich ausgebildet und eine schwere Beeinträchtigung dieser Fähigkeit kann als eine wesentliche Benachteiligung angesehen werden, die auszugleichen bzw. absehbare negative Folgen abzuwenden ein schulischen Eingreifen erfordert.

Deutliche Schwierigkeiten beim Erlernen des Lesens und Schreibens sind – ohne Intervention – sehr stabil und bleiben von der 2. Klasse Grundschule an bei der Mehrzahl der Kinder bis zum Ende des Schulbesuchs und wahrscheinlich darüber hinaus erhalten. Dabei nimmt das Ausmaß des Rückstands gegenüber den gleichaltrigen Kindern – absolut gesehen – mit zunehmendem Alter immer weiter zu (Klicpera & Gasteiger-Klicpera, 1995). Diese hohe Stabilität und der zunehmende Rückstand dürften zu einem guten Teil dadurch bedingt sein, dass die leseschwachen Schüler nicht nur langsamer lesen und damit pro Zeiteinheit Lesen weniger Kontakt mit der Schrift haben. Vor allem lesen sie deutlich weniger außerhalb der Schule, da das Lesen für sie anstrengend und weniger belohnend ist. Hinzu kommt wahrscheinlich noch, dass sich – ohne Intervention – ungünstige Lesestrategien einstellen, die den weiteren Fortschritt behindern.

Mit dem geringeren Buchkontakt stellen sich eine Reihe negativer Sekundärfolgen ein. Die sprachlichen Fähigkeiten der Kinder, am deutlichsten an der Entwicklung des Wortschatzes abzulesen, entwickeln sich weniger weiter, sodass sich neben den Problemen bei der Lesesicherheit und der Lesegeläufigkeit fast notwendigerweise auch Schwierigkeiten im Leseverständnis einstellen (Share & Silva, 1988). Ebenso kommen bei den meisten Kindern zu den Rechtschreibschwierigkeiten auch Probleme im schriftlichen Ausdruck hinzu.

Diese Aufgabe – die zusätzliche schulische Förderung von lese- und rechtschreibschwachen Kindern – hat in den letzten vierzig Jahren ein sehr wechselhaftes Schicksal in den deutschsprachigen Ländern und nicht nur hier gehabt. Alles in allem kann man – so glauben wir –

feststellen, dass diese Aufgabe an den meisten Orten bisher nicht sehr konsequent angegangen wurde. Österreich scheint auf den ersten Blick eine Ausnahme darzustellen, da es hier in einer Reihe von Bundesländern eine bis in die frühen 60-er Jahre zurückreichende Tradition schulinterner Legasthenikerhilfe gibt, die nicht der Rücknahme spezieller Maßnahmen für Legastheniker in den alten deutschen Bundesländern zum Opfer gefallen ist, die man in den 70-er Jahren beobachten konnte. Schulischen Maßnahmen kommt in Österreich allerdings auch deshalb eine besondere Bedeutung zu, weil es bislang nur relativ wenig Angebote außerhalb der Schule gibt und diese auch – im Unterschied zu Deutschland – rein privat finanziert werden müssen.

Daher scheint es uns ein wichtiges Anliegen, die Arbeitsweise der schulischen Fördermaßnahmen für Legastheniker zu analysieren, sie besser zu verstehen und weiterzuentwickeln. Ein wichtiges Instrument dafür sind Verlaufsuntersuchungen.

Wenn wir von Verlaufsuntersuchungen zur schulischen Förderung von Legasthenikern reden, so meinen wir nicht Untersuchungen zur Evaluation bestimmter Förderansätze, die von den Entwicklern bestimmter Programme oder den Proponenten eines bestimmten Förderkonzepts in der Schule durchgeführt und evaluiert wurden, sondern wir sprechen von Versuchen, die Realisierung und Wirksamkeit schulischer Fördermaßnahmen dann zu evaluieren, wenn die Programmentwickler das Schulgebäude wieder verlassen haben, wenn also die Förderung institutionalisiert worden und der Alltag eingekehrt ist. Eine derartige Untersuchung kann also in einem gewissen Sinn als Versuch einer Qualitätskontrolle der laufenden Arbeit betrachtet werden. Sie muß dabei natürlich die gesamte Organisation und Arbeitsweise schulischer Förderung berücksichtigen, die Rahmenbedingungen dieser Förderung (von der Auswahl der Kinder, den zur Verfügung stehenden Mitteln bis zu den personellen Ressourcen, auf denen sie beruht, wie etwa der Ausbildung und den Fortbildungsangeboten der Lehrerinnen) ebenso wie die eigentlichen Inhalte der Fördermaßnahmen.

Wir haben bisher zwei derartige Verlaufsuntersuchungen zur schulischen Legasthenikerförderung in Österreich durchgeführt, die ich in den Grundzügen darstellen und einige ihrer Ergebnisse berichten möchte.

Zuvor jedoch noch einige Worte zu den seitens der Schule in Österreich vorgesehenen Maßnahmen. In Österreich sind in den meisten Bundesländern sogenannte funktionell-therapeutische Übungen vorgesehen, in denen in Form von Kursen, die entweder außerhalb der Unterrichtszeit oder begleitend zum regulären Unterricht stattfinden können, Kinder mit speziellen Schwächen zusätzlich gefördert werden. Für diese Kurse sind bei einer Größe von 6-8 Kindern jeweils zwei Unterrichtsstunden pro Woche vorgesehen, wobei die Kurse jedoch geteilt werden sollen, sodass pro Kleingruppe eine Wochenstunde zur Verfügung steht. Die Zielrichtung der Kurse ist zwar oft allgemeiner formuliert, ihr wesentliches Anliegen ist jedoch die Förderung von lese- und rechtschreibschwachen Kindern. Deshalb werden diese Kurse vielfach auch traditionell Legasthenikerförderkurse genannt. Wie die Lehrer dieses Anliegen realisieren, ist – im Rahmen der Lehrfreiheit – Sache jedes einzelnen Lehrers, der jedoch eine spezielle Ausbildung – entweder bereits im Rahmen der Lehrerausbildung oder im Rahmen der Lehrerfortbildung – absolviert haben muß.

Erste Verlaufsuntersuchung von 1983 bis 1987

In den Längsschnittuntersuchungen, die wir in Wien von 1983 bis 1993 durchführen konnten, hatten wir die Gelegenheit, in zwei Stichproben den Einfluß der Förderung lese- und rechtschreibschwacher Kinder über einen längeren Zeitraum hinweg zu beobachten. Die umfangreichere Längsschnittuntersuchung betraf die Entwicklung von etwa 500 Kindern aus 10 Schulen, die von Beginn der 2. bis zum Ende der 4. Klasse Grundschule (1984-1987) verfolgt wurde (Klicpera, Gasteiger-Klicpera & Hütter, 1993). Von diesen Kindern besuchte etwa ein Viertel die speziellen Fördermaßnahmen für Legastheniker in Österreich, den Legasthenikerförderkurs, in der 2. und etwa ein Sechstel in der 3. Klasse, sodass die Entwicklung von über hundert Kindern, die an den Fördermaßnahmen teilnahmen, beobachtet werden konnte. Es wurden dazu regelmäßig Tests mit den Kindern durchgeführt, gleichzeitig wurden jedoch auch die Lehrer, die Eltern und die Kinder selbst befragt sowie die Aktivitäten im Klassen- und im Förderunterricht beobachtet.

Wir hatten natürlich gehofft, dass wir in dieser relativ großen Stichprobe bei einem insgesamt bedeutsamen Zuwachs an Lese- und Rechtschreibfertigkeit und einem Rückgang der Schwierigkeiten im Lesen und Rechtschreiben jene Bedingungen herausarbeiten könnten, die zu diesem Erfolg beitragen.

Die Untersuchung konnte allerdings insgesamt keine Angleichung der Leistungen der Kinder, die die Förderkurse besuchten, an den Leistungsstand der übrigen Kinder in den Klassen feststellen. Auch wenn die Leistungsentwicklung der lese- und rechtschreibschwachen Kinder, die am Förderkurs teilnahmen oder aber nicht teilnahmen, miteinander verglichen wurde, ergab sich kein wesentlicher Vorteil der Teilnahme an einem Förderkurs. Im Rechtschreiben mußte bei den schwachen Schülern, die am Förderkurs teilnahmen, sogar eine relative Verschlechterung über die Zeit gegenüber den nicht teilnehmenden Schülern festgestellt werden. Dieser Vergleich war dadurch möglich, dass – wie wir etwas später noch darstellen – trotz der relativ hohen Teilnehmerquote von etwa 25% aller Schüler in der 2.Klasse bei weitem nicht alle lese- und rechtscheibschwachen Kinder in die Förderkurse aufgenommen wurden.

Die Studie versuchte im weiteren – trotz der eher ungünstigen Gesamtsituation, da sich ja insgesamt kein positiver Effekt zeigte – jene Bedingungen herauszuarbeiten, die mit einem relativ günstigen Gesamtergebnis verbunden waren, und jene, die zu einem negativen Ergebnis beizutragen schienen. Schließlich versuchte die Studie aufzuzeigen, welche ungünstigen Rahmenbedingungen die Arbeit der schulischen Legasthenikerförderung insgesamt behinderten. Auf diese beiden Aspekte möchten wir später noch etwas näher eingehen.

Neue Verlaufsuntersuchung 1998-1999

Im vergangenen Jahr ergab sich für uns neuerlich die Gelegenheit, die Praxis und die Auswirkungen der Legasthenikerförderung in zwei österreichischen Bundesländern zu untersuchen. Motiviert zu der neuerlichen Studie wurden wir vor allem durch die Neugierde, ob sich die von uns beschriebene Situation verändert hätte.

An dieser Untersuchung nahmen 1850 Kinder der 2., 3. und 4. Schulstufe der Grundschule aus 19 Schulen in 4 Schulbezirken teil, die das erste Mal im November und das zweite Mal im Mai/ Juni des gleichen Schuljahrs getestet wurden. Zur Testung des Lesens und Rechtschreibens wurden Parallelformen der neuen Wiener Lese- und Rechtschreibtestbatterien verwendet, die einen individuell vorzugebenden mündlichen Lesetest von 90 Wörtern bzw.

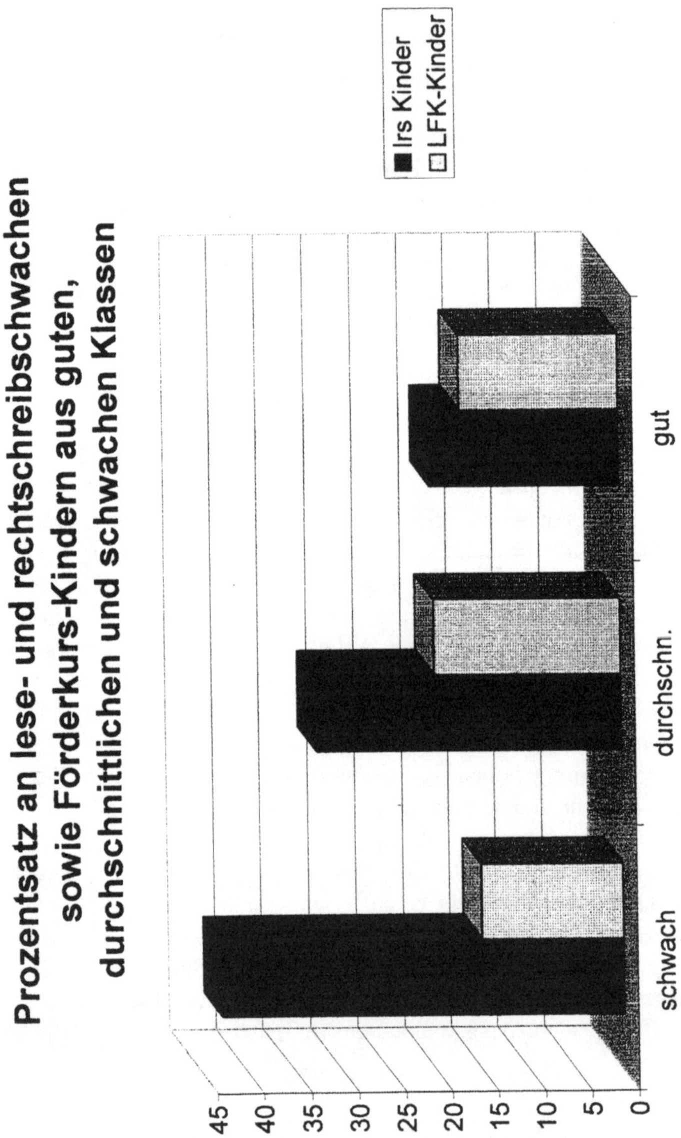

Abb.3.2.1 Leistungsentwicklung im Lesen und Rechtschreiben (T-Werte, wobei höhere Werte schlechtere Leistungen bedeuten) von Mitte der 2. bis Ende der 4. Klasse bei lese- und rechtschreibschwachen Kindern, die entweder an einem Legasthenikerförderkurs teilgenommen oder nicht teilgenommen haben (Längsschnittuntersuchung 1984-1987, nach Klicpera et al., 1993)

Pseudowörtern und verschiedene Rechtschreibtests mit insgesamt 180 Wörtern und Pseudowörtern, die teils als Diktat, teils als Wiedererkennungsaufgabe vorgegeben wurden, umfaßt.

Neuerlich wurden die Fortschritte im Lesen und Rechtschreiben jener Kinder bestimmt, die an den speziellen schulischen Fördermaßnahmen für Legastheniker teilnahmen, und mit jenen der nicht geförderten Kinder verglichen. Wie bereits bei der früheren Untersuchung war dies dadurch möglich, dass nur ein Teil der schwachen Kinder in den Förderkursen betreut wurde. Zur besseren Verständlichkeit wurden die Ergebnisse der Lese- und Rechtschreibtests für jeden Zeitpunkt und jeden Test in T-Werte transformiert, sodass die Werte über die Zeit und die Tests vergleichbar sind.

Wir sind mit der Dateneingabe des 2. Untersuchungszeitpunktes erst vor kurzem fertig geworden und konnten die Fehleranalyse noch nicht ganz abschließen, sodass ich ihnen vorläufige Ergebnisse mitteile. Um die Veränderungen über die Zeit zu analysieren, wurde eine Varianzanalyse mit wiederholten Messungen für die beiden Zeitpunkte und die drei Maße – Lesesicherheit, Lesegeschwindigkeit und Rechtschreibsicherheit – sowie in einem ersten Schritt für die interindividuellen Faktoren Klassenstufe (2., 3. und 4. Klasse) und Teilnahme an den Förderkursen gerechnet.

Dadurch, dass die Werte für jeden Zeitpunkt und für jede Klassenstufe getrennt T-normiert wurden, ergaben sich keine Unterschiede zwischen den beiden Zeitpunkten und zwischen den drei Klassenstufen. Es zeigten sich aber auch keinerlei Unterschiede in der Entwicklung zwischen jenen Kindern, die an den Fördermaßnahmen teilnahmen, und jenen, die nicht teilnahmen (Interaktion Zeit x Teilnahme: $F(1,1531)=0.01$, $p=0.95$) (Tab.1). Auch zwischen den verschiedenen Klassenstufen sind die Veränderungen über die Zeit vollständig miteinander vergleichbar. Die einzigen Unterschiede, die nachweisbar sind, betreffen einerseits das niedrigere Leistungsniveau der Kinder in den Förderkursen, das allerdings in der 2. und 3. Klasse nur etwas mehr als eine halbe Standardabweichung beträgt ($F(1,1531)=102.4$, $p<0.001$), andererseits das relativ geringere Leistungsniveau der geförderten Kinder im Rechtschreiben im Vergleich zum Lesen (Interaktion Maß x Teilnahme: $F(1,1531)=10.6$, $p<0.001$) und drittens die größeren Leistungsrückstände der geförderten Kinder in der 4.Klasse im Vergleich zum Leistungsniveau der Kinder, die nicht an den Förderkursen teilnahmen ($F(2,1531)=3.0$, $p=0.05$). Alle diese Effekte waren aber bereits zum ersten Testzeitpunkt nachweisbar und veränderten sich nicht mit der Zeit.

Sowohl bei den Kindern in den Förderkursen als auch bei den übrigen Kindern lag bereits bei der ersten Testung ein sehr unterschiedliches Leistungsniveau im Lesen und Rechtschreiben vor. Wenn wir dieses berücksichtigen und bei der statistischen Analyse als weiteren interindividuellen Faktor das Ausmaß der anfänglichen Schwierigkeiten im Lesen und Rechtschreiben (eingeteilt in drei Stufen – große, mäßige Schwierigkeiten und durchschnittliche bis gute Leistungen) miteinbeziehen, verändert sich das Bild bezüglich der Auswirkungen ein wenig. (Große Schwierigkeiten wurden im Rahmen dieser Untersuchung so definiert, daß die Kinder entweder in der Lesesicherheit, der Lesegeschwindigkeit oder der Rechtschreibsicherheit zu den schwächsten 15 Prozent der Klassenstufe zählen mussten. Dies war bei etwa 30% der Schüler der Fall. Um zu der Gruppe mit durchschnittlichen bis guten Leistungen zu zählen, mußten die Kinder auf der anderen Seite in allen drei Teilbereichen Leistungen mit einem Prozentrang über 30 erzielt haben. Kinder mit mäßigen Schwierigkeiten waren alle

Kinder zwischen den beiden Extremen, die also zwar keine sehr schwachen, aber auch keine durchgehend guten Leistungen erzielt hatten.)

	Keine Teilnahme				Teilnahme			
	November		Mai-Juni		November		Mai-Juni	
	Mw.	Std.	**Mw.**	Std.	**Mw.**	Std.	**Mw.**	Std.
Lesesicherheit:								
2. Klasse	**50,6**	9,5	**50,4**	9,9	**46,1**	11,8	**47,9**	10,4
3. Klasse	**50,7**	9,9	**50,7**	9,5	**47,1**	9,9	**46,6**	11,5
4. Klasse	**50,5**	9,3	**50,8**	7,7	**43,9**	15,3	**44,6**	10,3
Lesegeschwindigkeit:								
2. Klasse	**50,8**	10,1	**50,7**	9,9	**45,3**	8,3	**46,2**	9,8
3. Klasse	**50,9**	10,0	**50,9**	9,8	**46,4**	9,4	**46,1**	9,8
4. Klasse	**50,5**	9,8	**50,6**	9,8	**43,2**	10,6	**42,6**	9,6
Rechtschreiben:								
2. Klasse	**50,8**	9,9	**50,8**	9,8	**45,1**	9,5	**45,7**	10,1
3. Klasse	**51,1**	9,9	**51,2**	9,6	**45,2**	8,8	**43,4**	8,9
4. Klasse	**50,9**	9,5	**51,0**	9,7	**39,3**	10,1	**40,4**	8,5

Tabelle 3.2.1 T-Werte für die Lesesicherheit (Prozentsatz der korrekt gelesenen Wörter und Pseudowörter), die Lesegeschwindigkeit (Anzahl der pro Minute gelesenen Wörter) und Rechtschreibsicherheit (Prozentsatz der korrekt geschriebenen Wörter und Pseudowörter) (Mittelwerte sowie Standardabweichung): Vergleich der Entwicklung über die 2 Testzeitpunkte von Schülern der 2.-4. Klasse, die an den Legasthenikerförderkursen teilgenommen bzw. nicht teilgenommen haben.

Es wird deutlich, dass insgesamt über die Zeit eine leichte Angleichung der Leistungsgruppen stattfindet (Interaktion Zeit x Leistungsgruppen: F(2,1519)=19.2, p<0.001) (Tab.2). Wenn dies berücksichtigt wird, dann zeigt sich, dass bei Kindern, die an den Förderkursen teilgenommen haben, ein etwas geringerer Fortschritt als bei den Kindern, die nicht den Förderkurs besuchten (Interaktion Zeit x Teilnahme: F(1,1519)=7.0, p<0.01), festzustellen ist. Dies ist vor allem bei Kindern ohne besondere Schwächen im Lesen und Rechtschreiben, die an den Förderkursen teilgenommen bzw. nicht teilgenommen haben, deutlich, allerdings ist diese 3-Weg-Interaktion nicht ganz signifikant (Interaktion Zeit x Teilnahme x Leistungsgruppen: F(2,1519)=2.2, p=0.11). Im übrigen bestätigt diese Analyse die bereits beschriebenen Effekte.

Zu kritischen Fragen bezüglich der mangelnden Effektivität schulischer Fördermaßnahmen.

Mit diesen eher ernüchternden Befunden zur Effektivität der schulischen Fördermaßnahmen für Legastheniker stehen wir nicht allein, vielmehr entsprechen sie im Grundtenor nahezu allen bisher vorliegenden Untersuchungen (u.a. Rainer, 1982; Seyfried & Rop, 1985). Daher möchten wir im Folgenden die wesentlichen Kritikpunkte, die sich an die gegenwärtige Form der Realisierung bzw. Umsetzung schulischer Fördermaßnahmen richten, anführen und die Konsequenzen, die sich aus dieser Kritik ergeben, darstellen. Im weiteren möchten wir Alternativen zur derzeitigen Praxis aufzeigen.

Probleme bei der Auswahl für die Förderung

Als ersten Kritikpunkt müssen wir anführen, dass schulische Legasthenikerförderung Probleme hat, die Förderung zielgenau jenen Kindern anzubieten, die eine zusätzliche Hilfe benötigen. Dies scheint uns ein recht gewichtiges Problem zu sein, auf das wir bereits bei unserer ersten Untersuchung hingewiesen haben. In der damaligen Untersuchung konnten wir zeigen, dass auf der einen Seite nur die Hälfte der Kinder, die eine Förderung wegen ihrer besonderen Probleme beim Lesen- und Schreibenlernen brauchen, diese Hilfe bekommt, während auf der anderen Seite die Hälfte jener Schüler, die in die Legasthenikerförderkurse aufgenommen wurden, – selbst bei einer sehr weiten Definition von Lese- und Rechtschreibschwierigkeiten (wenn man nämlich alle Schüler, die beim Lesen und Rechtschreiben zu den schwächsten 30 Prozent zählen, als förderungswürdig betrachtet) –eine zusätzliche Förderung eigentlich nicht benötigt.

Die Untersuchung, die wir im vergangenen Schuljahr durchgeführt haben, hat diese Ergebnisse als noch immer gültig bestätigt, ja in der Tendenz sogar stärker ausgeprägt gefunden. Obwohl die Förderkurse in den von uns untersuchten Schulen noch immer einen relativ großen Teil der Schüler erreichen, nämlich etwa ein Sechstel, nimmt derzeit nur etwa ein Drittel der Kinder, die im Lesen und Rechtschreiben Schwierigkeiten haben, daran teil. Selbst wenn man die Schüler mit nicht-deutscher Muttersprache und mangelhaften Deutschkenntnissen ausschließt, wird der Anteil der schwachen Schüler, die der Förderkurs erreicht, nicht wesentlich größer. Auf der anderen Seite bestätigte sich, dass auch viele Kinder mit geringen Problemen im Lesen und Rechtschreiben, ja sogar Schüler mit durchschnittlichen Leistungen im Lesen und Rechtschreiben an den Förderkursen teilnehmen.

Was sind nun die Gründe für die mangelhafte Zielgenauigkeit. Hier sind vor allem drei Dinge zu nennen:

einmal die Tatsache, dass sich die Auswahlentscheidung weitgehend auf das Lehrerurteil und relativ unverlässliche Erhebungsprozeduren stützt. So werden kaum normierte Tests für die Auswahl der Kinder zu den Förderkursen verwendet, sondern zumeist von den Lehrerinnen selbst zusammengestellte Diktate, die zum Teil noch von Klasse zu Klasse variieren und durch unterrichtsnahes Material ergänzt werden. Zudem wird bei der Auswertung vielfach gar nicht die Fehleranzahl berücksichtigt, sondern nur die Art der Fehler.

zum Zweiten die Annahme, dass es bei der Auswahl der Kinder für die Legasthenikerförderkurse darum geht, Kinder mit simplen Lese- und Rechtschreibschwächen von Legasthenikern zu unterscheiden und dass dafür bestimmte Merkmale – vor allem das Fehlerprofil der Kinder – einen klaren Indikator darstellen. Hier spielen auch Vorurteile und stereotype Vorstellungen über das Wesen der Legasthenie eine beträchtliche Rolle, die sich in den Lehrereinstellungen trotz gegenteiliger Forschungsevidenz halten. Dies gilt – wie wir in der früheren Untersuchung im Detail aufzeigen konnten – etwa für Ansichten über die Händigkeit der Kinder, wodurch Linkshänder eine deutlich größere Chance zur Teilnahme an den Förderkursen haben als Rechtshänder, und für die Ansichten über die besondere Bedeutung von Reversionsfehlern, wodurch auch Kinder in die Förderkurse überwiesen wurden, bei denen die Lehrer meinten, Reversionsfehler beobachtet zu haben, auch wenn die Kinder durchschnittlich lesen und rechtschreiben konnten.

	Keine Teilnahme				Teilnahme			
	November		Mai-Juni		November		Mai-Juni	
	Mw.	Std.	**Mw.**	Std.	**Mw.**	Std.	**Mw.**	Std.
LRS sehr schwache Kinder								
Lesesicherheit:								
2.Klasse	**42,2**	13,1	**43,6**	13,4	**40,2**	13,8	**43,2**	11,8
3.Klasse	**40,8**	12,7	**42,5**	11,8	**41,4**	10,2	**42,0**	13,1
4.Klasse	**39,9**	11,6	**44,2**	10,1	**37,9**	14,7	**41,5**	10,8
Lesegeschwindigkeit:								
2.Klasse	**43,5**	8,3	**44,1**	8,5	**41,1**	6,0	**42,7**	9,5
3.Klasse	**42,0**	8,3	**42,1**	8,3	**40,3**	6,9	**39,7**	6,5
4.Klasse	**41,0**	7,5	**41,2**	6,8	**39,0**	7,4	**39,1**	7,9
Rechtschreiben:								
2.Klasse	**42,1**	9,0	**44,3**	9,2	**39,0**	8,7	**39,5**	9,3
3.Klasse	**41,0**	8,7	**41,8**	8,6	**39,8**	7,3	**39,4**	7,5
4.Klasse	**41,2**	9,5	**42,1**	10,1	**35,1**	7,4	**37,6**	7,1
LRS schwache Kinder								
Lesesicherheit:								
2.Klasse	**50,3**	4,5	**49,9**	7,1	**49,2**	4,4	**48,9**	7,7
3.Klasse	**48,4**	5,4	**49,5**	8,2	**49,9**	5,4	**49,0**	6,5
4.Klasse	**49,8**	5,2	**50,2**	5,7	**57,1**	4,6	**52,0**	5,1
Lesegeschwindigkeit:								
2.Klasse	**48,0**	7,2	**48,2**	8,3	**45,5**	6,0	**44,9**	7,6
3.Klasse	**48,1**	7,2	**48,7**	7,4	**47,5**	5,6	**48,1**	5,8
4.Klasse	**47,8**	6,7	**47,9**	6,8	**45,8**	6,4	**45,8**	5,2
Rechtschreiben:								
2.Klasse	**49,0**	7,7	**49,0**	9,1	**47,6**	6,1	**49,8**	6,1
3.Klasse	**48,4**	6,3	**48,8**	7,2	**46,6**	5,6	**45,3**	7,9
4.Klasse	**48,6**	6,5	**49,3**	7,1	**44,4**	6,3	**44,6**	5,6

	Keine Teilnahme				Teilnahme			
	November		Mai-Juni		November		Mai-Juni	
	Mw.	Std.	**Mw.**	Std.	**Mw.**	Std.	**Mw.**	Std.
durchschnittliche und gute Kinder								
Lesesicherheit:								
2.Klasse	**55,5**	3,6	**54,1**	6,1	**55,4**	3,3	**54,0**	5,1
3.Klasse	**56,1**	4,3	**54,7**	5,7	**55,2**	4,3	**51,6**	9,5
4.Klasse	**55,9**	3,8	**54,2**	4,5	**58,1**	2,0	**52,8**	3,6
Lesegeschwindigkeit:								
2.Klasse	**56,3**	8,8	**55,3**	8,5	**54,7**	8,0	**53,5**	8,5
3.Klasse	**55,9**	7,9	**55,4**	8,4	**56,9**	6,8	**55,4**	10,2
4.Klasse	**56,4**	7,8	**56,2**	8,0	**62,0**	9,8	**57,3**	8,3
Rechtschreiben:								
2.Klasse	**56,5**	6,9	**55,2**	8,2	**53,9**	5,6	**53,5**	6,8
3.Klasse	**57,0**	6,9	**56,3**	7,2	**54,2**	5,6	**48,7**	9,7
4.Klasse	**56,9**	5,7	**56,4**	6,6	**56,6**	6,1	**52,9**	5,3

Tabelle 3.2.2 T-Werte für die Lesesicherheit (Prozentsatz der korrekt gelesenen Wörter und Pseudowörter), die Lesegeschwindigkeit (Anzahl der pro Minute gelesenen Wörter) und Rechtschreibsicherheit (Prozentsatz der korrekt geschriebenen Wörter und Pseudowörter) (Mittelwerte sowie Standardabweichung): Vergleich der Entwicklung über die 2 Testzeitpunkte von Schülern der 2.-4. Klasse, die bei der Anfangstestung im November einen unterschiedlichen Leistungsstand im Lesen und Rechtschreiben hatten und an den Legasthenikerförderkursen teilgenommen bzw. nicht teilgenommen haben.

Drittens die großen Unterschiede zwischen verschiedenen Klassen der gleichen Schulstufe im Leistungsstand im Lesen und Rechtschreiben sowie die mangelnde Berücksichtigung dieser Unterschiede in der Zuweisung der Kinder zu den Förderkursen. Die Lehrer tendieren dazu, die für die Förderung zur Verfügung stehenden Plätze in den Förderkursen auszunutzen, ohne das – manchmal besonders gute, manchmal aber auch sehr schlechte – Leistungsniveau der Klasse zu berücksichtigen.

Bereits in der früheren Untersuchung wurde auf die mangelnde Übereinstimmung zwischen dem Leistungsstand der Klassen und der Zuweisung zu den Förderkursen hingewiesen. Die neue Untersuchung fand dies sehr eindrucksvoll bestätigt. Wenn wir die Klassen pro Klassenstufe nach dem Leistungsstand im Rechtschreiben in Drittel unterteilen, so können wir feststellen, daß in der 2. und 3. Klassenstufe in den Klassen, die zum schlechtesten Drittel gehören, doppelt so viele Kinder mit größeren Schwierigkeiten im Lesen und Rechtschreiben sind als in den Klassen des besseren Drittels, daß aber eher weniger Schüler in den Legasthenikerförderkurs überwiesen wurden (siehe Abb. 3.2.2).

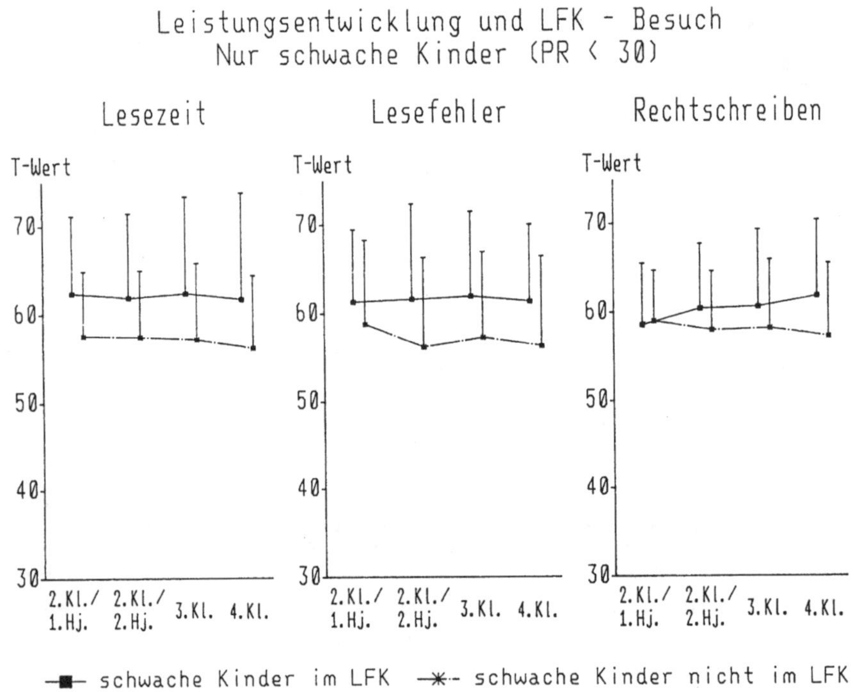

Abb. 3.2.2 Prozentsatz an lese- und rechtschreibschwachen Kindern in guten, durchschnittlichen und schwachen Klassen der 2. und 3. Klassenstufe Grundschule sowie Prozentsatz an Kindern, die aus diesen Klassen an einem Legasthenikerförderkurs teilgenommen haben (Längsschnittuntersuchung 1998-1999)

Diese Mängel bei der Zuweisung erscheinen uns aus mehreren Gründen relevant.

Sie führen dazu, dass die Förderung nicht sehr intensiv sein kann, weil zu viele Kinder identifiziert werden, die einer Förderung bedürfen, und eine intensive Förderung daher nicht mehr finanzierbar ist.

Sie führen weiter dazu, dass die Probleme der Kinder in den Legasthenikerförderkursen sehr unterschiedlich sind. Manche der Kinder haben größere Probleme beim Lesen, ja sind noch kaum über die Anfänge des Lesenlernens hinausgekommen. Andere sind recht gut im Lesen und haben nur beim Rechtschreiben Probleme. Einige Kinder haben sogar weder beim Lesen noch beim Rechtschreiben merkbar größere Schwierigkeiten als ihre Alterskollegen. Dies ergibt beträchtliche Schwierigkeiten bei der Vorbereitung und Durchführung der Förderkurse.

Unklarheit der Förderziele

Das zweite große Problem der schulischen Legasthenikerförderung in Österreich betrifft die Ausrichtung der Förderung auf wenigstens drei Ziele, die in eine unterschiedliche Richtung gehen und damit nur schwer unter einen Hut zu bekommen sind. Diese Vielfalt der Ziele führt dazu, dass die wenige zur Verfügung stehende Zeit nicht für das Erreichen von machbaren Zielen genutzt wird und damit für Kinder, Eltern und Lehrer merkbare Veränderungen bewirkt. Wenigstens in Teilen konnten wir vor allem in den recht zeitintensiven Begleituntersuchungen zur Legasthenikerförderung, die wir Anfang der 80-Jahre durchgeführt haben, einen Beleg dafür finden, dass das Ziel einer Förderung von basalen Teilleistungen neben der Förderung des Lesens und Rechtschreibens zu einer Reduktion der für das Üben des Lesens und Schreibens zur Verfügung stehenden Zeit geführt und damit den Fördererfolg beeinträchtigt hat.

Wir konnten zeigen, dass insgesamt relativ viel Zeit in den Förderkursen für Dinge verwendet wird, die nicht unmittelbar dem Lesen und Scheiben dienen, sondern für die Förderung von „basalen" Fertigkeiten (Funktionsübungen zur Verbesserung von angeblich für das Lesen und Schreiben grundlegenden Fertigkeiten wie etwa der Raum-Lage-Orientierung) gedacht sind. Weiters konnten wir zeigen, dass Förderkurse, die relativ erfolgreich waren, mehr Zeit für die Übung des Lesens und Rechtschreibens zur Verfügung stellten und weniger für Übungen in „basalen Teilleistungen" als Kurse mit einem geringeren Erfolg.

Auch in der neuen Verlaufsuntersuchung konnten wir einen Zusammenhang zwischen den Fortschritten beim Lesen und Rechtschreiben und der Konzentration der Förderung auf den Bereich des Lesens und Rechtschreibens feststellen. Wenn die Kinder auf Grund einer Regression der Ausgangs- auf die Schlußleistungen im Lesen und Rechtschreiben in jene geteilt wurden, die sich mehr bzw. weniger als der Durchschnitt verbessert hatten, und dann die Schwerpunkte der Förderprogramme für diese Kinder, die von den Kursleitern angegeben wurden, verglichen wurden, so zeigte sich, dass bei Kindern mit geringen Fortschritten Konzentrationsübungen und Übungen zur visuellen und akustischen Differenzierung einen signifikant größeren Stellenwert hatten als bei Kindern mit besseren Fortschritten. Ähnliches gilt auch (allerdings nicht signifikant) für Übungen in anderen Teilleistungsbereichen. Demgegenüber traten die Übungen im Lesen und Rechtschreiben bei Kindern mit geringeren Fortschritten eher zurück.

Damit wird ein Problem angesprochen, das wir als grundlegend für die schulische Förderung von Legasthenikern erachten, nämlich dass sich die Lehrerinnen von Förderkursen vielfach an Konzepten orientieren, die keine geeignete Grundlage für eine effiziente Förderung darstellen, ja einer solchen Förderung eher im Wege stehen, wie wir dies für Übungen zur Förderung von „basalen Teilleistungen" (für eine allgemeiner gehaltenere Kritik an solchen Funktionsübungen siehe auch Mann, 1979) und an anderer Stelle für kinesiologische Übungen (Klicpera & Gasteiger-Klicpera, 1996) zeigen konnten. Diese Möglichkeit ergibt sich aus der Lehrfreiheit und der freien Methodenwahl im Unterricht.

Dem kann nur entgegengewirkt werden, indem auf empirische Evidenz gesetzt und der Nachweis verlangt wird, dass die verwendeten Methoden ein probates Mittel zum Erzielen von Lernfortschritten in den Bereichen des Lesens und Schreibens bei den Kindern sind. Wege dazu sind neben der Intensivierung von Fortbildungsmaßnahmen auch Maßnahmen zur Effektivitäts- bzw. Qualitätssicherung. Dies können u.a. Verlaufsuntersuchungen wie die eben berichteten sein, deren Ergebnisse den Lehrerinnen rückgemeldet werden.

Ungünstige Rahmenbedingungen für den Förderunterricht in vielen Schulen

Trotz des relativ langen Bestehens von Fördermaßnahmen für legasthene Kinder in Österreich zeigt sich an einer Reihe an Merkmalen, dass die Fördermaßnahmen eine Randstellung im schulischen Leben führen. Dies gilt zu gutem Teil noch immer für die räumliche Situation, die das Abhalten von Förderkursen unter optimalen Bedingungen an vielen Schulen verhindert.

Zudem ist festzustellen, dass manche organisatorischen Bedingungen und manche Regelungen der Förderung von lese- und rechtschreibschwachen Kindern nicht sehr dienlich sind, wie wir dies etwa bei der Auswahl der Kinder aufgezeigt haben.

Allgemeinere Gefahren einer speziellen Trennung außerhalb des Regelunterrichts

Hinzu kommen negative Auswirkungen, die sich bei einer Trennung der Förderung vom regulären Unterricht fast unwillkürlich einschleichen (siehe auch Johnston & Allington, 1991) und die den erwartbaren Fördererfolg zusätzlich unterminieren.

Hierbei ist vor allem hervorzuheben, dass durch die Trennung des Förderunterrichts vom regulären Leseunterricht die Gefahr groß wird, dass Kinder mit Lese- und Rechtschreibschwierigkeiten allzu sehr mit dem Drill an Wortlisten und eher eintönigem Übungsmaterial beschäftigt werden und damit Probleme mit der Generalisation des Gelernten und seiner Übertragung in den regulären Unterricht haben.

Alternativen

Was sind nun die Alternativen für die derzeitige Gestaltung der schulischen Förderung von lese- und rechtschreibschwachen Kindern in Österreich? Sehr vereinfachend denken wir, dass folgende Richtung eine deutliche Verbesserung der Förderpraxis bedeuten würde: Die Förderung müßte früher erfolgen, sich auf eine kleinere Zahl von Kindern konzentrieren, aber dafür intensiver sein und sich klarer auf die Erhöhung der Lese- und Rechtschreibfertigkeit der Kinder konzentrieren, wobei das Entscheidende wohl die Verbesserung der Lesefertigkeit ist, die soweit gehen sollte, dass die Kinder einen für sie interessanten Text in für sie belohnender Weise sinnerfassend und mit ausreichender Leichtigkeit und Geläufigkeit lesen können.

Ein gutes Beispiel dafür, was schulische Förderung bringen kann, wenn sie mit hinreichender Intensität und relativ frühzeitig erfolgt, bietet das Förderprogramm des Reading Recovery, das ausgehend von Neuseeland in den letzten Jahren auch in den USA in mehreren größeren Längsschnittuntersuchungen erprobt wurde (Center, Wheldall, Freeman et al. 1995). Auch andere Programme mit einer etwas anderen Schwerpunktsetzung wie jenes von Vellutino und Mitarbeitern (Vellutino, Scanlon, Sipay et al. 1996) scheinen vielversprechend zu sein.

In diesen Programmen werden Kinder noch während des Erstleseunterrichts – im Fall von deutlichen Schwierigkeiten bei Lesen- und Schreibenlernen – soweit gefördert, dass sie dem regulären Unterricht wieder folgen können. Die Förderung erfolgt einzeln oder in einer kleinen Gruppe von 2-3 Kindern täglich etwa eine halbe Stunde lang. Sie ist damit zeitlich recht intensiv, dauert aber im Regelfall nur 3-4 Monate.

Wir müssen uns allerdings bei der Bewertung dieser Programme bewußt sein, was sie bringen können und was nicht. I.A. sind sie in der Lage, einige wesentliche Lernvoraussetzungen für das Lesenlernen vor allem bei jenen Kindern auszugleichen, die wegen unzureichender Förderung vor Schulbeginn mit mangelnden Lernvoraussetzungen in die Schule eingetreten und deshalb in Gefahr sind, soweit beim Lesenlernen zurückzubleiben, dass sie vom regulären Unterricht nicht mehr profitieren können. Solche Kinder können zu einem großen Teil durch das Reading Recovery Programm an den Durchschnitt der Klasse herangebracht werden. Es bleiben aber auch bei dieser Förderung einige Kinder – wahrscheinlich zwei bis drei Prozent, die eine noch intensivere und länger anhaltende Unterstützung benötigen.

Literatur

Center, Y., Wheldell, K., Freeman, L., Outhred, L. & McNaught, M. (1995). An evaluation of reading recovery. Reading Research Quarterly, 30, 240-263.

Johnston,P. & Allington,R.L. (1991). Remediation. In: R.Barr, M.L.Kamil, P.Mosenthal & P.D.Pearson (Eds.) Handbook of research on reading, Vol.II (pp 984-1012). New York: Longman.

Klicpera,C. & Gasteiger-Klicpera,B. (1995). Psychologie der Lese- und Schreibschwierigkeiten – Entwicklung, Ursachen, Förderung. Weinheim: Beltz & Psychologie Verlags Union.

Klicpera,C. & Gasteiger-Klicpera,B. (1996). Auswirkungen einer Schulung des zentralen Hörvermögens nach edu-kinesiologischen Konzepten auf Kinder mit Lese- und Rechtschreibschwierigkeiten. Heilpädagogische Forschung, 22, 57-64.

Klicpera,C., Gasteiger-Klicpera,B. & Hütter,E. (1993). Die Legasthenikerförderung in zwei Wiener Schulbezirken. Eine Evaluationsstudie einer schulinternen Fördermaßnahme. In: Bundesministerium für Unterricht und Kunst (Hrsg.) Was macht die Förderung effektiv? Kontroverse (?) Konzepte zur Legasthenikerbetreuung. Beiträge zur pädagogischen Psychologie Nr. 769-778 (S.41-147). Wien: Ketterl-Verlag.

Mann,L. (1979). On the trail of process: A historical perspective on cognitive processes and their training. New York: Grune & Stratton.

Mikulecky,L. & Drew,R. (1991). Basic literacy skills in the workplace. In: R.Barr, M.L.Kamil, P.Mosenthal & P.D.Pearson (Eds.) Handbook of research on reading, Vol.II (pp 669-689). New York: Longman.

Rainer,S. (1982). Legasthenikerbetreuung – eine pädagogische Verpflichtung. Beiträge zur Pädagogischen Psychologie Nr.627-632. Wien: Ketterl Verlag.

Seyfried,P. & Rop,I. (1985). Ergebnisse zur schulischen Legasthenikerbetreuung. Wien: Ketterl.

Share,D.L. & Silva,P.A. (1988). Language deficits and specific reading retardation: Cause or effect? British Journal of Disorders of Communication, 22, 219-226.

Vellutino,F.R., Scanlon,D.M., Sipay,E.R., Small,S.G., Pratt,A., Chen,R.S. & Denckla,M.B. (1996). Cognitive profiles of difficult-to-remediate and readily remediated poor readers: Early intervention as a vehicle for distinguishing between cognitive and experiential deficits as basic causes of specific reading disability. Journal of Educational Psychology, 88, 601-638.

3.3 Die Würzburger Längsschnittstudien zur frühen Prävention von Lese-Rechtschreibschwäche

Wolfgang Schneider

Es gibt inzwischen eine Vielzahl von Studien, die nur unbefriedigende Effekte bei der Förderung von Schulkindern mit spezifischen Lese-Rechtschreibdefiziten (sog. Legasthenikern) belegen. Dies ist insbesondere dann der Fall, wenn sich die Schüler schon in höheren Klassenstufen befinden (vgl. Mannhaupt, 1994; Scheerer-Neumann, 1988). Dies mag zum einen daran liegen, dass die verfügbaren Förderprogramme nicht hinreichend auf die Vielfalt möglicher Schwächen eingehen. Andererseits sind auch zweifellos Motivationsprobleme der älteren Schüler für die nur spärlichen Erfolge der Trainingsbemühungen mitverantwortlich. Aufgrund zahlreicher Mißerfolgserlebnisse hat sich eine ‚Sekundärsymptomatik' ausgebildet, die darin besteht, dass die Thematik Lesen und Rechtschreiben außerordentlich unbeliebt geworden ist. Diese negative Voreinstellung schränkt die Möglichkeit von Trainingserfolgen stark ein.

Obwohl eigene Trainingsansätze bei fortgeschrittenen Grundschülern mit Lese-Rechtschreibschwierigkeiten durchaus positive Wirkungen hervorriefen (z.B. Schneider & Springer, 1978), habe ich mich seit ca. 15 Jahren verstärkt mit der Frage beschäftigt, ob es nicht vergleichsweise lohnender ist, sich auf Möglichkeiten der frühzeitigen Verhinderung von Lese-Rechtschreibproblemen im Grundschulalter zu konzentrieren. Seit Beginn der achtziger Jahre beschäftigten sich Lese-Rechtschreibforscher zunehmend damit, den frühen Schriftspracherwerb genauer zu untersuchen. Man nahm nicht länger an, dass der Schuleintritt im Hinblick auf das Lesen- und Schreibenlernen die ‚Stunde Null' darstellte, sondern ging davon aus, dass schon im Vorschulalter wichtige Weichen für spätere Entwicklungsverläufe gestellt werden (vgl. Brügelmann, 1984; Schneider, Brügelmann & Kochan, 1990). So ließ sich etwa im Rahmen mehrerer Längsschnittstudien zeigen, dass Merkmale der sog. ‚sprachlichen Bewußtheit', also der Fähigkeit junger Kinder, Reime zu erkennen oder Silben in Wörtern zu unterscheiden, eine hohe prognostische Bedeutung für die späteren Lese- und Rechtschreibleistungen der gleichen Kinder hatten (z.B. Bradley & Bryant, 1985; Schneider & Näslund, 1993). Diese Fähigkeit zum Erkennen größerer Spracheinheiten wurde von Skowronek und Marx (1989) als ‚phonologische Bewußtheit im weiteren Sinne' bezeichnet und von der Fähigkeit abgegrenzt, einzelne Laute/Phoneme in Wörtern oder Silben wahrzunehmen. Letztere wurde für den späteren Schriftspracherwerb als vergleichsweise noch bedeutsamer eingestuft und als ‚phonologische Bewußtheit im engeren Sinne' bezeichnet.

Ergebnisse aus Trainingsstudien mit unausgelesenen (‚normalen') Kindergartenkindern.

Die Relevanz der frühen phonologischen Bewußtheit für den Schriftspracherwerb in der Schule wurde in einer Reihe von Trainingsstudien belegt, in denen die Auswirkungen vorschulischer Förderung im Bereich der phonologischen Bewußtheit für das Lesen und Schreiben im Grundschulalter untersucht wurden. Sicherlich am bekanntesten ist die skandinavische Langzeitstudie von Lundberg, Frost und Petersen (1988) geworden. Die Autoren entwickelten ein Trainingsprogramm, das bei einer Stichprobe von ca. 250 Kindergartenkindern (die sich im letzten Kindergartenjahr befanden) innerhalb eines Zeitraums von ca. 9 Monaten von den Erzieherinnen durchgeführt wurde. Es wurde dabei Wert darauf gelegt, dass in diesem Zeitraum das Training an jedem Wochentag für ca. eine Viertelstunde in kleinen Gruppen stattfand.

Die Befunde der Studie waren durchaus positiv. Die geförderten Kinder erwiesen sich im Vergleich mit einer Gruppe von nicht geförderten Kindern (der Kontrollgruppe) unmittelbar nach Abschluß des Trainings in allen erfaßten Maßen der phonologischen Bewußtheit als deutlich überlegen. Beide Gruppen hatten sich vor Trainingsbeginn in dieser Hinsicht nicht unterschieden. Auch bei einem ‚metalinguistischen Transfertest', über den vier Monate später (also kurz nach der Einschulung) langfristige Trainingseffekte mit neuen Aufgaben zur phonologischen Bewußtheit geprüft wurden, fand sich das gleiche Bild. Die Unterschiede zwischen den beiden Gruppen waren nicht nur statistisch signifikant sondern auch praktisch bedeutsam. Beeindruckend erschien auch der Tatbestand, dass sich die Vorteile der trainierten Gruppe im Bereich der sprachlichen Bewußtheit auch im späteren Schriftspracherwerb niederschlugen. So erwiesen sich die Kinder der Trainingsgruppe denen der Kontrollgruppe bis zum Ende der Untersuchung (dem Ende der dritten Klassenstufe) im Lesen und Rechtschreiben als deutlich überlegen.

Diese positiven Befunde wurden in der internationalen Forschung mit großer Aufmerksamkeit registriert. Es stellte sich bald die Frage, inwieweit diese Ergebnisse über unterschiedliche Orthographien hinweg verallgemeinerbar waren. Weiterhin blieb unklar, ob die für vergleichsweise ‚alte' und damit kognitiv schon insgesamt weit entwickelte dänische Kindergartenkinder (ca. 7 Jahre) erzielten Effekte auch für jüngere Kindergartenkinder Gültigkeit haben. Um die Übertragbarkeit dieser Befunde auf den deutschsprachigen Bereich zu überprüfen, führte ich in Zusammenarbeit mit Petra Küspert, Ellen Roth, Mechtild Visé und Marco Ennemoser ähnlich angelegte Studien im Würzburger Raum durch. Zunächst ging es darum, die Bedeutung des Trainings der phonologischen Bewußtheit für unausgelesene (‚normale') Gruppen von Kindergartenkindern zu bestätigen. Es wurden dazu zwei umfangreiche Studien durchgeführt (vgl. Küspert, 1998; Schneider, Roth & Küspert, 1999; Schneider, Visé, Reimers & Blaesser, 1994). Wie bei Lundberg und Kollegen wurde jeweils im letzten Kindergartenjahr eine größere Anzahl von Trainings- und Kontrollgruppenkindern rekrutiert (insgesamt jeweils ca. 350 Kinder). Es wurde darauf geachtet, dass die beiden Gruppen geographisch klar getrennt waren, um das ‚Risiko' von Kommunikationsvorgängen zwischen den Erzieherinnen der Trainings- und Kontrollgruppe zu minimieren. Im Trainingszeitraum nahm die Kontrollgruppe am regulären Kindergartenprogramm teil, erhielt also keine spezifische Förderung. Merkmale der phonologischen Bewußtheit im weiteren und engeren Sinne wurde in beiden Gruppen unmittelbar vor und nach der Trainingsphase erhoben, um die Auswirkungen der Förderung in der Trainingsgruppe genauer erfassen zu können. Das Training selber wurde von den Erzieherinnen durchgeführt, die von uns vorher ausführlich darauf vorbereitet und mit den einzelnen Schritten des Förderprogramms vertraut gemacht worden waren. Die Fördermaßnahmen erstreckten sich über einen Zeitraum von ca. 6 Monaten, wobei die Übungen und Sprachspiele täglich etwa 10-15 Minuten in Anspruch nahmen. Unser Team führte kontinuierlich Supervisionen durch, um sichergehen zu können, dass die Umsetzung des Programms angemessen erfolgte.

Inhaltlich betrachtet gliederte sich das Trainingsprogramm in sechs größere Einheiten, die aufeinander aufbauten und im folgenden kurz beschrieben werden (zu Details vgl.

Küspert & Schneider, 1999). Es wurde mit *Lauschspielen* begonnen. Die Kinder sollten hier lernen, ihre Aufmerksamkeit auf Geräusche und Laute in der Umgebung zu richten. Es wurde ihnen dabei vermittelt, dass Sprache etwas ist, worauf man genau hören muss. Im nächsten Schritt wurden dann *Reimspiele* eingeführt, bei denen es darum ging, die Kinder für die Lautstruktur der gesprochenen Sprache zu sensibilisieren. Es sollten zunächst Reime erkannt und später Reime produziert werden. Reimspiele wurden in den ersten Wochen des Trainingsprogramms intensiv praktiziert, kamen in der Folge jedoch nur noch sporadisch zum Einsatz. In der dritten Trainingsphase wurden die Kinder mit den sprachlichen Einheiten *Satz* und *Wort* vertraut gemacht. So sollte z.B. jedes Wort eines Satzes mit Legoklötzchen gelegt werden, um die Wortgrenzen in einem Satz bewußt zu machen. Es wurde weiterhin illustriert, wie zwei einzelnen Wörter zu einem umfassenderen Wort kombiniert werden können („Schnee" und „Mann" wird zu „Schneemann"), und wie ein zusammengesetztes Wort in zwei einzelne Wörter zerlegt werden kann („Kaffeemaschine" in „Kaffee" und „Maschine"). Spiele zum Umgang mit Silben bildeten die vierte Trainingseinheit und wurden ab der fünften Trainingswoche durchgeführt. Zunächst ging es darum, die Silbengrenzen durch rhythmisches Sprechen und Händeklatschen akustisch wahrzunehmen. Weitere Spiele bezogen die Motorik ein, so dass den Kindern die Silbengrenzen über die Bewegungen erfaßt wurden.

Die verbleibenden beiden Trainingseinheiten bezogen sich auf die Lautebene bzw. auf das *Phonem* und damit auf die kleinste sprachliche Einheit. Im Gegensatz zur Unterscheidung von Wörtern und Silben muß das Kind beim Erkennen und Unterscheiden von Einzellauten eine Abstraktionsleistung vollbringen, da die Phoneme fast gleichzeitig artikuliert werden und auf natürliche Weise wie etwa durch rhythmisches Sprechen kaum eindeutig identifiziert werden können. Die zentrale Aufgabe besteht also darin, einzelne Sprachlaute aus der Gesamtheit artikulierter Laute zu abstrahieren. Es steht außer Zweifel, dass dieser Teil des Programms die größten intellektuellen Anforderungen an die Kinder stellte. Um ihnen den Zugang zu diesem Problem zu erleichtern, wurden zunächst *Anlaute* im Wort identifiziert, wobei der erste Laut eines Wortes besonders betont und gedehnt gesprochen wurde. Nachdem dieser Schritt bewältigt worden war, ging es dann darum, den letzten Laut eines Wortes zu bestimmen. Die anspruchsvollste Stufe dieser Einheit stellte die *Manipulation von Anlauten* dar, bei der beispielsweise der erste Laut eines Wortes ignoriert und das verbleibende Wort benannt werden sollte. Die sechste und letzte Übungseinheit beschäftigte sich mit der *Synthese* und *Analyse von Phonemen*. Die Sensibilisierung der Kinder für die Identifikation einzelner Phoneme innerhalb eines Wortes verlangt eine intensive Übungszeit. Es wurde mit der Synthese begonnen, da diese Kindergartenkindern erfahrungsgemäß leichter fällt. Bei der Synthese wurden Wörter in einzelne Phoneme zerlegt (‚zerhackt'), und das Kind sollte die Einzellaute zu einem sinnvollen Wort zusammenfügen. Zeitlich verzögert fanden dann die Übungen zur Phonemanalyse statt. Zunächst wurde anhand von kurzen (einsilbigen) Wörtern gelernt, wie einzelne Laute in Wörtern unterschieden werden können. Im Verlauf der Übungseinheit wurden immer längere Wörter eingeführt, die in Einzellaute zerlegt werden sollten.

Die Ergebnisse der Förderung fielen wie bei Lundberg und Kollegen positiv aus. Der Vergleich der Vor- und Nachtestwerte zur phonologischen Bewußtheit ergab in beiden Studien deutliche Kompetenzgewinne der geförderten Kinder im Bereich der sprachlichen Bewußtheit. Während bei Lundberg et al. (1988) spezifische Effekte für die phonologische Bewußtheit im engeren Sinne (also den Umgang mit Phonemen) berichtet und keine Anstiege im Bereich der phonologischen Bewußtheit im weiteren Sinne registriert wurden, ergaben sich in unseren Studien deutliche Vorteile der trainierten Kinder in beiden Komponenten der phonologischen Bewußtheit. Die Unterschiede waren insofern substantiell, als die Leistungen der Trainingsgruppe im Mittel etwa eine Standardabweichung über der der Kontrollgruppe lagen. Der Trainingseffekt war insofern langfristig, als er auch noch im metalinguistischen Transfertest zu Beginn der Grundschulzeit nachweisbar war. Wie schon erwähnt, kamen bei diesem Test neue und schwierigere Aufgaben zur Phonemanalyse und –synthese zum Einsatz. Abgerundet wurde das positive Bild durch den Einbezug von Lese- und Rechtschreibtests zu Ende des ersten und zweiten Schuljahrs. Wenn auch die Gruppenunterschiede nicht mehr ganz so deutlich ausfielen wie bei der phonologischen Bewußtheit, so waren sie immer noch substantiell. Allerdings konnten wir insbesondere aus den Befunden unserer ersten Studie (Schneider et al., 1994) ableiten, dass der Erfolg der Förderung nicht zuletzt von dem Interesse und dem Engagement der Erzieherinnen abhing. Nur für die konsistent trainierten Kinder ließ sich nachweisen, dass das Training letztendlich langfristig fruchtete. Wenn Übungseinheiten ausgelassen wurden und gerade im letzten Programmteil nicht mehr kontinuierlich gefördert wurde, fanden sich schon im Transfertest keine signifikanten Unterschiede zwischen inkonsistent trainierten Kindern und den Kindern der Kontrollgruppe mehr.

Insgesamt kann aus den Befunden unserer Würzburger Studien mit unausgelesenen Kindergartenkindern gefolgert werden, dass sich die Befunde der skandinavischen Untersuchung von Lundberg und Kollegen auch für den deutschsprachigen Raum bestätigen lassen. Das ‚fortgeschrittene' Alter der dänischen Kinder war also nicht entscheidend für den Trainingserfolg. Die generell große Bedeutung früher Förderprogramme zur sprachlichen Bewußtheit für den späteren Schriftspracherwerb war damit eindeutig belegt.

Befunde zur Förderung von ‚Risikokindern'

In den Diskussionen um die praktische Relevanz der oben beschriebenen Befunde wurde häufig das Argument vorgebracht, dass Trainingserfolge bei Stichproben ‚normaler', also nicht vorselegierter Kinder nicht automatisch belegen, dass das Förderprogramm auch bei solchen Kindern Wirkung zeigt, die anfänglich sehr niedrige Niveaus sprachlicher Bewußtheit demonstrieren und von daher als ‚Risikokinder' im Hinblick auf den späteren Schriftspracherwerb einzustufen sind. Es ist in der Tat so, dass ein solcher Einwand genau überprüft werden muss, um den Wert des Förderprogramms für unterschiedliche Leistungsgruppen zu dokumentieren. Wir führten von daher zunächst eine ‚Sekundäranalyse' zu einer der beiden Studien durch, in der nachträglich Subgruppen von Kindern nach ihrem Leistungsvermögen im Bereich der phonologischen Bewußtheit gebildet und die Wirksamkeit des Trainings für jede dieser Gruppen genauer überprüft wurden (Schneider, Roth, Küspert & Ennemoser, 1998). Als wichtigster Befund dieser Sekundäranalyse konnte festgehalten werden, dass auch sog. ‚Risikokinder' deutlich vom Training profitierten. Ihr Leistungszuwachs im Bereich der phonologischen Bewußtheit entsprach in etwa dem Zugewinn der anfangs normalen bis überdurchschnittlichen Kinder der Trainingsgruppe. Weiterhin ließ sich zeigen, dass diese Subgruppe nach dem Training das Defizit in der phonologischen Bewußtheit so weit kompensiert hatte, dass sie im Vergleich zur ‚normalen' Kontrollgruppe nun sogar die besseren Leistungen in diesem Bereich zeigte. Die Risikogruppe wies auch später im Vergleich zur Kontrollgruppe kaum schlechtere Lese- und Rechtschreibleistungen auf. Wurde dagegen die Leistung der trainierten Risikokinder mit der einer Subgruppe von Risikokindern verglichen, die kein Training erhalten hatten, so zeigten sich nach anfänglicher Vergleichbarkeit der phonologischen Bewußtheits-Scores substantielle Vorteile der trainierten Risikokinder im Nachtest, die auch langfristig erhalten blieben und sich später in vergleichsweise deutlich besseren Lese- und Rechtschreibleistungen widerspiegelten.

Obwohl diese Nachuntersuchungen deutliche Hinweise auf die Nützlichkeit des Förderprogramms für anfänglich schwache Kinder ergab, blieb aus methodischer Sicht ein gewisses Problem. Als Risikokinder waren Kinder selegiert worden, die im Vortest zur phonologischen Bewußtheit sehr niedrige Punktwerte erzielt hatten. Da der Vortest vergleichsweise schwere Aufgaben enthielt (es sollte sich ja im Vorher-Nachher-Vergleich eine gewisse Entwicklung zeigen lassen), schnitt ein relativ großer Anteil der untersuchten Kinder hier schlecht ab. Es lag von daher die Vermutung nahe, dass nicht alle der als ‚Risikokinder' klassifizierten Kindergartenkinder wirklich ernsthafte Probleme im Bereich der sprachlichen Bewußtheit aufwiesen.

Aus diesem Problem ergab sich für uns der Schluß, eine weitere Trainingsstudie zur phonologischen Bewußtheit durchzuführen, bei der lediglich vorher sorgfältig ausgewählte Risikokinder im Bereich der sprachlichen Bewußtheit gefördert werden sollten. (für Details s. Roth, 1999; Schneider, Roth, Ennemoser & Küspert, in press). Aus ethischen Gründen schien es uns nicht akzeptabel, Risikokinder der unbehandelten Kontrollgruppe zuzuweisen. Stattdessen wurde die Entwicklung der Risikokinder mit der von unausgelesenen (‚normalen') Kontrollgruppenkindern verglichen. Gegenüber den beiden ersten Studien bestand eine weitere Neuerung darin, dass drei verschiedene Trainingsgruppen eingerichtet wurden, um die Gültigkeit der ‚phonological-linkage'-Hypothese zu prüfen. Dieser Annahme zufolge erbringt die Kombination eines Trainings der phonologischen Bewußtheit mit einem Training der Buchstaben-Laut-Verbindung den vergleichsweise größten Ertrag. Dahinter steht die Überlegung, dass Kinder zunächst die Fähigkeit zur Lautunterscheidung erworben haben müssen, bevor ein Buchstaben-Laut-Training fruchten kann. Um diese in anglo-amerikanischen Studien schon bestätigte Hypothese auch für den deutschen Sprachraum zu validieren, erhielt eine unserer drei Risikogruppen ein kombiniertes Trainingsprogramm, bei dem das oben beschriebene Training der phonologischen Bewußtheit mit einem Buchstaben-Laut-Zuordnungstraining verknüpft wurde. Eine weitere Gruppe erhielt lediglich das phonologische Training, während in der letzten Gruppe ausschließlich Buchstaben-Laut-Verknüpfungen geübt wurden. Die Risikokinder waren vorher in einer aufwendigen Screening-Prozedur (dem Bielefelder Screening von Jansen, Mannhaupt, Marx & Skowronek, 1998) selegiert worden, die vergleichsweise leichte Aufgaben zur phonologischen Bewußtheit, zur Informationsverarbeitungsgeschwindigkeit und zum sprachgebundenen Kurzzeitgedächtnis enthielt. Ein Versagen bei solch leichten Aufgaben kann als Indiz dafür gewertet werden, dass bei den betroffenen Kinder ein ernsthaftes Risiko hinsichtlich des späteren Schriftspracherwerbs besteht.

Erwartungsgemäß schnitten die Risikokinder der drei Trainingsgruppen im Vortest deutlich schlechter ab als die Kinder der unausgelesenen Kontrollgruppe. Dieses Ergebnismuster änderte sich jedoch nach Trainingsabschluß grundlegend. Die größten unmittelbaren und langfristigen Trainingseffekte im Bereich der sprachlichen Bewußtheit wurden für diejenigen Risikokinder festgestellt, die das klassische Training der phonologischen Bewußtheit absolviert hatten, gefolgt von den Kindern mit kombiniertem Trainingsprogramm. Ebenfalls erwartungsgemäß war der Befund, dass das alleinige Training der Buchstaben-Laut-Zuordnung nur geringe Effekte zeigte. Im Hinblick auf die spätere Lese- Rechtschreibentwicklung bestätigte sich die ‚phonologische Verknüpfungshypothese': diejenigen Kinder, die das kombinierte Training absolviert hatten, erwiesen sich den anderen Risikogruppen als überlegen und den ‚normalen' Kontrollgruppen-Kindern als annähernd ebenbürtig. Eine genauere Analyse der standardisierten Lese- und Rechtschreibleistungen gegen Ende der zweiten Klassenstufe ergab für die kombinierte Trainingsgruppe im Durchschnitt normale Leistungsniveaus. Während der Prozentrangwert (PR) für das Lesen bei 47 lag, wurde für das Rechtschreiben ein mittlerer PR von 53 registriert. Auch die durchschnittlichen Niveaus der beiden anderen geförderten Risikogruppen lagen noch in einem Bereich (PR zwischen 40 und 45), der von den üblichen Legastheniegrenzwerten (PR < 15) deutlich nach oben abwich. Allerdings fanden sich in diesen beiden Risikogruppen in der zweiten Klassenstufe deutlich mehr Legastheniker (ca. 20%) als in der kombinierten Trainingsgruppe (ca. 6%).

Zusammenfassend läßt sich festhalten, dass der Erfolg von Fördermaßnahmen im letzten Kindergartenjahr auch für ‚Risikokinder' eindrucksvoll bestätigt werden konnte. Wenn wir auch letztendlich nicht sagen können, wieviele dieser Kinder ohne gezielte Förderung auffällig geworden wären, so wissen wir doch aus früheren Längsschnittstudien, dass ein erheblicher Prozentsatz von Kindern mit ähnlich ungünstigen Ergebnissen im Kindergarten-Screening später in der Grundschulzeit erhebliche Lese-Rechtschreibprobleme entwickelten und diese meist auch beibehielt. Als Fazit unserer Studie kann also festgehalten werden, dass auch sog. Risikokindern effektiv geholfen werden kann, wenn frühzeitig interveniert wird.

Literatur

Bradley, L. & Bryant, P. (1985). *Rhyme and reason in reading and spelling.* Ann Arbor: The University of Michigan Press.

Brügelmann, H. (1984). Lesen- und Schreibenlernen als Denkentwicklung – Voraussetzungen eines erfolgreichen Schrifterwerbs. *Zeitschrift für Pädagogik, 30*, 69-91.

Jansen, H., Mannhaupt, G., Marx, H. & Skowronek, H. (1998). *Bielefelder Screening zur Früherkennung von Lese- Rechtschreibschwierigkeiten.* Göttingen: Hogrefe.

Küspert, P. (1998). *Phonologische Bewußtheit und Schriftspracherwerb zu den Effekten vorschulischer Förderung der phonologischen Bewußtheit auf den Erwerb des Lesens und Rechtschreibens.* Frankfurt a.M.: Lang.

Küspert, P. & Schneider, W. (1999). *Hören, lauschen, lernen. Sprachspiele für Kinder im Vorschulalter: Das Würzburger Trainingsprogramm zur Vorbereitung auf den Erwerb der Schriftsprache.* Göttingen: Vandenhoeck & Ruprecht.

Lundberg, I., Frost, J. & Petersen, O. P. (1988). Effects of extensive program for stimulating phonological awareness in preschool children. *Reading Research Quarterly, 23*, 253-284.

Mannhaupt, G. (1994). Risikokind Junge – Vorteile der Mädchen in Vorläufer- und Teilfertigkeiten für den Schriftspracherwerb. In S. Richter & H. Brügelmann (Hrsg.), *Mädchen lernen anders lernen Jungen* (S. 36-50). Konstanz: Libelle.

Roth, E. (1999). *Prävention von Lese- und Rechtschreibschwierigkeiten: Evaluation einer vorschulischen Förderung der phonologischen Bewußtheit und der Buchstabenkenntnis.* Frankfurt a.M.: Lang.

Scheerer-Neumann, G. (1988). *Rechtschreibtraining mit rechtschreibschwachen Hauptschülern auf kognitionspsychologischer Grundlage – eine empirische Untersuchung.* Opladen: Westdeutscher Verlag.

Schneider, W., Brügelmann, H. & Kochan, B. (1990). Lesen- und Schreibenlernen in neuerer Sicht: Vier Perspektiven auf den Stand der Forschung. In H. Brügelmann & H. Balhorn (Hrsg.), *Das Gehirn, sein Alfabet und andere Geschichten* (S. 220-234). Konstanz: Faude.

Schneider, W., Ennemoser, M., Roth, E. & Küspert, P. (1999). Kindergarten prevention of dyslexia: Does training in phonological awareness work for everybody? *Journal of Learning Disabilities, 32*, 429-436.

Schneider, W. & Näslund, C. (1993). The impact of early metalinguistic competencies and memory capacities on reading and spelling in elementary school: Results of the Munich Longitudinal Study on the Genesis of Individual Competencies (LOGIC). *European Journal of Psychology of Education, 8*, 273-288.

Schneider, W., Roth, E., Küspert, P. & Ennemoser, M. (1998). Kurz- und langfristige Effekte eines Trainings der sprachlichen (phonologischen) Bewußtheit bei unterschiedlichen Leistungsgruppen: Befunde einer Sekundäranalyse. *Zeitschrift für Entwicklungspsychologie und Pädagogische Psychologie, 30*, 26-39.

Schneider, W., Roth, E. & Küspert, P. (1999). Möglichkeiten der frühen Prävention von Lese-Rechtschreibproblemen: Das Würzburger Trainingsprogramm zur Förderung sprachlicher Bewußtheit bei Kindergartenkindern. *Kindheit und Entwicklung, 8*, 147-152.

Schneider, W. & Springer, A. (1978). Individualisierendes Rechtschreibtraining auf verhaltenstherapeutischer Basis. *Psychologie in Erziehung und Unterricht, 25*, 197-204.

Schneider, W., Visé, M., Reimers, P. & Blaesser, B. (1994). Auswirkungen eines Trainings der phonologischen Bewußtheit auf den Schriftspracherwerb in der Schule. *Zeitschrift für Pädagogische Psychologie, 8*, 177-188.

Skowronek, H. & Marx, H. (1989). The Bielefeld longitudinal study on the early identification of risks in learning to write and to read: Theoretical background and first results. In M. Bambring, F. Lösel & H. Skowronek (Eds.), *Children at risk: Assessment, longitudinal research, and intervention* (pp. 268-294). New York: de Gruyter.

4 Therapie und Förderung

4.1 Heutige Therapieverfahren bei Lese-Rechtschreibstörung im Überblick

Hedwig Amorosa, S. Baur, Michele Noterdaeme

1 Einleitung

Jeder, der mit Kindern mit Lese-Rechtschreibschwäche arbeitet, weiß, dass es nicht *den* Legastheniker gibt, sondern sehr unterschiedliche Kinder, die individuell verschiedene Schwierigkeiten zeigen, das Lesen und Schreiben zu lernen. Sie sind unterschiedlich weit im Leselernprozess, sie haben unterschiedliche Defizite und sehr unterschiedliche Fähigkeiten und Temperamente. So ist es nötig, aus der Beobachtung des Kindes, dem Wissen über den Leselernprozess und den vorhandenen Programmen und Übungen ein Training individuell zusammenzustellen.

2 Training von „Funktionsdefiziten"

Es wurde immer wieder versucht, die „Basisdefizite", welche als Ursache der Lese-Rechtschreibschwäche angesehen wurden oder werden, zu trainieren, in der Hoffnung, dass der Leselernprozess dann normal verlaufen würde. Diese Trainings führten aber nur begrenzt zu Erfolgen. Zur Zeit werden zwei Defizite speziell diskutiert: Die Schwierigkeiten im Bereich der phonologischen Bewusstheit und Störungen in der zeitlichen Auflösung von Sprache.

Zwei Ansätze, deren Training an diesen Defiziten ansetzt, sollen kurz vorgestellt und diskutiert werden. Es handelt sich zum einen um das vorbeugende Programm von Küspert und Schneider (1999) und zum anderen um das Training der auditiven Unterscheidungsfähigkeit von Merzenich und Tallal (Merzenich et al. 1996).

2.1 Vorschultrainingsprogramm von Küspert und Schneider

Aufbauend auf dem Bielefelder Screening Test (1999) zur Früherkennung von Risikogruppen bezüglich einer Lese-Rechtschreibstörung entwickelten Küspert und Schneider (1999) ein Vorschulprogramm, welches von Kindergärtnerinnen durchgeführt werden kann. Hierbei werden im Wesentlichen Fähigkeiten, die zur phonologischen Bewusstheit gezählt werden, trainiert. Dies sind Aufgaben wie Hinhören, Geräusche erkennen, Segmentieren von Sätzen in Wörter und von Wörtern in Silben. Es werden Reimspiele gemacht und das Hören von Lauten in Wörtern trainiert. Die Effektivität dieses Programms lässt sich steigern, wenn die Übungen, die ohne Schriftsprache durchgeführt werden, durch Buchstaben ergänzt werden.

Die Kinder lernen, dass Buchstaben Laute repräsentieren. Damit wird ein wichtiger Ansatz des alphabetischen Schreibens in die Vorübungen eingebaut. Es gibt Längsschnittstudien, in denen Schneider und Mitarbeiter zeigen konnten, dass Kinder, die im Screeningtest sehr schlecht abschnitten, d. h. die ein hohes Risiko hatten, eine Lese-Rechtschreibstörung zu entwickeln, am Ende der zweiten Klasse eine ausreichende Leistung im Lesen und Rechtschreiben erreichen konnten, wenn sie an einem solchen Training teilgenommen hatten. Dies spricht dafür, dass es mit dem Training gelingt, einen Teil der Kinder vor größeren Schwierigkeiten in der Schule zu bewahren. Weitere Untersuchungen und Überprüfungen in den 3. und 4. Klassen werden erforderlich sein, um die Möglichkeiten und Grenzen dieser vorbeugenden Maßnahmen bestimmen zu können.

2.2 Trainingsprogramm zu Störungen der zeitlichen Auflösung

Tallal und Mitarbeiter (Fitch, Miller, Tallal 1997) befassten sich seit vielen Jahren mit den Ursachen von Sprachentwicklungsstörungen. Ihre These besagt, dass diese Kinder Schwierigkeiten haben, Sequenzen von kurzen aufeinanderfolgenden Lauten richtig zu erkennen. Sie sind der Meinung, dass durch eine akustische Veränderung des Sprachsignals, d. h. durch eine Verlängerung einiger Anteile des Sprachsignals die Verarbeitung dieser kurzen Reize verbessert werden kann. Ihre Erklärungen der Befunde sind nicht unwidersprochen geblieben (Mody, Studdert-Kennedy 1997). Merzenich und Tallal (Merzenich et al. 1996) entwickelten ein Trainingsprogramm, das auf dieser Theorie aufbaut. Nach einem Training mit Videospielen mit akustisch veränderter Sprache 3 Stunden am Tag, an 5 Tagen der Woche, über einen Monat lang, holten elf 5- bis 10-jährige Kinder Entwicklungsrückstände in der Sprache von 1-2 Jahren auf. Eine Vergleichsgruppe, die Videospiele mit akustisch unveränderter Sprache hörte, machte dagegen keine Fortschritte. Dieses Training soll auch bei Kindern mit Lese-Rechtschreibstörungen sehr erfolgreich sein. Ob es sich dabei um den Teil der lese-rechtschreibgestörten Kinder handelt, die gleichzeitig unter einer Sprachstörung leiden oder auch um andere, ist unklar. Andere Arbeiten zeigten, dass nur ein kleiner Teil der Kinder mit einer Lesestörung eine solche Störung der zeitlichen Auflösung hat (Manis et al. 1997), die nach Meinung der Autoren möglicherweise durch das Lesedefizit mitbedingt ist.

Am psychologischen Institut der medizinischen Fakultät in München werden von Frau Dr. Steinbüchel und Mitarbeitern (Steinbüchel, Wittmann 1997) ähnliche Trainings durchgeführt. Nach den Pilotuntersuchungen scheint es, als könne man die Lauterkennung verbessern.

Wie sich dieses Training aber tatsächlich auf das Lesen selbst auswirkt, ist noch offen.

Diese kurze Zusammenfassung zeigt, dass es experimentelle Ansätze für ein Funktionstraining gibt. Das Training der phonologischen Bewusstheit sieht sehr vielversprechend für einen Teil der Kinder aus. Es enthält viele Komponenten, aber welche davon für das einzelne Kind die wirksamsten sind, ist unklar. Ob der Effekt, der zweifellos bis zum Ende der zweiten Klasse besteht, auch in höheren Klassen beibehalten werden kann, wird sich zeigen müssen.

Über den Erfolg des Trainings von Merzenich und Tallal gibt es keine neueren Arbeiten.

Die Funktionstrainings sind bei einzelnen Kindern wirksam, bei den meisten Kindern ist es aber nötig, das Lesen und Rechtschreiben zusätzlich zu allen „Basisdefiziten" zu üben. Auf diese Programme wird im Folgenden eingegangen.

3 Training von Lese- und Rechtschreibfähigkeiten

Für die Bereiche des Lesens und Rechtschreibens existieren unterschiedliche Programme. Ein Teil ist für den Schriftspracherwerb an Grundschulen oder für Kinder an Förderschulen gedacht, andere wurden speziell für Kinder mit Lese-Rechtschreibstörungen entwickelt. Bevor auf die Möglichkeiten der einzelnen Programme eingegangen wird, sollen kurz die verschiedenen Prozesse der Lese- und Rechtschreibentwicklung beschrieben werden. Hierbei werden Lesen und Rechtschreiben getrennt, auch wenn die beiden Prozesse sehr eng miteinander verknüpft sind.

3.1 Lesen

Buchstabe-Lautzuordnung: Laute sind „Namen“ für Buchstaben. Beim geübten Leser wird der Buchstabe sofort den dazugehörigen Laut aktivieren, d. h. den Namen. Manchen Kindern, insbesondere solchen mit Sprachentwicklungsstörungen, bereitet bereits dieser Schritt größte Schwierigkeiten. Sie wissen, dass sie den Laut zu dem gesehenen Buchstaben kennen sollten, aber er fällt ihnen nicht ein oder sie sind nicht sicher, welcher von mehreren er ist.

Zusammenlesen: Für das Zusammenlesen ist es notwendig, den Laut für den ersten Buchstaben zu erkennen, und ihn „im Mund zu behalten“ bis der Laut für den nächsten Buchstaben erkannt wird. Diese gedehnte Silbe muss dann auf die normale Länge verkürzt werden, damit die Sprechsilbe erkannt werden kann. Das Arbeitsgedächtnis wird erheblich belastet, denn die Laute und ihre Reihenfolge müssen behalten werden. Besonders schwierig ist das Zusammenlesen bei den Verschlußlauten wie „t“ oder „k“, weil beim Sprechen der nachfolgende Vokal bereits die Aussprache des Konsonanten beeinflusst.

Erkennen häufiger Wörter: Nach kurzer Übung erkennen Kinder einfache Wörter als Ganzes und sie müssen nicht mehr erlesen werden. Sie gehen vom visuellen Wortbild direkt zur Bedeutung, ohne dass notwendigerweise die phonologisch-artikulatorische Repräsentation aktiviert wird. Durch diese Strategie wird das Lesen erheblich schneller. Die Gefahr dieser Strategie ist bekannt. Kinder mit einem guten visuellen Gedächtnis merken sich ganze Fibelseiten auswendig und keinem fällt auf, dass sie sich ein Wort nicht erlesen können.

Erkennen von häufigen Buchstabenkombinationen und Silben: Aus einem Wort werden häufige Buchstabenkombinationen oder Silben als Ganzes erkannt und in einen phonologisch-artikulatorischen Code umgesetzt. Dies gilt besonders für Vor- und Nachsilben, was die Belastung des Kurzzeitgedächtnisses verringert und das Lesetempo erhöht.

Satzteile, Wörter oder Wortteile aus dem Kontext vorhersagen: Diese Fähigkeit, die wir beim Lesen ununterbrochen anwenden, wird als Ratestrategie negativ gewertet, wenn Kinder sie anwenden. (Man sagt dann, dass die Kinder raten würden, statt zu lesen.) Es ist aber eine wichtige Kompensationsstrategie besonders bei älteren Kindern mit einem sehr geringen Lesetempo, um das Lesetempo zu erhöhen.

Die verschiedenen Prozesse sind je nach Stadium des Leselernprozesses und nach der Art der Aufgaben mehr oder weniger aktiv. Sie laufen parallel ab, bis das Gesamtergebnis zufrieden- stellend ist, und dann wird der nächste Satz gelesen.

Tabelle 4.1.1 enthält eine Reihe von Programmen, die bei Kindern mit Lese-Rechtschreibschwäche eingesetzt werden. Die verschiedenen Prozesse, die eben dargestellt wurden, sind aufgeführt und es wird angegeben, welche Prozesse mit dem jeweiligen Programm besonders trainiert werden.

Lesen

Im Kieler Leseprogramm (Dummer-Smoch, Hacketal 1993) wird die Buchstabe-Laut- zuordnung über Lautgebärden eingeführt, ähnlich wie auch in dem Programm von Müller-Egloff und Pretzlik (1994; Amorosa et al. 1994). Es werden unterschiedliche Lautgebärden benutzt. Therapeuten in verschiedenen Ländern haben die Erfahrung gemacht, dass es den Kindern leichter fällt, sich die Buchstabe-Lautzuordnung zu merken, wenn die Zuordnung über eine Gebärde läuft. Die Lautgebärden müssen lange und konsequent eingesetzt werden, nicht nur für wenige Tage, wenn der Laut eingeführt wird, wie es in Förderschulen häufig passiert.

Programm	Buchstabe-Laut-zuordnung	Zusammen-lesen	Häufige Buchstaben-gruppen oder Silben	Häufige Wörter	Wörter aus dem Kontext vorhersagen
Kieler Lese-aufbau	XX	XX	XX	XX	
Grissemann 1998			XX		XX
Kossow	XX			XX	
Müller-Egloff, Pretzlik	XX	XX	XX	XX	
Kretschmann 1991-1996	XX	XX	XX		

Tabelle 4.1.1 Übersicht über die Schwerpunkte verschiedener Trainingsprogramme für das Lesen

In dem Programm von Frau Kretschmann (1995) wird ein anderer Weg eingeschlagen. Sie führt die Buchstaben als Hinweis auf eine bestimmte Mundstellung ein. Das „m" steht für die geschlossenen Lippen. Das „a" für den offenen Mund. Diese Mundstellungen werden für eine Reihe von Buchstaben intensiv z. T. auch vor dem Spiegel geübt. D. h. das Kind lernt die Sprechbewegung und damit indirekt den Laut zu dem Buchstaben. Sowohl das Programm von Müller-Egloff und Pretzlik als das von Frau Kretschmann beschränken sich zunächst auf wenige Buchstaben, um der Schwierigkeit bei der Buchstabe-Lautzuordnung Rechnung zu tragen. Das Zusammenlesen wird nur mit dieser kleinen Auswahl geübt. Der nächste Schritt, das Erfassen von ganzen Wörtern, von Buchstabenkombinationen und Silben, wird in einigen Programmen, wie z. B. dem von Grissemann (1998) sehr systematisch geübt. Oft werden die kurzen lautgetreuen Wörter aus dem Grundwortschatz der ersten Klasse zugrunde gelegt.

Das Vorhersagen von Wörtern und Silben aus dem Kontext wird bei Grissemann geübt, spielt aber in den anderen Programmen keine Rolle.

Dies waren nun alles Programme, die mit Papier und Bleistift bearbeitet werden. Inzwischen existieren zunehmend mehr auch Computerprogramme, um das Lesen zu üben (Tabelle 4.1.2).

Diese Aufzählung ist sicher nicht vollständig, zeigt aber deutlich, dass bei den Computerprogrammen die verschiedenen Bereiche unterschiedlich geübt werden. In den älteren Programmen ging es häufig um das Erkennen von ganzen Wörtern und mit einer frei wählbaren Darbietungszeit kann eine Erhöhung der Lesegeschwindigkeit erreicht werden. Die neueren Programme haben ein größeres Spektrum an Möglichkeiten. Diese Programme sind als Ergänzung in der Therapie und teilweise zum zusätzlichen Üben allein gut einsetzbar.

Das regelmäßige genaue Lesen ist ein wichtiger Faktor im Training der Kinder über sehr lange Zeit (Firnhaber 1992). Neben dem genauen Lesen ist aber von Anfang an auch das sinnentnehmende Lesen von entscheidender Bedeutung. Müller-Egloff (1994) beginnt damit bei den ersten Übungen zum Zusammenlesen. Es geht darum, bereits die ersten gelesenen Wörter einem Bild zuzuordnen. Dazu werden Bücher wie Bild-Wort-Zuordnung oder „sinnentnehmendes Lesen" aus dem Cornelsen Verlag eingesetzt. Von den Computer-programmen kommt z. B. „Mano mit dem Lesepfeil" in Frage. Sobald es möglich ist, werden kurze Sätze und kurze Texte gelesen. Bei der Auswahl des Lesestoffes ist es besonders bei den älteren Kindern wichtig, auf einen altersentsprechenden Inhalt wie auch auf die Aufmachung zu achten. Es kann kein 10-jähriges Kind motivieren, wenn eine Fibel für die erste Klasse zum Üben genommen wird. Häufig ist es nötig, eigene Texte anzufertigen. Hilfen dazu finden sich in dem Artikel von Baur, Endres und Löffler (1997).

Programm	Buchstabe Laut-zuordnung	Zusammen-lesen	Häufige Buchstaben-gruppen oder Silben	Häufige Wörter	Wörter aus dem Kontext vorher-sagen
TAO	XX	XX	XX	XX	
Cesar Lesen 1.0	XX		XX		
Wortkiste				XX	
Remo			XX	XX	
Sprechende Anlauttabelle	XX				
Alphabet Traeger	XX				
Lesen und Schreiben lernen		XX	XX	XX	

Tabelle 4.1.2 Übersicht über die Schwerpunkte verschiedener Computertrainingsprogramme für das Lesen

3.2 Rechtschreiben

Die einzelnen Schritte für den Erwerb des Rechtschreibens unterscheiden sich vom Lesen.

Segmentieren: Das Kind muss lernen, dass man eine Äußerung in einzelne Wörter und die Wörter wiederum in einzelne Silben und Laute segmentieren kann, bevor es diese aufschreiben kann.

Das Segmentieren in Silben gelingt den meisten Kindern bereits lange vor der Einschulung. Sie können z. B. die Silben eines Wortes klatschen.

Laute in Silben erkennen: Bevor es gelingt, ein Wort zu schreiben, d. h. die richtigen Buchstaben zu wählen, muss das Kind lernen, die einzelnen Laute in einer Silbe zu erkennen und deren Reihenfolge zu bestimmen. Einem Teil der Kinder mit Rechtschreibschwierigkeiten gelingt dies nur mit Mühe.

Die Laut-Buchstaben-Zuordnung: Wie beim Lesen muss auch für das Schreiben die Zuordnung des Lauts zum Buchstaben gesichert sein. Am Anfang kann man sich auf die eindeutigen Phonem-Graphem-Zuordnungen beschränken, später müssen dann auch komplexere Zuordnungen gelernt werden, z. B. dass ein kurzer und ein langer Vokal, die sich sehr verschieden anhören, durch den gleichen Buchstaben repräsentiert werden oder ein „schb“ als gehörtes „sp“ geschrieben wird.

Häufige Lautfolgen, Silben und Wörter schreiben können: Um ein höheres Schreibtempo zu erreichen, muss das Kind die Buchstabenfolge für bestimmte Lautfolgen auswendig beherrschen, ebenso die Schreibweise von häufigen Silben und Wörtern.

Schreibweise von Morphemen kennen: Ähnlich wie im Vorhergehenden erhöht sich das Schreibtempo, wenn immer wiederkehrende Morpheme, wie z. B. das „st“ für die zweite Person Singular bei den Verben, als solche erkannt und geschrieben werden können.

Ableitungsregeln: Häufig ist es notwendig, Wörter ableiten zu können, wie „Kämme“ von „Kamm“ oder „Hund“ und „Hunde“, um auf die richtige Schreibweise der Wörter zu kommen. Dazu gehört neben dem Wissen über Ableitungsregeln auch ein erhebliches linguistisches Wissen.

Rechtschreibregeln: Jede Sprache hat Rechtschreibregeln, die man kennen muss, wenn man nicht alle Wörter in seinem Gedächtnis mit der korrekten Schreibweise gespeichert hat. Das Einüben dieser Rechtschreibregeln nimmt einen großen Teil des Deutschunterrichts in der Grundschule und den ersten Klassen der weiterführenden Schulen ein. Welche Emotionen solche Rechtschreibregeln auslösen können, zeigte die Diskussion über die Rechtschreib-reform.

Auch beim Schreiben gilt, dass viele dieser Prozesse parallel ablaufen, und vom Stadium des Schreibenlernens und der Art der Aufgabe abhängig sind.

Die Programme für den Rechtschreiberwerb (Tabelle 4.1.3) sind wie die Leseprogramme auf unterschiedliche Schwerpunkte ausgerichtet. Bei Grissemann (1998), Walter (1996), Reuter-Liehr (1992) und Kretschmann (1995) spielt das Segmentieren eine große Rolle. Dabei geht es bei Grissemann und Walter sehr stark um das Segmentieren in Morpheme. Das Erkennen von Lauten wird in den auditiven Gliederungsübungen von Grissemann und in den Mundbewegungsübungen von Kretschmann besonders beachtet. Das Training der Laut-Buchstabenverbindung wird in den verschiedensten Programmen mit unterschiedlichen Mitteln sehr intensiv geübt, ebenso wie das Trainieren häufiger Silben und Wörter. Überwiegend werden lautgetreu geschriebene Wörter geübt. Die wenigen Ausnahmen betreffen sehr häufige Wörter, wie den Artikel „die“. Ableitungsregeln werden intensiv bei Kretschmann geübt (1996). Das Regeltraining steht in dem Marburger Programm von Schulte-Körne und Mitarbeitern (1997) ganz im Vordergrund.

Die Tabelle 4.1.4 enthält einige Rechtschreibprogramme für den Computer.

Es ist deutlich, dass es nicht *das* Programm gibt, sondern viele Programmteile, die man für das einzelne Kind und seinen gegenwärtigen Leistungsstand auswählen kann. Manchmal muss man das Vorhandene abändern und anpassen, damit es für die individuellen Schwierigkeiten eines Kindes geeignet wird.

3.3 Finden von Programmen

Eine wichtige Frage ist, wie man die entsprechenden Programme finden kann. Wichtig ist es sich immer wieder in den Buchhandlungen bzw. Verlagen mit Lernmitteln, auf Kongressen oder in den einschlägigen Katalogen über Neuerscheinungen zu informieren.

Für Computerprogramme gibt es aber auch die SODIS-Datenbank, in der man nach Stichwörtern suchen kann. So kann man Informationen über das Programm und eine Bewertung mit Angabe des Datums und des entsprechenden Instituts gewinnen. Diese Datenbank ist auch auf CD-ROM erhältlich (Internetadresse: http://www.sodis.de). Das Staatliche Institut für Bildungsforschung in München plant die Herausgabe einer ähnlichen Datenbank zum Ende des Jahres 1999.

Programm	Segmentieren	Laute in Silben erkennen	Laut-Buchstabenzuordnung	Häufige Silben, Wörter	Morpheme	Ableitungsregeln	Rechtschreibregeln
Kieler Rechtschreibaufbau			XX	XX			
Grissemann	XX	XX	XX		XX	XX	
Reuter-Liehr	XX		XX	XX			
Schulte-Körne						XX	XX
Kossow		XX	XX	XX		XX	XX
Walter	XX			XX	XX		
Kretschmann 1991-1996	XX		XX	XX		XX	XX

Tabelle 4.1.3 Übersicht über die Schwerpunkte verschiedener Trainingsprogramme für das Rechtschreiben

Autoren	Segmentieren	Laute in Silben erkennen	Laut-Buchstabenverbindung	Häufige Buchstabengruppen oder Silben	Morpheme	Häufige Wörter	Rechtschreibregeln
TAO		XX	XX	XX		XX	
Cesar Schreiben 1.0				XX		XX	
Wortkiste						XX	
Remo					XX	XX	
Lesen und Schreiben				XX			
Wortbaustelle				XX		XX	
Uniwort						XX	XX

Tabelle 4.1.4 Übersicht über die Schwerpunkte verschiedener Computertrainingsprogramme für das Rechtschreiben

3.4 Beurteilung von Programmen

Das Finden der verschiedenen Trainingsprogramme ist schon ein Problem, das größere Problem ist aber die Beurteilung ihrer Qualität. Scheerer-Neumann (1979) und Walter (1996) haben eine Reihe von Kriterien zusammengestellt. Die wichtigsten Merkmale guter Programme lassen sich folgendermaßen zusammenfassen:

Es werden keine schnellen „Wunderheilungen“ versprochen.

Es wird nicht versprochen, dass die Lese-Rechtschreibstörung durch „spielerisches" Üben allein zum Verschwinden zu bringen ist.
Die Übungen werden dem Entwicklungsstand des Kindes und dem Stadium des Leselernprozesses angepasst.
Es werden die für das Lesen und Rechtschreiben relevanten Teilprozesse geübt.
Die Integration dieser Teilprozesse und ihre Automatisierung wird trainiert.
Konzentration wird im Rahmen der Lese- und Rechtschreibübungen trainiert.
Durch die Verbesserung der Lese- bzw. Rechtschreibleistung werden Ängste und emotionale Blockaden abgebaut.

4 Schluss

Für die Behandlung von Kindern mit Lese-Rechtschreibstörungen ist es wichtig, sich immer wieder klarzumachen, dass das Lesen und Rechtschreiben sehr komplexe Prozesse sind.

Auch bei unauffälligen Kindern bedarf er einer langen und stetigen Übung, bis sie soweit automatisiert sind, dass sie nebenbei zur Übermittlung eines Inhalts herangezogen werden können.

Kinder mit Lese-Rechtschreibstörungen sind sehr unterschiedlich in ihren Fähigkeiten, aber auch in den Schwierigkeiten, die der Erwerb der Schriftsprache ihnen bereitet. Programme müssen dem Rechnung tragen. Einfache Lösungen gibt es nicht. Die neuen Programme, in denen das Training phonologischer Bewusstheit mit all ihren Teilfähigkeiten eine wichtige Rolle spielt, erscheinen vielversprechend insbesondere auch im vorbeugenden Einsatz bei Vorschulkindern. Aber auch damit können wir nicht erwarten, ein Allheilmittel gefunden zu haben.

Literatur

Amorosa, H.; Müller-Egloff, E.; Pretzlik, E.: Treatment approaches in dyslexia. Acta Paedopsychiatrica 56, 199-202, 1994

Baur, S., Endres, R., Löffler, B.: Schwierigkeitskategorien von Wörtern zum Erstellen von Lesetexten. Die Sprachheilarbeit, 4, 179-181, 1997

Dummer-Smoch, L.; Hacketal, R.: Handbuch zum Kieler Leseaufbau. Kiel, Veris Verlag, 1993, 3. Auflage,

Dummer-Smoch, L.; Hacketal, R.: Handbuch zum Kieler Rechtschreibaufbau. Kiel, Veris Verlag, 1993, 2. Auflage,

Firnhaber, M.: Legasthenie. Frankfurt/Main, Fischer Verlag, 1992

Fitch, R.; Miller, S.; Tallal, P.: Neurobiology of Speech Perception. Annual Revue of Neurosciences, 20, 231-253, 1997

Grissemann, H.: Psycholinguistische Lese- Rechtschreibförderung. Bern, Verlag Hans Huber, 1998, 2. Auflage

Grissemann, H.: Spätlegasthenie und funktionaler Analphabetismus. Bern, Verlag Hans Huber, 1984

Jansen, H.; Mannhaupt, G.; Marx, H.; Skrowronek, H.: Bielefelder Screening zur Früherkennung von Lese-Rechtschreibschwierigkeiten (BISC). Göttingen, Hofgrefe, Verlag für Psychologie, 1999

Klicpera, C.; Gasteiger-Klicpera, B.: Psychologie der Lese-Schreibschwierigkeiten. Weinheim, Beltz-Psychologie-Verlags Union, 1995, 2. Auflage

Kossow, H-J.: Leitfaden zur Bekämpfung der Lese- Rechtschreibschwäche, Berlin, Deutscher Verlag der Wissenschaften. 1991, 2. Auflage

Kretschmann, M.: Diktate. München, Ehrenwirth Verlag, 1991

Kretschmann, M.: Rechtschreibregeln sprachlogisch. München, EhrenwirthVerlag, 1996

Kretschmann, M.: So lernst du lesen und schreiben. München, Ehrenwirth Verlag, 1995

Küspert, P.; Schneider, W.: Hören, lauschen, lernen. Vandenhoeck & Ruprecht 1999

Manis, F.; McBride-Chang, C.; Seidenberg, M.; Keating, P.; Doi, L.; Munson, B.; Peterson, A.: Are Speech Perception Deficits Associated with Dyslexia? Journal of Experimental Child Psychology, 66, 211-235, 1997

Merzenich, M.M.; Jenkins, W.M.; Miller, S.L.; Schreiner, C.; Tallal, P.: Temporal processing deficits of language learning impaired children are remediated by training. Science 271:77-81, 1996

Mody, M.; Studdert- Kennedy, M.; Brady, S.: Speech Perception Deficits in Poor Readers; Auditory Processing or Phonological Coding. Journal of Experimental Child Psychology, 64, 199-231, 1997

Müller-Egloff, E.: Die Förderung teilleistungsgestörter Kinder in der Klinikklasse. In: J. Martinius, H. Amorosa (Hrsg) Teilleistungsstörungen. München, Quintessenzverlag, 1994.

Reuther-Lier, C.: Lautgetreue Rechtschreibförderung. Bochum, Verlag Dr. Winkler, 1992

Scheerer-Neumann, G.: Intervention bei Lese-Rechtschreibschwäche. Überblick Themen, Methoden und Ergebnisse. Bochum, Kamp, 1979

Schulte-Körne, G.; Schäfer, J.; Deimel, W. Remschmidt, H. Das Marburger Eltern-Kind-Rechtschreibtraining. Zeitschrift für Kinder- und Jugendpsychiatrie 25, 151-159, 1997

Schulte-Körne, J.; Deimel, W. Remschmidt, H. Das Marburger Eltern-Kind-Rechtschreibtraining – Verlaufsuntersuchung nach zwei Jahren. Zeitschrift für Kinder- und Jugendpsychiatrie 26, 167-173, 1998

v. Steinbüchel, N.; Wittmann,: Elementare zeitliche Informationsverarbeitung als Diagnoseinstrument zentralnervöser Störungen. In: E. Kasten, M.Kreutz, B. Sabel (Hrsg) Neuropsychologie in Forschung und Praxis. Jahrbuch der Medizinischen Psychologie 12. Göttingen, Hogrefe, 146-162, 1997

Walter, J. Förderung bei Lese- und Rechtschreibschwäche. Göttingen, Hogrefe, Verlag für Psychologie. 1996

Liste der Computerprogramme:

Alphabet. Eugen Traeger Lernsoftware-Verlag
Cesar Lesen 1.0 CES Verlag
Die Wortbaustelle. Eugen Traeger Lernsoftware-Verlag
Lesen + Schreiben lernen. Eugen Traeger Verlag
Mano und der Lesepfeil, Cornelsen Verlag
REMO (Rechtschreibpaket auf Morphembasis. J. Walter, Apparatezentrum Göttingen
Sprechende Anlauttabelle. Friedrich Verlag
TAO (Texte für Auge und Ohr) SWETS Test Services
Uniwort. Eugen Traeger Lernsoftware-Verlag
Wortkiste, Lehrinstitut für Orthographie und Schreibtechnik. I.S:B. trainmedia GmbH. Berlin

4.2 Welche schulische Förderung ist effektiv?

Was leistet Förderunterricht und wie könnte er noch erfolgreicher sein?

Peter May

1 Einleitung

Das seit 1994 durchgeführte Projekt „Lesen und Schreiben für alle" (PLUS) sieht vor, dass die schulische Förderung von Kindern mit Lese-Rechtschreib-Schwierigkeiten möglichst nach folgenden Prinzipien gestaltet wird:

(1) Die Förderung soll von Anfang an *präventiv* dazu beitragen, das Entstehen lang anhaltender Lernstörungen bei Kindern soweit wie möglich zu vermeiden.

(2) Die Förderung soll weitgehend *integrativ* im Rahmen des Klassenunterrichts oder eng auf ihn bezogen stattfinden, um eine Ausgrenzung von Kindern mit Lernschwierigkeiten zu vermeiden und die Anregungen der Lerngruppe zu nutzen.

(3) Die Förderung soll *kooperativ* stattfinden, indem eine zusätzliche Lehrkraft in die Klasse kommt, um die Klassenlehrerin bei der Förderung der Kinder mit Lernschwierigkeiten zu unterstützen und bei der Durchführung des Unterrichts zu beraten.

Als flankierende Maßnahme wurde in verschiedenen Standortschulen eine sog. Außerunterrichtliche Lernhilfe (AUL) eingerichtet, in der besonders qualifizierte Pädagogen und Psychologen spezielle Lernangebote für jene Kinder machen, die durch die integrative Förderung nicht genügend Lernfortschritte machen.

Im Rahmen der wissenschaftlichen Begleitung des PLUS wurde die schriftsprachliche Lernentwicklung von Kindern aus ca. 100 Klassen vom ersten bis zum vierten Schuljahr untersucht, darunter Kinder mit Lese-Rechtschreibschwierigkeiten, die verschiedene Formen schulischer Förderung erhielten. Verglichen wurden verschiedene Konzeptionen des Klassenunterrichts (direkte und offene Formen) sowie Formen des Förderunterrichts durch eine zusätzliche Lehrkraft (extern und integrativ) mit binnendifferenzierenden Maßnahmen durch die Klassenlehrer. Über erste Erfahrungen mit der integrativen Förderung wurde auf dem Darmstädter Kongress des Bundesverbands Legasthenie berichtet (May 1996b). Nach dem Abschluss der Evaluation kann nun an dieser Stelle über weiter gehende Ergebnisse des Projekts berichtet werden.

Insgesamt hat sich das PLUS-Förderkonzept und die damit einhergehende Verstärkung der Aufmerksamkeit für die Förderung lernschwieriger Kinder in den Schulen bewährt: Der Anteil von Kindern, die nach den gleichen Kriterien wie bei der Voruntersuchung im Jahre 1994 als lese-rechtschreib-schwach eingestuft werden müssen[1], hat sich im Laufe von fünf Jahren in der Gesamtstichprobe aller beteiligten Schulen um durchschnittlich ein Drittel verringert, und in den Klassen mit hohem Lernerfolg ging der Anteil leistungsschwacher Kinder sogar um ca. 70 Prozent zurück.[2] Dies muss angesichts der Berichte über ansonsten eher dürftige Erfolge schulischer Förderung (siehe Klicpera, Gasteiger-Klicpera & Hütter 1993 sowie Klicpera in diesem Band) als ein beachtlicher Erfolg gewertet werden, der beweist,

---

1 Als Kriterium für die Förderbedürftigkeit dient die Rechtschreibleistung in der Hamburger Schreibprobe (HSP 4/5), die einem Prozentrang 8 oder geringer entspricht (siehe May 1994c).

2 Siehe dazu auch den ausführlichen Gesamtbericht (May 1999c)

dass mit entsprechenden Anstrengungen der Anteil der Kinder mit Lernschwierigkeiten deutlich gesenkt werden kann.

Der folgende Bericht konzentriert sich auf die über das konkrete Projekt hinaus reichenden Fragestellungen, welche persönlichen Voraussetzungen der Kinder den Lernerfolg im Lesen und Schreiben begünstigen und unter welchen Bedingungen der schulische Klassen- und Förderunterricht effektiv ist. Dabei geht insbesondere um die Fragen, ob für Kinder mit Lernschwierigkeiten andere Akzente bei der Unterrichtsgestaltung gesetzt werden sollten als bei leistungsstärkeren Kindern und ob Klassen mit höherem Lernerfolg bei aller Vielfalt erfolgreicher unterrichtlicher Varianten nicht häufiger solche Unterrichtsmerkmale aufweisen, die besonders das Lernen von Kinder mit Lernschwierigkeiten fördern. Denn daraus ließen sich einige allgemeine Hinweise zur lernförderlichen Gestaltung des (Förder-) Unterrichts ableiten.

2 Welche Persönlichkeitsmerkmale unterscheiden Kinder mit guten und schwachen Rechtschreibleistungen?

Bevor auf lernförderliche Bedingungen des schulischen (Förder-)Unterrichts eingegangen wird, soll ein Blick auf die zu fördernden Kinder geworfen werden. In jeder Klasse gibt es Kinder, die sich die Schriftsprache schnell und sicher aneignen, und solche Kinder, die Lesen und Schreiben nur mühsam lernen und in ihren Ergebnissen schon bald hinter den anderen Kindern zurückbleiben. Es ist jedoch auch bekannt, dass die Gruppe der Kinder mit Lernschwierigkeiten keineswegs einheitlich ist. Einem Teil der zunächst im Lernprozess zurückbleibenden Kinder gelingt es, ihren Rückstand gegenüber den übrigen Kindern wenigstens teilweise aufzuholen. Dagegen stagniert der Lernprozess eines anderen Teils dieser Kinder weiterhin, ihre schriftsprachlichen Lernprobleme weiten sich häufig auch auf andere Lernbereiche, und nicht selten zeigen sie allmählich auch Verhaltensauffälligkeiten.

Um zu erkunden, welche Persönlichkeitsmerkmale erfolgreich lernende Kinder von solchen mit anhaltenden Lernschwierigkeiten unterscheiden, wurden in einer Längsschnittuntersuchung drei Gruppen von Kindern mit unterschiedlicher Lernentwicklung verglichen. Abbildung 4.2.1 zeigt die Leistungsentwicklung der drei Gruppen im Rechtschreiben anhand der mittleren Ergebnissen in der Hamburger Schreibprobe (HSP).

(1) „gute Rechtschreiber“:
Diese Gruppe umfasst Kinder, die von Anfang an und über die gesamte Grundschulzeit hinweg gute Leistungen im Lesen und Schreiben zeigen. Ihre mittlere Leistung in der HSP entspricht bereits in Klasse 1 dem Prozentrang 70 und steigt bis zur Klasse 4 auf einen Prozentrang 77. Diese leicht und erfolgreich lernenden Kinder eignen sich die Schriftsprache aufgrund günstiger Lernvoraussetzungen schnell und sicher an.

(2) „schwache Rechtschreiber mit hohem Lernerfolg“:
Diese Gruppe umfasst Kinder, die anfangs schwache Rechtschreibleistungen zeigen, diese jedoch im Laufe der Grundschulzeit steigern können, so dass sie Anschluss an den Leistungsstand ihrer Klasse finden. Ihre mittleren Leistungen in der HSP 1 entsprechen dem Prozentrang 4 und steigen im Laufe der Grundschulzeit auf einen Durchschnittswert, der dem Prozentrang 24 entspricht. Diese Gruppe repräsentiert jene Kinder, die ihre anfänglichen Lernschwierigkeiten allmählich überwinden und zum Leistungsdurchschnitt ihrer Klasse aufschließen können.

(3) „schwache Rechtschreiber mit niedrigem Lernerfolg“:
Diese Gruppe umfasst Kinder, die von Anfang an schwache Rechtschreibleistungen zeigen und diese auch bis zum Ende der Grundschule nicht nennenswert steigern können. Ihre mittleren Leistungen entsprechen durchweg dem Prozenträngen 5 oder darunter. Diese Gruppe repräsentiert die Kinder mit gravierenden und langanhaltenden Lernschwierigkeiten im Lesen und Schreiben.

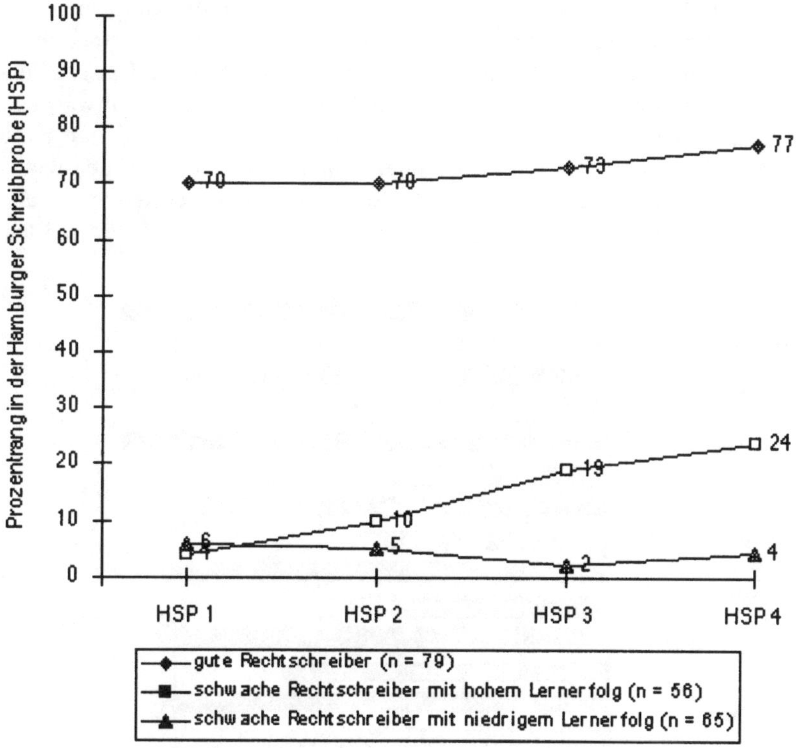

Abb. 4.2.1 Entwicklung der Rechtschreibung verschiedener Lerngruppen in der Grundschule

Von den Kindern aller drei Gruppen wurden neben den Rechtschreibergebnissen zahlreiche weitere Daten erhoben, darunter für die Schuljahre 2 bis 4 auch Einschätzungen ihrer Klassenlehrer zu verschiedenen Merkmalen der Lernerpersönlichkeit bzw. ihrer Lernvoraussetzungen. Abbildung 4.2.2 zeigt die Werte der verschiedenen Teilgruppen, die sich im Durchschnitt der drei Schuljahre 2 bis 4 ergeben. Die Werte der fünfstufigen Skala erstrecken sich von „sehr schwach“ (1) bis „sehr stark“ (5).

Erwartungsgemäß ergeben sich beträchtliche Unterschiede zwischen den Kindern mit gleichbleibend hohen Rechtschreibleistungen und den beiden Gruppen von Kindern mit anfänglichen Lernschwierigkeiten. Diese Unterschiede betreffen nicht nur die Schulleistungen (sowohl schriftsprachliche als auch allgemeine Schulleistungen) und das Lern- und Arbeitsverhalten, sondern auch emotionale und motivationale Aspekte der Lernerpersönlichkeit (Motivation, Selbstbild). Die Klassenlehrer schätzen auch diese nicht-kognitiven Persönlichkeitsmerkmale bei Kindern mit hohen Rechtschreibleistungen erheblich günstiger ein als bei Kindern mit Lernschwierigkeiten. Damit wird verdeutlicht, dass erfolgreiches Lernen in der Schule in der Regel auch mit günstigen Ausprägungen von Persönlichkeitsmerkmalen einhergeht, die ihrerseits das weitere Lernen positiv beeinflussen. Dagegen werden die Vorteile leistungsstarker Kinder hinsichtlich der sozialen Integration und der Regeleinhaltung sowie der häuslichen Unterstützung geringer eingeschätzt.

Weiteren Aufschluss liefern die Vergleiche zwischen den beiden Gruppen von Kindern mit anfänglichen Lernschwierigkeiten. Da die Gruppe mit hohem Lernerfolg ihre Rechtschreibleistung im Laufe der Grundschulzeit deutlich steigert, fällt die Einschätzung ihrer schrift-sprachlichen Leistungen durch die Klassenlehrer entsprechend positiver aus als bei den Kindern mit anhaltenden Lernschwierigkeiten. Dagegen unterscheiden sich die übrigen Schulleistungen beider Gruppen in den Augen ihrer Lehrer kaum. Das bedeutet, daß der Leistungsunterschied zwischen beiden Gruppen aus Sicht der Lehrer spezifisch ist, also nicht durch Unterschiede in den allgemeinen kognitiven Leistungsfähigkeiten erklärt werden kann.

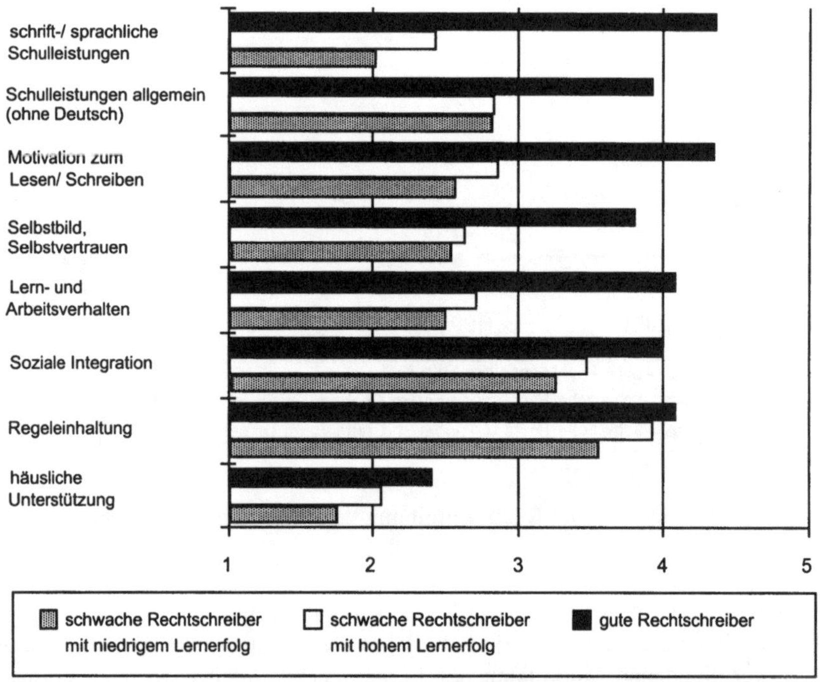

Abb. 4.2.2 Persönlichkeitsmerkmale von Kindern mit hohen bzw. niedrigen Lernerfolg aus Sicht der Klassenlehrer

Deutliche Unterschiede ergeben sich nach den Lehrereinschätzungen zudem bei den Bereichen „Motivation zum Lesen und Schreiben“, „Lern- und Arbeitsverhalten“ sowie „Selbstbild, Selbstvertrauen“, die für die Kinder mit höherem Lernzuwachs günstiger ausfallen. Diese Unterschiede bei den nicht-kognitiven Merkmalen der Lernerpersönlichkeit werden auch durch Selbsteinschätzungen der Kinder bestätigt: Kinder mit anfänglichen Lernschwierigkeiten und hohem Lernzuwachs nennen in den schriftlichen Befragungen im Vergleich zu Kindern mit anhaltenden Lernproblemen wesentlich häufiger Lesen und Schreiben bzw. Deutsch als Lieblingsfach (z.B. Klasse 3: 63 gegenüber 28 Prozent), und ein deutlich größerer Teil der erfolgreicheren Lerner ist von seinem eigenen schriftsprachlichen Leistungsvermögen überzeugt (Klasse 3: 27 gegenüber 11 Prozent).

Bei den weiteren Merkmalen, die von den Klassenlehrern eingeschätzt wurden, ergeben sich ebenfalls signifikante Unterschiede zwischen den beiden Gruppen von Kindern mit anfänglichen Lernschwierigkeiten, die in die zu erwartende Richtung zeigen. Die häusliche Unterstützung fällt demnach bei Kindern mit höherem Lernzuwachs höher aus. Weiter ergeben sich für die Kinder mit andauernden Lernschwierigkeiten deutliche Nachteile hinsichtlich der sozialen Integration und der Regeleinhaltung, die sich im Laufe der Grundschulzeit noch vergrößern. Dies weist auf eine mit der Dauer der Lernschwierigkeiten wachsende Sekundärsymptomatik bei diesen Kindern hin: Kinder mit anhaltenden Lernschwierigkeiten entwikkeln häufig mit der Zeit auch Verhaltensauffälligkeiten (z.B. Stören im Unterricht, Arbeitsverweigerung).

Aus beiden Vergleichen – sowohl aus dem Vergleich zwischen Kindern mit von Anfang an hohem Leistungsvermögen und den Kindern mit Lernschwierigkeiten als auch aus dem Vergleich der Gruppen lernschwieriger Kinder mit unterschiedlichem Lernzuwachs – ergeben sich deutliche Hinweise darauf, dass Lernerfolg bzw. Lernmisserfolg mit entsprechenden Merkmalsausprägungen in den Bereichen Motivation, Selbstbild, Lern- und Arbeitsverhalten sowie längerfristig auch Sozial- und Regelverhalten einhergehen. In diesem Zusammenhang wird immer wieder die Frage aufgeworfen, ob ein Kind aufgrund bestehender Verhaltensauffälligkeiten auch Lernschwierigkeiten bekommt, oder ob ein Kind Verhaltensauffälligkeiten aufgrund anhaltender Lernschwierigkeiten in der Schule entwickelt. Diese Frage „nach der Henne oder dem Ei“ wird nicht nur von Eltern und Lehrern je nach Standort unterschiedlich beantwortet. Auch in der wissenschaftlichen Lernpsychologie gibt es verschiedene Modellvorstellungen zur gegenseitigen Beeinflussung von kognitiven Fähigkeiten und nicht-kognitiven Persönlichkeitsmerkmalen.

Nach neueren Erkenntnissen ist allerdings davon auszugehen, dass längerfristig die sozial kontrollierten Leistungsergebnisse das Selbstbild als Lerner und weitere nicht-kognitive Lernermerkmale (Motivation, Ängstlichkeit usw.) nachhaltig beeinflussen (vgl. van Aken, Helmke & Schneider 1997). Jedoch kann auch angenommen werden, dass emotional-motivationale Merkmale ihrerseits das kognitive Lernen (positiv oder negativ) beeinflussen (vgl. Hofer, Pekrun & Zielinski 1986). In jedem Falle sollte ein lernförderlicher Unterricht diesen Zusammenhang berücksichtigen, indem er neben der Anregung kognitiver Lernfortschritte auch immer jenen nicht-kognitiven Bereichen der Lernerpersönlichkeit Beachtung schenkt, die einen indirekten Einfluss auf das Lernen haben. Und auch dann, wenn eine spürbare Wirkung im Sinne deutlich ansteigender Lernergebnisse dadurch nicht direkt erreichbar erscheint, sollte der Unterricht durch die bewusste Förderung günstiger emotionaler und motivationaler Zustände bei Kindern mit Lernschwierigkeiten verhindern, dass sich aufgrund ungünstiger Gefühle beim Lernen obendrein Verhaltensauffälligkeiten und psychische Beeinträchtigungen herausbilden.

3 Welche Art von Unterricht benötigen Kinder mit unterschiedlichen Schulleistungen?

Welche Unterrichtsmerkmale benötigen Kinder mit Lernschwierigkeiten? Unterscheidet sich ein Vorgehen im Unterricht, das günstig für lernschwache Kinder erscheint, von einem Unterricht, der vorwiegend an den Lerninteressen leistungsstarker Kinder ausgerichtet ist?

In der Hamburger Längsschnittuntersuchung wurde erkundet, welchen Aspekten des Unterrichts – aus Sicht der Lehrer – ein hoher Stellenwert für das Lernen verschiedener Lernergruppen zukommt. Dazu wurde den Klassenlehrern im zweiten Schuljahr eine Liste von Merkmalen der Unterrichtsgestaltung zur Beurteilung vorgelegt. Die Lehrer wurden gebeten, die einzelnen Merkmale nach der Bedeutung, die diese ihrer Ansicht nach für die Lernentwicklung der einzelnen Kinder haben, in eine Rangreihe zu bringen. Abbildung 4.2.3 zeigt die mittleren Rangplätze für die einzelnen Unterrichtsmerkmale hinsichtlich der beiden Schülergruppen. Auf den ersten Blick wird offenkundig, dass sich die einzelnen Unterrichtsmerkmale im Hinblick auf ihre Bedeutung für die beiden Teilgruppen deutlich unterscheiden.

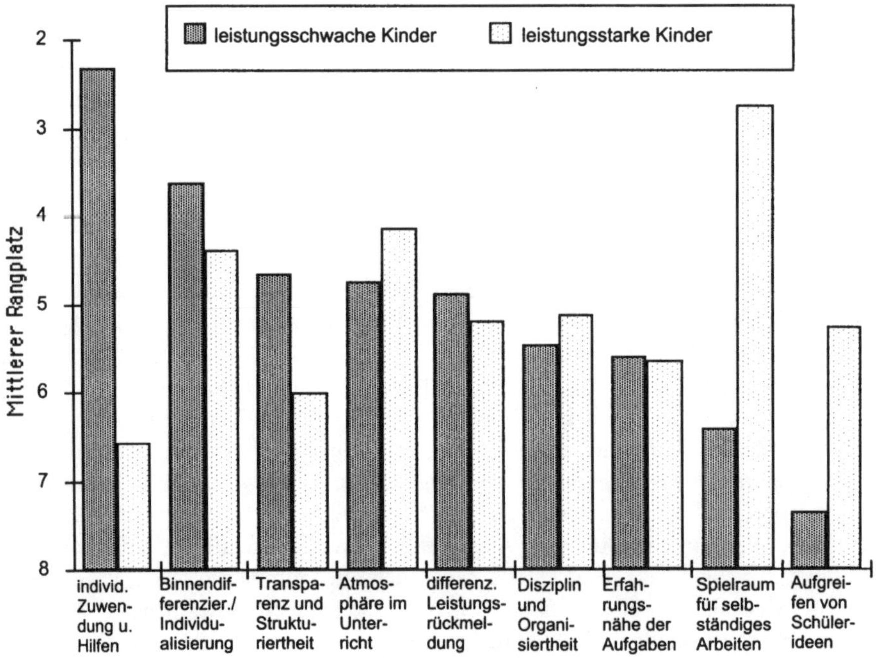

Abb. 4.2.3 Stellenwert von Merkmalen der Unterrichtsgestaltung für leistungsschwache bzw. leistungsstarke Kinder nach Einschätzung der Klassenlehrer (Klasse 2)

Besonders groß fallen die Unterschiede bezüglich des Merkmals „individuelle Zuwendung/ Hilfen während der Arbeit“ aus, das für die leistungsschwachen Kinder mit Abstand am wichtigsten eingestuft wird, für die leistungsstarken Kinder jedoch vollkommen nachrangig erscheint. Auch den Merkmalen „Binnendifferenzierung/ Individualisierung“ und „Transparenz und Strukturiertheit“ kommt nach Einschätzung der Lehrer eine deutlich höhere Bedeutung für das Lernen der Kinder mit schwachen Leistungen zu.

Auf der anderen Seite ordnen die Klassenlehrer im Hinblick auf die leistungsstarken Kinder dem Merkmal „Spielraum für selbständiges Arbeiten“ eindeutig den größten Stellenwert zu, während dieses Merkmal für die leistungsschwachen Kinder an zweitletzter Stelle erscheint. Auch bei den Merkmalen „Aufgreifen von Schülerideen“ und „Atmosphäre im Unterricht“ ergibt sich nach Ansicht der Klassenlehrer jeweils ein deutlich höherer Stellenwert im Hinblick auf die leistungsstarken Kinder.

Für die beiden Gruppen von Kindern mit unterschiedlichem Leistungsvermögen ergeben sich damit deutlich verschiedenartige Merkmalskonstellationen, die ein idealtypisch gestalteter Unterricht aufweisen sollte:

- *Für leistungsschwache Kinder* sollte nach Einschätzung der meisten Klassenlehrer ein Unterricht in erster Linie durch individuelle Zuwendung und Hilfe, durch Binnendifferenzierung und Individualisierung sowie durch Transparenz und Strukturiertheit gekennzeichnet sein. Das Aufgreifen von Schülerideen und der Spielraum für selbständiges Arbeiten erscheinen dagegen zunächst vollkommen nachrangig.
- *Für leistungsstarke Kinder* sollte der Unterricht hingegen vor allem einen Spielraum für selbständiges Arbeiten bieten, eine gute Atmosphäre aufweisen und auch Schülerideen aufgreifen. Individuelle Zuwendung und Hilfen sowie Transparenz und Strukturiertheit des Unterrichts erscheinen demgegenüber deutlich nachrangig.

4 Ausmaß des Lernerfolgs in verschiedenen Klassen

Die Frage, wonach der Lernerfolg einer Schulklasse beurteilt werden soll, lässt sich nach verschiedenen Gesichtspunkten beantworten: Lernzuwachs aller Kinder, Heranführen der lernschwachen Kinder an den Klassendurchschnitt, Verminderung der Leistungsstreuung u.a. (vgl. Treiber & Weinert 1985). Da in das Hamburger Projekt „Lesen und Schreiben für alle“ vorwiegend Schulen aus sozialen Brennpunkten mit einem relativ hohen Anteil von Kindern mit Lernschwierigkeiten einbezogen sind, wurden in der vorliegenden Längsschnittuntersuchung folgende Kriterien für den Lernerfolg herangezogen:

(1) durchschnittlicher Leistungszuwachs aller Kinder in der HSP von Klasse 1 bis Klasse 4
(2) Leistungszuwachs der Kinder mit ursprünglich schwachen Rechtschreibleistungen (Prozentrang = 15).

Nach diesen Kriterien wurden die Klassen in zwei Gruppen mit hohem bzw. niedrigem Lernerfolg eingeteilt.

Wie Abbildung 4.2.4 zeigt, unterscheiden sich die mittleren Leistungen der beiden Klassengruppen in der ersten Klasse nur wenig (Prozentrang 15 bzw. 20). Ab dem zweiten Schuljahr jedoch gehen die mittleren Leistungen in beiden Gruppen bis zur Klassenstufen 4 erkennbar auseinander. Während sich die Klassen mit hohem Lernerfolg zu einer durchschnittlichen Klassenleistung steigern, die dem Prozentrang 42 entspricht, liegt die mittlere Leistung der übrigen Klassen auf dem Prozentrang 27.

Gleichzeitig mit der Steigerung der Durchschnittsleistung sinkt in den Klassen mit hohem Lernerfolg die mittlere Zahl von Kindern mit schwachen Rechtschreibleistungen von Klasse 2 nach Klasse 4 von 20,1 Prozent auf 8,1 Prozent, während diese Zahl in den Klassen mit niedrigem Lernerfolg im gleichen Zeitraum im Mittel von 20,9 Prozent auf 27,1 Prozent steigt. Demnach gelingt es den erfolgreich lernenden Klassen, die Steigerung der Durchschnittsleistung mit einer Verringerung des Anteils rechtschreibschwacher Kinder zu verbinden.

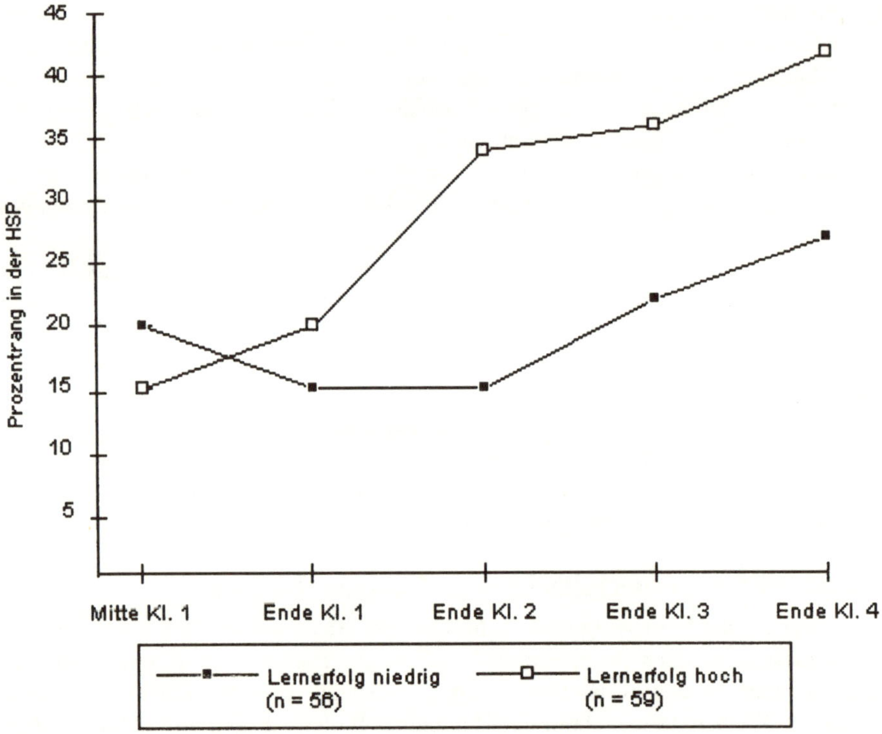

Abb. 4.2.4 Mittlere Rechtschreibleistungen in Klassen mit hohem bzw. niedrigem Lernerfolg

5 Bedingungen des (Förder-)Unterrichts erfolgreicher Klassen

Neben schriftlichen Lehrerbefragungen wurden zur Erfassung der Unterrichtsbedingungen in den Klassen Hospitationen durch geschulte externe Beobachter durchgeführt, die verschiedene Merkmale des Unterrichts protokollierten und einschätzten. Im Folgenden werden die Beobachtungsergebnisse zusammengefasst, die sich auf die zeitliche Ausdehnung und die Qualität der Lehrer- und Schüleraktivitäten im Unterricht beziehen. Um den Zusammenhang der verschiedenen Unterrichtsaktivitäten mit dem Lernerfolg zu untersuchen, wurden die Ergebnisse der Gruppen mit relativ hohem bzw. niedrigem Lernerfolg verglichen.

5.1 Ausmaß verschiedener Lehrer- und Schüleraktivitäten im Unterricht

Abbildung 4.2.5 zeigt die durchschnittlichen Zeitanteile für verschiedene Lehrer- und Schüleraktivitäten in Klassen mit hohem bzw. niedrigem Zuwachs der Rechtschreibleistungen. Die Graphik auf der linken Seite zeigt die Ergebnisse des auf mittlere Klassenleistungen zielenden Vergleichs; auf der rechten Seite sind die Ergebnisse abgebildet, die sich aus der gesonderten Analyse von Klassen ergeben, in denen die förderbedürftigen Kinder mit ursprünglich schwachen Rechtschreibleistungen einen hohen bzw. geringen Lernzuwachs zeigen.

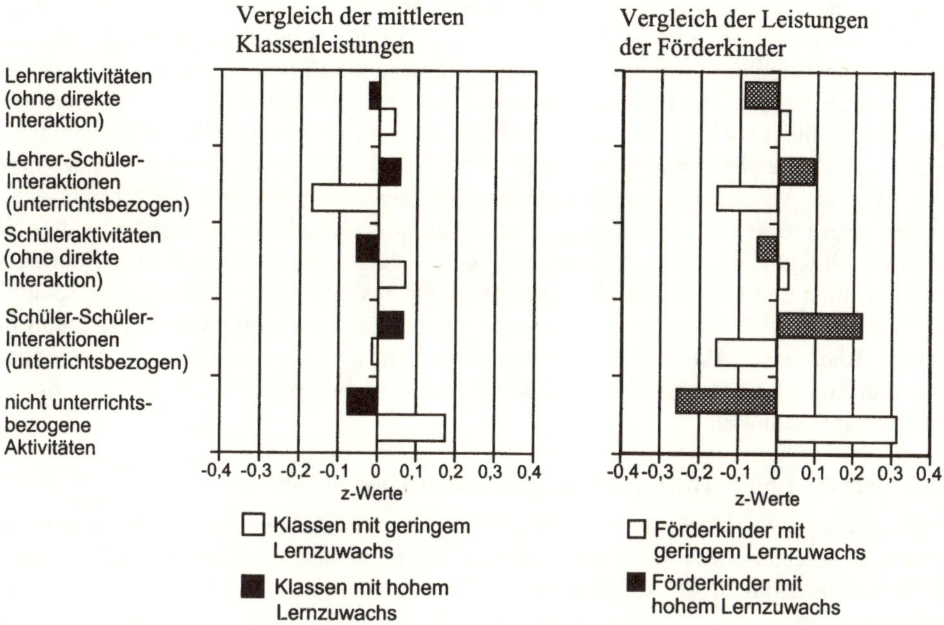

Abb. 4.2.5 Lehrer- und Schüleraktivitäten im Unterricht von Klassen mit hohem bzw. niedrigem Lernerfolg[3]

Beide Vergleiche – sowohl bezogen auf den durchschnittlichen Leistungszuwachs der Klassen als auch bezogen auf den Lernfortschritt der Förderkinder – ergeben dasselbe Beziehungsmuster zwischen Unterrichtsaktivitäten und Lernerfolg. Allerdings erweist sich dieser Zusammenhang bei den Förderkindern als deutlich stärker, d.h., die Unterschiede zwischen den Gruppen fallen bei den Förderkindern höher aus. Dies unterstreicht, dass der Lernfortschritt bei Kindern mit Lernschwierigkeiten stärker mit Merkmalen der Unterrichtsgestaltung zusammenhängt als die Lernentwicklung der übrigen Kinder. Kausal interpretiert bedeutet dies, dass der Lernerfolg der Kinder mit Rechtschreibschwierigkeiten stärker von den unterrichtlichen Bedingungen abhängt.

Hinsichtlich der zeitlichen Verteilung der Aktivitäten lässt sich ein lernförderlicher Unterricht idealtypisch beschreiben: Das Ausmaß der Lehreraktivitäten ohne direkte Interaktion mit den Kindern sollte relativ gering ausfallen, statt dessen sollte die Lehrerin so häufig wie möglich direkt mit den Kindern (einzeln oder in Gruppen) interagieren. Schüleraktivitäten, in denen die Kinder allein arbeiten, sollten zeitlich eng begrenzt werden. Statt dessen sollten Schüleraktivitäten häufiger in der Form stattfinden, dass die Handlungen der

3 Bei den Werten handelt es sich um Faktorwerte, die aufgrund der Ergebnisse der Faktorenanalyse jeweils mehrere Einzelvariablen zusammenfassen; Faktorwerte weisen stets einen Mittelwert von 0 und eine Standardabweichung von 1 auf.

Kinder aufeinander bezogen sind. Insbesondere sollte die Dauer der nicht unterrichtsbezogenen Aktivitäten soweit wie möglich eingeschränkt werden.

Das Muster dieser Vergleichsergebnisse lässt sich mit einschlägigen Erkenntnissen der pädagogischen Psychologie in Übereinstimmung bringen: Die Kinder profitieren beim Lernen von der Interaktion mit der Lehrerin – allerdings nur, wenn diese sich ihnen direkt zuwendet, indem sie ihnen gezielte Erklärungen, individuelle Hilfen, persönliche oder sachliche Rückmeldungen gibt. Verbringen die Kinder im Unterricht längere Zeit mit Einzelarbeit, bei der sie nicht direkt von der Erfahrung und Hilfe anderer Personen profitieren können und keine Rückmeldungen bekommen, sinken Motivation und Konzentration und damit der Lernerfolg. Von der Kooperation mit Mitschülern profitieren insbesondere die lernschwächeren Kinder, sofern diese unterrichtsbezogen ist. Zwar ist diese Schüler-Schüler-Interaktion nicht systematisch und pädagogisch ausgerichtet, jedoch stützt sie gerade bei Lernschwierigkeiten die Motivation und kann durch wertvolle Anregungen weiterhelfen, während die Kinder bei der Einzelarbeit sich selbst überlassen sind. Das Ergebnis, dass ein höherer Zeitanteil nicht unterrichtsbezogener Aktivitäten den potentiellen Lernzuwachs mindert, leuchtet unmittelbar ein, denn dadurch werden die Möglichkeiten zur lernproduktiven Nutzung der Unterrichtszeit unmittelbar beschnitten.

5.2 Art des Unterrichtsverhaltens von Lehrern und Schülern

Die qualitativen Merkmale des Unterrichtsverhaltens von Lehrern und Schülern beurteilten externe Beobachter mit Hilfe verschiedener Einschätzungsskalen. Abbildung 4.2.6 zeigt einige Verhaltensmerkmale der Klassen mit relativ hohem bzw. niedrigem Lernerfolg – auf der linken Seite bezogen auf den mittleren Zuwachs der Rechtschreibleistungen in der Klasse, auf der rechten Seite bezogen auf den Lernzuwachs der zu fördernden Kinder mit ursprünglich schwachen Rechtschreibleistungen.

Bis auf eine Ausnahme ergeben sich sowohl für den Vergleich der Klassenmittelwerte als auch für den Vergleich der Leistungen der Förderkinder gleichgerichtete Beziehungsmuster zwischen Unterrichtsmerkmalen und Lernerfolg. Fasst man die in Abbildung 4.2.3 dargestellten Ergebnisse zusammen, so lassen sich für die Klassen insgesamt als auch für die Förderkinder folgende Tendenzen ablesen, die den Unterricht der Klassen bzw. Förderkinder kennzeichnen, die einen höheren Lernzuwachs im Rechtschreiben aufweisen:

Auf Seiten der *Lehrerin* zeigt sich im lernförderlichen Unterricht

- ein höheres Ausmaß an Direktivität des Lehrerverhaltens
- eine höhere Aufmerksamkeit für die Abläufe in der Klasse
- ein höheres Ausmaß an Zuwendung an die Förderkinder, jedoch eher weniger Einzelzuwendungen an die übrigen Kinder
- eine stärkere Orientierung auf den Lehrstoff und ein stärkeres Einfordern von Disziplin

Diese Ergebnisse zum Lehrstil, die auf den Einschätzungen externer Beobachter beruhen, werden durch die Selbsteinschätzung ihres Unterrichtsstils durch die Klassenlehrer bestätigt: Nach den Ergebnissen schriftlicher Befragungen achten Lehrer in Klassen mit hohem Lernerfolg stärker auf sachliche Beiträge der Kinder, schenken Störungen im Unterricht stärkere Beachtung und beschreiben ihren Unterrichtsstil insgesamt stärker als direktiv. Diese Merkmale des Lehrerverhaltens bestimmen maßgeblich die Qualität ihres „Klassenmanagements“, dessen Wirkungen auf den Lernerfolg mehrfach empirisch nachgewiesen wurde (siehe Einsiedler 1997).

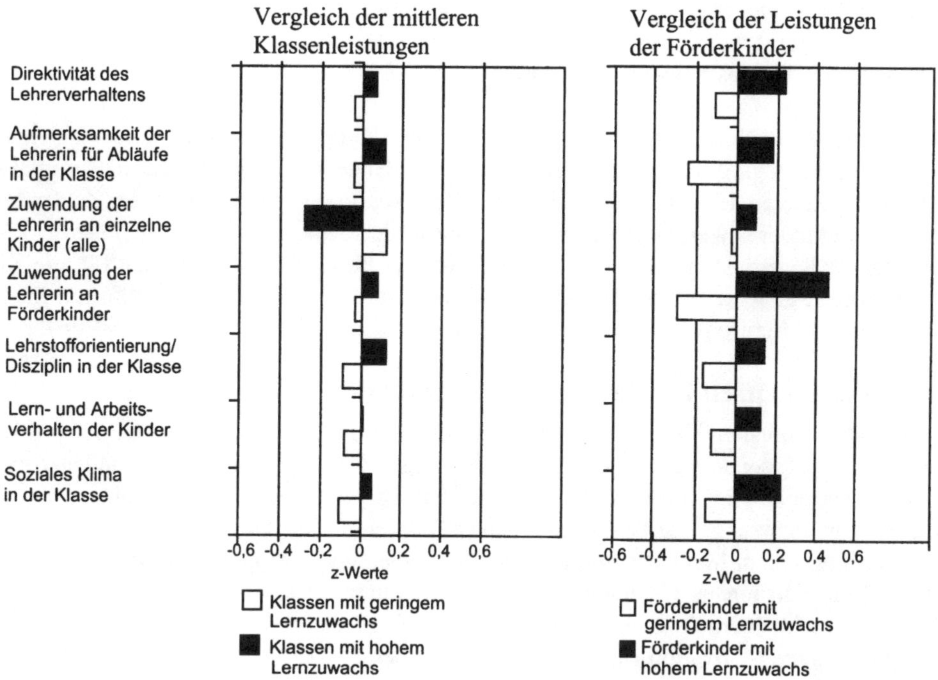

Abb. 4.2.6 Merkmale des Unterrichtsverhaltens und Lernerfolg

Auf den ersten Blick widersprüchlich erweist sich das Ausmaß der Zuwendung der Lehrerin an die übrigen Kinder in der Klasse: Während dieses Ausmaß im Vergleich der mittleren Klassenleistungen bei erfolgreicher lernenden Klassen eher niedriger ausfällt, ist im Vergleich der Förderkinder auch das Ausmaß an die übrigen Kinder im Unterricht der erfolgreicher lernenden Förderkinder geringfügig höher. Eine Erklärung für diesen Widerspruch wäre, dass die übrigen Kinder in der Klasse – im Gegensatz zu den Förderkindern – die individuelle Zuwendung der Lehrerin weniger benötigen, und dass ein sehr starkes Eingehen der Lehrerin auf die einzelnen Kinder den Lernfortschritt der gesamten Klasse dann eher hemmt, weil sie den meisten Kindern damit weniger zur Verfügung steht (mit ungünstigen Auswirkungen auf das Lernverhalten). Bemerkenswert erscheint, dass das Ausmaß der Zuwendung der Lehrerin an die Förderkinder nicht nur für diese selbst, sondern für die Klasse insgesamt lernförderlich zu sein scheint. Darin manifestiert sich offenbar die generelle Tendenz der Lehrerin, sich insbesondere den förderbedürftigen Kindern zuzuwenden, und dies ist auch für andere Kinder, die (zeitweise) Lernschwierigkeiten haben, von Gewinn. Zudem wirkt die Lehrerin damit als Modell für gegenseitige Unterstützung. Diese Förderorientierung der Lehrerin setzt eine relativ hohe diagnostische Kompetenz voraus, damit klare Schwerpunkte bei der Zuwendung gesetzt werden können – im Unterschied zur Tendenz, dass sich die Lehrerin den einzelnen

Kindern unabhängig vom Ausmaß ihrer Lernschwierigkeiten zuwendet. Letzteres scheint bezogen auf die Klasse – weniger lernwirksam zu sein.

Auf Seiten der *Kinder* zeigt sich im lernförderlichen Unterricht
- ein günstigeres Arbeits- und Sozialverhalten sowie
- ein besseres soziales Klima in der Klasse

Wiederum sind die Unterschiede zwischen den beiden Gruppen der Förderkinder insgesamt deutlicher ausgeprägt, d.h., der Lernfortschritt dieser Kinder zeigt einen engeren Zusammenhang mit Merkmalen des Unterrichts.[4] Dies betrifft insbesondere das Ausmaß der Zuwendung an die Förderkinder sowie die Ausprägung des Lern- und Arbeitsverhaltens und des sozialen Klimas in der Klasse. Dies zeigt, dass die Merkmale lernförderlichen Unterricht für alle Kinder weitgehend gleich zu sein scheinen, jedoch ist ihre Relevanz für den Lernfortschritt bei den Kindern mit Lernschwierigkeiten erheblich höher.

6 Konsequenzen für den (Förder-) Unterricht

Kinder mit langanhaltenden Lernschwierigkeiten weisen nicht nur Rückstände im kognitiven Lernergebnis auf, sondern zeigen auch weniger günstige Ausprägungen verschiedener emotional-motivationaler Persönlichkeitsmerkmale. Zudem erhalten sie häufig eine geringere häusliche Unterstützung. Die Wirksamkeit eines (Förder-)Unterrichts hängt daher wesentlich davon ab, in welchem Maße die Förderkinder über eine systematische Hilfe beim Erwerb kognitiver Strategien hinaus Unterstützung zur Entwicklung weiterer günstiger Merkmale der Lernerpersönlichkeit erhalten; dazu gehören insbesondere
- eine tragfähige Motivation zum Lesen und Schreiben,
- ein hohes Maß an Überzeugtheit von der eigenen Lernwirksamkeit (Selbstvertrauen),
- effektive Lern- und Arbeitsstrategien.

Während Kinder mit guten Lernergebnissen meist relativ stabile Persönlichkeitsmerkmale aufweisen, die ein eigenständiges und zielgerichtetes Lernen begünstigen, muss sich ein Förderunterricht auf die psychologischen Besonderheiten der Kinder mit Lese-Rechtschreib-Schwierigkeiten und auf ihre speziellen Lernbedingungen einstellen. Ein Unterricht, der sich in erster Linie an den Kindern mit günstigen Lernvoraussetzungen orientiert, ist daher für die Förderkinder mit hoher Wahrscheinlichkeit ineffektiv oder sogar schädlich, da er ihnen wirksame Hilfen, auf die sie viel stärker als die übrigen Kinder angewiesen sind, vorenthält.

Die Vielfalt verschiedener Varianten des Unterrichts, die die Lernfähigkeit von Kinder mit anhaltenden Lernschwierigkeiten wirksam unterstützen können, ist hoch. Dies kann nicht anders sein, denn zahlreiche weitere Faktoren (z.B. Lehrerpersönlichkeit, soziale Zusammensetzung der Klasse, außerschulische Lernbedingungen) beeinflussen den Lernerfolg in der Klasse. Daher kann es kein allgemeingültiges Rezept für lernförderlichen Unterricht geben. Jedoch sollte sich die Planung eines lernwirksamen Unterrichts an solchen Bedingungen ori-

---

4 Dies wird auch durch die Korrelation zwischen den Einzelmerkmalen und dem Ausmaß des Lernzuwachses bestätigt: Die multiple Korrelation zwischen den in die dargestellten Gruppenvergleiche eingehenden Variablen und dem Lernerfolg im Rechtschreiben ergibt für den mittleren Lernzuwachs der Klassen einen Wert von $R = .65$, d.h., ca. 43 Prozent des mittleren Lernzuwachses der Klassen sind auf diese Weise vorhersagbar. Für die Förderkinder beträgt der betreffende multiple Korrelationskoeffizient immerhin .77, d.h., die Unterschiede des Lernzuwachses innerhalb eines ganzen Schuljahres lassen sich damit sogar zu 59 Prozent aufklären (siehe May 1999c).

entieren, die der Unterricht in Klassen mit hohem Lernerfolg trotz aller Unterschiede in höherem Maße aufweist als weniger lernwirksamer Unterricht.

Mit Blick auf die lese-rechtschreibschwachen Kinder sollte ein lernwirksamer Unterricht u.a. folgende Merkmale aufweisen:

- differenzierte und individualisierte Aufgabenstellungen, um die persönliche Motivation zu berücksichtigen und Überforderungen zu vermeiden;
- Gestaltung von klar strukturierten Aufgabenstellungen und möglichst transparenten Lösungssituationen;
- Vermeidung längerer Phasen der Einzelarbeit mit komplexen und offenen Aufgabenstellungen, die den Förderkindern noch wenig vertraut sind;
- häufige individuelle Zuwendungen an die Förderkinder, um sie zu ermuntern sowie ihnen Erläuterung und Hilfen zu geben;
- möglichst unmittelbare Leistungsrückmeldung nach der Bewältigung von Teilschritten;
- Vermeidung von Leerlauf und unterrichtsfremden Aktivitäten

Derartige Bedingungen sind im Rahmen des Klassenunterrichts nicht beliebig herstellbar; häufig entsprechen andere Vorgehensweisen (z.B. offenere, mehr selbst bestimmte Lernarrangements) eher den Lernbedingungen der übrigen Kinder. Zudem mangelt es im regulären Klassenunterricht nicht selten an ausreichend Zeit für die besonders förderbedürftigen Kinder. In solchen Fällen sollte ein gezielter und auf die speziellen Bedingungen der lernschwierigen Kinder abgestimmter Förderunterricht eingerichtet werden. Dieser kann als externer Förderunterricht außerhalb der Klasse oder unter bestimmten Bedingungen auch als integrativer Förderunterricht innerhalb des Klassenunterrichts stattfinden. Aufgrund der Empfehlungen der Lehrer sowie aufgrund der Evaluationsergebnisse zur Effektivität des Förderunterrichts ergibt sich die Tendenz, dass im ersten (und evtl. noch im zweiten) Schuljahr ein integrativer Förderunterricht eher Vorteile aufweist, während in den höheren Klassenstufen zunehmend die externe Form der Förderung bevorzugt wird (siehe May 1999c).

Literaturhinweise

Einsiedler, W. (1997): Unterrichtsqualität und Leistungsentwicklung: Literaturüberblick. In: Weinert, F.E. & Helmke, A. (Hg.): Entwicklung im Grundschulalter. Weinheim: PsychologieVerlagsUnion, S. 226-240.

Hofer, M., Pekrun, R. & Zielinski, W. (1986): Die Psychologie des Lerners. In: Weidenmann, B., Krapp, A., Hofer, M., Huber, G.L. & Mandl, H. (Hg.): Pädagogische Psychologie. München: PsychologieVerlagsUnion, S. 219-276.

Klicpera, C., Gasteiger-Klicpera, B. & Hütter, E. (1993): Die Praxis der Legasthenikerförderung in zwei Wiener Schulbezirken. In: Bundesministerium für Unterricht und Kunst (Hg.): Was macht die Förderung effektiv? Kontroverse (?) Konzepte zur Legasthenikerbetreuung. Wien: Ketterl-Verlag, S. 41-147.

May, P. (1994c): Rechtschreibfähigkeit und Unterricht. Rechtschreibleistungen Hamburger Schüler/innen im vierten Schuljahr im Zusammenhang mit Merkmalen schriftsprachlichen Unterrichts. Ergebnisse der Voruntersuchung zum Projekt Lesen und Schreiben für alle (PLUS). Bericht der Wissenschaftlichen Begleitung Nr. 94/01. Hamburg: Behörde für Schule, Jugend und Berufsbildung.

May, P. (1996b): Integrative Förderung von Kindern mit Lernschwierigkeiten durch kooperativen Unterricht – Erfahrungen aus dem Hamburger Projekt „Lesen und Schreiben für alle". In: Bundesverband Legasthenie (Hg.): Legasthenie. Bericht über den Kongress 1995 in Darmstadt. Emden: Ostfriesische Beschützende Werkstätten.

May, P. (1997c): Diagnose orthographischer Kompetenz. Zur Erfassung der grundlegenden Rechtschreibstrategien mit der Hamburger Schreib-Probe. Unter Mitarbeit von Ulrich Vieluf und Volkmar Malitzky. Hamburg: Verlag für pädagogische Medien. 3., erweiterte Auflage.

May, P. (1999c): Lernförderlicher Unterricht. Schriftsprachlicher Klassen- und Förderunterricht und seine Wirkungen auf den Lernerfolg im Rechtschreiben und Textgestalten sowie auf die Motivation der Kinder. Bericht über die Evaluation des Projekts „Lesen und Schreiben für alle" (PLUS). Psychologisches Institut II der Universität Hamburg.

Treiber, B. & Weinert, F.E. (1985): Gute Schulleistungen für alle? Psychologische Studien zu einer pädagogischen Hoffnung. Münster: Aschendorff.

van Aken, M.A.G., Helmke, A. & Schneider, W. (1997): Selbstkonzept und Leistung – Dynamik ihres Zusammenspiels: Ergebnisse aus dem SCHOLASTIK-Projekt. In: Weinert, F.E. & Helmke, A. (Hg.): Entwicklung im Grundschulalter. Weinheim: Psychologie-Verlags-Union, S. 341- 350.

4.3 Die Bedeutung der alphabetischen Strategie für die Förderung lese-rechtschreibschwacher Kinder

Gerheid Scheerer-Neumann

Ich wurde vom Bundesverband Legasthenie gebeten, zu dem Thema „Die Bedeutung der alphabetischen Strategie bei der Förderung lese-rechtschreibschwacher Kinder" zu sprechen. Spontan fiel mir dazu folgender Satz ein:

„Wenn sie noch nicht beherrscht wird, muss die alphabetische Strategie, also das Erlesen bzw. lautorientierte Schreiben, im Zentrum der Förderung lese-rechtschreibschwacher Kinder stehen. Sie ist unverzichtbar."

Dies ist auch nach weniger spontanen Überlegungen das Fazit meines Beitrags; ich werde diese Aussage begründen und an Beispielen erläutern. Die Beschränkung auf wenige Seiten macht die Konzentration auf entweder Lesen *oder* Schreiben notwendig; ich habe das Lesen gewählt, werde aber kurz auch auf das Schreiben zu sprechen kommen.

1 Lesen als komplexer kognitiver Prozess

Zunächst ist zu präzisieren, was unter dem Begriff der „alphabetischen Strategie" zu verstehen ist. Dazu ein kleiner historischer Rückblick: Unser heutiges Verständnis der Prozesse beim Lesen und Schreiben wurde von der Kognitiven Psychologie angestoßen, die sich seit Ende der 60er Jahre daran gemacht hat, komplexe kognitive Prozesse in ihrer Mikrostruktur zu analysieren, d.h. der Frage nachzugehen, aus welchen unterscheidbaren modularen Teilprozessen komplexe kognitive Prozesse aufgebaut sind. Der Leseprozess war für diese Forschungsrichtung von Anfang an ein ganz wichtiges Teilgebiet (z.B. Gibson & Levin 1975, Coltheart 1978). Auch ohne formale Analyse wird schon deutlich, dass Lesen ein unglaublich komplexer Prozess ist: Lesen hat zu tun mit Bausteinen unterschiedlicher Größe, mit Buchstaben, Silben, Morphemen, Wörtern, Sätzen usw.; es gibt unterschiedliche Herangehensweisen: man kann sehr genau lesen, erlesen oder überfliegen usw. Das Entsprechende gilt für den Schreibprozeß: Auch hier ist es ein sehr komplexer Weg vom diktierten Wort oder dem Gedanken bis zum Niederschreiben auf dem Papier – oder in den Computer.

Ich glaube, dass es uns noch nicht gelungen ist, die Prozesse des Lesens und Schreibens in ihrer ganzen Komplexität zu entschlüsseln; aber es gibt in vielen Teilbereichen gute Ansätze, die zeigen, daß die Analyse nicht nur wissenschaftlich interessant, sondern auch von praktischer Relevanz ist. *Das heißt, sie gibt uns Einsichten in das Lesen und Schreiben und in die entsprechenden Lernprozesse – auch in verzögerte oder gestörte Lernprozesse – von denen sinnvolle Ansätze für die Lehre und Förderung abgeleitet werden können.*

2 Die Bedeutung des Wortlesens für den Leseprozess

Auch wenn Lesen als Ganzes – vom Erkennen eines Buchstabens zum Verstehen eines Buches – ein unglaublich komplexer Prozess ist, gibt es bestimmte Teilbereiche, die für den Gesamtprozess besonders wichtig sind, weil andere auf ihnen aufbauen und die deshalb didaktisch vorrangig zu berücksichtigen sind. Ein solcher Teilbereich ist das *Lesen einzelner Wörter,* das auch Worterkennen genannt wird, wobei das Wort durchaus im Satzzusammenhang stehen kann. Es gab vor Jahren eine internationale Tagung zum Lesen und zu Problemen des Lesens, auf der sich das Schlagwort entstand: „It´s all in the word“ – Es ist alles im Wort. Es ist das Nadelöhr im Leselernprozess. Das heißt natürlich nur, dass das effiziente Wortlesen zentral ist; es impliziert nicht, dass höhere Leseprozesse gerade auch *für die Analyse von Leseproblemen* unbedeutend sind.

Ich denke, die Bedeutung des schnellen, effizienten, automatisierten Worterkennens für den gesamten Leseprozeß ist intuitiv einleuchtend: *Falsch* gelesene Wörter behindern natürlich das Verständnis des ganzen Satzes, aber das Gleiche gilt auch für das *langsame* Worterkennen: Die Wörter müssen zur Sinnentschlüsselung des ganzen Satzes im Kurzzeitgedächtnis aufbewahrt werden. Wenn Kinder – oder auch Erwachsene – einzelne Wörter sehr mühsam lesen, reicht die Dauer der Zwischenspeicherung oft einfach nicht aus und die ersten Wörter sind schon wieder vergessen, wenn das Ende eines Satzes oder eines Teilsatzes erreicht ist. Eine positive Beziehung zwischen der Geschwindigkeit, mit der einzelne Wörter gelesen werden und dem Textverständnis konnte auch in empirischen Untersuchungen bestätigt werden und gilt nicht nur für Kinder, sondern mindestens bis ins Jugendalter. Wir führen zu dieser Frage zur Zeit selbst eine Untersuchung in den Klassen 5 und 6 durch, die noch nicht abgeschlossen ist.

3 Teilprozesse und Strategien des Wortlesens: Das Zwei-Wege-Modell und die Nutzung des Kontexts

Wenden wir uns nun den Prozessen beim Wortlesen zu. Obwohl in den letzten Jahren Netzwerkmodelle des Worterkennens entwickelt wurden, kann das von Coltheart (1978) formulierte „Zwei-Wege-Modell“ immer noch – auch innerhalb der Neuropsychologie – als valides Analysemodell gelten. Die zwei Wege sind zum einen das direkte Worterkennen ohne einen erlesenden, phonemorientierten Aufbau des Wortes, zum anderen das synthetisierende Erlesen, das den alphabetischen Charakter unserer Schrift nutzt und deshalb auch als „alphabetische Strategie“ bezeichnet wird.

Auch das direkte Worterkennen verläuft nicht ohne phonologische Anteile: Sie sind aber „postlexikalisch“, d.h. werden dem Wort erst dann zugeordnet, wenn die Bedeutung bereits erkannt ist. Dagegen erfolgt das Erkennen der Wortbedeutung beim indirekten, alphabetischen Weg zumindest unter Führung der beim Erlesen gewonnenen phonologischen Merkmale des Wortes, wenn es nicht sogar dem Erlesen völlig nachgeschaltet ist.

Abb. 4.3.1 stellt eine Erweiterung des Zwei-Wege-Modells dar; es bezieht neben den beschriebenen „Wegen“ bzw. Strategien als weitere wichtige Einflussgröße den *Kontext* mit ein, in dem das zu lesende Wort steht. Unter „Kontext“ werden sehr heterogene Informationsquellen verstanden, die alle eines gemeinsam haben: Sie beeinflussen die Auftretenswahrscheinlichkeit eines bestimmten Wortes. *Syntaktisch* ist z.B. an der Stelle:
In der Vase stehen ....
ein Nomen oder ein Adjektiv wahrscheinlich, aber nicht zwingend. Semantisch haben das Wort „Blumen“ oder eine bestimmte Blumenart (Tulpen, Rosen) sicher die höchsten Wahrscheinlichkeiten. Neben Assoziationen, die allen Benutzern einer Sprache mehr oder weniger gemeinsam sind, gibt es idiosynkratische Erwartungen, die auf individuellen Erfahrungen beruhen. So kennen Erstklässer ihre Fibeln oft so gut, dass sie genau wissen, welche Wörter auf den ersten Seiten überhaupt vorkommen können, an welcher Stelle oder bei welchem Bild ein Wort steht etc. Auch hier ist es sinnvoll, von Kontext zu sprechen.

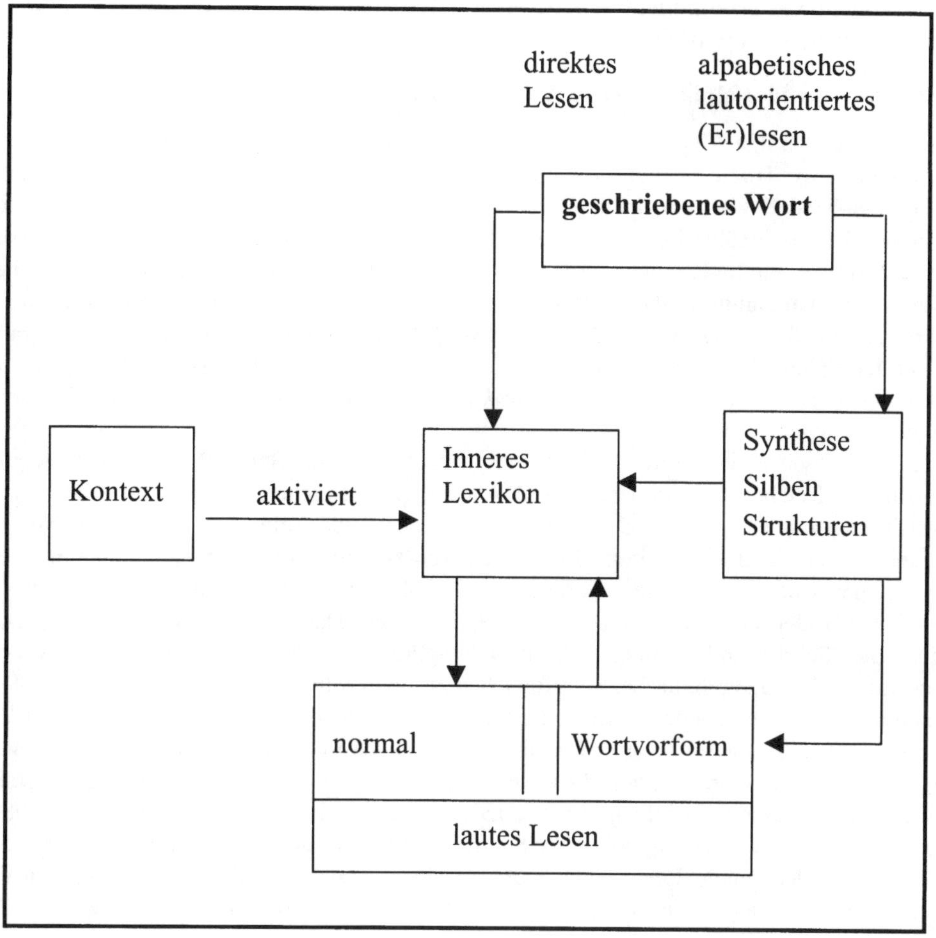

Abb. 4.3.1 Rahmenmodell zur Veranschaulichung von Lesestrategien

Im Folgenden sind nun vier Fragen zu klären:

Welche der beschriebenen Komponenten bzw. Wege oder Strategien sind für den erwachsenen Leser besonders wichtig?

Wie entwickeln bzw. verändern sich dieser Strategien bzw. Komponenten im Laufe der Leseentwicklung?

In welchen Strategien bzw. Komponenten liegen die Probleme lese-rechtschreibschwacher Kinder?

Was ergibt sich daraus für die Förderung?

3.1 Welche der Komponenten bzw. Wege oder Strategien sind für den erwachsenen Leser besonders wichtig?

3.1.1 Direktes oder alphabetisches Worterkennen?

Theoretische Ansätze, die das Worterkennen des erwachsenen Lesers modellieren, haben schon eine lange Tradition (vgl. H. Günther 1996). Im Zusammenhang mit dem skizzierten Zwei-Wege-Modell war man in den 70er Jahren vor allem im englischen Sprachraum der Meinung, dass der geübte Leser vor allem über das direkte Worterkennen liest und phonologische Prozesse nur eine untergeordnete Rolle spielen. Dies wird heute anders gesehen. Selbst wenn man annimmt, dass der erwachsene Leser viele Wörter oder Morpheme sozusagen als „Sichtwörter" erkennt, ist deutlich geworden, dass dies eigentlich immer in Interaktion mit der alphabetischen Strategie geschieht. *D.h. wir nutzen den Vorteil auch aus, den unsere alphabetischen Schrift bietet – die strukturelle Korrespondenz zwischen geschriebener und gesprochener Sprache.*

Das Lesen eines Wortes ist nicht das Gleiche wie das Benennen eines Bildes, auch wenn Jürgen Reichen dies immer wieder behauptet (z.B. Reichen 1998). Lesen erfolgt beim Erwachsenen immer schneller als das Benennen eines Bildes und es ist unabhängig von der Anzahl der verschiedenen Wörter, die gelesen werden sollen im Gegensatz zum Benennen, bei dem man schnelle Reaktionszeiten nur dann erhalten kann, wenn man die Anzahl der verschiedenen Bilder auf sehr wenige reduziert. Interessante Daten für den Vorteil einer phonographischen Schrift fand ich in einer Untersuchung aus Japan: Es gibt im Japanischen sowohl chinesische, also logographische, Schriftzeichen als auch Silbenschriften, bei denen eine Korrespondenz zur gesprochenen Sprache besteht. Farbwörter werden in der Regel mit chinesischen Schriftzeichen geschrieben; man kann sie aber auch mit Silbenzeichen umschreiben. Es zeigte sich nun, dass erwachsene Leser mit viel Erfahrung im Lesen der logographischen Zeichen die Farbwörter in Silbenschrift trotzdem schneller lasen (Feldman & Turvey 1980). Dies zeigt den Vorteil phonographischer Schriften, der offensichtlich auch genutzt wird. Natürlich erliest der geübte Leser nicht buchstabenweise, sondern in größeren Einheiten und gelegentlich auch in ganzen Wörtern; aber auch dann ignoriert er die Information aus den Graphem-Phonem-Beziehungen nicht.

3.1.2 Die Nutzung des Kontexts

Eine andere interessante Frage bezieht sich auf die Kontextnutzung. Auch in heutigen Veröffentlichungen kann man die Ansicht von Kenneth Goodman von 1967 finden: Reading: A linguistic guessing game – Lesen ist eine psycholinguistisches Ratespiel. Goodman beschrieb den Leseprozess als kontextgesteuert: Der Leser hat aus dem Kontext heraus Erwartungen an den Text und bildet nach dem Lesen jeweils weniger Wörter eines Satzes Hypothesen über dessen Fortgang. Das Lesen wird durch diese Erwartungen gesteuert und meistens bestätigt; gelegentlich muß der Leser die Hypothesen auch revidieren. Diese Meinung kann aufgrund einer ganzen Reihe von Untersuchungen heute nicht mehr aufrecht erhalten werden (vgl. Scheerer-Neumann 1981, Stanovich 1981), auch wenn man sie bei uns leider immer noch in didaktischen Kommentaren – mit den entsprechenden Konsequenzen in der Praxis – findet. Dass der Kontext das Worterkennen bzw. die Sinnentschlüsselung überhaupt beeinflussen kann, ist nicht zu bestreiten; mehrdeutige Wörter fordern dies geradezu, wie in dem folgenden Beispiel:

Es war die *Hochzeit* der Gotik.

Für sich alleinstehend würde <Hochzeit> eine andere Bedeutung attribuiert als im Kontext; aber – dies sind genau die Stellen, an denen auch der geübte Leser gelegentlich „hängen bleibt“ und den Satz ein zweites Mal lesen muss. Es wird noch viel Forschung nötig sein, um Kontexteinflüsse im Detail aufzuklären. Bezogen auf die ablaufenden Prozesse wird die Situation derzeit folgendermaßen gesehen:

Es gibt zwei Kontexteffekte, einen schnellen automatischen und einen, der mehr Zeit benötigt und die bewusste Vorhersage eines Wortes impliziert. Der schnelle automatische Effekt hat bei einem „besonders gut passenden“ Kontext einen positiven Effekt, führt also zum schnelleren Lesen als bei neutralen Wörtern; ist ein Wort eher unerwartet, ergibt sich kein negativer Effekt. So führt das Wortpaar <Gras> – <grün> zu einem schnelleren Lesen von <grün>; folgt auf <Gras> jedoch <blau> ist das Worterkennen im Vergleich zu einem „neutralen“ Wort wie <braun> nicht verzögert. Man kann sich diesen Effekt als eine Art *semantische Aktivierung* vorstellen, die ganz spontan abläuft, also auch didaktisch weder beeinflusst werden muss noch sollte. Der Effekt ergibt sich aus der Speicherung der Wörter in semantischen Netzen in unserem inneren Lexikon: „Gras“ hat eine semantische Nähe zu „grün“, „Weihnachten“ zu „Tannenbaum“, „Christkind“ usw.

Neben dieser automatischen semantischen Aktivierung gibt es eine bewusste Hypothesenbildung, die aber mehr Zeit benötigt, mindestens 700 msec; diese Zeit steht dem Erwachsenen normalerweise zwischen zwei Wörter nicht zur Verfügung; sie wäre höchstens zum übernächsten oder noch weiter entfernten Wort möglich. Bei dieser zweiten Art der Kontextnutzung, der bewussten Hypothesenbildung, gibt es nicht nur *Bahnung*, also eine Erleichterung des Lesens bei passenden Wörtern, sondern auch *Hemmung*, eine Verlängerung der Lesezeit bei nicht-passenden Wörtern, die nicht erwartet wurden. Hier liegt natürlich das Hauptproblem: Richtig vorhergesagt werden können nur wenige Wörter: Falsche Hypothesen, die zurückgewiesen werden müssen, verlängern aber die Lesezeit und die meisten Hypothesen müssen falsch sein, weil Wörter nur in wenigen Fällen tatsächlich mit Sicherheit vorhersagbar sind. Die Strategie des kontextgeleiteten Lesens mit Hilfe der aktiven Hypothesenbildung kann also nicht sehr effektiv sein. Ich war schon vor 20 Jahren dieser Meinung und sehe mich heute darin bestätigt. Vellutino & Scanlon halten das Wortlesen beim *geübten Leser* für einen schnellen und automatischen und modularen Prozess, der wenig von Kontextinformation abhängig ist... (Vellutino & Scanlon 1991).

Von besonderer Wichtigkeit ist hier der Begriff „modular“; modulare Prozesse sind relativ autonom und in sich abgeschlossen; eine Minderleistung kann kaum durch andere Prozesse kompensiert werden. Die Modularitätsannahme des Worterkennens ist wahrscheinlich richtig, wird derzeit aber noch diskutiert (vgl. Rayner & Pollatsek 1989, Kap. 7). Wenn Worterkennen tatsächlich ein kognitives Modul im komplexen Leseprozess ist, so bedeutet dies didaktisch, dass wir ihm besondere Aufmerksamkeit schenken müssen. Als Übung folgt jedoch nicht unbedingt das Erlesen einzelner Wörter. Dies kann allerdings unter Umständen notwendig sein, wenn nämlich die eigentlich relevanten Teilprozesse durch kompensatorische Kontextnutzung nicht ausreichend geübt werden.

3.2 Wie verändern sich die Lesestrategien bzw. Komponenten des Lesens im Laufe der Entwicklung?

Der entwicklungspsychologische Blick auf den Schriftspracherwerb ist eine der wichtigsten Veränderungen im Bereich der Erforschung des Lesen- und Schreibenlernens der letzten Jahrzehnte – auch für unser Verständnis der Lese-Rechtschreibschwäche (vgl. Scheerer-

Neumann 1989, 1996). Wir haben gute Gründe anzunehmen, dass sich Kinder nicht linear und kontinuierlich dem Lesen und Schreiben des Erwachsenen annähern, sondern die verschiedenen Strategien nach und nach mit unterschiedlichen Schwerpunkten erwerben. Wir sprechen auch von verschiedenen Phasen oder Stufen des Schriftspracherwerbs.

Für das Worterkennen gilt – bezogen auf das Zwei-Wege-Modell – in Stichworten etwa diese Abfolge, wobei ich hier auf die Vorstufen nicht eingehe:

Direktes, logographisches, „ganzheitliches" Lesen, Kontext wichtig
Dies ist das typische Lesen des *Vorschulkindes,* das seinen eigenen und andere Namen an wenigen Buchstaben oder Merkmalen erkennt („Omi ist das mit dem Punkt")

Beginnend lautorientiert – Kontext wichtig
Das beginnende lautorientierte Lesen kombiniert direktes und alphabetisches Lesen: Erste Einsichten in Graphem-Phonem-Korrespondenzen erleichtern das Wiedererkennen logographisch gespeicherter Wörter.

Reine alphabetische, indirekte Strategie des Erlesens – Kontext spielt kaum eine Rolle, wird oft regelrecht ausgeblendet
Dies ist das typische Erlesen des ersten Schuljahrs: „Derrr Bärrr und derrr Tigerr" –selbst frühere Sichtwörter werden erlesen. Kinder achten in dieser Phase oft kaum auf den Inhalt des Gelesenen, weil sie so sehr mit dem Einüben der Lesetechnik befasst sind. Wir sollten dies akzeptieren. Es ist wie „Fahrradfahren um den Block".

Alphabetisches Lesen unter Nutzung größerer Einheiten (z.B. Silben) und morphematischer und orthographischer Strukturen (Kind<u>er</u>, Mutt<u>er</u>)
Silben müssen schon auf der vorausgehenden Stufe zur Gliederung der Grapheme genutzt werden; jetzt werden die häufigen zu graphematischen Einheiten. Zu funktionalen Einheiten können auch Morpheme (-er, -en etc.) werden.

Lesen wird jetzt wieder wortspezifischer, „direkter"; Kontextnutzung wie beim Erwachsenen, beginnende Automatisierung.
Lesen wird jetzt wieder lexikalischer, wortspezifischer, direkter. Es unterscheidet sich vom logographischen Worterkennen durch die Merkmale der gespeicherten Repräsentation des Wortes im inneren Lexikon: Die innere Repräsentation des „gereiften" direkten Worterkennens basiert auf der Entsprechung zwischen Sprechschema und Schreibschema; die zu speichernden Merkmale entstehen auf der Basis der alphabetischen Strategie. Entsprechend besteht eine unmittelbare Abhängigkeitsbeziehung zwischen den Phasen 4 und 5: Das elaborierte direkte Worterkennen kann nur erreicht werden, wenn die alphabetische Strategie bereits beherrscht wird. Allerdings wird die alphabetische Strategie auch beim geübten Leser nie ganz ausgeblendet (s. o. S. 268).

3.3 In welchen Strategien bzw. Komponenten liegen die Probleme leseschwacher Kinder?

3.3.1 Probleme bei der alphabetischen Strategie

Hier stellt sich sofort die Frage nach der Definition von „Leseschwäche“. Ich beziehe mich zunächst auf alle Kinder, deren Leseleistungen deutlich vom Alters- bzw. Klassendurchschnitt abweichen ohne weitere Kriterien anzulegen. Es hat im Jahrbuch der Deutschen Gesellschaft für Lesen und Schreiben 1987 eine Kontroverse zwischen Lisa Dummer und Hans Brügelmann über die Frage gegeben, ob lese-rechtschreibschwache Kinder eher als entwicklungsverzögert oder als Problemkinder mit einem spezifischen Defizit gesehen werden sollten (Dummer & Brügelmann 1987). Brügelmann, der den Ansatz der Entwicklungsverzögerung vertritt, schrieb, dass lese-rechtschreibschwache Kinder nur „zu dem falschen Zeitpunkt normal“ seien, für Dummer stehen „Teilleistungsschwächen“ im Vordergrund. Beide Ansätze haben in gewisser Weise ihre Berechtigung. Ich sehe lese-rechtschreibschwache Kinder als entwicklungsverzögerte Kinder, deren Entwicklungsverzögerung aber durchaus eine spezifische Ursache haben kann. *Vor allem für die Förderung ist es wichtig, nicht nur auf spezifische kognitiven Minderleistungen zu achten, sondern den Entwicklungskontext beim Schriftspracherwerb mit einzubeziehen. Nur so können proximale („nahe“) Ziele der Förderung gegenstandsadäquat festgelegt werden.*

An welcher Stelle der Entwicklung werden leseschwache Kinder nun auffällig? Hierzu hat die Forschung in den letzten Jahren sehr eindeutige Ergebnisse erbracht: Das logographische, ganzheitliche Lesen gelingt in der Regel, vielleicht auch noch das lautunterstützte Worterkennen. Ein Teil der jüngeren Leseschwachen hat aber bereits Schwierigkeiten beim Erwerb von Graphem-Phonem-Korrespondenzen. *Massive Probleme gibt es aber bei der alphabetischen Strategie, vor allem bei Konsonantenclustern und bei der vollständigen Synthese und Analyse.* Je nach Grad der Entwicklungsverzögerung gelingt das Erlesen einfach strukturierter Wörter (z.B. Oma, Hase, Rabe). Das Lesen längere Wörter ist fast immer problematisch; Die Kinder haben Schwierigkeiten, die Silben- bzw. Morphemstruktur zu erkennen und ein Wort in diesen Einheiten zu erlesen. Manchmal sind von den Syntheseproblemen auch kurze Wörter betroffen: Häufig wird kein Unterschied gemacht zwischen:

ein	das	kein
eine	da	keine
einer	dann	keiner

Warum treten bei diesen vermeintlich einfachen Wörtern so viele Lesefehler auf? Ich denke, dies sind Anzeichen einer ganzheitlichen, logographischen Lesestrategie; die Kinder erkennen in den Beispielen das <ein>, <da> oder <kein> wieder und ignorieren die anderen Buchstaben. Dies kann auch dann auftreten, wenn ein Kind prinzipiell dazu in der Lage wäre, die zu den Graphemen korrespondierenden Phoneme zu synthetisieren: Der Rückgriff auf die logographische Strategie ist für das Kind eine Entlastung, wenn die Synthese ein hohes Maß an Konzentration und Anstrengung erfordert. Die beherrschten Lesestrategien können vom Kind in diesem Sinne flexibel eingesetzt werden. Die Aufgabe der Förderung besteht darin, das Kinder immer wieder zur alphabetischen Strategie „zurückzuholen“, bis diese ausreichend beherrscht wird.

Ein anderer Weg, das unzureichend beherrschten Erlesen zu kompensieren bzw. die alphabetischen Strategie zu vermeiden, ist die massive Nutzung des Kontexts, über die alle Förderlehrer berichten können. Leseschwache Kinder verbringen oft enorme Gedächtnisleistungen und wissen genau, an welchen Stellen im Buch welche Wörter stehen. Oder sie komplettieren nach dem Erlesen der Anfangsbuchstaben die Wörter oft inkorrekt – aber kontextkompatibel (vgl. Abb. 4.3.2).

Abbildung 4.3.2 Kontextkompatible Ersetzung der Wortes <fühlte> durch „fürchte“

Wie wir vorhin beim Schnelldurchlauf durch die Leseentwicklung gesehen haben, sind logographisches Worterkennen und Kontextnutzung durchaus „normal“ und können für eine gewisse Zeit auch akzeptiert werden, allerdings nur im Kontext eines geöffneten Unterrichts, der auch diesen Kindern zu einem späteren Zeitpunkt noch elementare Lernangebote macht. Wird dies versäumt, kann es leicht geschehen, dass das logographische Worterkennen verbunden mit einer hohen Kontextnutzung zu einer überdauernden kompensatorischen Strategie wird, von der sich die Kinder sehr schlecht wieder lösen können, weil sie metakognitiv als erfolgreich empfunden wird. Ältere Leseschwache sind in diesem Sinne in der Regel nicht einfach entwicklungsverzögert, sondern haben häufig solche kompensatorischen Lesestrategien entwickelt oder weisen ganz spezifische Probleme auf. Im übrigen haben ältere Leseschwache oft Probleme bei längeren Wörtern und sind in ihrer Lesegeschwindigkeit in der Regel sehr verlangsamt. Sie haben Schwierigkeiten, Pseudowörter zu lesen, also Wörter, die nur über die alphabetische Strategie gelesen werden können.

In diesem Zusammenhang erscheint mir das traditionelle „Lesenüben“, das ich in vielen Schulen beobachte, äußerst problematisch. „Lesenüben“ besteht meistens darin, den gleichen Text immer wieder zu lesen; er wird zu Hause geübt und dann wieder in der Schule gelesen. Manchmal schauen die Kinder gar nicht mehr ins Buch.

3.3.2 Phonologische Bewusstheit: Basis der alphabetischen Strategie auch schon im Vorschulalter

Entwicklungsverzögerungen treten in der Regel nicht plötzlich auf, sondern kündigen sich schon vorher an und tatsächlich lassen sich Vorläufer der Probleme mit der alphabetischen Strategie recht früh beobachten. Die alphabetische Strategie erfordert den Umgang mit den kleinsten Einheiten der gesprochenen Sprache, den Phonemen bzw. Lauten und deren Analyse aus dem komplexen gesprochenen Wort bzw. ihre Synthese; man spricht hier von „phonologischer Bewusstheit“ und bezieht im weiteren Sinn auch die Sensibilität für Reime, die Fähigkeit zur Gliederung von Wörtern in Silben und das Nachsprechen komplexer Wörter mit ein (vgl. Landerl und Schneider in diesem Band). Obwohl gerade Analyse und Synthese im Erstleseunterricht eingeführt und geübt werden, gibt es im Vorschulalter offensichtlich schon entsprechende rudimentäre Kompetenzen, auf die die Schule in der Regel aufbauen kann. Sind diese Vorläuferfähigkeiten nicht vorhanden, kann es leicht zu Verzögerungen im Lernprozess kommen, vor allem, wenn die Entwicklungsverzögerung nicht nur durch mangelnde Erfahrung im Umgang mit Sprache bedingt ist, sondern allgemeinere Schwächen in der phonologischen Verarbeitung vorliegen.

Es gibt vor allem zwei Gründe, warum phonemanalytische Fähigkeiten, die als Basis für die alphabetische Strategie gelten können, oft nur mit Mühe erworben werden:

Vorschulkinder achten vor allem auf die Bedeutung von Wörtern und weniger auf die sprachlich-formale Seite. Bosch entwickelte schon in den dreißiger Jahren d. J. eine Aufgabe, um die „Komplexbestimmtheit des kindlichen Verhaltens in Dingen der Sprache“ zu untersuchen. Auf die Frage: „Welches Wort ist länger: Kuh oder Piepvögelchen?“ antworten Kinder, die noch ganz in der Bedeutung der Wörter verhaftet sind: „Piepvögelchen“ (Bosch 1937, S. 82). Ich habe selbst beobachtet, wie erstaunt ein langsam lesen- und schreibenlernender Junge noch im 2. Schuljahr darüber war, dass ein so großes Gefährt wie ein Bus nur mit drei Buchstaben geschrieben wird!

Neben der Fokussierung der Bedeutung des Wortes, die zunächst andere Zugänge verstellt, gibt es in der Sprache selbst einen weiteren Grund, der erklärt, warum die Phonemanalyse für Schulanfänger eine so hohe Hürde darstellt. Die Silben der gesprochenen Sprache sind artikulatorische Einheiten und deshalb relativ leicht zugänglich – (allerdings wirklich nur relativ; lese-rechtschreibschwache Kinder tun sich oft hier schon schwer). Die Phonemanalyse ist weit schwieriger, weil die Laute innerhalb der Silben artikulatorisch und akustisch ineinander übergehen, also wirklich miteinander „verschmolzen“ sind. Es gibt beim Wort „Fisch“ keinen Zeitpunkt, bei dem das /f/ schon zu Ende wäre und das /i/ noch nicht angefangen hätte. Wir sprechen hier von der „Koartikulation“ der Laute innerhalb der Silben. Die Analyse eines Wortes in seinc Lautbestandteile entspricht also nicht einer linearen Abtrennung wie es die korrespondierenden Buchstaben nahe legen könnten. Gefordert wird dagegen eine echte Analyse der Laute aus einer größeren komplexen Einheit.

3.4 Implikationen für die Förderung

3.4.1 Schulische Förderung

Im Bild der grundlegenden Probleme leseschwacher Kinder ist also recht gut ein roter Faden erkennbar. Die Schwierigkeiten liegen eindeutig im Bereich des analytischen Umgangs mit der gesprochenen Sprache, später mit der alphabetischen Strategie. Inwiefern sollte die Leseförderung dies berücksichtigen? Es gibt prinzipiell zwei Möglichkeiten:

Förderung kompensatorischer Strategien, die die geschilderten Probleme umgehen
Förderung der unzureichenden Teilprozesse des Lesens bzw. ihrer Grundlagen.

Die erste Alternative – die Förderung kompensatorischer Prozesse zur Umgehung der bestehenden Schwierigkeiten, wird im englischen Sprachraum durchaus ernsthaft diskutiert. Wir haben jedoch weiter oben schon gesehen, dass die von den Kindern selbst gewählten kompensatorischen Strategien des logographischen Lesens und der Kontextnutzung nicht sehr erfolgreich sind. Könnte es andere kompensatorische Strategien geben? Vielleicht ist ein effektives direktes Worterkennen auch ohne vollständige Beherrschung und Automatisierung der alphabetischen Strategie in einer morphemarmen Sprache wie dem Englischen noch eher denkbar (vgl. <can> mit <kann, kannst, können, könnt>). Wie schwierig Lesen- und Schreibenlernen ohne den Bezug zwischen geschriebener und gesprochener Sprache ist, zeigen die großen Probleme, die Schwerhörige beim Schriftspracherwerb haben. Taubstumme können die strukturelle Ähnlichkeit zwischen gesprochener und geschriebener Sprache nicht nutzen und sind damit beim Schriftspracherwerb sehr behindert (Günther 1996). Das Ausklammern der alphabetischen Strategie kann also auf jeden Fall für die deutsche Schriftsprache kein sinnvoller Ansatz für die Förderung sein.

Die zweite Alternative bedeutet, eben jene Strategie, bei der die Probleme bestehen bzw. ihre Grundlagen zu fördern. Die bei uns derzeit vorliegenden wichtigen Ansätze zur Förderung setzen genau hier an (z.B. Kossow 1972, Scheerer-Neumann 1981, Dummer & Hackethal 1984, Reuter-Liehr 1993). Es wird in der Regel sehr kleinschrittig in die alphabetische Strategie eingeführt. Basis der Analyse ist die Silbengliederung; über die Korrespondenz zwischen Sprechsilbe und Schreibsilbe kann unter Verwendung sehr einfach strukturierter Silben (mi, ma, mo) gut in die alphabetische Strategie eingeführt und die Funktion der Phoneme verdeutlicht werden.

Der Kieler Leseaufbau und der Ansatz von Kossow verbinden die frühen Übungen mit Handzeichen, die jeweils für eine Phonem-Graphem-Beziehung stehen. Theoretisch ist die Funktion von Handzeichen noch nicht geklärt. Ich sehe den entscheidenden Vorteil von Handzeichen in der Möglichkeit, die Sukzessivität der Laute, die im gesprochenen Wort sehr flüchtig ist, in der Abfolge der Bewegungen zu konkretisieren. Im geschriebenen Wort sind die Buchstaben gleichzeitig präsent; die Sukzession entsteht erst durch den Prozess des Erlesens. Wenn die elementaren Gliederungs- und Syntheseprobleme überwunden sind, sollten die Synthese von Konsonantenclustern und die Silbengliederung bei längeren Wörtern eingeübt werden. Im konkreten Fall muss die Auswahl der Fördermaßnahmen, die hier ohnedies nur kurz umrissen werden können, immer von den spezifischen Problemen eines Kindes abgeleitet werden. D.h. Förderdiagnostik und Förderung sind eng miteinander zu verflechten. Neben den systematischen Übungen sollten gleichzeitig schon Leseangebote gemacht werden, die authentischen Lesesituationen entsprechen – d.h. Lektüre von Kinderbüchern, Briefen, Zeitungsmeldungen, etc. Ist das im Handel erhältliche Lesematerial noch zu schwierig, sollte man selbst Texte verfassen. Aus Bilderbüchern lassen sich durch Überkleben der alten Texte mit eigenen attraktive Leseangebote gestalten (vgl. Scheerer-Neumann 1994). Das Motto der Förderung sollte lauten:

So systematisch wie nötig
So authentisch wie möglich

3.4.2 Vorschulische Förderung

Überlegungen und Methoden zur vorschulischen Förderung des Schriftspracherwerbs sind schon seit Jahren in der Diskussion. In der DDR hatten Breuer & Weuffen ein diagnostisches Instrument zur Erfassung der „Verbosensomotorik" im Vorschuljahr entwickelt und für leistungsschwächere Kinder kompensatorische Übungen vorgeschlagen (Breuer & Weuffen 1986). Als Teilbereiche der Verbosensomotorik galten die optische, die phonematische, die kinästhetische, die melodische und die rhythmische Differenzierungsfähigkeit. In der Bundesrepublik wurde in den 70er Jahren in Zusammenarbeit mit der Stiftung Volkswagenwerk das Programm CIEL ins Lebe gerufen – ein Förderprogramm zur Elementarerziehung und seine wissenschaftlichen Voraussetzungen. Innerhalb dieses Programms wurde das Curriculum „Elementare Leseerziehung" (CELE) mit Elementen, die auf das Lesen vorbereiten, entwikkelt (vgl. Antrag Rüdiger in Garlichs et al. 1983). Es muss an dieser Stelle offen bleiben, warum dieser Ansatz nicht weiter verfolgt wurde. Die jüngsten Ansätze einer vorschulischen Förderung des Schriftspracherwerbs leiten sich unmittelbar aus der internationalen Forschung zur phonologischen Bewusstheit ab: Hier in Würzburg haben Prof. Schneider und Mitarbeiter das Trainingsprogramm von Lundberg et al. ins Deutsche übertragen und seine Wirkungen in mehreren Studien überprüft (vgl. ausführlich hierzu: Schneider in diesem Band). Das Programm ist für ein sechsmonatiges Training im Vorschuljahr angelegt und besteht bei täglichen kurzen Übungen (10-15 Minuten) in Kleingruppen aus insgesamt sechs unterschiedlichen didaktischen Einheiten, die mit der Identifikation von Umweltgeräuschen beginnen und bis zur Phonemanalyse- und Synthese fortschreiten.

Im ersten Durchgang (Schneider et al. 1994) war das Training insgesamt nur mäßig erfolgreich; eine detaillierte Analyse ergab jedoch eine starke Abhängigkeit von der Genauigkeit und Gründlichkeit, mit der das Training durchgeführt worden war. Die Kinder aus den Kindergärten, in denen das Training motiviert und konsequent zu Ende geführt worden war, zeigten nicht nur in den Aufgaben des Nachtests zur phonologischen Bewusstheit bessere Leistungen, sondern auch einen leichten Transfer auf den Anfangsunterricht. Eine zweite, vor allem in der Supervision verbesserte Studie (Schneider et al. 1997), war recht erfolgreich: Der Leistungsvorsprung beim Schriftspracherwerb war bei den geförderten Kindern auch nach zwei Schuljahren noch deutlich zu sehen. Bemerkenswert ist auch, dass insbesondere die im phonologischen Ausgangstest schwachen Kinder besonders profitiert haben: Ihre Differenz zu den „durchschnittlichen" Kindern wird durch das Training reduziert. Dies ist ein eindrucksvolles Ergebnis, das bildungspolitische Folgen haben sollte, wenn es auch von den Forschern „abgenabelt" Bestand hat.

4 Die alphabetische Strategie beim Rechtschreiberwerb

Zum Schluss ein paar Worte zum Rechtschreiben, das im vorliegenden Beitrag zu kurz kommen musste. Auch beim Schreiben gibt es verschiedene Strategien, deren Gewicht sich im Laufe der Entwicklung verschiebt. *Aber auch hier ist die alphabetische, die lautorientierte*

Strategie, von ganz entscheidender Bedeutung – und viele Kinder scheitern an dieser Stelle des Lern- und Entwicklungsprozesses. Ein wichtiges Zwischenziel bei der Förderung rechtschreibschwacher Kinder ist die weitgehend lautorientierte Verschriftung.

Zur Übung wählt man am besten lauttreue Wörter; beim freien Schreiben akzeptiert man zunächst lautorientiert korrekte und vollständig Schreibweisen, auch wenn sie orthographisch inkorrekt sind. Ich halte es für einen häufigen und groben didaktischen Fehler, wenn rechtschreibschwache Kinder des 2. und 3. Schuljahrs, die lautorientiert noch unvollständig verschriften, orthographisch schwierige Wörter für Diktate lernen müssen. Da ihnen die Korrespondenz zwischen Sprechschema und Schreibschema nicht oder zu wenig hilft, müssen Kinder mit sehr geringen phonemanalytischen Fähigkeiten die Buchstaben eines Wortes und ihre Reihenfolge (!) auswendig lernen, eine Strategie, die die weitere Entwicklung nicht fördert. Abbildung 4.3.3 zeigt Schreibprotokolle eines Mädchens aus dem dritten Schuljahr. Trotz häufiger Übung und großer Anstrengung gelang nur der Erwerb weniger Lernwörter – nicht sehr erstaunlich, wenn man die Entwicklungsstufe der eigenen Konstruktionen berücksichtigt, die noch lange nicht das Niveau lautorientierter Verschriftungen erreicht haben. Das gut beherrschte Abschreiben wird die weitere Entwicklung kaum fördern; es ist eher kontraproduktiv, weil hier das richtige Ergebnis dem Kind subjektiv das Gefühl gibt, eine angemessene Strategie zu verwenden.

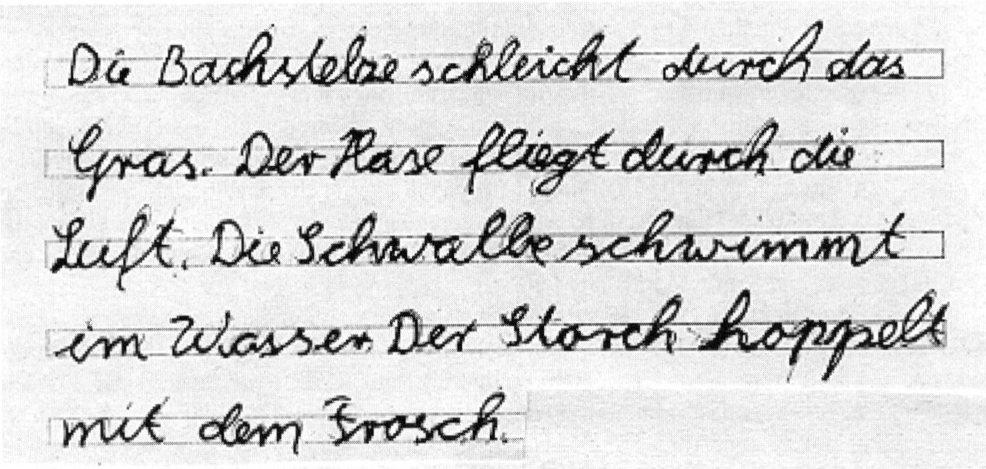

Abb. 4.3.3 a: Schreibproben Maria (3. Schuljahr) Abschrift

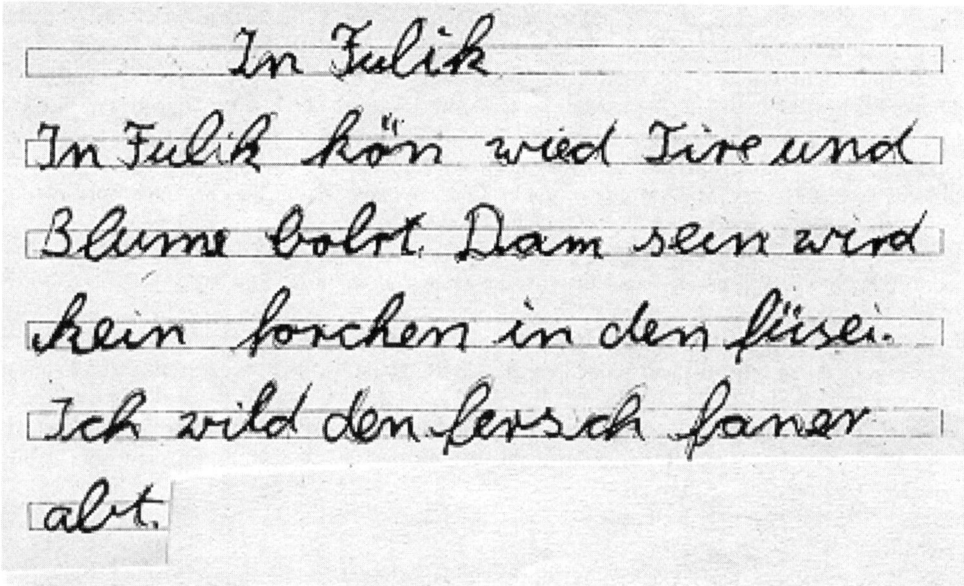

Abb. 4.3.3 b: Schreibproben Maria (3. Schuljahr) Diktat

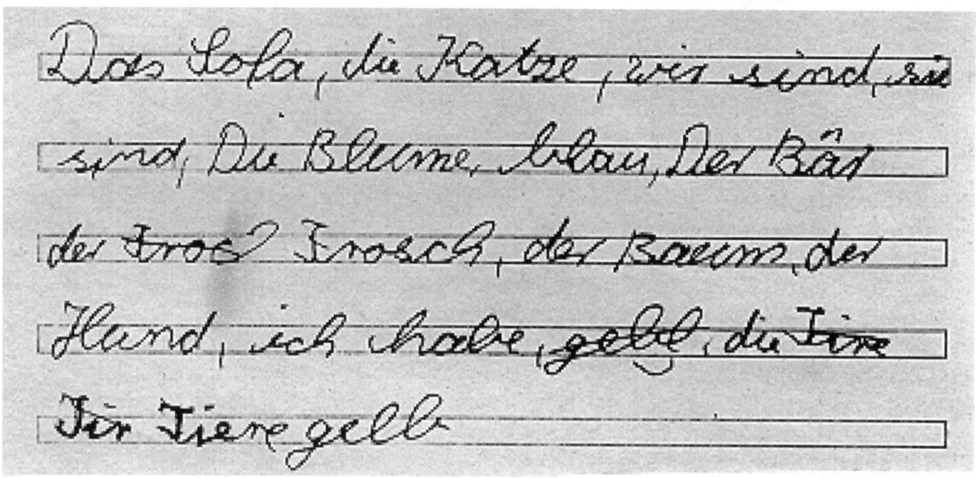

Abb. 4.3.3 c: Schreibproben Maria (3. Schuljahr) häufig geübte Lernwörter

Literatur

Bosch, B.: Grundlagen des Erstleseunterrichts. Zeitschrift für angewandte Psychologie und Charakterkunde. Beiheft 76 (1937)

Breuer, H. & Weuffen, M.: Gut vorbereitet auf das Lesen- und Schreibenlernen? Berlin: Deutscher Verlag der Wissenschaften, 1986

Dummer, L. & Brügelmann, H.: Vom <3lft> zum <Elefant>: Was heißt hier Leseschwäche? In: Balhorn,H. & Brügelmann H. (Hrsg.): Welten der Schrift in der Erfahrung der Kinder. Konstanz: Libelle 1987; Seite 110-121

Coltheart, M: Lexical access in simple readings tasks. In: Underwood, G. (ed.): Strategies of information processing. London: Academic press, 1978

Dummer, L. & Hackethal, R.: Handbuch zum Kieler Leseaufbau. Kiel: Veris, 1984

Feldmann, L. B. & Turvey, M.T.: Words writen in Kana are named faster than the same words written in Kanji. Language and Speech 23, 1980; Seite 141-147

Gibson, E. J. & Levin, H.: The psychology of reading. Cambridge MA: MIT Press, 1975

Goodman, K.. Reading: A psycholinguistic guessing game. Journal of the Reading Specialist, 6 (1967); Seite 126-135

Günther, H.: Historisch-systematischer Aufriß der psychologischen Leseforschung. In: Günther, H. & Ludwig, O. (Hrsg.), Schrift und Schriftlichkeit – Writing and its Use. Berlin, New York: Walter de Gruyter 1996; Seite 918-932

Günther, K.-B.: Die Schrift als kompensatorisches Mittel zum Verbalspracherwerb.In. In: Günther, H. & Ludwig, O. (Hrsg.), Schrift und Schriftlichkeit – Writing and its Use. Berlin, New York: Walter de Gruyter. 1996; Seite 1205-1216

Kossow, H.-J.: Zur Therapie der Lese- Rechtschreibschwäche. Berlin: Deutscher Verlag der Wissenschaften, 1972

Rayner, K. & Pollatsek, A.: The Psychology of reading Hillsdale, N. J.: Lawrence Erlbaum, 1989

Reichen, J.: Lesen und Schreiben von Anfang an? Nein!!! In: Balhorn, H., Bartnitzky, H., Büchner, I. & Speck-Hamdan, H.: Schatzkiste Sprache 1. Von den Wegen der Kinder in die Schrift. Hannover: Arbeitskreis Grundschule – Der Grundschulverband und DGLS – Deutsche Gesellschaft für Lesen und Schreiben, 1998; Seite 327-333

Reuter-Liehr, C.: Behandlung der Lese-Rechtschreibschwäche nach der Grundschulzeit: Anwendung und Überprüfung eines Konzeptes. In: Zeitschrift für Kinder- und Jugendpsychiatrie , 21(1993), Seite 135-147

Rüdiger¸ D.: Curriculum Elementare Leseerziehung (CELE). In: Garlichs, A., Knab, D. & Weinert, F. E. (Hrsg.): CIEL II. Fallstudie zu einem Förderungsprogramm der Stiftung Volkswagenwerk zur Elementarerziehung. Göttingen: Vandenhoeck & Ruprecht 1983, Seite 107-123

Scheerer-Neumann, G.: Prozeßanalyse der Leseschwäche. In: Valtin, R.; Jung, U. O. H. & Scheerer-Neumann, G.: Legasthenie in Wissenschaft und Unterricht. Darmstadt: Wissenschaftliche Buchgesellschaft, 1981

Scheerer-Neumann, G.: Lese- Rechtschreibschwäche im Kontext der Entwicklung. In Naegele, I. & Valtin, R. (Hrsg.). LRS in den Klassen 1-10. Weinheim: Beltz, 1989

Scheerer-Neumann, G.: Lesestrategien und ihre Entwicklung im 1. Schuljahr. In: Grundschule, 32 (1990); Seite 20-24

Scheerer-Neumann, G.: Der Erwerb der basalen Lese- und Schreibfertigkeiten. In: Günther, H. & Ludwig, O. (Hrsg.), Schrift und Schriftlichkeit – Writing and its Use. Berlin, New York: Walter de Gruyter, 1996; Seite 1153-1169

Scheerer-Neumann, G.: Texte für langsam lesenlernende Kinder. Überlegungen und Tips zum Selberschreiben. In: Grundschulunterricht 41 (1994) 11; Seite 13-16

Scheerer-Neumann, G.: Udo ist gemein. In: Balhorn, H.; Brügelmann H.; Kretschmann, R. & Scheerer-Neumann, G. (Hrsg.) Regenbogen-Bücher. Hamburg: Verlag für pädagogische Medien, 1986

Schneider, W.; Reimers, P.; Roth, E.; Visé, M. & Marx, H.: Short- and Long-term Effects of Training Phonological Awareness in Kindergarten: Evidence from Two German Studies. In: Journal of Experimental Child Psychology, 66 (1997); Seite 311-340.

Stanovich K. E: Attentional and Automatic Context Effects in Reading. In: Lesgold, A. M. & Perfetti, Ch. (Hrsg.): Interactive Processes in Reading. Hillsdale, N. J.: Lawrence Erlbaum, 1981; Seite 241-267

Vellutino, F. R. & Scanlon, D. M.: The Preeminence of Phonologically Based Skills in Learning to Read. In: Brady S. A. & Shankweiler, D. P. (Eds): Phonological Processes in Litercy. Hillsdale, N. J. Lawrence Erlbaum, 1991; Seite 237-252

4.4 Lautgetreue Rechtschreibförderung im Verbund mit der Methode des rhythmisch-silbierenden Sprechschreibens als Grundlage für weiteres Fördervorgehen

Carola Reuter-Liehr

Eine Falldarstellung

Anhand einer Falldokumentation möchte ich ein differenziertes, sprachsystematisch und kleinschrittig aufgebautes Behandlungsvorgehen (Reuter-Liehr, 1993) bei einer ausgeprägten legasthenen Störung exemplarisch beschreiben. Das Konzept habe ich in seiner Gesamtheit bereits auf dem 12. Fachkongress in Greifswald (Reuter-Liehr, 1997) vorgestellt. Ich weiß sehr wohl, dass eine Kasuistik jede Theorie stützen oder stürzen kann. Ich habe aber aus Gründen der Anschaulichkeit diese Falldarstellung vorgezogen. (Eine ausführlichere Fassung wird in Reuter-Liehr, 2000 veröffentlicht).

Vorgeschichte

Simon lernte ich im Februar 1992 kennen. Er war zu diesem Zeitpunkt 8; 9 Jahre und besuchte die 2. Klasse einer Waldorfschule. Seine Mutter bat mich, Simons Lese- und Schreibentwicklung zu überprüfen.

Dies war ihr besonders wichtig:
Ihr älterer Sohn leidet unter einer ausgeprägten Lese-Rechtschreibstörung. Ein kinder- und jugendpsychiatrisches Gutachten und – auf Grund schulphobischen Verhaltens – letztlich privat organisierter Schulunterricht (ab 4. Klasse) ermöglichten schließlich eine emotionale Entlastung für den Jungen. Seine Lese-Rechtschreibschwäche wurde jedoch nicht ausreichend therapeutisch angegangen. Der inzwischen junge Erwachsene leidet unter Depressionen bei Prüfungsdruck, dies trotz überdurchschnittlicher Begabung. Medikamentöse wie verhaltenstherapeutische Interventionen sind notwendig, haben aber noch keinen dauernden Erfolg gezeigt.

Bei seinem jüngeren Bruder Simon sollte deshalb nichts versäumt werden, die Mutter hatte bereits Anzeichen einer ähnlich ausgeprägten Lese-Rechtschreibstörung wahrgenommen.

Der Versuch, Simons Rechtschreibkompetenz mit dem Rechtschreibtest RST 1 (Rathenow, u. a, 1973) einzuschätzen, scheiterte. Er grübelte sehr lange und schien völlig ratlos zu sein. Schreiben bedeutete für ihn „abschreiben", beim Abschreiben malte er jeden Buchstaben einzeln. Mir wurde schließlich klar, dass er dabei das Bild des Wortes abmalte. Ohne Vorlage versuchte er das Wort aus seinem Gedächtnis zu malen, was ihn überforderte. Diesen Vorgang fand er nach eigener Aussage langweilig. Er hatte bisher nicht verstanden, welches hilfreichere Prinzipien der Schriftsprache sind, nämlich gehörte und gesprochene Laute in Schriftzeichen umzuwandeln und diese in einer bestimmten Reihenfolge als Wort aufzuschreiben. Das Lesen war bislang ebenso wenig entwickelt.

Simons Mutter ist Engländerin und sein Vater Amerikaner. Simon ist in Deutschland aufgewachsen. In der Familie wird überwiegend Englisch, außerhalb des Hauses wird Deutsch gesprochen. Simon selbst spricht völlig akzentfrei und fließend Deutsch.

Wir beschlossen gemeinsam, mit einer gezielten Therapie Simons Lese- und Rechtschreibentwicklung zu unterstützen. In der Schule waren Simons Probleme bisher nicht besonders aufgefallen. Diktate wurden noch nicht geschrieben. Inhalte dagegen konnte sich Simon gut merken. Es machte bereits in diesem Alter Freude, mit ihm über verschiedene Themen zu diskutieren. Ein zu einem späteren Zeitpunkt durchgeführter Intelligenztest (CFT 20, Weiß, 1987) bestätigte die Beobachtung einer überdurchschnittlichen Begabungsausstattung.

1 Therapiephase

Gehörten Lauten Buchstaben zuordnen und miteinander verschleifen

Gemäß dem in der therapeutischen Arbeit bewährten Prinzip „Erfolge von Anfang an...“, war ein Start mit wenigen einfach strukturierten „Mitsprechwörtern“ für Simon notwendig, hier sah ich seine „Nullfehlergrenze“ (Warnke, 1995).

Schritt 1: Lautgebärden anwenden

Wir begannen mit 4 Buchstaben, für die sprachtherapeutische Lautgebärden (Horn-Breul, 1974 u. Grässli 1980) zur Unterstützung des Sprechbewegungsablaufs bei der Lautbildung und des Gedächtnisses eingeführt wurden. Diese wandte Simon mit Begeisterung an. Die Wörter enthielten nur offene Silben (Beispiel: le-se – Konsonant/Vokal – Konsonant/Vokal), so dass das Zusammenschleifen einzelner Laute zur Silbe und somit das Erkennen der Silbengliederung beim Lesen langsam aufgebaut wurde. Anfangs produzierte Simon jeden Laut einzeln und erkannte die Silben im Wort nicht. Erst die verbindende Handbewegung zweier Lautgebärden mit gleichzeitigem Sprechen der Laute ermöglichte schließlich das Verschleifen von Lauten zu einer Silbe.

Mit den ersten 4 Buchstaben konnte Simon bereits 3 Wörter bilden.

Silbenkasten 1: Lautgebärden zu: m / a / l / e

ma	**me**
la	**le**

Mama

Lama

male

Dieser Silbenkasten erweiterte sich im nächsten Schritt um 2 weitere Buchstaben. Jetzt ergaben sich bereits 9 Silben, die zu 8 Wörtern zum Lesen mit Lautgebärden, zum rhythmisch-silbierenden Schwingen und zum synchronen Sprechschreiben zusammengesetzt werden konnten.

Silbenkasten 2: Lautgebärden zu: s / i

ma	me	mi
la	le	li
sa	se	si

Mama lese

Lisa Lama

male Same

lila Salami

Schritt 2: rhythmisch-silbierendes Schwingen

Mit wachsendem Buchstaben- und insofern auch Wortmaterial konnten immer mehr Schwungübungen im Silbenrhythmus unter Einsatz des ganzen Körpers nach Buschmann (Buschmann, 1986, Reuter-Liehr, 1997) integriert werden. Anschließend versuchte er sich die einzelnen gesprochenen Laute durch die Anwendung der entsprechenden Lautgebärden zu verdeutlichen und machte sich damit gleichzeitig die Reihenfolge der Buchstaben im Wort klar. Dabei sprach er wiederum ganz deutlich und laut artikuliert mit.

Das „Tanzen" von Wörtern im Silbenrhythmus bereitete Simon keine Koordinationsprobleme. Genaues Sprechen gelang ihm spontan. Die Lautgebärden nahm er schnell an, sie mussten aber häufig wiederholt werden. Auch entfiel ihm immer wieder die eine oder andere Buchstabengestalt. Das sofortige Verschleifen der einzelnen Laute zur Silbe gelang ihm am Anfang häufig nicht, er sprach jeden Laut einzeln aus und setzte zum Schluss schnell das Wort zusammen.

Schritt 3: synchrones Sprechschreiben

Anschließendes Mitsprechen beim Schreiben an der Tafel erbrachte dann in der Regel bereits fehlerfrei geschriebene Wörter. Dieses synchrone Mitsprechen beim Schreiben erfordert, dass der Laut so lange anhaltend gesprochen wird, wie der Schreibvorgang des Buchstabens andauert. Die Großschreibung ließen wir noch außer Acht. Ab der 8. Therapiestunde konnte Simon das synchrone Mitsprechen beim Schreiben sehr effektiv einsetzen.

Schritt 4: Silbenbögenlesen

Nach dem Schreibvorgang malte Simon unter jedes Wort Silbenbögen, bei denen er nochmals laut im Silbenrhythmus mitsprach. Noch einmal erfasste er damit den Sprechrhythmus und trainierte seine Auge-Hand-Koordination. Mit Hilfe dieses lauten Silbenbögenlesens übte Simon auch das genaue Lesen von unbekannten Wörtern aus dem Übungsbereich, was ihn zwar anstrengte – er wurde dabei stets besonders motorisch unruhig – aber zunehmend sicherer gelang.

Schritt 5: Silben"tanzen" auf dem Spielbrett

Das rhythmisch-silbierende Sprechen übten wir auch mit kleinen Wettrennspielen nach vorgegebenen Bildkärtchen, deren Abbildungen ein- bis viersilbige Wörter ergaben, für jede Silbe wurde ein Feld vorgerückt. Bald konnten die Bildkarten durch ein- bis viersilbige, später auch sechssilbige Wortkarten dem Lernstand entsprechend ersetzt werden. Dieses Spiel machte Simon erstaunlicherweise immer wieder viel Spaß und war gleichzeitig eine besonders motivierende Leseübung.

Der Silbenkasten wuchs, bis alle mitsprechbaren Vokale, Diphthong, Umlaute und dauerhaft sprechbaren Konsonanten eingeführt waren. Das zu benutzende Wortmaterial erweiterte sich parallel dazu. Es wurde bis zu diesem Zeitpunkt nur mit offenen Silben gearbeitet. Jetzt konnte Simon aber bereits kleine Satzteile lesen und richtig schreiben.

Satzteile mit nur offenen Silben der Phonemstufe 1:

Na, so eine schöne Rose.	So eine saure Limone!
So eine feine Reise!	So eine feine Nase!
Schau, meine neue Schere.	Rufe meine Oma.
Lese neue Reime.	Male eine Ameise.

Ein erster wichtiger Lernabschnitt war geschafft. Alle Laut/Buchstabenverbindungen der Phonemstufe 1 (Reuter-Liehr, 1997) waren durch den Einsatz der Lautgebärden gesichert. Simon konnte Wörter mit offenen Silben mühelos lesen und schreiben.

Aus der Schule berichtete er stolz, er habe bereits eigene Sätze aufgeschrieben. Beim Schreiben verfiel er allerdings gerne wieder in seine alte Strategie des Abschreibens, dies wurde besonders deutlich bei den eingeteilten häuslichen Trainingsaufgaben (5-10 Min. täglich) aus dem Übungsbereich. Es dauerte lange, bis Simon diese vollständig und sorgfältig erledigte, hier schien er am liebsten so wenig wie möglich zu machen. Strukturen einzuhalten fiel ihm zunächst sehr schwer.

Nach und nach wurden jetzt Wörter mit geschlossenen Silben, zunächst nach einem langen Vokal, dann nach einem Diphthong (au, ei, eu), hinzugenommen: Sch**af**, Sch**al**, eine M**aus**, m**ein** S**eil** (Lernschritte 4 und 5) (Reuter-Liehr, 1997). Rasch folgten Wörter mit den häufigen Endungen „en / er / es / el“: lauf**en**, Mal**er**, schön**es**, Schauf**el**, was Simon keine Probleme mehr bereitete. Fühlte sich Simon aber doch überfordert, so waren deutlich überschießende Bewegungen mit den Füßen unter dem Tisch zu beobachten, seine Körperhaltung war angespannt. Außerdem musste er beim Schreiben mehrfach seine Hand ausschütteln.

Durch das rhythmisch-silbierende Schwingen und synchrone Sprechschreiben mit dem bewussten Einhalten der Silbenpausen war es jetzt möglich, die hörbar zu machende Doppelung zwischen Vokalen einzuführen: We**ll**en, So**mm**er, So**nn**e, A**ff**e, Me**ss**er, scha**rr**en. Beim „Tanzen“ der Wörter in Silben gelang ihm die richtige Doppelung fast spontan. Beim Schreiben konnte der vorher erfahrene Silbenrhythmus wieder verloren gehen, so dass die Doppelung manchmal noch nicht erkannt oder auch übertrieben wurde.

Schließlich hatten wir den Aufbau der gesamten **Phonemstufe 1 (a e i o u – au eu ei – ö ü; m l s n f r w sch, ohne Konsonantenhäufung innerhalb einer Silbe)** nach 18 Std. abgeschlossen. Eine Überprüfung anhand eines lauttreuen Bildertests (LBT 1) (Reuter-Liehr, 1992b) der Phonemstufe 1 ergab von 24 Testwörtern 16 richtige Verschriftungen.

In weiteren 30 Std. erarbeiteten wir stückweise die **Phonemstufe 2** mit dem Einsatz der gleichen Methoden: Lautgebärden bei den neu hinzukommenden Buchstaben, rhythmisch-silbierendes „Tanzen" von entsprechenden Wörtern, synchrones Sprechschreiben und Silbenbögenlesen. Vielfach übten wir spielerisch und setzten dem erreichten Lernstand entsprechende Lernspiele statt langweiliger Übungen ein.

Es wurden zunächst die schwer akustisch und sprechmotorisch zu differenzierenden Dauerkonsonanten „h z j ch" buchstabenweise aufgenommen, um dann die eher weichen und mit wenig Luftstrom verbundenen Plosivlaute „d b g" hinzuzufügen, die nicht mehr dauerhaft sprechbar sind. Am schwierigsten erfassbar sind aber die Plosivlaute „t p k" mit herausspringendem Luftstrom.

Nachdem wir die Buchstaben „j und ch" eingeführt hatten, schrieb Simon mit viel Freude, da er sich durch den Inhalt angesprochen fühlte, folgende zwei Sätze nach Diktat. Er sprach beim Schreiben laut synchron im Silbenrhythmus mit, las alles noch einmal laut mit gleichzeitigem Malen der Silbenbögen vor und war sehr zufrieden mit seinem Ergebnis.

Simon, 9. 11. 92 28. Therapiestunde 1. Therapiephase
Phonemstufe 2 – h, z, j, ch eingeführt

Am Ende des Aufbaus der Phonemstufe 2 nach 48 Therapiestunden im Juni 1993, beherrschte Simon die Methoden des rhythmisch-silbierenden Schwingens („Tanzen"), des synchronen Sprechschreibens und des Silbenbögenlesens. Die Erfolgskontrolle mit dem LBT 2, einem lauttreuen Bildertest der Phonemstufe 2 (Reuter-Liehr, 1993a), ergab jetzt 23 richtige Wörter von insgesamt 24, lediglich das Wort „Schu-he" hatte er ohne h geschrieben, da er das „h" am Anfang der Silbe noch nicht beim Sprechen spürte.

In der Schule schrieb er erste ungeübte Kurzdiktate, deren Ergebnisse mit dem Durchschnitt der Klasse vergleichbar waren; denn er schrieb alles lautgetreu und hatte dadurch schon die meisten Wörter richtig. Seine Leseentwicklung war inzwischen so weit fortgeschritten, dass er im Übungsbereich – besonders mit Einsatz der Silbenbögen – sicher und richtig lesen konnte.

Seiner Mutter schrieb er, als diese im Krankenhaus lag, einen Brief in seiner bisher nur mündlich gelernten Muttersprache. Sie konnte ihn gut lesen, da ihr die Strategien unserer Therapie durch regelmäßigen Austausch bekannt waren. Simon hatte die englische Sprache versucht lautgetreu aufzuschreiben (Beispiel: „once" wurde zu „wans"). Daran wurde klar, dass er sich auf die gelernten Strategien voll eingelassen hatte, andere standen ihm bisher noch nicht zur Verfügung.

Simon hatte nun die 3. Klasse abgeschlossen. Wir mussten unsere Therapie unterbrechen, da die Familie aus beruflichen Gründen des Vaters für ein Jahr nach Washington ging. Er bedauerte unsere Unterbrechung, denn er stand Veränderungen stets skeptisch gegenüber.

Wir hatten uns relativ viel Zeit für den ersten grundlegenden Aufbau des Lesens, Schreibens und Rechtschreibens – alles im Verbund mit einer genauen Artikulation – genommen. Dies erscheint mir aber auch im Nachhinein sinnvoll und notwendig gewesen zu sein; denn Simon signalisierte mir meist nonverbal, wenn ich aus Ehrgeiz zu zügig voranschritt. Seine immer wieder auftretende Merkschwäche im Zusammenhang mit Buchstabenmaterial erforderte häufige Festigungsphasen. Sicherlich kam erschwerend hinzu, dass zu Hause Englisch gesprochen wurde, so dass er die deutsche Sprache nur außerhalb der Familie hörte und anwandte.

2 Therapiephase

Sicher rhythmisch-silbierend Mitsprechwörter schreiben

Simons Lese- und Rechtschreibentwicklung wurde nach seiner Rückkehr aus Amerika im Nov. 1994 kinder- und jugendpsychiatrisch untersucht. Simon besuchte jetzt die 5. Klasse der Waldorfschule. Es fiel während der Untersuchung auf, dass Simon immer noch motorisch unruhig auf Aufgaben mit Lesen und Schreiben reagierte und wiederholt Wortfindungsschwierigkeiten beim Erzählen bestanden, obwohl ihm das, was er vermitteln wollte, völlig klar war. Bei Testaufgaben, welche schriftunabhängig waren, zeigte Simon keinerlei Angespanntheit.

Zur Überprüfung der Rechtschreibentwicklung wurde der WRT 4/5 (Rathenow, 1979) eingesetzt. Das Ergebnis war mit RW 8, PR 4 weit unterdurchschnittlich. Die fehleranalytische Auswertung der einzelnen Fehlentscheidungen ergab 17 Phonemfehler, 23 Regelfehler, 13 Speicherfehler und 2 Restfehler (Reuter-Liehr, 1992a). Insgesamt kam es zu 55 Fehlentscheidungen in 26 falsch geschriebenen Wörtern, damit ergab sich ein hoher Mehrfachfehlerquotient von 2,12 pro falsch geschriebenem Wort (s. 1. Erfolgskontrolle).

Es bestand also weiterhin eine dringend therapiebedürftige Lese-Rechtschreibstörung. Das kinder- und jugendpsychiatrische Gutachten erbrachte jetzt die Kostenübernahme nach KJHG § 35a durch das Jugendamt. Die Familie hatte die vorherige 1. Therapiephase selbst finanziert. Wir konnten die Therapie aber erst im Februar 1995 (nach 20. Mon. Pause) wieder aufnehmen, vorher war die Kostenfrage nicht geklärt.

Schritt 1: Pilotsprache erfahren

Es galt jetzt, das Begonnene systematisch fortzusetzen. Die fehleranalytische Auswertung des Rechtschreibtests WRT 4/5 zeigte mir, dass Simon weiterhin Probleme im lautgetreuen Bereich hatte, was allerdings auch nicht anders zu erwarten war, da wir diesen Bereich noch nicht abschließend behandelt hatten. Bereits in der 1. Stunde schrieb Simon nach einer kurzen Trainingsphase der bisher gelernten rhythmisch-silbierenden Schreibstrategien, wobei wir die Lautgebärden nicht mehr einsetzen mussten, den für ihn unbekannten Text fehlerlos: „Die Chinesen haben das Porzellan erfunden..." (Reuter-Liehr, 1992).

Das Wortmaterial der Phonemstufe 2 erschien mir weiterhin gesichert zu sein. Jetzt galt es den nächsten wichtigen Schritt zu vollziehen, nämlich bewusst mit Wörtern umzugehen, deren Umgangssprache von der Hochlautung bzw. Schriftsprache abweicht, dazu ist vor dem Schreiben eine korrekte Sprechweise und/oder eine genaue Leseerfahrung notwendig.

Bei der Arbeit mit sogenanntem lautgetreuen Wortmaterial ist die wichtigste Schreibstrategie: **„Ich spreche genau mit" – und das immer laut!** Diese Mitsprechstrategie muss allerdings noch erweitert werden: **„Vielfach ist es notwendig, zunächst einmal genau so zu sprechen, wie ich schreibe, da unsere Umgangssprache oft recht verschleifend ist.“**

Diese fürs Rechtschreiben notwendige Präzision der gesprochenen Sprache wird als Pilotsprache – eine genau gesteuerte Aussprache – bezeichnet. Die pilotsprachliche Sprechweise bedeutet: Eine silbengliedernde Aussprache von Wörtern, die möglichst eng an die Schriftsprache angeglichen ist. Die lautgetreue Schriftsprache muss also bei einigen Wörtern mit Hilfe einer pilotsprachlichen – d.h. genau in Silben gesteuerten – Artikulation aufgebaut werden.

Umgangssprache	Pilotsprache
gen	ge-hen
Mutta	Mut-ter
intresant	in-te-res-sant

Häufig sind Eltern recht verzweifelt, wenn ihre Kinder derart umgangssprachlich verschriften: „Er schreibt einfach so, wie er spricht“. Es wird dabei übersehen, dass dies zunächst genau richtig ist. Das Kind hat das Prinzip der Schriftsprache – gesprochene Laute in Buchstaben umzuwandeln – verstanden. Jetzt gilt es, diese gesprochene Sprache durch deutliche Artikulation und viel Leseerfahrung zu präzisieren, um so viele Informationen wie möglich aus der gesprochenen Sprache fürs Schreiben zu gewinnen. Die genaue Artikulation wird spontan durch das rhythmisch-silbierende Schwingen und Schreiten von Wörtern in Schreibrichtung unterstützt. Ohne diese steuernde Methode, die den ganzen Körper im Verbund mit Sprache integriert und die Atmung aktiviert, ist ein Erfolg erfahrungsgemäß nur langsamer und viel mühseliger zu erreichen. Gerade die Möglichkeit Schreibweisen nicht ausschließlich kognitiv durchdringen zu müssen, sondern sich auf seinen eigenen erlebten Sprachrhythmus verlassen zu können, bildet ein wichtiges motivationserhaltendes und stressminderndes Moment und gleichzeitig eine Basis für weiteres aufbauendes orthographisches Schreiben.

Bei genau gesteuerter Artikulation und vorher erfahrenem Sprechrhythmus schrieb Simon auch Wörter mit pilotsprachlichen „Gefahrenstellen“ fehlerlos. Ohne diese hilfreichen Strategien gelang ihm das spontane Schreiben dieser Wörter allerdings erst nach einiger Zeit. Wir spielten sehr häufig das ihm immer noch so beliebte Lesespiel – inzwischen mit der SpielSpirale (Reuter-Liehr, 1992) – jetzt aber mit ein- bis sechssilbigen Pilotsprachewörtern der Phonemstufe 2.

Nach 6 Therapiestunden konnten wir zur **Phonemstufe 3 – Dauerkonsonantenpaare**: **schm schl schn schr schw / fl fr / zw wr** übergehen. Hier zeigte Simon beim Lesen keine Probleme, beim Schreiben gab es hin und wieder fehlende Buchstaben bei Konsonantenhäufungen. Erstaunlicherweise fand Simon aber diese Buchstabenauslassungen bei eigenständigem Lesen mit Silbenbögen, während er vorher seine Fehler in der Regel auf diese Weise nicht gefunden hatte.

In der 10. Therapiestunde fiel mir auf, dass Simon inzwischen gleichmäßig rhythmisch und in einem harmonischen Fluss schrieb, das synchrone Mitsprechen gelang ihm automatisch. Es war eine besondere Freude für mich zu erleben, wie die Anspannung beim Schreiben von ihm abfiel.

Zügig konnten wir in der 11. Therapiestunde zur **Phonemstufe 4 – Konsonantenhäufungen mit einem Plosivlaut: dr bl br gl gn gr tr pl pf pfl pfr pr kl kn kr** voranschreiten. Besonders mussten wir Wörter mit pf/pfl/pfr sprechen, „tanzen" und mitsprechend schreiben. Diese pilotsprachlichen Lautverbindungen waren für Simon bisher völlig unbekannt bzw. unerklärlich geblieben.

Schritt 2: Erste Regeln werden einbezogen

Als erste 100%ige Regel integrierten wir in das bisherige Mitsprechmaterial der Phonemstufe 4 **Qu/qu (Beispiele: Quatsch, quatschen).** Dem folgte sofort eine weitere 100%ige Regelhaftigkeit, das **St/st – Sp/sp zu Beginn einer Silbe (Beispiele: Steine / Spiele).**

Simon beherrschte die Silbengliederung jetzt so sicher, dass er mühelos den Beginn einer Silbe erkannte und diese Regelhaftigkeit auch umsetzen konnte. Er bemühte sich sehr, alles Gelernte anzuwenden. Seine innere Einstellung, die legasthene Schwäche zu überwinden, war deutlich zu spüren. Ich bestärkte ihn darin.

Großschreibung:

In der 15. Therapiestunde begannen wir erstmalig uns genauer dem Thema der Großschreibung zu widmen. Wir malten gemeinsam ein sehr schönes Bild. Es war erstaunlich, wie differenziert Simon malen konnte, wie ausgeprägt sein Sinn für Farben, Formen, Licht und Schatten war. Zum Schluss dieser Stunde hatten wir nur noch Zeit unser Werk zu betrachten und alles zu benennen, was wir gemalt hatten; denn schließlich werden alle diese Lebewesen, Gegenstände und Teile davon groß geschrieben.

Als Lernplakate visualisierten wir diese gewonnenen Regeln:

Alles, was ich anfassen kann, ist ein Nomen. Nomen schreibe ich immer groß! Anfassen kann ich Lebewesen, Gegenstände und Teile davon.

Manches kann ich nur sehen, aber auch malen oder fotografieren. Auch das sind Nomen. Nomen schreibe ich immer groß!

Simon zeigte im Gespräch immer wieder Wortfindungsschwierigkeiten. Wir begannen verstärkt Wörter zu suchen, Inhalte zu besprechen und uns viel zu erzählen. Gegen Ende der Stunde wirkte er dann jedesmal gelöster und freier in seiner Ausdrucksweise. Informationen konnte Simon gut mitteilen, aber über seine eigene Befindlichkeit fiel es ihm schwer zu sprechen. Manchmal wirkte er jetzt zögerlich, gelegentlich auch leicht depressiv. Er kam sichtlich in die Pubertät, seine Haare wurden fettig, sein Gesicht bekam viele Pickel, er schoss in die Höhe, wurde immer dünner und seine Körperhaltung war schüchtern und verklemmt. Dennoch wurde seine Schrift immer ausgeglichener, Lernstrategien wurden immer präziser eingesetzt. So gelang eine Erfolgskontrolle (Reuter-Liehr, 1992) in der 20. Therapiestunde zum Qu/qu und zum Erkennen konkreter Nomen fast fehlerfrei (einziger Fehler: Früchtfleisch statt Fruchtfleisch).

Simon, 25. 10. 95 20. Therapiestunde • 2. Therapiephase / Phonemstufe 4
Erfolgskontrolle „Quittenbrot"

Zum Abschluss der 1. Phase zum Erkennen der Großschreibung ergänzten wir:

Alles was ich innerlich fühlen kann, ist ein Nomen. Zur Sicherheit brauche ich den Begleiter: der/die/das/dem/den/des! Er gibt das Signal: Achtung gleich kommt ein Nomen. Nomen schreibe ich immer groß!

Es war erfreulich zu beobachten, wie präzise Simon für ihn logisch erfassbare Regelhaftigkeiten annehmen und umsetzen konnte. Ich gewann den Eindruck, dass ich inzwischen den Lernaufbau nur noch für ihn nachvollziehbar zu organisieren hatte, dazu das ausgewählte Wort- und Textmaterial bereitstellen musste und für eine angenehme Atmosphäre durch viel Erzählen und den Einsatz von Lernspielen zu sorgen hatte. Beim Lesen und Schreiben der jeweils dem Lernstand entsprechenden Texte fühlte er sich sicher und frei von Stress. Er machte dann nur wenige Fehler; denn Nicht-Gelerntes kam nicht vor. Diese ständig für das Kind erlebbare Sicherheit scheint eine wichtige Funktion für den Erhalt der Lernbereitschaft zu haben. Diese Erfahrung konnte ich bereits bei vielen meiner Therapien bestätigt finden.

Schritt 3: Durch „Tanzen" eine Regel erfassen

In der 23. Therapiestunde nahmen wir erstmals eine Regelhaftigkeit hinzu, deren Umsetzung nicht hundertprozentig ist, sondern nur einer Mehrheitsregel entspricht. Wir erweiterten das Wortmaterial der Phonemstufen 1-4 durch **Phonemstufe 5 – Wörter mit dem langen /i:/ verschriftet als ie**. Es wurden aber **nur Wörter mit offenen ie-Silben** benutzt.

Beispielsweise das Wort „Maschine" kam nicht mehr vor, um Interferenzen beim Lernen zu vermeiden. Die offene Silbe wird nach dem lang gesprochenen Vokal durch keinen Konsonanten geschlossen.

Wörter dieser Phonemstufe 5 sind beispielsweise:

Wie sen blu men – Lie bes brie fe – Zwie bel ku chen – Rie sen schrit te

Es versteht sich von selbst, dass Simon diese offenen ie-Silben nur erkennen konnte, wenn er die Silbengliederung sicher beherrscht. Zur Unterstützung „tanzte" Simon die Wörter und kennzeichnete die offene ie-Silbe mit einem Überschwung seines Schwungarmes, so dass beim Sprechen ganz deutlich wurde, die Silbe bleibt offen, es folgt kein weiterer Buchstabe nach dem „ie". Beim Silbenbögenlesen dieser Wörter setzte er zur besonderen Kennzeichnung auch einen überziehenden Silbenbogen ein. Simon hatte – wie ich inzwischen auch nicht anders erwartete – keinerlei Probleme mit der Übernahme dieser Schreibstrategie.

Schritt 4: Durch präzises Sprechen die s-Laute differenzieren

In weiteren 5 Therapiestunden bewältigten wir die **Phonemstufe 6 (Das Wortmaterial wird erweitert durch Wörter mit ß zu Beginn einer Silbe:** Kar tof fel klö ße).

Auch hierbei war Voraussetzung, dass Simon sicher den Beginn einer Silbe ortete. Die bewusste Unterscheidung des scharfen (stimmlosen) ß vom summenden (stimmhaften) s gelang Simon zunächst nur bei wenigen ihm bekannten Wörtern.

Auch schien ihm momentan die Kraft zu fehlen, diese Differenzierung bewusst vorzunehmen. Er wirkte müde, erzählte, er schlafe erst spät ein, konnte beim Spielen Reihenfolgen nicht einhalten, fragte ständig nach. Bei Ansprechen seiner Befindlichkeit kamen sogar Tränen. Hinzu kam offensichtlich, dass er erschöpft und aufgeregt war. Simon spielt Geige und sollte demnächst ein Stück von Vivaldi vor einem Auditorium spielen. Bei mir wollte er zu diesem Zeitpunkt lieber nur mechanisch üben statt Kraft einsetzen.

Nach der Weihnachtspause im Januar 1996 ging es ihm wieder besser. Die Differenzierung der s-Laute gelang, wenn ich präzise vorsprach, er beim Schreiben leicht übertrieben das „summende s" oder „scharfe ß" mitsprach. Auch hier unterstützte das „Tanzen" der Wörter die präzise Aussprache. Wir beendeten den Aufbau der 6 Phonemstufen in der 28. Therapiestunde der 2. Therapiephase.

Simon, 24. 1. 96 28. Therapiestunde • 2. Therapiephase / Phonemstufe 6
Erfolgskontrolle: „So hat alles begonnen."

Simon hatte von 125 Wörtern 123 richtig verschriftet. Statt „aufhörten" hatte er erst „aufheurten", dann verbessert zu „aufhürten" geschrieben. Seine Unsicherheit in der Unterscheidung von grammatischen Endungen (Dativ/Akkusativ) wurde in seinem zweiten Fehler sichtbar (schützendem statt schützenden).

Abschluss der 2. Therapiephase

Im Februar 1996, Simon besuchte jetzt die 6. Klasse der Waldorfschule, wurde erneut ein normierter Rechtscheibtest zur Überprüfung seiner Rechtschreibentwicklung eingesetzt. Dieses Mal schrieb Simon den WRT 6+ (Rathenow, 1980). Mit RW 15, PR 25 war er jetzt an der unteren Grenze des Durchschnitts im Vergleich zur Klassennorm angelangt (s. 2. Erfolgskontrolle).

Was allerdings noch viel erfreulicher war: Simon hatte nach fehleranalytischer Auswertung in den trainierten Bereichen O Fehler. Die lautgetreue Schreibung mit ersten integrierten Regeln (Qu/qu, St/sp) das Erkennen der offenen ie-Silbe sowie das Erkennen konkreter Nomen war gesichert. Bei allen Abweichungen vom Gelernten verschriftete Simon so, wie er sprach und dies ganz exakt. So kam es zu 26 Regelfehlern und 10 Speicher- bzw. Restfehlern. Seine Mehrfachfehlerhäufung im falsch geschriebenen Wort war von 2,12 im WRT 4/5 auf 1,44 im WRT 6+ gesunken.

3 Therapiephase

Regeln Stück für Stück ergänzen

Ziel unseres gesamten Trainings war der Transfer auf nicht-geübtes Wortmaterial; denn nicht das eingesetzte Wortmaterial wurde vorrangig geübt, sondern jeweils die dazu notwendige Rechtschreibstrategie. Das Ergebnis des Rechtschreibtests WRT 6+ bestärkte mich in dieser Zielvorstellung. Simon hatte jetzt nach **insgesamt 77 Therapiestunden** eine Automatisierung beim lautgetreuen Schreiben erreicht, die den Kopf langsam frei werden ließ, um kompliziertere Regelkenntnisse aufnehmen zu können. Von der Schule schien er aufgrund seiner ausgeprägten legasthenen Schwäche zu diesem Zeitpunkt noch wenig zu profitieren. Positiv zu sehen war aber in diesem Zusammenhang, dass die Waldorfschule Simon einen Schonraum bot. Diktate wurden wenig geschrieben, Lerninhalte wurden mündlich vorgetragen, der Unterricht beschäftigte sich vielfältig mit anderen Dingen. Simons sonstige gute Fähigkeiten wurden anerkannt. Seine Eltern boten ihm einen stabilen emotionalen Rückhalt, jede kleine Lernentwicklung wurde positiv begleitet, Rückschritte als normal angesehen.

Schritt 1: Wörter in Wortbausteine zerlegen

So galt es jetzt, die bisherige Einteilung in Sprechsilben (Sprechbarkeitseinheiten) durch die Einteilung in Wortbausteine (Bedeutungseinheiten, Morpheme) zu ergänzen. Ein Start mit den Anfangsbausteinen (bekannt als Vorsilben) (Reuter-Liehr, 1992, 1997) vermeidet Interferenzen zu den Sprechsilben, da sie der Silbengliederung entsprechen. Das Wort- und Textmaterial bleibt weiterhin lautgetreu, regelhafte Abweichungen werden kleinschrittig integriert. So konnten Simons Erfolgserleben und seine emotionale Sicherheit beim Schreiben in der Therapiesituation erhalten bleiben.

Simon erfuhr, dass diese Anfangsbausteine Wörter vielfach verändern können. So ist es etwas anderes, ob Besucher „empfangen“ oder „gefangen“ werden, ob Schüler beim Diktat „schreiben“ oder „abschreiben“. Die Bedeutungen der Wörter nahmen jetzt mehr Raum in der Therapiesituation ein. Wir konnten dabei vielfach spielerisch mit Sprache umgehen. Spielkärtchen der Anfangsbausteine waren gelb und wurden von den roten Stammwörtern unterschieden und im Lottospiel angelegt. Immer neue Kombinationen von Wörtern entstanden und wurden abgelegt. Sieger war, wer die meisten Wörter gesammelt hatte.

Bei eher ungebräuchlichen Wörtern im Umfeld Simons tauchten jetzt deutlich Schwierigkeiten auf, Simon kannte viele Möglichkeiten der Wortkombinationen nicht. In jeder Stunde erweiterte er seinen deutschen Wortschatz. Er ließ sich die Bedeutungen stets sehr genau erläutern, fragte nach, in welchen Zusammenhängen die Wörter benutzt werden und behielt erstaunlicherweise viel davon. Die Logik des deutschen Sprachaufbaus wurde ihm verständlicher, er erweiterte deutlich beobachtbar seine Sprachkompetenz. In 10 Therapiestunden war das Erkennen und Schreiben von Anfangsbausteinen in Wörtern gesichert.

Simon sah jetzt dem Ende der 6. Klasse entgegen. Zusammen mit seinen Eltern überlegte er ab der 7. Klasse auf ein Gymnasium zu wechseln, da die Waldorfschule ihm keinen adäquaten Rahmen mehr für seine Lernentwicklung bot. Ferner bestand in der ausgewählten Schule die Möglichkeit, die Fächer Geschichte, Erdkunde, Biologie und Sport auf Englisch erteilt zu bekommen. Nach anfänglicher Skepsis, die für Simon bei Veränderungen stets charakteristisch war, schien er sich darauf zu freuen. Ich erlebte ihn in dieser Zeit auffällig offen und gesprächig.

Das Gymnasium nahm ihn an und es fielen kleine sichtbare Veränderungen auf. Er hatte bisher eine schwere Brille getragen, die seine Augen stark vergrößerten, jetzt bekam er auf eigenen Wunsch Kontaktlinsen. Seine Frisur wurde schwungvoller. Er war immer noch eher schüchtern und zurückgenommen in seinem Verhalten, aber konnte seine Gedanken klar und für den Gesprächspartner interessant äußern.

Wir setzten die Einteilung von Wörtern in Wortbausteine fort. Es folgte das bewusste Erkennen von Endbausteinen. Als erstes lernte Simon die Endungen von Nomen (-heit, -keit, -nis/-nisse, -schaft, -sal, -tum, -.ung, -ling) (Reuter-Liehr, 1992, 1997). Damit verbindet sich eine

100-prozentige Regelhaftigkeit: Stehen diese Endbausteine am Ende eines Wortes, wird das Wort mit Sicherheit groß geschrieben. Eine Kontrolle mit dem Artikel erübrigt sich.

Wie zu erwarten war, bereitete Simon diese klare Regelhaftigkeit keine Probleme. So konnte er jetzt die Großschreibung von vielen abstrakten Nomen auch erkennen. Eine Erfolgskontrolle sah nach dem Diktat von Simon so aus:

Simon, 19. 8. 96 14. Therapiestunde • 3. Therapiephase
Anfangs- und Endmorpheme (Nomen)

Falschschreibungen sind markiert:

Gedanken über die Rechtschreibung
*Fragen wir Leute, welches das ödeste Problem der Welt sei, so hat die Rechtschreibung vermutlich gute Aussichten, an die erste Stelle zu gelangen. Aber bei kaum **E**twas anderem lodern die Leidenschaften so auf. Unsere Einstellung zu Regeln ist eigentlich unklar. Einerseits mögen wir sie nicht und **A**ndererseits werden wir in der Schule damit gezwiebelt. Bei allen Befragungen w**u**nschten sich die meisten Menschen eine Vereinfachung der geltenden Rechtschreibung. Haben wir aber eine Schreibung verinnerlicht und gerade diese möchten andere verbessern, so sind wir mit flammender Entr**u**stung dagegen und meinen, dieses sei eine Verst**u**mmelung unserer Muttersprache. Was wir eingeschliffen haben und automatisch verrichten, wollen wir nicht missen und werden damit zum Hindernis in unseren eigenen Angelegenheiten.*

insgesamt 120 Wörter, davon 118 richtig geschrieben zuzüglich 3 x fehlende Umlautzeichen

Simon hatte diesen noch immer überwiegend den 6 Phonemstufen entsprechenden Text fast fehlerfrei geschrieben. Das Weglassen der Umlautzeichen beim „ü" war zu diesem Zeitpunkt noch gelegentlich zu beobachten, evtl. nahm er dies nicht ganz ernst; denn in der englischen Sprache kommen sie nicht vor. Er hatte aber jedes Nomen erkannt, die Großschreibung bei zwei Wörtern jedoch übergeneralisiert. Er erklärte mir seine Überlegungen zu dieser Großschreibung: Das Wort „etwas" war für ihn als Gegenstand erfassbar, das Wort „andererseits" bezog er auf die „andere Seite", welche er sehen kann. Ich fand seine Überlegungen sehr klug und war mir sicher, dass ihm meine anschließende geplante 3. Phase zur Großschreibung weiterhelfen würde.

3. Phase zum Erkennen der Großschreibung

Diese Sequenz zur Großschreibung erweitert das grammatische Wissen um die Begleiter, welche als Signal für ein kommendes Nomen dienen. Neben bestimmten Artikeln (der, die, das, dem, den, des) gibt es unbestimmte (ein, eine, einer, eines, einem, einen) und versteckte Artikel in Präpositionen (beim / vom / zum / im / ins / zur etc.). Das Possessivpronomen (mein, dein, sein, unser, euer, ihr) sowie das Demonstrativpronomen (dieser, jener, solcher, derselbe, derjenige etc.) haben ebenfalls eine ankündigende Funktion. Wieder werden alle Regeln stückweise integriert und in der Anwendung trainiert.

In diversen Geschichten – in denen alles klein geschrieben war – unterstrich Simon diese Begleiter farbig, umrahmte das dazugehörige Nomen und verbesserte mit einem Rotstift die falsche Kleinschreibung. Die Geschichten waren wiederum so zusammengestellt, dass Simon jeweils nur die bekannten Begleiter vorfand, um nicht verwirrt zu werden.

Am Gymnasium wurden erste Arbeiten geschrieben. Während er in Französisch und Englisch die Noten 2-3 erhielt, schrieb er seinen ersten Aufsatz mit der Note 4. Es zeigten sich deutlich grammatikalische Mängel und 11 Rechtschreibfehler, ferner schrieb Simon lieber zu wenig als zu viel. Er gab zu, dass er zu Hause englische und nicht deutsche Bücher lese, die englische Sprache gefalle ihm besser.

Sein erstes Diktat wurde ihm zu schnell diktiert. Es kam zu 19 Rechtschreib- und 7 Zeichensetzungsfehlern, welche mitgezählt wurden. Er erhielt die Note 6. Von seinen Fehlern hätte Simon aber nach dem bisher erreichten Lernstand nur ca. 5 vermeiden können. Vielfach wurden Fremdwörter abverlangt, die Simon bisher nicht geschrieben hatte.

In dieser Zeit verwickelte er mich gerne in Gespräche, lenkte gerne ab, wollte Schreiben lieber vermeiden. Auch fiel mir auf, dass er seiner Mutter gerne Organisatorisches überließ. Sie suchte für ihn die beste Busverbindung zu mir heraus, sie sagte seine Termine ab, wenn er nicht konnte. Ich nahm mir vor diesbezüglich Gespräche zu führen, um ihn zu mehr Selbständigkeit zu bewegen.

Als er schließlich auch in einer Englischarbeit wegen etlicher Rechtschreibfehler eine Note 5 erhielt, wurde ihm im gemeinsamen Gespräch deutlich, dass er bei allen Schreibaufgaben wesentlich mehr Training als andere Schüler seines Alters benötigt. Auch in dem Fach Englisch bedurfte er einer erkennbaren Systematik, um hier gewinnbringend die Rechtschreibung zu erlernen. Seine Mutter half ihm dabei, aber letztlich musste Simon lernen, die Verantwortung für sein legasthenes Problem im Fach Deutsch und Englisch selbst zu übernehmen. Wir hofften, dass er es zunehmend schaffen würde, vermeidendes Verhalten aufzugeben und sich den Aufgaben zu stellen. Sein 1. Halbjahreszeugnis des Gymnasiums fiel dann doch zu seiner Zufriedenheit aus. Er hatte vorwiegend die Note 2 und nur im Fach Deutsch eine 4.

Nach 29 Std. in der 3. Therapiephase vervollständigten wir die Einteilung von Wörtern in Wortbausteine durch das Erkennen der Adjektivendbausteine (-ig, -lich, -ent(lich), -isch, -bar, -haft, -los, -sam) (Reuter-Liehr, 1992, 1997).

Diese Art der Wortbausteine erhielt die Farbe grün, so dass jetzt das Zusammenfügen von gelben (Anfangsbausteine), roten (Grundbausteine), blauen (Endbausteine von Nomen) und grünen Kärtchen (Endbausteine von Adjektiven) vielfältige Übungen und Spiele ergaben. Simon wusste nun, der letzte Baustein bestimmt die Groß- oder Kleinschreibung.

Schritt 2: Übergeordnete Ableitungsstrategien anwenden

Das Abtrennen von Anfangs- und Endbausteinen isoliert den Grundbaustein (Hauptmorphem), nur hier gibt es Ableitungsprobleme zu bewältigen. Es wurden Schritt für Schritt 4 übergeordnete Ableitungsstrategien eingeführt und in der Anwendung trainiert. Die im Vorfeld aufgebaute Fähigkeit zur Morphemsegmentierung hilft dem struktursuchenden Kind, den

Blick für die „Gefahrenstellen“ im Wort zu schärfen und logische Schlussfolgerungen zu ziehen.

Es wird mit der 1. Ableitungsstrategie am Beispiel des doppelten Konsonanten gestartet:

Ich leite ab:

1.	**durch Endverlängerung**	*Kniff*	-->	*Kniffe*
	auch ck:	*Schreck*	-->	*Schrecken*
	auch tz:	*Spatz*	-->	*Spatzen*

Für Simon war die Schreibweise des doppelten Konsonanten am Ende des Wortes noch nicht geläufig. Er schrieb das erste Testwort „Hauptgewinn“ nur mit einem „n“. Es bedurfte bei den nachfolgenden Verschriftungen mit Ableitungswörtern seiner vollen Konzentration, um das dazugehörige „lautgetreue Ursprungswort“ – wie wir es nannten – im richtigen Moment des Schreibens parat zu haben. Wieder traten starke Wortfindungsprobleme auf, sein Gesicht wurde rot und die Stirn legte sich vor Anstrengung in dicke Falten. Aber er schaffte es, auch die weiteren Ableitungsstrategien Stück für Stück beim Schreiben zu bedenken:

Ich leite ab durch Abtrennen:

2.	- bei zusammengesetzten Wörtern **und dann verlängern**	*Rennpferde —> rennen*
3.	- der grammatischen Endung **und dann Grundform bilden**	*er kommt —>kommen*
4.	- des Endbausteines **und dann verlängern**	*sinnlos —> Sinne*

Der eingeführte Ableitungspfeil unter die nicht mehr sprech- und hörbare Doppelung des Konsonanten symbolisierte für Simon das innere „Weiterschwingen“ und führte zum Bilden des „lautgetreuen Ursprungswortes“.

Die Verdoppelung des „k“ zum „ck“ und des „z“ zum „tz“ war eingeschlossen. In der 4. Std. im Umgang mit den neuen Ableitungsstrategien bewältigte er bereits mühelos die Strategie Nr. 3. Die Strategie Nr. 4 bereitete ihm durch die vielfältige Vorarbeit mit den Wortbausteinen keinerlei Schwierigkeiten. Wörter, deren Ableitungen nicht im direkten Zusammenhang zur Wortbedeutung standen – beispielsweise Schutt ---> schütten–, musste Simon sich erarbeiten. Wieder leisteten wir viel Spracharbeit, der Herkunftsduden wurde oft zu Rate gezogen. Simon gewann Freude an sprachgeschichtlichen Betrachtungen.

Das zweite Klassendiktat erbrachte auf Grund vieler Grammatikfehler eine 5. Simon empfand dies als Erfolg gegenüber der 6 im ersten Diktat. Seine Unsicherheit in der deutschen Grammatik kristallisierte sich langsam als sein Restproblem in der Bewältigung der deutschen Sprache heraus. Hier fehlte ihm meiner Meinung nach der ausreichend mündliche und schriftsprachliche Umgang mit deutschen Texten. Er las sie nicht und schrieb sie nur für die Schule.

Zu diesem Zeitpunkt diskutierte er häufig mit mir über den Therapietermin. Er wollte auf alle Fälle zu mir kommen, aber eigentlich passte ihm der von mir vorgeschlagene Termin fast nie. Ich gewann den Eindruck, dass wir jetzt langsam zu einem Abschluss kommen müssten. So plante ich, den Umgang mit den Ableitungsstrategien noch zu perfektionieren, dann aber die Therapie zu beenden.

In meiner therapeutischen Praxis bestätigte sich wiederholt die Erfahrung, dass sich nach der Einführung der vier Ableitungsstrategien am Beispiel des doppelten Konsonanten am Ende eines Wortes (1), bei zusammengesetzten Wörtern (2), vor der grammatischen Endung (3) oder vor einem Endbaustein (4) die gesamte Problematik der Auslautverhärtung (g, d, b) in einem Zuge problemlos anschließen lässt. Ebenso ist es erfahrungsgemäß notwendig, das „z" im Auslaut zu beweisen; denn „ H a l s " ist nicht von „ S a l z " zu unterscheiden. Dem folgt das Erkennen des „ableitbaren h", wie beispielsweise in den Wörtern: R e h – R e - h e / K u h g l o c k e – K ü h e / e r g e h t – g e h e n / a b s e h b a r - s e h e n , dessen Verschriftung ebenfalls nur den Einsatz der 4 Ableitungsstrategien als Beweis benötigt. Die trotz der neuen Rechtschreibreform weiterhin bestehende Problematik mit dem „ß" am Ende eines Wortes oder einer Silbe wird dann mit der kurzen Regel **„ß bleibt ß!"** angegangen. In der Schule wurde Simon mit der neuen Rechtschreibung der s-Laute konfrontiert. Wie so viele Schüler geriet er – sicherlich auch deswegen, weil hier sämtliche Informationen über die neue Schreibweise durch die Lehrerin auf einmal erteilt wurden – damit völlig durcheinander. Er rechnete sich aus, dass er die Schule bereits verlassen hat, wenn die neue Rechtschreibung nur noch allein gültig ist, und nimmt jetzt in Kauf, dass seine Lehrerin immer „veraltet" an den Rand schreibt, wenn er sich für die bisherige alte Schreibweise entschieden hatte, die ihm teilweise logischer erscheint.

Simon benötigte 6 Std. zum Erfassen der 4 Ableitungsstrategien und in weiteren 15 Std. festigten wir das Ableiten in vielfältiger Form. Schließlich schrieb er schon recht flüssig die diktierten Texte, musste aber die von der Lauttreue abweichenden Schreibweisen stets noch einmal überdenken. Schließlich integrierten wir in das Wort- und Textmaterial auch Wörter mit „ie" in der geschlossenen Silbe, die Simon mühelos ableiten konnte, dies entsprechend der Phonemstufe 5. Zum Abschluss unseres Ableitungstrainings befassten wir uns mit der Mehrheitsregel **„ä kommt von a"** (ebenso: äu von au).

Mit diesem Aufbau in der 3. Therapiephase hatte Simon einen weiteren wichtigen Teil der deutschen Orthographie bearbeitet und systematisiert erfahren. Die hauptsächliche Rechtschreibstrategie dieser Lernphase war gut verinnerlicht: ***Ich schreibe ein Wort nur dann anders als ich es mitsprechen kann, wenn ich eine Begründung dafür weiß (---> überprüftes Einsetzen von Regelwissen).***

Abschluss der 3. Therapiephase

Im Klassendiktat der 8. Klasse erhielt er jetzt die Note 5+. Er sah wiederum eine Verbesserung in diesem Ergebnis und schien zufrieden zu sein. Die Lehrerin hatte für ihn wieder viel schnell diktiert, so dass er nur unzureichend mitgekommen war. Es fehlten 4 Wörter, 8 Fehler waren auf Grund falscher grammatischer Endungen entstanden. Die restlichen Fehler hielten sich bereits sehr in Grenzen. Ich hatte den Eindruck, dass die Legasthenietherapie momentan keine weiteren Erfolge für ein Klassendiktat erzielen konnte. Die Ursache für diese Restproblematik sah ich nach wie vor im eingeschränkten Umgang mit der deutschen Schriftsprache.

Kurz vor Weihnachten 1997 wurde Simons Rechtschreibentwicklung erneut mit dem WRT 6+ (einer nach Testanalyse selbstentwickelten B-Form) untersucht. Nach der Norm für Anfang 7. Klasse erreichte er jetzt mit 29 richtig geschriebenen Wörtern PR 66, damit ein gut durchschnittliches Ergebnis. Die während unserer gesamten gemeinsamen Arbeit trainierten Bereiche schloss er mit 4 Fehlern ab. Seine Fehlerschwerpunkte lagen jetzt nur noch im Speicher- und Restfehlerbereich (insgesamt 8). Die Mehrfachfehlerhäufung war mit 1,09 ganz unbedeutend geworden.

1., 2. und 3. Erfolgskontrolle

Die Überprüfung der Lesefähigkeit mit dem Zürcher Lesetest ergab zwar noch eine etwas verlangsamte Lesezeit aber mit Prozentrang 51-75 eine gut durchschnittliche Leistung bei der Einordnung der Lesefehler. Es kam nur zu kleinen Verlesungen, die völlig unerheblich für die Sinnentnahme waren. Das Gelesene konnte er auf das Wesentliche beschränkt sehr präzise und sogar erläuternd wiedergeben.

4 Therapiephase

Umgang mit den Speicherwörtern

Simon und seine Mutter wollten die Therapie noch nicht beenden. Inzwischen waren insgesamt 127 Std. durchgeführt worden, dies allerdings in einem Zeitraum von 6 Jahren. Das Jugendamt bewilligte weitere 20 Std., dies aber erst nach 4 Monaten. Simons Terminschwierigkeiten wurden immer häufiger. Ich stand dem gelassen gegenüber, da für mich die Grenzen dieser Therapie erreicht waren.

Wir beschäftigten uns nunmehr mit dem weder hörbaren, noch ableitbaren Dehnungs-h. Die Anzahl der Wörter ist gering; denn in der Regel wird der lange a-Laut einfach a geschrieben, ebenso der lange e-, o-, u-Laut ohne Dehnungs-h. Inzwischen hatte Simon längst erfahren, dass „Grundbausteine“ (Hauptmorpheme) die Basis für Wortfamilien bilden. Die Besonderheit „Dehnungs-h“ im „Grundbaustein“ findet sich somit in der gesamten „Familie“, nach dem Motto „Wenn einer in der Familie den h-Tick hat, dann hat ihn auch die ganze Verwandtschaft.“. Noch viel seltener sind die Wörter, die einen doppelten Vokal enthalten.

Nach den Sommerferien rief mich Simon an, er würde gerne die Tanzstunde besuchen, der Termin wäre übereinstimmend mit unserem. Ich fand dieses Vorhaben sehr wichtig und stimmte dem freudig zu. Erst zu Beginn dieses Jahres, Februar 99, Mitte 9. Klasse setzten wir unsere Treffen auf ausdrücklichen Wunsch von Simon fort. Simon wirkte auf mich inzwischen recht souverän im Umgang mit Sprache und Schriftsprache. Die Schule belastete ihn nicht mehr; denn Diktate werden in der 9. Klasse nicht mehr geschrieben. In seinen letzten Aufsätzen schrieb er die Noten 2/3/2, er hatte jeweils nur noch maximal 5 Rechtschreib- und 2 Grammatikfehler.

Für Simon ist es so, als habe er einen tiefen Graben übersprungen, der ihm unüberwindbar erschienen war. In seinem letzten Zeugnis erhielt er erstmalig die Note 3 im Fach Deutsch.

In einer der letzten Therapiestunden schrieb er flüssig und ohne Probleme den Text „Das gefährliche Großhirn" von 273 Wörtern. Fehler bemerkte er selbst und korrigierte richtig. Als einziger Fehler verblieb: stendig, die Ableitung von „Stand" war ihm nicht geläufig.

Simon, 10. 3. 99 12. Therapiestunde • 4. Therapiephase / Speicherbereich (ah/aa/oh/oo)
Erfolgskontrolle: „Das gefährliche Großhirn"

Abschluss der 4. Therapiephase

Im Juli 1999 haben wir unsere gemeinsame Arbeit nach insgesamt 145 Therapiestunden beendet. Es waren 8 Jahre – mit zum Teil großen Unterbrechungen – , in denen ich Simon bei seinem schweren Weg, seine ausgeprägte legasthene Schwäche zu bewältigen, lerntherapeutisch begleiten konnte. Seine überdurchschnittlichen Lern- und Leistungsmöglichkeiten rechtfertigen den Besuch des Gymnasiums. Es ist unwahrscheinlich, dass Simon dies ohne diese systematische Behandlung seiner Teilleistungsschwäche geschafft hätte. Der Umgang mit der deutschen Sprache beginnt ihm Freude zu bereiten.

Zum Abschluss wagten wir den für heutige Schüler mit 65 Testwörtern sehr schweren und inzwischen 31 Jahre alten Rechtschreibtest „Moselfahrt" (Jäger, 1968) einzusetzen, der mit PR 62 den WRT 6+ bestätigte, dies trotz völlig veralteter Normen.

Abschlusstest nach insgesamt 145 Therapiestunden (4. Erfolgskontrolle)
„Moselfahrt" – 65 Testwörter

Seine Mutter berichtete mir, in welch disziplinierter Form er seine Englisch-Arbeiten vorbereite. Er schreibe sich vor der Arbeit die zu erwartenden Vokabeln auf, systematisiere sie unter bestimmten sprachlichen Gesichtspunkten, dabei beziehe er ihre Hilfe mit ein, und lerne die Schreibweisen auswendig. So erreichte er inzwischen die Note 1 im Fach Englisch.

Um diese doch recht aufwendige Vorbereitung durchzuhalten, musste Simon lernen, seine frühere Haltung aufzugeben, nämlich dem Unbequemen lieber auszuweichen. Er erfährt stattdessen, dass systematische Vorbereitungen zum Erfolg führen, während bloßes Vermeiden zu Misserfolg und somit zur Kränkung geführt hat. Er hat akzeptiert, dass er letztlich mehr tun muss als andere, um zu einem guten Ergebnis zu gelangen.

Darin sehe ich letztlich den entscheidendsten Erfolg der Therapie; Simon ist die Übernahme der Eigenverantwortung für sein legasthenes Problem gelungen.

Literatur

Buschmann, H. (1986) Die Methode des rhythmisch-dynamischen Sprechschreibens bei Legasthenikern, Hannover, unveröffentlichter Vortrag vom 7. Fachkongress des Bundesverbandes Legasthenie in Hannover

Grässli, B. (1980) Lesetraining 3 – Wörter, Huesmann und Benz

Horn-Breul, E. (1974) Kullerköpfe, Krumpelmurkse und der Club der Purzelkinder, Limburg Lahn

Jäger, A. O. (1968) Diktat C „Moselfahrt"; in Rechtschreibungstets R-T, 2. Auflage, Göttingen Hogrefe

Rathenow, P. u.a. (1973) Rechtschreibtest RST 1, Beltz Weinheim

Rathenow, P (1979) Westermann Rechtschreibtest 4/5, Westermann Braunschweig

Rathenow, P. (1980) Westermann Rechtschreibtest 6+, Westermann Braunschweig

Reuter-Liehr, C. (1992) Lautgetreue Rechtschreibförderung; (²2000/2001) Vollständig überarbeitete und erweiterte Neuauflage unter dem Titel: Lautgetreue Lese-Rechtschreibförderung (4 Bde.), Winkler Bochum

Reuter-Liehr, C. (1992a) Lautgetreue Rechtschreibförderung, Begleitbuch, Kap.: Die qualitative Fehleranalyse: Grundlage für Diagnose und Therapie, S. 9ff)

Reuter-Liehr, C. (1992b) Lauttreuer Bildertest der Phonemstufe 1. LBT 1, Göttingen, unveröffentlichte Materialien

Reuter-Liehr, C. (1993) Behandlung der Lese-Rechtschreibschwäche nach der Grundschulzeit: Anwendung und Überprüfung eines Konzeptes; in: Zeitschrift für Kinder- und Jugendpsychiatrie, Jg. 21, S. 135-147, Huber Bern

Reuter-Liehr, C. (1993a) Lauttreuer Bildertest der Phonemstufe 2. LBT 2, Göttingen, unveröffentlichte Materialien

Reuter-Liehr, C. (1997) Ein ganzheitlicher, sprachsystematischer Aufbau des Lesens und Rechtschreibens bei lese-rechtschreibschwachen Kindern; in: Legasthenie, Bericht über den 12. Fachkongress 1997 Greifswald, hrsg. v. Bundesverband Legasthenie e. V.

Reuter-Liehr, C. (2000), Vom Leichten zum Schweren und vom Häufigen zum Seltenen. Eine Falldarstellung; in: Haase, P. (Hrsg.), Schreiben und Lesen sicher lehren und lernen, borgmann Dortmund

Warnke, A. (1995) Umschriebene Lese-Rechtschreibstörung; in: Petermann, F. (Hrsg.), Lehrbuch der Klinischen Kinderpsychologie, Hogrefe Göttingen

Weiß, R.H. (1987) Grundintelligenztest Skala 2 CFT 20, Hogrefe Göttingen, 3. Auflage

4.5 Wie können wir das Selbstwertgefühl von Kindern – trotz Teilleistungsschwäche – erhalten und stärken?

Christina Krause und Christine Stückle

Zusammenfassung

Das Selbstwertgefühl des Kindes wird bis zum Schulbeginn in besonderem Maße von der emotionalen Sicherheit in der Familie, von den positiven Rückmeldungen durch Eltern und Verwandte, die die Entwicklung und die Fortschritte des Kindes mit Stolz und Freude erleben, bestimmt. Der Schuleintritt labilisiert in jedem Fall das normalerweise positive Selbstwertgefühl, wobei sich schon in relativ kurzer Zeit eine Veränderung ergeben kann. Da das Kind zunächst nicht zur selbständigen Bewertung seiner tatsächlichen Schul- und Lernkompetenzen in der Lage ist, ist es in großem Maße von der Reaktion seiner Bezugspersonen abhängig.

Ausgehend davon, dass Schule für nicht wenige Kinder Stress bedeutet und sie oft relativ unvorbereitet in diese Situation geraten, ist die Entwicklung von Fähigkeiten und Fertigkeiten zum kompetenten Umgang mit Belastungen eine wichtige Aufgabe der Schule. Das trifft erst recht zu für Kinder, die beim Erlernen des Lesens und Schreibens Schwierigkeiten haben.

In diesem Beitrag werden Ergebnisse aus einem vierjährigen Längsschnittprojekt, das über die Grundschulzeit hinweg durchgeführt wurde, vorgestellt. Ziel des Projektes war der Erhalt und die Stärkung des Selbstwertgefühls der Kinder. Zu diesem Zweck wurde ein Modell zur Gesundheitsförderung, insbesondere der psychischen Gesundheit, erarbeitet und erprobt. Der Erwerb von Kompetenzen, um mit den Belastungen kompetent umgehen zu können, war Hauptanliegen des Projektes „Ich bin Ich – Gesundheit fördern durch Selbstwertstärkung“.

1 Selbstwert als Gesundheitsfaktor

Die WHO-Gesundheitsdefinition aus dem Jahre 1946 enthielt zum ersten Mal den Begriff ‚Wohlbefinden‘, womit die positive Ausprägung einer emotionalen, subjektiv reflektierten Befindlichkeit gemeint war. Dieses Wohlbefinden ist ein komplexes Gefühl und kann auf der Grundlage unterschiedlicher Anteile – auch situationsbedingter – zustande kommen. Glück und Unglück, Freude und Trauer, Anspannung und Entspannung wechseln und bestimmen die emotionale Befindlichkeit, die sich auf einem Kontinuum von positivem bis negativem Befinden bewegen kann. Entscheidend jedoch ist, was letztlich überwiegt und zu einer allgemeinen Zufriedenheit führt. Eine der wesentlichen Voraussetzungen dafür, dass das Wohlbefinden überwiegt, ist neben der körperlichen Fitness vor allem das Selbstwertgefühl, das heisst die globale Wertschätzung, die man der eigenen Person entgegenbringt. Es ist die gefühlsmässig verankerte Beziehung bzw. Einstellung eines Individuums zu sich selbst und schliesst die Akzeptanz der eigenen Person sowie Zuversicht in die eigenen Möglichkeiten ein. Ein positives Selbstwertgefühl ist sowohl Quelle als auch Folge von Wohlbefinden und damit auch von Gesundheit.

Das Selbstwertgefühl ist ohne Zweifel eine der wichtigsten Ressourcen für die Bewältigung der zukünftigen Anforderungen, und es bestimmt gleichzeitig die emotionale Befindlichkeit des Kindes.

Das Selbstwertgefühl ist ein situationsübergreifendes Phänomen, es ist somit auch relativ stabil. Es ist die Wertschätzung, die das Individuum in bezug auf die eigene Person vornimmt. Personen, die sich selbst wenig zutrauen, unsicher sind, vielleicht sogar ängstlich und depressiv oder auch aggressiv, haben in den meisten Fällen ein niedriges Selbstwertgefühl.

Das Selbstwertgefühl ist sozusagen der affektive Teil des Selbst und entwickelt sich vom ersten Lebenstage an. Entscheidend für die Herausbildung eines positiven Selbstwertgefühls ist die Fürsorge und Liebe der Mutter oder einer anderen Bezugsperson, die dem Kind das Gefühl von Sicherheit, Geborgenheit und Angenommensein gibt.

Kinder, die sich von anderen anerkannt und angenommen fühlen, die erfolgreich die täglichen Anforderungen bewältigen können und in einer Atmosphäre aufwachsen, „in der individuelle Unterschiede gewürdigt werden, Liebe offen zum Ausdruck gebracht wird, wo die Möglichkeit besteht, aus Fehlern zu lernen, wo offen kommuniziert wird, Regeln flexibel gehandhabt werden, Verantwortlichkeit vorgelebt und Ehrlichkeit praktiziert wird" (Satir 1994, S.48), entwickeln ein positives Selbstwertgefühl.

In den ersten Lebensjahren können die meisten Kinder ein positives Selbstwertgefühl entwickeln, weil ihre Bedürfnisse nach Anerkennung und Geborgenheit befriedigt werden. Normalerweise erleben Eltern die Entwicklungsfortschritte ihres Kindes mit großer Freude, sie bringen ihr Erstaunen und ihren Stolz offen zum Ausdruck. Diese positiven Rückmeldungen sind eine Quelle des positiven Selbstwertgefühls, das die meisten Kinder haben. So kann davon ausgegangen werden, dass Schulanfänger ihren Schulweg mit Optimismus beginnen und sich in bezug auf die zu erwartenden Anforderungen kompetent fühlen.

Das Wohlbefinden wiederum entscheidet darüber, ob eine Person sich gesund fühlt. Wohlbefinden als ein Indikator von Gesundheit – das ist ein neuer Ansatz in der Beschäftigung mit Störungen aller Art. Die Gesundheitsdefinition der WHO aus dem Jahre 1946 war sozusagen der Einstieg in die Auseinandersetzung um das Verständnis von Gesundheit, womit auch die allmähliche Abkehr vom klassischen medizinischen Modell verbunden ist. Wohlbefinden kann ein eher aktuelles oder auch ein habituelles Gefühl sein. Immer aber ist es eine selbst getroffene Entscheidung, eine subjektive Bewertung der Person. Nimmt man das ernst, dann geben wir dem Individuum auch mehr Verantwortung für seine Gesundheit.

Die Abkehr vom klassischen medizinischen Modell wird noch deutlicher im salutogenetischen Konzept von Gesundheit. Antonovsky (1993) führte den Begriff „Salutogenese" – die Ursprünge der Gesundheit – als Gegenbegriff zur Pathogenese ein. Kernpunkt dieses Konzeptes ist die Annahme eines „Sense of Coherence", worunter Antonovsky eine Reihe „generalisierter Widerstandsressourcen" versteht. Ohne das hier weiter auszuführen, soll das wichtigste im Zusammenhang mit der Gesundheit von Kindern erläutert werden:

Antonovsky nennt drei Komponenten, die den „Sense of Coherence" bestimmen: „Sense of Comprehensibility", „Sense of Managebility", „Sense of Meaningfulness".

Das Vertrauen darauf, dass Anforderungen der Umwelt vorhersagbar und erklärbar sind (Sense of Comprehensibility), kann dem Kind Sicherheit geben und Mut machen. Legasthenie ist erklärbar und die sich daraus ergebenden Anforderungen an die besonders schwierige Gestaltung von Lernprozessen sind vorhersagbar.

Antonovsky meint, dass es nicht weniger wichtig sei, auf seine eigenen Ressourcen vertrauen zu können. Solange das legasthenische Kind daran glaubt, dass es das Lesen und Schreiben auch erlernen kann, dass es mit der Unterstützung der Familie, der Schule und anderer Institutionen (z.B. Legasthenieverband) rechnen kann und trotz aller Schwierigkeiten die Anforderungen bewältigen wird, können wir noch von einer ‚gesunden' Situation sprechen.

An dieser Stelle wird auch deutlich, dass das Selbstwertgefühl eine der wichtigsten Ressourcen des Kindes ist.

Mit der dritten Komponente (Sense of Meaningfulness) ist gemeint, dass die Person von der Bedeutsamkeit und Richtigkeit der eigenen Anstrengungen und des eigenen Engagements überzeugt ist. Diese motivierende Komponente setzt das Vorhandensein der ersten beiden voraus, andererseits darf sie aber auch nicht fehlen.

Die Erklärbarkeit und Vorhersagbarkeit der besonderen Anforderungen, die sich aus der Legasthenie ergeben, sowie das Wissen um die eigenen Ressourcen, die dem Kind die Bewältigung der besonderen Anforderungen ermöglichen, werden dann zu einem ‚Gesundheitsfaktor', wenn das Kind außerdem sicher ist, dass sich diese Anstrengungen lohnen.

Im Falle der Legasthenie ist das relativ klar, weil das Erlernen der Schriftsprache in jedem Falle einen Gewinn an Lebensqualität mit sich bringt.

Die Stärke des „Sense of Coherence" entscheidet darüber, wie eine Person den Anforderungen des Lebens begegnet und wie fähig sie sich fühlt, ihre Gesundheit in die eigenen Hände zu nehmen. Je mehr das gelingt, desto positiver ist das allgemeine Wohlbefinden, das Gefühl von Glück, Zufriedenheit und Gesundsein. Kinder müssen diese ‚Gesundheitsfaktoren' aber erst entwickeln. Genau das war die Zielstellung des Projektes „Ich bin Ich – Gesundheit fördern durch Selbstwertstärkung". Im Mittelpunkt stand die psychische Gesundheit der Kinder und die Erhaltung, Stärkung und Förderung des Selbstwertes während der Grundschulzeit sowie die Entwicklung ihrer Kompetenzen zum Umgang mit dem alltäglichen Streß, wozu auch die Schule gehört.

2 Schule und Selbstwert

Der Schuleintritt verändert die Lebensbedingungen des Kindes so umfassend, dass Selbstbildveränderungen in jedem Fall zu erwarten sind. Allein schon deshalb, weil sich die Struktur des Selbstbildes verändert, u. a. dadurch, dass eine völlig neue Substruktur entsteht.

Wenn das Kind zum Schulkind wird und die neue Rolle eines Schülers/einer Schülerin übernimmt, sich mit neuen signifikanten Bezugspersonen auseinandersetzen muß und neue Maßstäbe für das Bewerten der anderen und der eigenen Person erwirbt – wenn all diese Bedingungen bedeutsam werden – dann entsteht das ‚Schul- und lernbezogene Selbstbild'.

Wie bereits gesagt, besitzen Schulanfänger/innen normalerweise ein positives Selbstwertgefühl, das mit Freude auf die Schule und einer positiven Einschätzung ihrer Fähigkeiten verbunden ist. Die meisten Kinder fühlen sich wohl, d.h. ihre emotionale Befindlichkeit, ihre Gesundheit ist aus der eigenen Sicht gut. Das bedeutet, dass für den Beginn des neuen Lebensabschnittes günstige Voraussetzungen bestehen.

Dennoch kann der Schulanfang zu einem kritischen Lebensereignis werden. Kritische Lebensereignisse können die individuelle Entwicklung voran bringen, der Schulanfang zum Beispiel die Entwicklung der leistungsfähigen und emotional stabilen Kinder. Sie führen aber auch häufig zu schwerwiegenden Beeinträchtigungen der Entwicklung. Diese betreffen vor allem das Selbstwertgefühl der Kinder. „Der Schulanfang ist für die Prozesse der Selbstwahrnehmung von großer Bedeutung. Man nimmt an, dass in den ersten Schulmonaten die entscheidenden Weichen für die Entwicklung der verschiedenen Selbstkonzepte und der sie begleitenden Selbstwertgefühle gestellt werden“ (Einsiedler 1988, S. 21).

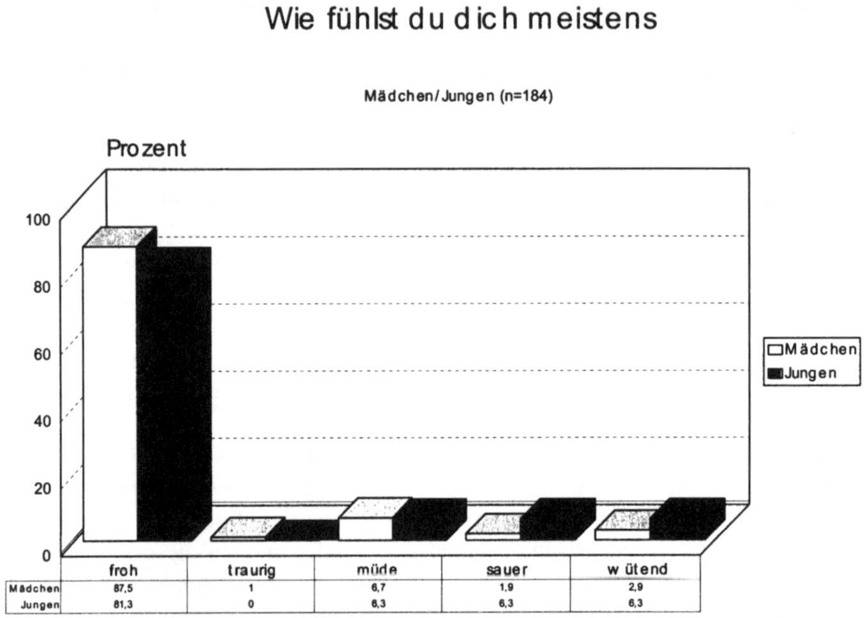

Abb. 4.5.1 Wie fühlst Du Dich meistens? Ergebnisse aus der Schuleingangsuntersuchung

Spätestens mit Schuleintritt freuen sich Eltern nicht mehr vordergründig über Entwicklungsfortschritte ihres Kindes. Während früher neu erworbene Fähigkeiten und Fertigkeiten des Kindes (das Erlernen neuer Wörter, neuer Fertigkeiten wie z.B. Klettern, Radfahren) und seine zunehmende soziale Kompetenz im Mittelpunkt bestärkender Rückmeldungen durch Eltern standen, ist es ab Schulbeginn zunehmend das Leistungsprodukt. Jopt (1987) spricht von einem „folgenschweren Reduktionismus der ursprünglichen Buntheit“ (S.63) der kindlichen Individualität. Folgenschwer deshalb, weil das Kind die Erfahrung macht, dass die Zuneigung der Eltern nunmehr von seinen schulischen Kompetenzen und seinen Lernerfolgen abhängt. Das bedeutet für Kinder mit Lernschwierigkeiten: Erleben von Liebesverlust, Erschütterung der im Vorschulalter erworbenen ursprünglichen Sicherheit, beginnende Zweifel an den eigenen Möglichkeiten, Veränderungen des Selbstwertgefühls mit den entsprechenden Auswirkungen auf die subjektive Befindlichkeit. Die Folgen dieser Verlusterlebnisse sind nicht selten somatische Beschwerden.

In der Schule erhalten die Jungen und Mädchen Rückmeldungen über ihre Kompetenzen (ihre Lernleistungen, aber auch ihr Lernverhalten) meist von der Lehrerin und zwar in Form direkter und indirekter Bewertungen und Zuweisungen. Aber auch durch ihr Verhalten zeigt sie, was sie von dem Schüler X oder der Schülerin Y hält. Ihre bewertenden und beurteilenden Handlungen bestimmen Glück oder Unglück des Kindes. Da die Lehrerin auch die Interaktion und Kommunikation in der Klasse lenkt und kontrolliert, beeinflusst sie auch die Beziehungen unter den Schülern und Schülerinnen. Sie trägt damit wesentlich dazu bei, ob das Kind sich angenommen fühlt oder nicht, ob es gern zur Schule kommt oder Schulangst entwickelt.

Es ist unbestritten, dass Schule über viele Jahre ein wichtiger Lebensraum für junge Menschen ist und damit auch die Chance bietet, ein gesundheitsförderlicher Bereich ihres Lebens zu werden. Für nicht wenige Kinder bringt Schule eher leidvolle Erfahrungen mit sich, denen sie ohne Hilfe nichts entgegensetzen können. Von 163 Göttinger Kindern der Längsschnittpopulation, die im dritten Schuljahr den „Fragebogen zur Erhebung von Streßerleben und Streßbewältigung im Kindesalter" von Lohaus et al. (1996) bearbeiteten, gaben fast alle Kinder an ein oder mehrmals in der Woche Stress zu haben. Davon waren 34% sogar dem hohen und 6% dem sehr hohen Niveau zuzuordnen.

kein Streß				**hoher Streß**
	niedrig	**∅**	**hoch**	
8%	20%	32%	34%	6%

Tabelle 4.5.1 Stresserleben von Drittklässlern (n=163)

Ein hohes Stressniveau fanden wir bei elf Jungen und bei einem Mädchen. Als Auslöser wurden vor allem schul- und leistungsbezogene Probleme genannt, aber auch Probleme im sozialen Umfeld, z. B. fehlende Anerkennung und Zuwendung, Konflikte in der Gruppe und zu hohe Erwartungen von Eltern. Alle in der Schule erfahrenen Handlungsanforderungen und Bewertungen, alle erlebten Konflikte und Misserfolge sind Belastungen, die Tag für Tag bewältigt werden müssen. Es ist nicht übertrieben zu behaupten, dass Schule ein Stressfaktor ist und das viele Situationen im Rahmen ‚Schule' für Kinder bedrohlich sind und nicht selten Angst auslösen. Tabelle 4.5.2 zeigt, welche Stresssymptome die befragten Kinder ein bzw. mehrmals in der Woche bei sich selbst wahrgenommen haben.

	Mädchen (n=83)	**Jungen (n=80)**	**Σ(n=163)**
Erschöpfung	63,75%	63,75%	63,8%
Schlaflosigkeit	39,75%	51,25%	45,3%
Appetitlosigkeit	44,55%	45,0%	44,7%
Kopfschmerzen	51,8%	36,5%	44,1%
Bauchschmerzen	45,75%	32,5%	39,3%

Tabelle 4.5.2 Stresssymptome bei Drittklässlern (n=163)

Kinder, die Leistungssituationen in der Schule immer wieder nicht erfolgreich bewältigen können oder der Abwertung durch ihre Mitschüler ausgesetzt sind, und dazu noch die Enttäuschung und den Ärger der Eltern ertragen müssen, kommen schon nach wenigen Schulwochen – spätestens aber am Ende des zweiten Schuljahres – zu dem Schluss, weniger wertvoll als andere Kinder zu sein. Das folgende Beispiel zeigt, wie sich das Selbstwertgefühl eines legasthenischen Jungen während der Grundschulzeit verändert hat

Satzanfang	**1. Klasse**	**2. Klasse**	**3. Klasse**	**4. Klasse**
Wenn ich etwas nicht schaffe	Dann schaffe ich es eben nicht.	dann mach ich es nach.	mache ich es morgen weiter.	dann probiere ich es noch mal.
Ich finde nicht schön	Nicht die echten Autos – die Vergaser, die müßten mal weg.	dass alle auf mir rumhacken.	dass meine Eltern sich manchmal streiten (wegen Kleinigkeiten).	wenn man mich am Wochenende früh wach macht.
Die anderen Kinder	Spielen gern.	hacken auf mir rum.	sind nett.	sind meistens nett.
Ich habe Angst	vor gar nichts.	in die Schule zu gehen (wegen Diktaten usw.).	abends wenn es gewittert.	wenn ich allein zu Hause und im Dunkeln bin.
Ich bin traurig	wenn mich andere schubsen.	manchmal.	wenn mein Bruder aufgebaute Sachen kaputt macht.	wenn mein Bruder wieder ins Internat geht.
Am meisten freue ich mich	über Tortenschlacht.	auf Judo.	auf meinen Geburtstag.	wenn ich gesund bin.
Ich ärgere mich	wenn ich nicht mitkommen darf.	über meine Dummheit.	wenn mal was daneben geht.	wenn ich eine schlechte Note geschrieben habe.
In der Schule	ist Rechnen gut.	finde ich die Pause gut.	bin ich gern auf dem Pausenhof.	finde ich Mathe schön.

Abb. 4.5.2 Satzergänzungen des Schülers K8

Zur Entwicklung des Selbstbildes und Selbstwertes im Grundschulalter kann zusammenfassend gesagt werden:

1. Bereits im ersten Schuljahr gibt es auffällige Veränderungen und eine starke Labilisierung des bis dahin entwickelten Selbstbildes.
2. Spätestens im dritten Schuljahr hat sich das schul- und lernbezogene Selbstbild entwickelt und hat für den weiteren Lernweg des Kindes handlungsorientierende und –regulierende Funktion. Diese Manifestierung eines negativen Selbstbildes fanden wir bei einigen Kindern schon am Ende des zweiten Schuljahres. In unserem Beispiel (s.o.) sagte der Junge bereits zu diesem Zeitpunkt: „Ich ärgere mich über meine Dummheit“.

Abb. 4.5.3 Wie Sandra die Reaktionen ihrer Eltern auf eine Diktatnote im zweiten, dritten und vierten Schuljahr zeichnerisch darstellte.

3. Die Erwartungen der Eltern und ihre Reaktion auf die Leistungen des Kindes bestimmen das Erleben des Kindes, vor allem auch deshalb, weil es zunächst seine Leistungen nicht selbst beurteilen kann.
   Die Abbildung 4.5.3 ist ein Beispiel dafür, wie die Kinder die erwarteten Reaktionen ihrer Eltern auf Schulleistungen zeichnerisch darstellten. Sandras Mutter scheint die Hoffnung zu haben, dass „viel üben“ die Situation verbessern könnte.
4. Die bewertenden und beurteilenden Handlungen der Lehrer/innen lenken die Interaktion unter den Kindern, sie bestimmen Glück oder Unglück des Kindes, entscheiden darüber, ob das Kind sich angenommen fühlt und gern zur Schule kommt oder nicht. Das Wohlbefinden wird zunehmend von Erfolgen und Misserfolgen in der Schule bestimmt. Die Abbildung 4.5.4 zeigt zum einen die Unterschiede in den Selbsteinschätzungen der Kinder und den Fremdeinschätzungen der Lehrerinnen und zum anderen die Unterschiede bezüglich der Selbst- und Fremdeinschätzungen in den Leistungsgruppen (L1 = Gruppe der erfolgreich lernenden Kinder, L3 = Gruppe der weniger erfolgreich lernenden Kinder).

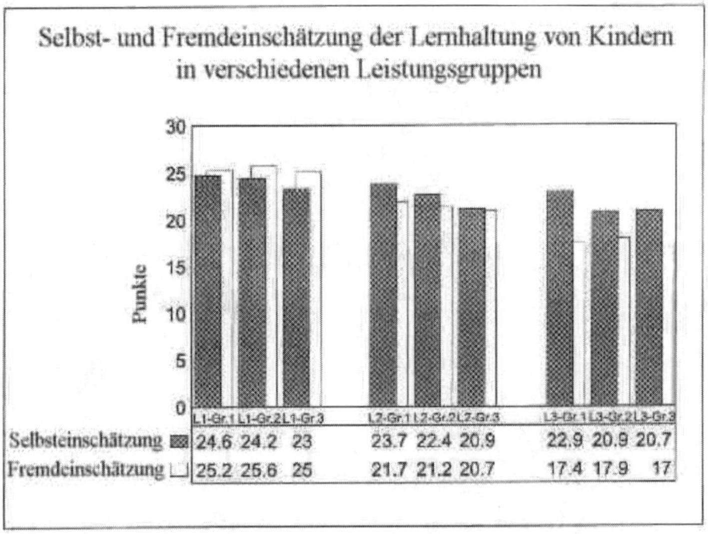

Abb. 4.5.4 Selbst- und Fremdeinschätzung in den Leistungsgruppen

Es ist zu sehen, dass

- die Fremdeinschätzungen der Lehrerinnen in den jeweiligen Leistungsgruppen relativ stabil sind und die Höhe dieser Einschätzungen von der Zugehörigkeit zur Leistungsgruppe abhängt;
- die Fremdeinschätzung erfolgreich lernender Kinder in allen drei Schuljahren höher ist als die Selbsteinschätzung dieser Kinder;
- bei den weniger erfolgreich lernenden Schülern und Schülerinnen eine große Diskrepanz zwischen Selbst- und Fremdeinschätzung besteht, die Fremdeinschätzung immer schlechter als die Fremdeinschätzung ist, die Kinder sich jedoch der Fremdeinschätzung allmählich annähern;

- das Fremdbild der Lehrerinnen sich schon im ersten Schuljahr entwickelt hat und in den folgenden Schuljahren relativ stabil bleibt.

5. Die Kinder erlernen Bewältigungsstrategien, um ihr Selbstwertgefühl zu erhalten. Die Prozesse laufen spontan ab, d.h. es ist bisher nicht Anliegen der Erziehung, entwicklungsfördernde Strategien bewußt mit den Kindern zu erarbeiten. Das, was den Kindern zur Konfliktlösung einfällt, äußert sich dann oft als ‚verhaltensauffällig', nicht normangepaßt und störend. Die Kinder selbst fühlen sich dabei immer weniger wohl, nicht wenige werden physisch und/oder psychisch krank.
6. Es sind vor allem die in der Schule erhaltenen leistungsbezogenen Bewertungen, die sowohl die Entwicklung des schul- und lernbezogenen Selbstbildes als auch das Selbstwertgefühl des Kindes beeinflussen. In welchem Ausmaß und mit welchen Folgen das geschieht, hängt zunächst mehr von den Reaktionen der Eltern und Lehrerinnen als von den konkret erbrachten Leistungen ab, weil die Kinder zunächst sich selbst nicht einschätzen können. Erhalten die Kinder vorwiegend negative selbstbezogene Informationen, dann werden diese gespeichert und der dann entstandene negative Selbstwert bewirkt, dass bei zukünftigen Informationen insbesondere die negativen wahrgenommen, wiederum gespeichert und später erinnert werden. Ein stabiles Selbstwertgefühl ist auch gegenüber widersprüchlichen Informationen resistent (vgl. Frey & Benning 1983, 165). Das ist besonders tragisch für Kinder mit negativem Selbstwertgefühl. Ein legasthenisches Kind mit negativem Selbstwertgefühl wird weniger bereit sein, eine positive Information zu akzeptieren. Es wird sie eher so interpretieren, dass das Selbstbild nicht verändert werden muss („Die Lehrerin hat ja es extra leicht für mich gemacht", „Das war Zufall" o.ä.). Auf diese Weise verschafft es sich ständig Misserfolg, der entmotivierend wirkt und die Wahrscheinlichkeit eines tatsächlichen Misserfolgs ständig erhöht. Wir haben es dann mit einem schwer zu durchbrechenden Teufelskreis zu tun. Leider gibt es die Erfahrung, dass manche die Tendenz, vor allem Negatives bezüglich ihrer Person wahrzunehmen, bis ins Erwachsenenalter nicht loswerden.

Kinder, die den Anforderungen nicht oder noch nicht gewachsen sind, geraten leicht in eine Stresssituation. Sie müssen sich mit dieser Situation auseinandersetzen und entsprechende Bewältigungsstrategien entwickeln. Dabei benötigen sie Hilfe, das heißt, dass die Schule durchaus der geeignete Platz ist, um die notwendigen Kompetenzen zu entwickeln. Bis heute ist das noch nicht oder nur in begrenztem Umfang möglich, weil sowohl die institutionellen Voraussetzungen als auch die notwendigen Voraussetzungen bei den Lehrkräften geschaffen werden müssen. Die gegenwärtigen Rahmenrichtlinien lassen jedoch durchaus das Erproben neuer Wege zu (vgl. Zubke 1999). Dabei kann das im folgenden dargestellte und erprobte Förderprogramm sicherlich hilfreich sein.

3 Selbstwertstärkung in der Schule?

Wenn junge Menschen durchschnittlich 15.000 Stunden ihres Lebens in der Schule verbringen und das in der Regel für jedes Mädchen und jeden Jungen zutrifft, dann bietet sich damit auch die einzigartige Möglichkeit, mit Programmen zur Gesundheitsförderung tatsächlich alle zu erreichen. Außerdem können solche Programme langfristig und komplex sein, sie können in früher Kindheit beginnen und in fester Partnerschaft von Lehrerinnen und Eltern erfolgen.

Wird Gesundheitsförderung nicht als Bearbeitung von Einzelproblemen verstanden, z.B. Verhinderung und Einschränkung von Nikotinmißbrauch, sondern als Möglichkeit, Kinder zu befähigen, mit Risiken, Problemen, Krisen und auch täglichen Anforderungen kompetent umgehen zu können, Kontrolle über ihr eigenes Handeln zu erlernen und das Bewußtsein des eigenen Wertes zu stärken, dann entspricht das den Zielen von Bildung und Erziehung. Gesundheitsförderung ist nichts Zusätzliches oder Schulfremdes, sondern vielmehr ein integrativer Bestandteil des Lernens und Lebens in der Schule.

Von der WHO wurde in den neunziger Jahren ein neuer Ansatz der Gesundheitsförderung propagiert, der sogenannte „Life Skills Ansatz". Lebenskompetenzen („Life Skills") sind nach Definition der WHO „... diejenigen Fähigkeiten, die einen angemessenen Umgang sowohl mit unseren Mitmenschen als auch mit den Problemen und Streßsituationen im alltäglichen Leben ermöglichen. Solche Fähigkeiten sind bedeutsam für die Stärkung der psychosozialen Kompetenzen" (WHO 1993).

Solche psychosozialen Kompetenzen zu entwickeln – an dieser Aufgabe wird Schule nicht vorbei gehen können. Wichtig ist zu beachten, dass diese Kompetenzen ebenso zielgerichtet ausgebildet werden müssen wie intellektuelle Kompetenzen. Gegenwärtig wird das in verschiedenen Einzelprojekten erprobt. Hier sollen Erfahrungen eines eigenen Projektes berichtet und vorgestellt werden.

4 Das Forschungsprojekt „Ich bin Ich – Gesundheit fördern durch Selbstwertstärkung"

Das Forschungsprojekt „Ich bin Ich – Gesundheit fördern durch Selbstwertstärkung" entstand 1994 als ein Gemeinschaftsprojekt von Wissenschaftler/n/innen der Universitäten Greifswald und Göttingen[1]. Es wurde als Längsschnittstudie von 1995 bis 1999 geplant.

In beiden Städten wurde in jeweils 4 Schulen, d. h. in 20 Schulklassen, ein Programm zur Gesundheitsförderung durchgeführt, dessen Schwerpunkt auf dem Erhalt und der Förderung des positiven Selbstwertgefühls der Kinder und dem Erwerb von Kompetenzen zum Umgang mit Stressoren liegt.

Wir haben nicht mit sogenannten ‚Risikokindern', sondern mit der ganzen Klasse gearbeitet. Dennoch sind wir der Meinung, dass Kinder, deren Selbstwertgefühl sich als Resultat von schulischem Leistungsversagen verändert, davon profitieren.

Das Förderprogramm wurde, beginnend im 1. Schuljahr und fortlaufend bis zum 4. Schuljahr, von Gesundheitsteams durchgeführt. Zu einem Gesundheitsteam gehörten die Projektmitarbeiter und –mitarbeiterinnen (meist Studierende), die Klassenlehrerinnen und gegebenenfalls interessierte Eltern.

Ausgangshypothese des Projektes war, dass Vorschulkinder in der Regel ein positives Selbstbild und Selbstwertgefühl haben und damit wichtigste Widerstandsressourcen besitzen. Dies bestätigte auch das Ergebnis der Schuleingangsuntersuchung (vgl. Abb. 4.5.1).

1 Die Projektleitung lag in den Händen von Frau Prof. Dr. Christina Krause (Georg-August-Universität Göttingen), Frau Dr. Christel Rohde und Herrn Prof. Dr. Hans-Joachim Hannich (Ernst-Moritz-Arndt-Universität Greifswald). Ende 1996 übernahm Herr Dr. Ulrich Wiesmann die Aufgaben von Frau Dr. Christel Rohde.

4.1 Ziele des Projekts

Im einzelnen hat das Forschungsprojekt folgende Ziele:

1. Ein Modell zur Stärkung gesundheitsförderlicher Faktoren und zur Befähigung von Grundschüler/innen, Belastungen kompetent bewältigen zu können erarbeiten und erproben.
2. Erhaltung und Förderung des positiven Selbstwertgefühls und des Wohlbefindens der am Projekt beteiligten Kinder.
3. Die Machbarkeit von Gesundheitsstunden und -tagen in der Grundschule erproben. Gesundheitsteams an den Projektschulen etablieren, zur Umsetzung des Programms anleiten und die Arbeit immanent evaluieren.
4. Erfahrungen aus der erweiterten Schuleingangsuntersuchung in Kooperation mit den Schulärztinnen analysieren und evtl. Forderungen ableiten.

Theoretische Grundlage für das Verständnis von Gesundheit ist dabei das salutogenetische Konzept von Antonovsky (1993), das die Entwicklung und Förderung von Kompetenzen zum Umgang mit Risiken in den Mittelpunkt stellt.

Gesundheitsförderung wird von uns als Möglichkeit verstanden, Kinder zu befähigen, mit Risiken, Problemen, Krisen und auch täglichen Anforderungen kompetent umgehen zu können, Kontrolle über ihr Handeln zu erlernen und das Bewußtsein des eigenen Wertes zu stärken.

4.2 Inhalte des Projekts

Unser Anliegen, eine der wichtigsten Widerstandsressourcen im Kindesalter – ein positives Selbstwertgefühl – zu stärken bzw. zu fördern, bestimmt auch die Inhalte des Programms, wobei wir uns auf fünf Schwerpunkte konzentrieren[2]:

- ***Selbstwertstärkende Selbstreflexion***
- ***Körpererfahrung und Körperbewußtsein***
- ***Gesundheitsförderliche Interaktion und Kommunikation***
- ***Freizeitverhalten und Gesundheit***
- ***Gesunde Ernährung***

Auf dieser Grundlage wurden im ersten Schuljahr 15 Gesundheitsstunden und im zweiten, dritten und vierten Schuljahr fünf Gesundheitstage mit je drei Stunden entwickelt.

2 Zur Beschreibung dieser Schwerpunkte vgl. „Bericht über den Fachkongreß 1997“, S. 233f. und Krause (1998).

1. Ich stelle mich vor	6. Manchmal bin ich traurig, manchmal bin ich froh (I)	11. Ich sehe fern (I)
2. Ich und mein Körper	7. Manchmal bin ich traurig, manchmal bin ich froh (II)	12. Ich habe Angst
3. Das bin Ich	8. Ich habe mich erkältet	13. Ich bewege mich (I)
4. Ich entspanne mich	9. Dann geht es mir wieder besser	14. Ich bewege mich (II)
5. Ich bin fröhlich	10. Was ich esse und trinke	15. Zirkusfest

Tabelle 4.5.3: Themen der Gesundheitsstunden im ersten Schuljahr

2. Klasse	**3. Klasse**	**4. Klasse**
1. Ich bewege mich (III)	1. Ich sehe, rieche, höre und fühle	1. Ich sehe fern (III) Gewalt im Fernsehen
2. Wir ernähren uns gesund	2. Ich bin Ich	1. Ich fühle mich nicht wohl
3. Manchmal bin ich traurig, froh, wütend oder ängstlich	3. Wie wir Konflikte lösen	2. Ich und meine Familie
4. Wie wir miteinander umgehen	4. Ich bin ein Junge..., ich bin ein Mädchen	3. Ich und die Natur
5. Ich sehe fern (II)	5. Wie ich mich einen Tag allein verpflege	4. Bleib gesund! (Abschiedsfest)

Tabelle 4.5.4 Themen der Gesundheitstage im zweiten, dritten und vierten Schuljahr

4.3 Organisation und Durchführung

Nach der Erarbeitung eines ersten Vorschlages für einen Gesundheitstag, wurde dieser mit den Lehrerinnen der beteiligten Projektschulen besprochen und diskutiert.

Der so entstandene Gesundheitstag wurde dann in allen beteiligten Klassen von Gesundheitsteams durchgeführt, wobei in jeder Schule ein Gesundheitsteam arbeitete.

Zu Beginn war die Einbindung der Gesundheitsstunden in den Stundenplan unterschiedlich. Es gab Schulen, die diese Gesundheitsstunden von Anfang an in den Stundenplan einbauten, es gab aber auch Schulen, die sie als zusätzliche Unterrichtsstunde an den Stundenplan anhängten.

Nach dem ersten Schuljahr hatte sich das Projekt so etabliert, dass dieser Zustand sich veränderte und alle Schulen die Gesundheitstage in den Stundenplan integrierten.

Ein wichtiges Element unserer Arbeit ist die Zusammenarbeit mit den Lehrerinnen und den Eltern. Schon bei der Konzipierung des Projektes haben wir die Zusammenarbeit mit den Eltern und Lehrerinnen als einen Schwerpunkt herausgearbeitet. So wurden z.B. noch vor Beginn der ersten Untersuchungen umfangreiche Gespräche mit den Lehrerinnen geführt.

Die Eltern wurden nicht nur informiert und um ihr Einverständnis gebeten, sondern auch zur aktiven Mitarbeit aufgefordert. Im Verlauf des Schuljahres wurde häufiger versucht, mehr mit den Eltern ins Gespräch zu kommen. Selbstverständlich war das ein Lernprozeß auf beiden Seiten.

Am Ende des Schuljahres wurde je ein Workshop in Göttingen und Greifswald durchgeführt, an dem die Projektmitarbeiter/innen und Lehrerinnen sowie Schulleiterinnen teilnahmen. Dabei wurden u.a. die Themen der Gesundheitstage für das darauffolgende Schuljahr erarbeitet.

Bei der *Durchführung* des Projekts haben wir von Anfang an großen Wert auf die Einführung und Einhaltung von Ritualen gelegt. Das sind vor allem:

➢ ***Die Entspannungsübung***

Der erste Teil der Gesundheitsstunde bzw. -tage gehört immer der Entspannungsübung. Die Kinder setzen oder legen sich auf ihre Matten und lernen, sich auf unterschiedlichste Weise zu entspannen.

➢ ***Begrüßung und Abschiedsritual***

Zur Begrüßung sitzen die Kinder im Kreis (ev. bereits auf den Liegematten für die Entspannungsübung). Sie werden mit „Gesundheit“ begrüßt und erhalten eine Einführung in den Gesundheitstag. An der Wand oder Tafel hängt das *Logo*, auf dem eine lachende Birne und ein lachender Apfel abgebildet sind.

Die letzten fünf Minuten der Gesundheitsstunde bzw. des Gesundheitstages werden dem Abschiedsritual, dem ‚Kleinen Tschüs‘, gewidmet: Die Kinder stehen im Kreis und fassen sich an den Händen. Ein Kind schickt das ‚Kleine Tschüs‘ auf die Reise. Es wird durch Händedruck weitergegeben. Wenn es beim ersten Kind wieder angekommen ist, sagt dieses laut „Tschüs“, und alle verabschieden sich.

➢ ***Die Arbeitsmappe***

Jedes Kind erhält in der ersten Gesundheitsstunde eine Arbeitsmappe (DIN A3 – Format). Alle während der Gesundheitsstunden bzw. –tage angefertigten Produkte werden darin gesammelt. Sie wird in der Schule aufbewahrt, die Eltern können jederzeit Einblick nehmen (z.B. am Elternabend).

➢ ***Kleingruppenarbeit***

Damit jedes Kind aktiv werden kann, sich angesprochen fühlt und seine Gefühle, Einstellungen und Wünsche mitteilen kann, wird möglichst viel in Kleingruppen gearbeitet. Ein sinnvoller Wechsel von Klein- und Großgruppe muß bereits bei der Planung mitbedacht werden.

4.4 Beispiel eines Gesundheitstages

Grundsätzlich sehen wir Selbsterfahrung und Selbsttätigkeit als wichtige Elemente, um der Zielstellung unseres Projektes gerecht zu werden. Daher ist die ***Förderung von Selbsterfahrung und Selbsttätigkeit*** ein weiterer wichtiger Baustein der Gesundheitsstunden bzw. –tage: Selbsttun und erfolgreich sein schafft positive Gefühle und stärkt das Selbstwertgefühl. Von positiven Gefühlen begleitetes Lernen unterstützt den Lernerfolg. Das, was man kann, tut man gern. Diese psychologischen Zusammenhänge versuchten wir bei den Überlegungen zu den einzelnen Stunden bzw. Tagen zu berücksichtigen. Es gibt keine Stunde, in der die Kinder nicht selbst etwas gestalten können.

Folgende Prinzipien waren bei der Gestaltung der Tätigkeit der Kinder an den Gesundheitstagen maßgeblich:

- Freiraum für selbsttätiges Handeln mit dem Ziel der Stärkung von Kompetenzen und Selbständigkeit ermöglichen.
- Die kindlichen Bedürfnisse, eigene Erfahrungen aktiv zu erleben, achten.
- Dem Streben nach Freiheit und der Neugierde, Neues zu entdecken, Zeit und Raum lassen.
- Altersgerechte Aufgaben unter Berücksichtigung des kognitiven, sozialen und emotionalen Entwicklungsstandes von Grundschulkindern formulieren.

Die Erwachsenen (Teamerinnen) geben als begleitende Betreuungspersonen den Kindern im Rahmen der jeweiligen Themen Denkanstöße, lassen ihnen jedoch Zeit und Raum für die Entwicklung eigener Ideen und Probelmlösungen.

Um Selbsttätigkeit und Selbsterfahrung in den Gesundheitstagen herauszufordern und zu fördern haben wir im wesentlichen folgende immer wiederkehrenden Bausteine verwendet:

➢ ***Entspannungsübungen,***
➢ ***Rollenspiele,***
➢ ***Malen bzw. Zeichnen und***
➢ ***Kreatives Gestalten.***

4.5 Untersuchungsmethoden und Evaluation

Wir untersuchten in unserem Projekt jedes Jahr das Selbstbild und die emotionale Befindlichkeit der Kinder. Im Mittelpunkt standen dabei folgende Fragen:

1. Wie entwickelt und verändert sich das Selbstbild und das Selbstwertgefühl der Kinder während der Grundschulzeit?
2. Welche Bewältigungsstrategien haben die Kinder und wie verändern sie sich über die Schuljahre?
3. Wie verändert sich die Befindlichkeit der Kinder?

Die erste Untersuchung fand nach der Schuleingangsuntersuchung, also am Ende der Kindergartenzeit statt. In der ersten, zweiten, dritten und vierten Klasse wurden die Kinder jeweils am Ende des Schuljahres befragt.

Der Gesundheitstag „Ich bin Ich“ (3. Klasse)

Zeit	Verlauf	Aktionsformen	Material
20 min	**Entspannungsübung**	Großgruppe	Logo, Kassetten-recorder, Text
15 min	**Wir hören die Geschichte vom „Ich bin Ich“** Die Teamerin zeigt zur Motivation der Kinder ein selbstgebasteltes „Ich bin Ich“. Die Kinder hören der Geschichte, die von einer Teamerin vorgelesen wird, die Kinder sehen zu und sehen sich dazu vorbereitete Farbfolien an.	vorlesen	„Das kleine Ich bin ich“ von Mira Lobe, OH-Projektor, Farbfolien
10 min	**Wir sprechen über die Geschichte** Die Kinder bilden Kleingruppen, in denen über das Geschehen in der Geschichte gesprochen wird. Dabei stehen das „Ich bin Ich“ und die Tiere, denen es begegnet, im Mittelpunkt: • Was ist dem „Ich bin Ich“ passiert? • Warum fragt das „Ich bin Ich“ wer es ist? • Wie hat sich das „Ich bin Ich“ verhalten? • Was ist das Besondere am „Ich bin Ich“? • Ihr habt nun gesehen wie das „Ich bin Ich“ in der Tierwelt auf die Suche gegangen ist. Könnt ihr euch vorstellen, dass (auch) wir Menschen nach jemandem suchen, der einem sagt, wer man ist und wozu und zu wem man gehört?	Kleingruppe Gespräch	
Pause			
45 min	**Wir basteln ein „Ich bin Ich“ (I)** Die Kinder basteln aus Stoffresten <u>ihr</u> „Ich bin Ich“.	basteln	Schere, Nadel, Faden, bunte Stoffreste (pro Kind 1mal 20x20, 1 mal 15x15, 1 mal 26x3), Füllwatte, Stifte, Klebstoff, Bastelanleitung
Pause			

10 min	**Weiterarbeit am „Ich bin Ich"**	basteln	s.o.
10 min	**Ich bin ein besonderes Kind unter vielen anderen Kindern** Hierbei werden Parallelen zwischen den Erlebnissen des „Ich bin Ich" in der Tierwelt und den Erfahrungen der Kinder in ihrer Umwelt gezogen. Dieses Gespräch bereitet die Kinder auf das folgende Malen eines Puzzles vor.	Gespräch	
20 min	**Wir gestalten ein Puzzle** Jedes Kind erhält 5 Puzzleteile: Auf das mittlere Puzzleteil malt das Kind sich selbst, auf die anderen vier Teile kann es das malen, was zu ihm gehört (z.B. bestimmte Dinge oder auch Eigenschaften). Anschließend werden die Puzzleteile mit einem Rand (versch. Farben, Muster) gekennzeichnet. Die Puzzleteile aller Kinder werden gesammelt und gemischt. Die Kinder erstellen dann gemeinsam ein „Klassenpuzzle", bei dem alle Teile auf einem großen Blatt Papier wieder zusammengefügt werden. Damit wird gewährleistet, dass sich jedes Kind sowohl mit seinem Puzzlefeld als auch mit der Klasse identifizieren kann.	malen, basteln Großgruppe, kleben	Puzzleteile (Anlage 2/2), Stifte, Klebstoff, Papier DIN A0
5 min	**Abschlußkreis** Das kleine „Tschüs" geht auf die Reise.	Kinder stehen im Kreis	

Tabelle 4.5.5. Ablauf des Gesundheitstages (3. Klasse)

Der *reine Längsschnitt*, d.h. die Population der Kinder, die an allen Befragungen teilgenommen haben, umfaßt *158 Kinder*. Darunter befanden sich im vierten Schuljahr 28 Kinder mit Lern- und Leistungsschwierigkeiten (LLS).

Die Kinder wurden jedes Jahr mit folgenden Instrumenten/Verfahren untersucht[3]:

➤ ***Fragebogen „Gesundheitsprofil"***

Der Fragebogen, der ähnlich wie ein mündliche Interview aufgebaut ist, enthält Fragen zur Befindlichkeit, Fragen zum Freizeitverhalten sowie zur Lebenswelt der Kinder.

Die Antwortkategorien sind mit passenden Bildern illustriert, die eine kindgerechte Beantwortung der Fragen ermöglichen.

➤ ***Bilderwahlverfahren***

Das Bilderwahlverfahren wurde von Krause entwickelt. Es erfaßt das subjektive Erleben von Kindern beim Betrachten alltäglicher Tätigkeiten, die von Kindern (oder Tieren) ausgeübt werden. In der ersten Untersuchung handelte es sich um 24 Tätigkeiten, in der ersten Klasse

3 Eine ausführliche Darstellung der Evaluationsmethoden findet sich im „Bericht über den Fachkongreß 1997", S. 237ff.

(2. Untersuchung) wurden zusätzliche schulspezifische Tätigkeiten, z.B. lesen, rechnen, schreiben, aufgenommen.

Die Kinder sollen dabei zu jeder Tätigkeit sagen, ob sie diese gern, manchmal gern oder gar nicht gern tun.

➢ ***Satzergänzungstest***

Beim Satzergänzungstest handelt es sich um ein halb-strukturiertes offenes Verfahren. Er erlaubt sowohl den intra- als auch den interindividuellen Vergleich. Durch die Vorgabe des Satzanfangs wird die Thematik festgelegt, dennoch kann durch die Vervollständigung der Sätze die subjektive Bedeutsamkeit und Betroffenheit der Proband/en/innen erhoben werden.

Die Kinder ergänzen dabei folgende acht Satzanfänge:

1. Wenn ich etwas nicht schaffe
2. Ich finde nicht schön
3. Die anderen Kinder
4. Ich habe Angst.
5. Ich bin traurig
6. Am meisten freue ich mich
7. Ich ärgere mich
8. In der Schule

Zusätzlich wurde im dritten Schuljahr der ***„Fragebogen zur Erhebung von Streßerleben und Streßbewältigung im Kindesalter“*** von Lohaus et al. (1996) und im vierten Schuljahr die ***„Aussagen-Liste zum Selbstwertgefühl“*** (ALS) von Schauder (1996) eingesetzt.

5 Ergebnisse

Im folgenden werden ausgewählte Ergebnisse der Kinder mit und ohne Lern- und Leistungsschwierigkeiten (LLS) vorgestellt.

1. Ergebnisse aus dem Satzergänzungstest

Der achte Satz „In der Schule...“ thematisiert die Schule, die als wichtiger Bereich im Leben des Kindes großen Einfluß auf das Selbstbild und Selbstwertgefühl des Kindes hat.

Zu Beginn der Längsschnittuntersuchung besuchten die Kinder noch den Kindergarten. Ihre Aussagen zum Satzanfang „In der Schule...“ beziehen sich daher auf theoretisches Wissen und Erwartungen bzw. Vorstellungen bezüglich der Schule. Aufgrund theoretischer Vorüberlegungen kann angenommen werden, dass sich die Mehrzahl der Kinder vor Schulbeginn auf die Schule freut und die Schule positiv bewertet (vgl. Knöfel 1990, S.58ff.; Speck-Hamdan 1990, S.27).

Das ‚Schul- und lernbezogene Selbstbild‘ entsteht in Auseinandersetzung mit den Anforderungen und Bedingungen der Schule. Es entwickelt sich im Verlauf der ersten zwei Schuljahre zur dominanten Substruktur und wird v.a. durch die schulische Leistung bzw. deren Bewertung durch Lehrer/innen, Eltern und Mitschüler/innen beeinflußt.

Abbildung 4.5.5 zeigt die Entwicklung der Aussagen bei den Kindern beider Gruppen.

Die Ergebnisse zeigen, dass die *Kinder mit LLS*

- ➢ in den ersten zwei Untersuchungen neutrale Aussagen zur Schule (ohne Bewertung) vorzogen (z.B. „In der Schule basteln wir“);
- ➢ ab dem dritten Schuljahr weniger positive Aussagen zur Schule machten (z.B. „In der Schule ist es schön“; „In der Schule gefällt es mir“);

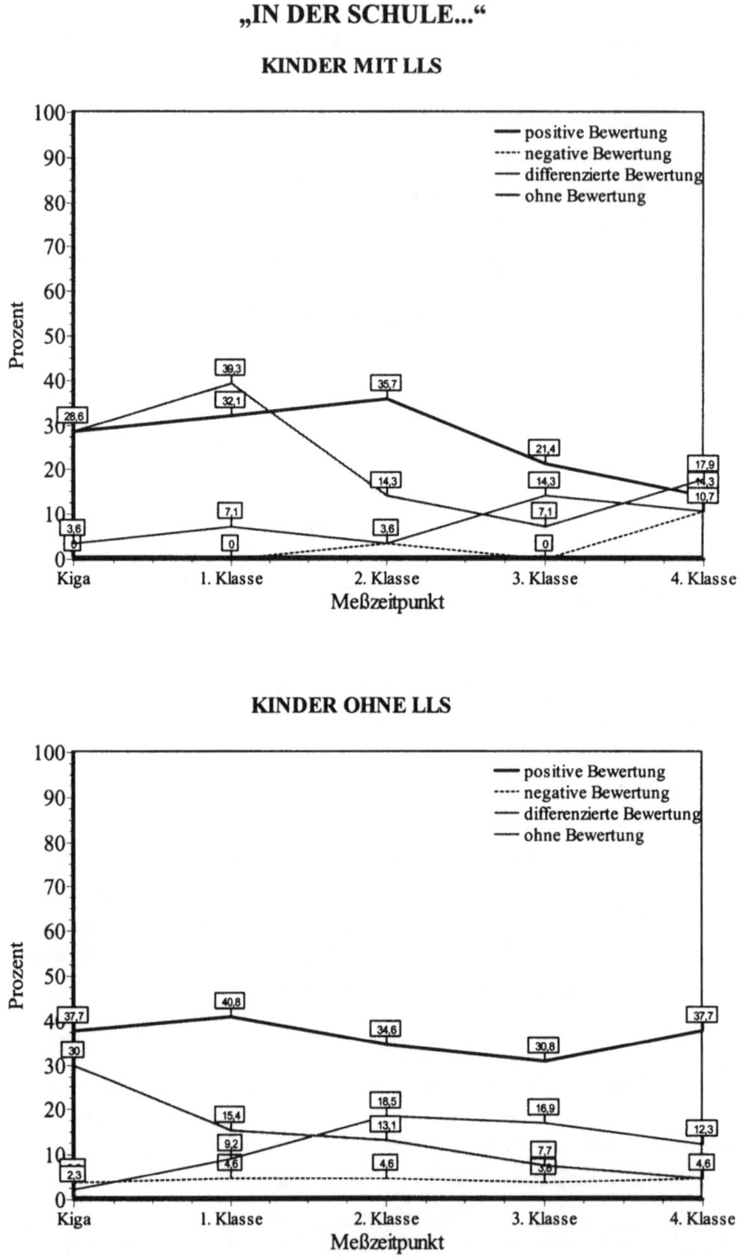

Abb. 4.5.5 Häufigkeit der Aussagen zu Satz 8 „In der Schule...“ bei Kindern mit LLS (n=28) und Kindern ohne LLS (n=130).

- im vierten Schuljahr am häufigsten (ca. 10%) negative Bewertungen der Schule vornahmen (z.B. „In der Schule finde ich es blöd").

Außerdem zeigt sich , dass die *Kinder ohne LLS*

- die Schule zu allen Untersuchungszeitpunkten positiv bewerteten;
- kaum negative Bewertungen der Schule vornahmen. Es waren pro Schuljahr vier bzw. fünf Kinder, die in dieses Kategorie einzuordnen waren;
- im Unterschied zu den Kindern mit LLS kontinuierlich immer weniger Kinder eine neutrale Aussage zur Schule (ohne Bewertung) machten.

Bemerkenswert ist, dass die ‚Differenzierten Bewertungen der Schule' (z.B. „In der Schule ist es manchmal gut und manchmal schlecht") in beiden Gruppen zunahmen.

Exemplarisch für eine zunehmend ‚negative Bewertung der Schule bzw. Befindlichkeit in der Schule' bei Kindern mit LLS werden die Satzergänzungen des Schülers K227 vorgestellt:

Satzanfang	**1. Klasse**	**2. Klasse**	**3. Klasse**	**4. Klasse**
Wenn ich etwas nicht schaffe	versuch ich´s nochmal.	versuch ich es nochmal.	hol ich jemanden der mir hilft.	dann versuch ich es wieder.
Ich finde nicht schön		keine Ahnung.	wenn mein Bruder mich ärgert.	dass es die Schule gibt.
Die anderen Kinder	spielen.	spielen mit mir Fußball.		
Ich habe Angst	ich laufe weg.	vor gar nicht.		vor nichts.
Ich bin traurig	ich weine.	niemals.		
Am meisten freue ich mich	wenn ich was geschenkt kriege.	wenn ich Fußball spiele.		wenn ich ein neues Computerspiel bekomme.
Ich ärgere mich	will ich meine Ruhe haben.	wenn mein Bruder mich ärgert.		über andere Erwachsene.
In der Schule	schreiben wir.	finde ich es nicht gut.		ist es Scheiße.

Abb. 4.5.6 Satzergänzungen des Schülers K227

2. Ergebnisse aus dem Gesundheitsprofil

WIE GEFÄLLT ES DIR IN DER SCHULE?

KINDER MIT LLS

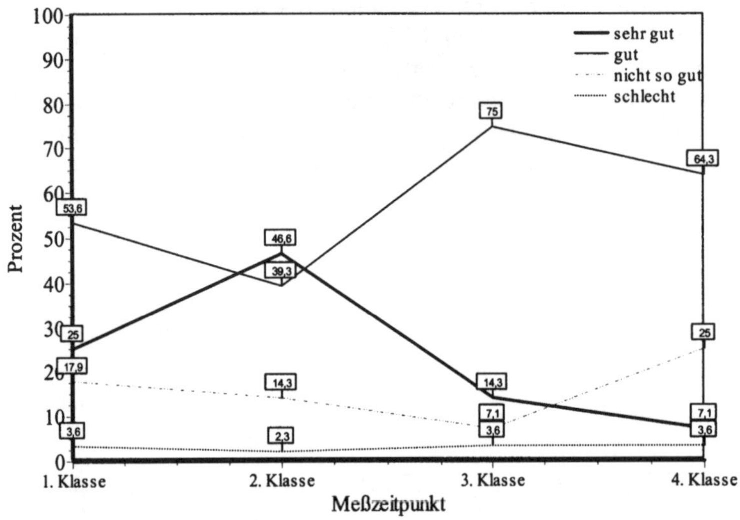

KINDER OHNE LLS

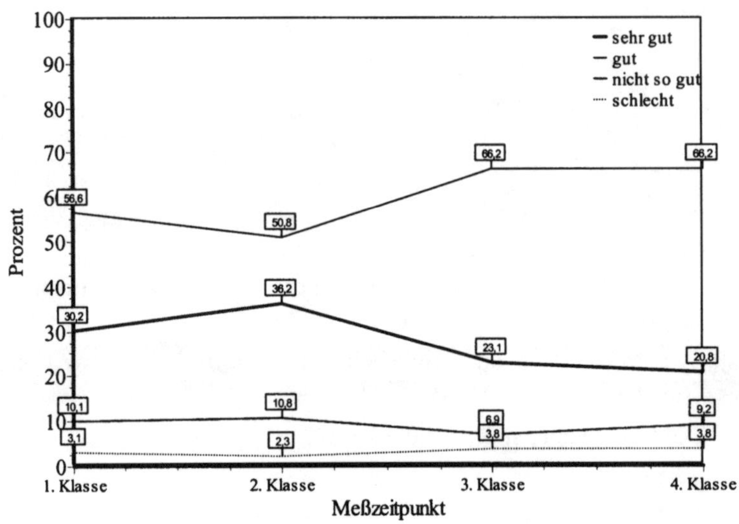

Abb. 4.5.7 Häufigkeit der Antworten zu „Wie gefällt es Dir in der Schule?“ bei Kindern mit LLS (n=28) und Kindern ohne LLS (n=130).

Der Fragebogen „Gesundheitsprofil" beinhaltet ein Item, das Auskunft über die Befindlichkeit der Kinder in der Schule geben soll. Es handelt sich um die Frage „Wie gefällt es Dir in der Schule?".

Abbildung 4.5.7 zeigt die Entwicklung der Antworten zu dieser Frage bei den Kindern mit und ohne LLS. Die Kinder hatten dabei die Möglichkeit, auf einer Skala von ‚sehr gut', ‚gut', ‚nicht so gut' und ‚schlecht' zu antworten.

In den Ergebnissen der Frage *„Wie gefällt es Dir in der Schule?"* kommt zum Ausdruck, dass sich die Mehrzahl der Kinder in der Schule wohl fühlt und eine positive Beziehung zur Schule hat; sie gaben an, dass es ihnen in der Schule ‚gut' bzw. ‚sehr gut' gefällt.

Die Befindlichkeit in der Schule sowie die positive Beziehung zur Schule steigt bei allen Kindern in der zweiten Klasse zunächst an, was in einer Zunahme der Antworten in der Kategorie ‚sehr gut' deutlich wird.

Dies stimmt auch mit an anderer Stelle gefundenen Ergebnissen, die zeigen, dass die emotionale Befindlichkeit der Kinder in der Schule in den ersten zwei Schuljahren hoch ist, überein (vgl. Knöfel 1990, S.106, Breuer & Weuffen 1996, S.19).

Unterschiede zwischen beiden Gruppen bestehen darin, dass sich die Befindlichkeit der Kinder mit LLS ab dem dritten Schuljahr auffällig verändert: ‚sehr gut' sinkt im dritten Schuljahr auf 14,3% ab, ‚nicht so gut' steigt im vierten Schuljahr auf 25% an (vgl. Stückle 1999, S.69ff.).

3. Ergebnisse aus dem Bilderwahlverfahren

Im Bilderwahlverfahren „Was ich gerne tue" können Ergebnisse, die Aussagen zum Selbsterleben des Kindes in der Schule ermöglichen, gewonnen werden.

Abbildung 4.5.8 zeigt die Entwicklung der Antworten der Kinder mit und ohne LLS in Bezug auf die Frage „Liest Du gern/ manchmal gern/ gar nicht gern?". Die meisten Kinder lesen in der Grundschulzeit ‚gern'. Es ist aber nicht zu übersehen, dass ca. 20% der Kinder mit LLS ‚gar nicht gern' lesen.

4. Auswirkungen auf das ‚Allgemeine Wohlbefinden'

Wie wirken sich diese Veränderungen im Selbstbild des Kindes, die im Zusammenhang mit schulischem Erfolg und Mißerfolg entstanden sind, auf das ‚Allgemeine Wohlbefinden' und das Selbstwertgefühl aus? Antwort darauf gibt die Frage „Wie fühlst Du Dich meistens?" aus dem Gesundheitsprofil. Den Kindern standen dabei die Antwortkategorien ‚froh', ‚traurig', ‚müde', sauer', und ‚wütend' zur Verfügung.

Abbildung 4.5.9 zeigt die Entwicklung der Antworten bei den Kindern mit und ohne LLS.

Es wird deutlich, dass sich die Mehrzahl der Kinder sowohl vor Schulbeginn als auch während der Schulzeit subjektiv wohl fühlt – sie gaben an sich meistens froh zu fühlen. Es werden jedoch Unterschiede zwischen den Kindern mit und ohne LLS deutlich: Während bei der Schuleingangsuntersuchung ca. 90% der Kinder ohne LLS angaben, sich meistens froh zu fühlen, gaben ‚nur' 70% der Kinder mit LLS eine entsprechende Antwort.

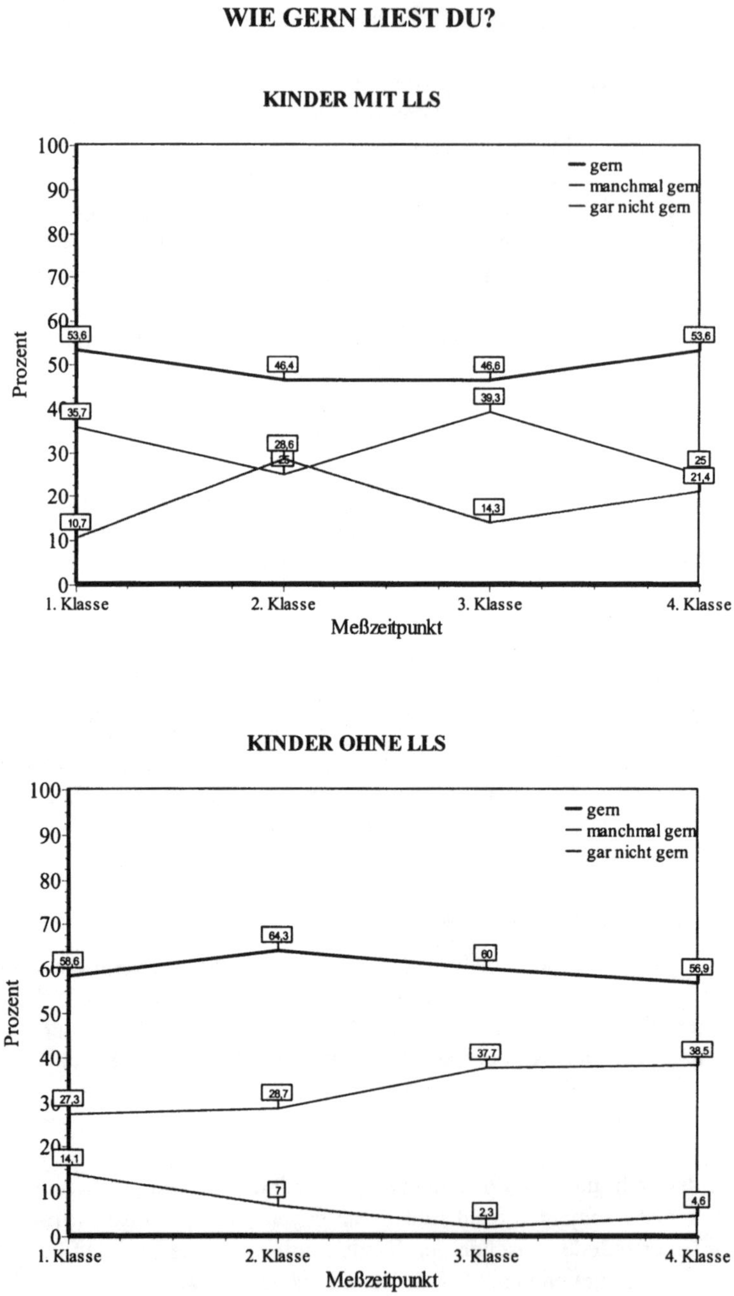

Abb. 4.5.8 Häufigkeit der Antworten zu „Wie gern liest Du?“ bei Kindern mit LLS (n=28) und Kindern ohne LLS (n=130).

WIE FÜHLST DU DICH MEISTENS?

KINDER MIT LLS

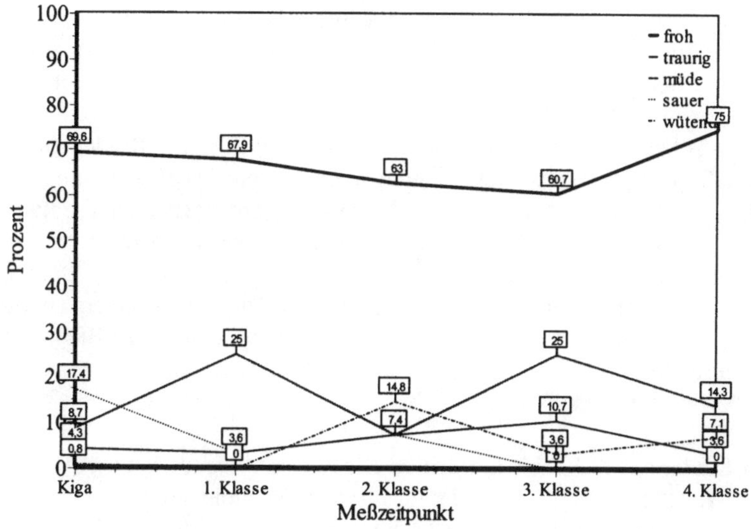

KINDER OHNE LLS

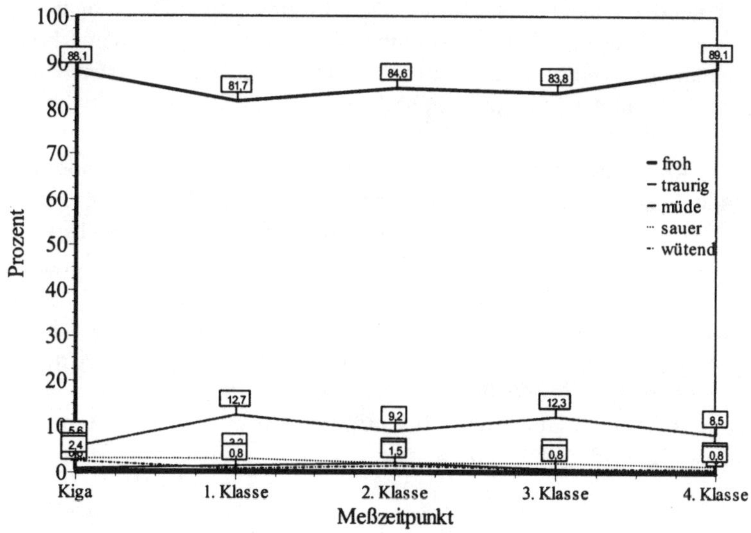

Abb. 4.5.9 Häufigkeit der Antworten zu „Wie fühlst Du Dich meistens?“ bei Kindern mit LLS (n=28) und Kindern ohne LLS (n=130).

6 Diskussion

Schon vor Schulbeginn hatten 30% der von uns befragten Kinder, die später Lernschwierigkeiten entwickelten, eine negative emotionale Befindlichkeit. Dies legt die Vermutung nahe, dass diese – zumindest bei einem Teil der Kinder – auslösend für die Probleme im schulischen Leistungsbereich waren. Daraus ergibt sich die Forderung in der Schuleingangsuntersuchung „zukünftig nicht nur medizinische Parameter zu erfassen, sondern den psychosozialen Entwicklungsstand der Kinder ebenfalls zu ermitteln, um den ‚gefährdeten' Kindern den Schulstart zu erleichtern".

Allerdings bedeutet dieses Ergebnis auch, dass bei 70% der Kinder mit LLS das Versagen im schulischen Leistungsbereich ‚unerwartet' eintrat. Da sich darunter einige Kinder vermuten lassen, deren Differenzierungsfähigkeiten nicht ausreichend entwickelt waren, könnten diese Probleme mit Hilfe der Differenzierungsprobe von Breuer & Weuffen (1996) erkannt und eine Frühförderung noch vor Schulbeginn eingeleitet werden. Denkbar wäre aber auch, die Förderung der Differenzierungsfähigkeiten in den Anfangsunterricht aufzunehmen. Dies würde ermöglichen, den Kindern schon vor Schulbeginn bzw. zu Beginn der Schulzeit zu helfen, diese Fähigkeiten ausreichend weiter zu entwickeln, so dass auch ihnen der Schulstart erleichtert werden könnte.

Die bei den Kindern mit LLS bis zur dritten Klasse stattfindende leichte Abnahme der Antworten in der Kategorie ‚froh', weist darauf hin, dass sich die subjektive Befindlichkeit und das Selbstwertgefühl einiger Kinder mit LLS im Verlauf der Grundschulzeit ‚verschlechtert'. In gleichem Maße steigen bei diesen Kindern die Antworten in der Kategorie ‚traurig' an. Grund dafür dürften die schlechten Schulleistungen der Kinder mit LLS und die damit verbundenen negativen Rückmeldungen sein.

Da auch bei den Kindern ohne LLS zu Schulbeginn eine leichte Abnahme der Antworten in der Kategorie ‚froh' deutlich wird, kann davon ausgegangen werden, dass der Schulanfang für alle Kinder eine belastende Situation bedeutet. Dies wird unterstrichen durch die Zunahme der Antworten in der Kategorie ‚müde', die in allen Schuljahren zwischen 9 und 13% liegen.

Insgesamt betrachtet handelt es sich bei den beobachtbaren Veränderungen hinsichtlich der Befindlichkeit der Kinder mit und ohne LLS nur um Tendenzen. Für die Mehrzahl der Kinder gilt, dass sie ihre positive Befindlichkeit und ihr positives Selbstwertgefühl während der Grundschulzeit beibehalten. Das gilt auch für Kinder, die in der Schule häufige Mißerfolge erleben.

Zusammenfassend können wir feststellen, dass die positive emotionale Befindlichkeit (‚subjektives Wohlbefinden') und das Vertrauen in die eigenen Kräfte bei den meisten Kindern erhalten geblieben ist. Möglicherweise hat auch das Projekt „Ich bin Ich – Gesundheit fördern durch Selbstwertstärkung" dazu beigetragen. Für eine genaue Analyse bleiben hier die Ergebnisse der Kontrollgruppe abzuwarten.

Literatur

Antonovsky, A. (1993). Gesundheitsforschung vs. Krankheitsforschung In Franke, A. & M. Broda (Hrsg.). *Psychosomatische Gesundheit*. Tübingen. DGfV, 3-14.

Breuer, H. & M. Weuffen (1996). *Lernschwierigkeiten am Schulanfang: Schuleingangsdiagnostik zur Früherkennung und Frühförderung*, 3. unveränderte Auflage. Weinheim & Basel: Beltz.

Einsiedler, W. (1988). Schulanfang und Persönlichkeitsentwicklung. *Grundschule*, 10, 20-23.

Frey, D. & E. Benning (1983). Das Selbstwertgefühl. In Mandl, H. & G.L. Huber (Hrsg.) Emotion und Kognition. München, Wien, Baltimore: Urban & Schwarzenberg.

Jopt, U.-J. (1987). Schulische Tüchtigkeitserziehung und Identitätsentwicklung – eine Gratwanderung. In Frey, H.P. & K. Haußer (Hrsg.). *Identität*. Stuttgart: Enke, 58-70.

Knöfel, A. (1990). *Selbstbildveränderungen beim Übergang vom Kindergarten zur Schule*. Dissertation. Ernst-Moritz-Arndt-Universität Greifswald.

Krause, Chr. (1998). Ich bin Ich – Gesundheit fördern durch Selbstwertstärkung: Bericht über ein Projekt zur Gesundheitsförderung in Grundschulen. Unter Mitarbeit von Meyer, V.; Rohde, Chr.; Stückle, Chr. & R.-K. Zimmermann. *Göttinger Beiträge zur erziehungswissenschaftlichen Forschung Nr. 15*. Göttingen: Pädagogisches Seminar.

Lohaus, A. et al. (1996). *Fragebogen zur Erhebung von Streßerleben und Streßbewältigung im Kindesalter*. Göttingen: Hogrefe.

Satir, V. (1994). *Kommunikation, Selbstwert, Kongruenz*. Paderborn: Jungfermann.

Schauder, T. (1996). *Die Aussagenliste zum Selbstwertgefühl für Kinder und Jugendliche*. Göttingen: BeltzTest.

Speck-Hamdan, A. (1990). Freude auf das Neue – Schulanfang aus der Sicht des Kindes. *Grundschule*, 22, 6, 26-28.

Stückle, Chr. (1999). *Entwicklung und Veränderung des Selbstbildes bei Grundschulkindern mit Lern- und Leistungsschwierigkeiten*. Magistraarbeit (unveröffentlicht). Sozialwissenschaftliche Fakultät, Georg-August-Universität Göttingen

Zubke, W. (1999) Gesundheitstage sind nie langweilig. *Grundschule*, 31, 5, 17.

World Health Organisation (1946). *Constitution*. Genf: WHOWorld Health Organisation (1993). *Life Skill education in schools* (WHO/MNH/PSF/93.AREV.1). Genf: WHO

4.6 Das Marburger Rechtschreibtraining

Gerd Schulte-Körne

Einleitung

In der Bundesrepublik Deutschland leben annähernd 200000 lese- und rechtschreibschwache Grundschüler. Nach dem Internationalen Klassifikationsschema für psychische Störungen (ICD-10) werden die Kinder, die im Gegensatz zur ihrer Intelligenz oder Klassenstufe extrem schlecht lesen und/oder schreiben als Kinder mit einer Lese- und/oder Rechtschreibstörung bezeichnet. Da diese Störung sehr oft bis ins Erwachsenenalter bestehen bleibt und entscheidend den Schulabschluss sowie die Berufsausbildung beeinflusst, ist es eine vordringliche Aufgabe, diesen Kinder möglichst frühzeitig und vor allem effektiv zu helfen. Denn nicht nur die Schullaufbahn wird durch diese Störung entscheidend beeinflusst sondern auch die emotionale und persönliche Entwicklung des betroffenen Kindes. So können diese Kinder häufig eine Reihe von psychischen Störungen, wie z. B. depressive Verstimmungen, Emotionalstörungen, Störungen des Verhaltens in Form von Hyperaktivität und Aggressivität entwickeln.

Bereits in den 70er Jahren wurde die Lese-Rechtschreibstörung intensiv erforscht, in Folge dessen zahlreiche Trainingskonzepte entwickelt wurden. Eine sehr ausführliche Übersicht über Förderprogramme findet sich bei Scheerer-Neumann (1979). In den letzten Jahren sind in Folge neuer Erkenntnisse zur Ursachenforschung weitere Trainingsmethoden hinzu gekommen, insbesondere das Training phonologischer Fertigkeiten[1].

Nach Dumont (1990) lassen sich 3 Gruppen von Förderprogrammen bei der Lese-Rechtschreibstörung unterscheiden:

- Training basaler kognitiver Funktionen (z. B. visuell-räumliche Wahrnehmung, Blickbewegungstraining)
- Re-Programmieren neurologischer Defizite (z. B. Lateralitäts- und Hörtraining, Tonschwellenunterscheidung)
- Symptomspezifische Trainings (z. B. Förderung von phonologischer Bewusstheit, Rechtschreibregeltraining)

Symptomspezifische Trainings sind solche, die einen direkten Bezug zur Symptomatik (Lese- und Rechtschreibstörung) erkennen lassen. Hierunter werden im wesentlichen Regeltrainings und Trainings zur Ausbildung und Förderung von phonologischer Bewusstheit gefasst (Amorosa et al. 1994).

Für die ersten beiden Kategorien (s. o.) liegt bis heute kein Wirksamkeitsnachweis vor, hingegen ist die Effektivität der symptomspezifischen Trainings gut belegt (Dummer & Hakketal 1984, Reuter-Liehr 1993, Schneider & Springer 1978; Übersichten bei Scheerer-Neumann 1993 und Tacke 1987).

---

1 Phonologische Fertigkeiten sind z. B. Benennen von vorgegebenen lautlichen Segmenten und das Verschmelzen dieser zu einer größeren sprachlichen Einheit. Im weiteren Sinne gehört der indirekt erschlossene Zugang zu phonologischen Regelhaftigkeiten, wie z. B. das Reimerkennen, zur phonologischen Bewusstheit (Schulte-Körne 2001).

Für eine theoretische Einordnung der Trainingskonzepte ist das Phasenmodell von Frith (1985) relevant (siehe Abbildung 4.6.1). Danach durchlaufen Kinder beim Schriftspracherwerb drei aufeinander aufbauende Phasen: die logographische, die alphabetische und die orthographische Phase. Die erste Phase ist im wesentlichen durch ein ganzheitliches Malen von Wörtern gekennzeichnet, in der zweiten Phase lernen die Kinder die Zuordnung von Laut- und Schriftsprache, und in der dritten Phase wird zunehmend orthographisches Wissen berücksichtigt.

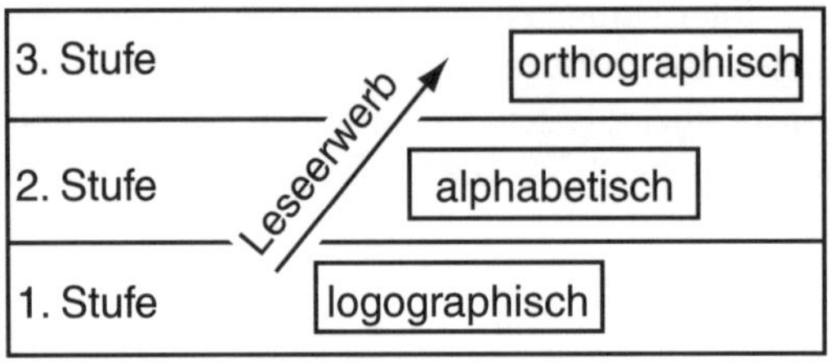

Abb. 4.6.1 Phasenmodell des Schriftspracherwerbs nach Frith (aus: Schulte-Körne 2001)

Phonologische Trainings lassen sich der alphabetischen Phase zuordnen, Regeltrainings der orthographischen Phase. Das bedeutet, dass von phonologischen Trainings vor allem jüngere Kinder profitieren sollten, die die orthographische Phase noch nicht erreicht haben. Für diese Annahme spricht, dass positive Effekte von phonologischen Trainings im Kindergartenalter auf die Lese- und Rechtschreibleistungen im frühen Schulalter nachgewiesen wurden (Schneider et al. 1997, 1998). Allerdings fanden Wimmer & Hartl (1991) mit einem Phonologietraining bei Zweitklässlern und Schulte-Körne und Mitarbeiter (2001a) bei Dritt- und Viertklässlern keine bedeutsamen Therapieeffekte, da die Kinder die trainierten Fertigkeiten zum großen Teil bereits beherrschten. Mannhaupt (1994) folgert aus seiner Metaanalyse, dass phonologische Trainings bis einschließlich der ersten Klasse sinnvoll seien, während ab der zweiten Klasse Regeltrainings zu bevorzugen sind.

Der Einsatz von Regeltrainings kann sinnvollerweise erst stattfinden, wenn die Kinder sich die Laut-Buchstaben-Beziehungen angeeignet haben und auch von ihrer kognitiven Entwicklung her in der Lage sind, Regeln zu lernen und anzuwenden. Regeltrainings sind somit etwa ab der 2. bis 3. Grundschulklasse einsetzbar (Scheerer-Neumann 1979).

Die Konzeption eines Rechtschreibtrainings sollte den Entwicklungsstand von Zweit- und Drittklässlern hinsichtlich der Lese- und Rechtschreibfertigkeit berücksichtigen. Drittklässler haben häufig keinerlei Regelwissen oder können bei ausreichender Regelkenntnis die Regeln oft nicht anwenden (Scheerer-Neumann 1988). Rechtschreiboperationen, die in Einzelprozessen richtig durchgeführt werden (z. B. Mitlautverdopplung nach kurzem Selbstlaut), können nicht auf den gesamten Schriftsprachprozess übertragen werden (z. B. wenn zusätzlich die Entscheidung über Groß- und Kleinschreibung getroffen werden muss). Das Ziel eines Rechtschreibtrainings sollte daher über die reine Vermittlung von Regelwissen auch die Vermittlung von Lösungsstrategien beinhalten (Scheerer-Neumann 1988).

Dass ein Rechtschreibregeltraining erfolgreich sein kann, zeigen mehrere Therapiestudien. Müller (1969) und Reith und Weber (1973) konnten bei Dritt- und Viertklässlern durch ein gezieltes Rechtschreibregeltraining die Zahl der Regelfehler erheblich reduzieren. Scheerer-Neumann (1988) untersuchte den Einfluss eines verhaltenstherapeutisch orientierten

Regeltrainings auf die Rechtschreibleistung von Hauptschülern der 5. und 6. Klassenstufe. Im Vergleich zu einer Kontrollgruppe erreichte die Experimentalgruppe signifikant bessere Ergebnisse beim Schreiben von Wörtern einer Prüfliste. Auch Schulte-Körne und Mitarbeiter (1997, 1998, 2001a) fanden einen bedeutsamen Therapieeffekt beim Einsatz des Marburger Rechtschreibtrainings bei Zweit-, Dritt- und Viertklässlern.

Ein weiterer positiver Aspekt von Regeltrainings ist, dass sie sich gut in den Schulalltag integrieren lassen. Die Abgrenzung vom normalen Förderunterricht besteht zum einen darin, dass der Bereich Rechtschreibregeln, der im normalen Unterricht nur einen verschwindend geringen Raum in Anspruch nimmt (weniger als 1%, Gasteiger-Klicpera und Klicpera 1988), in den Vordergrund rückt. Dies erscheint besonders sinnvoll, da bei Zweitklässlern 66% der Rechtschreibfehler Regelfehler sind (Glogauer 1970). Zum anderen werden im Regeltraining auch gezielt Lösungsstrategien vermittelt. Dies trägt der Tatsache Rechnung, dass rechtschreibschwache Kinder nicht einfach nur intensiveren, sondern tatsächlich andere Förderung benötigen. Das mehr oder weniger "intuitive" (automatisiert ablaufende) Schreibenlernen steht ihnen nicht zur Verfügung, weshalb sie dazu angeleitet werden müssen, "bewusst" zu schreiben.

Konzept des Trainingprogramms

Das Marburger Rechtschreibtraining besteht aus 12 Kapiteln, die in einen *Anleitungs-*, einen *Lern-* und einen *Übungsbereich* gegliedert sind. Zusätzlich sind im *Anhang* Arbeits- und Lernmaterialen zusammengestellt (siehe Tabelle 4.6.1). Zu jedem Kapitel des Lern- und Übungsbereichs werden in der Anleitung Detailinformationen gegeben. Das Wortmaterial des Trainings ist in einem *Wortindex* zusammengefasst.

Die 12 Kapitel bauen aufeinander auf. Jedoch besteht die Möglichkeit, dass einzelne Kapitel zu bestimmten Themen (z. B. Ableitungen) aus diesem Training genommen und zu anderen Übungsverfahren ergänzt werden.

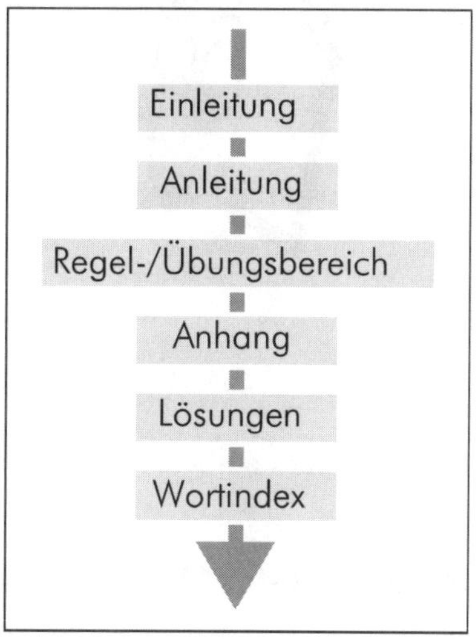

Tab. 4.6.1 Struktur des Trainings

Das Training ist so angelegt, dass es nicht allein durch das rechtschreibschwache Kind durchführt wird. Das Prinzip dieses Programms besteht in dem gemeinsamen Erarbeiten der einzelnen Lern- und Übungsbereiche. Nach dem Durcharbeiten der einzelnen Kapitel sollen die Kinder die Rechtschreibregeln, zunächst mit Hilfe der Lern- und Regelkarten, z. B. bei den Hausaufgaben anwenden.

Dieses Rechtschreibtraining ersetzt keine Grammatik. Daher können nicht alle Rechtschreibprobleme gelöst werden. Im wesentlichen werden die wesentlichen Rechtschreibprobleme von lese-rechtschreibschwachen Kinder der 2.- 4. Grundschulklasse bearbeitet.

Ziel des Trainings ist die Vermittlung von Lösungsstrategien. Den rechtschreibschwachen Kindern stehen Lösungswege, die nicht-rechtschreibschwache Kinder anwenden, nicht zur Verfügung. Daher werden in diesem Training neue Lösungsstrategien angeboten. Um diese neuen Strategien anwenden zu können, wurden spezielle Rechtschreib-Algorithmen (Kathi, siehe Abbildung 4.6.3) entwickelt. Anhand dieser Algorithmen gelangen die Kinder Schritt für Schritt zur richtigen Rechtschreibung.

Durch die graphische Gestaltung des Programms besteht eine gute Strukturierung und Übersichtlichkeit der Lern- und Übungsbereiche. Z. B. leitet das Ausrufezeichen **Anton** die Kinder durch das gesamte Programm und weist auf wesentliche Lerninhalte hin (siehe Abbildung 4.6.2).

Abb. 4.6.2: Das Ausrufezeichen Anton weist auf wesentliche Lerninhalte des Trainings hin

Untersuchungen zur Wirksamkeit des Marburger Rechtschreibtrainings

Die Überprüfung der Wirksamkeit (Evaluation) eines Förderprogramms stellt eine Grundanforderung dar. Allerdings werden insbesondere im Bereich der Lese- und Rechtschreibförderung Evaluationsstudien kaum durchgeführt. Somit ist für viele Programme bisher unklar, ob sie helfen, die Rechtschreibleistung zu verbessern.

Im Rahmen von drei Studien wurde das vorliegende Rechtschreibtraining evaluiert. Die Ergebnisse sind bisher in drei Fachartikeln veröffentlicht (Schulte-Körne et al. 1997, 1998, 2001a).

In einer ersten Studie wurde untersucht, inwieweit Eltern in der Lage waren, unter Anleitung die Rechtschreibfähigkeit ihres Kindes zu verbessern. Zwei Jahre wurden die Eltern regelmäßig zur Durchführung des Marburger Rechtschreibtrainings angeleitet. An diesen Abenden, die einmal im Monat stattfanden, wurden den Eltern gezeigt, wie das Trainingsprogramm durchzuführen sei. Außerdem wurde das aktuelle Lern- und Übungsmaterial ausgeteilt und besprochen. An diesen Abenden hatten die Eltern ausreichend Gelegenheit, sich gegenseitig über die aktuellen schulischen Probleme und Schwierigkeiten bei der Durchführung des Trainingsprogramms auszutauschen.

Diese Eltern-Kind-Trainings-Studie erbrachte zwei wesentliche Ergebnisse: Die Eltern waren in der Lage, mit Hilfe des Marburger Rechtschreibtrainings die Rechtschreibleistung ihres Kindes signifikant zu verbessern. Nach einem Jahr zeigte sich ein signifikanter Therapieeffekt im Bereich der spezifischen Rechtschreibfehler. D. h., dass die Kinder in der Lage waren, die gelernten Rechtschreibregeln anzuwenden. Allerdings zeigte sich eine Verbesserung der gesamten Rechtschreibleistung erst nach zwei Jahren.

Das Selbstvertrauen der Kinder konnte durch das Training signifikant gesteigert werden. Die Kinder hatten mehr Spass und Interesse am Lesen und Schreiben gewonnen, sie trauten sich eher, am Unterricht mündlich teilzunehmen. Die Eltern lernten hingegen, die Rechtschreibschwäche ihres Kindes anders zu bewerten und den Umgang miteinander zu verändern.

In einer weiteren Studie wurde das Marburger Rechtschreibtraining in der Einzelförderung durch eine Medizinstudentin unter Anleitung evaluiert (Schulte-Körne et al. 2001a). Zweimal pro Woche (jeweils 45 Minuten, 30 Minuten Förderung, 25 Minuten Spiel und Bewegung) wurden 10 rechtschreibschwache Kinder einzeln gefördert. Bereits nach 12 Wochen intensiver Förderung zeigte sich eine signifikante Verbesserung der Lese- und Rechtschreibleistung. Jedoch konnte innerhalb dieser kurzen Zeit keine Veränderung des Selbstvertrauens der Kinder nachgewiesen werden.

In der dritten Studie wird zur Zeit der Einsatz des Marburger Rechtschreibtrainings in der Schule evaluiert. Im Rahmen eines Modellprogramms (MONA) wird in der Grundschule Höchst im Odenwald mit der Unterstützung des Hessischen Kultusministeriums und der Deutschen Forschungsgemeinschaft diese Evaluationsstudie durchgeführt. Jeweils fünf bis sieben Kinder mit Schwierigkeiten im Schriftspracherwerb aus der 2. und 3. Klasse wurden in acht Gruppen mit maximal 5-7 Kinder zusammengefasst und anhand des vorliegenden Trainingsprogramms oder einem eigenen schulischen Programm 2 Jahre lang gefördert. Die Förderstunden werden parallel zum Regelunterricht erteilt und sind über die Vormittage verteilt. Pro Woche werden zwei Förderstunden erteilt. Jeweils eine Lehrerin arbeitet mit den Kindern. Die bisher vorliegenden Ergebnisse zeigen, dass die Kinder sehr gern an dem Förderprogramm teilnehmen, auch wenn sie dafür teilweise eine Stunde eher zur Schule kommen müssen. Die Lese- und Rechtschreibleistung der Förderkinder hat sich bereits deutlich verbessert. Nach 1.5 Jahren Förderung liegen die Rechtschreib- und die Leseleistung der Förderkinder im Normalbereich. Auch diese Studie belegt die Wirksamkeit des Marburger Rechtschreibtrainings.

Aufbau des Trainings

Lerninhalte

Die einzelnen Kapitel des Trainings bauen aufeinander auf. Beginnend mit der Einführung der Selbstlaute wird die Unterscheidung von lang und kurz gesprochenem Selbstlaut im Wortstamm geübt. Tabelle 4.6.2 gibt eine Übersicht über die Inhalte des Programms.

Themen
Selbstlaute erkennen
Unterscheidung von lang und kurz gesprochenen Selbstlauten
Mitlaute erkennen
Unterscheidung von Selbst- und Mitlauten
Verschriftlichung der Mitlaute nach lang und kurz gesprochenem Selbstlaut
Hauptwörter erkennen
Groß- und Kleinschreibung
Wortstamm erkennen
Verschriftlichung von Wortstämmen
Verschriftlichung von Wortendungen
Verschriftlichung der Mitlaute nach lang und kurz gesprochenem Selbstlaut in zusammengesetzten Hauptwörtern
Verschriftlichung von Wortendungen in zusammengesetzten Hauptwörtern
Verschriftlichung der Mitlaute nach lang und kurz gesprochenen Umlauten
Vorsilben erkennen
Tuwörter erkennen
Verschriftlichung von Endungen in Tuwörtern
Verschriftlichung der Mitlaute nach lang und kurz gesprochenem Selbstlaut in Tuwörtern
Stumme-h erkennen
Verschriftlichung des stummen-h
Wiewörter erkennen
Verschriftlichung der Mitlaute nach lang und kurz gesprochenem Selbstlaut in Wiewörtern
Verschriftlichung der Ausnahmen von der Stumme-h-Regel bei verschiedenen Wortarten
Erkennen des lang gesprochenen Selbstlautes *i*
Erkennen des Dehnungs-e
Verschriftlichung des lang gesprochenen *i* mit Dehnungs-e
Selbstlaute-trennende-h bei Hauptwörtern und Tuwörtern erkennen
Erkennen und Verschriftlichung von Mitlauten bei Selbstlautpaaren
Ableitung zu gleichklingenden Umlauten bei Hauptwörtern, bei Tuwörtern und bei Wiewörtern
Ableitung zur Auslautverhärtung bei Hauptwörtern, bei Tuwörtern und bei Wiewörtern

Tabelle 4.6.2 Übersicht über die Lerninhalte des Marburger Rechtschreibtrainings

Regeln

Die Regeln stellen ein wesentliches Grundgerüst des Rechtschreibtrainings dar. Insgesamt 8 Regeln enthält das Programm. Anhand dieser Regeln können jedoch nicht alle Rechtschreibprobleme gelöst werden, da es eine Reihe von Wörtern gibt, die anhand dieser Regel nicht richtig verschriftlicht werden können. Diese Ausnahmen sind aber vergleichsweise selten.

Lösungsstrategien

Anhand von sog. **Algorithmen** (Abbildung 4.6.3) wird den Kindern vermittelt, zu der richtigen Verschriftlichung eines Wortes zu gelangen. Die Struktur der Algorithmen ist immer gleich, d. h. ausgehend von einer Problemstellung werden über einen Entscheidungsbaum mit Ja/Nein-Antworten die Lösungsschritte vermittelt. Zu jedem Lernbereich gibt es einen Algorithmus, der graphisch als **Kathi** umgesetzt ist. Die Algorithmen bauen aufeinander auf (siehe Abbildung 4.6.3).

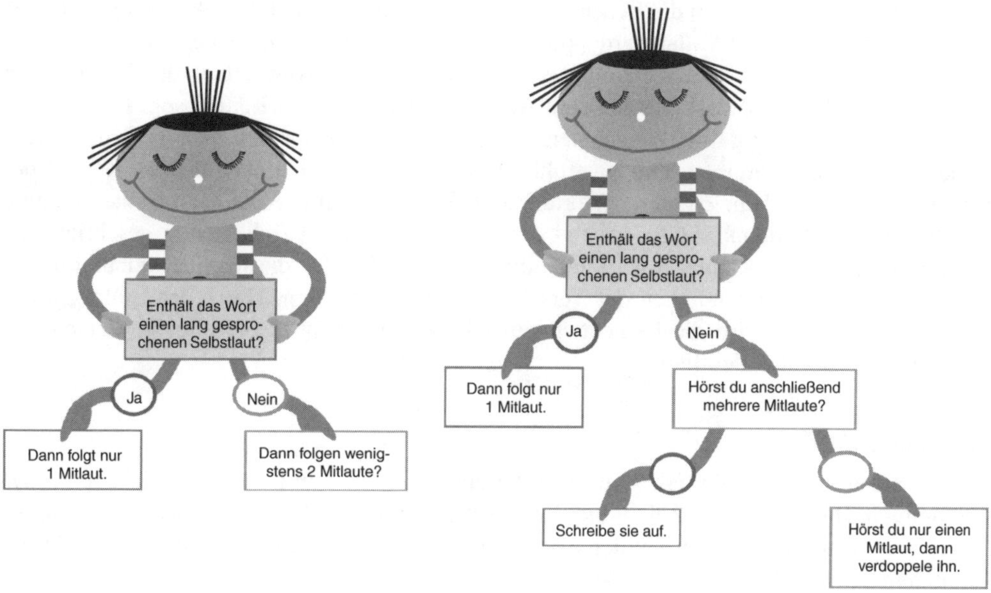

Abb. 4.6.3 Darstellung der Algorithmen

Eine weitere Lösungsstrategie besteht in der Visualisierung von weitestgehend auditiven Problemen. Da eine Reihe von Kindern insbesondere Schwierigkeiten bei der Unterscheidung von lang und kurz gesprochenen Selbstlauten hat, wird eine Lösungsstrategie vermittelt, die auf der Visualisierung und grapho-motorischen Umsetzung aufbaut. So werden für den kurz gesprochenen Selbstlaut ein Punkt, für den lang gesprochenen Selbstlaut ein horizontal verlaufender Strich unter dem Selbstlaut eingeführt (Abbildung 4.6.4). Für einen auf einen Selbstlaut folgenden Mitlaut wird ein senkrechter Strich, für 2 auf einen Selbstlaut folgenden Mitlaute 2 Striche. Auch bei den Regeln werden auf diese Techniken der Markierung der Länge der Selbstlaute und der folgenden Anzahl von Mitlauten zurück gegriffen.

Abb. 4.6.4 Lernstrategie zur Unterscheidung von lang und kurz gesprochenem Selbstlaut

Lerneffekt/Erfolgskontrolle

Gut belegt ist die Tatsache, dass erst die regelmäßige Wiederholung von Lerninhalten zu einem andauernden Lernerfolg führt. Dazu werden in diesem Programm regelmäßig Wiederholungsübungen angeboten, die auf bereits dargestellte Lerninhalte aufbauen. Teilweise werden in den Wiederholungsübungen verschiedene Lerninhalte gemeinsam überprüft. Diese Überprüfung entspricht der Anforderungssituation in der alltäglichen Schreibpraxis. Für die Verschriftlichung von Wörtern ist eben nicht nur die Kenntnis von einem ausgewählten Problembereich erforderlich, sondern die Beachtung recht verschiedener Schwierigkeiten (z. B. Groß- und Kleinschreibung und Mitlautverdopplung nach einem kurz gesprochenem Selbstlaut).

Eine wesentliche Voraussetzung des Lernerfolges ist die Anwendung der Regeln beim Schreiben. Zu diesem Zweck werden zum Abschluss der einzelnen Kapitel sog. **Erfolgskontrollen** (siehe Abbildung 4.6.5) angeboten. Anhand eines Lückentextes wird das Kind aufgefordert, Wörter zu schreiben. Die Auswahl der Wörter richtet sich nach den im Kapitel behandelten Lernbereichen. Zu diesen Wortdiktaten finden Sie immer eine Geschichte und eine Graphik (siehe Abbildung 4.6.5), anhand derer die Kinder die Anzahl richtig geschriebenen Wörter eintragen. Ab Kapitel 9 wird auch die benötigte Zeit für die Rechtschreibung protokolliert, um die Geschwindigkeit der Verschriftlichung zu fördern. Durch das Eintragen der aktuellen Ergebnisse wird die Lernentwicklung für das Kind, aber auch für die Person, die mit dem Kind arbeitet, deutlich.

Wortmaterial

Das Wortmaterial des Trainings ist aus dem Grundwortschatz von Pregel und Rickheit (1987) entnommen. Dies ist die zur Zeit aktuellste, für den Grundschulbereich repräsentative vorliegende Sammlung. Die Wörter wurden aus dem Corpus des schriftlichen Wortschatzes für die zweiten und dritten Klassen ausgewählt.

Schrift

Um eine sehr gute Lesbarkeit des Trainings zu erreichen, wurde eine 16-Punkt-Schriftgröße verwendet. Ferner wurde eine serifenlose Schrift gewählt, die insbesondere im Erstleseunterricht verwendet wird.

Dauer und Häufigkeit der Übungs- und Lerneinheiten

Die Übungs- und Lerneinheiten sollten auf zwei Einheiten pro Woche verteilt werden. Ein häufigeres Üben kann zur Überforderung der Kinder führen. Außerdem benötigen die Kinder ein ausreichendes Maß an Freizeit, deren Beschneidung auch die Motivation negativ beeinflussen würde.

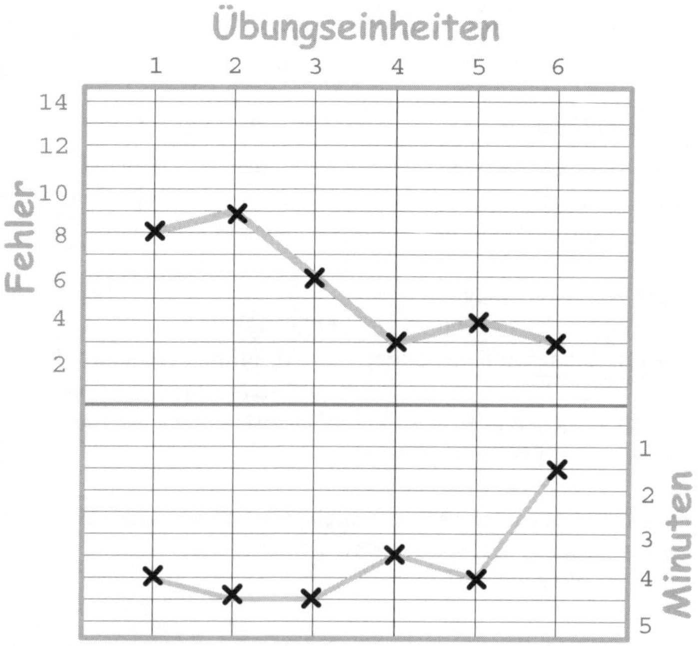

Abb. 4.6.5 Die Erfolgskontrolle

Die Dauer der einzelnen Übungseinheiten sollte 45 Minuten nicht überschreiten. Allerdings bedeutet 45 Minuten nicht reine Lern- und Arbeitszeit, sondern auch Spiel- und Erholungszeit. Die effektive Lern- und Übungszeit beträgt dann maximal 20-30 Minuten.

Generell richtet sich die Dauer der Übungseinheiten nach der individuellen Belastbarkeit des Kindes. Für manche Kinder erscheint es sinnvoll, die Lerneinheiten auf mehr als zwei Wochentage zu verteilen. Es sollte darauf geachtet werden, dass Lernzeiten nicht auf die Abendstunden gelegt werden und ein ruhiger Ort zum Lernen und Üben zur Verfügung steht.

Für die schulische Förderung ist eine zweistündige Förderung pro Woche sinnvoll. Die Förderung sollte zumindest einmal pro Woche am frühen Vormittag erfolgen. Förderung in den letzten Schulstunden sind wenig effektiv und sollten möglichst vermieden werden.

Einzel- und Gruppenförderung

Das Training sollte wenn möglich, als Einzeltraining durchgeführt werden. Im Rahmen schulischer Förderung ist allerdings oft nur eine Förderung in der Gruppe möglich. Die Gruppe sollte nicht mehr als 5 Kinder umfassen. Es sollten nur lese- und/oder rechtschreibschwache Kindern zusammen gefördert werden. Die Kombination von lese- und/oder rechtschreibschwachen mit Kindern mit anderen Entwicklungsstörungen (z. B. Dyskalkulie) oder Kindern, die aufgrund einer anderen Muttersprache Schwierigkeiten beim Erlernen der deutschen Schriftsprache aufweisen, ist zu vermeiden. Die Zusammensetzung der Gruppe sollte an dem individuellen Leistungsniveau der Kinder ausgerichtet sein. Heterogene Leistungsgruppen, d. h. die Kombination von Kindern mit einer relativ guten mit Kindern mit einer sehr schlechten Rechtschreibleistung, ist nicht sinnvoll.

Voraussetzung zur Durchführung des Trainings

Verschiedene Voraussetzungen vor Beginn des Trainingsprogramms sollten überprüft werden.

Voraussetzungen beim Kind

Das Trainingsprogramm ist für Kinder entwickelt worden, die Schwierigkeiten beim Erwerb der Rechtschreibfähigkeit haben. Diese Schwierigkeiten sollen nicht auf folgende Faktoren zurückführbar sein, da ansonsten keine Aussagen über die Wirksamkeit des Programms gemacht werden können.

- Vorliegen einer Lernbehinderung.
- Vorliegen einer Hör- und Sehstörung, die nicht korrigiert ist.
- Mangelnde Unterrichtung im Rechtschreiben z. B. infolge von unregelmäßigem Schulbesuch.
- Vorliegen einer psychischen oder neurologischen Erkrankung, die den Erwerb der Rechtschreibfähigkeit wesentlich beeinträchtigt hat.

Nachdem die Faktoren genannt wurden, die **nicht vorhanden sein sollen,** werden nachfolgend die Kriterien vorgestellt, anhand derer entschieden werden kann, ob dieses Programm sinnvoll für das betreffende Kind ist.

Entscheidend ist, ob tatsächlich besondere Probleme im Rechtschreiben vorliegen. Diese Probleme sollten nicht nur einmalig bei einem Diktat auftreten, sondern mehrmals über einen längeren Zeitraum zu beobachten sein.

Überprüfung der Voraussetzungen beim Kind

Eingangsuntersuchung

Die Überprüfung der Voraussetzungen setzt psychologische und medizinische Spezialkenntnisse voraus. Daher wird empfohlen, dass die Kinder vor Beginn des Trainings erst eingehend untersucht werden. Untersuchungen können bei Fachärzten und in Ambulanzen in Kliniken für Kinder- und Jugendpsychiatrie und Psychotherapie und bei in der Diagnostik erfahrenen Psychologen durchgeführt werden. Angebote zur psychologischen Untersuchungen finden Sie auch in Erziehungsberatungsstellen, psychologischen Beratungsstellen und teilweise bei schulpsychologischen Diensten. Da die Durchführung der Diagnostik sehr unterschiedlich ist, werden nachfolgend Empfehlungen zum Aufbau der Überprüfung gegeben.

Die Untersuchung sollte folgende Faktoren erfassen:

- Intelligenztest (möglichst ein Verfahren auswählen, das insgesamt oder zumindest in Teilen sprachfrei ist, z. B. Kaufman Assessment Battery for Children (K-ABC), Hamburg-Wechsler-Intelligenztest für Kinder III (HAWIK-III), Grundintelligenztest Skala 1, 20 (CFT 1, 20).
- Standardisierter Rechtschreibtest (z. B. Weingartener Rechtschreibtest 1+, 2+, 3+ (WRT 1+, 2+, 3+), Diagnostischer Rechtschreibtest für zweite und dritte Klassen (DRT 2, DRT 3), Grundwortschatz Rechtschreib-Test für 4. und 5. Klassen (GRT 4+).
- Standardisierter Lesetest (Salzburger Lese-Rechtschreibtest (SLRT), Würzburger Leise Leseprobe (WLLP).

- Überprüfung der Emotionalität.
- Neurologische Untersuchung einschließlich der Überprüfung der Hör- und Sehfähigkeit.

Wir empfehlen das Training für Kinder, die besondere Schwierigkeiten beim Erlernen des Rechtschreibens haben. Es wird in der Praxis erst dann von einer Rechtschreibstörung gesprochen, wenn die Leistung im Rechtschreibtest unter dem Klassendurchschnitt liegt und die Intelligenz mindestens im Durchschnittsbereich liegt (d.h. > 85 ist). Aus überwiegend methodischen Gründen empfehlen wir ein diagnostisches Vorgehen, dass das Verhältnis von aktueller Rechtschreibleistung zur Intelligenz berücksichtigt. Es sollte erst dann von einer Rechtschreibstörung gesprochen werden, wenn die aktuelle Rechtschreibleistung deutlich schlechter ist als aufgrund der Intelligenz zu erwarten wäre. Das genaue Vorgehen ist in einem Artikel beschrieben (Schulte-Körne et al. 2001b) oder kann bei den Autoren nachgefragt werden (siehe homepage: http://www.kjp.uni-marburg.de/kjp/legast/Index.htm).

Ab welcher Klassenstufe kann das Programm eingesetzt werden?

Das Training ist nicht für Kinder der ersten Klasse geeignet, da die Buchstabenkenntnis und Laut-Buchstabenzuordnung häufig noch nicht sicher erworben werden konnte. In den bereits durchgeführten Studien zur Wirksamkeit des Trainingsprogramm konnte ein Erfolg für Kinder der 2.-5. Klasse gezeigt werden. Der Einsatz in höheren Klassen ist bisher nicht untersucht, allerdings ist anzunehmen, dass bei Vorliegen einer ausgeprägten Rechtschreibstörung auch in höheren Klassen sinnvoll mit dem Programm gearbeitet werden kann.

Emotionalstörung und Hyperaktivität

Einige Kinder mit einer Lese- und Rechtschreibstörung haben erhebliche Probleme sich zu konzentrieren, still zu sitzen und ihre Aufmerksamkeit über einen längeren Zeitraum aufrecht zu erhalten. Diese Probleme können die Durchführung und den Erfolg des Trainingsprogramms stark beeinflussen. Bei einzelnen Kindern sind diese Probleme so ausgeprägt, dass bereits in der Eingangsuntersuchung von einer **Aufmerksamkeits-Hyperaktivitätsstörung** (oder **Hyperkinetischen Störung)** gesprochen wird. In diesem Fall empfehlen wir, dieses Problem fachärztlich zu behandeln, um die Voraussetzungen für die Durchführung des Trainingsprogramms zu schaffen. Das Vorliegen einer Hyperkinetischen Störung ist unter der Voraussetzung einer entsprechenden Behandlung kein Ausschlussgrund für die Durchführung des Trainings.

Manche Kinder haben möglicherweise als Folge der nicht erkannten Rechtschreibstörung verschiedene Probleme entwickelt, z. B. häufig traurig zu sein und an sich selbst zu zweifeln. Bauch- und Kopfschmerzen in Zusammenhang mit Anforderungen an die Rechtschreibleistung oder Schulangst treten häufig auf. Wenn emotionale Probleme vorliegen, sollte auf jeden Fall ein Kinder- und Jugendpsychiater oder ein Psychologe mit psychotherapeutischer Zusatzqualifikation aufgesucht werden. Auch emotionale Störungen sind kein Ausschlussgrund für die Durchführung des Trainings, wenn eine entsprechende Behandlung erfolgt.

Wer kann das Training durchführen?

Das Training ist so konzipiert, dass es von Eltern und Fachkräften (Pädagogen, Psychologen, Ergotherapeuten, Logopäden, Ärzten) durchführt werden kann. Allerdings sind bestimmte

Voraussetzungen zu überprüfen, die in Abhängigkeit von der beruflichen Ausbildung und spezifischen Fördersituation (zu Hause, bei einer/m Therapeutin/en, in der Schule) unterschiedlich sind.

Voraussetzungen beim Trainer/in

Es wird hier unterschieden, ob das Training durch Eltern oder durch Fachkräfte durchgeführt wird.

Voraussetzungen, wenn Eltern des Training durchführen

Als erstes sollte überprüft werden, ob das Verhältnis zwischen Kind und einem Elternteil so entspannt ist, dass ein regelmäßiges Üben mindestens zweimal wöchentlich sinnvoll durchgeführt werden kann. Dieser Aspekt ist von großer Bedeutung. Nicht selten haben Eltern, bevor die Lese-Rechtschreibstörung festgestellt wurde, häufig intensiv und nicht selten vergeblich mit ihrem Kind geübt. Das wiederholte Schreiben von Diktaten führte zwar kurzfristig zu einer Fehlerreduktion, jedoch am nächsten Tag in der Schule zeigte sich dieser Übungseffekt nicht mehr. Diese Misserfolge, vor allem wenn sie über einen längeren Zeitraum erlebt wurden, haben oft das Verhältnis zwischen übendem Elternteil und Kind verschlechtert. Wenn von vornherein absehbar ist, dass aufgrund der negativen Vorerfahrungen das Eltern-Kind-Verhältnis durch ein gemeinsames Üben belastet wird, ist die Durchführung des Trainings durch eine Fachkraft zu empfehlen.

Die Konzeption des Trainings sieht vor, dass Eltern bei der Durchführung des Trainings angeleitet werden, z. B. durch Anbindung an eine psychologische Beratungsstelle oder Erziehungsberatungsstelle. Außerdem können sich die Eltern in Elterngruppen zusammenschließen und regelmäßig (z. B. einmal monatlich) durch eine Fachkraft angeleitet werden (vergleichbar dem Vorgehen in der Evaluationsstudie, siehe Schulte-Körne et al. 1997, 1998). Ohne Unterstützung sollten Eltern das Programm nicht durchführen.

Voraussetzungen, wenn Fachkräfte das Training durchführen

Generell setzt die Durchführung des Trainingprogramms eingehende Kenntnisse über die Lese- und Rechtschreibstörung voraus. Zusätzlich wäre eine psychotherapeutische Zusatzqualifikation empfehlenswert, da nicht selten bei den betroffenen Kindern psychische Probleme vorliegen. Insbesondere kann der Einsatz von verhaltenstherapeutischen Methoden bei der Durchführung des Trainings sinnvoll sein (siehe hierzu Scheerer-Neumann 1988).

Literaturverzeichnis

Amorosa, H., Müller-Egloff, E., Pretzlik, E.: Treatment approaches in dyslexia. Acta Paedopsychiatrica, 56, 199-202, 1994.

Dummer, L., Hackethal, R.: Kieler Leseaufbau, Veries, Kiel 1984.

Dumont, J.J., Oud, J., van Mameren-Schoehuizen, G., Jakobs, M., van Herpen, M., van Bekerom, F.: Effectiveness of dyslexia treatment. In Pavlidis, G.T. (Hrsg.) Perspectives on dyslexia, vol 2, 293-325, Wiley, Chichester 1990.

Frith, U.: Beneath the surface of developmental dyslexia. In Patterson, K.E., Marshall, J.C., Coltheart, M. (Hrsg.) Surface dyslexia: Neuropsychological and cognitive studies of phonological reading. L. Erlbaum, London 1985.

Gasteiger-Klicpera, B., Klicpera, C.; Legasthenieförderkurse an den Grundschulen: Ein geeignetes Fördermodell? In Dummer-Smoch, L.: Legasthenie. Bericht über den Fachkongress 1988. Bundesverband Legasthenie e.V. 1988.

Glogauer, W.: Die quantitative und qualitative Rechtschreibfehler-Analyse bei 7/8 jährigen Schülern. Schule und Psychologie, 17, 225-234, 1970.

Mannhaupt, G.: Deutschsprachige Studien zu Intervention bei Lese-Rechtschreibschwierigkeiten: Ein Überblick zu neueren Forschungstrends. Zeitschrift für Pädagogische Psychologie, 8, 123-138, 1994.

Müller, R.: Erfolgskontrolle eines gezielten Rechtschreibtrainings in homogenen Förderungsgruppen. In W. Siersleben (Hrsg.): Lernen heute. Beltz, Weinheim 1969.

Pregel, D., Rickheit,G.: Der Grundwortschatz im Grundschulalter. Olms, Hildesheim 1987.

Reith, D., Weber, R.: Ist die Rechtschreibschwäche überwindbar. Westermanns Pädagogische Beiträge, 25, 493-498, 1973.

Reuter-Liehr, C.: Behandlung der Lese-Rechtschreibstörung nach der Grundschulzeit: Anwendung und Überprüfung eines Konzeptes. Zeitschrift für Kinder- und Jugendpsychiatrie, 21, 135-147, 1993.

Scheerer-Neumann, G.: Intervention bei Lese-Rechtschreibstörung. Überblick über Theorien, Methoden und Ergebnisse. Kamp, Bochum 1979.

Scheerer-Neumann, G.: Rechtschreibtraining mit rechtschreibschwachen Hauptschülern auf kognitionspsychologischer Grundlage: Eine empirische Untersuchung. Westdeutscher Verlag, Opladen 1988.

Scheerer-Neumann, G.: Interventions in developmental reading and spelling disorders. In Grimm, H., Skowronek, H. (Eds.): Language acquisition problems and reading disorders: aspects of diagnosis and intervention, 319-360. Walter de Gruyter, Berlin 1993.

Schneider, W., Springer, A.: Individualisierendes Rechtschreibtraining auf verhaltenstherapeutischer Basis. Psychologie in Erziehung und Unterricht, 25, 197-204, 1978.

Schneider, W., Küspert, P., Roth, E., Vise, M., Marx, H.: Short- and long-term effects of training phonological awareness in kindergarten: evidence from two German studies. Journal of Experimental Child Psychology, 66, 311-340, 1997.

Schneider, W., Roth, E., Küspert, P., Ennemoser, M.: Kurz- und langfristige Effekte eines Trainings der sprachlichen (phonologischen) Bewusstheit bei unterschiedlichen Leistungsgruppen: Befunde einer Sekundäranalyse. Zeitschrift für Entwicklungspsychologie und Pädagogische Psychologie, XXX (1), 26-39, 1998.

Schulte-Körne G. Lese-Rechtschreibstörung und Sprachwahrnehmung. Psychometrische und neurophysiologische Untersuchungen zur Legasthenie. Waxmann Verlag 2001.

Schulte-Körne, G., Schäfer, J., Deimel, W., Remschmidt, H.: Das Marburger Eltern-Kind-Rechtschreibtraining. Zeitschrift für Kinder- und Jugendpsychiatrie und Psychotherapie, 25, 151-159, 1997.

Schulte-Körne, G., Deimel, W., Remschmidt, H.: Das Marburger Eltern-Kind-Rechtschreibtraining – Verlaufsuntersuchung nach 2 Jahren. Zeitschrift für Kinder- und Jugendpsychiatrie und Psychotherapie, 26, 167-173, 1998.

Schulte-Körne, G., Deimel, W., Hülsmann, J., Seidler, T., Remschmidt, H.: Das Marburger Rechtschreib-Training – Ergebnisse einer Kurzzeit-Intervention. Zeitschrift für Kinder- und Jugendpsychiatrie und Psychotherapie, 29 (1), 7-15, 2001a.

Schulte-Körne, G., Deimel, W., Remschmidt, H.: Zur Diagnostik der Lese-Rechtschreibstörung. Zeitschrift für Kinder- und Jugendpsychiatrie und Psychotherapie, 29 (2), 2001b.

Schulte-Körne, G., Mathwig, F.: Das Marburger Rechtschreibtraining. Ein regegeleitetes Rechtschreibtraining für rechtschreibschwache Kinder, Verlag Dr. Winkler, Bochum, 2001.

Tacke, G., Nock, H., Staiber, W.: Rechtschreibförderkurse in der Schule: Wie erfolgreich sind sie, und welche Faktoren tragen zu Leistungsverbesserungen bei? Zeitschrift für Pädagogische Psychologie, 1, 45-52, 1987.

Wimmer, H., Hartl, M.: Erprobung einer phonologisch, multisensorischen Förderung bei jungen Schülern mit Lese-Rechtschreibschwierigkeiten. Heilpädagogische Forschung, XVII, 74-79, 1991.

4.7 Spezifische Förderung in einem Lehrgang über zwei Jahre in LRS-Klassen durch engagierte Grundschullehrer

Monika Szaszi

1 LRS-Klassen in Sachsen

Schon in der damaligen DDR gab es Kleinklassen mit Schülern, bei denen eine Lese-Rechtschreib-Schwäche diagnostiziert wurde. Prof. Ralph Weigt entwickelte damals einen spezifischen Lehrplan, Lehrbücher und Arbeitshefte. Damit wurde in allen LRS-Klassen gearbeitet.

Nach der Wende konnten die LRS-Klassen bei uns in Sachsen erhalten werden. Während es zuvor im Bezirk Karl-Marx-Stadt nur 8 LRS-Klassen gab, wurde die Anzahl nach der Wende im Regierungsbezirk auf 64 erhöht. Man kann nun sagen, dass wir ein flächendeckendes Netz an LRS-Klassen haben.

1.1 Meldung und Begutachtungsverfahren für Schüler mit Lese-Rechtschreib-Schwäche

Die Verwaltungsvorschrift des Sächsischen Staatsministeriums für Kultus zur Förderung von Schülern mit Schwierigkeiten im Lesen und Rechtschreiben in LRS-Klassen an Grundschulen im Freistaat Sachsen regelt die Vorgehensweise.

Die Grundschulen melden uns die Schüler, die in Klasse 2 besonders auffällig in Lesen und Rechtschreiben sind. Es wird ein Antrag zur Teilnahme am LRS-Begutachtungsverfahren gestellt. Der Schulleiter schreibt mit dem entsprechenden Schüler ein Überprüfungsdiktat. Dieses wird uns mit allen notwendigen Unterlagen unkorrigiert zugeschickt. Gleichzeitig wird ein Termin beim Psychologen und beim Logopäden beantragt, damit ein psychologisches und ein logopädisches Gutachten erstellt werden kann. Im März erfolgt dann das Begutachtungverfahren, das von den Grundschullehrern durchgeführt wird, die in LRS-Klassen unterrichten. Begleitet wird es durch einen Logopäden und einen Psychologen. An zwei aufeinander folgenden Tagen kommen die gemeldeten Schüler von 08.00 bis 12.00 Uhr in unsere Schule. In Lektionen und durch Einzelüberprüfungen werden die mathematischen Fähigkeiten, das Schreiben nach Diktat, das Abschreiben, die Lernfähigkeit, das Lesen, die Buchstabenkenntnisse, das Zusammenziehen von Lauten, die Merkfähigkeit und das Nachzeichnen von geometrischen Formen in ein Punktegitter überprüft. Alle Tests werden genau analysiert und ausgewertet. Durch eine normierte Bewertungstabelle wird die LRS-Stufe für jeden Teilbereich festgelegt. Es gibt die LRS-Stufen I bis V. Ein Team von besonders erfahrenen Personen (z.B. Lehrer, die in LRS-Klassen unterrichten, ein Psychologe, ein Logopäde, ein Vertreter des Regionalschulamtes) legen nach Beendigung des Begutachtungsverfahrens die Gesamtstufe des Schweregrades der LRS fest und nach gründlicher Sichtung aller Unterlagen entscheiden sie, wer die Empfehlung für die Aufnahme in eine LRS-Klasse erhält. Wenn die Eltern ihre Zustimmung geben, erfolgt im August eine Umschulung in eine LRS-Klasse 3/I. Zwei Jahre besucht dann das Kind die Klasse 3. Es wird also ein Dehnjahr eingeschoben. Im ersten Jahr wird in der LRS-Klasse der gesamte Lehrplanstoff Klasse 1 und 2 der Grundschule wiederholt, aber mit spezifischen Methoden und in Klasse 3/II wird dann der Lehrplanstoff der Klasse 3 der Grundschule behandelt. Nach Beendigung des 2-jährigen Zykluses wird das Kind dann in Klasse 4 wieder an die Heimatschule umgeschult.

1.2 Der Unterricht in Klasse 3/I

Die ersten Schulwochen sind dadurch geprägt, dass sehr intensiv die phonematische, optische, sprechmotorische und rhythmisch-melodische Differenzierungsfähigkeit geschult wird. Um den Schülern die Angst vor erneutem Versagen zu ersparen, werden anfangs kaum schriftliche Leistungen abverlangt. In spielerischer und abwechslungsreicher Form werden die Übungen gestaltet. Wichtig ist für uns, dass die Schüler Freude dabei haben, Erfolgserlebnisse verzeichnen können und so bereit sind, die nächste Schwierigkeitsstufe zu meistern. Dazu gehört dann zum Beispiel das Lösen schriftlicher Übungen. Methodische Anregungen dazu können sich die Lehrer aus der Broschüre „Handreichung für Lehrer zur Lese-Rechtschreib-Schwäche“ entnehmen, die vom Comenius-Institut für den Freistaat Sachsen herausgegeben wurde.

In dieser Anfangsphase nutzen wir auch methodische Anregungen, die wir dem Kieler Lese-und Rechtschreibaufbau entnommen haben. Alle Laute und Buchstaben werden noch einmal neu erarbeitet. Dabei berücksichtigen wir die Schwierigkeitsstufen, die der Kieler Lese- und Rechtschreibaufbau vorgibt:

Schwierigkeitsstufe I → leicht hörbare Laute (lange Vokale, dehnbare Konsonanten)

Schwierigkeitsstufe II → nicht dehnbare Konsonanten (vor allem Verschlusslaute)

Schwierigkeitsstufe III → alle übrigen Laute, vor allem solche, die durch zwei oder mehr Buchstaben repräsentiert werden (z.B. pf, ch)

Zu jedem neu erarbeiteten Laut und Buchstaben werden intensive Übungen zur Schulung des phonematischen Gehörs und zur sprechmotorischen Gliederungsfähigkeit durchgeführt. Dabei nutzen wir gerne die Signalkarten. Das methodische Vorgehen beschreibt Prof. Weigt auf S. 114–121 in seinem Buch „Lesen- und Schreibenlernen kann jeder?“.

Als zusätzliche Unterstützung nutzen wir auch die Lautgebärden des Kieler Lese- und Rechtschreibaufbaus. Für einige Kinder ist es ein wichtiges Hilfsmittel, um sich Laute und Buchstaben besser einzuprägen und das Zusammenziehen von Lauten zu unterstützen. Alle Kinder nutzen sie mit viel Freude. Auch das ist ein wichtiger Aspekt.

Bei der Erarbeitung der Buchstaben werden weiterhin alle vier Buchstabenformen gelernt, da den Kindern diese aus den ersten Schuljahren bereits bekannt sind.

Der Leselernprozess muss noch einmal ganz von vorn begonnen werden, da viele Kinder, wenn sie zu uns kommen, nicht in der Lage sind, zwei Laute zu einer Silbe zusammen-zu-ziehen. Deshalb beginnen wir bei der Einführung von Lautverbindungen und Buchstaben-ver-bindungen auf der Silbenebene. Gut angenommen werden dabei die Marsmännchengeschichten und der Silbenteppich vom Kieler Leseaufbau. Die Verschmelzung zweier Laute zu einer Silbe gelingt den meisten Kindern besser, wenn sie zur Unterstützung die Lautgebärden nutzen.

Um gut schreiben und lesen zu lernen, müssen größere Einheiten wahrgenommen werden. Deshalb sind Übungen zur Erfassung der Silbenstruktur eines Wortes wichtig. Dabei nutzen wir gern die Silbenbogen oder Silbenboote. Zur Unterstützung der rhythmischen

Wahrnehmung wird das Sprechen der Silben mit Körperbewegungen verbunden. Auch dazu bietet das Material zum Kieler Lese- und Rechtschreibaufbau methodische Anregungen.

Als Übungsmaterial für die Hand des Kindes nutzen wir in Klasse 3/I die LRS-Hefte 1 und 3 „Üb mit mir" vom Verlag Dürr und Kessler Regensburg.

Von entscheidender Bedeutung für das richtige Schreiben von Wörtern ist das konsequente Lautieren und deshalb täglicher Bestandteil des Unterrichtes. Prof. Weigt hat dazu sechs Grundsätze erarbeitet, die zum erfolgreichen Lautieren beitragen. Sie sind nachzulesen in seinem Buch „Lesen- und Schreibenlernen kann jeder !?" Seite 183-185.

Alle LRS-Schüler sollen systematisch an die Gesetzmäßigkeiten der Rechtschreibung herangeführt werden, deshalb sollen sie durch das kommentierte Lautieren befähigt werden, Laut– und Schriftbild miteinander zu vergleichen (Weigt 1994 S. 188/189).

Beim kommentierten Schreiben werden vorher festgelegte rechtschreibliche Besonderheiten angesagt (Weigt 1994 S. 190-201). Diese Kommentare finden in dem LRS-Arbeitsheft 2 „Üb mit mir" Berücksichtigung. Um bei allen Schülern zu überprüfen, ob die rechtschreiblichen bzw. die grammatischen Besonderheiten erfasst wurden, habe ich das Kommentarbrett entwickelt. Die Anfertigung dieses Kommentarbrettes wird in dem Ergänzungsmaterial (Kopiervorlagen) zum LRS-Heft 2 „Üb mit mir" beschrieben.

Durch meine langjährigen Erfahrungen im Unterricht bei Schülern mit einer Legasthenie weiß ich, dass sich durch die speziellen Methoden, wie z.B. die intensive Schulung der phonematischen und optischen Wahrnehmungsfähigkeit oder durch konsequentes Lautieren Auslassungs-, Umstellungs-, Hinzufügungs– und Verwechslungsfehler reduzieren. Dagegen halten sich Regelfehler hartnäckiger. Aus diesem Grund bin ich dazu übergegangen, bewusster mit den Rechtschreibregeln zu arbeiten. Ich habe mir fünf Rechtschreibregeln zusammengestellt und sie durch Symbole verdeutlicht. Dadurch soll das Einprägen erleichtert werden.

Eine wichtige Voraussetzung bei der Nutzung der Regeln ist, dass der Schüler mit den Begriffen Selbstlaut (S), Mitlaut (M), Wortstamm, Endung und Stammselbstlaut umgehen kann.

Außerdem sind im Vorfeld intensive Differenzierungsübungen zum Erkennen der Länge und Kürze der Vokale notwendig.

Das sind die fünf Rechtschreibregeln:

1. Regel:
   S (kurz) MM → wie in „Keller" – nach kurzem Selbstlaut folgen zwei gleiche Mitlaute
2. Regel:
   S (kurz) M***M*** → wie in „Kerze" – nach kurzem Selbstlaut folgen zwei verschiedene Mitlaute
3. Regel:
   S (lang) M → wie in „schmal, Schere" – nach langem Selbstlaut folgt ein Mitlaut
4. Regel:
   S (lang) ***h*** vor l,m,n,r → wie in „Stuhl, nehmen" – nach langem Selbstlaut folgt meist vor l, m, n, r ein Dehnungs-h.
5. Regel:
   S (lang) ***h*** am Stammende → wie in „Reh, gehen"

Besondere Fälle der Rechtschreibung, also Wörter, bei denen die Regeln nicht genutzt werden können, müssen mit den Kindern besonders besprochen werden.

Genauere Erläuterungen zum bewussten Einsatz dieser Regeln gibt es in den Handreichungen für Lehrer zur Lese- Rechtschreib-Schwäche des Freistaates Sachsen Seite 46/47.

Durch diese vielfältigen Methodenkombinationen ist es uns Lehrern besser gelungen, die Lese- Rechtschreib- Schwäche bei den Schülern abzubauen.

Besonders glücklich sind wir, wenn wir erfahren, dass Schüler von uns in ein Gymnasium aufgenommen wurden und dort erfolgreich lernen. Wir kennen auch Schüler, die erfolgreich ein Studium absolviert haben und nun mit beiden Beinen fest im Leben stehen. Das gibt auch uns Kraft.

1.3 Fortbildungsmaßnahmen für Lehrer, die in LRS-Klassen unterrichten

Alle LRS-Klassen in Sachsen sind einer Grundschule zugeordnet und werden ausschließlich von Grundschullehrern unterrichtet. Von Seiten des Schulamtes ist man bemüht, engagierte und interessierte Lehrer für den Unterricht in LRS-Klassen zu finden. Regelmäßig treffen sich diese Lehrer zu Fortbildungsveranstaltungen, um sich immer tiefgründiger und umfassender mit der gesamten LRS-Problematik auseinanderzusetzen.

Außerdem gibt es seit Februar 1999 eine 2-jährige berufsbegleitende Fortbildung für Lehrer, die in LRS-Klassen unterrichten. Zur Zeit nehmen 50 Lehrer daran teil. Jeweils eine Woche im Februar, Mai, Juli und Oktober nutzen sie das umfangreiche Angebot an Vorlesungen und Seminaren in Meißen. Die Fortbildungsteilnehmer erhalten Studienaufträge und müssen als Abschlussbeleg eine umfassende Dokumentation über einen Schüler mit einer vermuteten oder diagnostizierten LRS erstellen.

Wenn dieser Kurs erfolgreich beendet wird, bekommen die Lehrer ein Zertifikat des Kultusministeriums. Dieser Kurs erteilt die Befähigung, mit LRS-Schülern auf den Gebieten der Beratung, Diagnostik und Förderung zu arbeiten und als Multiplikator zu wirken.

Literatur

Brose, B./Dummer-Smoch, L./Renatus, K./Szaszi, M./Weigt,R.Handreichung für Grundschule, Förderschule, Mittelschule und Gymnasium Lese- Rechtschreib- Schwäche Sächsisches Staatsinstitut für Bildung und Schulentwicklung, Comenius Institut, 1996, Stoba-Druck GmbH, Lampertswalde

Dummer-Smoch,L./Hackethal,R.: Handbuch zum Kieler Leseaufbau Veris Verlag, Kiel 1994

Dummer-Smoch,L.,/Hackethal,R.: Handbuch zum Kieler Rechtschreibaufbau Veris Verlag, Kiel 1996

Sächsisches Staatsministerium für Kultus: Verwaltungsvorschrift zur Förderung von Schülern mit Schwierigkeiten im Lesen und Rechtschreiben in LRS-Klassen an Grundschulen im Freistaat Sachsen. Vom 05.10.1992, Amtsblatt Nr. 15, S. 10 f., vom 28.01.1993, Amtsblatt Nr. 3, S. 101, vom 11.03.1994, Amtsblatt Nr. 8, S. 201

Szaszi,M./Braun,P./Jerusel,H.: Üb mit mir! Arbeitshefte 1,2,3, Fördermaterial Deutsch LRS Verlag Dürr und Kessler, Regensburg 1995

Weigt, R.: Lesen- und Schreibenlernen kann jeder!? Methodische Hilfen bei Lese-Rechtschreib-Schwäche, Luchterhand, Wied/Kriftel/ Berlin 1994

4.8 Spielen statt üben – Kompensationshilfen durch geeignete Spiele in der Förderung

Barbara Seidel-Steffen

Übungshilfen für Eltern

1 Die Bedeutung des Spiels

„Peter ist noch zu verspielt." „Moni hat den Ernst der Schule noch nicht begriffen." So oder ähnlich steht es in Zeugnissen. „Das Lesen muss er noch tüchtig üben." „ Bei mehr Übung würde sie weniger Rechtschreibfehler machen." Jeder sieht es ein: Bei derartigen Schwierigkeiten muss *mehr getan werden!* Lehrer entwickeln neue Übungsformen , oftmals Arbeitsblätter. Eltern verbringen Stunde um Stunde, um ihre Kinder für Diktat- oder Leseübungen zu motivieren. Häufig bleibt der Erfolg aus. Die Kinder möchten lieber spielen. Lassen wir sie doch einmal spielen und beobachten wir dabei, was sie tun, wirklich tun!

„**Spiel,...:** eine lustbetonte, von äußeren Zwecken freie, ungezwungene, vorwiegend von der Phantasie geleitete und sie anregende biologisch bedingte Tätigkeit, die große soziale, kulturelle und pädagog. Bedeutung besitzt." (Bertelsmann Lexikon, Band 13, Bertelsmann Lexikothek Verlag GMbH Gütersloh, 1985 A, S. 320). In weiteren Erklärungen wird daraufhingewiesen, dass das Spielen in psychologischer Sicht **Arbeit** bedeutet und **mit Anstrengung verbunden** sein kann.

Wir wissen, dass die Tätigkeiten, die uns Spaß bereiten, von uns gerne wiederholt werden. Wiederholungen **festigen unser Wissen**, unsere Geschicklichkeit bei geistigen und körperlichen Aufgaben. Also lassen wir die Kinder doch spielen!

Grundsätzliche Kriterien für die Auswahl der Spiele

Für mein Schulkind, das übend im Lese- und / oder Rechtschreibprozess sicherer werden soll, muss ich die obengenannte Definition von „Spiel" einschränken. **Neben** der freien, unverplanten Zeit für jedes Kind, **muss ich zweckgebundene Spiele** anbieten, weil die für Lesen und Schreiben nötigen Tätigkeiten (Teilleistungen) sonst vermieden werden. Trotzdem sollte man den Spielcharakter hervorheben.Im Vordergrund steht die Suche nach **dem** Spiel, das **von dem Kind** als lustbetont empfunden wird. Für die Auswahl des Angebots ist es unabdingbar, die **Stärken** und die **Schwächen meines Kindes** sowie die **Leistungsanforderungen des Spiels** zu kennen. Was es gut kann, wird es gerne mögen bzw. sich überreden lassen, es zu tun. Alle Tätigkeiten, bei denen sich eine Schwäche auswirkt, werden vermieden.

„Memory" wird von Kindern mit einer Schwäche hauptsächlich im Behalten von Gesehenem (visuelle Speicherschwäche) eher abgelehnt. „ Kofferpacken" ist für diejenigen eine Zumutung, die vornehmlich Schwierigkeiten im Behalten von Gehörtem (auditive Speicherschwäche) haben. Als Faustregel kann gelten: **Sehen, Hören, Sprechen und Handeln sollten anteilig in jedem Spiel vorhanden sein,** damit die Stärken des Kindes **zur erfolgreichen Spielbeeinflussung** eingesetzt werden können. Für das oben genannte **visuell schwache Kind** wird das „ **Memory**"- Spiel verändert: Die beiden aufgedeckten Bild- oder Wortkarten müssen angetippt und mit dem Wort benannt bzw. vorgelesen werden. Die Karten verbleiben aufgedeckt, bis der nächste Mitspieler sie wieder umdreht und dann seine beiden Karten aufdeckt. „**Kofferpacken**" **mit auditiv schwachen Kindern** ist möglich, wenn die Dinge, die aus dem Gedächtnis wiederholt werden müssen, als Bildkarten (Gegenstand oder Wortkarten?) vorhanden sind. Sie werden beim „Einpacken" nach und nach unter eine Decke, Tablett o.ä. geschoben und auf Wunsch eines jeden Mitspielers kurz für alle sichtbar in der richtigen Reihenfolge angetippt und benannt. Die Gewissheit nachschauen zu können lässt die Sicherheit und das **Vertrauen in die eigene Gedächtnisleistung** stetig wachsen. Gleiches gilt für Schreibspiele. **Fehlervermeidend** können Wortlisten sein, die neben dem Spielplan liegen und zur Kontrolle benutzt werden können.

Der mitspielende Erwachsene kann zum gleichgestellten Spielpartner werden, indem er erschwerte Bedingungen bekommt, z.B. keine Unterstützung durch das wiederholende Sehen, keine Wortliste usw.

Ein **Reiz zur Anstrengungsbereitschaft** kann durch **„Hilfe-Knöpfe"** (aus Omas Knopfkiste o.ä.) gegeben werden. Für jeden Spielvorgang werden drei Knöpfe pro Kind ausgegeben. Durch Abgabe eines Knopfes erhält der Spieler eine Hilfestellung, die ihm zur Lösung der Aufgabe verhilft. Die nicht „verbrauchten" Knöpfe können in einer Schachtel gesammelt und nach vorher festgelegten Bedingungen eingetauscht werden. Das **Tauschobjekt** (z.B. ein besonderer Stift) muss nur begehrlich genug sein und in einem zumutbaren Zeitabschnitt (z.B. in einer Woche) erreicht werden können.

Spiele und ihr Einsatz in verschiedenen Phasen der Lese- und Schreibentwicklung

Die Spiele, die ich Ihnen nun nahebringen möchte, sind vielen von Ihnen nicht neu. Die Ideen finden Sie in vielen praxisbezogenen Büchern, von denen ich einige im Anhang nenne. Vielfach habe ich Spiele dahingegen abgewandelt, damit sie die oben genannten Kriterien erfüllen. Manches entstand durch Anregungen von Kolleginnen und Kollegen. Meine Auswahl habe ich getroffen für Eltern, die mit ihren Kindern zusätzlich zu den Hausaufgaben kleine spielerische Übungseinheiten gestalten müssen.

1.1 Spiele für die Basisfunktionen Gleichgewicht, Körperbewusstsein, Sehen und Hören finden Sie in Ihrer Erinnerung an Ihre eigene Kindheit und in allen Elternratgebern für die Zeit vor der Schule (Hinker-Spiele, Ball-Probe, Halli-Hallo u.ä.) **Das Holzfällerspiel** (verändert nach: „Spiel mit am Strand", Fischer Verlag) **15 DINA4-Bögen** (schön ist farbiges Tonpapier) werden – die schmalen Seiten aneinander – in eine Reihe gelegt (=Baumstamm). **Spieler A und Spieler B** (= Holzfäller) stellen sich **jeweils mit einem Würfel** in der Hand auf die Endstücke. Nun wird abwechselnd gewürfelt und so viele Bögen vorgerückt, wie Punkte gewürfelt wurden. Versperrt der Gegner den Weg, muss der Spieler um die restliche Punktzahl rückwärts gehen. Sieger wird, wer den Gegner über den Start hinausdrängt.

1.2 Spiele zur Lautunterscheidung

1.2.1 Anlaut-Spiele (jeweils ca.5 Minuten):

„Ich sehe was, was du nicht siehst und das fängt mit „P"an. (Unbedingt lautieren und nicht „Pe" sagen!). Für jedes richtig genannte Ding bekommt der „Rater" einen Muggelstein, auch wenn es nicht das Objekt des „Sehers" ist. Für jedes Wort mit falschem Anlaut muss der „Rater" einen Stein an den „Seher" abgeben. Wurde das Objekt genannt, wird gewechselt. Sieger ist, wer nach der vereinbarten Zeit die meisten Steine hat. Memory mit Bildkarten, bei denen jeweils zwei mit gleichem Anlaut gesucht werden sollen. Material in Dr.Dummer-Smoch,L. Laute- Silben- Wörter, Schülerarbeitsheft Echo-Spiel: Die Grundlage dieses Spiels bilden Wortkarten, die unter verschiedenen Gesichtspunkten gesammelt oder zusammengestellt wurden: z.B. Wörter, die einmal falsch geschrieben wurden (Sammelwörter), Lernwörter einer Rechtschreib-Problematik (z.B. lautgetreu, Konsonanten-Dopplung oder Konsonanten-Häufung in der Mitte des Wortes, Wörter mit unterschiedlicher Silbenzahl). Der Spielverlauf kann variiert werden: Zwei Spieler sitzen Rücken an Rücken, a.) Spieler A liest die obere Wortkarte seines Stapels vor, Spieler B wiederholt ohne Anlaut. Ist die Antwort richtig, erhält Spieler B die Karte und steckt sie als letzte Karte unter seinen Stapel. War die Antwort falsch, steckt Spieler A die Karte unter seinen Stapel. Dann liest Spieler B vor usw. Sieger ist, wer nach einer vorher abgemachten Zeit die meisten Karten hat.b) Spieler A liest das Wort ohne Anfangslaut vor. Spieler B muss raten, wie das ganze Wort heißt.Geeignetes Material finden Sie in den Wörter-Listen des Kieler Lese-und Rechtschreibaufbaus.

1.2.2 Buchstabenformen unterscheiden

Spiel-Idee: Meister, H."Stibitz", Otto Maier Verlag Ravensburg, 1991 10 verschiedene Motive sind jeweils viermal als Pappbilder vorhanden.Sie fertigen sich also von 10 Buchstaben jeweils vier Kärtchen an (unbedingt die Schreiblinie kennzeichnen!). Schreiben Sie gleiche Buchstaben in gleicher Farbe. Die Karten werden gemischt und offen ausgelegt. Während sich die Mitspieler umdrehen, nimmt ein Spieler eine Buchstabenkarte weg und deckt sie zu. Die Mitspieler versuchen nun herauszufinden, welcher Buchstabe fehlt. Für die richtige Antwort darf der Spieler einen von drei vorher ausgegebenen Chips abgeben, für eine falsche Antwort bekommt er einen Chip aus dem Topf dazu. Sieger ist, wer zuerst keinen Chip mehr hat. Die Aufgabe des Aufdekkens geht reihum.

1.2.3 Laute aus einem Wort heraushören

Spiel-Idee: „Pferderennen", ein Jahrmarktspiel, nach Renate HackethalPro Spieler (Jockey) gibt es, einschließlich Start und Ziel, linear angeordnet 15 Stationen. Die Spielsteine stehen auf dem ihm zugehörigen Startfeld bereit. Für das anstehende Rennen wählt jeder Mitspieler einen Laut/ Buchstaben des Alphabets als Signal aus. Wortkarten werden gemischt und von den Spielern abwechselnd vorgelesen. So häufig wie der ausgewählte Buchstabe vorkommt, so viele Stationen darf der Spieler vorrükken. Hört er es nicht heraus, darf er einen Helfer-Knopf einsetzen. Sieger ist, wer zuerst über die Ziellinie geht. Spiel-Idee: „Vorwärts oder rückwärts?", Regelein, Lernspiele im Deutschunterricht, Oldenbourg Verlag GmbH, München. Für dieses Würfelspiel benötigt man ein lineares Spielfeld mit Start und Ziel. Die einzelnen Stationen bestehen aus Wörtern und ihren Abbildungen, die in willkürlicher Reihenfolge angeordnet sind. Spieler A setzt seinen Spielstein entsprechend seiner Würfelzahl. Kommt er auf ein Wort, muss er sich auf das dazugehörige Bild – vorwärts oder rückwärts – begeben. Kommt er auf ein Bild , geht er entsprechend auf das Wort. Sieger ist, wer das Ziel zuerst direkt erreicht.Frau Regelein hat einen Spielplan mit Wörtern der Konsonanten-Dopplung entworfen. Hildegard Roosen stellt einen Plan mit auffälligen Buchstabenkombinationen und Abbildungen vor („all"/ Ball), Roosen in Niemeyer (Hg.), Kommunikation und Lese-Rechtschreibschwäche, Verlag Dr. Dieter Winkler, Bochum 1995.

1.3 Silben erkennen

Spiel-Idee: „Dübelspiel“, ein Würfelspiel aus dem Spielehandel. Es besteht aus einer schmalen Holzkiste mit einem dicken Schiebedeckel, in den linear fünf Kuhlen und ein Loch gebohrt sind. Ich ersetze die Würfel durch eine Anzahl Wortkarten mit unterschiedlich langen Wörtern. Alle Spieler bekommen die gleiche Anzahl an Dübeln (z.B. 7). Es wird reihum gewürfelt. Der Spieler mit der höchsten Punktzahl beginnt. Er nimmt die obere der verdeckt liegenden Wortkarten, liest sie vor und besetzt – vom Start ausgehend – die Kuhle (oder das Loch) der Silbenanzahl. Bei einem Wort mit sechs Silben fällt der Dübel in die Kiste. Der Spieler darf solange Wortkarten aufnehmen, bis er ein Wort mit einer Silbenzahl bekommt, dessen Kuhle schon durch einen Dübel besetzt ist. Diesen Dübel muss er nun wieder zu seinen verbliebenen legen und der nächste Spieler ist an der Reihe. Sieger ist derjenige, der als erster keinen Dübel mehr hat. Spiel-Idee: „Mensch-ärgere-dich-nicht“, statt des Würfels bringt mich die unterschiedliche Anzahl der Silben von Wortkarten voran, die gemischt verdeckt neben dem Spielplan liegen. Die Spieler heben abwechselnd die jeweils zuoberst liegende Karte ab und setzen ihre Figur, indem sie deutlich die einzelnen Silben des Wortes sprechen, für jede Silbe ein Feld weiter. Einzelheiten der Regeln müssen zu Spielbeginn abgesprochen werden (z.B. Rauswerfen). Mit vorher markierten Ereignisfeldern kann das Spiel abwechslungsreicher gestaltet werden. Wer auf ein solches kommt, muss eine Ereigniskarte lesen und die Aufgabe erfüllen. Das können reine Bewegungsaufgaben sein („Hüpfe auf deinem linken Fuß einmal um deinen Stuhl herum“) oder eine Rechtschreibübung beinhalten („Schreibe drei Wörter mit –ah- auf!“).Zur Erstellung eines Spielplans eignen sich auch sehr gut Straßenkarten der heimatlichen Region, eine Deutschlandkarte o.ä. Der Weg wird dann durch Kreise oder Rechtecke markiert, die man mit farbigen Stiften aufträgt. Spiel-Idee: „Schiffe – versenken“ oder „Marsmännchen-Spiel“ aus“ Hackethal R., „Praxis zum Kieler Leseaufbau und Kieler Rechtschreibaufbau“,Veris Verlag, oder auch als „Mäuschen-Spiel“ von R.Hackethal bekannt:

Jeder Mitspieler bekommt einen Spielplan, der aus einem Raster besteht, z.B. sechs Kästchen breit und vier Kästchen hoch.Das linke obere Feld wird nicht beschriftet. Daneben schreibt man in die einzelnen Felder die Vokale a, e, i, o, u. Die linke senkrechte Spalte wird mit Konsonanten beschriftet z.B. K, P, T oder kr, tr, pr.Ein Spieler malt nun –für die anderen nicht sichtbar- drei Mäuschen einzeln in die freien Kästchen seiner Wahl.Die anderen versuchen nun reihum durch Fragen die Mäuschen zu finden: „Ist ein Mäuschen in „kra“ versteckt? Ist das nicht der Fall, schreiben alle Mitspieler „kra“ in das entsprechende Feld. Befindet es sich aber in dem erfragten Feld, darf der „Frager“ ein Mäuschen in seinen Plan zeichnen und die anderen kennzeichnen das Feld mit einem Strich von der linken unteren bis zur rechten oberen Ecke. Sieger ist, wer die meisten Mäuschen gefunden hat.

1.4 Wortstämme, grammatische Strukturen:

Spiel-Idee: „Schiffe-versenken“, s.o., Konsonannten-Dopplung in Verben : Schreiben Sie in nur drei waagerechte Kästchen entsprechende Verben im Infinitiv (Grundform) – z.B. kennen, trennen, beginnen. In die linke senkrechte Spalte gehören untereinander die Personalpronomen: ich, du, er, sie, es, wir, ihr, sie. Kennzeichnen Sie Einzahl und Mehrzahl durch besondere Farben. Beim Aufschreiben der Wörter im Spiel werden die Veränderungen bei den Endungen deutlich.

Thema: Zeiten. Den gleichen Spiel-Plan können Sie verwenden, um die Zeitformen zu üben. Legen Sie zu Beginn fest, welche Zeitform gebildet werden soll. Der Unterschied zwischen regelmäßigen und unregelmäßigen Verben springt bei diesem Spiel ins Auge, ohne dass Sie viel erklären müssen.

1.5 Gedächtnis

„Coco Crazy“, von H. Bücken, Ravensburger Spieleverlag GmbH, 1998: Auf einem runden Spielplan stehen sechs undurchsichtige – aus zwei Teilen zusammengesteckte – „Kokosnüsse“. In ihnen befinden sich jeweils soviel gleichfarbige Affen-Figuren, wie Personen mitspielen. Zu Beginn schaut jeder verdeckt in eine Nuss und merkt sich die Farbe. Nun wird gewürfelt. Die Würfelbilder geben an, ob die Spieler in eine Nuss schauen, oder alle nacheinander zwei Nüsse vertauschen dürfen, den Spielplan um 90° drehen, auf eine Nuss zeigen, die Farbe benennen und bei der richtigen Angabe eine Figur entnehmen dürfen. Bei dem Joker darf sich der Spieler aussuchen, was er machen möchte. Sieger ist, wer als erster von jeder Farbe einen Affen vor sich stehen hat.Spielen Sie dieses geliebte Spiel, indem Sie in jeder Nuss eine farbige Figur belassen. Jetzt schreibt jeder Mitspieler auf sechs kleine Papierstreifen sechs Wörter, die irgendetwas gemeinsam haben z.B. schwimmt, kommt, musst, brüllt, rennt, kennt; oder fahren, gefahren, fuhr, die Fahrt, die Fährte, gefährlich. Gleiche Wörter werden zusammen in eine Nuss gesteckt und nun wird nach den angegebenen Regeln gespielt. Spiel–Idee: „Pfad-Finder“, Schmidt Spiele 03073, D-8057 Echingen. Zwischen der Start-Karte und der Ziel-Karte wird mit verschiedenen Weg-Karten(Feld, Wald, Weide usw.) nach Lust und Laune ein Weg gebaut. Zehn Standfiguren werden beliebig an die Weg-Karten gestellt. Der erste Spieler versucht sich nun in einer Minute den Wegverlauf, d.h. die Reihenfolge der Weg-Karten, einzuprägen, schließt dann die Augen und gibt aus dem Gedächtnis die Reihenfolge wieder. Nennt er eine falsche Karte, wird sein Spielstein auf die letzte richtige Karte gesetzt. Nun ist der nächste Spieler an der Reihe. Sieger ist, wer als erster das Ziel erreicht hat. Ich spiele das Spiel mit Lernwörtern einer bestimmten Rechtschreibproblematik, z.B. –ah-Wörter (Lernwörter-Übersichten findet man bei Loubier, E., „Richtig schreiben mit System“, Pagenstecher, Beethovenweg 5,23795 Bad Segeberg). Die Weg-Karten können aus kleinen Karteikarten hergestellt werden. Wir schreiben ein Lernwort an die untere lange Seite, drehen die Karte und wiederholen das Wort wiederum an der unteren Kante. So entsteht der „Weg“ zwischen den Worten und es kann von beiden „Spielerseiten“ gelesen werden. Als Anfang und Ende kann jeweils eine lustige Figur aufgestellt werden. Das Spiel folgt den Regeln wie oben beschrieben."Luftwörter“, Spiele für Zuhause, Treff, Velber Verlag GmbH, 2/99. Dieses Spiel trägt ebenfalls zur Festigung von Lernwörtern bei. Ein Spieler stellt sich hinter den anderen, nimmt dessen Hand und schreibt ein Wort aus einer vorher verabredeten Wortliste (vielleicht die Vokabeln?) in die Luft. Rät der geführte Spieler das Wort, bekommt er die Karte und führt nun die Hand des Partners. Sieger ist, wer die meisten Wortkarten hat.

Auswahl des Wortmaterials: Eltern bekommen oft den Hinweis aus der Schule mehr mit ihren Kindern üben zu müssen. Voraussetzung ist, dass es Ihnen gelingt, die richtige Balance zwischen Anforderungen und großzügigem Übergehen von Fehlern zu finden. Das „Wie“ und allgemein auch „Was“ habe ich oben in einer unvollständigen Auswahl dargestellt. Das „Wie“ ist von den Vorlieben Ihres Kindes abhängig und das „Was“ von der Art der Fehler, die

Ihr Kind macht. Ein Realschüler der 5. Klasse – ich nenne ihn Tom – bringt seinen Biologie-Test mit nach Hause. Unter anderem steht da: „Der Igel macht einen Winterschlaff er frisst sich eine dicke Speck schicht an und dann ...geht er in den Bau und Schlaft seinen Winterschlof er ernert sich nur fon der Speck schicht. Die Körpertemper-atur singt auf 5 Grad. Er wacht im Frühling wieder auf.“ Drei Wörter würde ich in ein kleines Heft untereinander schreiben und mit Tom Wörter suchen, die zu diesen „passen“: Winterschlaf / schla-fen / Schlafmütze / Schlafzimmer / Tiefschlafernährt / Nahrung / Ernährung / Nahrungssuche / nahrhaft / ernähren, **oder** die 12 Lernwörter mit „äh“(Loubier,L.,“Richtig schreiben mit System) sinkt / sinken / trinkt / trinken / blinkt / blinken. Und nun müssen wir uns nur noch auf eine Wortgruppe und **ein Spiel** einigen!

Literatur

„Bertelsmann Lexikon“, Band 13, Bertelsmann Lexikothek Verlag GMbH Gütersloh, 1985 A. Blank, H. , „Hüpfekästchen“, Coppenrath Verlag, 1993

Breuer,H./Weuffen,M., „Lernschwierigkeiten am Schulanfang“, Beltz Weinheim und Basel 1993

Dummer-Smoch, L. „Laute- Silben- Wörter“, Schülerarbeitsheft, Veris Verlag 1997

Hackethal, R., „Praxis zum Kieler Leseaufbau und Kieler Rechtschreibaufbau“,Veris Verlag,1990

Hackethal, R., „Zehn Schritte zur Rechtschreibung“, Megalopolis-Verlag 2.Auflage 1996

Heitmann,F., „Wörterspiele für Grundschule und Sekundarstufe 1“, Die Arbeitsmittelwerkstatt Thorsten Schmidt, Lehrmittelverlag, 25358 Horst/Holstein, 1999

Heuß,E., „Sehen/Hören/Sprechen, Lesevorbereitung 1 und 2“, Ravensburger Buchverlag 1973

Loubier, E., „Richtig schreiben mit System“, Pagenstecher, Beethovenweg 5, 23795 Bad Segeberg

Niemeyer (Hg.), Kommunikation und Lese-Rechtschreibschwäche, Verlag Dr. Dieter Winkler, Bochum 1995.

Nitsch, C., „Quatsch mit Kindern“, Rowohlt Taschenbuchverlag Reinbek 1992

Regelein, Lernspiele im Deutschunterricht, Oldenbourg Verlag GmbH, München

Schlender, B., „Krims-Krams-Spiele“, Bastei Lübbe 1991“Spiel mit am Strand“, Fischer Verlag

Blank, H. , „Hüpfekästchen“, Coppenrath Verlag, 1993

Spiele

Bücken, H. „Coco Crazy“, Ravensburger Spieleverlag GmbH, 1998

Meister, H.“Stibitz“, Otto Maier Verlag Ravensburg, 1991

„Pfad-Finder“, Schmidt Spiele 03073, D-8057 Echingen

„Spiele für Zuhause“, Treff, Velber Verlag GmbH, 2/99

4.9 Kieler Lsesaufbau und Kieler Rechtschreibaufbau (zwei getrennte Werke mit unterschiedlicher Zielsetzung aber ähnlich rotem Faden)

Renate Hackethal

Oft wird übersehen, dass der KIELER LESEAUFBAU und der KIELER RECHTSCHREIBAUFBAU zwei getrennte methodische Werke mit unterschiedlicher Zielsetzung sind.

Wenn die Kinder nach dem KIELER LESEAUFBAU lesen gelernt haben, schreiben viele noch sehr fehlerhaft.

Einige Kollegen meinen dann, die Wörter aus dem KIELER LESEAUFBAU noch einmal intensiv üben zu müssen. Die Wörter aus dem KIELER LESEAUFBAU dienen aber allein nur zum Erlernen des Lesens. Es sind keine Wörter dabei wie z.B. Suppe, Kartoffel, Mehl, Autofahrt, also keine Wörter mit Dopplung oder Dehnung.

Treten diese Wörter beim Lesen auf, können sie in der Regel im Textzusammenhang richtig gelesen werden. Es ist nicht schwierig, einen Satz wie „Wir helfen beim Kartoffelschälen." zu lesen. Wer diesen Satz aber schreiben will, wird zunächst sicher Fehler machen.

Der KIELER RECHTSCHREIBAUFBAU hat zum Ziel, die Rechtschreibung durch einen nach Schwierigkeiten gestuften Aufbau zu vermitteln.

Aufgrund der bisher erworbenen Fertigkeiten im Lesen werden sich lautgetreue, alphabetische Schreibungen am besten festigen lassen, denn Rechtschreiben besteht nicht in der zeichnerischen Wiedergabe eines „Wort-Bildes", sondern in der Rekonstruktion der Buchstabenfolge in enger Anlehnung an die Lautfolge. Diese Basisleistung muss anderen Rechtschreibleistungen vorausgehen.

Die Fähigkeit zur Lautdiskrimination ist bei den meisten Zweitklässlern so weit entwickelt, dass auch einfache Konsonantenverbindungen in ihre Lautkomponenten aufgelöst werden können. Wörter mit Konsonantenverbindungen am Anfang (Glaube, Bruder) und in der Mitte (Fragen, Wolke) gehören daher auch zum Übungsstoff am Anfang der Rechtschreiberziehung (Anfang Klasse 2) .

Auslaut- und Umlautschreibungen (Korb, Hand, Wald – Wälder) lassen sich durch die Technik der Verlängerung von Wörtern ebenfalls zu diesem Zeitpunkt anbahnen. Diese Probleme können noch als Spezialfälle lautgetreuer Schreibung gelten.

Auch die Dopplung kann schon in der zweiten Klasse mit der Strategie der „Pilotsprache" eingeübt werden, zunächst allerdings mit zweisilbigen Wörtern wie „Kof-fer" oder „Son-ne" (hörbare Dopplung), noch nicht im Auslaut, wie bei „rollt" (nicht hörbare Dopplung).

Wenn zunächst die „Basisleistungen" (Zuordnung von Lauten zu Buchstaben) beim Schreiben lautgetreuer einfacher und dann schwieriger Wortstruktur und die Dopplung gesichert sind, muss man sich dem orthographischen Bereich zuwenden.

Als Orthographischer Bereich im engeren Sinne werden alle Schreibungen, die nicht durch lautgetreue Zuordnung von Lauten/Buchstaben und auch nicht durch die Pilotsprache korrekt gelöst werden können, sondern nur durch zusätzliches Rechtschreibwissen. Dieser Bereich umfasst im einzelnen, nicht hörbare Dopplung, Dehnung, die Schreibung der S-Laute, schwierige Konsonantenverbindungen (z.B. x, chs, ks, chz, qu und andere), sowie Fremdwortschreibungen (z.B. ph, th, v u.a.)

Die beschriebene Stufung des Rechtschreibaufbaus gilt im Prinzip sowohl für den Deutschunterricht in der Grundschule als auch für die individuelle Förderung im Anschluss an den Leseaufbau. In einer solchen Förderung kommt es nicht darauf an, welche Klassenstufe das Kind besucht, sondern allein auf den tatsächlich erreichten Leistungsstand im Lesen und Schreiben.

Darüber hinaus kann man diesem Aufbau in allen Schularten folgen. Lediglich die Auswahl der Wörter innerhalb der Stufen wird sich je nach Schultyp unterschiedlich gestalten.

In höheren Klassenstufen sollte daneben eine individuelle Wörterkartei geführt werden. Der Schüler, die Schülerin sammeln in dieser Wörterkartei (oder in einem Sammelheft) die Wörter, die sie öfter falsch geschrieben haben und mit denen sie zu Hause z.B. in Form von Tonband-Diktaten üben können.

Wir beginnen also mit Wörtern aus dem alphabetischen Bereich und üben nach Schwierigkeitsstufen.

Die Kinder müssen jede Schwierigkeitsstufe gesondert üben, zuerst mit Wörtern, dann mit Sätzen. Es ist wichtig, nach jeder Schwierigkeitsstufe mit langen Wörtern zu üben, um die Strategie zu festigen.

Nach ca. 50 Rechtschreibeinheiten (für eine Rechtschreibeinheit rechnen wir ca. 15 Minuten) werden dann Wörter aus dem Orthographischen Bereich (Klecks, Frühling, Wohnung, Erwachsener, Ochse, Apotheke, Theater) geübt und zwar der Reihe nach: nicht hörbare Dopplung (z.B. er rennt, Schwimmhalle, Geschirr), Dehnung (Stuhl, Bahn, Frühling) und Fremdwörter (Apotheke, Mathematik, Gymnasium, Leichtathletik) geübt.

Zusammenfassung:

Wörter wie „Frühling, Ruderboot, Wohnung, er schwimmt, er rennt, es quiekt" dürfen erst dann geübt werden, wenn Wörter wie „Kirche, Birne, Pinsel, Gurke oder Verkäuferin „ relativ sicher geschrieben werden können.

Wenn nach einem bestimmten Grundwortschatz vorgegangen werden soll, müsste dieser zunächst nach den Schwierigkeitsstufen geordnet werden.

Spätestens am Ende der 1. Klasse beginnen die Kinder mit dem Aufbau der Rechtschreibung und zwar in der Schwierigkeitsstufe 1. Bei den Schwierigkeitsstufen ist die Beachtung der Wortstruktur am wichtigsten.

Zeichenerklärung:
K = Konsonant, V = Vokal (k) = am Ende eines Wortes kann ein Konsonant stehen.
Der Einfachheit halber werden auch Diphthonge (AU, EI, EU, ÄU) mit V abgekürzt.
z.B. Krankenhaus = KKVK KEN KVK

Wortstruktur nach dem KIELER RECHTSCHREIBAUFBAU:
Im Stamm eines Wortes sind die Vokale lang und dadurch gut hörbar.
Nur am Ende des Wortes kann ein kurzes e in -e, -en, -er und -el stehen.

A. Die Schwierigkeitsstufen im Rechtschreibaufbau

Schwierigkeitsstufe 1:

Einfach strukturierte Wörter:
In Verbindung mit dehnbaren Konsonanten sind Wörter mit Silben nach der Wortstruktur KV am leichtesten zu schreiben, weil man sie gut hörbar machen kann.
Es handelt sich um Silben der folgenden Wörter:
KV KV NA SE, RO SE, HU PE, DO SE,
KV KVK MA LER, RU FEN, PU DEL, BA DEN, RE GEN,
HO BEL, LE DER, LEBER, DAU MEN, SCHU LE
(In all diesen Wörtern endet die Anfangssilbe auf einen Vokal oder auf einen Diphthong, (SEI, LAU, SCHU, FEU, RO, NA, MO, GA). Die Endsilben enthalten das kurze e in -e, -er, -en, oder -el)

Wörter wie KINDER, HILFE, GURKE, KIRCHE werden auf dieser Stufe noch nicht verwendet.

Wenn die Kinder auf dieser Stufe relativ sicher in der Laut-Buchstabenzuordnung sind. Das ist eigentlich schon am Ende der 1. Klasse, wenn das Kind lesen kann, zu erwarten, wird die 2. Schwierigkeitsstufe durchgenommen. Muss noch einmal mit dem Rechtschreibaufbau begonnen werden, so schalten sie ca. 20 Rechtschreibeinheit vor, in denen Wörtern der Schwierigkeitsstufe 1 geübt werden.

Schwierigkeitsstufe 2:

Wörter mit einfachen Konsonantenverbindungen am Wortanfang – aber immer noch langem Vokal im Stamm!
KKV KV(k) FRA GEN, BRU DER, FREU DE, KREI DE, TRAU BE
Hier sollen die Kinder die beiden Anfangslaute deutlich gedehnt sprechen, damit die Aufmerksamkeit auf den zweiten Laut gerichtet wird.

Diese Stufe kann nach ca. 8 Rechtschreibeinheiten verlassen werden und sollte am Anfang der 2. Grundschulklasse geübt werden..

Schwierigkeitsstufe 3:

Die Schwierigkeitsstufe 3 muss am sorgfältigsten (und am länsgetsn!) geübt werden; denn hier entstehen die meistens Fehler.

Es ist außerordentlich schwer, die Lautfolge herauszuhören, wenn kurze Vorkale oder Auslautverhärtung die Lautstruktur schwer hörbar machen. Deshalb unterscheiden wir hier auch 3 verschiedene Ebenen:

3a. Die Stammsilbe endet auf einen Konsonanten: KVK.

Durch den Konsonanten am Ende der Silbe wird der Vokal kurz und kann deshalb nicht mehr genau genug erkannt werden (Birne – die Silbe BIR wird am Anfang in der Regel als BER geschrieben, ebenso Turm und Hund in der Regel Tom und Hot). Andere Beispiele: WOL

KE, KIN DER, GUR KE, TUR NER, BIR NE, KIR SCHE (Übungszeit ca. 12 Rechtschreibeinheiten)

3b Jetzt werden Wörter mit hörbarer Dopplung geschrieben:

HIM MEL, WOL LE, SUP PE, RET TER, SCHWIM MER, REN NEN, ROL LEN, BREN NEN (Auf dieser Stufe sollen die Verben im Plural gebraucht werden. Das bedeutet, dass die Satzgegenstände mehere Personen sind oder in der Mehrzahl stehen: „Katzen klettern auf den Baum.“ „Uma und Opa schwimmen in der Halle.“
Auch in diesen Wörtern endet die erste Silbe auf einen Konsonanten.
Diese Stufe sollte zum ersten Halbjahr in der 2. Klasse sehr genau geübt werden.
Übungszeit ca. 15 Rechtschreibeinheiten.

3c. Das in der Regel (einsilbige) Wort hört mit einer Auslautverhärtung auf:

Es muss also die Verlängerung bzw. die Ableitung geübt werden: HAND – Hände, HUND – Hunde, GELD – Gelder, KORB – Körbe, BERG – Berge)
Übungszeit ca. 8 Rechtschreibeinheiten

Für die Schwierigkeitsstufe 3 veranschlagen wir mindestens 40 Rechtschreibeinheiten.
Jede Stufe muss gesondert geübt werden.

Wenn die Wörter der Stufen 3a-3c relativ sicher geschrieben werden können, sollen die Kinder Sätze mit Wörtern der Schwierigkeitsstufe 3a-c noch mindestens für die Dauer von 15 Rechtschreibeinheiten geübt werden.

Die Kinder sollen zeigen, dass sie einzelne Schwierigkeiten auch im Zusammenhang aller Wörter im Basisbereich schreiben können. Wenn das der Fall ist, kann der Orthographische Bereich geübt werden.

B. Grundsätze und Aufbau der Übungen

Es hat sich gezeigt, dass das bloße visuelle Vorstellen eines Wortes für den dauerhaften Aufbau der Rechtschreibleistung nicht ausreicht.

Wichtig ist bei allen Übungen das Ansprechen möglichst vieler Sinne:
Das Wort muss angesehen, zugleich silbenweise deutlich gesprochen und dann unter Mitsprechen jeden einzelnen Lautes aufgeschrieben werden. Beim Mitsprechen sollte besonders auf Pausen zwischen den Silben geachtet werden.

Das Mitsprechen insbesondere verhindert, dass den Kindern beim Aufschreiben Buchstaben entfallen.

Erst die Verbindung von Artikulationsmotorik, innerem Sprechen und Hören und dem schreibmotorischen Vollzug bietet eine Voraussetzung für einen störungsfreien Aufbau und einen dauerhaften Bestand der Rechtschreibung.

Jede Rechtschreibeinheit sollte 10-15 Minuten umfassen. Sie kann grundsätzlich zu Beginn in jeder Deutschstunde eingeplant werden.

Folgender Übungsaufbau:

Zu empfehlen sind folgende Übungen:

Die Kinder haben ein Übungsheft, in dem jede zweite Reihe beschrieben wird. An den Anfang der Übung ist stets das Datum zu setzen. Die Schüler schreiben zu Beginn der Übungseinheit 6-8 Wörter in dieses Heft, während ein Mitschüler an der verdeckten Tafel mitschreibt.

Anschließend vergleicht jeder Schüler seine Wörter mit denen an der Tafel. Die richtig geschriebenen Wörter erhalten einen dicken Punkt (unter das Wort). Falsch geschriebene Wörter werden einmal durchgestrichen und in die leere Zeile über das Wort richtig hingeschrieben. Wenn ein Kind im Laufe des Schreibens einen Irrtum bemerkt, soll es das angefangene Wort einmal durchstreichen und das ganze Wort richtig dahinter schreiben. Achten Sie bitte auch darauf, dass nicht Buchstabe für Buchstabe sondern silbenweise unter Mitsprechen geschrieben wird.

Nach ca. 6 Rechtschreibeinheiten (je 15 Minuten) sollen die Kinder dann außer den 5-8 Wörtern einen – später zwei – Sätze mit Wörtern derjenigen Stufe auf der gerade geübt wird, aufschreiben.

Auf Stufe 1 sind das Sätze wie z.B.: „Oma und Opa kaufen Tomaten. Uli und Sabine schreiben an die Tafel. Chinesen kochen Reis."

Später dann in der Schwierigkeitsstufe 3:

„Britta streicht Quittenmarmelade auf das Roggenbrötchen. Im Medikamentschrank lag eine Klapperschlange neben den Wattetupfern." Diese Sätze entsprechen der geübten Struktur und dürften den Kindern daher keine Schwierigkeiten bereiten.

Weitere Tipps:

- Übungen im silbenweisen Sprechen sind sehr wichtig. Kar – tof – fel – sa –lat.Das Wort wird in Pilotsprache (alle Laute einer Silben werden so hörbar gemacht) langsam gesprochen. Dazu beschreiben die Kinder mit den Armen die Silbenbögen in die Luft oder mit der Hand Silbenbögen auf dem Tisch oder mit den Beinen Silbenbögen tanzend zur Seite.
- Die Pilotsprache dient dazu, die Umgangssprache in die Schriftsprache zu übersetzen. In Bayern oder in Schwaben sind solche Übungen verständlich, aber in Schleswig-Holstein denkt man leicht, die Kinder müssen eben deutlich sprechen, dann können sie diese Laute auch in die Schriftsprache übernehmen. Das ist ein Trugschluß!
- Wichtig sind auch *lange Wörter* aus den einzelnen Schwierigkeitsstufen aufzuschreiben. Zunächst meinen die Kinder, sie könnten solche langen Wörter nicht schreiben. Nach den ersten Erfolgen mit: „Panamakanalsachleusentor oder Bananenschale" etc. haben die Kinder viel Spaß beim Schreiben solcher Wörter. Die Strategie ist erlernt.
- Lassen Sie die Kinder auch *„Wörter ohne Hinzugucken"* schreiben. Das zu schreibende Wort wird mit dem Kind zunächst besprochen mit der Frage: Was ist an diesem Wort schwierig?. Dann darf das Kind auf einem Probeblatt versuchen, das Wort zu schreiben. Falls ein Fehler auftritt, wird dieser besprochen. Danach schreibt das Kind nochmals auf das Übungsblatt. Sobald das Wort einmal richtg geschrieben wurde, erfolgt die Probe durch das „Schreiben ohne Hinzugucken" Das Kind schließt die Augen und schreibt gewissermaßen „blind". Dabei muss es sich Silbe für Silbe jeden einzelnen Buchstaben vergegenwärtigen ehe es ihn schreibt.
- *Sprechen Sie mit den Kindern über Wörter.* Woher kommt das Wort „während"? Im Duden finden Sie als Erklärung „währen = dauern, von diesem Wort wird nur noch das Par-

tizip Präsens – während – gebraucht.Was ist schwer an dem Wort und woher kommt es: „gefährlich" – von Gefahr und deshalb mit Umlaut.Was steckt in den Wörtern „Schiedsrichter"? „entscheiden" und Richter" – „Gefängnis" „gefangen" und Endung „nis".

- Die Wörter, die falsch oder zunächst falsch, dann verbessert, geschrieben wurden, sollten in einem Sammelheft (ein Wort pro Zeile in der Mitte eines DIN A5 Heftes) geschrieben werden. Man sollte jeweils nach 5 oder 6 Wörtern die Farbe des Schreibstiftes wechseln und auch einmal ein paar Zeilen frei lassen, damit die Hefte übersichtlich bleiben. Mit den Wörtern des Sammelheftes können auch Eltern zusätzlich üben. Ältere Schüler führen am besten eine individuelle Wörterkartei.
  In dieses Sammelheft sollten Eltern auch Wörter aus den Diktatheften oder Hausheften der Kinder in deutlicher Schrift für zusätzliches häusliches Üben hineinschreiben. Das Heft heißt ja „Sammelheft" und da kommt es darauf an, dass möglichst viele Wörter gesammelt werden.
- Es hat sich bewährt, Bildkarten von Wörtern mit gleichen Rechtschreibschwierigkeiten zu sammeln und die Kinder zu den Bildern schreiben zu lassen. Sie können in diesem Fall allein auf Grund der eigenen Artikulation schreiben. Dabei kommt es darauf an, dass sich die vollständige Lautstruktur des Wortes durch deutliches Sprechen bewußt machen. Solche Bilder können auch zu längeren Wörtern zusammengesetzt werden (Nagelschere, Fingerhut, Autoschlüssel).
- Eine besondere Übung für Wörter der Wortstruktur KVK z.B. MAN, KAR, BEN, KIR und der Dopplung kann man mit Kärtchen durchführen auf die die Silben solcher Wörter geschrieben sind: MAN, KAR, WEN, KIR .Wie bei einem Memory liegen die Wörter verdeckt auf dem Tisch. Der Spielleiter deckt eine Karte auf und das Kind, das als erstes ein Wort mit dieser Silbe ruft, erhält die Karte. Wenn in dieser Form länger geübt wurde und die Kinder mit der Anforderung vertrauter sind, bekommt das Kind das ein längeres Wort gefunden hat, die Karte, auch wenn ein anderes Kind schon vorher ein Wort genannt hat.

Ein letzter Hinweis:

Vergessen Sie nicht mit den Kindern täglich über Wörter zu sprechen (woher kommt das Wort? Was ist schwer an dem Wort? Wie kann man es sich merken? Eselsbrücken, Verwandte etc.

Die Kinder sollen auch täglich Wörter und Sätze schreiben. Wiederholen sie einen Teil der besprochenen Wörter (Was war schwer an „Gurke", „Sprachbuch", „Verkäuferin"?) bei der nächsten Rechtschreibeinheit! Vermeiden Sie Arbeitsbögen bei denen nur Buchstaben eingesetzt werden müssen.

Rechtschreiben lernt man am besten durch Schreiben!

Literatur mit entsprechenden Übungswörtern:

Dummer-Smoch, L. Hackethal, R.: Handbuch zum KIELER RECHTSCHREIBAUFBAU 3. überarb. Auflg. (umfangreiches Wortmaterial zum Üben)Veris, Kiel 1996 ISBN 3-924 173-16-8

Hackethal, R.: Zehn Schritte zur Rechtschreibung 2. Aufl. (umfangreiches Wortmaterial zum Üben) Megalopolis, Schwerin, 1996 ISBN 3-939679-03-5

Hackethal, R.: Dreizehn Stationen auf dem Weg zum Lesen (umfangreiches Wortmaterial zum Üben) Megalopolis, Schwerin ISBN 3-939679-04-3

4.10 Lautgebärden sind motorische, kinästhetische und visuell deutlich wahrnehmbare Lautzeichen und bieten gute Kompensierungsmöglichkeiten

Renate Hackethal

Die Lautgebärden richten die Aufmerksamkeit des Lesers auf die Lautfolge des Wortes. Damit unterstützen sie die Wahrnehmung und Wiedergabe der Sequenz und verhelfen dem Leser zu einem hohen Maß an Selbständigkeit und Eigenaktivität im Leselernprozess.

Wie der Name schon sagt, erhält grundsätzlich jeder Laut eine Gebärde, die zugleich als Hinweis auch auf den entsprechenden Buchstaben dient. Bedingt durch die deutsche Schriftsprache müssen bei Lauten, die durch zwei verschiedene Zeichen repräsentiert werden (f-w, ß – ss) zusätzlich am Buchstaben orientierte Zeichen benutzt werden. Die beiden CH-Laute erhalten dagegen nur ein Zeichen. Dem Buchstaben Q wird keine Lautgebärde zugeordnet. Stattdessen gibt es für die Lautverbindung „KW", geschrieben als QU eine einzige Gebärde.

Eine genaue Beschreibung der Lautgebärden findet sich im Handbuch zum KIELER LESEAUFBAU (Dummer-Smoch/Hackethal, 5. überarbeitete Auflage, Kiel 1989)

Die Lautgebärden dienen also nicht der Isolierung der einzelnen Laute, sondern der bewussteren Wahrnehmung der Laute im gesprochenen Wort und der bewussteren Zuordnung von Laut- und Buchstabenzeichen beim Dehnlesen. Sie stellen nicht nur eine -Merkhilfe- dar, sondern eine Koordinationshilfe für die im Leseakt beteiligten sensorischen und motorischen Teilleistungen. **Lesen ist ein psychomotorischer Prozess.**

Die Lautgebärden einzuführen bedeutet keinen besonderen Aufwand. Der Schüler sagt täglich wenigstens zweimal 3 Reihen mit den Lautgebärden auf.

> MA ME MI MO MU in den ersten 7 Unterrichtseinheiten
> später dazu dann die Silben MAU MEI MEN MER MEL
> wobei der Laut –en- (-er-, -el-) für die geschriebenen Buchstaben e und n (r, l) immer **nur am Ende eines Wortes** steht.

Es ändert sich jeweils nur der Anfangskonsonant. Die Aufgabe heißt beispielsweise: „Sage die Reihe mit (Konsonant) „ Antwort: (PA, PE, PI, PO, PU, PAU, PEI, PEN, PER, PEL etc.

Es ist wünschenswert, dass die Kinder die Reihen auswendig aufsagen können.

Dabei dürfen die Kinder die Laute der Silbe nicht einzeln nennen und zeigen sondern müssen die Laute beim gedehnten Sprechen (Dehnsprechen oder Dehnlesen) sofort zur Silbe verschmelzen. Beim Dehnlesen lässt man dann die Lautgebärden zeigen. Hier kommt es wieder auf die Koordination der Leistungen: **Sprechen, Buchstaben anschauen und Lautgebärden zeigen** an und zwar silbenweise und unter Beachtung der Reihenfolge der Silben im Wort.

Gelegentlich haben Kinder größere Schwierigkeiten, die Laute zur Silbe zu verschmelzen. Im Handbuch zum KIELER LESEAUFBAU sind mehrere Übungsformen als Hilfe bei diesem Problem angegeben.

Es empfiehlt sich, mit den Konsonanten M, R, S, N, L, F zu beginnen, weil diese Konsonanten beim Dehnlesen leichter verschmolzen werden können. Bei den Verschlusslauten (Konsonanten P, T, K und B, D, G) ist es eine Hilfe, den Kindern zu raten, die Reihe zunächst stumm mit Mundbewegungen zu sprechen, damit das Verschleifen besser gelingt.

In den Lese-Intensivmaßnahmen (ca. 30 Tage täglich zwei Stunden Einzelunterricht) erlebe ich, wie den Kindern durch den Einsatz der Lautgebärden entscheidend geholfen werden kann und sie sehr bald Erfolge erleben. Dadurch motiviert, kann das Tempo mit den Lautgebärdenreihen gesteigert werden.

Ich beginne grundsätzlich bei allen Kindern, deren Leseleistung nicht durchschnittlich ist, noch einmal mit dem Leselernprozess und zwar mit den 6 Konsonanten M, R, S, N, L, F. Oft sind die Kinder so sehr entmutigt, dass sie sich nichts mehr zutrauen. Dann sage ich zu ihnen: „Wir tun so, als ob du gar nichts kannst und fangen noch einmal ganz von vorne an.“

Der KIELER LESEAUFBAU ist speziell für diesen Personenkreis konzipiert.. Er hebt Entmutigungen auf und ist in erster Linie erfolgsorientiert.

Der KIELER LESEAUFBAU gliedert sich in 10 aufeinander aufbauende Stufen mit je drei neuen Konsonanten (bzw. Doppellauten und Endungen wie –en, -er und –el) pro Stufe und vier zusätzliche Übungsstufen.

Auf den ersten beiden Stufen werden möglichst nur lange Vokale in der ersten und zweiten Silbe zweisilbiger Wörter verwendet (O ma, ro sa, li la, Mo fa) verwendet. Da aber viele einfach strukturierte Wörter auf das kurze e enden und die Zahl der Wörter auf diesen ersten Stufen ohnehin klein ist, wurden Wörter mit kurzem e am Ende (Ro se, Na me, Na se) dennoch zugelassen.

Bis zur 10. Stufe sind die Wörter in den ersten, zwei- dreisilbigen Wörtern auch in den zweiten Silben, grundsätzlich lang (Me lo ne, Sa la mi, Ro si ne, To ma te, Re na te, Ra ke te)

Erst die 12. Stufe bringt in Wörtern wie „Wolke“ oder „Lampe“ den kurzen Vokal auch in der ersten Silbe des Wortes.

Wörter mit Dopplungen (Himmel, Puppe, kommt), Dehnungen (Frühling, Liebe) und schwierigen Konsonantenverbindungen (Fuchs, Klecks, Keks) sind im KIELER LESEAUFBAU nicht enthalten, sondern gehören zum KIELER RECHTSCHREIBAUFBAU.

Der KIELER RECHTSCHREIBAUFBAU ist ein gesondertes Werk mit ähnlich rotem Faden wie der KIELER LESEAUFBAU. Er setzt dann ein, wenn die Kinder den Leselernprozess verstanden und einfach strukturierte Sätze lesen können.

Praktische Übungen:

Wir beginnen mit den Silbenreihen zu den Konsonanten M, R, S, N, L und F.

1. Sage die Reihe mit dem F (...)
2. Lies die Silbenkarten (MA, RO ...)
3. Hole mir die Silbe (SA, NI ...)
4. Ziehe zwei Silbenkarten und schaue ob du eine „Perle“ (ein sinnvolles Wort) gefischt hast (z.b. NO, KI = KI NO)

Auf den ersten Stufen soll schnell vorangeschritten werden, so dass die Kinder nach etwa 5 Tagen in der Lese-Intensivmaßnahme bereits die Reihen mit den Konsonanten M, R, S, N, L, F, P, T, K auswendig mit den Lautgebärden zeigen können.

Dann wird auf der Silbenebene geübt: Dabei bedienen wir uns der Spielmotivation als Kompensationshilfe.

An dieser Stelle verweise ich auf ein Spiel, dass für die anfänglich etwas ermüdenden Übungen mit den Silben inzwischen unverzichtbar geworden ist, das Marsmännchenspiel oder die kleinen grünen Männchen vom Mars.

Zuerst erklärt man den Kindern „Bei den Marsmännchen ist alles anders. Zum Beispiel kommt der Familienname zuerst und der Vorname danach. Sie heißen nicht Peter Laufer, sondern Laufer, Peter. Der Familienname besteht auch nur aus einem Buchstaben, z.B. M, R oder S. Auch der Vorname ist nur ein Buchstabe. A, E, I, O, U. Es gibt außerdem noch die Vornamen AU und EI.

Die Mitglieder der Familie M können also MA, ME, MI, MO, MU später auch MAU und MEI heißen.

Nun kommen die Marsmännchen eines Tages mit ihrem Luftschiff zur Erde geflogen. Als Luftschiff nehmen wir eine Streichholzschachtel, die mit grünem Metallpapier umkleidet und mit goldenen oder silbernen Sternen verziert ist. Sie werden durch ihre Pässe, kleine Pappkärtchen, symbolisiert, auf denen die Namen stehen.

Die Marsmännchen haben vorher mit einem Hotel auf der Erde Kontakt aufgenommen, in dem sie wohnen wollen. Dem Hotelbesitzer haben sie erklärt, dass jede Familie in einem Stockwerk für sich wohnen muss, und alle Leute mit gleichem Vornamen müssen übereinander wohnen. Der Hotelbesitzer hat infolgedessen die Räume (ein Gitternetz auf einer Plakatpappe) vorbereitet. In der obersten Zeile stehen über den darunter liegenden Kästchen die Türschilder A, E, I, O und U, später auch AU und EI und vor den Stockwerken die Familiennamen M R und S.

Mit dem Fortschreiten im Leseaufbau werden die Türschilder (Konsonanten) entsprechend ausgetauscht und/oder ergänzt, so dass bald ein „Marsmännchen-Wolkenkratzer" entstehen kann.

Sobald das Raumschiff auf der Erde gelandet ist, gehen die Marsmännchen in ihre Zimmer. Dabei ruft ein Kind in der Gruppe das Marsmännchen auf, das das Raumschiff gerade verlässt. Ein „Hotelbesitzer" geleitet das Marsmännchen in sein Zimmer. Auf diese Weise wird das Hotel allmählich gefüllt.

Am folgenden Morgen entdecken die Marsmännchen zunächst den Spielplatz und vergnügen sich dort. Abends wollen sie wieder in das Hotel zurückkehren. Der Hotelbesitzer erklärt, dass in drei Zimmern Mäuschen sind. Drei Marsmännchen können also ihr Zimmer nicht beziehen. Der Spielleiter schreibt – von den Kindern ungesehen – drei Namen für die von Mäuschen besetzten Zimmer auf und fordert die Kinder auf, die Mäuschen zu fangen. Sie müssen raten und dabei die Lautgebärden benutzen: „Ist ein Mäuschen im Zimmer von MA?" Verneint der Spielleiter, so sortieren die Kinder ihr „MA"-Männchen in das entsprechende Zimmer ein. Bejaht der Spielleiter die Frage, dann stellen alle Kinder einen Halmastein in das entsprechende Zimmer. Erst, wenn alle drei Zimmer mit Mäuschen ausfindig gemacht worden sind, kommt der Kammerjäger und entfernt die Mäuschen. Die letzten drei Mäuschen können nun wieder einziehen.

Entsprechend kann man mit den Pappen „Spielplatz“, „Prater“ oder „Kirmes“ bzw. „Zoo“ entsprechend spielen.

Um von der Silbe zum Wort zu gelangen, setzen wir das „Tanztee-Spiel“ ein. Eines Tages feiern die Marsmännchen ein Fest. Sie trinken Brause, eine Kapelle spielt und sie tanzen miteinander.

Zur Tanzparty kommt auch die kleine Hexe Hadula. Sie ist eine liebe Hexe, die mit ihren Zaubereien immer nur das Beste will. Leider macht sie manchmal etwas falsch, weil sie nämlich nicht so gut lesen kann. Sie möchte den Marsmännchen-Paaren, die gut zusammen passen, helfen auch zusammen zu bleiben. Jedes Mal, wenn nun ein Paar an ihr vorüber tanzt, tippt sie das Paar mit ihrem Zauberstab an. Da sie aber noch nicht so gut lesen kann, tippt sie manchmal auch Paare an, die nicht zusammen passen (das sind die Silben, die kein sinnvolles Wort ergeben). Nun müssen die beiden „entzaubert“ werden, weil sie sonst nicht auf den Mars zurück kehren können. War z.B. KI mit SE verbunden, so können die Kinder mit den Silben NO (KI NO), LO (KI LO), RO (RO SE) oder NA (NA SE) den Zauber wieder lösen.

Schließlich können die Marsmännchen heiraten. Sie gehen zum Standesamt und tauschen dort ihre „Pässe“ gegen einen gemeinsamen Familiennamen ein (statt „Ro“ und „SE“ heißen sie nun ROSE.

Alle diese Spiele haben das Ziel, das Kind mit den Silben auf den ersten Stufen des Leseaufbaus so vertraut zu machen, dass die Schwierigkeiten beim Zusammenziehen der Laute zur Silbe überbrückt werden und ihm das Silbensprechen ganz selbstverständlich wird. Fragen wie „Lesen Ameisen? – Rufen Hasen? – Malen Maler?“ „Laufen Hasen?“ können sehr bald mit den Lautgebärden erlesen und richtig beantwortet werden.

Wörterlisten nach der Wortstruktur des KIELER LESEAUFBAUs erleichtern den Schülern die ersten Lernschritte. Dadurch erlebt der Schüler von Anfang an Lernerfolge, die er auch selbst wahrnehmen kann. Mit diesen Übungsformen ist schon ein großer Schritt zum Automatisieren der psychomotorischen Fertigkeiten beim Lesen getan. Kinder, die täglich mehrmals die Reihen mit den Lautgebärden aufsagen, haben dabei zusätzlich große Vorteile.

In den ersten Wochen sollte auf die Silbenpause geachtet werden. Wörter, die Silbenpausen enthalten, können mit den Lautgebärden schneller erlesen werden. Es gibt Kinder, die die zu erlesenden Wörter nicht gliedern können Sie versuchen z.B. TOMATEN zunächst bis TOM zu lesen und bei AT wieder neu zu beginnen. Auf diese Weise gelangen sie nur schwer zur Wortbedeutung.

Kinder, die diese Hilfe nicht brauchen, lernen sie im doppelten Sinne spielend. Schüler mit Schwächen in den Leselernvoraussetzungen haben es da etwas schwerer. Bei ihnen muss besonders im Anfang auf das konsequente Verschleifen geachtet werden.

Wenn aber alle Kinder an den Lautgebärdenspielen beteiligt werden. In Partner- und Gruppenarbeit und mit Spielen unterschiedlicher Schwierigkeitsstufen – wird keine Gruppe diskriminiert. Für den Rechtschreibaufbau sind die Lautgebärden auch für die problemlos lernenden Schüler von Vorteil, sie können nach dem Aufschreiben kontrollieren, ob alle Buchstaben vorhanden sind und keine Lautvertauschungen vorkamen.

Literatur

Dummer-Smoch, L.: Laute – Silben – Wörter Übungsbuch zum Lesenlernen mit Lautgebärden, Kiel: Veris-Verlag 1996

Dummer-Smoch, L.: Kompensatorische Leselernhilfen für Legastheniker – Konzeption und Erfahhrungen mit dem KIELER LESEAUFBAU in Forum Logopädie, Heft 1, Februar 1993 S. 14 ff

Dummer-Smoch, L.: Hackethal, R.: Handbuch zum KIELER LESEAUFBAU, Kiel: Veris-Verlag, 1984, 1988, 1993, 1994, 1999 (5. überarbeitete Auflage 1999)

Hackethal, R.: Praxis zum KIELER LESEAUFBAU und zum KIELER RECHTSCHREIBAUFBAU, Kiel: Veris Verlag 2. Auflage 1995 (aktualisierte Neuauflage)

4.11 Integrative Legasthenie-Therapie

Reinhold Komnick

1 Gesetzliche Grundlagen

Die Jugenddorf-Christophorusschule erhielt 1977 nach Überprüfung durch das hessische Kultus- und Sozialministerium die staatliche Anerkennung als geeignete Einrichtung zur Behandlung von Legasthenikern.

Auf der Grundlage rechtlicher Vorgaben werden zur Zeit 80 Kinder betreut, wobei als Orientierung die Grenze von 10 Prozent der Gesamtschülerzahl gilt. Dieses ist notwendig, um einen geregelten Schulbetrieb aufrecht zu erhalten, die im Lehrplan vorgesehen Unterrichtsziele zu erreichen und einen staatlich anerkannten Schulabschluß zu gewährleisten.

Die Rechtsvorschriften aus dem Hessischen Schulgesetz:
Auszug aus den Richtlinien zur Förderung von Schülerinnen und Schülern mit besonderen Schwierigkeiten beim Lesen, Schreiben und Rechtschreiben vom 15. Dezember 1995: „Misserfolge und Schwierigkeiten beim Erlernen der grundlegenden Fertigkeiten Lesen, Schreiben und Rechtschreiben haben gravierende Beeinträchtigungen nicht nur des gesamten schulischen Lernens, sondern auch der Persönlichkeitsentwicklung zur Folge:

- durch Beeinträchtigung des Selbstwertgefühls bis zu Verhaltensauffälligkeiten und körperlichen Störungen,
- in sozialer Hinsicht durch den Verlust von Ansehen und Zuwendung,
- im Unterricht durch Leistungsrückgang bis zum völligen Schulversagen,
- im häuslichen Bereich durch Belastungen der Beziehungen zwischen den Familienmitgliedern,
- im späteren beruflichen Rahmen durch verminderte Ausbildungs- und Arbeitsmöglichkeiten.

In Extremfällen können diese Störungen zu einer übergreifenden Entwicklungsbehinderung im Sinne des § 39 des Bundessozialhilfegesetzes führen."

Daraus ergibt sich, dass es (zu definierende) Extremfälle gibt, bei denen schulische Fördermaßnahmen nicht ausreichen. An dieser Stelle findet die Überleitung zur Sozialgesetzgebung statt.

Sozialgesetzbuch VIII (Kinder- und Jugendhilfegesetz) § 35 a

Eingliederungshilfe für seelisch behinderte Kinder und Jugendliche"Kinder und Jugendliche, die seelisch behindert oder von einer solchen Behinderung bedroht sind, haben Anspruch auf Eingliederungshilfe. Die Hilfe wird nach dem Bedarf im Einzelfall

- in ambulanter Form,
- in Tageseinrichtungen für Kinder oder in anderen teilstationären Einrichtungen,
- durch geeignete Pflegepersonen und
- in Einrichtungen über Tag und Nacht sowie sonstigen Wohnformen geleistet.

Für Aufgabe und Ziel der Hilfe, die Bestimmung des Personenkreises sowie die Art der Maßnahme gelten § 39 Absatz 3 und § 40 des Bundessozialhilfegesetzes .....“ Mit diesem Gesetz ist geregelt, dass der Anspruch und die Form der Hilfe in der Zuständigkeit der Jugendhilfe verankert ist. Das Ziel der Hilfe gibt das Bundessozialhilfegesetz vor.

§ 39 Bundessozialhilfegesetz (BSHG)

Personenkreis und Aufgabe

„Aufgabe der Eingliederungshilfe ist es, eine drohende Behinderung zu verhüten oder eine vorhandene Behinderung oder deren Folgen zu beseitigen oder zu mindern und den Behinderten in die Gesellschaft einzugliedern ...“

Die Art der Maßnahmen regelt der § 40 BSHG.

Maßnahmen der Eingliederungshilfe sind vor allem:

„Ambulante oder stationäre Behandlung oder sonstige ärztliche oder ärztlich verordnete Maßnahmen zur Verhütung, Beseitigung oder Milderung der Behinderung. Hilfe zu einer angemessenen Schulbildung, vor allem im Rahmen der allgemeinen Schulpflicht und durch Hilfe zum Besuch weiterführender Schulen einschließlich der Vorbereitung hierzu. Hilfe zur Teilnahme am Leben in der Gemeinschaft.“

Zusammenfassend lässt sich feststellen, dass durch die Sozialgesetzgebung nicht die Behandlung von Teilleistungsschwächen, sondern deren Auswirkung geregelt ist. Das bedeutet, es muss bereits eine seelische Behinderung vorliegen oder zumindest drohen, bevor ein Anspruch auf Hilfe vorliegt. Für die Praxis lassen sich daraus folgende Schlüsse ziehen:

- bevor die Förderung in einem Internat zum tragen kommt, muss das Kind bereits „in den Brunnen gefallen sein“,
- die Kinder haben mit vielen negativen Vorerfahrungen zu kämpfen, leben unter einem enormen Leidensdruck,
- einzelne Auffälligkeiten sind inzwischen so ausgeprägt, dass eine ambulante oder stationäre psychiatrische Behandlung nötig wird.

Daraus ergibt sich, dass Erfahrungen mit internatsmäßig geförderten Kindern nicht repräsentativ für die allgemeine Legasthenie-Diskussion sein können.

Bei der Ausgestaltung des § 35 a gilt **für die Kosten:**

Die öffentliche Jugendhilfe trägt ambulante Kosten ohne Beteiligung durch Kinder oder Eltern. Bei Tageseinrichtungen oder teilstationären Einrichtungen erfolgt eine Heranziehung zu den Kosten.

Zum Nachweis der seelischen Behinderung:Für die Feststellung, ob ein junger Mensch seelisch behindert ist, wird eine medizinisch-psychologische Stellungnahme erforderlich. Diese wird üblicherweise von Kinder- und Jugendpsychiatern erstellt.

Die im § 40 BSHG vorgegebenen Hilfemaßnahmen finden im ganzheitlichen Ansatz unserer Einrichtung ihren Niederschlag.

2 Das integrative pädagogische Wirkungsgefüge

In der Schule

Integration in die Realschule (Klassen 5-10) und das Gymnasium (Klassen 5-13). Zur Berücksichtigung und Aufarbeitung spezifischer Defizite sind in den Bereichen Methodik und Didaktik therapieverstärkende Elemente in den Unterricht eingebaut (Fachkonferenzen). In Kooperation aller am Erziehungsprozess beteiligten Pädagogen werden spezielle Förderprogramme festgelegt (pädagogische Konferenzen). Weitere spezielle Lernhilfen werden unseren Schülern in der täglichen Lernzeit gegeben. Ein umfangreiches Angebot an musischen und sportlichen Aktivitäten trägt ganz wesentlich zur Persönlichkeitsgestaltung und Stabilisierung bei.

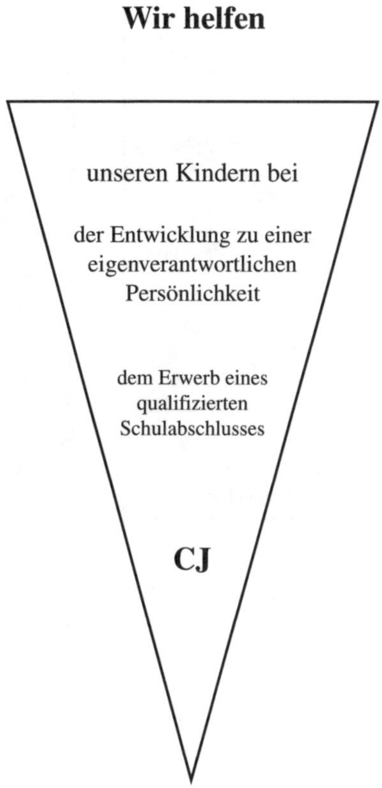

Im sozialpädagogischen Wohnbereich

Als grundlegende Hilfe bei der Persönlichkeitsentwicklung unserer Kinder dienen Maßnahmen, die emotional stabilisieren und Störungen beseitigen, damit positive Selbsterfahrungen zu einem verantwortlichen Umgang mit sich und der Umwelt führen: Hilfen zur eigenverantwortlichen Lebensführung und zum Erwerb sozialer Kompetenzen. Schwerpunkte unserer Arbeit sind: der Erlebnissport, die Religionspädagogik, die musische Bildung, die Mitverantwortung, die politische Bildung. Wir leisten Erziehungshilfen, die die Verselbständigung unserer Kinder fördern, um damit den Schulabschluss und den Einstieg in die berufliche Ausbildung zu ermöglichen.

Abb. 4.11.1

Im Legastheniezentrum

Der Ausprägung der Legasthenie entsprechend werden Übungen in den Bereichen

Wahrnehmung (visuell, auditiv)
Motorik (Steuerung, Koordination)
Konzentration
Kognition (Merkfähigkeit, Anwendung von Rechtschreibregeln) durchgeführt.

Für die im Legasteniezentrum durchgeführten Trainingseinheiten gilt als Orientierung der von Rathenow vogestellte Stufenplan:

3 Stufenplan für die Förderung lese-rechtschreibschwacher Kinder

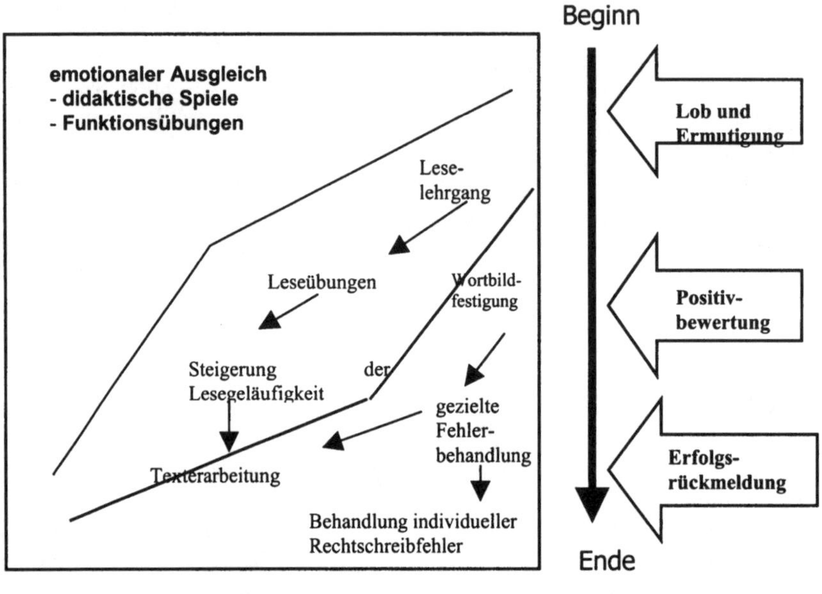

Abb. 4.11.2: Waagrechte Linien durch diese schematische Darstellung gezogen markieren für Gruppen oder einzelne Kinder unterschiedliche Ausgangslagen für die Förderung und geben Hinweise für die momentane Gewichtung einzelner Förderelemente.
Die eingesetzten Materialien entstammen zum großen Teil den Empfehlungen und Aufstellungen des Bundesverbandes und der Landesverbände Legasthenie.

Literatur:

P. Rathenow, J. Vöge „Erkennen und Fördern lese- rechtschreibschwacher Schüler“, Fuldatal/Kassel, Hessisches Institut für Lehrerfortbildung 1979

G. Happe, H. Saurbier, Kinder- und Jugendhilfegesetz 19. Auflage, Verlag W. Kohlhammer 1993

Neufassung des Bundessozialhilfegesetzes vom 10. Januar 1991, Bundesgesetzblatt Jahrgang 1991

Verordnung und Richtlinien des Hessischen Kultusministeriums vom 22. Oktober 1985 und 15. Dezember 1995, Amtsblatt 1/96

4.12 Einsatz von Computerprogrammen in der LRS-Therapie

Ute Laue

1 Einleitung

Computer sind aus unserem Leben nicht mehr wegzudenken. Wenn wir unsere Kinder heute auf das Leben von morgen vorbereiten wollen, müssen wir sie auch den Umgang mit dem Computer lehren. Leider sind deutsche Schulen häufig nur sehr mäßig mit Hard- und Software ausgestattet. Nichtsdestotrotz gibt es viele Lehrer, die Computer in ihren Unterricht einbinden und gute Erfahrungen damit machen. Es gibt Programme, die schon im Anfangsunterricht in Deutsch und Mathematik eingesetzt werden können und durch die gesamte Grundschulzeit begleiten. Insbesondere für Kinder mit Schwierigkeiten beim Erlernen des Lesens und Rechtschreibens oder Rechnens kann die Arbeit am Computer eine große Erleichterung sein.

Wir können davon ausgehen, daß auch rechtschreibschwache Kinder schreiben wollen, die Orthografie aber bald als unüberwindliche Hürde erfahren. Wenn die Aneignung der Schriftsprache scheitert, ist ihr Gebrauch bei diesen Kindern schnell angstbesetzt. Wegen der vielen Misserfolge, die sie ständig im Deutschunterricht erleben, sind viele von ihnen überhaupt nicht mehr bereit, einen Stift in die Hand zu nehmen, geschweige denn, damit zu schreiben. Bei diesen Kindern versagen oft auch herkömmliche Therapiemethoden, sie blokkieren total und wollen mit dem Vorgang des Schreibens nicht mehr konfrontiert werden.

Nicht nur in der Schule sondern ganz besonders in der außerschulischen Therapie bietet der Computer Kindern die Möglichkeit ihre Angstbarriere zu überwinden, ihre Motivation zu wecken und somit ihre Arbeitshaltung zu verbessern. Denn der Computer ist so ganz anders als die Schreibwerkzeuge, die sie bisher kennengelernt haben. Er fasziniert die meisten Kinder so sehr, dass sie ihr Tun keineswegs als Anstrengung empfinden und bereitwillig lesen und schreiben.[1]

Der Computer verliert niemals die Geduld, auch nach der zehnten Falscheingabe 'verzieht er nicht das Gesicht'. Weder Therapeut noch Lehrer oder Eltern können so neutral sein. Bei guten Programmen kann man Falscheingaben verhindern. Somit werden den Kindern nur Erfolgserlebnisse rückgemeldet, was natürlich motivierender ist als das Aufzeigen und Zählen von Fehlern. Aber wiederum brauchen Kinder mit Teilleistungsstörungen (und nicht nur die) Lob auch für ihre Anstrengungen, nicht nur für richtige Ergebnisse. Dies kann ein Computer im Normalfall nicht leisten, ebensowenig, wie er kleine Fehler von gravierenden unterscheiden kann. Hier ist wieder der Lehrer/Therapeut gefordert als 'Moderator' aufzutreten.

Diese Kinder, die auch im sozialen Umfeld, in der Klasse, häufig schlechte Erfahrungen wegen ihrer vielen Fehler gemacht haben, brauchen keine Angst zu haben, vom Computer wegen falscher Antworten ausgelacht zu werden. Außerdem kann ihnen der Zeitdruck genommen werden, da die Zeitvorgaben individuell eingestellt werden können. Wir wissen inzwischen aus vielen Lehrererfahrungen, dass LRS-Schüler durchaus die vom Lehrplan verlangten Leistungen erbringen können, wenn man ihnen denn nur genügend Zeit einräumt.

---

1 Arenhövel, Computereinsatz, S. 80

Viele Schüler, nicht nur LRS-Kinder haben motorische Probleme, ihr Schriftbild ist unleserlich. Auf dem Monitor dagegen erscheint es immer gut lesbar und strukturiert. Die Kinder müssen nicht gleichzeitig das Wortgedächtnis und die visuomotorische Steuerung in Anspruch nehmen. Das Tastaturschreiben entlastet von der physischen Anstrengung und ermöglicht dem Kind, sich mehr auf den Inhalt zu konzentrieren. Es kann sich dadurch viel ausführlicher mitteilen.

Entscheidungen, die beim Schreiben mit der Hand alle gleichzeitig getroffen werden müssen, können am Computer nacheinander bedacht, geprüft und gegebenenfalls korrigiert werden. Mit wesentlich geringerem Aufwand kann das Kind Wortwahl, Satzbau, Gliederung, Orthografie überarbeiten.

Kinder schreiben am Computer langsamer, durchgliedern genauer und lautieren leise mit. Phonematische Fehler wie Buchstabenauslassungen, Hinzufügungen und Verdrehungen kommen seltener vor; Regelfehler (Dehnungs-h, s-Laute) aber genauso häufig wie beim Schreiben mit der Hand.[2]

Fehler sind am Monitor leichter zu entdecken als in einem handschriftlichen Text und sind einfach und spurenlos zu verbessern.[3] Die Kinder strengen sich an, um ein perfektes Ergebnis zu erreichen. Der sichtbare Erfolg spornt sie an. Ein gutes Textverarbeitungsprogramm und etwas Fantasie des Therapeuten genügen, um Lernerfolge zu erzielen. Lernspiele können eingesetzt werden zur Unterstützung und Ergänzung des Unterrichtes. Sie können visuelle und auditive Wahrnehmung und Logik fördern: Rate- und Geschicklichkeitsspiele, Memories, Herstellung von Kreuzworträtseln. Beispiele sind: (dreidimensionales) Tetris, Mahjongg, Sokoban (Übung der Lateralität), Soundmemory. Es gibt auch spezielle Programme zur Verbesserung der Wahrnehmungsfähigkeiten auf dem Markt: Traeger: Wahrnehmung, Hören-Sehen-Schreiben, Audio; goodgame lernsoftware: Basis, Logic.

Beim computerunterstützten Lernen zeigen die Schüler ein hohes Maß an Durchhaltevermögen und Ausdauer. Aufmerksamkeit und Konzentrationsfähigkeit werden wirkungsvoll unterstützt. Selbst hyperaktive und konzentrationsschwache Kinder können am Computer sitzen bleiben und arbeiten.[4]

Wenn man Kinder, die zu zweit oder dritt daran arbeiten, beobachtet, kann man feststellen, dass sie sich sehr intensiv und aufgabenbezogen unterhalten. Es finden lernzielorientierte Interaktionen statt, kommuniziert wird eher mit dem 'Mitarbeiter' als mit dem Lehrer. Leider gibt es noch kein 'ideales' Lernprogramm auf dem Markt. Aber:

Das ideale Programm soll folgende Bedingungen erfüllen:

- einfache Installation (auch für Laien)
- einfacher Programmstart
- kein Absturz bei falscher Bedienung
- bedienerfreundliche Oberfläche
- übersichtliche grafische Oberfläche
- verständliches Handbuch
- es muß sich aus sich selbst erklären
- hoher Motivationsgrad
- angemessene Animation (nicht zu viel)

2 Arenhövel, Fördern macht Spaß, S. 100

3 Kochan/Herz

4 Arenhövel, Computereinsatz, S. 49

- Anpassung des Schwierigkeitsgrades
- individuelle Aufgabengestaltung: veränderbare Buchstabengröße und Farbe von Hintergrund und Buchstaben, einfache Eingabe eigener Wort- und Textdateien
- spielerische Komponente als Belohnung
- Lösung nach 2-3 Falscheingaben, mit – auch für Legastheniker – verständlicher Erklärung
- Protokolle sollten enthalten: alle Falschangaben, Lösungszeit
- Arbeitsblättererstellung
- Ermittlung von Lernfortschritten
- Beachtung der *Ranschburgschen Hemmung* (Ähnlichkeitshemmung)
- Anlage von Fehlerdateien
- in jeder Phase muss Stop und Ausstieg möglich sein
- angemessener Preis

Wünschenswert wäre es zusätzlich, wenn dieses Programm so konzipiert wäre, dass die Kinder selbstbestimmte Erfahrungen machen können. Sie sollten mit Sprache und Schrift experimentieren können und Freiräume für eigene Entscheidungen haben.

Man sollte sich aber immer darüber im Klaren sein, dass der Computer nur ein Lernmittel von vielen ist. Er darf nie als alleiniges Werkzeug eingesetzt werden. Und : *Computer können Lehrer nicht ersetzen und die Anstrengung des Lernens nicht beseitigen.*

2 Der Computereinsatz zu Hause

Ganz besonders begrüßenswert ist es, wenn in der Schule/Therapie und zu Hause dasselbe Programm benutzt werden kann. Hierfür ist das Programm Uniwort von Traeger geeignet. Eltern sollten nicht davon ausgehen, dass sie ihr Kind an den Computer 'abgeben' können. Sie müssen ihr Kind auch hier begleiten. Nur in Ausnahmefällen sollte es allein vor dem Computer sitzen um zu lernen. Ein großes Manko ist eben noch, dass er zwar sprechen, aber nicht gut hören kann. (Es gibt zwar Spracherkennungsprogamme. Bei denen muss jedoch sehr genau artikuliert werden. LRS-Kinder haben häufig Sprachprobleme, welche die Kommunikation mit dem Computer fast unmöglich machen.) Bei diesen Kindern muss ständig kontrolliert werden, ob sie richtig lesen und das Gelesene auch verstehen und sich nicht etwa nur visuell eine Buchstabenreihenfolge eingeprägen, die sie dann reproduzieren, ohne die Bedeutung des Wortes erfasst zu haben.

Beim Lernen von Englischvokabeln kommt es auf die genaue Aussprache an, die der Computer noch nicht kontrollieren kann.

3 Software

Leider gibt es nicht viele Programme auf dem Markt, die annähernd die Voraussetzungen für lerngerechte Software erfüllen, was uns aber nicht daran hindern soll, die vorhandenen Programme zu nutzen und das Beste aus ihnen herauszuholen. Man sollte aber auch bedenken, dass ungeeignete Lernprogramme frustrieren und keineswegs Erfolge erzielen.

AUSGEWÄHLTE PROGRAMME FÜR COMPUTERUNTERSTÜTZTES LERNEN

Deutsch und Rechtschreibung

Wortbaustelle	Traeger	2.-7. Klasse
Universelles Worttraining	Traeger	ab 3. Klasse
ULK – Rettung für den Zeitreisenden	Cornelsen	5.-9. Klasse
Lese-u. Rechtschreibmeister	Auer	ab 2. Klasse
Karolus	Veris	ab 1. Klasse
Budenberg		1.-6. Klasse
Gut 1	Computer und Lernen	2.-7. Klasse

Mathematik

Die Zahlenwaage	Traeger	1.-2. Klasse

Englisch

Vokabeltrainer	Traeger	
Wortbaustelle	Traeger	

3.1 Überblick über Computerprogramme für die LRS-Therapie

3.1.1 Deutsch und Rechtschreibung

Wortbaustelle Traeger 2.-7. Klasse

11 Unterprogramme, u.a.:

- Wortvergleich: sind 2 kurz eingeblendete Wörter identisch?
- Vorsilben und Endungen: zu einem vorgegebenen Wort(baustein) müssen aus mehreren Möglichkeiten die passenden Vorsilben bzw. Endungen ausgewählt werden.
- Silben ordnen
- Wörter in Silben zerlegen
- Baustelle: *Reparieren*: bxckxn (= backen)
- Elektroblinker-Wortspiel (Kontakt)

mit Übungen zum Thema Silben, Morpheme und Wortbausteine. Der Editor gestattet Einflussnahme auf den Programmablauf. Zwei Spieler können gegen- bzw. miteinander spielen. Protokoll.

Beurteilung: didaktisch sehr gut aufbereitet, abwechslungsreiche, einfache Gestaltung; wenig Animation

Universelles Worttraining Traeger ab 3. Klasse

Zur gezielten Bearbeitung von Problemschwerpunkten

- Blitzwort: Aufmerksamkeits- und Worterfassungstraining, ein Wort erscheint nur ganz kurz, muss dabei gelesen und dann aus dem Gedächtnis geschrieben werden
- Fehlbuchstabe: fehlender Buchstabe muß eingesetzt werden (zum Üben spezifischer Fehlerschwerpunkte wie d-t oder g-k). Ranschburgsche Hemmung beachten!
- Tachistoskop: Steigerung des Blitzwortes, ein Wort erscheint nur so kurz (Dauer einstellbar), dass es nicht mehr erlesen werden kann. Dabei soll die schnelle ganzheitliche Erfassung von Wörtern trainiert werden.
- Lesen, Abschreiben
- Diktat (mit Partner)
- Spiegelschrift: umgedrehte Reihenfolge der Buchstaben, die selber aber nicht gespiegelt sind. Jeder Buchstabe muss einzeln gelesen und in der richtigen Reihenfolge zu einem Wort zusammengesetzt werden. Hilft bei visuellen Laterationsschwierigkeiten (problematisch für Linkshänder).
- Halbschrift : von oben beziehungsweise unten horizontal abgeschnittene Schrift, die gelesen werden muß. Förderung von Merkfähigkeit (Form der Buchstaben)
- Eigene Wortdateien können (z.B. nach Schulbuch oder Therapieerfordernissen) sehr einfach erstellt werden, falsch geschriebene Wörter in eine Fehlerdatei aufgenommen und somit ganz gezielt geübt werden.

140 Wortdateien sind schon eingegeben, unter anderem untergliedert in solche, bei denen besondere pädagogische Betreuung notwendig ist und in solche, die auch von Eltern ohne pädagogische Vorbildung genutzt werden können.

5 große Grafikschriften u.a. lateinische Ausgangsschrift und die neue vereinfachte Ausgangsschrift sind wählbar und Zeugnisausdrucke ebenso möglich wie Arbeitsblätter.

Beurteilung: didaktisch sehr gut aufbereitet; übersichtliche, nüchterne Grafik, die das Lernziel in den Mittelpunkt stellt; nicht alle eingegebenen Wortdateien entsprechen den Anforderungen in der Legasthenie-Arbeit (Ranschburgsche Hemmung) . Kaum Animation, keine Spiele zur Belohnung

In der Therapie sehr sinnvoll, wenn man das Programm intensiv betreut

Nicht so schwer betroffene Legastheniker können auch allein damit arbeiten. Die Programme von Traeger sind geeignet, gleichzeitig zu Hause, in der Schule und in der Therapie angewendet zu werden.

ULK – Rettung für den Zeitreisenden Cornelsen 6.-9. Klasse

Abenteuerwelt, in der ein notgelandetes Raumschiff repariert werden muß. Das Kind greift interaktiv in das Geschehen ein und hilft ULK bei der Reparatur. In einem Testdiktat werden die Fehlerschwerpunkte des Kindes ermittelt, so dass individuell nach Vorkenntnissen und Lernproblemen geübt werden kann. Es unterhält sich mit den Robotern des Schiffes (Sprachausgabe), muss Fragen stellen, Anweisungen geben und ihre Antworten lesen. 'Zerstörte Texte' aus den Datenspeichern des Raumschiffs müssen in einer Werkstatt repariert werden (Wortstamm, Vorsilbe, Endung).

Das Programm enthält außerdem einen Karteikasten, mit dem spezifische Rechtschreibschwierigkeiten besonders geübt werden können:

- Groß-Kleinschreibung
- Konsonantenverdopplung

- Dehnungs-h
- Wörter mit v; s, ss, ß; b/p, d/t, g/k; z, tz, ä, e, äu, eu
- das oder dass
- ie

Um Hilfe bei der Raumschiff-Reparatur zu bekommen, braucht man Taler. Diese kann man sich durch Rechtschreibübungen und kleine Berichte erarbeiten. Der grünhaarige 'Brauser' überprüft mit seinem knatternden Motorrad Zeile für Zeile die Texte und weist auf Fehler hin.

Spielerische Übungen im Pausenraum wie Puzzle und Memory müssen mit erarbeiteten Talern bezahlt werden. Wenn alle Reparaturen durchgeführt sind, kann das Raumschiff auf seinen Heimatplaneten zurückkehren.

Beurteilung: Gute Animation, gute Ausnutzung des Mediums Computer; pädagogisch sinnvoll aufgebaut, motivierend, spielerisches Lernen wird mit diszipliniertem Üben verknüpft, wobei auch Partnerarbeit möglich und sogar wünschenswert ist. Die Anlässe zu lesen und zu schreiben haben für das Kind Spielcharakter, sind nicht vergleichbar mit dem schulischen Lernen. Das Ziel, der Start des Raumschiffes, soll so schnell wie möglich erreicht werden. Dafür sind mehrere Stunden, also mehrere Sitzungen notwendig und genügend Ausdauer nötig. Dabei kann gelernt werden, sich eine Arbeit vernünftig einzuteilen. Die Lösung der Aufgaben ist nicht immer einfach.Eigene Dateien sind leider nicht möglich, ein Protokoll kann nicht erstellt werden.Deshalb ist das Programm weniger für Schule oder Therapie geeignet, kann aber zu Hause unterstützend eingesetzt werden.

Budenberg **ab 1. Klasse**

40 Programme: Lesen, Schreiben, Diktat, Rechnen (bes. gut!), Erdkunde, Rätsel, Spiele,.

Die Budenberg Lernspiele wurden für den Förderunterricht an Sonderschulen konzipiert, sind aber im gesamten Grundschulbereich einsetzbar, um auch grundlegende Probleme (z.B. Zehnerübergang) anzugehen. Die Aufteilung des Programmes in Übungsgruppen lässt eine dem Leistungsstand des Kindes angepaßte Strukturierung des Lernstoffes zu. Verständliche Hilfen, Protokoll, Arbeitsblätter.

Für zu Hause gibt es Schülerdisketten nach Jahrgangsstufen.

Beurteilung: unterhaltsame, didaktisch gut strukturierte Programme; die klaren, zeitlich begrenzten Übungseinheiten sind für Kinder sehr ansprechend; die Darstellungen sind anschaulich; einzelne Programme zur Wahrnehmungsförderung geeignet; kleine Schritte sichern Lernerfolg; Protokolle, Kopiervorlagen

Diese Programme können Kinder auch mal allein bearbeiten.

Lese-u. Rechtschreibmeister **Auer** **ab 2. Klasse**

7 Übungen:

- Silbenrätsel: ungeordnete Silben müssen zu Wörtern zusammengesetzt werden. (Lautanalyse und -synthese)
- Buchstaben-Salat: bei Hilfe-Anforderung erscheint das Wort in richtiger Schreibweise
- Geheimschrift: Wörter werden durch Striche symbolisiert: soll das Einprägen von Wortbildern fördern
- Lückentext: vorgegebene und eigene Texte der Kinder, können auch vom Mitschüler bearbeitet werden

- Diktat (Sprachausgabe): ein Wort (oder ein Satz) wird eine festlegbare Zeit dargeboten. Das Wort verschwindet und das Kind muss es aus dem Gedächtnis nachschreiben.
- Tachistoskopisches Lesen: individuelle Wörterlisten können erstellt werden.
- 2 Spiele zur Belohnung: Glücksrad, Satz-Tetris (nach einer einstellbaren Menge erfolgreicher Übungen),

differenzierte Protokolle, Eingabe eigener Wörterlisten und Textdateien notwendig, auch schwerpunktmäßig möglich

Beurteilung: einfache Bedienung, individuelle Anpassung an Rechtschreibprobleme sehr gut möglich, Übungen sind abwechslungsreich, didaktisch gut aufbereitet, bedarf Einarbeitung und Begleitung.

Gut 1 Computer und Lernen 2.-7. Klasse

Das Programm simuliert eine Lernkartei im Computer. Ein Satz wird eingeblendet. Nach dem Lesen wird ein Wort davon ausgeblendet, das dann nachgeschrieben werden muss. Dabei sind 3 Hilfestufen möglich – 1. ohne Hilfe, 2. Wort wird noch einmal eingeblendet und verschwindet dann wieder, 3. Wort bleibt stehen und kann abgeschrieben werden. Richtig geschriebene Wörter kommen in den Beutel des 1.Kängurus, nach zweimaliger Wiederholung, wobei das Wort jeweils in den nächsten Beutel wandert, in die Schatzkiste im Baumhaus, falsch geschriebene in den Beutel des ersten Kängurus zurück und erst nach viermaliger Wiederholung in die Schatzkiste. Mit dem erworbenen Schatz kann der Schüler das Baumhaus einrichten, Urkunden, Poster und Bastelbögen drucken.

Für jeden Schüler wird eine eigene Diskette erstellt. Im Lernprotokoll werden gewählter Wortschatz, Hilfestufe, Datum, Zeit, Anzahl richtiger Schreibungen und Gesamtzahl der Schreibungen festgehalten. Die enthaltenen Wortschätze beinhalten die wichtigsten Wörter unserer Sprache, schwierige Wörter, Lautverbindungen, fehlerträchtige Konsonantenfolgen, Groß- und Kleinschreibung u.a.. Gleichzeitig wird ein Transfer angestrebt durch Übertragung der Wortstämme und Anwendung grundlegender Regeln.

Beurteilung: gut durchdachtes Programm, die Mischung von Arbeit und Spiel ist ausgewogen; die Anreize, die Schatzkammer zu füllen und sich daraus zu bedienen, sind hoch. Die Ranschburgsche Hemmung wird beachtet. Die Protokolle enthalten alles Notwendige. Grafisch ansprechend, phantasievoll gestaltet (auch wenn Kängurus selten im Urwald anzutreffen sind, aber ihr Beutel eignet sich nun einmal gut als Karteikasten.) Leider können keine eigenen Wortdateien eingegeben werden, was den Anforderungen in der Therapie nicht entspricht. Für Schule, wenn Lehrer nicht nach eigenen Konzepten arbeiten, und zu Hause ist es geeignet. Nur ab Windows 95! Die alte Version ist nicht empfehlenswert.

Gut 2 Computer und Lernen 2.-7. Klasse

Mit Diktatlisten werden noch zu lernende Wörter herausgefiltert. Zu diesen werden Karteikärtchen gedruckt, mit denen dann konventionell gelernt wird. Eigene Kärtchen können gestaltet werden. Dieses Programm ist für den Einsatz in der Schule bestimmt. Es erleichtert sehr die ‘Karteiarbeit’.

3.1.2 Mathematik

Die Zahlenwaage Traeger 1.-2. Klasse

Zahlenbereiche 10 / 20 / 100; Addition und Subtraktion. 7 Programme:
- eine Zahlenwaage muss ins Gleichgewicht gebracht werden
- es wird mit Stäbchen gerechnet
- Nachbarzahlen müssen gefunden werden (als Lern- oder Spielprogramm)
- Zahlenstrahlübungen
- Thermometer (mit Nullübergängen)
- Geheimzahl (Zahlenratespiel)
- Wieviele Mäuse sind im Karton?

Beurteilung: didaktisch sehr gut aufbereitet, abwechslungsreich, einfache, übersichtliche Graphik; für die Dyskalkulie-Therapie empfehlenswert

3.1.3 Fremdsprachen

Elektronische Vokabeltrainer haben in den letzten Jahren den Markt geradezu überschwemmt. Die meisten sind nur stupide Frage- und Antwortspiele (d*rill and kill)*

Vokabeltrainer Traeger

Spezielle Lernmethode zur Einführung neuer Vokabeln:
- Blitzvokabel
- Fehlbuchstabe
- Übersetzung
- Diktat
- Redewendungen
- Konjugationen unregelmäßiger Verben in dt., eng., frz., sp., it., lat.

Fehlerdatei.

Beurteilung: didaktisch sehr gut aufgebaut, wenig Animation, Methodenwechsel festigt den Lernstoff.

Wortbaustelle Traeger

Dieses Programm (s. unter Deutsch) ist auch für den Englischunterricht geeignet.

3.1.4 Edutainment-Programme

sind nicht für Therapie gedacht, da sie nicht modifizierbar sind, viel Spiel- und wenig Lernanteil haben; können aber gut zu Hause eingesetzt werden, um den Kindern ein bisschen Spaß bei dem Umgang mit Wörtern und Zahlen zu bringen und ihre Ängste abzubauen.

Die Abenteuerwelt der Wörter Sunflowers ab 2. Klasse

6 Spiele: Erkennen von Buchstaben und Wörtern, Groß- und Kleinschreibung, Reimen, Wortpuzzle; verschiedene Schwierigkeitsstufen; es können auch eigene Wörter eingegeben werden! Sehr unterhaltsam

Die Abenteuerwelt der Zahlen Sunflowers ab 2. Klasse

Aufwendig animiertes Programm, 10 Schwierigkeitsstufen, Grundrechenarten, Kopfrechnen, Bruchrechnen, Zahlenstrahl, Uhr, Kalender, Reihen

Meisterdetektive jagen Lork Cornelsen ab 3. Klasse

Fürst Marigor und die Tobis Cornelsen ab 3. Klasse

Auch **Grafikprogramme** bieten viele Lernmöglichkeiten u.a. Bearbeitungsmöglichkeiten für Texte, so dass der Fantasie keine Grenzen gesetzt sind. Ein Farbdrucker wäre hierbei wünschenswert

3.2 Anbieter

Cornelsen Software, Postfach 330109, 14171 Berlin
Eugen Traeger Lernsoftware Verlag, 49504 Lotte, Tel./ Fax 05404 71858
Budenberg Lernsoftware, über K. Emmig, An der Wielermaar 74, 51143 Köln
Memory-Shareware, R. Bartkowiak, Weststr.31, 47929 Grefrath
Veris Verlag GmbH, Kiel
Auer, Postfach 1152, 86601 Donauwörth
Computer und Lernen, Im Eichelgarten 49, 76530 Baden-Baden
Sunflowers, Infogrames, Robert-Bosch-Str. 18, 63303 Dreieich-Sprendlingen
goodgame lernsoftware, Altensdorf 6, 84088 Neufahrn

Literatur

Arenhövel, F.:Computereinsatz in der Grundschule. Donauwörth: Verlag Ludwig Auer, 1994 (1.Auflage)

Arenhövel, F./Ringbeck, B.(Hrsgb): Fördern macht Spaß. Ganzheitliche Fördermaßnahmen für Kinder mit Lernschwierigkeiten. Donauwörth: Verlag Ludwig Auer,1995 (1.Auflage)

Feibel, T.: Großer Kinder Software-Ratgeber 1999.Haar bei München: Markt und Technik

Kochan.B./Herz.G.: Schreibprozesse am Computer. In: Grundschule 12/1988

Schwinghammer, H.: Legasthenie. So helfe ich meinem Kind. Augsburg: Weltbild Verlag,1999

4.13 Kinder mit Teilleistungsschwächen im heutigen Schulsystem

Manfred Bönsch

1 Einleitung

Viele, ja die meisten Veranstaltungen dieses Fachkongresses geben Auskunft über das Phänomen „Legasthenie“, über Ursachen, Begleitphänomene und Bearbei-tungsmöglichkeiten. Das ist gut so. Mein Ansatz ist ein anderer: wie steht es eigentlich mit den Reaktionen der Schule, wie geht sie mit Legasthenie um, wie ernst ist es ihr? Entlastet sie sich schnell mit Stigmatisierungen, setzt sie vor allem organisatorische Fördermaßnahmen mit dem faktischen Effekt der Aussonderung oder setzt sie intelligente Lösungen ein, um mit integrativer Förderung LRS-Kindern zu helfen? Man kann in den Fragen unschwer die implizite Antwort erkennen. Da ist offensichtlich ein Entwicklungsfeld!

1.1 Die Bereitstellung von hilfreichen Ausgangstexten und Grundgedanken einer Pädagogik des Förderns

Die Schulgesetze der Bundesländer sprechen vom Recht auf Bildung und davon, dass Unterschiede in den Bildungschancen nach Möglichkeit durch besondere Förderung der benachteiligten Schüler/innen auszugleichen seien. Erziehungsberechtigte können schulische Fragen mit erörtern.

Die Grundschulerlasse weisen darauf hin, dass die Grundschule den Schüler/innen erfolgreiches Lernen zu ermöglichen habe und sich bemühen müsse, Lernfreude zu erhalten. Die Erlasse zur Förderung von Schüler/innen mit besonderen Schwierigkeiten beim Erlernen des Lesens und Rechtschreibens entwickeln Fördermöglichkeiten.

Nicht immer wird eine umfassende Pädagogik des Förderns deutlich. Deren Grundaxiome sind:

Die Person des Schülers / der Schülerin ist wichtiger als eine Teilleistungsschwäche. Letztere darf nicht zur Charakterisierung der Person insgesamt führen.

Der Grundgedanke des ganzheitlichen Förderns bedeutet die Umkehrung der Leistungserwartungen. Die Person ist das Wichtige und die Leistungen sind das zweite Wichtige. Das ist deshalb so wichtig, weil die sozialen und psychischen Prozesse eine fatale Entwicklung nehmen können, wie das an der Sekundärsymptomatik und deren Teufelskreis nach Betz/Breuninger immer wieder sehr schön deutlich zu machen ist.

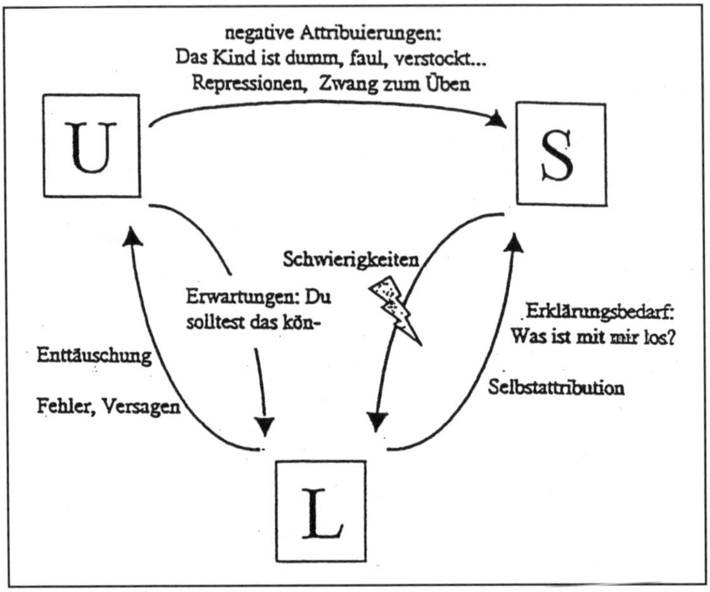

Abb. 4.13.1 Schematische Darstellung des 1. Stadiums, angelehnt an Betz/Breuniger 1996, S.34

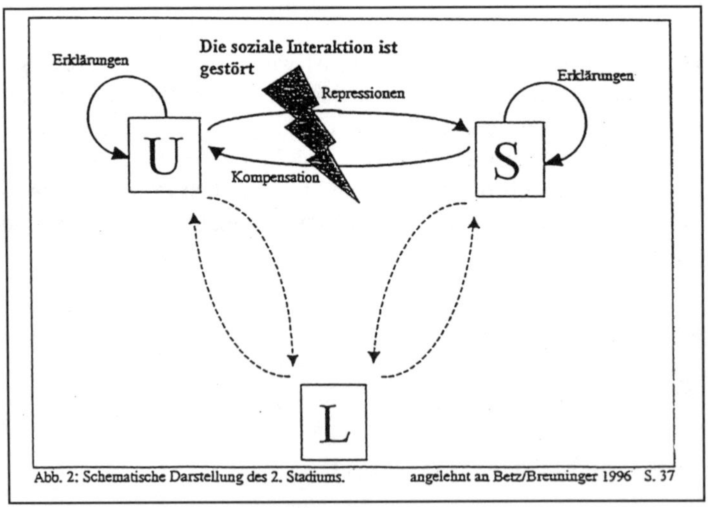

Abb. 4.13.2 Schematische Darstellung des 2. Stadiums, angelehnt an Betz/Breuniger 1996, S.37

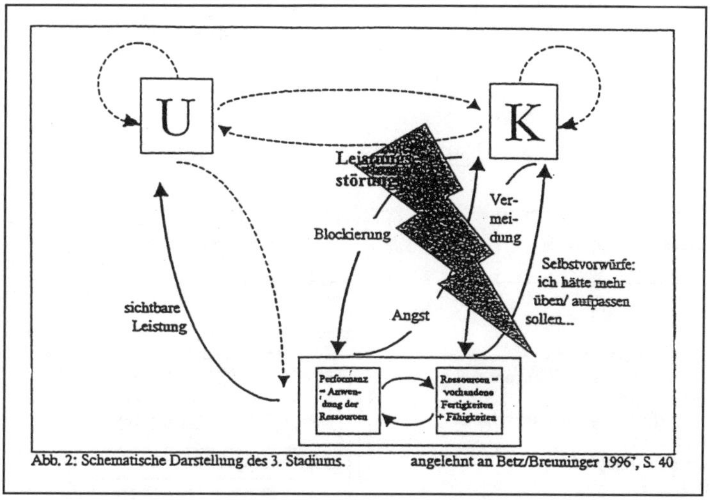

Abb. 4.13.3 Schematische Darstellung des 3. Stadiums, angelehnt an Betz/Breuniger 1996, S.40

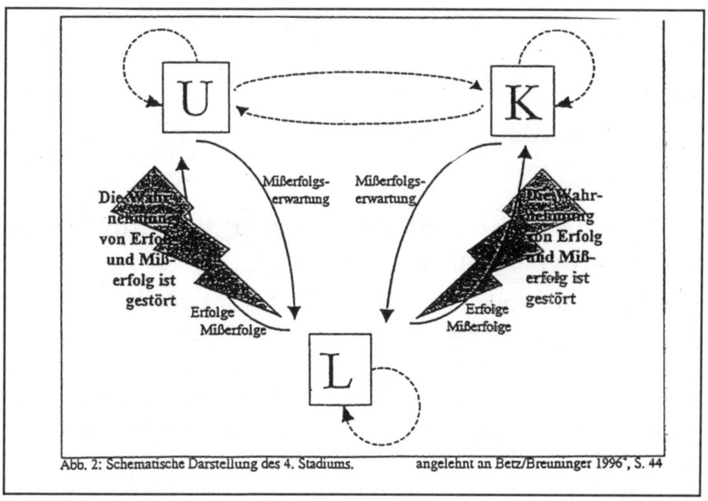

Abb. 4.13.4 Schematische Darstellung des 4. Stadiums, angelehnt an Betz/Breuniger 1996, S.44

Die organisatorischen Lösungen sind erst die halbe Antwort

Die Fördererlasse entwickeln in der Regel ein Repertoire, das vor allem organisatorische Maßnahmen vorsieht. Die folgende Übersicht soll dies im knappen Überblick zeigen:

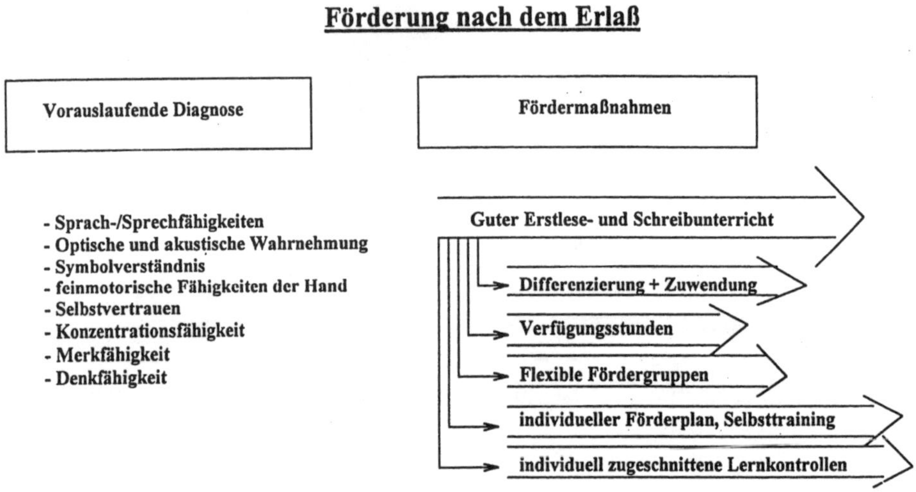

Abb. 4.13.5 Förderung nach dem Erlass

2 Ein Paradigmenwechsel für die Konstruktion von Unterricht ist für integrative Förderung nötig

Bisher ist das dominante Konstruktionsprinzip das der Linearität. Das heißt, es wird ein Unterrichtsverlauf geplant, der in seinem Vermittlungs- und Bearbeitungsanspruch an einem angenommenen Durchschnitt orientiert ist und immer zwei Gruppen vernachlässigt, die der schneller und die der langsamer Lernenden (Abb. 6). Dies führt ständig zu unvollständig bleibenden Lernprozessen bei denjenigen, die aus irgendeinem Grunde Durchschnitterwartungen nicht entsprechen können.

Der Paradigmenwechsel zielt auf das Konstruktionsprinzip der kontrollierten Variabilität. Die folgende Übersicht zeigt den jeweiligen Zeitpunkt der Bearbeitung in einem Viereck, innerhalb dessen Spielräume für variable Lernwege gegeben werden können, Langsamkeiten, Überholungen, Umwege, Abweichungen, Varianten werden möglich.

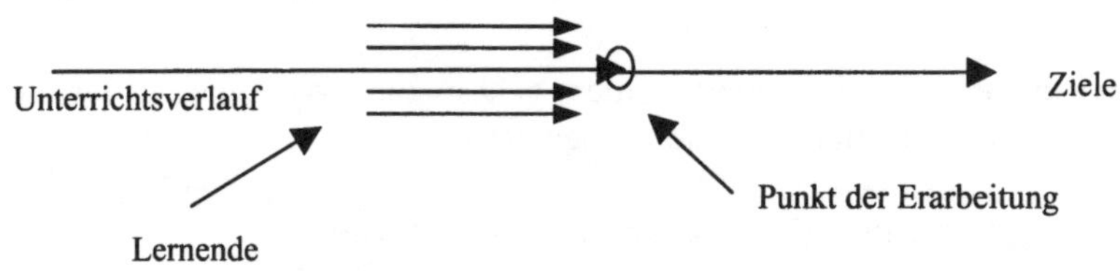

Abb. 4.13.6 Linearität als Konstruktionsprinzip des Unterrichts

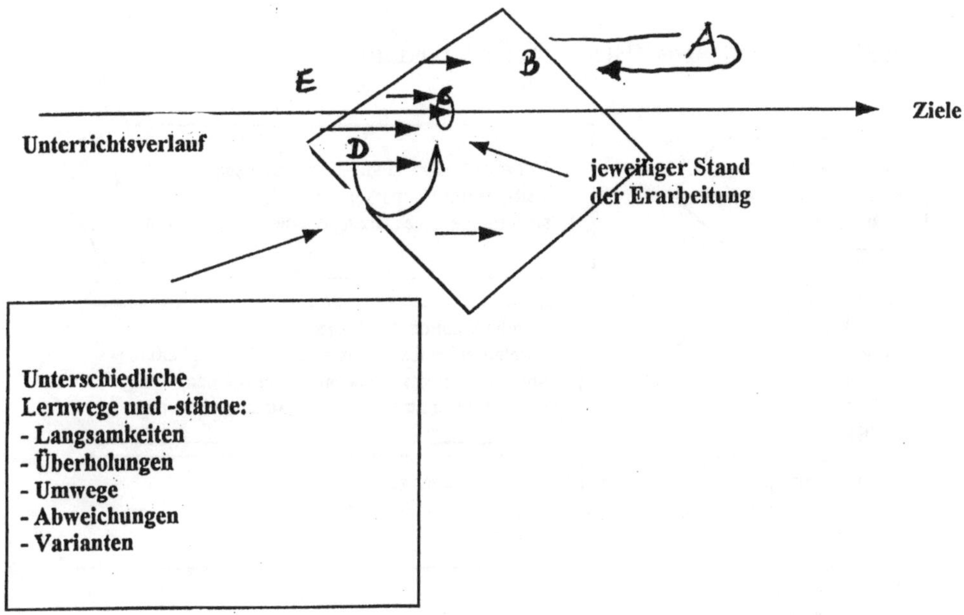

Abb. 4.13.7 Unterrichtsverlauf

3 Sechs Bauelemente für einen Unterricht der kontrolliertenVariabilität

Kann dieser Paradigmenwechsel akzeptiert werden, geht es um Konsequenzen für die Konstruktion des Unterrichts. Sechs Bauelemente werden entwickelt.

3.1 Differenzierungsstrategie „Optimierung von Lernprozessen“

Während der Lehrplan/das Lehrbuch die planmäßige Erarbeitung des für notwendig Erachteten angeben, kommt als zweites Bestimmungsmoment hinzu, was in der Übersicht „Abholstation“ genannt wird. Je nach den Gegebenheiten sind dann drei Konstruktionsvarianten für individuelle Lernprozesse möglich. Sie werden in der Übersicht (Abb. 4.13.8) angegeben.

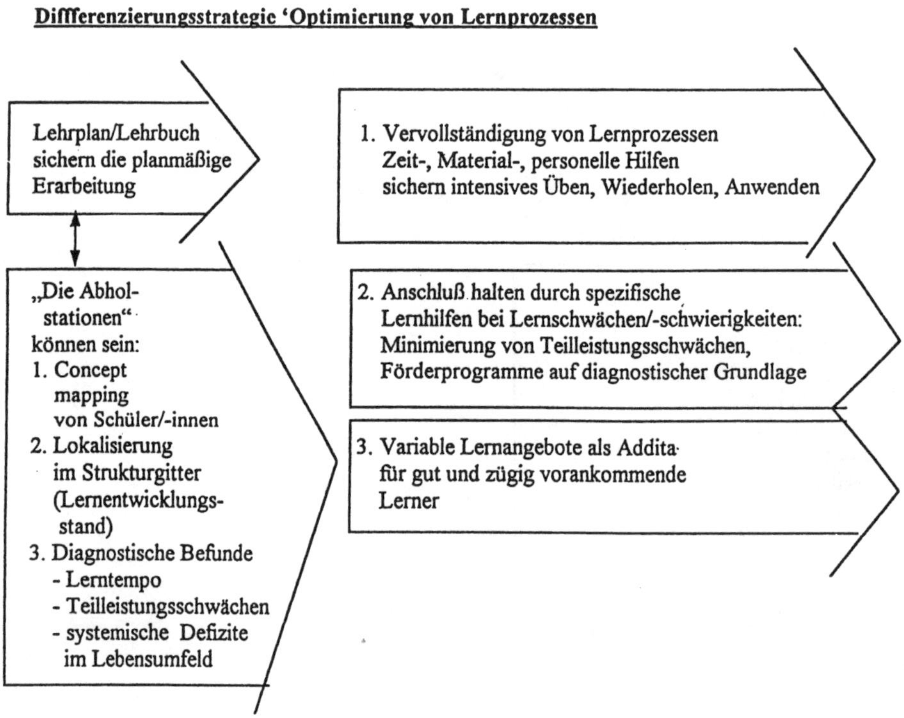

Abb. 4.13.8 Differenzierungsstrategie „Optimierung von Lernprozessen“

3.2 Die Hintergrundfolie „Sachstruktur“

Um die jeweiligen Sachstrukturen verlässlich zu sichern, ist die nächste Übersicht als Folie zu verstehen, mit deren Hilfe die jeweiligen Lernprozesse auf dem Weg von einfachen zu komplexen Strukturen nach unterschiedlichen Niveaustufen (von konkreten Handlungen zu Denkoperationen) verortet werden können. Normalweg und Varianten sind eingefügt.

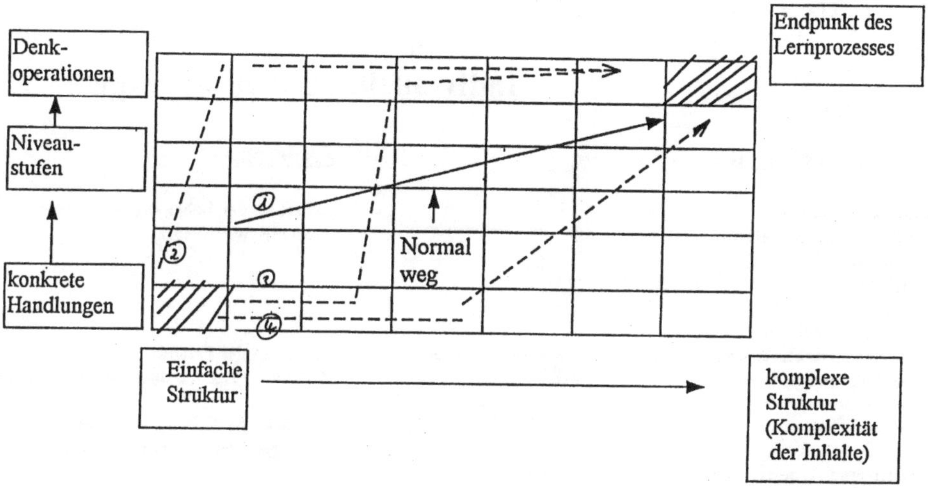

Abb. 4.13.9 Lernprozesse

3.3 3 D-Differenzierung als Lernprozessoptimierung

Die folgende Übersicht (Abb.4.13.10) gibt drei Differenzierungsansätze an. Die didaktische Differenzierung ist am ehesten bekannt. Die diagnostische Differenzierung zielt auf eine genauere Lerndiagnostik, von der aus Lernangebote konzipiert werden. Die dialogische Differenzierung rechnet mit dem Lerner und seinem Wissen um seine Schwierigkeiten. Wenn er den Lernweg kennt, kann er selbst beginnen, die für ihn notwendigen Lernhilfen zu suchen.

3 D - Differenzierung
zur Lernprozeßoptimierung

	1. Didaktische Differenzierung	2. Diagnostische Differenzierung	3. Dialogische Differenzierung
Intention:	Stufung der Schwiergkeiten von den Lernzielen/-inhalten her	Stufung der Anforderungen nach den aktuellen Lernmöglichkeiten/ -schwierigkeiten	Stufung der Lernaufgaben nach lerntyporientierten Präferenzen durch den Lerner
Vorgehensweise:	Differenzierte Lernangebote bieten eine 'Treppe' zu den gesetzten Lernzielen	Lerndiagnosen identifizieren aktuelle individuelle Lernstockungen, -schwierigkeiten Lernangebote werden darauf abgestellt.	Der Lerner kennt den Lernplan. Er kann seinen Lernweg in Abstimmung mit ihm nach Beratung selbst gestalten.
Jeweiliges Logo	Differen-zierte Lern-ange-bote → Das Insgesamt des zu Lernenden	Individuelle Lerndispo-sitionen/ -schwierig-keiten → Lern-inhalte/ -anfor-derungen	Lernpräferenzen/ -ressourcen / Zugriffe Zeit Materialien Hilfen / Lern-anforderungen/ - Inhalte

Abb. 4.13.10 3 D-Differenzierung zur Lernprozessoptimierung

3.4 Der individuelle Entwicklungsplan

Da integrierte Förderung auf individuelle Förderung bei gemeinsamer Arbeit zielt, sind individuelle Entwicklungspläne zu entwickeln, die folgendes Basisfeld haben können (Abb.4.13.11):

Individueller Entwicklungsplan

Diagnostische Zugriffe		**Förderpläne**
Lebenssituation (Familie, Wohnsituation, materielle Situation, Erziehung)	→	**Arbeit an der Lebenssituation (systemischer Ansatz)**
Entwicklungsstand		
1. Motorik, Basiskompetenzen (Gleichgewicht, Ausdauer, Kraft, Gelenkigkeit), Sensorik	→	**Arbeit an der Person (Stärken stützen, Schwächen minimieren)**
2. Selbstkonzept + Körperleben	→	**Arbeit an partiellen Insuffizienzen (Übungen, verändernde Praxis fördern)**
3. Sozialverhalten	→	
4. Lern- und Arbeitsverhalten	→	
5. Sprach- und Kommunikationsverhalten (Dialogfähigkeit, Artikulation, Grammatik, Semantik)	→	**Arbeit an Lernproblemen (gezielte Förderprogramme)**
6. Unterrichtsbereiche (Mathematik, Schriftsspracherwerb, ästhetisch-kreative Fähigkeiten u.a.m. Teilleistungsschwächen (z.B. LRS, Dyskalkulie u.a.m.)	→	

Abb. 4.13.11 Individueller Entwicklungsplan

3.5 Adäquate Unterrichtskonzepte

Da das ständig gemeinsame Fortschreiten bei dem hier vorzustellenden Ansatz nicht mehr möglich ist, müssen korrespondierend Unterrichts(-teil)konzepte zur Realisierung kommen, die das individuelle Arbeiten möglich machen. Aus der nun folgenden Übersicht sind besonders die Teilkonzepte „Wochenplanarbeit“ und „Freie Arbeit“ wichtig. Sie sind aus der Diskussion im offenen Unterricht bekannt (Abb.4.13.12).

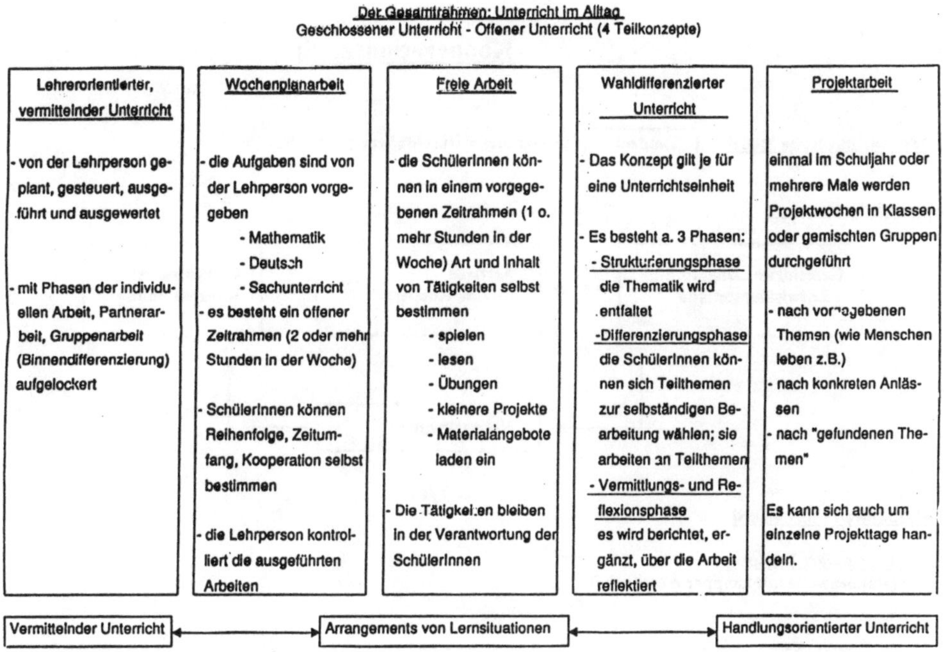

Abb. 4.13.12 Der Gesamtrahmen: Unterricht im Alltag

3.6 Kooperationsmodi von Lehrer/innen

Die Förderung von LRS-Kindern wird nicht immer in der Hand der Klassenlehrerin / des Klassenlehrers liegen können. Hier kann schnell eine „Bruchstelle“ des vorgestellten Ansatzes liegen. Sie liegt ggf. darin, dass in speziellen Förderstunden eine zweite Lernperson die Förderung übernimmt und aus Alltagsgründen (Zeit, Belastung u. a. m.) wenig Absprachen erfolgen (siehe Variante 3). Die folgende Übersicht (Abb. 4.13.13) zeigt daher in den Varianten zwei und eins Optimierungen der Kooperation zwischen Lehrer/innen.

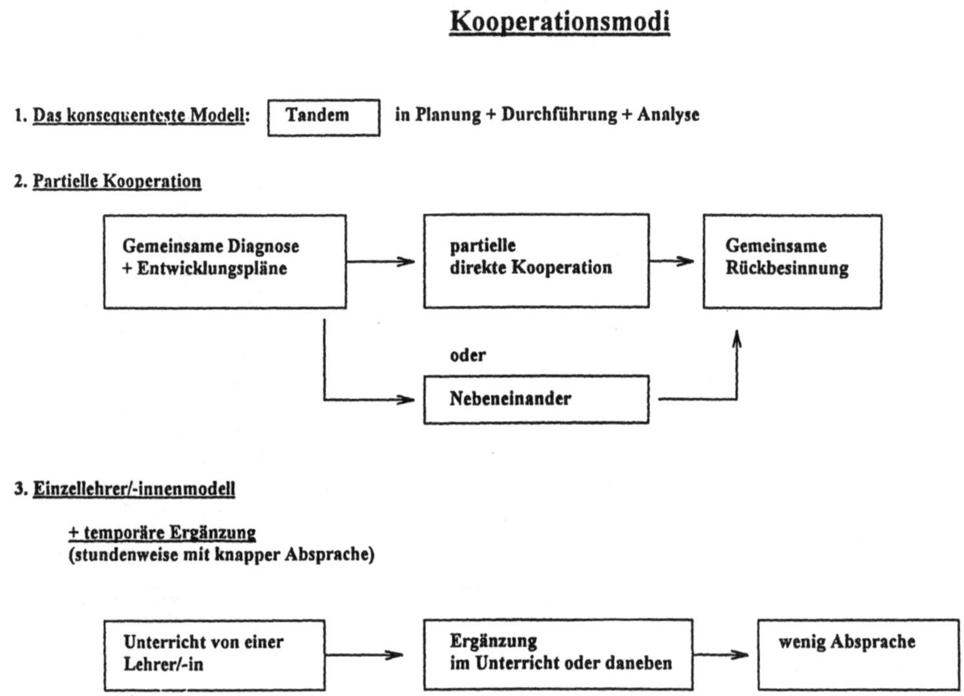

Abb. 4.13.13 Kooperationsmodi

Fazit: Intelligente Unterrichtsstrukturen

Wenn auf dem skizzierten Weg fortgeschritten werden kann, entstehen sog. intelligente Unterrichtsstrukturen.

Sie erlauben gemeinsames Arbeiten und gleichzeitig die Verfolgung individueller Lern-/Förderpläne, sie setzen bei verbesserten Diagnosefähigkeiten an (das ist das dringende Desiderat!), sie benötigen dann konsequent die individuelle Buchführung der Lernschwierigkeiten und –fortschritte, sie sind insgesamt gesehen die angemessene Antwort auf die Heterogenität der Leistungen und auf den Ansatz, Teilleistungsschwächen nicht zu Stigmatisierungen werden lassen!

Literatur

Akademie für Lehrerfortbildung Dillingen: Rechenstörungen: Diagnose, Förderung, Materialien; ein Fortbildungsmodell der Akademie f. L.D., Donauwörth, 1995

Arenhoevel, Franz; Buigbeck, Bernhard (Hrsg.): Fördern macht Spaß:ganzheitliche Fördermaßnahmen für Kinder mit Lernschwierigkeiten, Donauwörth, 1995

Arenhoevel, Franz: Fördern – einmal anders! In: Grundschulmagazin, 11 (1996) 10, S. 4 – 6

Bach, Heinz: Schulintegrierte Förderung bei Verhaltensauffälligkeiten: Konzept und Praxis, Berlin, 1987

Betz, Dieter; Breuninger, Helga: Teufelskreis Lernstörungen, theoretische Grundlagen und Standardprogramm, Weinheim, 1998[5]

Manfred Bönsch: Schüler aktivieren. Hannover: Hahnsche Buchhandlung, 1994[3]

Manfred Bönsch: Schule verbessern. Hannover, Hahnsche Buchhandlung, 1990

Manfred Bönsch (Hrsg.): Offener Unterricht in der Primar- und Sekundarstufe I.Hannover, 1993

Manfred Bönsch: Üben und Wiederholen im Unterricht. München: Verlag Ehrenwirth, 1993[2]

Manfred Bönsch: Variable Lernwege. Ein Lehrbuch der Unterrichtsmethoden.Paderborn; Verlag Schöningh, 1995[2]

Manfred Bönsch: Differenzierung in Schule und Unterricht. München: Ehrenwirth Verlag, 1995

Manfred Bönsch: Didaktisches Minimum. Prüfungsanforderungen für LehramtsstudentInnen, Neuwied: Luchterhand Verlag, 1996

Manfred Bönsch: Didaktisches Additum. Prüfungsanforderungen für LehramtsreferendarInnen, Neuwied: Luchterhand Verlag, 1998

Manfred Bönsch: Lerngerüste. Didaktik 2000 für die Primarstufe. Baltmannsweiler, Schneider Verlag Hohengehren, 1998

Bundesministerium für Unterricht und Kunst (Hrsg.): Was macht die Förderung effektiv?: Kontroverse(?) Konzepte zur Legasthenikerbetreuung, Wien, 1993

Burk, Karlheinz: Brauchen wir ein neues Förder-Verständnis? In: Arbeitskreis aktuell, 15 (1994) 45, S. 1 - 4

Dumke, Dieter: Förderung lernschwacher Schüler: Theoretische Grundlagen verschiedener Fördermodell und ihre Erprobung in der Praxis, München et. al., 1980

Dunkermühle, Ludger: Förderunterricht in der Grundschule. Frankfurt/M. et. al., 1985

Ehl, Axel: Förderung benachteiligter Schüler in der Hauptschule. In:Schulverwaltung. Ausgabe NRW, 8 (1997) 4, S. 123 – 125

Engelbrecht, Arthur et. al.: Lernbehinderungen verhindern: Anregungen für eine förderorientierte Grundschule, Frankfurt/M., 1991

Fischer, Monika: Drei Projekte zur integrativen Behandlung von Lernstörungen (Themenheft). In: Doppelpunkt (1996) 1, S. 2 – 20

Frey-Flügge, Elke: Kinder mit Teilleistungsschwächen in der Schule für Sprachbehinderte: Modellversuch Diagnose- und Förderklassen, München, 1989

Fritz, Annemarie: Erfolgreicher im Lernen: ein Förderprogramm für lernschwache Kinder, Berlin, 1986

Fritz, Annemarie et. al.: Schule zum Anfassen: ein Förderkonzept zum Aufbau von Anstrengungsbereitschaft, Sozialfähigkeit und Handlungsfähigkeit in der Grundschule, Heidelberg, 1989

Geppert, Klaus: Förderunterricht in der Grundschule. In: Schule heute, 22 (1982) 3, S. 13 – 14, 25

Guder, Rudolf: Fördern und Differenzieren in der Grundschule: Schwerpunkte:Mathematik, Hildesheim, 1994

Grad, Claus Dieter: Lesen – links, rechts, links. Förderunterricht auf anderem Wege. In: Beispiele: In: Niedersachsen Schule machen, 14 (1996) 4, 60 – 64

Hager, Willi (Hrsg.): Programme zur Förderung des Denkens bei Kindern: Konstruktion, Evaluation und Metaevaluation, Göttingen, 1995

Hefner, Norbert: Stütz- und Förderunterricht aus pädagogischer Sicht. In: Lehren und Lernen, 15 (1989) 11, S. 68 – 79

Henze, Godehard: Fördern in der Orientierungsstufe: eine empirische Untersuchung zur Förderung lernschwacher Schüler in Kleingruppen, Bad Heilbrunn, 1996

Jacobs, August Bernhard: Mit Geduld zum Erfolg: Erfahrungen, Hinweise und Hilfen für die Förderung von Schülern bei besonderen Schwierigkeiten im Erlernen des Lesens und Rechtschreibens (LRS) in der Sekundarstufe I, Boenen, 1995

Jeske, Werner: Lernstörungen und Leistungshemmungen: pädagogische Stützmassnahmen; Neuwied et. al., 1995

Kludt, Anette: Förderunterricht. Aufgabe und Herausforderung der Hauptschulen. In: Schulmanagement, 28 (1997) 5, S. 36 – 37

Landesinstitut für Schule und Weiterbildung: Lernwege entdecken: Entwicklungsförderung in Grund- und Sonderschulen; Boenen, 1996

Lange, Inge: Fördern ist mehr ... In: Grundschulunterricht, 45 (1998) 6, S. 25 – 26

Laschkowski, Werner, Schepek, Albert: Die Organisation des Förderunterrichts. Eine neue Aufgabe für den Beratungslehrer an Förderschulen. In: Förderschulmagazin, 19 (1997) 3, S. 5 – 8

Mackel, Andreas: Lese-Schreibschwäche als didaktisches Problem, Bad Heilbrunn, 1977

McAllen, Andrey: Zeichen- und Bewegungsübungen für Kinder mit Schwierigkeiten in Schreiben, Lesen und Rechnen, Stuttgart, 1996

Mend, Johannes: Neue Methoden der Rechtschreibförderung für Schüler mit Lernbehinderungen, Kempen, 1999

Nauck, Joachim: Fördern statt Auslesen: Pädagogisches Handeln im selektiven Schulsystem, Bad Heilbrunn/Obb., 1983

Nock, Helmut: Kognitionspsychologisch begründete Interventionen bei rechtschreibschwachen Schülern: eine vergleichende Studie, Tübingen, 1990

Reinhard, Andreas (Hrsg.): Förderung besonderer Schülergruppen in Bayern: aktuelle Herausforderung für die Schulpädagogik, München, 1989 (Aufsatzsammlung)

Reiser, Helmut et. al.: Sonderschullehrer in Grundschulen: Ergebnisse eines Schulversuchs zur integrativen Betreuung bei Lern- und Verhaltensstörungen, Weinheim-Basel, 1984

Riezinger, Beate: Legasthenieprävention: Fördermaßnahmen im Schuleingangsbereich, Frankfurt/M. et. al., 1998

Schulz, Andrea: Lernschwierigkeiten im Mathematikunterricht: grundsätzliche Überlegungen zum Erkennen, Verhindern und Überwinden von Lernschwierigkeiten – dargestellt am Beispiel der Klassenstufe 3, Berlin, 1995

Sandfuchs, Uwe: Förderunterricht für lernschwache Grundschüler. In: Grundschulunterricht, 45 (1998) 6, S. 2 – 5

Schulz, Andrea: Fördern im Mathematikunterricht: was kann ich tun? Berlin et. al., 1997

Seitz, Oskar: Schule umfassenden Lernens, in: Unterrichten, erziehen, 17 (1998) 3, S. 4 – 9

Walter, Jürgen: Förderung bei Lese- und Rechtschreibschwäche: Grundlagenforschung, methodische Konsequenzen, Praxisbeispiele und mediendidaktische Anregungen auf der Basis empirischer Forschungsmethoden, Göttingen et. al.,1996

4.14 Förderung in Intensivkursen

Hanspeter Orth

Zunächst möchte ich mich bei den Damen und Herren des Bundesvorstandes Legasthenie dafür bedanken, dass sie mir durch ihre Einladung die Möglichkeit geben, über die Förderarbeit in der 'Mannheimer Leseschule' zu berichten.

Die nachfolgenden Ausführungen geben meine Erfahrungen als Grundschullehrer, als Schulleiter einer Grundschule in Mannheims Norden, als Beratungslehrer, als Mitverantwortlicher für die Fortbildung der Multiplikatoren LRS im Oberschulamtsbereich Karlsruhe und nicht zuletzt als Vater eines inzwischen 21 jährigen jungen Mannes wieder, der seine Rechtschreibschwäche inzwischen weitgehend überwunden hat.

Ich hoffe sie mit meinem Praxisbericht zu ermutigen, sich in ähnlicher Weise mit ihren Fähigkeiten für die betroffenen Kinder zu engagieren. Es sind die uns anvertrauten Kinder mit besonderen Bedürfnissen, denen wir eine Chance für eine zufriedenstellende berufliche Laufbahn erhalten müssen.

Nachdem ich zusammen mit Frau Anita Leuschner anlässlich des Bundeskongresses 1997 in Greifswald die Möglichkeit hatte, unsere Förderkonzeption vorzustellen (vgl.: Schwarz M., Leuschner A., Orth Hp., Förderung durch LRS-Schulen in Mannheim oder der Werdegang eines lese- und rechtschreibschwachen Kindes, Bericht über den Fachkongress Legasthenie 1997, Bundesverband Legasthenie e. V. , Hannover, 1998), möchte ich, ermutigt durch die vielfältigen positiven Erfahrungen bei meiner Fortbildungsarbeit in Baden-Württemberg, insbesondere in Mannheim, in meinen Ausführungen die weitere inhaltliche und organisatorische Ausgestaltung unsrer Fördereinrichtungen darstellen.

Nachfolgend referiere ich die Textauszüge aus der in Baden-Württemberg gültigen Verwaltungsvorschrift zur Förderung von Kindern mit Schwächen im Lesen und/oder Rechtschreiben, weil sie die gesetzliche Grundlage für die Arbeit in unseren Fördereinrichtungen darstellen, die quantitative Ausdehnung und konzeptionelle Weiterentwicklung der Fördereinrichtungen, die Diagnosemappe zur Erfassung der betroffenen Kinder, den Fortbildungsmodus mit dem die Kollegien mit der Diagnosemappe fortgebildet werden, und die bisher erprobten und erarbeiteten Fördermaterialien, erste Ergebnisse unserer Förderarbeit im Hinblick auf die Kinder, die Kollegien, Schulverwaltung und die außerschulischen Beratungs- und Fördereinrichtungen.

Grundlage der konzeptionellen Weiterentwicklung unsrer Förderarbeit bildet die oben genannte Verwaltungsvorschrift (**Förderung von Schülern mit Schwierigkeiten im Lesen und/oder Rechtschreiben Verwaltungsvorschrift vom 10. Dez. 1997, Kultus u. Unterricht. Nr. 1, Januar 1998**), die die seit 1988 gültige Verwaltungsvorschrift ersetzt.

In dieser ist fest gehalten, dass **Lesen- und Schreibenlernen** zu den **Hauptaufgaben der Schule** gehört; **Früherkennung der betroffenen Kinder Aufgabe der Schule ist**.

„Ausgangspunkt für die Einleitung besonderer Fördermaßnahmen ist eine differenzierte Lernstandsbeschreibung des Deutschlehrers im Laufe des 1. Schj....

Dazu gehören Beobachtungen zum laut- und schriftsprachlichen, kognitiven, emotionalen, sozialen und motorischen Entwicklungsstand sowie zur Sinnestüchtigkeit des Kindes...

Fördermaßnahmen sind bereits während Kl. 1 möglich...

Dieser Förderunterricht ist in klasseninternen oder klassenübergreifenden, in jahrgangs- oder schul- bzw. schulartübergreifenden Gruppen durchzuführen. In der Regel sollen diese Gruppen mindestens vier Schüler umfassen. Die Förderung einzelner Schüler ist grundsätzlich möglich...

Falls auf einer Jahrgangsstufe mindestens zehn Schüler besonderer Fördermaßnahmen bedürfen, kann für sie eine eigene Klasse gebildet werden. Derartige Klassen können auch an einer zentral gelegenen Schule für Schüler mehrerer Schulen eingerichtet werden. Eingeschlossen ist damit auch die Bildung von Intensivkursen...

Förderbedürftige Schüler

Schüler während der Klassen 1 u. 2, denen die notwendigen Voraussetzungen für das Lesen und /oder Schreiben noch fehlen...

Schüler der Klassen 3 bis 6, deren Leistungen im Lesen und /oder Rechtschreiben dauerhaft geringer als „ausreichend" beurteilt wurden...

Die Kluft zwischen Verwaltungsvorschrift und schulischer Realität- oder die subjektive Bestandsaufnahme der Ausgangssituation

Es vergeht zu viel Zeit (zum Teil über ein Jahr), bis ein Kind mit einer Lese-Rechtschreibschwäche einer kompetenten Beratung vorgestellt wird. In dieser Zeit werden von den Eltern meist mehrere außerschulische Beratungseinrichtungen konsultiert, die unabhängig voneinander, eine Diagnose erstellen. In der Mehrzahl der Fälle schließt sich an die Diagnose kcine Therapie der Lese-Rechtschreibschwäche an. LehrerInnen stehen dem Phänomen Lese-Rechtschreibschwäche auch oft hilflos gegenüber. Sie suchen ebenfalls außerhalb der Schule Hilfe, weil sie einfache Diagnosemöglichkeiten nicht kennen, oder unsicher sind, ob sie diese anwenden dürfen. Außerschulische Beratungseinrichtungen sind überlastet und verweisen die Aufgabe zurück zur Schule. Damit schließt sich für das betroffene Kind der Teufelskreis.

Fazit:

Schule ist derzeit nur vereinzelt in der Lage, den geltenden LRS-Erlass umzusetzen.

Gleichzeitig sind die BeratungslehrerInnen derart überlastet, dass sie wegen anstehender Testungen kaum zu ihrer eigentlichen Aufgabenstellung, der Beratung, kommen.

Verzweifelte LehrerInnen oder Eltern bemühen private Hilfseinrichtungen.

Gleichzeitig werden vermehrt die Sozial-, Jugendämter um Kostenübernahme. gebeten.

Damit sind mit der Problematik wieder öffentliche Einrichtungen befasst. Ein langer kostenintensiver Weg für die Betroffenen; meist ein verlorenes Jahr für die Kinder.

Damit Schule einer ihrer Grundaufgaben gerecht werden kann, muss verschüttete Kompetenz neu belebt, wo nicht vorhanden, Grundwissen vermittelt werden.

Dies gilt umso mehr, da Schulen künftig mit der Tatsache der Früh- oder zweimaligen Einschulung betroffen sein werden (Schulanfang auf neuen Wegen!).

So betrachtet leidet das System Schule an der gleichen Symptomatik wie ein Teil der betroffenen Kinder um die es hier geht. Es ist wahrnehmungsbeeinträchtigt!

Die LehrerInnen sehen und erleben die Kinder jeden Tag in ihren Klassen. Sie können deren Problematik aber oftmals nicht erkennen, weil das erforderliche Wissen dazu nicht oder nur teilweise vorhanden ist.

Ich greife für die LehrerInnen das gleiche Schlagwort auf, wie es für die Schüler formuliert wurde. Es geht darum die LehrerInnen zu fordern und sie gleichzeitig zu fördern!
- in einer effizienten Fortbildungsform,
- möglichst schnell und flächendeckend,
- weitgehend kostenneutral und
- lehrer- und kindorientiert

Die praktische Umsetzung

Im Schj. 1996/97 hat Frau Monika Schwarz, Beratungslehrerin, mit nachfolgend skizziertem Fortbildungskonzept gute Erfahrungen gemacht:

Den Grundschulen, die Frau Schwarz und mir als Beratungslehrer oder als Leiter der Leseintensivmaßnahmen „Problemkinder" angemeldet haben, oder deren Kinder wir unterrichteten, bot Frau Schwarz die kontinuierliche Zusammenarbeit in Form einer „Patenschaft" an. Das heißt, dass ca. drei- bis viermal im Laufe des Schuljahres eine „Pädagogische Konferenz" mit den Erst- und ZweitklasslehrerInnen unter Beteiligung der Schulleiterin oder des Schulleiters stattfand. (Dauer ungefähr zwei Zeitstunden.) Gegenstand dieser Konferenzen war die Vermittlung und konkrete praktische Umsetzung der zeitlichen und inhaltliche Schritte zur Erfassung von Kindern mit Lernleistungsstörungen, insbesondere mit Lese-Rechtschreibproblemen. (siehe Broschüre: 'Lesen und Schreiben, o große Not', Ministerium für Kultus, Jugend und Sport Baden-Württemberg, gemeinsam mit dem Landesverband Legasthenie Baden-Württemberg e.V.).

Nach einem Schuljahr war damit dieses Kollegium in der Lage, die Verwaltungsvorschrift umzusetzen. Gleichzeitig wurden die betroffenen Kinder erfasst, Eltern und LehrerInnen über mögliche Hilfen für das Kind informiert. Im Mittelpunkt der Beratung standen dabei die Vermittlung von Unterrichtsmethoden und -techniken zur Prävention einer möglichen Lese-Rechtschreibschwäche zum Beispiel:
- durch den Einsatz der Lautgebärdensprache nach R. Hackethal, im Anfangsunterricht;
- dem Einsatz des Kieler Lese-und Rechtschreibaufbaus,
- der Vermittlung der Methode Buschmann,
- dem Einsatz geeigneter Übungsformen bei der Diktatvorbereitung,
- Hilfen zur Durchführung von differenzierten Diktaten,
- Beratung über die Teilnahme an möglichen außendifferenzierenden Angeboten wie Leseambulanz oder Leseschule
- Aufklärung über die Möglichkeiten und Grenzen außerschulischer Therapieeinrichtungen wie Ergotherapie Logopädie usw.

Die kontinuierliche Begleitung von Frau Schwarz wirkte sich sehr motivierend auf die Kollegien und vertrauensbildend (im Hinblick auf die Eltern) für die Schulen aus, so dass Frau Schwarz und ich daran dachten, diese Erfahrungen an die Multiplikatoren für LRS und an die Beratungslerer weiterzugeben, um sie so in das Fortbildungskonzept, auf freiwilliger Basis, einzubeziehen. Durch dieses Konzept werden die Beratunglslehrer bzw. die Leiter einer Fördermaßnahme, von zeitraubender Diagnose entlastet, das betroffene Kind rascher erkannt, verloren gegangenes oder nicht vorhandenes „know how" wird an die Schule zurückgebracht, die Beratungslehrer kommen ihrer eigentlichen Zweckbestimmung wieder näher, die von dem Kind erhobenen Daten zu gewichten und die Ratsuchenden zu beraten.

Wie konnte dieses Modell möglichst schnell und kostengünstig umgesetzt werden?

Ausgangspunkt und Ausbildungsinhalt war eine ‘Diagnosemappe’, deren Inhalt wir mit der Unterstützung, fachlichen Begleitung und Beratung von Herrn Günter Schultheiß (Schulpsychologische Beratungsstelle Mosbach), von Frau Renate Hackethal u. Frau Dr. Lisa Dummer-Smoch (und deren Einverständnis zur Verwendung ihres geistigen Eigentums), und den MitarbeiterInnen der ‘Mannheimer Leseschule’ zusammengestellt haben. Dank der ideellen und finanziellen Unterstützung des Oberschulamtes Karlsruhe konnte jedem Multiplikator für LRS und BeratungslehrerIn in diesem Oberschulamtsbezirk ein Exemplar für die Lehrerfortbildung zur Verfügung gestellt werden.
Ihren Inhalt möchte ich an nachfolgender Übersicht erläutern:

Inhaltsübersicht

weiß	**Früherkennung von Lernbeeinträchtigungen** - Diagnostische Möglichkeiten der Schule Informationen für Eltern und Lehrer und Einverständniserklärung - am Beispiel der „Leseschule" Mannheim–	2 Seiten
	Beobachtungshilfen zur Früherkennung von Lernschwierigkeiten	1 Seite
	Formblatt: **Zusammenstellung der Überprüfungsergebnisse Einschulungsverfahren**	1 Seite
	Formblatt: **Zusammenstellung der Beobachtungsdaten** (Klasse 1 u. 2)	1 Seite
	Zusammenfassung: **Pragmatische Verfahren zur Diagnostik sprachbezogener Wahrnehmungsstörungen** (Grundlagen der Differenzierungsprobe)	2 Seiten
	Protokollblätter zur Differenzierungsprobe I und II	7 Seiten
	Zusammenfassung: **Zusammenhänge zwischen zentraler Fehlhörigkeit und anderen Wahrnehmungsstörungen**	3 Seiten
	Protokollblatt: **Buchstabenkenntnis**	1 Seite
	Vorwerker Leseprobe	1 Seite
	Malauftrag	1 Seite
	Testanweisungen für die Diagnostischen Bilderlisten	2 Seiten

rosa	**Anweisungen zur DBL-AS**	1 Seite
	Kopiervorlage: **Alphabetische Schreibprobe (DBL-AS)**	2 Seiten
	Muster: **Diagnostische Bilderliste –Frühform (DBL-F)**	2 Seiten
	Muster: **Diagnostische Bilderliste (DBL-1),** Form A und B, **Ende Kl. 1; und**	2 Seiten
grün		
	Ende 1. Quartal Kl. 2	2 Seiten
	Muster: **Diagnostische Bilderliste (DBL-2), Mitte Kl. 2**	2 Seiten
weiß	**Auswertungshilfen** zu den Diagnostischen Bilderlisten mit **Beispielblatt**	2 Seiten
	Zusammenfassung: **Wie können Eltern und Lehrer Kindern mit Wahrnehmungsstörungen helfen?**	4 Seiten
	Literaturangaben/Bezugsquellen	2 Seiten

Anmerkungen:
weiß: für Überprüfung in der 1. und in der 2. Klasse, abhängig vom Leistungsstand
rosa: für Überprüfung in der 1. Klasse
grün: für Überprüfung in der 2. Klasse

Die Vorlagen der Diagnostischen Bilderlisten Frühform (F), 1 und 2 werden in der Lehrerfortbildung aus Gründen des *Copyright* nur mit ausgefüllten Testbeispielen wiedergegeben. Es war eine Entscheidung der Autorengruppe, die Diagnosemappe nur auf dem Weg der Lehrerfortbildung weiterzugeben. Sie ist und wird deswegen nicht veröffentlicht. Weil wir der Annahme sind, dass sich einzelne Diagnoseinstrumente weiterentwickeln werden, wurde die Form einer Heftmappe gewählt, um so überalterte diagnostische Maßnahmen durch neuere oder praktikablere zu ersetzen.

Wie konnte dieser Inhalt in einem Fortbildungskonzept flächendeckenden und möglichst kostengünstig, umgesetzt werden?
In der Zusammenarbeit mit dem Ministerium für Kultus, Jugend und Sport Baden-Württemberg und dem Oberschulamt Karlsruhe konnte nachfolgend aufgeführtes Fortbildungskonzept (Abb. 4.14.1 + 4.14.2) im genannten Oberschulamtsbereich verabredet und mit der Unterstützung der Staatlichen Schulämter, den Multiplikatoren LRS und den beteiligten Schulleitungen probeweise umgesetzt werden.

Organisationsschritte	Zeitrahmen
➢ Erscheinen des neuen LRS-Erlasses	Januar 1998, KuU 1/98
➢ Informationsveranstaltung des OSA über das Konzept Adressatenkreis: Staatliche Schulämter, Schulpsychologische Beratungsstellen, Leiter der Beratungslehrer AG	April '98
➢ Vorabinformation der BeratungslehrerInnen durch die Schulpsychologischen Beratungsstellen im Rahmen der Fall-AG	ab Januar '98
➢ Dienstbesprechung der einzelnen Schulämter mit den BeratungslehrerInnen und den Multiplikatoren LRS zur Information über das Fortbildungskonzept	April/Mai '98
➢ Dienstbesprechung der einzelnen Schulämter mit den Schulleitern (Schulleitertagung) zu Information über das Fortbildungskonzept	April/Mai/Juni '98
➢ Regionale Fortbildung der BL durch die Multiplikatoren LRS: Fortbildungseinheit (Vorschlag: freie Beobachtung)	bis zu den Sommerferien
➢ Kontaktaufnahme BeratungslehrerIn-Grundschule Fortbildungsvereinbarung , Terminabsprache Für den/die BeratungslehrerIn bieten sich an: Fortbildungsangebote für die eigenen Schule oder für eine Schule, die dafür aus organisatorischen Gründen und auf Grund gewachsener Zusammenarbeit besonders in Frage kommt. Günstige Voraussetzung: Die Lehrkräfte der 1. Klassen des neuen Schuljahres sind schon vor den Sommerferien bekannt.	vor den Sommerferien/ in der ersten Schulwoche
➢ Beginn der Fortbildung BeratungslehrerIn-Grundschule 1. Fortbildungseinheit (freie Beobachtung)	bis Ende September
➢ Die Planung der weiteren Einheiten (Multiplikator-BeratungslehrerIn- Grundschule nach Absprache und Bedarf	Schuljahr 98/99 u. 99/00

Abb. 4.14.1 Zeitplan für das vorgeschlagene Fortbildungskonzept zur *Früherkennung von Lernschwierigkeiten, insbesondere LRS,* durch die Multiplikatoren-LRS des Oberschulamtes Karlsruhe, Zielgruppe Beratungslehrer für deren Zusammenarbeit mit den Grundschulen

Beispiel meines Anschreibens an interessierte Schulen

Liebe/r Kollege/in
Sie haben den Wunsch geäußert, dass ich Ihr Kollegium im Rahmen der „LRS-Patenschaften" fortbilde.
Dazu sind 3x 2 Zeitstunden notwendig.

1. Einheit: Von der freien zur gezielten Beobachtung (Breuer/Weuffen)
2. Einheit: Lese- und Schreibstandsdiagnose
3. Einheit: Welche Maßnahme für das Kind? (Inner- und außerschulischen Hilfen)

Der Inhalt jeder Einheit wird handlungsorientiert mit den Teilnehmern erarbeitet.
Diese bekommen nach jedem Termin die **verbindliche Aufgabe** den Inhalt der erlernten Einheit an u. mit ihren 'Problemkindern' durchzuführen.
Zu Fortbildungsbeginn jeder nachfolgenden Einheit werden die vorliegenden Ergebnisse gemeinsam gesichtet und die Kollegen beraten, damit diese wiederum Eltern beraten können.
Damit ist nach drei Bausteinen das 'know how' an der Schule **und** die entsprechenden Kinder sind überprüft.
Grundlage der Fortbildung ist die '**Diagnosemappe'**, die Sie bitte rechtzeitig vor Beginn der Veranstaltung für jeden der teilnehmenden Kollegen/innen kopieren.
(Entweder ein Kollege/in holt die Mappe bei mir ab, oder Sie fordern sie bei mir an und ich schicke sie mit der Dienstpost.)
Für die Fortbildung benötige ich noch eine **Videogerät** und einen **Overheadprojektor**.
Zur praktischen Arbeit ist die Anschaffung folgender Literatur für die Lehrerbibliothek notwendig:

1. Breuer, H.; Weuffen, M.: Lernschwierigkeiten am Schulanfang, Beltz, Weinheim und Basel 1993, ISBN: 3-407-62170-1 **(Differenzierungsproben zur Überprüfung der Wahrnehmung)**
2. Dummer-Smoch, L.: Die Diagnostischen Bilderlisten, **Handanweisung,** Veris Verlag GmbH Kiel, ISBN 3-89493-0-13-6
3. Dummer-Smoch, L.: Die Diagnostischen Bilderlisten, **Testmaterial,** Veris Verlag GmbH Kiel, ISBN 3-89493-0-16-0
4. Dr. Pischner, E.: Prävention schriftsprachlicher Lernschwierigkeiten im Vor- und Grundschulalter, Reha Verlag, Bonn 1993, **(Ergänzung zur Differenzierungsprobe 1 nach Breuer/Weuffen)** ISBN 3-88239-180-4
5. Milz I.: Sprechen, Lesen, Schreiben, Edition Schindele, Heidelberg 1994,
(Unterlagen zur Kontrolle der Hand/Augen-Dominanz, Fragebogen zum Hören)
ISBN 3-89149-200-6
6. Kleinmann, K.: Verstehen, Beobachten und gezieltes Fördern von LRS-Schülern, Ein Leitfaden für die Praxis, Borgmann Verlag, Dortmund, 1999, **(Beobachtungs- und Praxishilfen auch für ältere Schüler)** ISBN 3-86145-168-9

Endziel: Die TeilnehmerInnen sind in der Lage den neuen LRS-Erlass umzusetzen:
Lernschwierigkeiten frühzeitig erkennen und 'Erste-Hilfe' zu leisten.

Ich schlage folgende Fortbildungstermine vor und **bitte um Bestätigung und Vereinbarung der Anfangszeiten**. (Ich wäre dankbar, wenn es grundsätzlich bei diesen Terminen bleiben könnte, da es sachlogisch sinnvoll ist und ich auch noch landesweit tätig bin.)

Ich bitte Ihre/n zuständige/n BeratungslehrerIn von diesen Terminen zu informieren und einzuladen.

Ihre Anwesenheit als SchulleiterIn setze ich selbstverständlich voraus.

	Pfingstberg-GHWRS	**Käthe-Kollwitz-GS**	**Schiller-GHWRS**	**Mozart-GS**	**Albrecht-Dürer-GS/SO**
1. Termin					
2. Termin					
3. Termin					

Ich freue mich, Ihrem Kollegium helfen zu können!
Mit kollegialen Grüßen

Hanspeter Orth, R

Abb. 4.14.2

Ergebnisse:

- Es wurden viel mehr 'Risikokinder' von den LehrerInnen erkannt als zuvor vermutet. Die Wartezeiten für eine LRS-Diagnose verkürzten sich.
- Außerschulische Beratungseinrichtungen wurden zunächst häufiger, dann weit weniger frequentiert.
- BeratungslehrerInnen und die Schulpsychologischen Beratungsstellen wurden von der Testdiagnostik in vielen Fällen entlastet.
- Die Zusammenarbeit mit Kinderärzten, Logopäden, Ergotherapeuten, Mitarbeitern des Gesundheitsamtes erhielt eine sachkompetente Basis, die dem Gesundheitssytem Kosten spart und allen Beteiligten interdisziplinäres Lernen ermöglicht.
- Den Kindern konnte schneller und nachhaltiger als bisher geholfen werden!
- Schule hat neben Kompetenz auch das Vertrauen der Eltern wiedergewonnen, wo es verloren gegangen war.
- Die LehrerInnen erwarben mit der neu oder wieder entdeckten Kompetenz auch neue Berufszufriedenheit und Motivation im Umgang mit den betroffenen Kindern.
- Der Zeitplan zum verabredeten Fortbildungskonzept konnte auf freiwilliger Basis aller an der Fortbildung Beteiligten in der überwiegenden Mehrzahl der Fälle umgesetzt werden.
- Zuweilen erwies es sich als sinnvoll, mit dem Inhalt der 2. Einheit zu beginnen und die 1. Einheit anschließend zu behandeln (Das trifft vorwiegend auf das Interesse der ZweitklasslehrerInnen)
- Der Fortbildungsmodus stieß auf große Akzeptanz.

- Es wurden Kollegen gewonnen, die sich für die weitergehende inhaltliche Arbeit zur Verfügung stellten und Förderangebote im Sinne unseres Modells an ihrer Schule anbieten.

So erklärt sich auch die Ausweitung der Fördermaßnahmen.

Die Abbildungen 4.14.3 und 4.14.4 zeigen die beiden Standorte der 'LRS-Schulen' und die angegliederten 'LRS-Ambulanzen' in Mannheim-Mitte und Mannheim-Nord. Sie richten sich mit ihrem Förderangebot ausnahmslos, im Sinne der Prävention, an Kinder der Klassenstufen 1 und 2.

(Zur Unterscheidung von LRS-Schule und LRS-Ambulanz verweise ich auf meinen gleichnamigen Aufsatz im Kongressbericht des Bundesverbandes Legasthenie von 1997)

Der Vergleich der beiden Übersichten macht zum einen die quantitative Ausweitung der LRS-Fördereinrichtungen in Mannheim deutlich, zum anderen aber auch deren qualtitative Fortentwicklung.

Es ist das Verdienst von Frau Monika Schwarz und der von ihr fortgebildeten und kontinuierlich betreuten Kollegien, dass sich die Förderung der Kinder nicht wie bisher auf die Klassenstufen 1 und 2 beschränkt, sondern auch auf die Klassenstufen 3/ 4 und die Klassen 5/ 6 der Orientierungsstufe ausgedehnt werden konnte.

Es nehmen sich vermehrt Haupt- und Realschule der 'LRS-Kinder' an, indem sie ihre Kollegien im Rahmen unsrer Fortbildungsmaßnahme ausbilden lassen und Förderkurse einrichten. Auch für die weiterführenden Schulen in Baden-Württemberg erarbeitet eine Autorengruppe unter Leitung des Ministeriums für Kultur, Jugend und Sport Baden-Württemberg eine 'LRS-Broschüre' mit praktischen Handreichungen zur Umsetzung des LRS-Erlasses. Desweiteren ist zu beobachten, dass Schulleitungen zusammen mit ihrem Kollegium an der vereinfachten Handhabung der LRS Diagnose und inhaltlichen Ausgestaltung der LRS-Förderung arbeiten. Anregungen und Kritik wird in jährlich zweimal stattfindenden Besprechungen von Förderteam, der jeweiligen Schulleitung und Vertreter des Schulamtes unter Leitung der Schulpsychologischen Beratungsstelle ausgetauscht und in die Weiterarbeit integriert.

Weitere Voraussetzungen unter denen die organisatorische Weiterentwicklung möglich war:

- Sie ist zunächst abhängig von den Möglichkeiten des Staatlichen Schulamtes, aus seinem sog. Ergänzungsbereich die hierfür erforderlichen Lehrerwochenstunden zur Verfügung zu stellen.
- Sie ist abhängig von der finanziellen Unterstützung durch den Schulträger, der in Mannheim die zusätzlichen Kosten für die 'Leseschulen' bereitstellt. Dies sind Kosten für Lehr- u. Lernmittel, und auch Fahrtkosten zum Transport der Kinder. (Für die 'LRS-Ambulanzen ist die jeweilige Schulleitung zuständig! Fahrtkosten fallen dort nicht an.)
- Sie ist abhängig vom Konsens innerhalb der Schule, dass die Einrichtung einer Fördermaßnahme vom gesamten Kollegium akzeptiert und unterstützt wird.
- Sie ist abhängig von der Kompetenz, mit der die LRS-Förderung durchgeführt wird. In Mannheim werden nur an solchen Schulen LRS-Ambulanzen eingerichtet, von denen ein Kollege der eine Kollegin mindestens 10 Doppelstunden in eine der drei 'Leseschulen' hospitiert hat. Die so fortgebildeten Kollegen erhalten darüber ein Testat.

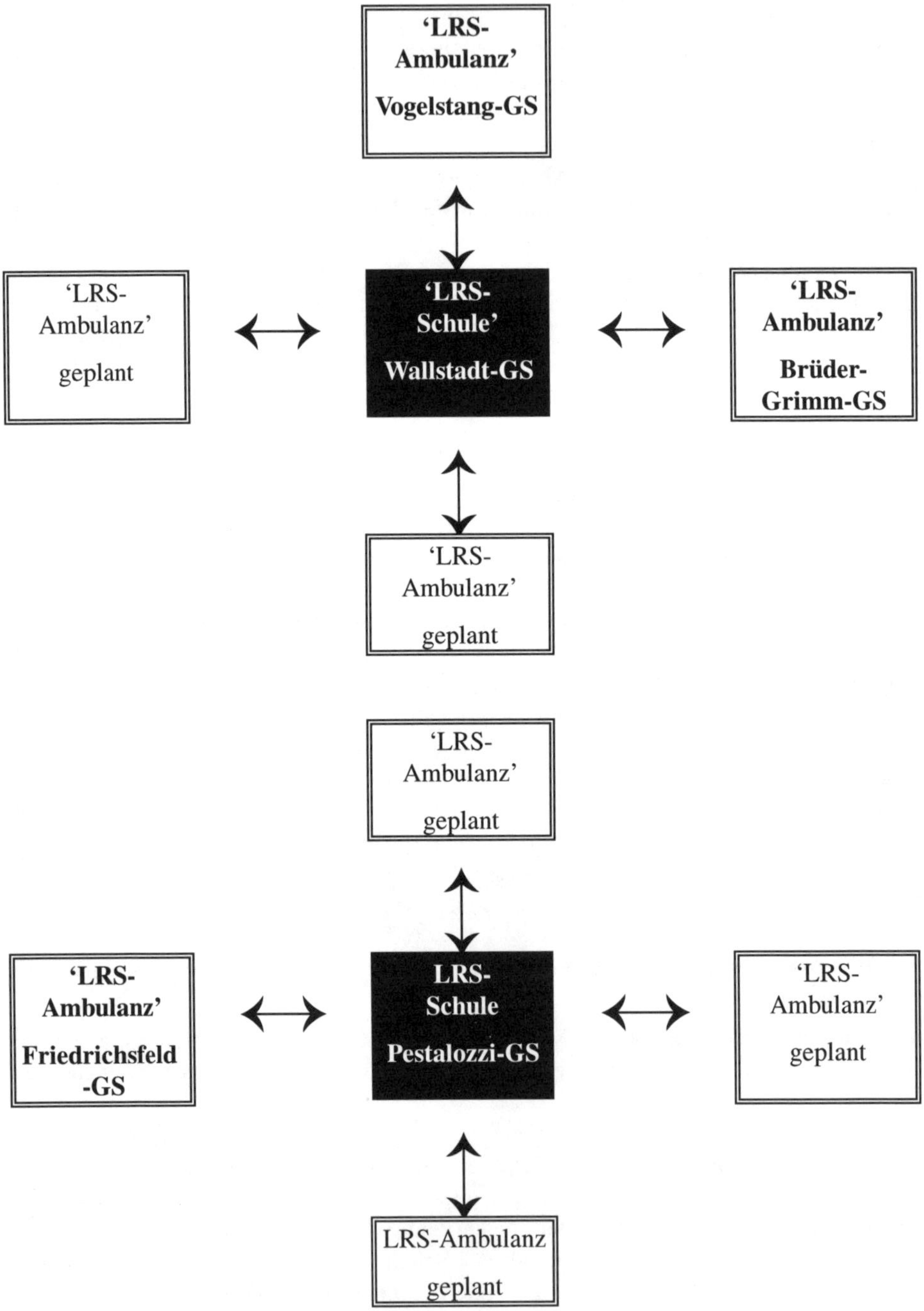

Abb. 4.14.3 Standorte der Mannheimer LRS-Schulen (auch 'Leseschule' genannt) LRS-Ambulanzen Schj. 1996/1997

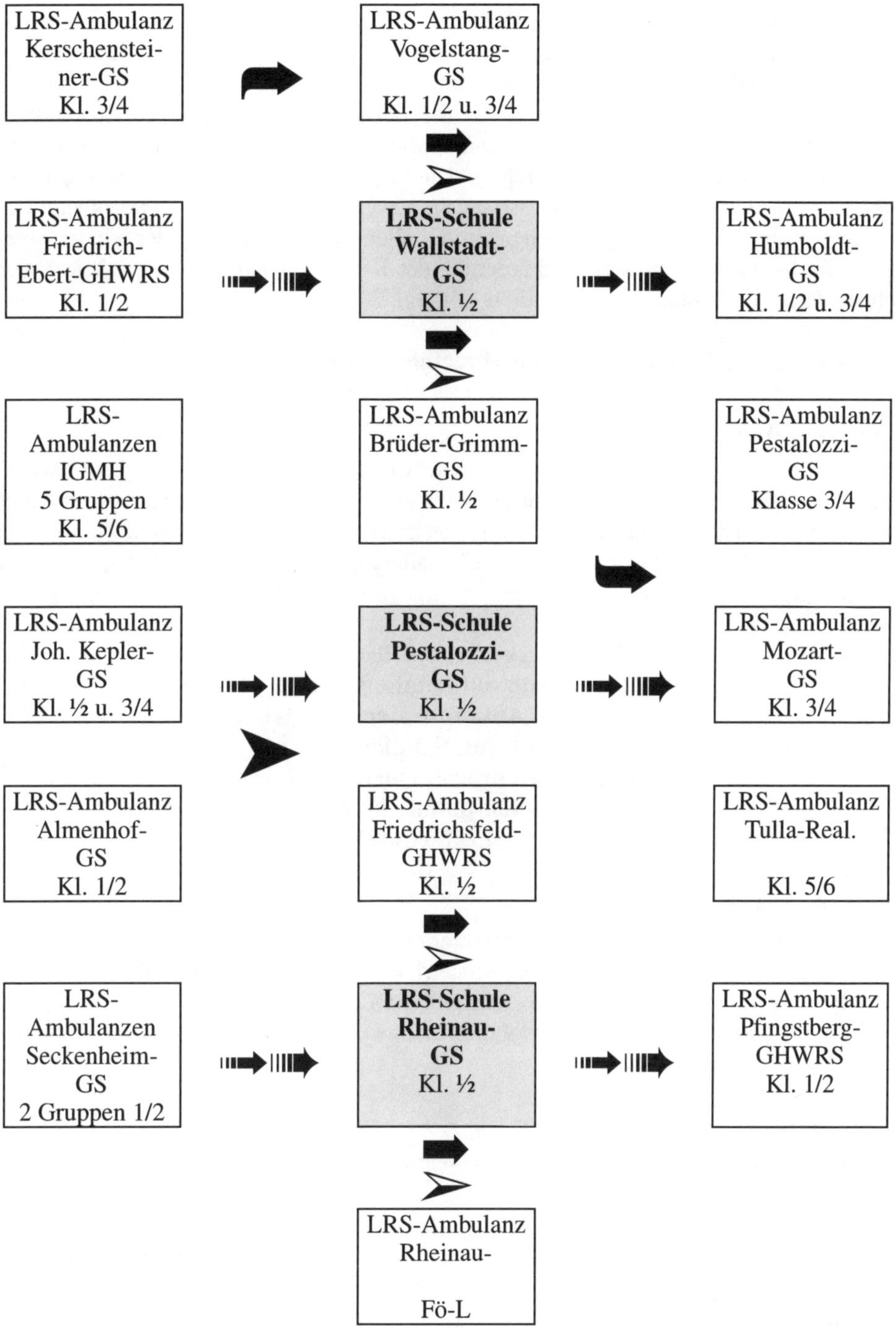

Abb. 4.14.4 Standorte der Mannheimer LRS-Schulen (auch 'Leseschule' genannt) LRS-Ambulanzen Schj. 1998/1999

- Sie ist abhängig von einer kontinuierlichen Fortbildung der KollegInnen, die eine Fördereinrichtung verantwortlich führen. Hierzu werden von Frau Schwarz und von mir mindestens drei Fortbildungsnachmittage im Schuljahr angeboten: Die Fortbildungsinhalte werden von den KollegInnen mit uns abgestimmt.
- Sie ist abhängig von der Vergleichbarkeit der Lernerfahrungen der FörderlehrerInnen. Hierzu haben die FörderlehrerInnen die Durchführung einer Eingangs- und Ausgangskontrolle bei den Förderkindern durchzuführen. Die Ergebnisse werden von der Schulpsychologischen Beratungsstelle zentral erfasst und ausgewertet. Ihre Ergebnisse gehen zum Beispiel in die oben erwähnten Besprechungen mit allen an der Förderung der Kinder Beteiligten ein. Desweiteren basiert die Förderung der Kinder auf nahezu identischem Unterrichtsmaterial, das nun auch veröffentlicht vorliegt.

Auf welches Material können die FörderlehrerInnen zurückgreifen?

Das Unterrichtsvideo

Seit Januar 1999 steht das nachfolgend skizzierte Unterrichtsvideo zur Verfügung. Als beschränkter Ersatz für eine Unterrichtsmitschau dokumentiert es dennoch unsere momentane inhaltliche und methodisch-didaktische Arbeitsweise.Neben diesem Fortbildungszweck leistete das Video auch gute Überzeugungsarbeit bei allen, die unserer Arbeit eher skeptisch bis misstrauisch gegenüberstehen.

„Unterricht 2000"
Unterrichtsdokumentation Grundschule, Deutsch, Anfangsunterricht, Kl. 2, Förderung von Schülern mit Lese-Rechtschreibproblemen durch eine Leseintesivmaßnahme im Rahmen der 'Leseschule'

Angaben zu den Lehrern

Beide Lehrer haben langjährige Unterrichtserfahrungen (vorwiegend im Bereich der Grundschule). Die Qualifikation für diesen Förderunterricht haben sich die Lehrkräfte zum einen über die Beratungslehrerausbildung und -tätigkeit, zum anderen über zusätzliche schulische und außerschulische Fortbildungsveranstaltungen sowie Unterrichtshospitationen in ähnlich organisierten Einrichtungen erworben.

Angaben zur Klasse

Es handelt sich um eine Gruppe von höchstens sechs Kindern aus der 2. Klasse. Sie kommen aus mehreren Grundschulen Mannheims an ein zentrale Grundschule, an der die 'Leseschule' als Leseintensivmaßnahme organisatorisch angegliedert ist. Auf der Grundlage der geltenden Verwaltungsvorschrift zur Förderung von Schülern mit Problemen im Lese- und Rechtschreiben („LRS-Erlass", 10.12.1997) besuchen die betroffenen Kinder über einen Zeitraum von 10 Wochen (täglich 3 Unterrichtsstunden; 2 Std. Deutsch, 1 Std. Mathe.) diese Klasse. Nähere Informationen zur Organisation dieser Maßnahme in der Broschüre „Lesen und Schreiben, o große Noit".

4.15 Hilfestellungen durch Augenärztin und Orthoptistin bei Legasthenie

Hilke Oberländer

Sehen im Sinne von Augenfunktionen – das ein- und beidäugiges Sehen – ist nur ein Teil dessen, was erforderlich ist, um lesen zu können. Zusätzliche Hirnfunktionen müssen voll funktionstüchtig sein. Nachfolgend werden neben dem ein- und beidäugigen Sehen Begriffe wie visuelle Wahrnehmung, Raumwahrnehmung und Äugigkeit erklärt. Des weiteren werden Hilfestellungen beim Lese- und Schreibvorgang – die Sehanwendungsberatung – besprochen.

Sehen im Sinne von Augenfunktionen – ein- und beidäugiges Sehen

Beim einäugigen Sehen handelt es sich um die volle Funktionstüchtigkeit der Netzhaut. Dabei wird unterschieden in das zentrale Sehen – die Stelle des schärfsten Sehens (Fovea) und das periphere Sehen (intaktes Gesichtsfeld). Des weiteren müssen die Augen in alle Blickrichtungen frei beweglich sein (Motorik) und eine normale Zusammenarbeit zwischen beiden Augen bestehen. Bei der Gesamtheit der geschilderten Sehfunktionen spricht man vom ein- und beidäugigen Sehen (Abb.4.15.1). In der Abbildung wird die Beziehung zwischen den verschiedenen Sehverarbeitungsprozessen und den entsprechenden Hirnarealen dargestellt. Das Modell wurde nach Roth, „Das Gehirn und seine Wirklichkeit" entwickelt.

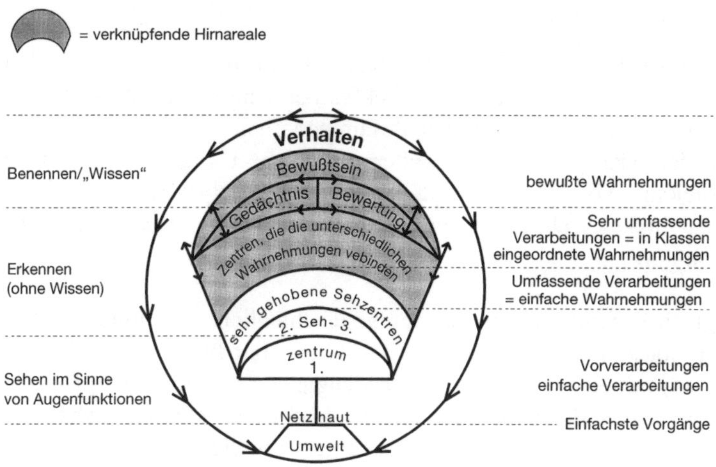

Abb. 1: Beziehung zwischen Hirnarealen und Verarbeitungsprozessen
(Oberländer, nach Roth, 1995)

Abb. 4.15.1 Zu einem intakten beidäugigen Sehen gehört auch das stereoskopische Sehen.

Definition plastisches/stereoskopisches Sehen (Meyers großes Universal-Lexikon, Bd. 11, S. 64, 1984) „dreidimensionale visuelle Wahrnehmung von Objekten aufgrund des beidäugigen Sehens"

Augenärztin und Orthoptistin sprechen bei dieser Sehfunktion vom dreidimensionalen Sehen, Tiefensehen oder „räumlichen" Sehen. Das dreidimensionale Sehen wird im 2. und 3. Sehzentrum verarbeitet (Abb. 4.15.1). Es handelt sich um einen *Teilaspekt* der Fähigkeit, Entfernung und Tiefe wahrzunehmen. Dies ist die Wahrnehmung der Entfernung von Objekten zum Betrachter und der Entfernung von Objekten untereinander. Diese Wahrnehmungsfähigkeit ist wiederum ein *Teilaspekt* der Raumwahrnehmung.

Untersuchung des ein- und beidäugigen Sehens

Die Qualität des zentralen Sehens findet ihren Ausdruck in der festgestellten Sehschärfe. Dabei ist zu bedenken, daß die verschiedenen Sehschärfentests sehr unterschiedliche Anforderungen an das Sehsystem stellen. Zum Beispiel werden mit Kinderbildern überwiegend Formerkennbarkeit und intellektuelle Fähigkeiten geprüft; bei Lesetexten erfährt man etwas über das Leseverständnis, wenig über die Sehschärfe.

Weiterhin sind die Abstände der Prüfsymbole untereinander zu berücksichtigen. Häufig stehen die Symbole der Sehtests zu weit auseinander – man erfährt dann nichts über die Fähigkeit, sehr dicht beieinander stehende Symbole zu unterscheiden – die Lesesehschärfe. Dies ist nur mit dem sprachfreien C-Test von Haase und Homann (1981) möglich.

Sehr wichtig ist die Prüfung der optischen Verhältnisse: liegt eine Fehlsichtigkeiten vor? Dabei kann es sich um eine Weitsichtigkeit, Kurzsichtigkeit oder Stabsichtigkeit (Hornhautverkrümmung) handeln. Des weiteren gehört zur Diagnostik des einäugigen Sehen die Prüfung der Augenbeweglichkeit. Die obligatorische allgemeine augenärztliche Untersuchung beinhaltet die vorderen und mittleren Augenabschnitte und die Inspektion des gesamten Augenhintergrundes.

Die Diagnostik des beidäugigen Sehens beinhaltet die Prüfung der Augenstellung in der Ferne, der Nähe und in den verschiedenen Blickfeldbereichen: besteht eine Abweichung vom Parallelstand der Augen? Die Qualität der Zusammenarbeit beider Augen wird mit den unterschiedlichsten Methoden getestet. Des weiteren wird die Fähigkeit überprüft, ob die Augen sich ohne Probleme von der Ferne auf die Nähe und umgekehrt einstellen können (Nahanpassungsfähigkeit). Dies muß bei angestrengter und nicht angestrengter Sehweise untersucht werden.

In der beidäugigen Diagnostik wird aus den unterschiedlichsten Gründen mit ganz verschiedenen Tests das sogenannte Führungsauge bestimmt. Hier handelt es sich zum Beispiel um das Auge, das am besten sehen kann, im beidäugigen Sehen das führende oder dominante Auge ist. Dabei werden Hirnfunktionen auf der Ebene des 1. bis 3. Sehzentrums überprüft (Abb. 4.15.1). Je nach Testmethode kann es zu unterschiedlichen Ergebnissen kommen.

Bei der gesamten Diagnostik ist zu bedenken, daß die Untersuchungssituation und -methoden nur Kunstprodukte sind. Sie entsprechen nicht unbedingt den Sehbedingungen im täglichen Leben. Berücksichtigt werden muß die <u>sehr kurze</u> Untersuchungssituation. Sie stellt lediglich eine Momentaufnahme dar und spiegelt in keiner Weise das längere Sehen – zum Beispiel beim Lesen – wider. Es ist zu bedenken, daß Kinder und Jugendliche – im Gegensatz zu Erwachsenen – häufig kurzfristig ein- und beidäugige Defekte kompensieren können; sie sind dann für die Untersucher *unter Umständen nicht feststellbar.* Ziel der Diagnostik muß es sein, diese Kompensationsmechanismen außer Kraft zu setzen.

Fehlsichtigkeiten können mithilfe der Nahanpassungsfähigkeit kompensiert werden. Sie sind in ihrem gesamten Ausmaß nur meßbar, wenn die Fähigkeit zur Brechkraftveränderung der Augenlinse aufgehoben wird. Daher müssen zur Diagnostik grundsätzlich pupillenerweiternde, akkommodationslähmende Medikamente eingesetzt werden. Diese Untersuchung hat bei der Erstuntersuchung obligatorisch zu sein und wird in Verbindung mit der Kontrolle des Augenhintergrundes von der Augenärztin durchgeführt.

Um beidäugige Kompensationsmechnismen außer Kraft zu setzen, ist bei bestimmten Auffälligkeiten, zum Beispiel Kopf- und Augenschmerzen, Tränen, Kneifen, Verschwommensehen beim Lesen, bestimmte Lesefehler (zum Beispiel: iene statt eine) der Augen-Belastungstest durchzuführen (Oberländer, 1989). Dabei handelt es sich um die Untersuchung des beidäugigen Sehens unter Belastung des Sehens (Nachempfinden der Schulsituation mit Lesen, Schreiben, Rechnen und ähnliches).

Untersuchung der Augen durch Augenärztin und Orthoptistin

Fallen Kinder durch Lernprobleme auf, gilt es die besten Grundvoraussetzungen für das Sehen und damit auch für das Lernen zu schaffen. Das bedeutet, daß bei jedem auffälligen Kind vor Beginn einer Legasthenietherapie – besser noch vor der Legastheniediagnostik – die peripheren Aufnahmeorgane Augen und Ohren untersucht werden sollten. Dabei muß sichergestellt sein, daß die *Gesamtheit* des ein- und beidäugigen Sehens untersucht wird. Dazu ist ein vielschichtiges Untersuchungsprogramm notwendig. Jede einseitige Untersuchung würde den betroffenen Kinder und Jugendlichen schaden.

Für die exakte Abklärung der aller Augenfunktionen sind die Kinder der Augenärztin *und* Orthoptistin vorzustellen. Weder Kinder- und Schulärztin noch Augenoptikerin können eine vollständige Diagnostik vornehmen.

Werden nur Teilfunktionen des ein- und beidäugigen Sehens – im Sinne eines Screening oder Untersuchungen zum Beispiel nur am Polatest – durchgeführt, kann damit in keinem Fall die Gesamtheit der möglichen Störungen festgestellt werden. Entsprechend ist die Beurteilung über ein belastungsfreies Sehen nicht möglich!

Korrektur ein- und beidäugiger Abweichungen

Legasthene Kinder und Jugendliche sind häufig überfordert. Sie benötigen für die Aufgaben, die die Umwelt an sie stellt, mehr Anstrengung. Vieles ist nicht so perfekt automatisiert und dauert dadurch länger. Nur mit einem Übermaß an Konzentration können viele Kinder den Anforderungen nachkommen. Schularbeiten, die länger dauern und erforderliche Therapien belasten die Kinder.

Des weiteren stehen sie unter einem ganz erheblichen Druck, da sie ihr eigenes Unvermögen sehr häufig spüren. Bei isolierten Leistungsschwächen sind die Kinder sehr wohl in der Lage, ihre Schwächen zu bemerken. Nur verstehen können sie diese Schwächen nicht. Sie müssen sich wesentlich mehr anstrengen als die nichtbetroffenen Kinder, sie erreichen jedoch weniger. Dies führt sehr häufig zu Reaktionen, die für die Umwelt kaum verständlich sind.

Für die betroffenen Kindern ist es daher besonders wichtig, daß das ein- und beidäugige Sehen belastungsfrei funktioniert. Nichtkorrigierte Abweichungen können Beschwerden auslösen (Tab. 4.15.1). Dadurch kann das Sehen und die Lernsituation erheblich erschwert werden.

- Kopfschmerzen, besonders im Laufe des Tages, nach Naharbeiten
- Unlust zu Naharbeiten
- Augenreiben, -kneifen, -tränen, -schmerzen, -zwinkern, besonders in Verbindung mit Naharbeiten
- Verschwommensehen beim Distanzwechsel beim Fixieren von der Ferne zur Nähe und umgekehrt
- Doppelbilder/Schattensehen

Aussagen zum Leseakt

- kann keine kleinen Texte lesen
- muß Texte mehrfach lesen, um ihn zu begreifen – kein sinnzusammenhängendes Lesen möglich
- kann nicht lange lesen
- lese nur noch kurze Texte
- muß beim Lesen
  - alles weit weg halten
  - dicht herannehmen
- wenn ich beim Lesen alles deutlich sehen will, wird der Text sehr klein
- muß mich anstrengen, um deutlich zu sehen
- das Sehen kommt und geht
- Buchstaben und/oder Zahlen wackeln, springen, rutschen ineinander, verschwimmen
- das Sehen und/oder Lesen strengt an
- Augen müssen beim Lesen aufgerissen oder zusammengekniffen werden

Tab. 4.15.1 Beschwerden, die eine augenärztliche und orthoptische Untersuchung erfordern

Da Beschwerden nicht vom Befundausmaß, sondern von der individuellen Belastbarkeit abhängig sind, müssen unter Umständen auch geringe Abweichungen des ein- und beidäugigen Sehens ausgeglichen werden (Böker, Oberländer, 1986). So werden die besten Voraussetzungen für das Sehen geschaffen. Dies kann positive Auswirkungen auf den Leseakt, den Leselernprozeß und das gesamte Lernverhalten haben. Die Heilung einer Legasthenie ist durch diese Maßnahmen jedoch *nicht* möglich.

Visuelle Wahrnehmung

Wird von visueller Wahrnehmung gesprochen, sind Verarbeitungsschritte in Hirnarealen gemeint, die dem Sehen im Sinne von Augenfunktionen – dem ein- und beidäugigen Sehen- *nachgeordnet* sind (Abb. 4.15.1).

Auch wenn es sich um scheinbar komplexe Geschehnisse handelt, sind es besonders zu Beginn dieser Verarbeitungen lediglich einfache Wahrnehmungsprozesse. Diese Prozesse sind bedeutungslose Ereignisse innerhalb der automatisch und unbewußt ablaufenden präkognitiven Phase der Gesamtwahrnehmung; das heißt, sie sind nicht unserem direkten Willen zugänglich und noch *nicht* mit „Wissen" belegt. Aspekte wie Gedächtnis, Aufmerksamkeit, Problemlösen spielen hier noch keine Rolle (Kognition). Dazu sind massive Verbindungen zu vielen anderen Hirnarealen erforderlich (Abb. 4.15.1).

Zu den einfachen Wahrnehmungen gehören unter anderem Konstanzmechanismen (Form-, Größen- und Farbkonstanz) und die Figur-Hintergrund-Unterscheidung (Roth, 1995).

Folgende visuelle Wahrnehmungsleistungen sind nach Marianne Frostig (1973) für den Schriftspracherwerb von besonderer Bedeutung:

- visuo-motorische Koordination
  die Fähigkeit, Auge und Hand gut koordiniert und punktgenau zusammen zu bewegen
- Figur-Hintergrund-Unterscheidung
  die Fähigkeit, ein Objekt von einem komplexen Hintergrund zu isolieren
- Formkonstanz-Beachtung
  die Unabhängigkeit der Wahrnehmungserlebnisse von Abbildungen auf der Netzhaut – das Erkennen und Beachten einer konstanten Form (zum Beispiel einen Kreis vom Oval, formähnliche Buchstaben zu unterscheiden: I-F-L-E)
- Erkennen der Lage im Raum
  die Fähigkeit des Unterscheidens und Identifizieren von gestaltähnlichen Objekten (zum Beispiel ist bei Buchstaben die Anordnung der Form im Raum bedeutungsvoll: q-b-d-g)
- Erfassen räumlicher Beziehungen
  die Fähigkeit, Beziehungen zwischen Objekten herzustellen (zum Beispiel das Erkennen der Anordnung der Buchstaben innerhalb eines Wortes)

Raumwahrnehmung

Die Raumwahrnehmung darf nicht mit dem „räumlichen Sehen" der Augenfunktionen – besser: dem dreidimensionales Sehen – verwechselt werden. Hier werden zwei unterschiedliche Hirnfunktionen ähnlich bezeichnet.

Die Raumwahrnehmung ermöglicht die Orientierung des Körpers in Raum und Zeit. Dies bedeutet, Objekte im Raum zu lokalisieren, räumliche Beziehungen zwischen diesen Objekten herzustellen, Objekte im Außenraum in Beziehung zum eigenen Körper zu setzen, räumlich und zeitlich zu denken und zu fühlen, Tätigkeiten durchzuführen – Handlungen zu planen. Raum beinhaltet also alle Dimensionen: die zweite, dritte und vierte Dimension!

> Raumwahrnehmung (Roche Lexikon Medizin, 1987, S. 1450) Definition: „Fähigkeit, zu bewußter Empfindung der Lage des Körpers im Raum oder einzelner Teile zueinander (Effekt des Zusammenwirkens mehrerer Sinne)"

Die Raumwahrnehmung verfügt nicht über einen eigenen Sinneskanal. Es wird Wissen aus allen Sinneskanälen in Wissen über den Raum umgesetzt. Durch Integration und richtige Interpretation vieler sensorischer Daten entsteht eine Vorstellung von Raum und Zeit. Das geschieht in Hirnarealen, die die verschiedenen Wahrnehmungen verbinden (Abb. 4.15.1).

Die wichtigsten Informationen kommen aus dem motorischen und kinästhetischen Bereich (Eigenwahrnehmung). Neben Informationen über das beidohrigen Hörens, vermittelt auch visuelle Sinneskanal einen Raumbegriff. Dazu gehört wie oben beschreiben als Teilaspekt auch das dreidimensionale Sehen. Entsprechend ist es nicht zwingend notwendig. Menschen ohne intaktes beidäugiges Sehen (keine normale Zusammenarbeit zwischen beiden

Augen – nur einäugiges Sehen vorhanden) verfügen aufgrund der obengenannten Informationen aus den anderen Sinnesbereichen über eine ungestörte Vorstellung des Raumes.

Entsprechend der Darstellungen wird die Raumwahrnehmung üblicherweise nicht von Augenärztin und Orthoptistin überprüft.

Äugigkeit/Augendominanz

Bei der Äugigkeit oder Augendominanz handelt es sich nicht um das Führungsauge im beidäugigen Sehen. Hier wird ein ähnlicher Begriff für zwei verschiedene Hirnfunktionen benutzt.

Für ein ungestörtes Lernen ist eine normale Hirnentwicklung und -reifung erforderlich. Das Endprodukt dieser Vorgänge ist eine ausgeprägte Lateralität. Um festzustellen, ob eine gute Lateralität vorliegt, wird überprüft, ob eine Körperhälfte bevorzugt wird. Diese Bevorzugung wird Dominanz genannt. Es gibt eine Dominanz für Hände, Füße, Ohren und Augen.

Bei der Überprüfung der Äugigkeit (zum Beispiel mit Kaleidoskop, Schlüsselloch) handelt es um die Feststellung der globalen visuellen Verarbeitung des gesamten Zentralnervensystems. Überlicherweise gehört diese Untersuchung nicht in den augenärztlichen und orthoptischen Bereich.

Hilfestellungen beim Lese- und Schreibvorgang – Sehanwendungsberatung

Legasthene Kinder sind schnell überfordert. Sie benötigen klare, für sie überschaubare Anweisungen und Arbeitsvorlagen. Auch zeitlich dürfen sie nicht überfordert werden. Häufig sind sie nicht in der Lage, das aktuell Wichtige vom Unwichtigen zu trennen.

Diese Kinder sollten wie Sehbehinderte behandelt werden. Sehbehinderte können nicht ausreichend sehen. Es muß ihnen gezeigt werden, wo und was das „Wichtige“ ist. Kinder mit Lernproblemen können sehen, haben aber unter Umständen Schwierigkeiten, das Gesehene richtig einzuordnen.

Augenärztin und Orthoptistin können helfen, indem sie beratend tätig werden. Ist geklärt, daß die vorhandenen Beschwerden nicht durch Abweichungen des ein- und beidäugigen Sehens verursacht werden, sind weitere Maßnahmen erforderlich.

In einer Sehanwendungsberatung werden Eltern, Kinder und gegebenenfalls Pädagogen und Therapeuten über mögliche Hilfestellungen informiert.

Es ist zu beachten, daß unbewußte Dinge den gesamten Sehprozeß und damit auch das Lesen und Schreiben beeinflussen. So können für das einzelne Kind zu kleine Schriftzeichen – trotz guter Sehschärfe, sehr eng bedruckte Schulbuchseiten, Schreiben auf Umweltpapier, schlechte Kopien u. ä. die Lernsituation zusätzlich erschweren. Entsprechend erleichtern u. a. große Schrifttypen, Schreibpapier mit hohem Kontrast, Schreiblinien und Rechenkästen im Fettdruck, Abschreiben vom Arbeitsblatt – nicht von der Tafel – das Lernen. Besonders in den ersten Schuljahren sollte in den Schreibheften Figur-Grund durch einen farbigen Hintergrund eindeutig definiert sein (zum Beispiel von der Firma Landrè, 31022 Gronau, zu beziehen in großen Kaufhäusern).

Die verwendeten Schriften sollten möglichst von klarer Struktur und Serifen aufweisen (kleine Striche an den Buchstaben.

(Beispiel für Buchstaben ohne Serifen).

SCHRIFTEN AUSSCHLIESSLICH MIT GROSSDRUCKBUCHSTABEN SIND SCHWERER LESBAR.

Auch eine kursive Schriftweise ist zu vermeiden; sie lassen kein ermüdungsfreies, längeres Lesen zu.

Unterschiedliche Schriftgrößen und -typen auf einer Seite können die Wahrnehmung erschweren.

Auch dürfen die Buchstaben im Wort nicht zu eng zusammenstehen.

Unter Umständen können die Zeilen- und Buchstabenabstände zusätzlich vergrößert werden.

Es sollte kein Überangebot auf dem Arbeitsblatt herrschen. Hier hilft ein Abdecken mit einem neutralen Blatt. Statt DIN A 4-Heften können DIN A 5-Hefte genutzt werden. Aus Gründen der Übersichtlichkeit kann nur jede zweite Reihe oder Rechenkasten beschrieben werden.

Hilfreich kann auch die Vergrößerung der Textvorlagen mit optischen Hilfsmitteln sein (zum Beispiel Lesestab von Eschenbach Nr.: 2605 – zu beziehen beim Augenoptiker).

Literatur

Böker, E., Oberländer, H.: Asthenopische Beschwerden bei Kindern und Jugendlichen. orthoptik/pleoptik, 83-90, 13/1986

Frostig, M.: Developmental Test of Visual Perzeption. Palo Alto: Consulting Psychologist Press, 1963

Homann, A. und Haase, W.: Entwicklung der Sehschärfe beim Menschen. Ein neuer Test mit standardisierten Einzel- und Reihenoptotypen. In: Arbeitskreis Schielen 13 (Dr. Freigang), S. 131-136 (1981)

Meyers gro§es Universal-Lexikon, Hrsg. von d. Lexikonred. d. Bibliograph. Inst. Mannheim, Wien, Zürich, Bibliographisches Institut, 1984

Oberländer, H.: Der okuläre Belastungstest – Überlegungen zur augenärztlichen Diagnostik bei Kindern mit Lernstörungen. In: Legasthenie (L. Dummer-Smoch), 371-374, BV Legasthenie, Hannover, 1989

Roche-Lexikon Medizin, Hrsg. von Hoffmann-La Roche u. Urban und Schwarzenberg. Urban und Schwarzenberg, München; Wien; Baltimore,1987

Roth, G.: Das Gehirn und seine Wirklichkeit: Kognitive Neurobiologie und ihre philosophischen Konsequenzen. Suhrkamp, Frankfurt am Main, 1995

5 Recht

5.1 Eingliederungshilfe nach § 35a SGB VIII bei jungen Menschen mit legasthenen Störungen

Heinz Steffen

Wesentliche Punkte aus der Sicht des BVL:

1. Wir müssen aufgrund der Rechtslage akzeptieren, dass **nicht in jedem Fall** von Legasthenie oder Dyskalkulie ein **Anspruch** auf Eingliederungshilfe oder auch auf Hilfe zur Erziehung gegeben ist.
   Aber:
   Die **Schwelle** bei der Interpretation der durch Gesetz und Verordnung formulierten Voraussetzungen für Hilfemaßnahmen im Rahmen der Jugendhilfe dürfen **nicht zu hoch gelegt** werden, nicht so hoch, dass irreparable Schäden in der Psyche dieser jungen Menschen erst eintreten müssen, somit die Fähigkeit zum Umgang mit dieser Teilleistungsstörung schwindet, die dem individuellen Leistungsvermögen entsprechende Eingliederung in das Berufsleben genommen wird.
2. Die **Gefährdung der Eingliederungsfähigkeit** ist **keine eigenständige, zusätzliche Antragsvoraussetzung**, die fachlich besonders zu untersuchen und zu bestätigen wäre. Es ist vielmehr bei der Bewertung von Auffälligkeiten und Persönlichkeitsstörungen als Folge von Legasthenie oder Dyskalkulie die vielfache Erfahrung zu berücksichtigen und in die verantwortliche Entscheidung des Jugendamtes einzubeziehen, dass eine solche Gefahr zumindest dann besteht, wenn bereits Auffälligkeiten und Persönlichkeitstörungen in einem Maße festzustellen sind, dass eine „seelische Behinderung" zumindest „droht".
3. Der BVL appelliert an alle Eltern, Personensorgeberechtigte und Fachkräfte, die hier ihre Leistungen anbieten, mit diesem **Hilfe-Instrumentarium sehr vorsichtig und verantwortungsbewußt umzugehen.** Wir dürfen den Fortbestand dieser gesetzlichen Möglichkeiten – vor allem jetzt in Zeiten von weitgehenden staatlichen und kommunalen Sparprogrammen – nicht durch zu weit gehende Forderungen gefährden.
4. Wir müssen zwar Verständnis dafür haben, wenn die kommunalen Träger der Jugendhilfe mit Sorge steigende Aufwendungen im Bereich der Kinder- und Jugendhilfe beklagen, von „Kostenexplosion" sprechen und deshalb nach Ursachen suchen und um Kostenreduzierung oder -begrenzung bemüht sind.
   Wir müssen aber in der Diskussion und in der täglichen Auseinandersetzung in Antragsverfahren darüber „wachen" und notfalls darauf bestehen, daß die „Grundgedanken" des Gesetzgebers für diese Regelungen dennoch weiter gewürdigt und berücksichtigt werden: **Den jungen Menschen mit Störungen in der (seelischen, körperlichen oder geistigen) Entwicklung oder Verfassung ist so rechtzeitig, d.h. frühzeitig, durch fachlich qualifizierte Hilfen zu gewähren, so dass die Eingliederung in unsere Gesellschaft und damit in unser Berufsleben nicht gefährdet wird. Eine dem Wohl des Kindes oder Jugendlichen entsprechende Erziehung ist zu gewährleisten.**
5. Daraus folgt für uns, dass wir die *Bemühungen der kommunalen Körperschaften und deren Jugendämter*, Kostensteigerungen in diesem wichtigen Bereich zu *begrenzen*, so weit akzeptieren, als der **Anspruch** auf die im Einzelfall nach sorgfältiger Prüfung erforderli-

che Hilfe **nicht unterlaufen** wird.Verbale Beteuerungen in diese Richtung allein reichen da nicht.

6. **Schule / Jugendamt**
Die Jugendämter dürfen Anträge nicht abstrakt mit dem Hinweis auf die Schule und deren Aufgabe ablehnen.
Richtig ist: Die **Schule ist – zunächst – vorrangig gefordert**, alle pädagogischen Möglichkeiten zu nutzen, um im Rahmen des gesetzlichen Bildungsauftrages jungen Menschen zu helfen, ihre legasthenie- oder dyskalkulie-bedingten Probleme zu bewältigen und dazu beizutragen, dass sie das ihrem individuellen Leistungsvermögen entsprechende Schulziel erreichen und so auch – gesamtgesellschaftlich gesehen – die Voraussetzungen für den Weg in unser Gesellschaftsleben gegebenen werden.Wenn die Schule aber nicht oder nicht genügend aktiv ist, muß auch das Jugendamt akzeptieren, dass dann – erfahrungsgemäß Auffälligkeiten und Persönlichkeitsstörungen als Folge der legasthenie- oder dyskalkulie-bedingten Probleme auftreten, – früher eine seelische Behinderung droht, – früher eine dem Wohl des Kindes oder Jugendlichen entsprechende Erziehung nicht mehr gewährleistet ist, und somit – früher die Verpflichtung des Jugendamtes zum Helfen eintritt.
(In der kommunal- und landespolitischen Auseinandersetzung um diesen Punkt wollen wir den Jugendämtern gern argumentativ in diesem Sinn zur Seite treten; nur dürfen bis zu einer Klärung und Verbesserung der Schulsituation die Betroffenen nicht darunter leiden). In den Antragsverfahren ist deshalb die tatsächliche schulische Hilfe darauf zu prüfen, ob sie in den jeweiligen Einzelfall ausreicht. Absprachen zwischen Jugendamt und Schule und/oder Schulamt können nur unter diesem Aspekt akzeptiert werden.

7. Auch die „**Hilfe zur Erziehung** „ nach § 27 SGB VIII (ein wesentlich länger praktiziertes Instrument der Jungendhilfe) kommt in diesem Bereich – alternativ – in Betracht. Dies ist umstritten, auch unter den Jugendämtern und in der Fachpresse. Der BVL weist dennoch in seinem neugefassten Merkblatt auf diese gesetzliche Möglichkeit hin und empfiehlt, diese in die Antragsverfahren mit einzubringen. Der BVL beruft sich bei seiner Argumentation auf ein Urteil des Urteil des VGH Baden-Württemberg. Dieses Instrument bietet die Möglichkeit, Hilfe nicht erst einsetzen zu lassen, nachdem sich deutliche Auffälligkeiten und Persönlichkeitstörungen als Folge von Legasthenie oder Dyskalkulie zeigen.

8. **Krankheit / Krankenkassen / SGB V**
Trotz gegenteiliger Auffassung der Spitzenverbände der gesetzlichen Krankenkassen vertreten wir weiterhin folgenden Standpunkt: Wenn die Folgen der legasthenie- oder dyskalkulie-bedingten Probleme Krankheitscharakter im Sinne des SGB V haben, sind die gesetzlichen Krankenkassen auch zu Leistungen für eine umfassende Therapie oder Fachbehandlung, die pädagogische Elemente einschließt, verpflichtet, zumindest dann, wenn ärztlich die Notwendigkeit festgestellt und im Rahmen einer ärztlichen Behandlung einer diagnostizierten Krankheit auch verordnet. Da sich diese Rechtsauffassung aber bisher – auch in Rechtsverfahren vor den Sozialgerichten – noch nicht durchgesetzt hat, dürfen die Jugendämter Antragsteller nicht auf die Krankenkassen verweisen und so die Hilfe im Rahmen der Jugendhilfe unvertretbar verzögern oder gar ablehnen.

Überblick „Sozialrecht“ der Bundesrepublik Deutschland
Sozialgesetzbuch (SGB)

SGB I	- Allgemeiner Teil
SGB III	- Arbeitsförderung - (Ausbildungsbegleitende Hilfen der Arbeitsämter) nach der Anordnung des Verwaltungsrates der Bundesanstalt für Arbeit über die Förderung der Berufsausbildung von ausländischen Auszubildenden sowie von lernbeeinträchtigten oder sozial benachteiligten deutschen Auszubildenden vom 16.03.1988 (Dienstblatt/RdErl der BAA 100/88)
SGB IV	- Gemeinsame Vorschriften für die Sozialversicherung
SGB V	**- Gesetzliche Krankenversicherung** § 27 – Krankenbehandlung (u.a. ärztliche Behandlung, medizinische Leistungen zur Rehabilitation) i.V.m. Art. 2 Psychotherapeutengesetz von 1998
SGB VI	- Gesetzliche Rentenversicherung
SGB VII	- Gesetzliche Unfallversicherung
SGB VIII	**- Kinder- und Jugendhilfe** § 27 – Hilfe zur Erziehung *(wenn „eine dem Wohl des Kindes oder des Jugendlichen entsprechende Erziehung nicht gewährleistet...“)* § 35a – Eingliederungshilfe *(„Kinder und Jugendliche, die seelisch behindert oder von einer seelischen Behinderung bedroht sind...“)* § 41 – Hilfe für junge Volljährige *(„...Hilfe für die Persönlichkeitsentwicklung und zu einer eigenverantwortlichen Lebensführung...., i.d.R. bis ...21. Lebensjahr“, längstens bis 27. Lebensjahr)*
SGB X	- Verfahrensfragen, Sozialdaten, Zusammenarbeit der Leistungsträger und ihre Beziehungen zu Dritten
SGB XI	- Soziale Pflegeversicherung

BSHG	- Bundessozialhilfegesetz (noch nicht in das SGB eingeordnet, gilt aber neben 21 anderen Gesetzen als „besonderer Teil“ des SGB, s. Art. II § 1 SGB I) *Auch hier noch von Bedeutung, weil § 35a SGB VIII auf §§ 39 Abs. 3 und 40 BSHG sowie auf die EinglHVO verweist.*

5.2 Eingliederungshilfe nach SGB VIII § 35 a bei jungen Menschen mit legasthenen Störungen

Doris Lau

1 Vorbemerkung

Durch die Beschäftigung mit dem § 35 a des Kinder- und Jugendhilfegesetzes (KJHG) im Zusammenhang mit meiner Tätigkeit im Niedersächsischen Landesjugendamt erlebe ich, dass die Umsetzung der Eingliederungshilfe für seelisch behinderte Kinder und Jugendliche noch viele Fragen mit sich bringt. Diese beziehen sich sowohl auf den vollstationären Bereich der Jugendhilfe – auf den ich hier nicht näher eingehe – als auch auf das Gebiet der ambulanten Eingliederungshilfe.

Ich möchte versuchen, Ihnen einen Einblick in die Verfahrensweisen der Jugendhilfeträger zu geben, die bei ambulanten Eingliederungshilfen gemäß § 35 a KJHG auf Grund von legasthenen Störungen angewandt werden.

Ich möchte meinen Beitrag mit dem § 1 Abs. 1 des KJHG beginnen: „Jeder junge Mensch hat ein Recht auf Förderung seiner Entwicklung und auf Erziehung zu einer eigenverantwortlichen und gemeinschaftsfähigen Persönlichkeit."

Die ursprünglich vom Gesetzgeber angedachte Absicht, alle Minderjährigen in die Jugendhilfe zu übernehmen, d.h., auch Kinder und Jugendliche mit einer Behinderung, hat sich auf die Minderjährigen beschränkt, die seelisch behindert oder von einer seelischen Behinderung bedroht sind. Als gesetzliche Grundlage hierzu wurde der § 35 a in das SGB VIII, das Kinder- und Jugendhilfegesetz, eingeführt. Anspruchsberechtigte nach § 35 a KJHG sind die Minderjährigen selbst, nicht die Eltern, wie bei den Hilfen zur Erziehung.

2 Ambulante Eingliederungshilfen gemäß § 35 a KJHG – eine Aufgabe der Jugendhilfeträger

Der überwiegende Teil der Jugendhilfeträger, die ich im Folgenden kurz Jugendämter nennen werde, hat sich seit der Einführung des § 35 a KJHG mit einer ständig ansteigenden Anzahl von Anträgen auf Gewährung von Eingliederungshilfe für Kinder und Jugendliche gemäß § 35 a KJHG auseinander zu setzen. Insbesondere sind hier die ambulanten Maßnahmen bei einer umschriebenen Entwicklungsstörung schulischer Fertigkeiten zu nennen.

Von dem Flächenland Niedersachsen weiß ich, dass es regionale Unterschiede bei der Quantität von Anträgen gibt. Dies hängt zum einen von der Größe des Einzugsgebietes ab. Es ist aber auch zu beobachten, dass sich in einigen Gegenden, in denen eine größere Anzahl Therapeuten zu finden ist, die Anträge auf ambulante Eingliederungshilfe bei den Jugendämtern häufen.

3 Entwicklung einer seelischen Behinderung durch das Vorhandensein einer Teilleistungsstörung

Die umschriebenen Entwicklungsstörungen schulischer Fertigkeiten bedeuten an sich noch keine Behinderung, sondern sind Beeinträchtigungen bei bestimmten kognitiven Prozessen. Ein Kind mit Teilleistungsstörungen wird häufig als „dumm", „faul", „schwierig" angesehen und verkannt. Anstrengungen der Kinder bleiben ergebnislos, sie fühlen sich minderwertig, weil sie oftmals die an sie gestellten Erwartungen nicht erfüllen können. Ermahnungen, Bestrafungen, psychische und vielleicht auch physische Verletzungen führen dazu, dass lebensphasentypische soziale Beziehungen so stark beeinträchtigt werden können, dass das Kind an psychosomatischen Störungen leidet und sich Verhaltensauffälligkeiten und Erziehungsprobleme einstellen.

Aus dieser Beeinflussung heraus kann sich für den Minderjährigen eine seelische Behinderung manifestieren oder mit hoher Wahrscheinlichkeit zumindest drohen. In diesem Fall reichen schulische Mittel der Förderung nicht mehr aus, das Kind oder den Jugendlichen in die Gemeinschaft zu integrieren.

4 Verantwortung der Schule

An dieser Stelle möchte ich darauf hinweisen, dass für die Vermittlung schulischer Fertigkeiten die Schule zuständig ist und sicherzustellen hat, dass allen Schülern das Erlernen der Kulturtechniken wie Lesen, Schreiben und Rechnen ermöglicht wird und sie ihren Fähigkeiten entsprechend gefördert werden. In Niedersachsen gibt es hierzu das Niedersächsische Schulgesetz sowie entsprechende Erlasse des Kultusministeriums zum Förderunterricht. Danach sind die Schulen verpflichtet, entsprechende Förderunterrichte für Kinder zu gewährleisten. Das ist besonders wichtig, weil bei frühzeitigem Erkennen einer Störung und entsprechender Reaktion darauf oftmals einer Verfestigung der sekundären Beeinträchtigung entgegengewirkt oder sie sogar verhindert werden könnte. Störungen schulischer Fertigkeiten sind bei genauer Beobachtung im Laufe der ersten Grundschuljahre erkennbar und sollten schnellstens angegangen werden. Hier liegt eine besondere Verantwortung bei den GrundschullehrerInnen, die meiner Meinung nach viel stärker darin aus- und fortgebildet werden müssten, eine Lese- und Rechtschreib- bzw. Rechenschwäche zu erkennen.

Die Schule ist daher in der Pflicht nachzuweisen, welche Fördermaßnahmen von ihrer Seite ergriffen wurden. Allein die Auskunft, dass kein Förderunterricht erteilt werden konnte, genügt nicht. Erst wenn nachweisbar die schulischen Angebote nicht ausreichen, setzt der Anspruch auf Jugendhilfe ein. Zur Zusammenarbeit zwischen Schule, Schulbehörde und örtlichem Träger der Jugendhilfe bei Anträgen auf Gewährung von Eingliederungshilfe nach § 35 a KJHG ist in Niedersachsen gerade ein Erlass in Arbeit, der klare Verfahrenswege der Zusammenarbeit zwischen Schule und Jugendamt regeln soll.

5 Antragsverfahren zur Eingliederungshilfe gemäß § 35 a KJHG

Die Bedarfsfeststellung zur Behandlung einer Teilleistungsstörung erfolgt entweder durch die Eltern selbst oder durch die Schule (s. Abb. 5.2.1). Durch das Bekanntwerden beim Jugendamt, bei dem ein Antrag auf Eingliederungshilfe für das Kind gemäß § 35 a durch die Personensorgeberechtigten gestellt wird, wird das Jugendamt zum Entscheidungsträger über das Verfahren und muss ermitteln, ob und in welchem Umfang Eingliederungsmaßnahmen notwendig sind. Hierzu muss das Jugendamt mit anderen Fachdisziplinen kommunizieren und kooperieren.

Gemäß § 36 Abs. 3 KJHG soll bei der Aufstellung und Änderung eines Hilfeplanes sowie bei der Durchführung der Hilfe ein Arzt, der über besondere Erfahrungen in der Hilfe für Behinderte verfügt, beteiligt werden. Ziel dieses Hilfeplanes ist, Art, Umfang, Dauer und Zielsetzung der Maßnahme festzulegen. Diese Erkenntnisse dienen als Grundlage für die Entscheidung des Jugendamtes.

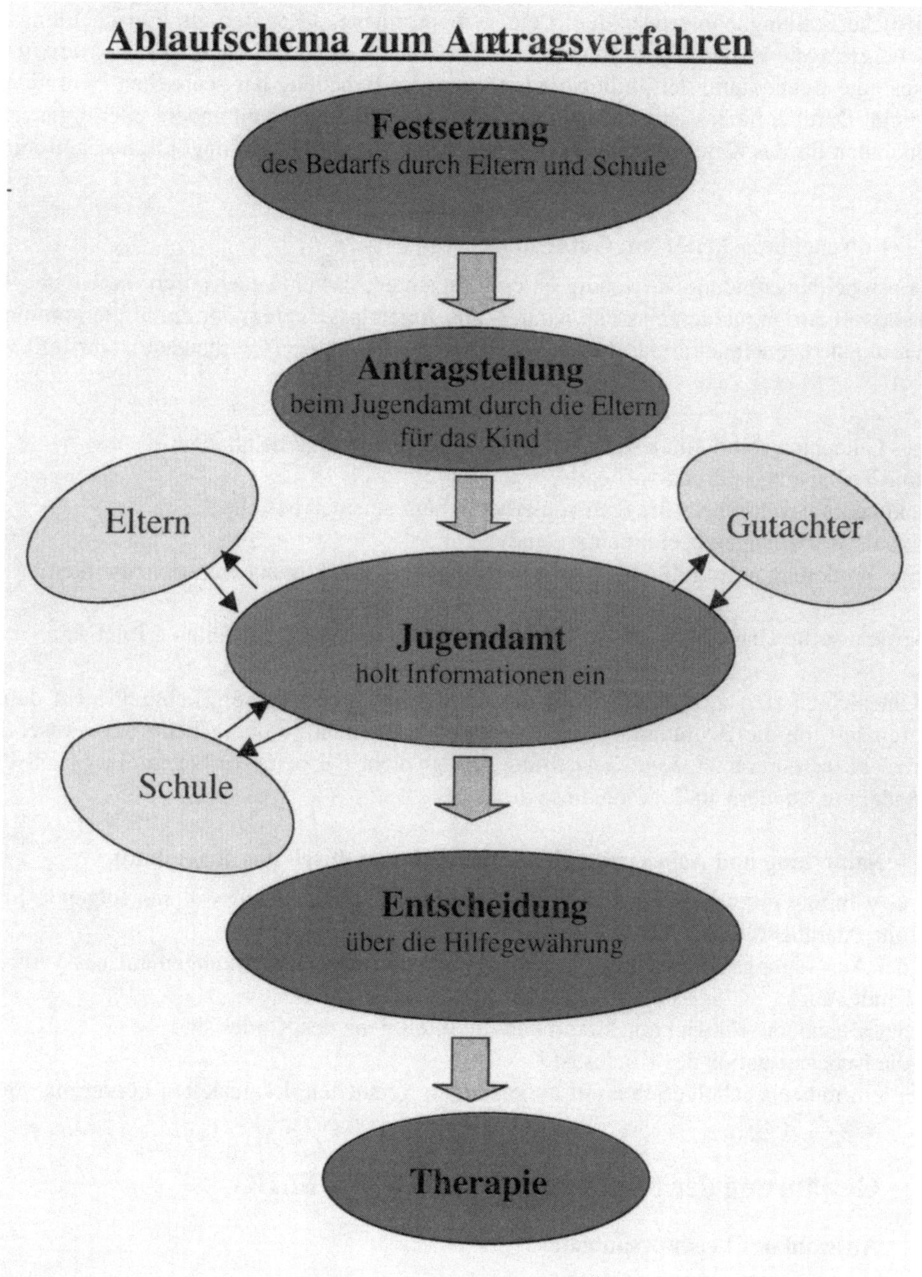
Ablaufschema zum Antragsverfahren
Festsetzung
des Bedarfs durch Eltern und Schule
Antragstellung
beim Jugendamt durch die Eltern
für das Kind
Eltern
Gutachter
Jugendamt
holt Informationen ein
Schule
Entscheidung
über die Hilfegewährung
Therapie

Abb. 5.2.1

Da die Form eines Hilfeplanverfahrens nicht vorgeschrieben ist, kann durch eine schriftliche Stellungnahme oder durch ein gemeinsamenes Gespräch zur Entscheidungsfindung beigetragen werden. Diese Entscheidung kann bedeuten, dass nach Meinung des Jugendamtes eine Behandlung der Teilleistungsstörung zur Behebung der seelischen Behinderung ausreicht. Darüber hinaus ist aber auch denkbar, dass das Jugendamt andere oder ergänzende Maßnahmen für das Kind für sinnvoll erachtet, wie z.B. die Sozialpädagogische Familienhilfe.

5.1 Entscheidungskriterium Gutachten

Zur Entscheidungsfindung notwendig ist ein Gutachten, das entweder durch die Kinder- und Jugendpsychiatrien, niedergelassene Kinder- und Jugendpsychiater oder durch die kommunalen Gesundheitsämter, sofern dort die notwendige Fachkompetenz vorhanden ist, erstellt wurde.

Dieses Gutachten sollte mindestens folgende Aussagen darüber beinhalten:
ob eine Teilleistungsstörung vorliegt
ob sekundäre psychische Störungen von erheblichem Ausmaß bestehen
ob soziale Beziehungen beeinträchtigt sind
ob eine Förderung notwendig und geeignet ist der Beeinträchtigung entgegenzuwirken.

Außerdem sollte eine Abklärung der allgemeinen Hör- und Sehfähigkeiten erfolgt sein.

Im Unterschied zum § 39 BSHG wird hinsichtlich der Leistungsverpflichtung nicht danach differenziert, ob die Behinderung vorübergehend oder nicht vorübergehend bzw. wesentlich oder nicht wesentlich ist. Eine Gewährung erfolgt nicht nur beim Vorliegen einer seelischen Behinderung, sondern auch, wenn diese droht.

5.2 Sammlung und Auswertung der Informationen durch das Jugendamt

Vor Gewährung einer individuellen Hilfe durch das Jugendamt muss dieses folgende Informationen darüber haben:
wie der Ausprägungsgrad der Legasthenie ist und wie deren Auswirkungen auf das Verhalten des Kindes sind
wie der allgemeine Entwicklungsstand und die Intelligenz des Kindes sind
wie die Lebenssituation des Kindes ist
außerdem müssen Schulberichte mit aufgezeigten Versuchen der gezielten Förderung vorliegen.

6 Gewährung der Maßnahme gemäß § 35 a KJHG

6.1 Auswahl des Leistungsanbieters

Nachdem eine Entscheidung über die Gewährung durch das Jugendamt getroffen wurde, sollten den Eltern Leistungsanbieter benannt werden, die die Kriterien für eine geeignete Therapie erfüllen.

Wie schon erwähnt, gibt es in Niedersachsen Gebiete, in denen kein Therapeut zu finden ist, aber auch Orte, in denen ein Überangebot an Therapeuten besteht. Für Jugendämter ist es oftmals schwierig, einen geeigneten Therapeuten zu finden, sofern noch keine Erfahrungen mit diesem Anbieter gemacht wurden.

In jedem Fall ist zur Verhinderung von Interessenkollisionen zu vermeiden, dass diagnostizierende und therapierende Stelle identisch sind.

Vom Niedersächsischen Landesjugendamt in Zusammenarbeit mit der Arbeitsgemeinschaft der Jugendämter der Länder Niedersachsen und Bremen sind im Juli 1998 Empfehlungen zur Durchführung geeigneter Eingliederungshilfen für Minderjährige, bei denen der Anspruch nach § 35 a SGB VIII u.a. durch das Vorhandensein umschriebener Entwicklungsstörungen schulischer Fertigkeiten begründet ist, herausgegeben worden. Diese enthalten unter anderem Aussagen zu den Zielen und den Inhalten der Hilfen sowie zu den Anforderungen an die Leistungsanbieter.

6.2 Dauer der Therapie

Die Behandlung einer Legasthenie-Therapie zieht sich in der Regel über einen Zeitraum von ein bis zwei Jahren hin. Meist wird anfangs eine Therapie-Einheit von 40 Stunden bewilligt, die circa ein Jahr dauert. Sollte darüber hinaus noch eine weitere Behandlung notwendig sein, wird in einem erneuten Hilfeplanverfahren unter Beteiligung der zuvor schon gehörten Fachdisziplinen und zusätzlich dem/der Therapeuten/Therapeutin, eine weitere Hilfegewährung festgelegt, die in der Regel nochmals 20 bis 40 Stunden dauert. In jedem Fall sollte die Gewährung Einzelfall abhängig sein und sich an dem Bedarf des Kindes orientieren.

Kosten

Über die Höhe der Kosten einer Therapiestunde, sollte sinnvollerweise zwischen dem Jugendamt und dem Anbieter eine Leistungsvereinbarung getroffen werden. Die Grundlage für diese Leistungsvereinbarung bietet eine vom Anbieter zu erstellende Leistungsbeschreibung.

7 Zusammenfassung

Wie schon eingangs erwähnt, sind die Kommunen als Entscheidungs- und Kostenträger durch die ständig steigende Anzahl von Anträgen und Gewährungen einer ambulanten Eingliederungshilfe gemäß § 35 a KJHG einem hohen Leistungs- und Kostendruck ausgesetzt. Die meisten Kommunen haben inzwischen ihren Weg gefunden, mit der Situation zurechtzukommen. Das gelingt nicht immer so, wie von allen Beteiligten gewünscht. Eine im Interesse des Kindes kooperative Zusammenarbeit funktioniert aber nur, wenn die beteiligten Stellen Eltern, Schule, Jugendamt und Fachärzte die jeweiligen Kompetenzen anerkennen und nutzen.

Literatur

Wiesner, u.a., SGB VIII, Kinder- und Jugendhilfe, Beck-Verlag, München 1995

Prof. Dr. Viola Harnach-Beck, Fachhochschule Mannheim – Hochschule für Sozialwesen, Eingliederungshilfe gemäß § 35 a SGB VIII bei Lese-Rechtschreibstörungen?, aus: Nachrichtendienst des Deutschen Vereins, August 1998

Wyrwoll, M., § 35 a KJHG aus der Sicht der Jugendhilfe, Hameln 1998 (unveröffentlichtes Manuskript)

Niedersächsisches Landesjugendamt, § 35 a, Hannover 1995

6 Rechnen

6.1 Neuropsychologie und Psychopathologie der Rechenstörungen im Kindesalter

Michael von Aster

1 Einleitende Übersicht

Die umschriebenen Entwicklungsstörungen schulischer Fertigkeiten, zu denen die Rechenstörungen und die Störungen des Schriftspracherwerbs zählen, werden ebenso wie die Sprachentwicklungsstörungen und die motorischen Entwicklungsstörungen auf der zweiten Achse des multiaxialen Klassifikationsschemas der Internationalen Klassifikation für Psychische Störungen der WHO (ICD-10; Remschmidt und Schmidt, 1994) erfasst. Ihre spezifische Bedeutung für das Fachgebiet der Kinder- und Jugendpsychiatrie ergibt sich aus dem besonders häufigen Zusammentreffen von schulischen Lernstörungen und anderen klinisch-psychiatrischen Symptomen (von Aster, 1996a). Diese Kombinationen sind es, die den langfristigen Verlauf besonders belasten.

Gemäss ICD-10 werden die schulischen Entwicklungsstörungen als Störungen zentralnervöser Reifungsvorgänge verstanden, die von früh an bestehen und einen kontinuierlichen Verlauf zeigen. Sie sind abzugrenzen von Leistungsdefiziten infolge unzureichender Beschulung, geringer allgemeiner Begabung oder erworbener Hirnschädigung. Das Kriterium für die Diagnosestellung gilt als erfüllt, wenn eine signifikante Diskrepanz zwischen der gemessenen, und der, aufgrund des Alters und der allgemeinen Intelligenz, erwarteten Schulleistung besteht.

Entgegen früheren Annahmen scheinen die Rechenstörungen mit 2-6% etwa ebenso häufig zu sein wie die Lese- und Rechtschreibstörungen (LRS) mit einer Prävalenz von 2-8%. Rechenstörungen gelten bislang als die einzige Entwicklungsstörung, von der Mädchen eher häufiger betroffen sind als Knaben (Klauer, 1992; Gross-Tsur et al., 1996). Bei der LRS sind, wie bei allen anderen Entwicklungsstörungen, Jungen bekanntermassen etwa dreimal häufiger betroffen als Mädchen.

Bezüglich der psychiatrischen Komorbidität ist bei der LRS der im Langzeitverlauf zunehmende Zusammenhang mit primär externalisierenden Störungen des Sozialverhaltens, d.h. Aggressivität, Dissozialität und Delinquenz seit längerem bekannt und gut belegt (Esser, 1991). Im Gegensatz dazu werden bei Kindern mit Rechenstörungen häufiger internalisierende psychische Auffälligkeiten berichtet, insbesondere Ängste und depressive Symptome (Rourke & Fuerst, 1991). Da Knaben aber generell häufiger von Störungen des Sozialverhaltens, und Mädchen häufiger von Ängsten und depressiven Symptomen betroffen sind, ist unklar, ob die erwähnten Zusammenhänge zwischen Lernstörungen und psychopathologischen Merkmalen nur Ausdruck der unterschiedlichen Geschlechterverteilungen in der Gruppe von Kindern mit LRS bzw. Rechenstörung sind, oder aber einen spezifischen syndromatischen Zusammenhang darstellen. Bei beiden Teilleistungsstörungen bestehen im übrigen auch häufig Aufmerksamkeits- und Hyperaktivitätsstörungen (Shalev, et al., 1995).

Hinsichtlich der neuropsychologischen Funktionen unterscheidet man bei den Lese-Rechtschreibschwächen im wesentlichen zwei Subtypen: Am häufigsten liegen dysphonetische, sprachbezogene Verarbeitungsstörungen vor, seltener dagegen visuelle, auch dyseidetisch genannte Störungen. Die neuropsychologischen Bedingungen für Rechenstörungen sind weit weniger gut erforscht. Man nahm bislang in erster Linie Störungen visuell-räumlicher Syntheseleistungen als ursächlich an. Das bekannteste Modell das solche primär auf die rechte Hirnhälfte zu beziehenden Verarbeitungdefizite postuliert ist das von Rourke (1989) beschriebene sogenannte 'non-verbal learning disability syndrome' (NLD). Es hat sich aber gezeigt, dass längst nicht bei allen Kindern mit Rechenstörungen solche nonverbalen Verarbeitungsdefizite bestehen und dass umgekehrt Kinder mit NLD nicht immer auch Schwierigkeiten beim Rechnenlernen haben (vgl. von Aster, 1994).

Wegen ihrer besonderen Relevanz für den Verlauf und die Therapie soll im Folgenden über zwei Ergebnisse aus einer Zürcher Untersuchung berichtet werden (von Aster, 1996b). Dabei geht es erstens um psychopathologische Auffälligkeiten bei Kindern mit Lernschwierigkeiten, und zweitens um spezifische kognitiv-neuropsychologische Befunde bei Kindern mit Rechenstörungen.

2 Ergebnisse einer Zürcher Studie

Lernstörungen und psychopathologische Auffälligkeiten

Mittels eines Fragebogens wurden die Klassenlehrer von knapp 300 Zürcher Schulkindern der 2.—. Primarstufe zu spezifischen Lernschwierigkeiten ihrer Schüler und zu allfälligen psychopathologischen Auffälligkeiten befragt.

Insgesamt wurde bei nicht ganz einem Drittel der Schüler von Lernschwierigkeiten berichtet. In der Gruppe der Kinder mit Rechenproblemen waren die Mädchen überrepräsentiert, während in der Gruppe der Kinder mit Lese-Rechtschreibproblemen und in der Gruppe der Kinder, die sowohl im Rechnen wie auch im Lesen und Schreiben Probleme hatten die Jungen überwogen.

Bezüglich der Häufigkeit psychopathologischer Auffälligkeiten unterschieden sich alle drei Gruppen sehr deutlich von der Gruppe jener Kinder, die gemäss Einschätzung ihrer Lehrer keinerlei Lernschwierigkeiten hatten:

Bei den drei besonders interessierenden Merkmalen 'Aufmerksamkeitsprobleme', 'externalisierende Probleme' (z.B. Aggressivität) und 'internalisierende Probleme' (z.B. Depressivität) fanden sich sowohl Gruppen- als auch Geschlechtseffekte.

Aufmerksamkeitsprobleme waren zum einen bei Knaben insgesamt häufiger als bei Mädchen, und zum anderen bei Kindern mit kombinierten Lernschwierigkeiten häufiger als bei Kindern mit isolierten Lernschwierigkeiten im Rechnen oder im Lesen und Schreiben. Bei den externalisierenden Auffälligkeiten lagen zwar ebenfalls die Werte der Knaben höher als die der Mädchen, hier gab es aber keine Unterschiede zwischen den gemäss Lehrerurteil teilleistungsschwachen und den unauffälligen Kindern, was am ehesten auf das vergleichsweise junge Alter und auf mögliche Selektionseffekte in Sonderklassen für Verhaltensauffällige zurückgeführt wurde.

Bei den internalisierenden Problemen wurden die Jungen im Mittel als weniger auffällig eingeschätzt als die Mädchen. Dies galt aber nicht für Kinder mit Lernschwierigkeiten im Rechnen. Hier zeigten die Jungen sogar noch deutlich höhere Werte als die Mädchen, und insgesamt erreichte die Gruppe rechenschwacher Kinder bei den internalisierenden Auffälligkeiten die höchsten Werte. Dies spricht dafür, dass neben dem erwarteten Geschlechtseffekt auch die Art der Lernschwierigkeiten (Rechnen vs Lesen und Schreiben) einen spezifischen Einfluss auf die Entwicklung psychopathologischer Symptome hat.

Neuropsychologische Subtypen von Rechenstörungen

Das Rechnen und der Umgang mit Zahlen stellt eine sehr komplexe kognitive Tätigkeit dar. Störungen des Rechnens und der Zahlenverarbeitung wurden früher zumeist auf zugrundeliegende umfassendere Störungen der Sprachverarbeitung oder visuell-räumlicher Funktionen bezogen. Die Erkenntnis aber, dass bei erwachsenen Patienten nach Hirnverletzungen sehr unterschiedliche Teilaspekte im Umgang mit Zahlen betroffen sein können (sogenannte Dissoziationen) hat wesentlich zu der Entwicklung von Modellen beigetragen, die ein autonomes, modular gegliedertes Funktionssystem für Zahlenverarbeitung und Rechnen postulieren (McCloskey et al., 1985; Dehaene, 1992). So konnte beispielsweise gezeigt werden, dass bestimmte Patienten nach einem Schädel/Hirntrauma kaum mehr in der Lage waren, Zahlen zu verarbeiten, wenn sie in der gesprochenen oder in alphabetisch geschriebener Form dargeboten wurden, dagegen aber keine Probleme hatten, wenn arabische Zahlen präsentiert wurden. Auch das umgekehrte Muster ist beschreiben, nämlich ein Verlust der Fähigkeit, Arabische Zahlen zu verarbeiten bei einer erhaltenen Fähigkeit, gesprochene Zahlen zu verstehen und mit ihnen rechnerisch umzugehen. Bei wieder anderen Patienten war die Fähigkeit des Schätzens und Überschlagens numerischer Grössen als einzige erhalten, während die Fähigkeiten zur exakten Verarbeitung von Zahlen sowohl in der sprachlichen wie in der arabischen Form schwer beeinträchtigt war. Des weiteren kennen wir aus der Literatur Fallbeschreibungen von geistig behinderten Menschen, die über ungewöhnliche Zahlenkenntnisse verfügen (z.B. Primzahlen, kalendarische Fakten) und dennoch kaum in der Lage sind, auch nur die allereinfachsten rechnerischen Operationen auszuführen.

Das von Dehaene (1992) vorgeschlagene 'Triple Code Model' geht von einem modular gegliederten System zahlenverarbeitender Hirnfunktionen bei Erwachsenen aus, das sich über beide Grosshirnhälften erstreckt und das drei Funktionseinheiten (Module) unterscheidet, in denen die Zahlen in unterschiedlichen Kodierungen repräsentiert sind (Dehaene und Cohen, 1995): 1. als gesprochenes oder geschriebenes Zahlwort, 2. als Arabische Zahl und 3. als analoger örtlicher Bereich auf einem inneren Zahlenstrahl. Das Modell geht davon aus, dass diese Module auch für unterschiedliche zahlenbezogene Fertigkeiten zuständig sind: So ist das Zählen und das Anlegen von Zahlenfaktenwissen an die sprachliche Repräsentation gebunden, das Operieren mit mehrstelligen Zahlen an das arabische Notationssystem und das Schätzen und Überschlagen von Mengengrössen und Beziehungen an eine räumlich-analoge Zahlenstrahlvorstellung. Erste Untersuchungen mit bildgebenden Verfahren konnten zeigen, dass beim Lösen von Rechenaufgaben bei denen eine Schätzantwort gefragt war (approximatives Rechnen) andere Hirnareale aktiviert waren als bei Aufgaben, bei denen das exakte Lösen einfacher Additionen verlangt war (Dehaene et al., 1999).

Man kann nun davon ausgehen, dass diese Module zu unterschiedlichen Zeitpunkten im Verlaufe der Kindheit reifen. Ausgehend von Erkenntnissen, wonach bereits bei wenigen

Monaten alten Säuglingen bestimmte Fähigkeiten der Mengenverarbeitung vorhanden sind, kann angenommen werden, dass eine genetische Anlage für die Fähigkeit des Einschätzens und Vergleichens von Mengen gegeben ist, die den Kern für die Reifung der semantisch-analogen Zahlenstrahl-Repräsentation (3. Modul) darstellt. Die Zahlwortrepräsentation (1. Modul) entwickelt sich im Zuge der vorschulischen Sprachentwicklung und die Arabische Repräsentation (2. Modul) erst mit Eintritt in die Schule und dem Beginn systematischer Unterrichtung.

Vor dem Hintergrund solcher Modellvorstellungen wurde eine Testbatterie entwickelt und normiert, mit der verschiedene auch kodierungsspezifische Elemente der Zahlenverarbeitung bei Kindern erfasst werden sollen. Die Testbatterie enthält 12 Untertests und prüft Aspekte des Zählens, das Transkodieren in die arabische und in die Wortform, das Vergleichen von Zahlen in Wort- und in Ziffernform, das Kopfrechnen mit Addition, Subtraktion und auch Textaufgaben, sowie das Schätzen und Beurteilen von Mengen, und das Zuordnen von Zahlen zu analogen Positionen auf einem Zahlenstrahl (von Aster, 1996b; von Aster, et al., 1997).

Auf der Basis von 93 Testprotokollen von Kindern mit Lernschwierigkeiten im Rechnen, zusammengesetzt aus einer Primarschülerpopulation und einer klinisch-kinderpsychiatrischen Population, wurde eine Personenclusteranalyse durchgeführt (ein statistisches Analyseverfahren, mit dem sich Ähnlichkeiten zwischen Personengruppen anhand ihrer Testleistungen feststellen lassen). Im Ergebnis konnten vier Gruppen unterschieden werden. Bei drei von diesen vier Gruppen lagen die mittleren Testresultate in mehr als einem Subtest um mindestens 1,5 Standardabweichungen unterhalb der Norm. Die grösste Gruppe bildeten jedoch Kinder, deren mittlere Testleistung in keinem Untertest um mehr als eine Standardabweichung unter der Norm lag. Gemäss den Diagnosekriterien der ICD-10 kann man bei den Störungen der Kinder der zuerst genannten drei Gruppen von 'Subtypen von Rechenstörungen' sprechen, während die vierte grosse Gruppe als 'subklinisch' bezeichnet werden kann. Die drei Subtypen von Rechenstörungen wurden mit den Begriffen 'sprachlicher Typ', 'arabischer Typ' und 'tiefgreifender Typ' gekennzeichnet.

Der Begriff 'sprachlich' wurde deshalb gewählt, weil die Kinder dieser Gruppe markante Schwierigkeiten hatten, korrekt abzuzählen, was zur Folge hat, dass ihre Zählprozeduren beim Kopfrechnen fehleranfällig sind und das Anlegen von Faktenwissen erschwert wird. Viele dieser Kinder zeigten im Übrigen Symptome eines Hyperkinetischen Syndroms.

Der 'arabische' Subtyp erhielt seinen Namen, weil die betroffenen Kinder in erster Linie Probleme beim Transkodieren in und aus der arabischen Kodierung hatten. In dieser Gruppe war der Anteil nicht muttersprachlich deutschschweizerischer Kinder deutlich erhöht, was übrigens auch für die subklinische Gruppe zutraf. Dies spricht dafür, dass die spezifischen zahlenlinguistischen Besonderheiten der deutschen Zahlwortsequenz (Zehner-Einer Inversion) einen gewissen Risikofaktor insbesondere für fremdsprachige Kinder darstellt (vergl. von Aster, et al., 1997).

Bei dem Subtyp schliesslich, der als 'tiefgreifend' bezeichnet wurde, lagen beträchtliche Minderleistungen in beinahe allen Subtests vor. Hier scheint bereits die grundlegende, analoge Mengenverarbeitung stark beeinträchtigt zu sein, was vermutlich den späteren Erwerb der sprachlichen und arabischen Zahlensyntax sowie die hiervon abhängigen prozeduralen, rechnerischen Fähigkeiten behindert. Bei den betroffenen Kindern lagen sehr häufig auch bedeutsame Probleme beim Lesen und Schreiben sowie im Verhalten und Erleben vor.

In diesen drei Gruppen (Subtypen Rechenstörungen) überwogen die Jungen etwa im Verhältnis 3:2, während das Geschlechterverhältnis in der subklinischen Gruppe ausgeglichen war. Die geschätzte Häufigkeit von Rechenstörungen betrug nach diesen Ergebnissen etwa 4,7%, was im Einklang steht mit Ergebnissen anderer Studien jüngeren Datums (s.o.).

3 Fazit

Primarschulkinder mit Lernschwierigkeiten werden von ihren Lehrern im Verhalten als auffälliger beschrieben als Kinder ohne Lernschwierigkeiten, und zwar insbesondere im Hinblick auf Aufmerksamkeitsprobleme sowie Ängste und depressive Symptome. Die Art der schulischen Lernschwierigkeiten und das Geschlecht haben offenbar einen Einfluss auf die Art und das Ausmass psychopathologischer Symptome.

Bei Rechenstörungen können verschiedene Unterformen beschrieben werden, bei denen unterschiedliche Aspekte der Zahlenverarbeitung und des Rechnens beeinträchtigt sind. Dies erscheint für eine differenzielle Förderung und Therapie bedeutsam.

Fremdsprachigkeit stellt ein Risiko für Schulschwierigkeiten im Rechnen dar. Dieser Umstand verdient besondere Beachtung bei der gezielten schulischen Förderung.

Literatur

Dehaene S (1992): Varieties of numerical abilities. *Cognition,* 44, 1-42.

Dehaene S & Cohen L (1995): Towards an anatomical and functional model of number processing. *Mathematical Cognition, 1, 83-120.*

Dehaene S, Spelke E, Pinel P, Stanescu R & Tsivkin S (1999): Sources of mathematical thinking: Behavioural and brain-imaging evidence. *Science,* 284, 970-974

Esser G (1991): Was wird aus Kindern mit Teilleistungsschwächen? Der langfristige Verlauf umschriebener Entwicklungsstörungen. Stuttgart: Enke.

Gross-Tsur V, Manor O & Shalev RS (1996): Developmental dyscalculia: Prevalence and demographic features. *Developmental Medicine and Child Neurology,* 38, 25-33.

Klauer KJ (1992): In Mathematik mehr leistungsschwache Mädchen, im Rechnen und Rechtschreiben mehr leistungsschwache Jungen? Zur Diagnostik von Teilleistungsschwächen. *Zeitschrift für Entwicklungspsychologie und Pädagogische Psychologie,* 24, 48-65.

Mc Closkey M, Caramazza A & Basili A (1985): Cognitive mechanisms in number processing and calculation: Evidence from dyscalculia. *Brain and Cognition,* 4, 171-196.

Remschmidt H & Schmidt MH (Hrsg., 1994): Multiaxiales Klassifikationsschema für psychische Störungen des Kindes- und Jugendalters nach ICD-10 der WHO. Huber, Bern.

Rourke BP & Fuerst DR (1991): Learning disabilities and psychosocial functioning. New York: Guilford Press.

Rourke BP (1989): Nonverbal learning disabilities. The syndrome and the model. New York: Guilford Press.

Shalev RS, Auerbach J & Gross-Tsur V (1995): Developmental dyscalculia behavioural and attentional aspects: A research note. *Journal of Child Psychology and Psychiatry,* 36,1261-1268.

von Aster MG (1994): Developmental Dyscalculia in Children: Review of the literature and clinical validation. *Acta Paedopsychiatrica*, 56, 169-178.

von Aster MG (1996a): Psychopathologische Risiken bei Kindern mit umschriebenen schulischen Entwicklungsstörungen. *Kindheit und Entwicklung*, 5, 53-59.

von Aster MG (1996b): Die Störungen des Rechnens und der Zahlenverarbeitung in der kindlichen Entwicklung. Habilitationsschrift, Universität Zürich.

von Aster MG, Deloche G, Dellatolas G & Meier M (1997): Zahlenverarbeitung und Rechnen bei Schulkindern der 2. und 3. Klassenstufe: Eine vergleichende Studie französischsprachiger und deutschsprachiger Kinder. *Zeitschrift für Entwicklungspsychologie und pädagogische Psychologie*, 29, 151-166.

7 Verzeichnis der Referentinnen und Referenten

Amorosa, Prof. Dr. med. Hedwig, Heckscher Klinik, Außenstelle Solm, Wolfrathshauser Str. 350, Haus 5, 81479 München

Aster, Priv. Doz. Dr. Michael von, Psychiatrische Univ.-Poliklinik für Kinder und Jugendliche, Freie Straß 15, CH-8028 Zürich

Becker, Michael, Buttelstr. 15, 17033 Neubrandenburg

Behrndt, Dr. Selma-Marie, Gang 4, 17509 Hanshagen

Bertrand, Dr. Lucien, Service Re-Educatif Ambulatoire, 64 Rue Ch. Martel, L-2134 Luxembourg

Blanz, Prof. Dr. Bernhard, Klinikum der Friedrich-Schiller-Universität Jena, Klinik für Kinder- und Jugendpsychiatrie, Postfach, 07740 Jena

Boensch, Prof. Dr. Manfred, In der Bebie 54, 30539 Hannover

Breitenbach, Dr. Erwin, Felix-Dahn-Straße, 97072 Würzburg

Breuer, Prof. Dr. Helmut, Maxim-Gorki-Str. 3 B, 17491 Greifswald

Buchhorn, Ingrid, Linckestr. 45, 59069 Hamm

Buschmann, Renate, Brettenburger Str. 5, 24975 Hürup

Dummer-Smoch, Dr. Lisa, Wildhofstr. 49, 24582 Bordesholm

Ebel, Volker, Ootmasumer Weg 32, 48527 Nordhorn

Firnhaber, Mechthild, Mangoldweg 25, 64287 Darmstadt

Goswami, Prof. Usha, Institut of Child Health 30, Behavioural Sciences Unit, Guildford Street, London WC1N 1EH (England)

Hackethal(†), Renate

Klipcera, Prof. Dr. Christian, Institut für Psychologie der Universität Wien, Neutorgasse 13 A, A-1010 Wien

Komnick, Reinhold, Jugenddorf-Christopherusschule Oberurff, 34596 Bad Zwesten

Krause, Prof. Dr. Christina, Hasenwinkel 43 a, 37079 Göttingen

Kruse, Prof. Dr. Eberhard, Abt. für Phoniatrie und Pädaudiologie, Universität Göttingen, Robert-Koch-Str. 40, 37075 Göttingen

Küspert, Dr. Petra, Würzburger Institut für Lernförderung, Balthasar-Neumann-Promenade 11, 97070 Würzburg

Lau, Doris, Bezirksregierung Hannover, Dezernat 407 - Niedersächsisches Landesamt, Postfach 203, 3002 Hannover

Landerl, Univ. Ass. Magister Dr. Karin, Institut für Psychologie der Universität Salzburg, Hellbrunnenstr. 34, A-5020 Salzburg

Laue, Ursula, Eichestr. 42, 64372 Ober-Ramstadt

May, Dr. Peter, Henriettenstr. 45, 20259 Hamburg

Oberländer, Hilke, Wegzoll 28, 22393 Hamburg

Orth, Hans-Peter, Hagenauer Str. 23, 68229 Mannheim

Ptok, Prof. Dr. Martin, Abt. für Phoniatrie und Pädaudiologie, Medizinische Hochschule Hannover, 30623 Hannover

Reuter-Liehr, Carola, Stiftsplatz 1, 37176 Nörten-Hardenberg

Rumsey, Prof. Judith M., National Institut of Mental Health, Child Psychiatrie Branch, Building 10, Room 6 N240, Bethesda, MD 20892 USA

Schäfer, Prof. Dr. W. D., Universitäts-Augenklinik, Josef-Schneider-Str. 11, 97800 Würzburg

Scheerer-Neumann, Prof. Dr. Gerheid, Am Gottesberg 59, 33619 Bielefeld

Schneider, Prof. Dr. Wolfgang, Institut für Psychologie der Universität Würzburg, Wittelsbacher Platz 1, 97074 Würzburg

Schulte-Körne, PD Dr. med. Gerd, Klinik für Psychiatrie und Psychotherapie des Kindes- und Jugendalters, Philipps-Universität Marburg, Hans-Sachs-Str. 6, 35039 Marburg

Scygiel, Christine, Hallstattstr. 2, 97265 Hettstadt

Seidel-Steffen, Barbara, Wischkamp 41, 24211 Preetz

Specht, Prof. Dr. med. Friedrich, Keplerstr. 3, 37085 Göttingen

Steffen, Heinz, Wischkamp 41, 24211 Pretz

Steffen, Dr. Martina, Schlehdornweg 6, 17493 Greifswald

Strehlow, Prof. Dr. Ulrich, Klinik für Kinder- und Jugendpsychiatrie, Berta-von-Suttner-Str. 1, 77654 Offenburg

Szaszi, Monika, Riedstr. 40, 09117 Chemnitz

Trauzettel-Klosinski, Priv. Doz. Susanne, Panoramastr. 65, 72116 Mössingen

Warnke, Prof. Dr. Andreas, Klinik für Kinder- und, Jugendpsychiatrie, Universität Würzburg, Füchsleinstr. 15, 97080 Würzburg

Witruk, Prof. Dr. Evelin, Institut für Angewandte Psychologie, Seeburgstr. 14-20, 04103 Leipzig